"A-List helped me improve my scores with their uniqu
techniques...Thank you so much A-List for making m
-Marcelle B.
Accepted into NYU

"I loved my experience with A-List... I couldn't be more appreciative of all the help that A-List has provided for me, and would strongly recommend A-List to any future SAT or ACT takers!"
-Evan S.
Accepted into University of Pennsylvania

"A-List prepared me for both the SAT and ACT better than I thought imaginable...I recommend A-list to anybody trying to get a great score."
-Adam G.
Accepted into University of Florida

Working with A-List helped me to realize my potential in standardized testing, and gave me the confidence I needed for the college process and the future... A-List taught me skills that have tremendously improved my comprehension, writing and general intelligence. I give A-List an A+!"
-Alex B.
Accepted into Northwestern University

"My scores jumped way up after A-List."
-Sam V.
Accepted into Bowdoin College

"I was given the necessary materials in order to raise my SAT/ACT score. I felt confident and prepared walking into the test."
-Lindsay P.
Accepted into Tulane

"I definitely enjoyed my experience with A-List. I found the materials excellent; the vocabulary flash-cards had sentences that had very helpful context clues and even better word groupings. The Book of Knowledge taught me so many things. I was more than satisfied with my final score on both the SAT and ACT exams... I would definitely recommend A-List to anyone."
-Dara B.
Accepted into University of Michigan

A-List

The Book of Knowledge ACT

5th Edition

ISBN 978-0-9891605-5-1

Cover photo by Sarah Scott-Farber

A-List Services LLC

363 7th Ave, 13th Floor

New York, NY 10001

(646) 216-9187

www.alisteducation.com

www.vocabvideos.com

Table of Contents

English

Math

Reading

Science

Writing

Appendices

INTRODUCTION TO THE ACT

Welcome to the ACT! This book will show you everything you need to conquer the test. We'll run through the content you need, show you tricks and shortcuts specific to ACT-style questions, and warn you about traps and common mistakes. This book is the product of the sum total of A-List's expertise, combining the knowledge gained from hours of research into thousands of actual ACT questions with the practical experience of successfully increasing countless students' scores.

FORMAT

The ACT is composed of 4 sections (called "tests"), plus an optional 5th, presented in this order:

TEST	NUMBER OF QUESTIONS	TIME	DESCRIPTION
ENGLISH	75	45 minutes	Multiple-choice grammar and usage questions.
MATH	60	60 minutes	Multiple-choice math questions.
READING	40	35 minutes	Multiple-choice reading comprehension questions.
SCIENCE	40	35 minutes	Multiple-choice data interpretation questions.
WRITING	*1 essay*	*30 minutes*	***Optional**. One 1–4 page essay.*
TOTAL	**215**	**2 hours 55 minutes**	
with essay	*215 + essay*	*3 hours 25 minutes*	

- You will get a score from **1 to 36** on each of the four main tests.*
- Your **Composite Score** is the *average* of your four test scores, rounded to the nearest whole number.
- The English, Math, and Reading tests also have **subscores** in different categories. Each subscore ranges from 1 to 18.
- The ACT score is calculated by taking the number of right answers (the "raw score"), and translating that score into a final score using a special scoring table. Each test has its own unique scoring table in order to adjust for slight difficulty differences among tests.
- **The ACT does not take off points for wrong answers**. This means that random guessing will not count against you. A wrong answer counts the same as a blank.
- Most multiple-choice questions have four choices, except for questions on the Math Test, which have five choices. The letters of the answer choices alternate ABCD / FGHJ every other question. On the Math test, the five choices alternate ABCDE / FGHJK
- If you choose to take the Writing test, you will get three scores together:
    - your English multiple-choice score (1–36),
    - your Writing essay score (0–12),
    - and a combined English/Writing score (1–36) that factors the first two scores together via a complicated formula.

  All three of these scores will be reported to colleges, but only the English score will be averaged into your ACT Composite score.

* See Appendix E at the end of this book for information about comparing SAT and ACT scores.

Point values

As we said, each test has a different scoring table. On one test, a raw math score of 31 might correspond to a final math score of 19. But on another, a raw score of 31 gives you a final score of 21 and a raw score of 29 gives you a 19. This is done in order to adjust for differences in difficulty among different tests. No two tests are exactly the same, so it's inevitable that any given test will be slightly easier or harder than another. If the test is easier than normal, its scoring table will be a bit harsher; if it's harder, the table will be more lenient. This way, the test is *standardized*—scores will be comparable no matter which actual test you took.

But the differences between scoring tables are never very drastic. No scoring tables will be different by more than 2 points. Therefore, we can get an approximate sense of how much each question is worth on your actual final score

SECTION	POINTS PER Q	QS PER POINT	WHAT DOES THAT MEAN?
ENGLISH	0.40	2.50	5 right answers give you about 2 points on your final score.
MATH	0.40	2.50	5 right answers give you about 2 points on your final score.
READING	0.75	1.33	4 right answers give you about 3 points on your final score.
SCIENCE	0.66	1.50	3 right answers give you about 2 points on your final score.

How can this table help you?

- This table shows the **value of each question on your final score**. On average, getting one English question right adds about 0.4 points to your final score. Getting 2.5 questions right adds 1 point to your final score, which means that getting 5 questions right adds 2 points. (Questions on the Reading and Science tests are worth more because the tests have fewer questions than English and Math Tests.)
- The values listed show the points on your **final score *of each test,*** *not* your Composite Score. The Composite Score is the average of your scores on the four tests. Therefore, 1 point on any of the tests will increase your Composite Score by 0.25 on average.
- You can use this table to figure out how many more questions you need to get a **target score**. Multiply the number of points you want by the questions per point to see how many questions you need.

  For example, say you've currently got a 21 on the Science Test and you want to score a 25. You want 4 more points on your score. 4 × 1.50 = 6, so you'll need to get about 6 more questions than you're getting now.
- Furthermore, this can give you a sense of how your mistakes are actually affecting your score. It can **quantify your mistakes**. On any given test, you can count up the number of questions you missed *that you should have gotten right.*[*] Multiply by the values in the table above to see what you should have scored on that test.

  For example, say you got a 23 on a Math Test and you missed 3 Plug-In questions, 2 Backsolve questions, and made 3 RTFQ mistakes.[†] That's 8 questions you should have gotten right: 8 × 0.40 = 3.2 points. You should have gotten another 3 points on this test, so you should have gotten a 26.

---

[*] It's important to note: we're not talking about *every* question you missed, just the ones that you *should've gotten right*. Some questions are legitimately hard. Some may involve weird concepts, or concepts that you haven't gotten to yet. Here we're just talking about the questions that involve concepts you've studied and that you are fully capable of getting.

[†] Don't worry if you don't know what these terms mean. We'll explain them soon enough in the Math Techniques chapter.

A few cautions about these numbers:

- Obviously, **this is an approximation**. This is not an exact exchange rate. You can't get a 22.4 on your Reading test. In reality, getting one more Reading question right might increase your score 1 whole point. Or it might not increase your score at all. But we're looking at the test *as a whole* here. Adding 4 right Reading questions *on average* increases your score 3 points. Adding 5 right math questions *on average* increases your score 2 points.
- Remember that the range of scores on the ACT is small, so **score improvements that sound low may actually be significant**. You might work really hard to improve your score and think, "oh, I didn't do too well. I only went up 5 points." Are you kidding? *Five points is huge!* Moving your Composite Score from a 20 to a 25 means moving from the 50th percentile to the 80th percentile. That's a substantial improvement.
- While these approximations hold up most of the time, things get a little messed up at the **very top of the scale**. Because so few students score so highly, once scores get above 31, questions are worth more than the values above. For example, 5 math questions will give you about 2 points on the Math Test, so moving your raw score from 30 to 35 will move your final score from 20 to 22. But at the top of the range, moving your raw score from 55 to 60 would increase your final score *four* points, from 32 to 36. Again, all these numbers are approximations, and the approximations start to fail at the extreme endpoints.
- Not every change in your scores constitutes a **significant** increase or decrease. There are many other factors that contribute to your test score besides the scoring table, including random chance and luck. Even if you do no work between practice tests, you're not going to get *exactly* the same score every time. You might score 1 point higher or lower just by pure chance.
- In fact, a difference of 1 point might just be a **rounding** issue. Your Composite Score is the average of your scores on the four tests, *rounded to the nearest whole number*. If your average score goes from 21.25 to 21.5, that's hardly a significant change. But the first score is rounded down to 21 and the second is rounded up to 22, so it seems like you went up a full point. And you know what? Colleges know that too. Your school isn't going to reject you because of 1 point. So don't sweat the small points.
- On the other hand, *do* sweat the big points. Doing a lot of little things better can quickly add up to big score increases. Substantial increases are well within your reach.

The Guessing Rule

As we already mentioned, **the ACT does not take off points for wrong answers.** A wrong answer will simply get you zero points, the same as a blank. Therefore, **you should always fill in an answer for every question**. If you are about to run out of time and there are questions you haven't done yet, guess something. We can't say this enough times:

NEVER LEAVE ANY BLANKS FOR ANY REASON!

Why, you ask? Well, why not? If wrongs are treated the same as blanks, then even if you guess wrong on every question, it won't hurt your score. But even when you guess totally randomly, you'll guess correctly a few times by accident. That means you'll pick up a couple of extra points for those guesses.

There's no secret method for guessing. If you want to always guess C and J or B and H, whatever. Some people like to pick choices they've chosen the least in that section so far. Some people have a set letter combination they always guess. There's no real pattern here, no secret code of answer choices. **Don't spend time thinking about it.** Just guess something.

It's important to note that we *don't* mean to say you should haphazardly guess on *every* question. **Accuracy is still more important than bulk**. Don't be afraid to take your time and be sure of your answers on all the questions you get to. Our point is that *if you do* run out of time, or if you are unsure of an answer, just pick something. No blanks.

THE TESTS

Before we get to the nitty-gritty, here is a quick overview of each Test in the ACT. For more information (probably more than you really need), skip ahead to the relevant chapters in this book.

English

You will be given 5 short passages, each of which has 15 questions that ask about the grammar, usage, style, and rhetoric of the passage.

In addition to your overall English score (1–36), you will get two subscores (1–18) in these areas:

- **Usage and Mechanics** (40 Questions): These questions ask you to correct errors in grammar, usage, and punctuation. For most questions, there will be a word or phrase underlined, and you will be given four options to either rewrite the word or phrase to correct an error, or to make no change.
- **Rhetorical Skills** (35 Questions): These questions ask about the style, writing strategy, or logical progression of the passage. Questions may ask you what the author should do to improve the passage.

Math

You will be given one section with 60 questions. The questions are ordered by difficulty, so the first ones should be easy and the last ones should be hard. Again, this is the only section on the ACT in which the questions have 5 choices instead of 4.

In addition to your overall Math score (1–36), you will get three subscores (1–18) in these areas:

- **Pre-Algebra & Elementary Algebra** (24 questions)
- **Intermediate Algebra & Coordinate Geometry** (18 questions)
- **Plane Geometry & Trigonometry** (18 questions)

Calculators are allowed for the Math Test, but not required. Every question can be done by hand if necessary, but you don't really want to do that. Get a calculator. You will be expected to know certain definitions and formulas, but if a question requires a more difficult formula, it may be given to you.

Figures on the test are *not necessarily* drawn to scale. That means that it's possible a figure is not drawn to scale. But in practice, figures are almost always actually drawn to scale.

Reading

You will be given 4 passages, each of which has 10 questions that ask about the content of the passages, inferences or conclusions that can be drawn from the passages, or the author's rhetorical strategies.

The four passages will be in the following topics: Prose Fiction, Social Science, Humanities, Natural Science, They will always be in that order, and the passage will state which type it is.

In addition to your overall Reading score (1–36), you will get two subscores (1–18) in these areas:

- **Art & Literature** (20 questions) covers the Prose Fiction and Humanities passages
- **Social Studies & Sciences** (20 questions) covers the Social Sciences and Natural Sciences passages

The nice thing about the questions is that they are very grounded in the passages. You don't need outside information and you won't have to do too much complex interpretation. It's mostly about understanding what the passage says. The bad thing is that timing is tight and the questions don't always tell you where to find the information you need in the passage.

Science

You will be given 7 passages, each followed by 5–7 questions. Each passage consists of a description of a set of situations, experiments, or hypotheses. There will usually be some set of tables, graphs, or other figures accompanying the text.

You will only get one Science score. You will not get any subscores.

The passages will be one of three types:

- **Data Representation** (3 passages, 5 questions each) These will present a set of data describing a situation or phenomenon and ask you to interpret the figures provided.
- **Research Summary** (3 passages, 6 questions each) These will present a series of experiments on a common theme or topic. In addition to interpreting data, these questions will ask about the design of the experiment or conclusions that can be drawn from the data.
- **Conflicting Viewpoints** (1 passage, 7 questions) This will present a situation or occurrence, followed by two or more conflicting hypotheses that seek to explain it. The questions will ask you to compare the different viewpoints.

Writing

The Writing Test consists of one 30-minute essay, always the last section of the test. It's a relatively recent addition to the ACT. It is optional, so you do not have to take it if you don't want to. But be advised that some colleges do require you to take the Writing Test.

The essay will be read by two readers, each giving the essay a score from 1 to 6, meaning your final essay score will range from 2 to 12 (or 0 if you write off-topic, leave it blank, or write illegibly.)

You will receive three scores: an English score, a Writing score, and a Combined English/Writing score. Only your English score will be factored into your Composite ACT score, *not* your Combined English/Writing score.

The topics are generally fairly specific. You're presented with a specific issue or debate in which you must take a side. This issue will be something "relevant to students", such as "Should high schools adopt dress codes?"

The nice thing about these topics is that they do not require any outside knowledge. The topic should be something easily understandable and familiar to you, and you'll be given all the information you need. The bad thing is that you must be rigorous in constructing a real argument. You only have 30 minutes to write. That's not much time, and it can be tough to come up with a logical argument that quickly.

ACT English

INTRODUCTION TO ACT ENGLISH

The ACT English Test will test you on effective writing strategies and the rules of Standard Written English. The test is composed of 5 short essays, each with 15 questions. Questions may ask you to correct grammatical errors, re-phrase awkward sentences, add or delete phrases, or understand the purpose of a paragraph, among other things.

One of the biggest difficulties with the ACT English test is that it's **long**. You have 45 minutes to do 75 questions: that's only **36 seconds per question**. Yikes! But don't worry, it's not so bad. This time constraint also means that individual ACT English questions tend to be pretty simple. The passages aren't like passages on the Reading Test; they're written to resemble a high school essay, and they don't involve any complex ideas or subtle imagery. The sentences are generally straightforward and the same mistakes are tested over and over again. Additionally, there are only four answer choices to choose from, so a little bit of elimination can go a long way. Work quickly.

The questions fall into two large categories—Usage/Mechanics and Rhetorical Skills—each of which has three subtypes. These categories are fixed by the test makers, so every test will always have the same number of questions of each type, though they will be mixed up in any order. Your Writing Score will include two subscores, each out of 18 points, showing your performance in the two main categories.

Below is a chart outlining how many questions will appear for each type:

CATEGORY	QUESTION TYPE	NUMBER OF QUESTIONS
Usage/Mechanics	Grammar & Usage	12
	Sentence Structure	18
	Punctuation	10
	Total	**40**
Rhetorical Skills	Style	12
	Organization	11
	Writing Strategy	12
	Total	**35**

Don't worry too much about these categories. Questions on the test won't say if they're Usage/Mechanics or Rhetorical Skills.* But this is a convenient way to organize the material. The more tests you take, the more you'll start to notice patterns in the types of things they ask you about. Once you start to notice the patterns, you'll be able to answer the questions much more quickly.

The test-makers lay out definitions of what sort of concepts belong to which category, but questions don't always fit into these categories neatly.† There will often be overlap: for example, a question may have three choices dealing with a verb issue and one with a comma issue. Even the concepts themselves are often closely related—you can't talk about run-on sentences without talking about punctuation. Nevertheless, here are the major concepts you'll see on the English Test:

* When you get your results, questions will be labeled as Usage/Mechanics or Rhetorical Skills, but the subcategories will not be labeled.

† All these categories come straight from the ACT makers themselves (via *The Real ACT Prep Guide*, 2008). The coming chapters are roughly organized according to the types listed here, but we've switched some of them around in order to make the material easier to follow. For example, the ACT considers Verb Tense to be a Sentence Structure issue, but we discuss it with Grammar & Usage so that we can discuss all verb issues in one section.

USAGE/MECHANICS

Usage/Mechanics questions ask you to identify **errors in a sentence**. Generally, a word or part of a sentence will be underlined and you will be asked to choose how to rewrite the phrase according to rules of grammar, usage, and punctuation. Choice A or F will usually be "NO CHANGE", meaning you can leave the phrase as it was originally written.

There are three types of Usage/Mechanics questions: **Punctuation**, **Grammar & Usage**, and **Sentence Structure**.

Grammar & Usage: These questions test relationships between single words and phrases within a sentence, relationships such as subject and verb, or pronoun and antecedent.

Sentence Structure: These questions deal with the way larger parts of sentences are connected, such as the way to properly connect clauses and where to place long phrases.

Punctuation: These questions will usually present four choices that differ *only* in their punctuation. You will be tested on when to use (and when *not* to use) commas, apostrophes, and other common punctuation marks.

RHETORICAL SKILLS

Rhetorical Skills questions focus less on writing *grammatically* and more on writing *effectively*. It tests you on how to choose the best way to word a sentence, the best way to structure a paragraph, or the best way to accomplish your goal as a writer. Unlike Usage/Mechanics questions, Rhetorical Skills questions may ask you about the essay as a whole, not just single words or phrases.

There are three types of Rhetorical Skills questions: **Style**, **Organization**, and **Writing Strategy**.

Style: These questions ask about the choice of language in the essay, as well as errors that are stylistic instead of grammatical or structural. You will be asked to trim wordy sentences, make phrases more specific, or ensure the language accurately reflects the essay's tone.

Organization: These questions ask about the logic and organization of the essay. You will be asked about the location and ordering of sentences and the transitions between sentences or paragraphs.

Writing Strategy: These questions ask about what the author should do to the essay to improve it. In fact, most Writing Strategy questions will explicitly phrase the question that way, asking what action the author should take. Common questions include whether the author should add or delete a sentence and whether the essay fulfills a certain goal.

GENERAL STRATEGIES

In the coming chapters, we'll talk more about the specific rules you'll encounter, but here are a few general strategies that can be applied to the test as a whole.

1. Read the whole sentence.

One of the most common reasons students don't notice grammatical errors is that they miss the big picture. Students often focus too much on just the words that are underlined. But there are often key words at the *beginning* of a sentence that tell you there's an error at the *end* of the sentence.

2. Read the whole paragraph.

Even though these questions usually ask about a single sentence, these sentences aren't islands—they're part of a larger passage. The sentences before it can be important to understanding the meaning of this sentence. If you're not sure which form of a word to use—which pronoun to use, say, or what tense the verb should have—the answer may be somewhere else in the paragraph.

3. **Read the whole passage.**

Most questions will deal either with parts of a single sentence or the relationship between two sentences. But there will also be questions that deal with the passage as a whole. You will have to know what the passage was about. You don't have to worry about it as much as you would on a Reading passage, but it will matter.

4. **Read all the choices.**

The following chapters are going to present a lot of material. Learning all these new rules can often seem overwhelming—how are you supposed to know which rules to check on which questions? You're in luck! Often, the question will tell you *exactly* what to look for.

Grammatical questions usually have short choices, each having only a few words. That means it's relatively easy to see the **differences between the choices**. The differences between the choices will give you clues about what grammatical errors you should be looking for in the sentence.

Let's say that a question gave you these four choices:

A. hope to
B. hope for
C. hopes to
D. hopes for

There are two differences between these choices—"hope" versus "hopes" and "to" versus "for"—so we know right away that those are the two things to check. In this example it's pretty clear what to look for, but sometimes it can be more subtle. Make sure to scan all the choices when you first read a question; it will be easier to home in on the important words in the sentence.

5. **Eliminate and Guess.**

As we've mentioned, there's no penalty for wrong answers on the ACT, so *you should never leave a question blank for any reason*. But you are on a tight time limit, and of course there will be some tricky questions. This makes it all the more important to **eliminate quickly**.

Look for differences in forms of words in the choices. Once you spot a rule violation in an answer choice, eliminate **all** choices that make that mistake. There may be more than one reason why a choice is wrong, but you don't have to understand all of them. Once you find one thing wrong with a choice, it's *out*.

If you're down to two choices but you can't figure out which one is better, don't dawdle: **just pick one**. Again, there's no penalty for wrong answers on the ACT, so there's no harm in guessing. You've got a lot of questions to do. If you're stuck, just pick a choice and move on quickly.

USAGE/MECHANICS: GRAMMAR & USAGE

Grammar and Usage questions on the ACT generally ask about the relationship between individual words in a sentence. Many of the errors we'll see here are about making sure one word properly goes with another. Does this verb agree with its subject? Does this pronoun agree with this antecedent? Does this adjective properly modify a noun? Is this the right preposition to use? Is this word spelled correctly? All of these questions will be discussed here.

If you don't have a lot of experience with English grammar—*that's okay*. A lot of students have very little exposure to grammar in high school. We're not going to discuss everything there is to know about English grammar—there's a lot to know, way more than we need for the ACT.* Nor will we cover every single rule that has ever shown up on an ACT. If a rule has shown up on one question in the past *10 years*, we're not going to talk about it. You probably won't see it when you take the test, and even if you do, it would only be one question and won't significantly affect your score.

Instead, we're going to focus on the big picture. We're going to discuss **the rules that appear most frequently on the ACT**. We've done all the legwork for you—we've pored over past real tests to find out which rules matter and which ones don't.

I. VERBS

A verb is traditionally defined as an **action word**, like *jump*, *go*, or *bake*. That's not entirely accurate; not every verb is an "action". These underlined words are verbs—*I like cats; the book sat on the table; Pittsburgh is in Pennsylvania*—even though none describes an "action". But a lot of verbs do describe actions, so this definition will help you develop a sense of which words are verbs.

Before we begin, here's a quick outline of the basic forms all verbs take, demonstrated with three different verbs. All the verb constructions we'll see use some combination of these forms.

FORM	"BAKE" (REGULAR)	"EAT" (IRREGULAR)	"BE" (IRREGULAR)
Simple present	He bakes cookies. They bake cookies.	He eats chicken. They eat chicken.	I am rude. He is rude. They are rude.
Simple past	He baked cookies. They baked cookies.	He ate chicken. They ate chicken.	He was rude. They were rude.
Past participle	He has baked cookies. The cookies were baked.	He has eaten chicken. The chicken was eaten.	He has been rude.
Present participle	He is baking cookies. Baking cookies is fun.	He is eating chicken. Eating chicken is fun.	He is being rude. Being rude is fun.
Infinitive	He should bake cookies. He likes to bake cookies.	He should eat chicken. He likes to eat chicken.	He will be rude. He likes to be rude.

* One of the most definitive books about English is *The Cambridge Grammar of the English Language*. It's over 1,800 pages long. We will not be discussing all of it.

Any time a verb is underlined, check the following things:

1. Agreement

Every sentence contains at least one main verb, and that verb will have a **subject**. The subject is a noun that identifies who performs the action of the verb.*

In present tense verbs, the verb will be in a different form depending on whether the subject is *singular* or *plural*. That is, the subject and verb must **agree in number**: †

✓ ***THE DOG* eats meat.**	× ***THE DOG* eat meat.**
✓ ***THE DOGS* eat meat.**	× ***THE DOGS* eats meat.**

If a verb is a multi-word phrase, only the first word (called an "auxiliary verb") agrees with the subject, so we can ignore the second word (for now).

✓ ***THE DOG* is barking.**	× ***THE DOG* are barking.**
✓ ***THE DOGS* are barking.**	× ***THE DOGS* is barking.**
✓ ***THE DOG* has barked.**	× ***THE DOG* have barked.**
✓ ***THE DOGS* have barked.**	× ***THE DOGS* has barked.**

If a verb underlined, find the subject and see that it agrees with the verb. To find the subject, ask yourself:

Who is performing the action?

Sound easy? Well, it's not. Sentences often describe abstract concepts where it's hard to identify actors and actions. Furthermore, there are a number of ways the subject can be *hidden* so that the subject isn't what you think it is. So how can you tell which word is the subject?

The core sentence

On the ACT, the subject may not be the word immediately in front of the verb. In fact, it probably isn't. In real life, sentences are rarely simple statements like "The dog is barking." There are usually a lot of extra words that modify, describe, or elaborate on the words and concepts.

> Note that the verb here is "*is* barking", not just "barking". An "-ing" verb alone cannot be the main verb of a sentence.

✓ **The dog *in the yard* is barking.**

✓ **The dog *that I got from the pound last week* is barking.**

✓ **The dog, *which I bought for my ex-girlfriend Jessica in a pathetic attempt to win her affection back after she dumped me—right in front of everyone in the hallway outside math class—a little over three months ago,* is barking.**

But in every sentence, you can strip away all the extra stuff and find a **core sentence**, a simple statement composed of just the subject and verb: **the dog... is barking**. Once you pull out the subject put it next to the verb, you can easily tell by ear whether the verb agrees with the subject.

Interrupting clauses

If you see a phrase **surrounded by commas**, the subject won't be in there. Take a look at this sentence:

➤ **The Queen, who has absolute power over her subjects as well as all the dukes and other aristocrats, are rich.**

---

* Unless it's a *passive* verb. More on those in a second.

† Confusingly, nouns and verbs have the opposite rules of formation: *plural nouns* take an "s" at the end ("dogs"), but *singular verbs* take an "s" ("eats"). Once you find the subject and verb, you can use your ear to tell if they match: "The dogs eats meat" just sounds wrong.

All that stuff between the commas isn't part of the core sentence. It's like a parenthetical phrase or a footnote, an extra chunk of information thrown in the middle of the sentence. But it doesn't affect the *core sentence*. So let's get rid of it.

× ***THE QUEEN*, ~~who has absolute power over all her subjects as well as all the dukes and other aristocrats~~, are rich.**

We can see the core sentence is "The Queen are rich." Does that sound right? Of course not. It should be:

✓ ***THE QUEEN*, ... , is rich.**

In the original sentence, the verb might have sounded okay to you because there are a lot of plural nouns in between the subject and the verb—"subjects", "dukes", and "aristocrats". Those words trick your ear into thinking we need a plural verb. If you **literally cross out** comma phrases like this until all you have left is the subject, it's much easier to hear whether the verb is correct.*

> Each sample sentence in this lecture will be marked with an × if it's wrong, a check (✓) if it's right, and a chili pepper (🌶) if we don't know yet.

Phrases surrounded by **dashes** work the same way:

🌶 **The sequel's budget—estimated to be over 100 million dollars—is more than double that of the original movie.**

✓ **The sequel's *BUDGET*~~—estimated to be over 100 million dollars—~~is more than double that of the original movie.**

The punctuation marks make these interrupting phrases easy to spot. However, a sentence might also have long interrupting clauses like this without any punctuation at all:

✓ ***THE DOG* that I got from the pound last week is barking.**

Prepositional phrases

Prepositions are small words like *of*, *in*, or *on* that show a relationship between two words (usually two nouns). In the phrase "**the dog in the yard**":

🌶 The word "in" is a *preposition* and "the yard" is its *object*.

🌶 The phrase "in the yard" is a *prepositional phrase*. It describes (or *modifies*) "the dog".

The subject cannot be the **object of a preposition**. For example:

✓ ***THE QUEEN* of England is rich.**

The phrase "of England" is a prepositional phrase: "of" is a preposition and "England" is its *object*. The phrase "of England" describes the Queen—it tells us *which* Queen we're talking about. *The Queen* is the subject of the verb "is", not *England*. She's the one who's rich.†

> "Of" is by far the most common preposition on verb agreement questions. The subject will be *before* "of", not after. We'll talk more about prepositions later in this section.

This holds true for *all* prepositional phrases—they are not part of the core sentence. So if you see a prepositional phrase, **cross it out**. The subject *cannot* be in there:

✓ ***THE DOGS* ~~in the yard~~ are barking.**

✓ ***THE MAN* ~~with three children~~ is married.**

✓ ***ALL FLIGHTS* ~~to Denver~~ have been delayed.**

✓ ***THE MOVIE* ~~about vampires~~ is scary.**

Of course, there may not be just one prepositional phrase. There could be a whole string of them.

---

* The grand majority of ACT verb agreement questions require you to change the verb. But occasionally you might have to change the subject instead. In the sentence "*The work of Monet are beautiful*," the subject "the work" doesn't agree with the verb "are". But we can't change the verb because it isn't underlined. Instead, we'll make the subject plural to match the verb: "*The works of Monet are beautiful*."

† Strictly speaking, the *entire* phrase "The Queen of England" is the subject of "is". But the verb only has to agree with the *head* of the phrase—the core noun that everything else in the phrase is describing. Since "Queen" is the word that agrees with the verb, that's all we care about, so we'll call it the subject as a shorthand description.

☛ **The construction of several groups of townhouses across the street from the complex of office buildings <u>have improved</u> the neighborhood.**

What improved the neighborhood? The groups? The townhouses? Let's cross out the prepositional phrases:

× ***THE CONSTRUCTION* (~~of several groups~~) (~~of townhouses~~) (~~across the street~~) (~~from the complex~~) (~~of office buildings~~) <u>have improved</u> the neighborhood.**

The core sentence is "the *construction* have improved the neighborhood". That doesn't match.

✓ ***THE CONSTRUCTION* ... <u>has improved</u> the neighborhood.**

You can see how the sentence tried to fool you: the actual subject is singular, but there are several plural words after it, so the verb sounded okay. Don't be fooled. The subject will **not** be in a prepositional phrase.

Multiple subjects and multiple verbs

It's easy to see that the subject is plural when it's a plural noun:

✓ ***THE DOGS* <u>are</u> barking.**

But sometimes the subject is a compound of *two singular nouns* joined by "and". Even though each of these words is singular, the two of them together make a plural subject:

× ***THE BULLDOG AND THE BEAGLE* <u>is</u> barking.** ✓ ***THE BULLDOG AND THE BEAGLE* <u>are</u> barking.**

Similarly, a single subject can have two verbs joined by "and":

✓ ***THE DOG* <u>eats</u> meat and <u>loves</u> bones.**

Here, *each* verb, "eats" and "loves", agrees with the same subject "the dog". We could write the same sentence as two separate clauses (though it would sound a bit repetitive):

✓ ***THE DOG* <u>eats</u> meat, and *THE DOG* <u>loves</u> bones.**

TRY SOME: *In each of the following sentences, circle the appropriate verb form.*

☛ The temperature and humidity **[has / have]** been rising for the past week.

☛ The chef who started all three of these restaurants **[was / were]** trained at a school in France.

☛ Dave's new invention, a set of rocket-powered rollerblades that can propel you 100 yards in just three seconds, **[are / is]** both pointless and unsafe.

☛ The veterinarian said that the problems with my dog's skin **[come / comes]** from a genetic condition rather than an infection.

☛ Mayor Black's announcement of the addition of four new bridges to the city's redevelopment designs **[was / were]** met with mixed reactions from the public.

2. Tense

A verb's *tense* tells us *when* the action takes place. Tense can be scary; if you've ever taken a foreign language, you've probably been through some of the misery of studying tenses. However, tense questions on the ACT are usually fairly straightforward. The main goal is **consistency**. When events happen in the past, present or future, the verbs should reflect that. If events happen at the same time, the verbs should be in the same tense. So how can you tell what tense the verb should be in?

The easiest way is to look for words that **literally refer to time**. If you see any such words, the tense of the verb should match the time they refer to.

× ***IN 1776*, America <u>is declaring</u> independence.**	✓ ***IN 1776*, America <u>declared</u> independence.**
× ***NEXT YEAR*, our team <u>has won</u> 30 games.**	✓ ***NEXT YEAR*, our team <u>will win</u> 30 games.**

More frequently, you can look at the tense of **other verbs in the sentence**. Verbs should be *consistent* within the sentence; if events happen at the same time, the verbs should be in the same tense.

× **Dave <u>sees</u> several museums when he *WENT* to Belgium.**

× **Mrs. Jones <u>made</u> us sit in the corner whenever we *ARE* bad.**

In the first sentence, the verb "went" is in the past, so we know his trip to Belgium happened in the past. Since the museum trips occurred *while* he was in Belgium, "sees" must also be put into the past. Similarly, in the second sentence, "are" is in the present. The word "whenever" tells us that the act of sitting in the corner happens *at the same time* as being bad, so "made" should be put into the present. *

✓ **Dave <u>saw</u> several museums when he *WENT* to Belgium.**

✓ **Mrs. Jones <u>makes</u> us sit in the corner whenever we *ARE* bad.**

Similarly, you can look at the tense of verbs **in other sentences nearby**. Most of the time, the passage as a whole will be set in a particular tense, so you can check the larger context to see which tense is appropriate. For example, by itself this sentence seems fine just the way it is:

✓ **The waiter <u>took</u> their orders.**

But put into a larger context, that tense may not be appropriate:

× **The restaurant workers always *FOLLOW* the same routine. First, the hostess *SHOWS* the guests to their table. Then, the chef *COMES* out and *TELLS* them about the specials. Finally, the waiter <u>took</u> their orders.**

Here, "took" is in the past, but all of the other verbs in this paragraph are in the present tense.† That doesn't match. The last sentence should also be in the present: **the waiter <u>takes</u> their orders**.

Perfect verbs

The majority of ACT tense questions just test whether the verb should be *present* or *past*. There are lots of other verb categories in English that won't be tested on the ACT. However, you still might see these forms used, so it's helpful to know a little about them. Look at this:

✓ **Bob <u>was</u> class president *IN 2006*.**

This sentence is the **simple past**. It refers to a specific time in the past and only the past. Compare it to this:

✓ **Bob <u>has been</u> class president *SINCE 2006*.**

---

* This does NOT mean that *all* verbs in a sentence must be in the same tense—only verbs that refer to the same time. Sentences often have multiple verbs in different tenses: "Bob *went* to the zoo yesterday, and Scott *will go* tomorrow."

† Note that just because a verb is present tense doesn't mean it's referring to an action that's occurring right now. In this paragraph, all the present tense verbs refer to repeated actions that occur *generally*. But don't worry about this; you don't have to understand the finer points to see that "took" doesn't match the other verbs here.

This sentence is in the **present perfect**. Not only was Bob president in the past, but he's *still* president now. The present perfect is used for time periods that extend *from the past up to the present.*

> The present perfect is formed with the present tense of the verb "to have", plus the past participle of the main verb.

Additionally, you may see verbs in the **past perfect**. This structure is used for *the past of the past*, when an event happened before another past event:

✓ **Lucas <u>had read</u> the book *BEFORE HE SAW* the film adaptation.**

> The past perfect is formed with past tense of the verb "to have", plus the past participle of the main verb.

Both the reading of the book and the watching of the movie are past events, but the reading was *further* in the past, so "had read" is in the past perfect.

The past perfect is often interchangeable with the simple past, however, so we could also say:

✓ **Lucas <u>read</u> the book before he saw the film adaptation.**

Would

Would is a special kind of verb that has several different uses.* It isn't tested on the ACT very frequently, but it does show up every once in a while, so it's good to know a little about it.

First of all, *would* is simply the past form of *will.* It can be used to describe events occurring in the future *from a point in the past.*

✓ **Dave *TOLD* Jennifer that he <u>would go</u> to the store.**

From Dave and Jennifer's perspective, his trip to the store will occur in the future. But the act of telling Jennifer occurred in the past. So his trip to the store is set in the future from that moment.

Second, *would* can be used to describe *habitual* actions in the past.

✓ ***WHEN HE WAS* a child, Dave <u>would go</u> to the park every Saturday.**

This sentence is set in the past, when Dave was a child. But it doesn't refer to any specific event in the past—it refers to events in the past that would happen *repeatedly.*

Finally, *would* can occur in *conditional* sentences—sentences containing an "if" clause. Conditional sentences can use several different tenses. The tense of the verb in the second clause is determined by the tense of the first.†

✓ **If you *ASK* me to the dance, I <u>will go</u> with you.**

✓ **If you *ASKED* me to the dance, I <u>would go</u> with you.**

✓ **If you *HAD ASKED* me to the dance, I <u>would have gone</u> with you.**

(Note that the verb in the last sentence is "would ***have*** gone", not "would ***of*** gone". "Would of" is *never* right in any context. We'll talk more about this in the "Commonly Confused Words" section.)

* If you're interested, the fancy name for this kind of verb is "*modal auxiliary verb*". *Will, can, could, should,* and *must* are other examples of modal auxiliaries.

† Conditional statements don't occur often on the ACT, so don't worry too much about the difference between these sentences.

TRY SOME: *In each of the following sentences, circle the appropriate verb form.*

- My dog | **sleeps / slept** | on my bed every night when he was a puppy.
- The war is finally over, but its effects | **were felt / will be felt** | for many years to come.
- Larry | **brings / brought** | some nuts and a loaf of bread when he goes to the park so he can feed the ducks and the squirrels.
- We worked together to speed up the preparations for the party: I | **cooked / will cook** | dinner while Naomi cleaned the dining room.
- Whenever I went fishing with my mother we | **buy / would buy** | bait from the same shop about a mile from the lake.

3. Irregular verbs and past participles

Most verbs form the past tense simply by adding "-ed". Some verbs, however, have special forms for the past. Others even use the same form for past and present. We call these verbs **irregular verbs**:

REGULAR:	✓ **I walk the dog.**	✓ **I walked the dog.**	
IRREGULAR:	✓ **I catch the fish.**	✓ **I caught the fish.**	× **I catched the fish.**
IRREGULAR:	✓ **I hit the ball today.**	✓ **I hit the ball yesterday.**	× **I hitted the ball.**

The "perfect" forms mentioned above were compound tenses that require more than one verb: a form of the verb "to have" plus the **past participle** of the verb. For regular verbs—and even some irregular verbs—the past participle looks exactly the same as the simple past:

✓ **I walk the dog.**	✓ **I walked the dog.**	✓ **I have walked the dog.**
✓ **I catch the fish.**	✓ **I caught the fish.**	✓ **I have caught the fish.**
✓ **I hit the ball today.**	✓ **I hit the ball yesterday.**	✓ **I have hit the ball.**

However, some irregular verbs have distinct past participles—they use *different* words in the simple past and perfect tenses. Here are a few examples:

PRESENT	SIMPLE PAST	PERFECT FORM
begin	began	had/have begun
choose	chose	had/have chosen
freeze	froze	had/have frozen
grow	grew	had/have grown
give	gave	had/have given
take	took	had/have taken

When a verb has different forms like this, don't confuse the two. The past participle must be used only in compound forms, not by itself.*

✓ **I chose an outfit for the dance.**	× **I chosen an outfit for the dance.**
✓ **I have chosen an outfit for the dance.**	× **I have chose an outfit for the dance.**

* That is, the past participle can't be used by itself *as a main verb*. But it *can* appear by itself in a modifier: *Begun in 1887, the Eiffel Tower was completed in 1889.* We'll talk about modifiers in the Sentence Structure chapter.

4. Active vs. Passive

There's one more distinction we can make among verb forms: *active voice* and *passive voice.*

An **active** verb is one in which the *subject* of the verb is the person or thing *doing* the action. A **passive** verb is one in which the *subject* is the person or thing *receiving* the action.

ACTIVE: A car hit Chapman. **PASSIVE: Chapman was hit by a car.**

> The passive is formed with a form of the verb "to be", plus the past participle of the verb.

See the difference? Both these sentences *mean* the same thing: the car *did* the hitting, and Chapman *received* the hitting. But in the first sentence, the "car" is the subject of the verb "hit", and in the second, "Chapman" is the subject of the verb "was hit".

How can you tell whether the verb should be active or passive? First, look at the **context:**

× **Because Roger sold the most toasters, he gave a prize.**

The underlined verb is *active* here: it tells us that Roger was the one who did the giving. But the first part tells us that Roger did something special,* so it's more likely that he *received* a prize. Therefore, we should use the passive:

✓ **Because Roger sold the most toasters, he was given a prize.**

Some people will tell you that the passive is *always* wrong, but that's a myth. Passive verbs are *not wrong*; they're just another way to say something. Just like every other verb form, sometimes it's right, and sometimes it's wrong. The important thing is to understand the context.

Passive verbs can be handy if the order of the words matters to us. For example, if we want the receiver of the action to come at the beginning of the sentence:

✓ ***WHILE CROSSING THE STREET*, Chapman was hit by a car.**

Here, we need "Chapman" to be the subject of the sentence so we can connect him directly to the phrase "while crossing the street".†

Passives are also useful if we don't know who performed the action:

✓ **Scott was fired yesterday.**

We don't know who actually performed the firing here. But we don't really *care* who did the firing. So the passive voice works perfectly.‡

However, the passive can become a problem when we *do* know who performed the action.

× **After Paolo read the menu, a sandwich was picked.**

The second clause is passive: the noun "sandwich" is the subject of "was picked", but the sandwich didn't *do* the picking. The second clause doesn't tell us who did the picking. But wait! We know who did the picking—Paolo did. So why don't we say that?

✓ **After Paolo read the menu, he picked a sandwich.**

We could leave the clause in the passive and add a prepositional phrase to tell us who the performer is, but sentences like that often sound ugly and weird:

× **After Paolo read the menu, a sandwich was picked by him.**

---

* It's hard to sell toasters. He deserves that prize.

† If we didn't, we'd have a *dangling modifier*. More on that in the Sentence Structure chapter.

‡ Don't confuse "passive" with "past"—*any* tense can be put into the passive voice by adding a form of "to be" and the past participle: "Scott will be fired tomorrow." "These toys are made out of wood." "The neighborhood has been improved by the construction of townhouses."

VERB SUMMARY

When a verb is underlined, check the following:

1. **Agreement**
   - Subject and verb must agree in **number**, singular or plural.
   - To find the **subject**, ask: Who is **performing** the action of verb?
   - Ignore **interrupting phrases** and **prepositional phrases**.
   - One verb can have **multiple subjects**; one subject can have **multiple verbs**.
2. **Tense**
   - Look for **time words**. Verbs must refer to the right time.
   - Look at **other verbs** in the sentence. Verbs that occur at the same time must be in the same tense.
   - Look at verbs in **nearby sentences**.
   - Watch out for special tenses: **present perfect, past perfect, would**.
3. **Irregular forms**
   - Some verbs need **irregular** past tense forms.
   - Some irregular verbs' **past participles** are different from their **simple past** forms.
4. **Active vs. Passive**
   - In a passive verb, the **subject does not perform the action**.
   - In general, if we **know** who the actor is, **don't** use the passive.

VERB DRILL

*All the questions in this exercise deal with **verbs**. Unlike the real ACT, the sentences in this exercise do not make up a full passage—each question refers to a single stand-alone sentence.*

Gerald went to three different grocery stores before he finally <u>finds</u> [1] the brand of cereal he was looking for.

1. **A.** NO CHANGE
   B. found
   C. will find
   D. has found

The room is a mess: the desk is covered with papers, and a pile of dirty clothes <u>are lying</u> [2] on the floor.

2. **F.** NO CHANGE
   G. is lying
   H. had been lying
   J. have been laid

Although the overall crime rate is much lower this year, the number of car thefts in suburban areas <u>are</u> [3] rising.

3. **A.** NO CHANGE
   B. were
   C. is
   D. have been

Before he became a children's book author, Dr. Seuss <u>is making</u> [4] training films for the U.S. Army during World War II.

4. **F.** NO CHANGE
   G. makes
   H. has made
   J. made

The possibility of the existence of black holes <u>were proposed</u> [5] by the geologist John Michell in 1784 in a letter to Henry Cavendish.

5. **A.** NO CHANGE
   B. have been proposed
   C. was proposed
   D. proposes

One of the biggest surprises in the former governor's memoirs <u>was</u> [6] the news that he did not seek reelection because he had fallen ill.

6. **F.** NO CHANGE
   G. were
   H. are
   J. have been

A joint organization of teachers and library workers <u>have agreed to</u> [7] sponsor a fundraiser to raise money for the museum.

7. **A.** NO CHANGE
   B. has agreed to
   C. are agreed on
   D. are in agreement about

The increasing use of smart phones has made it [8] much easier for companies to do business on the road.

8. F. NO CHANGE
G. make
H. have made
J. are making

Whenever my family and I go to the movies, my father gets an extra-large popcorn and will refuse [9] to share it with any of us.

9. A. NO CHANGE
B. would refuse
C. refuses
D. refused

The orangelo—a hybrid fruit resulting from a cross between an orange and a grapefruit—have grown [10] naturally in Puerto Rico.

10. F. NO CHANGE
G. has grew
H. grow
J. grows

Measuring over ten feet long, the Mekong giant catfish seems frightening, but it actually has no teeth and has ate [11] only algae and small plants.

11. A. NO CHANGE
B. eats
C. ate
D. would eat

Once a reliable method for measuring degrees of longitude were discovered [12], cartographers were able to draw accurate maps of the oceans.

12. F. NO CHANGE
G. discovers
H. was discovered
J. would have discovered

My fascination with science begins [13] on my eighth birthday when I received a simple toy microscope as a present from my grandmother.

13. A. NO CHANGE
B. had began
C. begun
D. began

When we started this company, we believed that it takes [14] at least five years of growth for it to become profitable, but it only took two.

14. F. NO CHANGE
G. would take
H. will take
J. took

Both the wildlife in the area and the population of a nearby village was [15] seriously damaged after a factory spilled toxic chemicals into the river.

15. A. NO CHANGE
B. have
C. has been
D. were

II. Pronouns

Pronouns are words like *they*, *it*, or *her* that take the place of nouns. They work like abbreviations; they refer to some other noun in the sentence so you don't have to repeat that noun. The noun a pronoun refers to is called the **antecedent**.

> A chart outlining all the different pronoun forms can be found at the end of this section.

✓ ***THE SNAKE* swallows <u>its</u> prey whole.**

"Its" is a pronoun and "the snake" is its antecedent; "its" refers to "the snake".

✓ ***THE SNAKE* swallows <u>[the snake's]</u> prey whole.**

Just like with verbs, there are several different ways pronouns can change their form, so there are a few things you'll want to check whenever a pronoun is underlined on the ACT.

Any time a pronoun is underlined, check the following things:

1. Agreement

Just like verbs, pronouns must **agree in number** with their antecedents: match singular to singular and plural to plural.

✓ ***THE SNAKE* swallows <u>its</u> prey whole.**

✓ ***SNAKES* swallow <u>their</u> prey whole.**

✗ ***THE SNAKE* swallows <u>their</u> prey whole.**

✗ ***SNAKES* swallow <u>its</u> prey whole.**

Any time you see a pronoun underlined, find its antecedent and make sure they agree in number. The best way to find the antecedent is to ask:

Who or what does the pronoun refer to?

That is, if you replaced the pronoun with another word in the sentence, which would you use?

✗ **This new mobile phone looks great, but <u>they</u> can break very easily.**

"They" is a pronoun, so let's find the antecedent. What does "they" refer to? What can break? *The phone* can break easily. "Phone" is singular, so we must say "it".

✓ **This new mobile *PHONE* looks great, but <u>it</u> can break very easily.**

Sometimes there may be more than one noun the pronoun could refer to, so you'll have to use the context to figure out which one the pronoun is supposed to refer to.

✓ **The *AGE* of some *TREES* <u>is</u> determined by counting <u>their</u> rings.**

Note that the subject of the verb may or may not be the same word as the antecedent of a pronoun. Here, the subject of the verb "is" is "age", but the antecedent of the pronoun "their" is "trees". Unlike the subject, the antecedent *can be* inside a prepositional phrase. The antecedent can be anywhere in the sentence, or even in a previous sentence. Take it slow. What *is determined*? The *age* is determined. But what has *rings*? *Trees* have rings.

Vague pronouns

✗ **Scott and Bob were partners until <u>he</u> quit.**

Here we have two options for who quit: Scott or Bob. How can you tell which it is? You can't; that's the problem. In this case, we can't use a pronoun at all. We have to specify who quit.

✓ **Scott and Bob were partners until <u>Bob</u> quit.**

Of course, if they *both* quit, then we'd have to say "they".

Mystery pronouns

× **In gymnastics, they take off points for bad dismounts.**

Sounds fine? Well, it's not. Who's "they"? Gymnastics? *Gymnastics* take off points? Are you kidding me? The problem here is that there isn't any word in the sentence that could possibly be the antecedent of the pronoun.* "They" is a *mystery pronoun*—we have no idea what it refers to. The only way to correct it is to not use a pronoun at all: we must specify who we're talking about.†

✓ **In gymnastics, judges take off points for bad dismounts.**

Generic pronoun shift

It's okay for a pronoun to lack a specific antecedent when we're not talking about any specific people. "One", for example, is a pronoun that basically means "anyone" or "someone". "You" works the same way:

✓ **If *ONE* is sick, one should go to the hospital.**

✓ **If *YOU* are sick, you should go to the hospital.**

These sentences mean the same thing (the only difference is that "one" is more formal). Neither "one" nor "you" has an actual antecedent—you can't point to anything in the sentence that they refer to. That's okay because they refer to people in general—they're *generic pronouns*. In these cases, either "one" or "you" would be fine. But you can't use *both* of them:

× **If *ONE* is sick, you should go to the hospital.**

If "one" and "you" show up in the same sentence, one of them is probably wrong. Furthermore, any time you see a generic pronoun, **check the other sentences in the passage**. If a generic pronoun was used earlier in the paragraph, you must keep using that pronoun throughout the passage.

This rule doesn't just apply to "one" and "you". You must be consistent with *all* generic pronouns:

× **If *WE* examine this painting closely, one can tell that the artist was left-handed.**

× **When *PEOPLE* spend all day typing, your hands get tired quickly.**

✓ **If *WE* examine this painting closely, we can tell that the artist was left-handed.**

✓ **When *PEOPLE* spend all day typing, their hands get tired quickly.**

Noun agreement

Just as pronouns must agree with antecedents, sometimes *nouns* have to agree with the words they refer to.

× **Scott and Bob want to be an astronaut.**

Here, the subject "Scott and Bob" is plural, but "astronaut" is singular. They don't match. Scott and Bob don't want to be *one astronaut*. They're two people! What we really mean is:

✓ ***SCOTT AND BOB* want to be astronauts.**

---

* It's okay for a pronoun to refer to a word in a previous sentence. So before you declare a pronoun to be a mystery pronoun, check the previous sentence for any words that might be the antecedent.

† Mystery pronouns and vague pronouns actually occur more frequently on Rhetorical Skills questions than on Usage and Mechanics questions. But while you're taking the test, you have no idea what category a question belongs to. All you see is an underlined pronoun, so check that it has a definite antecedent.

TRY SOME: *In each of the following sentences, circle the appropriate pronoun form.*

- Cucumbers are generally considered to be vegetables, but **[its / their]** structure more closely fits the botanical definition of fruit.

- Despite our growing interest in the processes of the brain, there is still much that **[they / we]** don't understand about the way we think.

- The construction of the towers had to be delayed because the architect decided to alter the materials with which **[it / they]** would be built.

- The naked mole rat is unique among mammals in that, due to the lack of a chemical called "Substance P", **[it / they]** cannot feel pain.

- A well-written magazine article should be easily accessible for all readers, regardless of **[its / their]** knowledge of the subject.

2. Case

Pronouns also take different forms depending on what they do in the sentence. We call that the pronoun's **CASE**.

Subject and object

✓ **I love Derek Jeter.** ✓ **Derek Jeter loves me.**

In these two sentences, "I" and "me" refer to the same person, but in different roles. Therefore, we put the pronouns in different *cases*: we use "I" when the person is *the subject* (performing the action) and "me" when the person is the *object* (receiving the action). So when you see a pronoun underlined, ask yourself: is the person *performing* the action (subject) or *receiving* the action (object).

The object case is also used if the pronoun is the object of a preposition:

✓ ***I* am talking to him.** ✓ ***HE* is talking to me.**

If the pronoun is next to another person, it can be hard to tell whether the pronoun is in the right form:

- **The studio loved the screenplay Roger and him wrote.**

In cases like this, if you delete the other person, it's much easier to see whether the pronoun is correct.

× **The studio loved the screenplay ~~Roger and~~ him wrote.**

That sounds wrong. "Him" is the subject of the verb "wrote", so we need the subject pronoun, "he":

✓ **The studio loved the screenplay he wrote.**

Reflexive pronouns

As we saw, pronouns have different forms depending on whether they are the subject or object:

✓ **I love Derek Jeter.** ✓ **Derek Jeter loves me.**

But when the subject and object refer to the same person, the object pronoun needs the **reflexive** form:*

* Reflexive pronouns are also sometimes used for emphasis, as in "I *myself* have never been a gardener, but I hear it's quite relaxing." Or "Ulysses S. Grant *himself* couldn't grow a beard that big."

✓ *I* love myself. ✓ *Derek Jeter* loves himself.

✓ *You* love yourself. ✓ *The Yankees* love themselves.

These forms can be confusing since some of them are formed from the possessive pronoun (myself, yourself, ourselves) but others are formed from the object pronoun (himself, themselves). Don't mix them up: *hisself* and *theirselves* are not words.

Contractions and possessive pronouns

All nouns have **possessive** forms, usually formed by adding an **apostrophe** and an "s" to the end:

✓ ***Bob*** **has a *cat*. This is Bob's cat. The cat's name is Gretchen.**

We'll talk more about apostrophes and possessive forms in the Punctuation chapter.

But pronouns do not take *'s*. They have special possessive pronoun forms:

✓ ***Bob*** **has a *cat*. This is his cat. Her name is Gretchen.**

HOWEVER, pronouns *do* use apostrophes for **contractions**. Contractions are when two words are stuck together into a single word. An apostrophe takes the place of the missing letters.

✓ **I'm Swedish. = I am Swedish.** ✓ **We're Swedish. = We are Swedish.**

✓ **He's Swedish. = He is Swedish.** ✓ **She's Swedish. = She is Swedish.**

Several pronouns have possessive and contraction forms that sound the same, so it can be **very** confusing to tell them apart. Just remember this simple rule:

Pronouns use CONTRACTION apostrophes, but NOT POSSESSIVE apostrophes.

1. **It's vs. Its vs. Its'**

☛ *It's* means *it is*.	**It's a beautiful day!**	[= It is a beautiful day!]
☛ *Its* shows **possession**.	**The dog wagged its tail.**	[The tail belongs to the dog.]
☛ *Its'* is never correct.	**NEVER USE *ITS'* FOR ANY REASON.**	

2. **You're vs. Your**

☛ *You're* means *you are*.	**You're a jerk.**	[= You are a jerk.]
☛ *Your* shows **possession**.	**Your fly is open.**	[The fly belongs to you.]

3. **They're vs. Their vs. There**

☛ *They're* means *they are*.	**They're going to win.**	[= They are going to win.]
☛ *Their* shows **possession**.	**I like their uniforms.**	[The uniforms belong to them.]
☛ *There* shows **location**.	**Put it over there.**	[I'm telling you where to put it.]

"There" isn't a pronoun at all, but it sounds the same as the other two, so it's easy to confuse all three. You can remember that *there* is the direction word because it looks like other direction words, *here* and *where*.

If you're not sure whether to use an apostrophe, try **switching it with a different pronoun**:

☛ **The snake swallows it's prey whole.**

Not sure if that's right? What if it was a girl snake? Would we use an apostrophe? No, we'd say *her*.

✗ **The snake swallows she's prey whole.** ✓ **The snake swallows her prey whole.**

Since we *don't* use the apostrophe with *her*, we shouldn't use an apostrophe with *its*.

✗ **The snake swallows it's prey whole.** ✓ **The snake swallows its prey whole.**

Try this one:

☛ **Your going to the zoo today.**

If we change the sentence from *you* to *me*, we can easily see the pronoun should be *I'm*, not *my*.

× **<u>My</u> going to the zoo today.** ✓ **<u>I'm</u> going to the zoo today.**

Since we *do* use the apostrophe with *I'm*, we should also use an apostrophe with *you*.

× **<u>Your</u> going to the zoo today.** ✓ **<u>You're</u> going to the zoo today.**

TRY SOME: *In each of the following sentences, circle the appropriate pronoun form.*

- A pronoun must always agree in number with **[its / it's]** antecedent.

- **[You're / Your]** lucky that you weren't in school today: you missed a pop quiz in math class.

- Mr. and Mrs. Walsh are a little dim-witted, but **[their / they're]** children are actually quite bright.

- I hope Professor Rodchenko will give Sherwyn and **[I / me]** a good grade on our art project even though we turned it in late.

- Located above the 23rd parallel, the Florida Keys are technically in a subtropical zone, but **[their / there]** climate is nonetheless considered tropical.

3. Relative pronouns

The ACT frequently tests a special kind of pronoun called **relative pronouns**: words like *who*, *which,* or *that.* Relative pronouns act like regular pronouns in that they refer to nouns in the sentence, but they also can connect different clauses together.

Verb agreement

Relative pronouns **use the same form for singular and plural**. That means they don't have to agree with their antecedents like regular pronouns. But we do still care about their antecedents. Take a look at this:

- **Bob is talking to a man <u>who is</u> from Cincinnati.**

The subject of the verb "is" is the pronoun "who". Is that right? Do we say "who is" or "who are"?

It depends. When a relative pronoun is the subject of a verb, the **verb must agree with the antecedent** of the pronoun. In this sentence the antecedent of "who" is "the man", which is singular. "A *man* <u>is</u> from Cincinnati" sounds fine, so "a *man* <u>who is</u> from Cincinnati" is fine, too.

> The antecedent of a relative pronoun is usually the word directly before it.

If the antecedent is plural, we use a plural verb:

✓ **Bob is talking to some *PEOPLE* <u>who are</u> from Cincinnati.**

Who vs. *Whom*

Just like other pronouns, *who* has a special form when it's an object: *whom*.

✓ **I met a man <u>who</u> likes French people.** ✓ **I met a man <u>whom</u> French people like.**

In the first sentence, "who" is the *subject* of the verb likes: this man likes French people. But in the second sentence, "whom" is the *object* of "like" and "French people" is the subject: French people like this man.

> Relative pronouns do not have reflexive forms. There's no such word as *whoseself.*

This is exactly like the case issues we saw with other pronouns:

✓ **<u>He</u> likes French people.** ✓ **French people like <u>him</u>.**

Similarly, "whom" is used as the object of a preposition:

✓ **The judges will give a prize *TO* the best *SINGER*.**

✓ **Roger is the *SINGER TO* whom the judges gave the prize.**

Do you want to know a secret? On the ACT, ***WHOM* IS ALMOST NEVER RIGHT**. In our research into over 10 years' worth of past real tests, we found that when "whom" is given as an answer choice, it's wrong **over 95% of the time**. So if you're not sure whether "whom" is correct on an ACT question, chances are that it's probably not.*

Who's vs. *Whose*

Just like other pronouns, relative pronouns have confusingly similar possessive and contraction forms. And just like other pronouns, relative pronouns take apostrophes with *contractions*, but *not* with possessives:

- ***Who's*** means **who is** — **the man who's buying my car** [= the man who is buying my car]
- ***Whose*** shows **possession** — **the man whose car I'm buying** [= the car belongs to the man]

Who vs. *Which*

Besides "who", the other common relative pronoun is "which". The difference is that "who" can only refer to **people**, and "which" can only refer to **non-people**.

✓ **Audrey is the girl who ate all the cookies.** × **Audrey is the girl which ate all the cookies.**

✓ **Audrey ate the one which had chocolate chips.** × **Audrey ate the one who had chocolate chips.**

Note that "which" can be used as the subject or object. But it does not have any possessive form: **"whose" is the only possessive relative pronoun.**

That

"Which" is often interchangeable with ***that***:†

✓ **Audrey ate the one which had chocolate chips.** ✓ **Audrey ate the one that had chocolate chips.**

✓ **This is the cookie which Audrey ate.** ✓ **This is the cookie that Audrey ate.**

"That" can be used as a subject ("that had chocolate chips") or object ("that Audrey ate").‡ But "that" cannot be the object of a preposition. You must use "which" instead:

✓ **This exhibit contains the pen with which George Washington signed the Constitution.**

× **This exhibit contains the pen with that George Washington signed the Constitution.**

"That" is a confusing word because it has two other uses besides the relative pronoun.

First, it can be used as a "pointing" word, similar in meaning to "this" or the plural "those":

✓ **I want that car.** ✓ **I want this car.** ✓ **I want those cars.**

✓ **That guy is a jerk.** ✓ **This guy is a jerk.** ✓ **Those guys are jerks.**

Note that these words are *not* relative pronouns and *cannot* be used to link clauses together:

× **She ate the cookie this had chocolate chips.** × **She ate the cookies those had chocolate chips.**

---

* "Whom" is a bit of an odd word. In real life, people *often* say "who" in places where they're "supposed" to say "whom". Not just in lazy, slang-filled teenager speech—in political speeches, in college lectures, and in heavily edited books and newspapers. Many people still cling to "whom", and knowing how to use it properly is still a sign of a careful writer. But frankly, "whom" is dying out. This might be why it's so rarely correct on the ACT.

† In fact, some people will tell you "that" is *required* in these sentences because they're *restrictive* clauses. These people are wrong: "which" can be used in restrictive clauses. More on restrictive clauses in the Punctuation chapter.

‡ When used as an object, you can even omit the relative pronoun entirely: "This is the cookie Audrey ate."

Second, "that" can connect certain kinds of verbs with full clauses:

✓ **I said <u>that</u> I want the red car.** ✓ **I think <u>that</u> you are a jerk.**

TRY SOME: *In each of the following sentences, circle the appropriate pronoun form.*

- The factory employs over thirty workers **[who are / who is]** well trained in woodworking.

- The guy **[who's / whose]** renting my apartment for the summer is a visiting student from France.

- Yesterday I got a chance to meet the district's superintendent of schools, **[which / who]** was a very friendly and charming person.

- After living in a dump for three years, I'd be happy to find an apartment **[that's / whose]** walls are perpendicular to the floor.

- Once a bill is approved by both houses of Congress, it is passed along to the President, **[who / whom]** can veto it or sign it into law.

Pronoun Chart

Here's an outline of all the different pronoun forms we discussed in this section:

	SUBJECT	OBJECT	POSSESSIVE	CONTRACTION	REFLEXIVE
Singular	I	me	my	I'm (I am)	myself
	you	you	your	you're (you are)	yourself
	he	him	his	he's (he is)	himself
	she	her	her	she's (she is)	herself
	it	it	its	it's (it is)	itself
Plural	we	us	our	we're (we are)	ourselves
	you	you	your	you're (you are)	yourselves
	they	them	their	they're (they are)	themselves
Relative	who	whom	whose	who's (who is)*	---
	which	which	whose	---	---
	that	that/which	whose	that's (that is)	---

* We mentioned that relative pronouns can be singular or plural. When "who" and "that" are plural, they take the verb "are" instead of "is". But the contractions "who're" or "that're" are very rare and would never show up on the ACT. (Perhaps partly because, without its apostrophe, the former resembles an unfortunate word.)

PRONOUN SUMMARY

When a pronoun is underlined, check the following:

1. Agreement

- Pronouns and antecedents must agree in **number**, singular or plural.
- To find the **antecedent**, ask: Who or what does the pronoun **refer to**?
- Watch for **vague pronouns**, when the antecedent is unclear.
- Watch for **mystery pronouns**, when there is no antecedent.
- Be consistent with **generic pronouns**.
- Sometimes **nouns must agree** with each other, too.

2. Case

- Pronouns have different forms depending on their **role** in the sentence.
- **Subjects and objects** use different forms.
- Use **reflexive** pronouns when subject and object refer to the same thing.
- **Contractions** use apostrophes, **possessive** pronouns do not.

3. Relative pronouns

- Relative pronouns are words like *who*, *which*, or *that*.
- **Verbs** agree with the **antecedent** of the relative.
- Relatives have **cases** just like regular pronouns.
- **Who** is for people, **which** is for non-people.
- **That** is generally interchangeable with *which*.

Pronoun Drill

All the questions in this exercise deal with ***pronouns****. Unlike the real ACT, the sentences in this exercise do not make up a full passage—each question refers to a single stand-alone sentence.*

When you listen to the music of early rock bands, one [1] can hear the influence of the blues in their guitar melodies.

1. A. NO CHANGE
   B. you
   C. we
   D. they

Public safety groups are concerned about the injuries an airbag can cause from the force with which they are [2] deployed.

2. F. NO CHANGE
   G. they were
   H. those are
   J. it is

Many of the people who [3] went to our annual holiday party last year have decided not to go this year.

3. A. NO CHANGE
   B. whom
   C. whose
   D. which

Some paleontologists believe the *Tyrannosaurus* was a scavenger, eating animals that were already dead rather than hunting it's [4] own prey.

4. F. NO CHANGE
   G. its
   H. its'
   J. their

Although their [5] still experiencing financial difficulties, the investment firm has shown significant growth in the past year.

5. A. NO CHANGE
   B. there
   C. its
   D. it's

The proposed new contract provides higher wages for employees which have worked [6] at the company for over three years.

6. F. NO CHANGE
   G. whom has worked
   H. who has worked
   J. who have worked

Because of their [7] magnificent plumage and exotic origins, peacocks were often kept in European gardens to flaunt the wealth of the king.

7. A. NO CHANGE
   B. they're
   C. it's
   D. its

Lindsay got an extension on the report that her and her lab partner [8] should have finished by today.

8. F. NO CHANGE
   G. she and her lab partner
   H. her lab partner and herself
   J. her lab partner and her

An architect has designed a new skyscraper who's [9] top floors house giant wind turbines that generate much of the building's power.

9. A. NO CHANGE
   B. thats
   C. whose
   D. which

In the event of a fire drill, employees must immediately evacuate the building and should not return to his or her desk [10] until the alarm stops.

10. F. NO CHANGE
    G. their desks
    H. they're desks
    J. it's desk

Marie Curie performed many experiments on radioactive elements without realizing that one's exposure to it [11] was slowly killing her.

11. A. NO CHANGE
    B. her exposure to them
    C. a person exposed to them
    D. their exposure to it

Before my trip to Europe, I asked for travel advice from my friend Paul, whom [12] grew up in Austria and frequently flies internationally.

12. F. NO CHANGE
    G. whose
    H. who's
    J. who

When the movie first opened, critics loved its' [13] stunning and innovative visual effects, but they were turned off by its formulaic plot.

13. A. NO CHANGE
    B. their
    C. it's
    D. its

The field of vision produced by our eyes is actually curved, but we experience it [14] as being straight because our brains reinterpret the images.

14. F. NO CHANGE
    G. we experience them
    H. they experience it
    J. one experiences them

Its [15] difficult to predict exactly where hurricanes will hit, but forecasters can give the probabilities of various scenarios.

15. A. NO CHANGE
    B. They're
    C. It's
    D. Ones

III. Other Topics

Verbs and pronouns make up the bulk of the grammatical errors you'll see on the ACT. But of course, there are other parts of speech in English. Here are a few more rules that you may encounter on the test.

Adjectives and Adverbs

An adjective describes a noun. An adverb describes a verb, adjective, or other adverb.

> Adverbs usually look just like adjectives with "-ly" stuck on the end.

ADJECTIVE: This is an easy *TEST*. ("Easy" describes "test")

ADVERB: I easily *PASSED* the test. ("Easily" describes "passed")

It's easy to tell when this concept is being tested. Just scan the choices; if some choices contain adjectives and others contain adverbs, you know it's an issue. To figure out which one you want, ask yourself:

What is the word describing?

If it's describing a *noun*, it should be an **adjective.*** If it's describing *anything else*, it should be an **adverb**.

× **He died of a previous unknown disease.**

What is "previous" here? The disease? It's a previous disease? No, the disease was *previously* ***unknown***. "Unknown" is an adjective, not a noun, so we need an adverb to describe it:

✓ **He died of a previously *UNKNOWN* disease.**

Look at this one:

× **He had an extraordinarily method for preparing pork chops.**

What is extraordinarily supposed to describe here? It's not "preparing"—it's his ***method*** for preparing. "Method" is a noun, so we need an adjective to describe it:

✓ **He had an extraordinary *METHOD* for preparing pork chops.**

Comparatives and Superlatives

Adjectives can have different forms when they're used for comparisons. When you compare **two** people or things, use the **comparative**—either an "-er" word or the word "more".

> The word "than" is a sign that you need the comparative form.

✓ **Alaska is larger than Texas.**

✓ **Of the *TWO* candidates, Julio is more qualified for the position.**

When you compare **three or more** things, use the **superlative**—either an "-est" word or the word "most".

✓ **Alaska is the largest of the *FIFTY* states.**

✓ **Of the *THREE* candidates, Julio is the most qualified for the position.**

Don't mix up these forms. If a sentence uses a comparative or superlative form, check how many people or things it's talking about.

× **Alaska is the larger of the *FIFTY* states.**

× **Of the *TWO* candidates, Julio is the most qualified for the position.**

* Adjectives almost always describe nouns with one exception: adjectives can also act like the object of certain verbs like *is*, *feel*, or *seem*: "I am sad," "I feel happy," or "She seems nice." You wouldn't say: "I am sadly," "I feel happily," or "She seems nicely."

And don't mix up the different ways of forming them: use *either* "more/most" *or* "-er/-est", not both.*

× **Alaska is <u>more larger</u> than Texas.**

× **Alaska is <u>the most largest</u> of the fifty states.**

Adverbs can also be modified this way, but they can only take "more" and "most":

✓ **Bob *CHOPPED* wood <u>more quickly</u> than Dave did.**

✓ **Out of everyone in the class, Bob *CHOPPED* the wood <u>most quickly</u>.**

Prepositions

We've already mentioned prepositions in the discussion of Verb Agreement. They're small words that connect words with regard to direction, location, or some other relationship. We saw some examples of prepositional phrases that describe nouns:

✓ ***THE QUEEN* <u>of England</u> is rich.**

✓ ***THE DOGS* <u>in the yard</u> are barking.**

✓ ***THE MAN* <u>with three children</u> is married.**

✓ ***THE MOVIE* <u>about vampires</u> is scary.**

Prepositional phrases don't have to modify nouns. They can also refer to verbs:

✓ **I am *GOING* <u>to Kansas City</u>.**

✓ **I *LOOKED* <u>at the baby</u>.**

✓ **I am *TRAVELING* <u>with three children</u>.**

✓ **I was *BITTEN* <u>by a vampire</u>.**

While it's sometimes difficult to define a pronoun—how do you explain what "to" means?—it's usually clear from the context which preposition you should use:

✓ **Dave complained (<u>*TO* his mother</u>) (<u>*ABOUT* his sister</u>).**

This sentence has two prepositional phrases performing two jobs: "to my mother" tells us who Dave was talking to, and "about his sister" tells us the topic of the complaint. If we use the wrong prepositions, the sentence won't make any sense:

× **Dave complained (<u>*ON* his mother</u>) (<u>*BY* his sister</u>).**

> Here are some examples of prepositions:
>
> - To
> - Of
> - In
> - For
> - On
> - With
> - As
> - At
> - By
> - From

Sometimes a word can take multiple prepositions, but our choice of preposition changes the meaning of the sentence. Compare:

I have <u>heard</u> the song.	= I actually listened to the song.
I have <u>heard of</u> the song.	= I know that the song exists.
I have <u>heard about</u> the song.	= Someone talked to me about the song.

Other times, certain words will even *require* certain prepositions to follow them:

× **Dave is <u>listening at</u> the radio.**

✓ **Dave is <u>listening to</u> the radio.**

The prepositions "at" and "to" are very similar in meaning. But the word "listen" must be followed by the preposition "to". Why? That's just the way it is. We call this kind of rule an **idiomatic** rule: you can't figure out by knowing the meanings of the individual words—you just have to know the rule.

Sometimes, your choice of preposition will affect the verb that follows it. For example:

× **In times of danger, an ordinary person is *CAPABLE* <u>to perform</u> extraordinary acts.**

✓ **In times of danger, an ordinary person is *CAPABLE* <u>of performing</u> extraordinary acts.**

In this sentence, the word "capable" must be followed by the preposition "of" and the "-ing" form of the verb (the present participle); you *cannot* use the "to" form of the verb (the infinitive). The key to determining which verb form to use here has nothing to do with the word "perform"; it depends on the word that comes before it, "capable".

---

* Most adjectives require one form: either *more/most* or *-er/-est*. You usually can't mix and match. In general, shorter words take -er/-est (larger/largest) and longer words take more/most (more qualified/most qualified).

Of course, some words work the other way; they *have* to take the infinitive, *not* the participle:

× **An ordinary person is *ABLE* <u>of performing</u> extraordinary acts.**

✓ **An ordinary person is *ABLE* <u>to perform</u> extraordinary acts.**

This is an idiomatic rule: "capable" and "able" mean *exactly the same thing*, but one takes the "to" form and one takes the "-ing" form. Why? That's just the way it is.

Often you'll be able to "hear" idiomatic errors—a preposition will sound weird in a certain sentence. But they can sometimes be hard to spot. If you're not sure which preposition to use in a sentence, first eliminate any choices that make *other* errors that are easier to spot (verb tense, pronoun agreement, etc.) Then make sure you understand the intended meaning of the sentence. And if all else fails, *guess*.

Commonly Confused Words

English has a lot of words that sound very similar to each other but are spelled differently and mean different things. These words are easy to mix up, and the ACT frequently tests your knowledge of the differences between them.

Pronouns

We've already seen an example of spelling confusion: the difference between contraction and possessive pronoun forms. Here's a summary of the forms we discussed:

It's means ***it is.*** ***Its*** shows **possession.** ***Its'*** **is <u>never</u> correct.**	**<u>It's</u> a beautiful day!** **The dog wagged <u>its</u> tail.** **Never use its' for any reason.**	[= <u>It is</u> a beautiful day!] [= The tail <u>belongs to</u> the dog.]
You're means ***you are.*** ***Your*** shows **possession.**	**<u>You're</u> a jerk.** **<u>Your</u> fly is open.**	[= <u>You are</u> a jerk.] [= The fly <u>belongs to</u> you.]
They're means ***they are.*** ***Their*** shows **possession.** ***There*** shows **location.**	**<u>They're</u> going to win.** **I like <u>their</u> uniforms.** **Put it over <u>there</u>.**	[= <u>They are</u> going to win.] [= The uniforms <u>belong to</u> them.] [= I'm telling you <u>where</u> to put it.]
Who's means **who is.** ***Whose*** shows **possession.**	**the man <u>who's</u> buying my car** **the man <u>whose</u> car I'm buying**	[= the man <u>who is</u> buying my car] [= the car <u>belongs to</u> the man]

Would *have* vs. Would *of*

We've already seen some verb forms that use "have".

✓ **If you had asked me to the dance, I <u>would have gone</u> with you.**

Verb forms using "would have" can be contracted to "would've".

✓ **If you had asked me to the dance, I <u>would've gone</u> with you.**

The contraction *sounds* a lot like "would **of**". But don't be fooled: **"would of" is never correct.**

× **If you had asked me to the dance, I <u>would of gone</u> with you.**

The same is true for any other verbs that use "have".

✓ **I <u>might have gone</u> with you.** ✓ **I <u>could have gone</u> with you.** ✓ **I <u>will have gone</u> with you.**

× **I <u>might of gone</u> with you.** × **I <u>could of gone</u> with you.** × **I <u>will of gone</u> with you.**

It may not always be clear which tense or verb form you need in any given sentence. **But you should NEVER say "would of"**. There is no legitimate English sentence in which "would" is followed by "of".*

---

* Except for the sentence, "You should never say 'would of'".

Than* vs. *Then

Than is used for *comparisons*. Don't confuse it with **then**, which means "*next*" or "*following*".

✓ **I am better <u>than</u> you.** × **I am better <u>then</u> you.**

✓ **I went to the store, and <u>then</u> got a snack.** × **I went to the store and <u>than</u> got a snack.**

While "then" is a legitimate English word, **"then" is almost always wrong on ACT questions**. If both are given as choices, when in doubt, pick "than".

Other Commonly Confused Words

Here are a few examples of commonly confused words. None of these will show up very frequently on the ACT, but you may see one every once in a while.

To is a preposition used with infinitive verbs. **Too** means "more than necessary".	**I am <u>too</u> tired <u>to</u> go out.** **I tried <u>to</u> solve the problem, but it was <u>too</u> hard.**
Affect is a *verb* meaning "produce a change". **Effect** is a *noun* meaning "a change".	**The accident <u>affected</u> me deeply.** **I still feel those <u>effects</u> today.**
Accept means to receive. **Except** is a preposition meaning "but not".	**I will <u>accept</u> any currency…** **… <u>except</u> Canadian Dollars.**
Principal means "main or primary". **Principle** means "guiding rule".	**I am the <u>principal</u> officer in the company.** **I live by one <u>principle</u>: always be polite.**

GRAMMAR & USAGE SUMMARY

Here are the key rules to look out for on ACT Grammar questions

1. Verbs

- The verb must **agree** in number with the subject.
- The verb must be in the appropriate **tense**.
- **Irregular** verbs may have special forms.
- Don't confuse active and **passive** voice.

2. Pronouns

- A pronoun must **agree** in number with its antecedent.
- A pronoun's **case** is determined by its role in the sentence.
- Don't confuse **contractions** and **possessive** pronouns.
- **Relative** pronouns behave similarly to regular pronouns.

3. Other issues

- **Adjectives** describe nouns. **Adverbs** describe all other words.
- **Comparatives** compare two things, **superlatives** compare three or more.
- Make sure to use the correct **prepositions**.
- Your choice of preposition may affect the form of the **verb** that follows.
- Beware of **commonly confused words**:
    - Use "would **have**", not "would of".
    - Use "**than**" for comparisons, not "then".

GRAMMAR & USAGE EXERCISE

This exercise contains a full passage with 15 questions, just like an ACT passage. Unlike a real ACT passage, it only features ***Grammar & Usage*** *questions. Look out for all the rules discussed above.*

PASSAGE I

Bicycling the Copenhagen Way

Last summer, while my parents and I spent a few weeks in Copenhagen, I developed [1] a new fascination with bicycles. We noticed that bicycle culture there was far different from what we were used to in America. The number of bicycles on the city streets were [2] astounding. Almost every block in the center of town had a bike rack filled with them, sometimes overflowing onto the street. The city even had a free bicycle sharing program. You [3] could pick up a bike from an outpost in one part of the city and drop it off at our destination.

Americans don't use bicycles this way. Back home, people whom [4] cycle usually do so for recreation or fitness. People associate bikes with memories of Dad running alongside them the first time they had took off [5] their training wheels, or teenagers wild [6] riding mountain bikes down homemade ramps. Others think of triathlons or cardio machines at the gym. But places like Copenhagen engage in "utility cycling": locals use bikes simply as a way to get around town. About 500,000 residents of the city—over a third of its [7] population—commutes [8] by bicycle every day.

1. **A.** NO CHANGE
   B. develop
   C. am developing
   D. would of developed

2. **F.** NO CHANGE
   G. was
   H. is
   J. are

3. **A.** NO CHANGE
   B. People
   C. We
   D. One

4. **F.** NO CHANGE
   G. who
   H. whose
   J. which

5. **A.** NO CHANGE
   B. had took in
   C. took off
   D. take to

6. **F.** NO CHANGE
   G. wild and
   H. wilding
   J. wildly

7. **A.** NO CHANGE
   B. it's
   C. they're
   D. there

8. **F.** NO CHANGE
   G. commuted
   H. will commute
   J. commute

Utility cycling had[9] many advantages over commuting by car, both for individuals and for the community as a whole. Cycling is a more cleaner[10] form of transportation because it produces no emissions. Cycling is safer than driving, both for passengers and for pedestrians. It's[11] also more economical than driving—bicycles are cheap to own and only requires[12] the fuel you need to run your body. On top of all that, it's great exercise and promotes a healthy lifestyle.

If utility cycling is so great, why don't more Americans do it? One problem is that American cities are not well equipped for bike travel. Most American cities are dominated by suburban areas which[13] neighborhoods are far from each other, making commutes too long and often too dangerous for bike travel. European cities have smaller, interconnected streets that are more bicycle-friendly.

While utility cycling in the United States are[14] still far less common than in Europe, more and more people have started using[15] bicycles for transportation. Cities from New York to Seattle have launched initiatives to encourage utility cycling. They have even contemplated bike sharing programs like the one in Copenhagen. "All big cities should promote bicycle use," one transit official said. "Bicycles take cars off the road, which is a big win for everyone."

9. A. NO CHANGE
   B. has
   C. will have
   D. would have

10. F. NO CHANGE
    G. more cleanly
    H. cleanest
    J. cleaner

11. A. NO CHANGE
    B. Its
    C. Its'
    D. Their

12. F. NO CHANGE
    G. required
    H. were required by
    J. require

13. A. NO CHANGE
    B. whom
    C. whose
    D. who's

14. F. NO CHANGE
    G. were
    H. is
    J. was

15. Which of the following alternatives to the underlined portion would NOT be acceptable?
    A. begun to use
    B. started with using
    C. started to use
    D. begun using

USAGE/MECHANICS: SENTENCE STRUCTURE

Each ACT will contain 18 Sentence Structure questions, making it the largest of the six subcategories of ACT English questions. The Grammar & Usage rules we already saw dealt with the relationship between individual words, while Sentence Structure questions deal with the relationships between larger parts of a sentence—how to join clauses, where to place modifiers, etc.

That means that, while Grammar & Usage questions tend to have only one or two words underlined, Sentence Structure questions are more likely to have an entire phrase underlined. Since the rules we discuss in this chapter deal with larger parts of a sentence, it's important to remember to **read the entire sentence**, not just the underlined portion, before picking an answer choice.

Still, there's a lot of overlap between these categories, and the rules discussed in this chapter are still "rules of grammar and usage". On the real test, you may see a question that has a Fragment in one choice and a Verb Agreement error in another. *Everything is important, and everything is connected.*

I. WHAT'S A CLAUSE?

We'll start by defining a few basic parts of a sentence. Several of the common errors on Sentence Structure questions deal with the same concepts, so everything will be clearer if we lay some groundwork first.

Sentences are made up of **clauses**. A clause is any phrase that contains a subject and a verb. There are two main types of clauses that we're concerned with here.

Independent clauses

An **independent clause** is a clause that can stand alone as a complete sentence:

✓ **Chapman is a doctor.**

The subject is "Chapman" and the verb is "is". It's "independent" because it doesn't *need* anything else; it sounds fine as it is. However, we could add another clause if we wanted:

✓ **Chapman is a doctor, and he cured my acne.**

This sentence has two independent clauses, linked together with the word "and". We happened to put them together in the same sentence, but either of the underlined phrases would sound fine all by itself, with or without the "and".

✓ **Chapman is a doctor.**	✓ **He cured my acne.**
✓ **Chapman is a doctor.**	✓ **And he cured my acne.***

Dependent clauses

A **dependent clause** is a clause that *cannot* stand alone as a complete sentence.

✓ **After he cured my acne, I felt much better.**

✓ **When I go out, I am no longer embarrassed by my skin.**

Each of these sentences contains one dependent clause followed by an independent clause. In each case, the dependent clause cannot stand by itself as a sentence. They *describe* the main clauses, *dependent* on them.*

---

* Some people may have told you it's wrong to start a sentence with "and" or "but". That is a lie. When teachers tell you not to do this, they really mean that you shouldn't do it *a lot* because it makes you sound like a five year old ("I went to the zoo. And then I went to the park. And then I went to lunch. And then I got a sandwich.") But don't worry about this rule—it won't be tested on the ACT.

× **After he cured my acne.** ✓ **I felt much better.**

× **When I go out.** ✓ **I am no longer embarrassed by my skin.**

The second clauses here sound fine as sentences, but the first ones do not. "After he cured my acne" is not a complete sentence: what happened after he cured my acne? It *depends* on the main clause to tell us what it's talking about.

Relative clauses

Relative clauses are special kinds of dependent clauses that use **relative pronouns**. We talked about relative pronouns in the Grammar & Usage chapter, remember?[†] They're words that can connect clauses, but they're also pronouns that have specific antecedents.

✓ **Chapman is the doctor <u>who cured my acne</u>.**

In this sentence, "who cured my acne" is a relative clause: its subject is "who" and its verb is "cured". "Who" is a relative pronoun whose antecedent is "the doctor", so the whole clause "who cured my acne" describes "the doctor". The antecedent of a relative pronoun is almost always the word directly before it.

> Relative clauses begin with relative pronouns– words like ***who, which,*** or ***that.***

Relative clauses are different from other dependent clauses because *they are directly connected to a word in the main clause*. In the earlier example, the dependent clause "after he cured my acne" didn't refer to any one word in the main clause—it referred to the whole situation. But here, the clause is specifically linked to "the doctor."

But the relative clause is still dependent because "who cured my acne" cannot stand alone as a sentence.[‡]

✓ **Chapman is the doctor.** × **Who cured my acne.**

It's not a complete thought; it's a description of someone. Thus it *depends* on the independent clause "Chapman is a doctor" to tell us what it's talking about.

Here are some more examples of dependent and independent clauses. The first three sentences contain relative clauses, the last two do not. In each of these examples, the independent clause would sound fine as a sentence all by itself, but the dependent clause would not—it needs the independent clause to tell us what it's talking about.

SENTENCE	INDEPENDENT CLAUSE	DEPENDENT CLAUSE
I want to meet a woman <u>who loves fishing</u>.	I want to meet a woman	who loves fishing
Harold got a new bike, <u>which he really liked</u>.	Harold got a new bike	which he really liked
The team <u>that scores the most points</u> will win.	The team will win	that scores the most points
You have been a real jerk <u>since you got your promotion</u>.	You have been a real jerk	since you got your promotion
<u>Once you finish your broccoli</u> you can have dessert.	you can have dessert	Once you finish your broccoli

---

[*] Dependent clauses are also called *subordinate* clauses. "Subordinate" means *submissive, subservient,* or *less important*. These clauses are *servants* to the main clauses.

[†] Do you remember? Do you?

[‡] Unless it's a question: "Who cured my acne?" But that's a whole different issue. Don't worry about questions.

Modifiers

Both clause types we've seen have a subject and verb. But what about phrases that don't have a subject and verb? Take a look at this:

✓ **<u>Hoping to cure my acne</u>, Chapman gave me a special herb.**

This sentence contains an independent clause, "Chapman gave me a special herb," and a separate opening phrase, "Hoping to cure my acne." The opening phrase is clearly not an independent clause, since it clearly can't stand by itself as a sentence. But it's not a dependent clause either, since it doesn't have a subject-verb pair. Nor does it have any kind of connecting word to link it to the main clause.

We'll call this kind of phrase a **modifier**, because it modifies the main clause. "Modifies" is just a fancy word for "describes". So any bunch of words that isn't a clause we'll call a modifier. There are lots of different types of modifiers. Often, they start with a verb without a subject:*

✓ **<u>Hoping to cure my acne</u>, Chapman gave me a special herb.**

✓ **<u>Known only to a few specialists</u>, this herb grows naturally in Asia.**

✓ **<u>To obtain it</u>, you need to know the right people.**

Or they could just be long noun phrases without a verb:

✓ **<u>A brilliant doctor</u>, Chapman cured my acne.**

And they don't have to come at the beginning of a sentence:

✓ **Chapman gave me a special herb, <u>hoping to cure my acne</u>.**

✓ **Chapman, <u>hoping to cure my acne</u>, gave me a special herb.**

So there are three things of interest to us: independent clauses, dependent clauses, and modifiers.

---

* Notice that the verbs here—"hoping", "known", and "to perform"—are the present participle, past participle, and infinitive forms (the last three rows of the verb chart at the beginning of the Grammar & Usage chapter). These forms (called "non-finite verbs" by fancy people) cannot be the main verb of an independent clause, but they can occur in modifiers like this.

II. FRAGMENTS

As we mentioned earlier when we were talking about verb agreement, every sentence must have a **subject** and a **verb**. If it *doesn't*, it's not a sentence—it's a **sentence fragment**. That is:

Every sentence must have at least one independent clause.

Back in the Grammar & Usage chapter, we talked about the idea of a *core sentence*—the main subject and verb of a sentence stripped of all the extra descriptive stuff. We found the core sentence by deleting prepositional phrases and phrases set off by commas.*

We can do exactly the same thing to find an independent clause. Sentences can often have very complicated structures, jumbles of commas and modifiers and clauses. But no matter how long and complicated a sentence is, if you can't find a core sentence with a subject and a verb buried in there, it's a fragment.

FRAGMENTS ARE THE MOST COMMON ERROR ON THE ACT ENGLISH.

<u>**Fragments are the most common error on the ACT English test**</u>, so it's important to learn how to spot them. Luckily, fragment questions usually fall into the same patterns.

There are three main ways to fix a fragment:

1. Change the verb

Here's an example of a fragment:

× **Riding the bus.**

See that? That's not a sentence. First of all, it has no subject. Who's riding the bus? We don't know. Okay, so let's **add a subject**:

× **<u>Bob</u> riding the bus.**

Hmm. That's better, but it's still not a sentence. It sounds like something a caveman would say. This is a fragment because it has **no main verb**. That's bad.

Wait, isn't "riding" a verb? Yes, but it's only **part of a verb**. A word like "riding" is a *participle* and *cannot stand by itself as a main verb*. It can be in a modifier, and it can be part of a multi-word verb phrase (like "is riding"). But it can't be the main verb by itself in an independent clause.

We can fix it by changing the verb to a form that can be a main verb:

✓ **Bob <u>is riding</u> the bus.** ✓ **Bob <u>rides</u> the bus.**

Much better.

2. Remove a connector

Take a look at this sentence:

Dr. Steve, who studies cell biology and is trying to develop new cancer drugs.

Hmmm. It *kinda* sounds like a sentence. We have a subject, "Dr. Steve". And we actually have two verbs: "studies" and "is trying". So what's wrong here?

The problem is that the verbs are stuck behind "who". *Everything* after the comma is a *dependent clause*:

who studies cell biology and is trying to develop new cancer drugs.

See that? It can't stand alone as a sentence. That means it's a dependent clause (more specifically, a relative clause). **Dependent clauses and modifiers are not part of the core sentence**. So let's ignore it and see what we're left with.

* We talked about this in the Grammar & Usage chapter. Don't you remember? Of course you don't. Look it up.

× **Dr. Steve, ~~who studies cell biology and is trying to develop new cancer drugs~~.**

"Dr. Steve" is definitely not a sentence. This is a fragment.

The problem is that the word "who" *starts* a relative clause, but there's nothing to *stop* it until the end of the sentence. "Who" is the subject of both verbs, so there's no verb to go with "Dr. Steve".

There are two ways we could fix it. First, we could *delete the relative pronoun*:

✓ **Dr. <u>Steve studies</u> cell biology and is trying to develop new cancer drugs.**

Now, there's no dependent clause at all. We just have one subject with two verbs: *Dr. Steve <u>studies</u>... and <u>is trying</u>*. That's an independent clause.

Second, we could *end the relative clause* with a comma and *remove the conjunction* "and":

✓ **Dr. Steve, who studies cell <u>biology, is</u> trying to develop new cancer drugs.**

Now the relative clause is just "who studies cell biology". If we ignore that clause, we're left with an independent clause:

✓ **Dr. Steve, ~~who studies cell biology~~, *IS TRYING* to develop new cancer drugs.**

Our main clause is *Dr. Steve... is trying*. That's a complete sentence. Excellent.

3. Join another sentence

Of course, the easiest way to fix a fragment is to link it to the sentence next door:

× **While riding the bus. My father lost his wallet.**

The second sentence is fine, but the first one is a fragment. It's just a modifier; it can't stand by itself. But it *can* be linked to the second sentence:

✓ **While riding the bus, my father lost his wallet.**

In the above example, we replaced the period with a comma. But sometimes we might not need a comma to connect them:

× **Dave got a tutor. To help him with his math homework.**

✓ **Dave got a tutor to help him with his math homework.**

We'll talk more about how to use commas in the Punctuation chapter.

Fragment Drill

Take a look at these examples and see if they are complete sentences or sentence fragments. If it is a complete sentence, ***circle the subject and verb*** *of each independent clause. If it is a fragment, write a corrected sentence below it. If there are two sentences, make sure* ***BOTH*** *are complete and circle the subject and verb of each of them.*

1. I am going to the library to study, and I will come back at six.

2. Sacramento, which is the capital of California but is only its seventh largest city.

3. The motorcycle, weaving from lane to lane and quickly darting between cars, was being followed by a pack of police cruisers.

4. Produced thirty years after the original film. The sequel was made with sophisticated computer technology that has only recently been developed.

5. Moe Berg, who held degrees from two Ivy League schools, an education that was, to say the least, unusual for a baseball player of his era.

6. The double agent running up and down the labyrinthine hallways of the National Security Agency, keeping a tight grip on the flash memory card that held the schematics of the doomsday machine.

7. Because Gary was worried about losing everything he owns. He decided that getting fire insurance would best protect his assets.

8. Thomas Paine was an outspoken supporter of American Independence. His pamphlet, *Common Sense,* was a harsh denouncement of British rule over the colonies.

9. Eddy Merckx, who is perhaps the greatest cyclist of all time and is one of the most famous people in Belgium.

10. Plato and Aristotle are still the most widely read ancient Greek philosophers on college campuses today. Despite the recent surge in interest in earlier thinkers such as Heraclitus and Empedocles.

11. The nineteenth-century French writer Gustave Flaubert spending almost six years writing the novel *Madame Bovary* because of his meticulous method of composition.

12. Every year, countries around the globe sponsor ultra-marathons, races that can last over 24 hours and stretch across a track 60 miles or longer—more than twice as long as a traditional marathon.

13. Having already revolutionized the scientific world with his theory of relativity, Albert Einstein spent the remainder of his life searching for a unified field theory. Which he ultimately was unable to discover.

14. The founder of Lego, Ole Kirk Christiansen, first making toys in the early 1930s. It was not until 1949, however, that he started producing the famous plastic bricks that bear the name today.

15. Upset by the barrage of news stories about recent scandals at Harvard, Mr. Bennett, who has been one of the most generous donors to the University since he graduated from its undergraduate engineering school in 1982, began to have doubts about the amount of his annual donation.

III. RUN-ON SENTENCES

We said that every sentence must have *at least one* independent clause. But what if we have two independent clauses in the same sentence? Take a look at these sentences:

✓ ***I AM GOING* to the game. *SCOTT WILL MEET* me there.**

These two sentences are fine; each is an independent clause with a subject and verb. However, there are rules about how you can combine them into *one* sentence. If you don't follow the rules, you get a **run-on sentence**.

First, you can't just shove one clause next to the other **without any connection at all**. This is sometimes called a *fused sentence*:

× ***I AM GOING* to the game *SCOTT WILL MEET* me there.**

Second, you cannot combine independent clauses **with a comma alone**. This is sometimes called a *comma splice* or *comma fault*.

× ***I AM GOING* to the game, *SCOTT WILL MEET* me there.**

The key to spotting run-on sentences is to ***look for subject-verb pairs***. As we saw with Fragments, the subject-verb pair makes up the core of an independent clause. If you see two subject-verb pairs with no connection between them, or with only a comma between them, then it's a run-on.*

There are three main ways to fix a run-on:

1. Use a period

Since independent clauses, by definition, can stand alone as sentences, the easiest way to fix a run-on is to simply make two separate sentences:

✓ ***I AM GOING* to the game. *SCOTT WILL MEET* me there.**

Nice. Just make sure that both your clauses are independent clauses before you separate them with a period.

> Run-on sentences on the ACT are corrected by using a period more frequently than by any of the other methods below.

Other punctuation

Some punctuation marks can directly connect independent clauses without making separate sentences.†

Dash	✓	**I am going to the game—Scott will meet me there.**
Colon	✓	**I am going to the game: Scott will meet me there.**
Semicolon	✓	**I am going to the game; Scott will meet me there.**

However, unlike a colon or a dash, *a **semicolon** must separate independent clauses.*

✓ **I am going to one game this year—the Super Bowl.**

✓ **I am going to one game this year: the Super Bowl.**

× **I am going to one game this year; the Super Bowl.**

---

* There is one case in which you can join subject-verb pairs directly. A relative pronoun is often optional: instead of "Dave watched the movie that I made" you can say "Dave watched the movie I made." Here we have two subject-verb pairs with nothing connecting them, but it's implied that the second pair "I made" directly modifies "the movie". You may see sentences like this on the ACT, but they're usually pretty easy to distinguish from fused sentences.

† The different punctuation marks do create slightly different meanings in these sentences, but don't worry about that right now. We'll talk more about these marks in the Punctuation chapter.

"The Super Bowl" is not an independent clause (it has no verb), so we *cannot* connect it to the main clause with a semicolon. But we can use a dash or a colon (or even a comma).

2. Add a conjunction

You could also use a **comma with a conjunction.***

✓ ***I AM GOING* to the game, <u>and</u> *SCOTT WILL MEET* me there.**

Conjunctions are words like "and", "but", or "or" that can be used to directly join independent clauses.† We saw this construction earlier when we were talking about independent clauses, remember?

✓ ***CHAPMAN IS* a doctor, <u>and</u> *HE CURED* my acne.**

Conjunctions usually come between clauses, but they don't have to:

✓ ***CHOCOLATE IS* my favorite, <u>but</u> *I'M GOING* to get vanilla.**

✓ **<u>Although</u> *CHOCOLATE IS* my favorite, *I'M GOING* to get vanilla.**

> Here are some examples of conjunctions:
>
> - and
> - but
> - or
> - although
> - because
> - while

The second clause means (roughly) the same thing as the first, but it puts its conjunction at the beginning of the sentence instead of between the clauses. That's totally fine.

Remember to use only *one* conjunction at a time:

× **<u>Although</u> *CHOCOLATE IS* my favorite, <u>but</u> *I'M GOING* to get vanilla.**

Furthermore, each conjunction can *only* link two clauses. What if the sentence has more than two clauses?

× ***I WILL ARRIVE* at the game at three o'clock, although *SCOTT WILL MEET* me there, *HE WON'T ARRIVE* until four.**

We've got three clauses here, but only one conjunction: "although". The conjunction can connect the first and the second, or it can connect the second and the third, but it can't do both. Either way, there is one clause that isn't properly connected. This is a run-on.

Sentences this long are usually best corrected by splitting them up with a period:

✓ ***I WILL ARRIVE* at the game at three o'clock. Although *SCOTT WILL MEET* me there, *HE WON'T ARRIVE* until four.**

3. Change one clause

The run-on rule deals with the connection between *two or more* independent clauses. Therefore, we could fix a run-on by **getting rid of one of the independent clauses**.

× **I WENT to a game at Wrigley Field, IT IS one of the oldest stadiums in America.**

This is a run-on because it has two independent clauses linked with a comma alone. We could fix it with a semicolon or a conjunction. But instead, let's change the second clause so it's no longer independent:

---

* Can I use a conjunction *without* a comma? Well, sometimes. It's usually not against the rules (especially if the clauses are short). But on the ACT, a choice like that is usually wrong (albeit for other reasons). If you see independent clauses joined with a conjunction and no comma, there's probably a better choice somewhere else.

† There are actually two different kinds of conjunctions. Words like "and", "but", and "or" are *coordinating* conjunctions, while "although", "because", or "while" are *subordinating* conjunctions. You can use either kind to join independent clauses. But technically, if you put a subordinating conjunction before a clause, it becomes a dependent clause. Either one will fix the run-on problem, so it doesn't matter.

✓ **I went to a game at Wrigley Field, <u>one of the oldest stadiums in America</u>.**

✓ **I went to a game at Wrigley Field, <u>which is one of the oldest stadiums in America</u>.**

In the first sentence, the second half is a modifier describing "Wrigley Field". In the second, it's a relative clause. In both cases, we avoid the run-on because there simply aren't two independent clauses anymore.

> Relative clauses behave a lot like modifiers: a relative clause must describe the noun that comes before it.

You can even sometimes combine the two clauses into a *single* clause with two verbs:

× ***DR. STEVE HAS BEEN DEVELOPING*** **new cancer <u>drugs, *HE HAS MADE*</u> a breakthrough.**

This is a run-on. It has two subject-verb pairs, "Dr. Steve *has been trying*" and "he *has made*", with only a comma between them. But the subject of the second clause, "he", is the same person as the subject of the first clause, "Dr. Steve". So let's combine them into one clause with two verbs:

✓ **Dr. Steve *HAS BEEN DEVELOPING* new cancer <u>drugs and *HAS MADE*</u> a breakthrough.**

RUN-ON DRILL

All the questions in this exercise deal with ***run-on sentences****. Unlike the real ACT, the sentences in this exercise do not make up a full passage—each question refers to a single stand-alone sentence.*

I tried to go to the <u>library, it was</u>[1] closed.

1. A. NO CHANGE
   B. library it was
   C. library, but it was
   D. library but was

Travis is very excited about the science fair next <u>week; hoping</u>[2] that his experiment about crickets will win the top prize.

2. F. NO CHANGE
   G. week, hoping
   H. week, he hopes
   J. week. Hoping

The board of directors will name a wing of the hospital after Dr. <u>Robinson, since it</u>[3] was his donation that made the new construction possible.

3. Which of the following alternatives to the underlined portion would NOT be acceptable?
   A. Robinson. It
   B. Robinson; it
   C. Robinson, it
   D. Robinson—it

Professor Fullington teaches the introductory course on <u>thermodynamics, it is</u>[4] one of the hardest classes in the department.

4. F. NO CHANGE
   G. thermodynamics it is
   H. thermodynamics. Which is
   J. thermodynamics,

While hiking on a mountain trail through the state park, Frank noticed a strange type of large, blue flower he had never seen anything like it [5] before.

5. A. NO CHANGE
   B. flower. Never having seen anything like it
   C. flower, they were unlike anything he had seen
   D. flower that was unlike anything he had seen

Although the bicycle was not the color she wanted, Lauren bought it anyway it was [6] the last one in stock, and the next shipment wouldn't arrive for six months.

6. F. NO CHANGE
   G. anyway. It was
   H. anyway, it was
   J. anyway. Because it was

In the fifteenth century, Johannes Gutenberg invented the mechanical printing press, a device that [7] would vastly change the course of history.

7. A. NO CHANGE
   B. press, it was a device that
   C. press, this device
   D. press, it

The football team and the soccer team both want to use the main field this Saturday the [8] director of athletics can't decide what to do about it.

8. F. NO CHANGE
   G. Saturday, the
   H. Saturday, and the
   J. Saturday, it is a problem that the

Karl has been the leading advocate for animal cruelty cases in the district; he [9] has helped rescue hundreds of abused animals.

9. Which of the following alternatives to the underlined portion would NOT be acceptable?
   A. district, and he
   B. district and
   C. district he
   D. district. He

Douglas hates using his debit card, believing that someone could easily steal it and gain access to his account, he prefers [10] using cash whenever he can.

10. F. NO CHANGE
    G. account. He prefers
    H. account he prefers
    J. account. Preferring

Harold returns from the store, then [11] we can begin to prepare all the food for the dinner party.

11. A. NO CHANGE
    B. When Harold returns from the store,
    C. As soon as Harold returns from the store;
    D. Harold returns from the store then

New research has confirmed that the medication is effective, according to the scientists who conducted the study, proper dosages of the serum can both relieve symptoms and treat the underlying cause of the disease.

12. F. NO CHANGE
G. effective according,
H. effective according
J. effective. According

All the woodworking skills that Brian has today were gained in his childhood his father was a carpenter and taught him everything he knows.

13. A. NO CHANGE
B. childhood, his
C. childhood, which his
D. childhood: his

The state government is horrendously over budget; this is a problem that will only get worse over the next four years.

14. Which of the following alternatives to the underlined portion would NOT be acceptable?
F. budget, this problem
G. budget; this problem
H. budget, a problem that
J. budget, which is a problem that

The new director of marketing, who previously ran a major advertising campaign for one of our competitors, had some radical ideas about how to promote our main product line, as a result, our sales in the first year of implementation almost doubled.

15. A. NO CHANGE
B. line. As a result,
C. line, as a result
D. line, the result was that

IV. MODIFIERS

Dangling Modifiers

Remember: modifiers are phrases that aren't clauses, but describe something else in the sentence. When a sentence *begins* with a modifier, the thing that phrase describes must come *immediately after the comma*, as the *subject* of the main clause. Otherwise, it's a *dangling modifier*. Observe:

× **Sitting close to the field, *A FOUL BALL* hit Bob.**

Who is sitting close to the field? *Bob*. The opening phrase is supposed to describe "Bob". But here, "a foul ball" comes after the comma. We call this a **dangling modifier**. That's bad. We need "Bob" to be the subject of the main clause:

✓ **Sitting close to the field, *BOB* was hit by a foul ball.**

Finding a dangling modifier error is essentially the same process as checking pronoun agreement. The opening phrase refers to something, so we'll figure out what it refers to and put it after the comma. Ask yourself:

Who or what does the modifier refer to?

× **An excellent salesman, MS. LEVINSON gave Roger a raise.**

Who is an excellent salesman? *Roger* is—that's why he got the raise. This sentence makes it sound like *Ms. Levinson* is the salesman. That's a dangling modifier. Here, we can't re-write the main clause because it isn't underlined, so we have to change the modifier. If we make the first part a *clause*, then there won't be any modifiers at all, thus there'll be no danger of a dangling modifier:

✓ **Because he is an excellent salesman, Ms. Levinson gave Roger a raise.**

¡Perfecto!

Modifiers at the end of a sentence

Modifiers that open a sentence describe the subject of the sentence, which is usually the noun right next to it. But if a modifier comes at the *end* of a sentence, the noun right next to it isn't the subject. What should we do?

Sometimes, an ending modifier will describe the word right before it:

× **A cake was made by *THE CHEF* covered in chocolate.**

This sentence suggests that the chef was covered with chocolate. That's probably not what we meant to say.* Let's rewrite the main clause to fix it:

✓ **The chef made *A CAKE* covered in chocolate.**

But other times, modifiers describe the **subject** of the main clause. This is true when the modifier is separated by *a comma*:

✓ ***CHAPMAN* sat in the park, eating an apple.**

Here, it's clear that it was Chapman who was eating the apple, not the park. There's none of the weird confusion that the chocolate sentence had. If the modifier is separated by a *comma*, it still describes the **subject** of the sentence, not the word next to it. It's just like adding a second verb to the subject:

✓ ***CHAPMAN SAT* in the park and *ATE* an apple.**

---

* To say nothing of the fact that this clause is *passive* and sounds awkward. The active version is more direct and concise. Remember when we talked about active and passive verbs? All this stuff is connected!

If you don't use a comma, a modifier can describe the word directly before it:*

✓ **Chapman walked through *A CLOUD OF STEAM* spewing from the subway grate.**

Here, it's clear that the cloud of steam was spewing from the grate, not Chapman. This is just like using a relative clause. Remember: *relative clauses always describe the words right before them.*

✓ **Chapman walked through a cloud of steam *THAT WAS* spewing from the subway grate.**

And as we saw before, modifiers don't need verbs at all; they can be simple noun phrases, too. **Noun phrases are always separated with a comma**, and they must always be right next to the words they describe, no matter where that noun is in the main clause:

✓ **A brilliant doctor, Chapman cured my acne.**

✓ **My acne was cured by Chapman, a brilliant doctor.**

Prepositional phrase placement

Modifier questions are all about making sure a phrase is in the right place so it describes the right word. But that's also true of *prepositional phrases.*

> Unlike modifier questions, questions about prepositional phrase placement often *explicitly* ask, "where should this be placed?"

We mentioned prepositional phrases several times in the Grammar & Usage chapter. Remember that prepositional phrases are made up of a preposition and its object. Prepositional phrases act very much the same way as modifiers in that they describe other words in a sentence.

Prepositional phrases often have very strong connections with words they describe. You must be careful to put the prepositional phrase **directly after** the word it's supposed to describe:

✓ ***THE BOY* in short pants likes dogs.** × **The boy likes *DOGS* in short pants.**

In the first sentence, the prepositional phrase "in short pants" describes the boy. In the second sentence, it describes the dogs.†

Some prepositional phrases have stronger connections than others. Take a look at this sentence:

✓ **The Queen of England drinks tea in the afternoon.**

There are two prepositional phrases in this sentence, "of England" and "in the afternoon". The phrase "of England" directly describes "the Queen", so it must be placed directly after "the Queen". But the phrase "in the afternoon" doesn't have that strong a connection to any particular word in the sentence. So we can move it around if we want:‡

✓ **In the afternoon, the Queen of England drinks tea.**

✓ **The Queen of England in the afternoon drinks tea.**

But we can't put it between "the Queen" and "of England":

× ***THE QUEEN* in the afternoon *OF ENGLAND* drinks tea.**

Now it sounds like "of England" describes "afternoon". Notice that the reason this is wrong has nothing to do with the underlined phrase itself—it's just that we can't separate "the Queen" from "of England" with *any* phrase.

So how can you tell whether a prepositional phrase is allowed to move around? Ask yourself:

---

* This is an oversimplification: in real life modifiers are quite a bit more complicated. But this rule generally holds for sentence-final modifiers *on ACT questions*, which is all we're concerned with right now.

† To be fair, the second sentence isn't wrong, per se. Who *doesn't* like dogs that wear short pants?

‡ Not all of these options are equally good. Putting the prepositional phrase in the middle sounds a bit weird in this case. The point is that there are places where it *can* go and places where it *can never* go.

Does the prepositional phrase* directly *describe a word in the sentence?

If it does, put it directly after that word. If it doesn't, you can put it almost anywhere as long as you don't split up other prepositional phrases that have strong connections.

V. Parallelism

Parallelism applies to several different concepts, but the overall point is *matching*. When you have two or more elements in a sentence that are similar to each other in some way, their forms must match.

It's easy to see this when you have a **list** of three items.

✓ **I like jogging, fishing, and hiking.**

✓ **I like to jog, to fish, and to hike.***

× **I like *JOGGING*, *FISHING*, and <u>to hike</u>.**

Either the "to" form or the "-ing" form can be okay here. What's not okay is mixing them up: if we start a list using one form, we must *repeat* that form for every element of the list.

> The key word for parallelism is the word "**AND**". Any words joined by "and" should be in parallel forms.

Similarly, don't repeat the subject if you don't have to:

× **Fred Astaire could *SING*, *DANCE*, and <u>he could act</u>.**

✓ **Fred Astaire could *SING*, *DANCE*, and <u>act</u>.**

We started with simple verbs, so we should end it with simple verbs. We don't have to repeat the subject.

When we make a list, we use commas alone between all the first terms and the word "and" between the last two. So as soon as we see those two verbs connected with a comma alone ("...sing, dance...") we know that we're starting a list.

This doesn't apply just to verbs, but to any type of list:

× **This book is about *PATIENCE*, *HARD WORK*, and <u>how to be a leader</u>.**

✓ **This book is about *PATIENCE*, *HARD WORK*, and <u>leadership</u>.**

Here, we started a list of nouns, "... patience, hard work, ..." so we should end it with another noun, "leadership".

Why do we have to do this? Because when things aren't parallel, they sound nasty. Parallelism makes your sentences beautiful and catchy. I mean, which of these sounds better?

× **A government *OF THE PEOPLE*, *BY THE PEOPLE*, and <u>it is meant for those people, too...</u>**

✓ **A government *OF THE PEOPLE*, *BY THE PEOPLE*, and <u>for the people...</u>**

See? We didn't make this up. Parallelism has been around for a while.

But besides just sounding pretty, parallelism falls under the larger concept of **coordination**. Coordination is a fancy word for joining words or phrases using a conjunction like *and*, *or*, or *but*.† Of those three, "and" is by far the most common one on the ACT.

Any words or phrases joined with the word "and" must be in parallel forms.

---

* We repeated the "to" here to make the parallelism more obvious, but when all items of a list take the same preposition, you don't have to repeat it. We could also say "I like to jog, fish, and hike."

† The key to coordination is that the elements being coordinated are *of the same importance*. That's obvious in a list of three things—there's nothing to indicate whether any one of" jogging, fishing, and hiking" is any more important than the other two. This is different from *subordination*. When one clause is subordinate, it is less important than the main clause. This is the difference between using "but" and using "although".

This doesn't just apply to lists of three terms. If a sentence has *two* elements linked with "and" they must be in parallel forms:

- ✓ **I have <u>cleaned the windows</u> *AND* <u>scrubbed the tiles</u>.**
- ✓ **I take this woman to be my wife <u>in sickness</u> *AND* <u>in health</u>.**
- ✓ **I use <u>my debit card</u> <u>for personal expenses</u> *AND* <u>my credit card</u> <u>for business expenses</u>.**
- ✓ **I think <u>that you're wrong</u> *AND* <u>that you're acting like a jerk</u>.**

Of course, the converse is also true: if you *don't* have parallel forms, don't use "and":

- ✗ **Chapman *SAT* in the park, <u>and</u> *EATING* an apple.**

Here, the word "and" connects "*sat* in the park" with "*eating* an apple". That's no good, because "sat" is not the same form as "eating". We could fix it by matching the verb forms (*sat... and ate*), but in this question the verbs aren't underlined, so we can't change them. So instead, we have to change the connection. We can just omit the underlined portion entirely, making "eating an apple" a modifier:

- ✓ **Chapman sat in the park, eating an apple.**

Much better.

SENTENCE STRUCTURE SUMMARY

Here are the key rules to look out for on ACT Sentence Structure questions:

1. Definitions

- An **independent clause** *can stand by itself* as a sentence.
- A **dependent clause** *cannot stand by itself* as a sentence.
- A **relative clause** is a dependent clause with a *relative pronoun* that *describes a single word* in the sentence.
- A **modifier** is a phrase with *no main verb* that modifies something in the sentence.

2 Fragments

- Every sentence *must have at least one independent clause*, or else it's a **fragment.**
- Fix a fragment by:
    - Turning a *partial verb* into a **main verb.**
    - **Removing unnecessary connectors** or relative pronouns.
    - **Joining it to another sentence** by *removing the period.*

3. Run-on sentences

- **Don't** connect independent clauses with a **comma alone**, or with **no connection** at all.
- Fix a run-on by:
    - Separating the clauses with a **period**.
    - Using a **comma with a conjunction**.
    - Making one of the independent clauses a **dependent clause or modifier**.

4. Modifiers

- A modifier at the *beginning of a sentence* must describe the *subject of the main clause* (the word right after the comma) or else it's a **dangling modifier**.
- A modifier at *the end of a sentence* may describe:
    - the **subject**, if there's a *comma.*
    - the **word next to it**, if there's *no comma.*
- *Prepositional phrases* must be **placed right after** the words they describe.

5. Parallelism

- Use **parallel forms** for **parallel ideas.** Any words or phrases joined with the word "and" must be in parallel forms.
- **Don't** use "and" if the forms **aren't parallel**.

SENTENCE STRUCTURE EXERCISE

This exercise contains a full passage with 15 questions, just like an ACT passage. Unlike a real ACT passage, it only features ***Sentence Structure*** *questions. Look out for all the rules discussed above. Enjoy!*

PASSAGE II

Scraping the Sky

As long as people have known how to build, people have tried to build tall structures. Skyscrapers as we know them are a modern invention, but we can find [1] examples of very tall buildings throughout ancient history. The Romans lived in *insulae*, high-rise apartment buildings, and [2] could rise to heights over 10 stories. Some medieval Italian cities featured stone towers over 200 feet tall. Such as [3] the Towers of Bologna or the Tower of Pisa. In Yemen, the walled city of Shibam, which was built in the sixteenth century and [4] consists entirely of buildings with five to eleven stories.

Buildings that tall, however, were rare until the nineteenth century. Because older buildings were made of materials like stone and brick, the outer walls bore the brunt of the building's weight, this limited [5] the maximum height that a tower could safely be built. However, once engineer Henry Bessemer discovered a process for cheap steel production, [6] buildings could be made with skeletal steel construction. A network of steel beams would distribute the weight of the building away, allowing taller construction from the outer walls [7] on relatively small plots of land.

1. A. NO CHANGE
   B. invention, we can find
   C. invention. But finding
   D. invention we can find

2. F. NO CHANGE
   G. buildings that
   H. buildings, they
   J. buildings, but they

3. A. NO CHANGE
   B. tall, some examples are
   C. tall; such as
   D. tall, such as

4. F. NO CHANGE
   G. Shibam, built in the sixteenth century,
   H. Shibam was built in the sixteenth century, it
   J. Shibam, a sixteenth century building that

5. A. NO CHANGE
   B. weight. Limiting
   C. weight. This design limited
   D. weight. Thus limiting

6. F. NO CHANGE
   G. a process for cheap steel production, engineer Henry Bessemer discovered that
   H. engineer Henry Bessemer, a process for cheap steel production, discovered
   J. the discovery by engineer Henry Bessemer of a process for cheap steel production,

7. The best placement for the underlined portion would be:
   A. where it is now.
   B. after the word *away* (but before the comma).
   C. after the word *plots*.
   D. after the word *network*.

Another problem was that tall buildings were inconvenient; no one [8] likes climbing ten flights of stairs every day. Elevators had existed in primitive form since the time of the Greek mathematician Archimedes, but they were cumbersome and dangerous. In 1852, Elisha Otis created the first safety elevator it was [9] equipped with a braking system to stop the car if the cables snapped. Furthermore, innovations in hydraulic and electric power made these new elevators practical to install and they were maintained [10] in urban environments.

These advancements, along with a few others like central heating and electric water pumps, made modern skyscrapers possible. Inspired by these developments, a construction boom was started by engineers at the turn of the century. [11] Soon, taller and taller skyscrapers popped [12] up in cities like Chicago and New York at an incredible rate. From 1890 to 1913, the record for the world's tallest skyscraper was broken eight times.

New designs in engineering continue to push the limits of human achievement, this [13] race to be the tallest has not stopped. In 2010, the city of Dubai celebrated the opening of the Burj Khalifa. A huge tower that stands [14] at 2,717 feet tall—over twice as tall as the Empire State Building. As we [15] continue to create new technologies and building techniques, we will keep rising to new heights.

8. Which of the following alternatives to the underlined portion would NOT be acceptable?
   - F. inconvenient: no one
   - G. inconvenient. No one
   - H. inconvenient, no one
   - J. inconvenient—no one

9.
   - A. NO CHANGE
   - B. elevator, it was
   - C. elevator, which was
   - D. elevator and

10.
   - F. NO CHANGE
   - G. for maintenance
   - H. maintaining
   - J. to maintain

11.
   - A. NO CHANGE
   - B. engineers started a construction boom at the turn of the century.
   - C. a boom in construction at the turn of the century was started by engineers.
   - D. the turn of the century saw a construction boom started by engineers.

12.
   - F. NO CHANGE
   - G. that popped
   - H. popping
   - J. to pop

13.
   - A. NO CHANGE
   - B. achievement, and this
   - C. achievement the
   - D. achievement, the

14.
   - F. NO CHANGE
   - G. Khalifa and is a huge tower standing
   - H. Khalifa, a huge tower stands
   - J. Khalifa, a huge tower that stands

15.
   - A. NO CHANGE
   - B. Later we would
   - C. Moreover, we
   - D. We

USAGE/MECHANICS: PUNCTUATION

Punctuation questions on the ACT are easy to spot: their choices will all be worded identically and differ only in their punctuation. Of course, as we've already seen, Grammar & Usage or Sentence Structure questions may also involve issues of punctuation—fixing run-on sentences, for example, requires you to look at comma and periods. But correcting these errors often requires changes in the wording of the sentence, too. Punctuation questions will *only* test you on punctuation marks.

In some ways, punctuation is one of the trickier concepts on the ACT because punctuation isn't *pronounced.* Grammatical errors will often "sound" wrong to you. You can tell that the sentence "The dog have being barking" *sounds really messed up*, even if you don't understand exactly why. But you can't really *hear* whether a comma is in the right place.

Thankfully, there are only a few rules of punctuation that you'll need to know for the ACT. Once you learn to recognize the basic rules, you'll speed through these questions.

I. COMMAS

There are a lot of different rules for comma use. It can be overwhelming to try to remember all these rules. To help guide you, keep two simple rules in mind:

First, many of the comma rules have the same motivation at heart:

DO use commas between words with WEAK connections.
DON'T use commas between words with STRONG connections.

For example, there's a strong connection between a subject and verb, so you should not separate them with a comma. But there's a weak connection between a parenthetical phrase and the rest of a sentence, so you should separate it with commas:

STRONG: <u>Dave likes</u> cats. (No comma between the subject and verb.)

WEAK: Dave, <u>who is from Ottawa</u>, likes cats. (Commas around the parenthetical phrase.)

This is more of a guideline than a rule—it won't apply to every single situation. But it does connect a lot of situations that might otherwise seem unrelated to each other.

Second, people usually use too many commas, not too few. So in general, a comma is more likely to be wrong than right. **Commas on the ACT are wrong over twice as often as they're right.** If you're really not sure whether a certain spot needs a comma, better to guess that it doesn't. Remember, a comma literally divides a sentence into parts. Don't split up the sentence unless you've got a good reason for doing so.

> ON THE ACT, COMMAS ARE WRONG OVER TWICE AS OFTEN AS THEY'RE RIGHT.

When should we use commas? More importantly, when should we *not* use them?

When *can* I use a comma?

1. Between independent clauses joined with a conjunction

We already discussed this at length in the Sentence Structure chapter. You can use a comma and a conjunction to separate independent clauses.* But don't use a use a comma between independent clauses without a conjunction—that's a run-on.

---

* A comma is not always *required* before the conjunction here. Commas are used here more often than not, but they are sometimes optional if the clauses are short. So "She thinks you're ugly and I agree" would be acceptable.

✓ **I am going to the <u>game, and</u> Scott will meet me there.**

✓ **I wanted to go to the <u>movies, but</u> the show was sold out.**

× **I am going to the <u>game, Scott</u> will meet me there.**

Run-on issues appear on Sentence Strategy questions more frequently than on Punctuation questions, because fixing them often involves changing the wording of the sentences. So we won't discuss them at length here.

2. Around parenthetical phrases

We mentioned earlier that dependent clauses and modifiers are not part of the "core sentence". If the sentence **would still make sense without the phrase**, you can put commas on *both sides* of the phrase. This relates directly to our first rule: phrases with *weak connections* take commas. These phrases can take many different forms:

✓ **Ottawa, <u>the capital of Canada</u>, is very beautiful in the wintertime.**

✓ **Ottawa, <u>established in 1850</u>, is very beautiful in the wintertime.**

✓ **Ottawa, <u>if you ask me</u>, is very beautiful in the wintertime.**

✓ **Ottawa, <u>which is known for its 5-mile skating rink on the Rideau Canal</u>, is very beautiful in the wintertime.**

In each of these sentences, the underlined phrase gives extra information that doesn't affect the main clause. We could delete each phrase and still be left with a complete sentence.

✓ **Ottawa, <u>...</u> , is very beautiful in the wintertime.**

There are several things to keep in mind when dealing with parenthetical phrases. First, if you start a parenthetical, make sure to end it. The phrase needs commas **on both sides**:

× **Ottawa, the capital of <u>Canada is</u> very beautiful in the wintertime.**

Second, when you do end it, make sure you end it in the right place.

× **Ottawa, the <u>capital, of</u> Canada is very beautiful in the wintertime.**

If you're not sure whether a parenthetical has its commas in the right place, try ignoring the words between the commas to see if the sentence still makes sense.

× **Ottawa, ... , of Canada is very beautiful in the wintertime.**

Of course, phrases like this can also appear at the beginning or end of a sentence. Then they just need one comma to separate them from the main clause. We've already seen tons of examples like this in the Sentence Structure chapter.

✓ **<u>The capital of Canada</u>, Ottawa is very beautiful in the wintertime.**

✓ **Ottawa is very beautiful in the wintertime, <u>if you ask me</u>.**

Parenthetical phrases can be particularly tricky when dealing with people's names and titles:

× **<u>Former Minnesota governor, Jesse Ventura,</u> has appeared in ten films.**

This kinds sounds okay. But since "Jesse Ventura" is surrounded by commas, it's a parenthetical phrase. So we should be able to delete it. Let's try:

× **Former Minnesota governor, ... , has appeared in ten films.**

"Former Minnesota governor has appeared" sounds weird. So "Jesse Ventura" is *not* a parenthetical phrase—it's the core subject of the verb "has appeared", and no comma should separate the subject and verb. "Former Minnesota governor" is Ventura's *title*, sort of like a long adjective.

✓ **<u>Former Minnesota governor Jesse Ventura</u> has appeared in ten films.**

Of course, we could also phrase the sentence differently so that there *is* a parenthetical:

✓ **The former Minnesota governor, <u>Jesse Ventura</u>, has appeared in ten films.**

✓ **The former Minnesota governor, … , has appeared in ten films.**

✓ **Jesse Ventura, <u>former governor of Minnesota</u>, has appeared in ten films.**

✓ **Jesse Ventura, … , has appeared in ten films.**

3. Between items of a list with three or more items

Any list of three or more should have commas alone separating the first items and the word "and" separating the last item.*

✓ **<u>Dave, Ted and Roger</u> all like cats**

✓ **<u>Dave, Ted, and Roger</u> all like cats.**

× **<u>Dave Ted and Roger</u> all like cats.**

This applies to *any* list of three: nouns, verbs, prepositional phrases, or even clauses. This is the only time you can legally combine independent clauses without a conjunction—when they're the first two in a list of three.

✓ **Dave went to market, Ted stayed home, and Roger ate roast beef.**

4. Between coordinate adjectives

If a noun has two adjectives that are of *equal importance* and each adjective directly describes the noun *in the same way*, use a comma to separate the adjectives:

✓ **Cindy just got a <u>happy, healthy</u> cat.**

Here are two quick tests: if you can **switch the order** of the adjectives, or if you can **insert "and"** between the adjectives without changing the meaning of the sentence, use a comma:

✓ **Cindy just got a <u>healthy, happy</u> cat.** ✓ **Cindy just got a <u>happy and healthy</u> cat.**

Compare to this sentence:

✓ **Cindy just got a <u>healthy Siamese</u> cat.** × **Cindy just got a <u>healthy, Siamese</u> cat.**

The adjectives "healthy" and "Siamese" are not coordinate. "Siamese" is more closely tied to "cat" than "healthy" is. So we should **not** use a comma. If we switch the adjectives or insert "and", the sentence is clearly nonsense:

× **Cindy just got a <u>Siamese, healthy</u> cat.** × **Cindy just got a <u>healthy and Siamese</u> cat.**

5. Before a direct quote

Use a comma before a **direct quote.**

✓ **Darth Vader <u>said, "Luke,</u> I am your father."†**

But **DO NOT** use a comma before a **description** of a quote.‡

✓ **Darth Vader <u>said he</u> was Luke's father.** × **Darth Vader <u>said, he</u> was Luke's father.**

---

* The comma before the "and" at the end of a list is *optional*. Some people love it, some hate it. This kind of comma is sometimes known as a "serial comma" or an "Oxford comma". This will not be tested on the ACT.

† Yes, yes, yes, I'm well aware that Vader doesn't actually say this quote in the movie. I wanted to include Luke's name in order to show the comparative structures of the different example sentences here. I'm quoting a *different* instance of Vader saying this. It was off-camera, you didn't see it. Please stop sending angry emails.

‡ This is actually just a "that" clause with a missing "that": *Darth Vader said <u>that</u> he was Luke's father.*

6. **Around sentence adverbs**

These are adverbs that modify the *entire* sentence, sometimes connecting it to the previous sentence:

✓ **Luckily, Dave decided not to sue.**

✓ **I like cats. I do not, however, like dogs.**

But **DO NOT** use a comma after **conjunctions**, like *and*, *or*, or *but*.

✓ **I like cats, but I do not like dogs.** × **I like cats, but, I do not like dogs.**

When should I *not* use a comma?

1. **Between the subject and verb or between the verb and object**

✓ **Dave likes cats.** × **Dave, likes cats.** × **Dave likes, cats.**

This rule ties back to our first rule: *Don't use commas for strong connections*. There are no stronger connections in a sentence than those between subject, verb, and object. Don't interrupt them with commas.

Unless of course *something else* comes between them:

✓ **Dave, who is from Ottawa, likes cats.**

Here, there's a *parenthetical phrase* stuck between the subject, "Dave", and the verb, "likes". So we need the commas for the parenthetical phrase, even though they come between the subject and verb.

Similarly, we can separate the verb and the object if there's a *list:*

✓ **Dave bought a cat, a dog, and a monkey.**

In this sentence, we have three objects of the verb *bought*: "a cat, a dog, and a monkey". Since that's a list of three, we need commas between the list items. But **don't** use a comma to **introduce the list**:

× **Dave bought, a cat, a dog, and a monkey.**

Now there's a comma separating the verb from its three objects. That's no good.

So if you see any comma between a verb and its subject, or between a verb and its object, check to see if it's used for a parenthetical phrase or a list. If it's not, then the comma probably shouldn't be there.

2. **Before infinitives**

Remember that infinitives are the form of a verb that begin with "to". Infinitives behave sort of like the objects of verbs. They have strong connections to the verbs, so they should not be separated by commas:

✓ **I want to go home.** × **I want, to go home.**

UNLESS the infinitive phrase comes **at the beginning** of a sentence.

✓ **To get home, walk ten blocks south on Broadway and turn right.**

3. **Around prepositional phrases**

We've mentioned prepositional phrases several times, so you should be able to identify them by now. In general, you should not separate them with commas:

✓ **Many people in Ottawa speak French.** × **Many people, in Ottawa, speak French.**

✓ **Many people speak French in Ottawa.** × **Many people speak French, in Ottawa.**

UNLESS the phrase comes **at the beginning** of the sentence.*

✓ **In Ottawa, many people speak French.**

Additionally, do not use a comma **between a preposition and its object**.

✓ **Many people in Ottawa speak French.** × **Many people in, Ottawa speak French.**

4. In a two-part list (a compound with a conjunction)

We mentioned that you should use commas to separate items in a list of three or more. But if you're only listing *two* things, just use a conjunction with no comma.

✓ **Dogs and cats are prohibited.** × **Dogs, and cats are prohibited.**

✓ **Gretchen is a small but fierce kitten.** × **Gretchen is a small, but fierce kitten.**

Unless, of course, you're combining two independent clauses with a conjunction. Then you need a comma:

✓ **I am going to the game, and Scott will meet me there.**

But if you're linking anything else, don't use a comma. Similarly, don't use a comma to separate **two verbs with a single subject**.

✓ **The dog *EATS* meat and *LOVES* bones.** × **The dog *EATS* meat, and *LOVES* bones.**

And as we mentioned earlier, you should never use a comma *after* a conjunction.

× **I like cats, but, I do not like dogs.** × **The dog eats meat and, loves bones.**

5. With a "that" clause

In general, you should not use a comma before or after "that":†

✓ **I think that the Rockets will win it all this year.**

× **I think, that the Rockets will win it all this year.**

× **I think that, the Rockets will win it all this year.**

6. With restrictive clauses or modifiers

We mentioned before that parenthetical phrases and modifiers can be separated by commas. But not *every* dependent clause or modifier is a parenthetical.

A **restrictive** (or *integrated*) clause is one that identifies or defines what we're talking about.

A **nonrestrictive** (or *supplementary*) clause is one that gives additional information about the topic. This is what we mean by "parenthetical phrases".

- RESTRICTIVE: **Our professor told us to buy the book that he wrote.**
- NONRESTRICTIVE: **Our professor told us to buy his book, which was expensive.**

* These rules are a bit fluid. It is sometimes okay to separate a prepositional phrase with commas if you intend it to be a parenthetical statement. And sometimes it's okay to not use a comma with a prepositional phrase at the beginning of the sentence. But on the ACT you'll rarely see either of those situations.

† As we mentioned in the Grammar & Usage chapter, "that" has several very different uses. So it is *possible* to have a sentence that needs a comma before or after "that". But you probably won't see any on the ACT.

In these sentences we know two things about the book: the professor wrote it, and it was expensive. The clause "that he wrote" identifies exactly which book we should buy. The clause "which was expensive" gives an additional characteristic about the book but doesn't *define* the book. The professor didn't tell us to buy the expensive book. He told us to buy *his* book. It just happened to be expensive.

This ties back to our first guideline: restrictive clauses are *strongly* connected to the main clause (so we *don't* use a comma), while nonrestrictive clauses are *weakly* connected (so we *do* use a comma). If the clause is *necessary information* that identifies the noun, don't use a comma. If it is *additional information* describing the noun, use a comma.

RESTRICTIVE	**NONRESTRICTIVE**
There was a big fire in the town where I was born.	There was a big fire in Cleveland, where I was born.
The man running down the street is my father.	Running down the street, my father tried to catch the bus.
The one who gets the most votes wins the election.	The president, who was just re-elected, is still a jerk.

Comma Drill

*All of these questions deal with **commas** and only commas. Have fun!*

PASSAGE III

The Rise of Punctuation

Every student of grammar knows that the English language has a series, of specific complex rules about proper use of punctuation marks. Today's rules, however, have not existed since the birth of writing. Punctuation has radically evolved over the centuries.

The earliest writing had no punctuation whatsoever. Even worse, there weren't even any spaces between words. Texts were dense blocks of uninterrupted letters. Ancient, Greek playwrights, began using simple punctuation marks in their texts so that actors, reciting their lines would know when to pause. Even through the start of the Middle Ages, books were meant to be tools for reading aloud, and punctuation continued to be used primarily to regulate the rhythm of speech.

Books gradually started to become more widespread, and, puctuation began to apply to grammatical structures not just to spoken units. But because books were copied and produced by hand, the shapes, and meanings of these symbolsstill varied, often drastically, from book to book. The shapes of punctuation marks became

1. A. NO CHANGE
   B. series, of specific, complex rules
   C. series, of specific complex rules,
   D. series of specific, complex rules

2. F. NO CHANGE
   G. rules however
   H. rules, however
   J. rules however,

3. A. NO CHANGE
   B. Ancient, Greek playwrights
   C. Ancient Greek playwrights
   D. Ancient Greek playwrights,

4. F. NO CHANGE
   G. so that actors reciting
   H. so, that actors reciting
   J. so that, actors reciting

5. A. NO CHANGE
   B. widespread and punctuation began
   C. widespread, and punctuation began
   D. widespread, and punctuation began,

6. F. NO CHANGE
   G. shapes, and, meanings of
   H. shapes and meanings of
   J. shapes and meanings of,

7. A. NO CHANGE
   B. symbols, still varied often
   C. symbols, still varied, often
   D. symbols still varied often

standardized, with the invention, of the printing press. Printers could now mechanically reproduce the same punctuation marks over and over again. The Italian publisher, and printer Aldus Manutius was the source of several important innovations. In a manuscript printed in 1494, Manutius took an earlier mark called the *virgula suspensiva* a mark that resembled a forward slash, curved it and lowered it to produce the mark we know today as the comma. Manutius was also one of the first printers to use semicolons round parentheses and, italic type.

Even after the shapes of punctuation marks became uniform, it still took several, hundred years for their uses to become fixed. Commas for example, were far more widespread in the seventeenth and eighteenth centuries than they are today. Try reading the U.S. Constitution as it was originally written and you'll be overwhelmed by seemingly unnecessary commas. Today, while there is some variation between British and American usage, English punctuation marks have been standardized into well-defined roles. But who knows? Maybe in another two hundred years, a different set of new barely recognizable marks, will be standard.

8. F. NO CHANGE
G. standardized, with the invention of
H. standardized with the invention of,
J. standardized with the invention of

9. A. NO CHANGE
B. publisher and printer Aldus Manutius
C. publisher, and printer Aldus Manutius,
D. publisher and printer Aldus Manutius,

10. F. NO CHANGE
G. *suspensiva* a mark that,
H. *suspensiva*, a mark, that
J. *suspensiva*, a mark that

11. A. NO CHANGE
B. use, semicolons, round parentheses, and
C. use semicolons, round parentheses, and
D. use, semicolons, round parentheses, and,

12. F. NO CHANGE
G. several hundred years
H. several hundred years,
J. several, hundred years,

13. A. NO CHANGE
B. Commas, for example, were
C. Commas, for example were,
D. Commas for example were,

14. F. NO CHANGE
G. usage, English punctuation marks,
H. usage English, punctuation marks
J. usage English punctuation marks,

15. A. NO CHANGE
B. set, of new, barely recognizable marks
C. set of new, barely recognizable marks
D. set, of new barely recognizable marks,

II. APOSTROPHES

Possession

Use *s* for **plurals:**

✓ **One dog** ✓ **Two dogs**

Use *'s* for **possessives:**[*]

✓ **This is my dog.** ✓ **This is my dog's bed.**

Use *s'* for **plural possessives:**

✓ **I have two dogs.** ✓ **This is my dogs' room.** ✓ **These are my dogs' beds.**

Note that we are adding an apostrophe to an already-plural noun, so we should keep any spelling changes that occur in the plural form:

✓ **Dave has one puppy.** ✓ **This is his puppy's bed.**

✓ **Linda has two puppies.** ✓ **These are her puppies' toys.** × **These are her puppys' toys.**

Plurals that don't end in *s* take *'s* for plural possessives:

✓ **Dave has one child.** ✓ **This is his child's bed.**

✓ **Linda has two children.** ✓ **These are her children's toys.**

Not sure if you need a possessive form? Try rewriting it as an **"of" phrase**. Possessives can usually be rewritten as a prepositional phrase starting with "of":

✓ **This is my father's boyhood home.** **= This is the boyhood home of my father.**

✓ **I am moving into my parents' basement.** **= I am moving into the basement of my parents.**

Notice also that possessive nouns should have something to possess: my father's *home*, my parents' *basement*.

Contractions

Apostrophes can also be used in **contractions**. When two words are stuck together, an apostrophe takes the place of the missing letters.

✓ **That's my dog.** **= That is my dog.**

✓ **He's a jerk.** **= He is a jerk.**

✓ **They're great!** **= They are great!**

✓ **Dave's going to win.** **= Dave is going to win.**

✓ **My dog's cute.**[†] **= My dog is cute.**

Contractions aren't just for forms of "to be". They can also be used for forms of "to have":

✓ **He's been to Paris.** **= He has been to Paris.**

✓ **I've never heard of it.** **= I have never heard of it.**

---

[*] This form has sometimes been called *the Saxon genitive*, presumably because derives from a case ending from Old English. However, some linguists now consider *'s* to be a *clitic*, not a true inflectional ending. None of this matters to you, but "Saxon genitive" and "clitic" are both really awesome terms.

[†] Contractions like this, with regular nouns instead of pronouns, are often considered colloquial, informal, or nonstandard.

Or negation:

✓ **He isn't Swedish.** **= He is not Swedish.**

✓ **They aren't Japanese.** **= They are not Japanese.**

Or any time a word has omitted letters:

✓ **y'all = you all** ✓ **'bout = about**

✓ **'tis = it is** ✓ **fo'c's'le = forecastle**[*]

Pronouns

We already discussed pronoun forms in the Grammar & Usage chapter. To review:

Pronouns DO NOT use possessive apostrophes.

Pronouns have special forms for possessives:

My feet	**His feet**	**Its feet**	**Our feet**
Your feet	**Her feet**	**Their feet**	**Whose feet?**

Pronouns DO use contraction apostrophes:

✓ **I'm French.** **= I am French.** ✓ **It's French.** **= It is French.**

✓ **You're French.** **= You are French.** ✓ **We're French.** **= We are French.**

✓ **He's French.** **= He is French.** ✓ **They're French.** **= They are French.**

✓ **She's French.** **= She is French.** ✓ **Who's French?** **= Who is French?**

Remember: pronouns use CONTRACTION apostrophes but *NOT* POSSESSIVE apostrophes.

It's means ***it is.*** ***Its*** shows **possession.** ***Its'*** **is never correct.**	**It's a beautiful day!** **The dog wagged its tail.** **Never use its' for any reason.**	[= It is a beautiful day!] [= The tail belongs to the dog.]
You're means ***you are.*** ***Your*** shows **possession.**	**You're a jerk.** **Your fly is open.**	[= You are a jerk.] [= The fly belongs to you.]
They're means ***they are.*** ***Their*** shows **possession.** ***There*** shows **location.**	**They're going to win.** **I like their uniforms.** **Put it over there.**	[= They are going to win.] [= The uniforms belong to them.] [= I'm telling you where to put it.]
Who's means **who is.** ***Whose*** shows **possession.**	**the man who's buying my car** **the man whose car I'm buying**	[= the man who is buying my car] [= the car belongs to the man]

[*] Yes, *fo'c's'le* is a real word. It's pronounced <FOX-ll>, as in "the fox'll eat the chicken". It's a nautical term.

III. Other Punctuation Marks

Semicolon (;)

A semicolon is basically the same thing as a period. They follow the same rules. Why bother with the semicolon, then? Because it puts the two clauses into *the same sentence*. Therefore, it connects the ideas more strongly than if they were separate sentences with a period.

In fact, a semicolon is exactly what it looks like—a combination of a period and a comma. It separates independent clauses as a period does, but it separates parts of a single sentence as a comma does.

Because a semicolon works just like a period, a semicolon **must** be used to separate **independent clauses**. If you're not sure whether you can put a semicolon somewhere, try replacing it with a period. A semicolon should always be **interchangeable with a period** without making any other changes to the sentence (except capitalization). If you can't replace it with a period without changing the words, you can't use a semicolon.

- ✓ **Dave has been studying more; his grades have improved as a result.**
- ✓ **Dave has been studying more. His grades have improved as a result.**
- × **<u>While riding the bus</u>; my father lost his wallet.**
- × **<u>While riding the bus</u>. My father lost his wallet.**

The semicolon can be a nice tool, and using it properly can help you improve your writing. However, for some reason, **on the ACT semicolons are almost always wrong**.* In our research of past tests, semicolons were wrong **90% of the time**. So if you're not sure whether a semicolon is correct, it probably isn't.

Occasionally, semicolons can be used instead of commas to separate items in a list when those items contain commas. But this does not occur often.

- ✓ **I've met three people at the conference: Dave, who likes cats; Roger, the man from Portland, Oregon; and a third man whose name, I think, was Jesse.**

Colon (:)

A colon **strongly connects** two clauses. Use a colon when what follows is a quotation, an elaboration on, or a direct example of what precedes it.

- ✓ **Steve is a bibliophile: he spends all his time reading.**

In this example, the colon separates independent clauses. But unlike semicolons, colons don't *have to* separate independent clauses:

- ✓ **I am going to one game this year: the Super Bowl.**

Here, "the Super Bowl" is not an independent clause, but the colon is just fine.

A colon may be used to introduce a list, especially a list of long, wordy items:

- ✓ **He had several tasks ahead of him: hiking the trail from the campsite down the side of the mountain, collecting enough firewood to last the evening, then hiking back up the mountain while carrying the wood.**

But you can't use a colon between the verb and its object, even if it's a list:

- × **Dave bought: a cat, a dog, and a monkey.**

---

* One exception (kinda) is in questions that ask you which choice is NOT acceptable. In those questions, the semicolon almost always is an acceptable alternative. But of course, these questions ask for the choice that's not acceptable, so the semicolon still wouldn't be the correct answer.

Dash (—)

Dashes may be used to surround a parenthetical remark or aside, just like commas.* They often give greater emphasis than commas would:

✓ **The sequel's budget—estimated to be over 100 million dollars—is more than double that of the original movie.**

✓ **This dress—if you ask me—is not the right color for your skin tone.**

✓ **He accidentally revealed his home address—a mistake that would cost him his life!**

Dash phrases at the end of a sentence only need one dash, but phrases in the middle need dashes on both sides. If you open a phrase with a dash, don't forget to close it with another dash.

× **This dress—if you ask <u>me is</u> not the right color for your skin tone.**

And like colons, dashes can be used to join independent clauses:

✓ **Steve is a bibliophile—he spends all his time reading.**

Sentence-final marks

Period (.)

A period is used to separate **complete sentences**. We discussed this in the section on sentence fragments. A complete sentence must have at least one independent clause with a subject and verb.

✓ **Since Dave has been studying more, his grades have improved as a result.**

× **<u>Since Dave has been studying more</u>. His grades have improved as a result.**

✓ **My father was running down the street, trying to catch the bus.**

× **My father was running down the street. <u>Trying to catch the bus</u>.**

Besides periods, there are several other marks we can use to end a sentence.

Question mark (?)

A question mark indicates that a sentence is a question. It *cannot* be used for non-questions.

✓ **What did you have for dinner?**

Exclamation point (!)

An exclamation point works just like a period that shows excitement or surprise.

✓ **I got a four-pound hamburger and ate the whole thing!**

Interrobang (‽)

An interrobang is a combination of an exclamation point and a question mark. It's used for questions that show excitement or surprise.

✓ **You ate a *what*‽**

Okay, that last one probably won't show up on the ACT.† But the other three might.

---

* There are several kinds of dashes, and usage among them can vary. This one is called an *em-dash*. An *en-dash* is shorter than an em-dash and is used for ranges of values, as in "1910–1918" or "pages 22–35". A *hyphen* is even shorter than an en-dash and is used to connect words and parts of words, as in "en-dash". You will not be tested on hyphens or en-dashes on the ACT.

† Maybe it won't be on the ACT, but the interrobang is all too real. It was invented in 1962 by advertising agent Martin Speckter to replace the clumsy practice of alternating question marks and exclamation points ("You ate a what?!?!") Sadly, the interrobang never quite caught on.

PUNCTUATION SUMMARY

Here are the key rules to look out for on ACT Puctuation questions

1. **DO use commas:**

   - between **independent clauses** with a **conjunction.**
   - around **parenthetical phrases**.
   - in a list of **three or more**.
   - with **coordinate adjectives**.
   - before a **direct quote**.
   - around **sentence adverbs.**

2. **DON'T use commas:**

   - between **subject and verb** or **verb and object**.
   - before **infinitives**.
   - before or in the middle of **prepositional phrases**.
   - with a **two part list** (two nouns or verbs with a conjunction).
   - with a **"that" clause**.
   - before **restrictive** clauses.

3. **Apostrophes**

   - **Plurals** take -s, **possessives** take -'s, **plural possessives** take -s'.
   - **Contractions** use apostrophes for missing letters.
   - **Pronouns** take **contraction** apostrophes but **not possessive** apostrophes.

4. **Other marks**

   - A **semicolon** separates *independent clauses* (interchangeable with a period).
   - A **colon** *strongly* connects phrases.
   - A **dash** connects *independent clauses* or *parenthetical phrases.*
   - Don't mix up **sentence-final marks**: *periods*, *question marks*, and *exclamation points.*

Punctuation Exercise

Here it is! Another passage! ***Punctuation*** *only! Wheeee!*

PASSAGE IV

My Dream Home

I recently moved into the apartment of my dreams. It's tiny, its inconveniently located, and, it's too [1] expensive. But the best thing about my apartment is, the fact that it sits above [2] a wonderful place called Emily's Bakery.

All independent bakeries [3] have a certain small-town charm to them, and this one is no different. The store actually owned, by a woman, named Emily [4] is a very cute place, but proximity to a bakery is not the sort of thing one usually makes living decisions around. Living above a bakery, though [5] is more important to me than having walk-in closets or beautiful wood, floors. [6]

There's one thing that makes life above Emily's so great; the [7] smell. Nothing in the world is better than the smell of fresh bread coming into your apartment first thing in the morning. Because the store starts baking when I get up in the morning, I don't even need an alarm clock, the aroma [8] of warm rolls nudges me awake and eases me into the day. I can't imagine a more pleasant way to get up.

1. A. NO CHANGE
   B. tiny it's inconveniently located, and
   C. tiny, it's inconveniently located, and
   D. tiny, it's inconveniently located; and

2. F. NO CHANGE
   G. is the fact, that it sits above
   H. is the fact that it sits above
   J. is the fact that it sits, above

3. A. NO CHANGE
   B. bakeries'
   C. bakery's
   D. bakerys'

4. F. NO CHANGE
   G. store, actually owned by a woman named Emily,
   H. store, actually owned by a woman named Emily
   J. store actually owned by a woman, named Emily

5. A. NO CHANGE
   B. bakery though,
   C. bakery though
   D. bakery, though,

6. F. NO CHANGE
   G. beautiful, wood floors.
   H. beautiful, wood floor's.
   J. beautiful wood floors.

7. A. NO CHANGE
   B. great? The
   C. great! The
   D. great: the

8. F. NO CHANGE
   G. clock—the aroma
   H. clock, the aroma,
   J. clock the aroma;

By now I can even distinguish all the different rolls scents. [9] I can tell what's coming out of the oven without leaving my bedroom. Baguettes, have a rich [10] dense aroma. Surprisingly, the sourdough loaves smell more sweet than sour, almost like maple syrup. My favorites, are, [11] the croissants. They're nice and buttery, and it's easy to detect the chocolate ones.

9. A. NO CHANGE
   B. rolls' scent's.
   C. roll's scents'.
   D. rolls' scents.

10. F. NO CHANGE
    G. Baguettes have: a rich
    H. Baguettes have a rich,
    J. Baguettes have, a rich

11. A. NO CHANGE
    B. favorites, are
    C. favorites are,
    D. favorites are

People are amazed to learn that, despite my obsession, I rarely keep any bread in the apartment. Why would I? If I want bread, I can just go downstairs and pick up something fresh. When I first moved in, this convenience made me a bit concerned about my weight. Fresh cupcakes and doughnuts, sit [12] literally steps away from my bedroom all day and much of the night! I've done a good job of staying in shape—I've actually lost weight since moving here but, [13] I have to be careful not to indulge myself too often.

12. F. NO CHANGE
    G. cupcakes, and doughnuts sit
    H. cupcakes and doughnuts sit
    J. cupcakes and, doughnuts, sit

13. A. NO CHANGE
    B. weight, since moving here but
    C. weight since moving here—but
    D. weight—since moving here but,

I was also worried that, [14] constant exposure to the bakery's smell might desensitize me until I no longer noticed it. Even worse, I might start to resent the smell or even hate it. My friend Paul used to love Indian food before he moved next to an Indian restaurant. After three months there, the smell drove him so crazy that he had to move. But I've been here over a year now. The smell is still as wonderful as it was on the first day and, I have [15] no intention of ever leaving.

14. F. NO CHANGE
    G. worried, that
    H. worried, that,
    J. worried that

15. A. NO CHANGE
    B. day, and I have
    C. day, and I have,
    D. day and I have,

RHETORICAL SKILLS

So far we've spent just about all our time talking about the rules of *grammar*. These are the rules that an English sentence must follow in order to be considered English. If you've mastered these by now, congratulations! You no longer sound like a poorly dubbed kung fu movie.

But wait! It turns out that following all the rules of grammar isn't enough to actually make you a *good writer*. So your sentence has the right verb, and the clauses are properly connected, and the commas are all in the right places. Your sentence is *acceptable*. But maybe we could make a *better* sentence.

Furthermore, we've only been discussing individual words and sentences. What about the paragraph? What about the whole essay? Are the sentences in the right order? Does it make the point it was trying to make?

These are all questions about *Rhetorical Skills*. "Rhetoric" refers to the art of using language persuasively. In this chapter we will go beyond grammar and look at rules for composing the most *effective* essay. Thankfully, Rhetorical Skills questions fall into a few easily identifiable categories, so it won't be too hard to figure out what we want.

Rhetorical Skills questions fall into three subcategories: ***Style, Organization,*** and ***Writing Strategy***.

I. STYLE

Style questions deal with saying things the right way. In order for a sentence to be most effective, we want it to convey exactly the right information—enough that we know what it's talking about, but not so much that the sentence weighs us down.

These three guidelines will help you with most Style questions:

1. Be concise

Redundancy

Take a look at this sentence:

× **Picking the right equipment is an <u>essential and important</u> step before you climb a mountain.**

Why does the sentence say "essential" *and* "important"? Those words mean the same thing! This phrase is **redundant**—that's a fancy word for *saying the same thing twice*. Using both words doesn't add any new information; it just makes the sentence unnecessarily longer. So let's get rid of one of them:

✓ **Picking the right equipment is an <u>important</u> step before you climb a mountain.**

Redundancy is the most common error among *all* Rhetorical Skills questions.

Much simpler; much better. Sometimes you can even OMIT the underlined phrase entirely.

× **Greek geometry was more advanced than *earlier* forms of mathematics <u>that came before it</u>.**

We already said we're talking about "earlier" forms of math. That *means* they "came before". The last phrase doesn't add any information to the sentence. So let's get rid of it.*

✓ **Greek geometry was more advanced than earlier forms of mathematics.**

This is another reason why it's important to **read the whole sentence**. The redundancy may not be apparent from the underlined portion alone—the phrase "that came before it" seems perfectly reasonable if you didn't see the word "earlier". If a choice is redundant, there are words *somewhere in the sentence* that

* "OMIT the underlined portion" doesn't show up as a choice too often, but when it does, it's correct about half the time. When it's right, it's usually because of redundancy. When it's wrong, it's usually for a grammatical reason. Like, you can't just omit the verb from the sentence.

mean exactly the same thing as the words in the underlined portion. Those other words might be earlier or later in the sentence, but you have to read the whole sentence to find them.

Most of the time, the key words will be fairly close to the underlined portion. But they might not even be in the same sentence:

× **Samantha was pleased with her decision. <u>Her choice made her happy.</u>**

The second sentence here means *exactly the same thing as the first sentence!* The second sentence literally adds no new information. So why say it twice?

✓ **Samantha was pleased with her decision.**

If you don't notice a redundant phrase right away, the answer choices can tip you off: if, say, three choices are all roughly the same length, but one is significantly shorter. Or if all the choices contain words that mean the same thing, but one doesn't. For example:

The first crafts sent into space were unmanned <u>rockets without any people in them.</u> 1

1. A. **NO CHANGE**
   B. **rockets that did not carry astronauts.**
   C. **rockets lacking human passengers of any kind.**
   D. **rockets.**

Notice that the first three choices all contain long phrases that refer to people, but the last choice does not. Perhaps, then, we don't *need* to refer to people here. Sure enough, the word just before the underlined portion, *unmanned*, means "without people".

Wordiness

There are other ways that a sentence can have too many words. Look at this one:

× **Steven helped <u>in the establishment of</u> the organization.**

There's nothing *redundant* about this phrase—it doesn't *repeat* anything. But it's still longer than it needs to be. Instead of using those four words, we can get the same meaning from just one word:

✓ **Steven helped <u>establish</u> the organization.**

That's more concise and more direct. Much better.

Many students think that it's better to use more words because it makes your writing sound fancier or more adult. **<u>That's backwards.</u>** It's *much* better to use *fewer* words. Using too many words makes it harder to pick apart what you're trying to say.*

I mean, which of the following do *you* prefer?

× **The bake sale was organized by Steve, <u>the person who, at the time of the event, was leading</u> the club.**

✓ **The bake sale was organized by Steve, <u>the leader of</u> the club.**

Redundancy and wordiness together make up about 20% of all Rhetorical Skills questions (and therefore about 10% of all ACT English questions). Since conciseness is so important, when in doubt, **check the shortest choice**. A shorter sentence is almost always preferable to a longer sentence, as long as it doesn't violate any rules.

* It is true that a lot of adults write long, wordy, and complicated sentences. But a lot of adults are *terrible* writers.

2. Be specific

Word count alone does not make a good sentence. Sometimes a sentence won't give *enough* information. The sentence may not contain any errors, but it doesn't give us enough detail.

✗ **My cat left <u>something</u> on my doorstep.**

This sentence is **too vague.** I can think of any number of things that a cat could leave on my doorstep. Can we be more specific?

✗ **My cat left <u>something awful</u> on my doorstep.**

Hmm. That doesn't help. Now I'm kind of scared.

✗ **My cat left <u>an object—something so disgusting it made me sick—</u>on my doorstep.**

Oh no! What is it? This is longer, but it's not actually more specific. It's more *vivid.* That's good: vivid sentences can be effective. But it's not *detailed.* It doesn't give us any more *information.* We still don't know what it was, only that it was something awful.

✗ **My cat left <u>a large, sticky hairball</u> on my doorstep.**

Now we know exactly what it was. Much better. Gross, but better.

How will you know when a choice is too vague? Often a question will *explicitly* ask you for a more specific choice:

When a tornado hit my town, it <u>significantly damaged everything</u> on my street.
2

2. **Which choice provides the most specific and detailed information?**
   F. **NO CHANGE**
   G. **caused a lot of destruction**
   H. **knocked down many trees and houses**
   J. **left everything in great disarray**

We can see here that three choices are vague, talking about "damage", "destruction", or "disarray" without actually saying *what happened.* Only choice H gives a specific example of what the damage was.

Vague pronouns

This idea of vagueness relates back to something we said about pronouns in the Grammar & Usage chapter. Remember that a pronoun is a word that refers back to another word in the sentence. You have to make sure that it's clear which word the pronoun refers to.

× **Scott and Bob were partners <u>until he quit</u>.**

Here we have two options for who quit: Scott or Bob. How can you tell which it is? You *can't*—that's the problem. In this case, we can't use a pronoun at all. We have to specify who quit.

✓ **Scott and Bob were partners <u>until Bob quit</u>.**

Of course, if they *both* quit, then we'd have to say "they".

3. Choose the right word

Often there are many different ways of saying the same thing. But words that seem to have the same meaning may have slight differences. We must use the word that *precisely* gives the meaning we intend.

The candidate gave a <u>forceful</u> speech thanking his supporters for helping him win the election.
(3)

3. **A.** NO CHANGE
   B. harsh
   C. passionate
   D. violent

All of the choices here have similar meanings: all imply that the speech was given with a lot of energy. But what kind of energy do we want here? What kind of speech is it? He's *thanking his supporters*. So it should be a *positive* speech. He's saying nice things. "Forceful", "harsh", and "violent" are all *negative* words. Only "passionate" could be used to describe positive energy.

Obviously, context is important here. Don't just read the words in the choices, and don't just rely on which one "sounds" best. Look at the whole sentence, the whole paragraph, or even the rest of the essay to find clues about what sort of word you want.*

Tone

Sometimes words will mean the same thing but differ in *tone*. There's a difference between *formal* and *informal* speech, for example. Many of the things you say to your friends you would never write in a school essay.† But sometimes the line between formal and informal speech is hard to judge. Take a look at this:

This chimpanzee has been observed engaging in behavior that is <u>atypical</u> for its species.
(4)

4. **F.** NO CHANGE
   G. messed up
   H. way out there
   J. totally freaky

All choices here mean the same thing, but choices G, H, and J are all informal phrases. The sentence, however, is very formal, so only choice F has the appropriate tone for the sentence.

That's not to say that informal language is *never* allowed. In fact, some ACT passages are personal narratives that have a slightly relaxed tone. You don't want the language to be *too* formal:

✗ **I was at the mall when all of a sudden my girlfriend <u>terminated our romantic affiliation.</u>**

✓ **I was at the mall when all of a sudden my girlfriend <u>broke up with me.</u>**

The important thing is for the language to be **appropriate**, for it to match the tone of the rest of the essay.

* Even in this example, we'd want to take a look at the rest of the paragraph, just to be safe. Maybe he *did* give a violent speech thanking people. Maybe he's a werewolf. Maybe he's just kind of a jerk. But the rest of the paragraph should give us all the clues we need.

† We're not talking about *vulgarity* here. I'm sure there are some terrible, *terrible* things you say to your friends that you wouldn't even say to your parents, let alone use on a school essay. You won't see any cursing on the ACT.

II. ORGANIZATION

Organization is all about the flow of information in the essay. Sentences and paragraphs should be put into a logical order and the transitions between them should be appropriate.

Transition words

Questions about transition words *between sentences* occur more frequently than those about transition words *between clauses in a single sentence.*

About half of all Organization questions deal with *transitions* between sentences. Transition words are words that connect parts of sentences or that connect different sentences. The key to picking the right transition word is to understand the **relationship** between the sentences.

Let's look at a few examples:

When sentences have **contrasting** meanings, the connecting word should reflect that contrast.

× **Johnny has never been a very good athlete. Additionally, he has won his last five races.**

✓ **Johnny has never been a very good athlete. However, he has won his last five races.**

Obviously, these two sentences are different: if Johnny's not a good athlete, we wouldn't expect him to win any races. So we want to connect the sentences with a contrast word like "however", not a similarity word like "additionally".

Other sentences may show **similarity**, or they may be a **continuation** of an idea in the previous sentence.

× **Sergio has never liked cats. On the other hand, he refuses to be in the same room as one.**

✓ **Sergio has never liked cats. In fact, he refuses to be in the same room as one.**

"On the other hand" shows contrast, but both sentences have similar meanings—Sergio hates cats. The second sentence is an *elaboration* on the first one. It gives an example of the *great extent* of Sergio's hatred.

A special kind of similarity is a **cause-and-effect** relationship:

× **Kristen needed a lot of different colors for her project. Nevertheless, she bought the large box of crayons.**

✓ **Kristen needed a lot of different colors for her project. Therefore, she bought the large box of crayons.**

The first sentence gives a reason for the second sentence. Kristen's need for a lot of colors *explains why* she bought the large box.

Of course, you don't need transition words between *every* two sentences. Sometimes the best transition is **no transition**. Observe:

× **Robinson completed his study on cat ownership. However, it found that cat owners were more likely to be happy than those without cats.**

× **Robinson completed his study on cat ownership. Additionally, it found that cat owners were more likely to be happy than those without cats.**

Neither of these transitions makes much sense here. "However" doesn't make sense since there's no contrast. But "additionally" doesn't make sense either: the second sentence isn't making a *new* point. It's giving details about the study mentioned in the first sentence.

We might be able to come up with a transition word that would work. But we don't really need a transition word here at all.

✓ **Robinson completed his study on cat ownership. It found that cat owners were more likely to be happy than those without cats.**

Here are some examples of transition words that show different relationships:

Contrast	*although, in contrast, instead, nevertheless, on the other hand, while, yet*
Cause and effect	*as a result, because, consequently, since, so, therefore, thus*
Similarity or continuation	*additionally, finally, for example, furthermore, indeed, in fact, that is*

These words don't all have exactly the same meaning. And these lists are not exhaustive—you'll almost certainly encounter other transition words that aren't listed here. But don't worry about the nuances; for most ACT questions, all you have to know is the *general* kind of word you need. If there's no contrast, don't use a contrast word. If there is contrast, don't use a similarity word.

Transition sentences

Transitions don't have to be simple words. Sometimes a clause or a full sentence can provide a transition:

Joy used to think sudoku puzzles were impossible. [5] She can now solve the hardest puzzles in just a few minutes.

5. Given that all the choices are true, which provides the most effective transition from the preceding sentence to the next one:

A. Once she learned a few tricks, though, they became easy for her.
B. Sudoku puzzles were invented in Japan.
C. The newspaper prints a new sudoku puzzle every day.
D. She loves crossword puzzles, but these things confused her.

What's the relationship between these sentences? The first sentence says that Joy has trouble with the puzzles. The next one says she can solve the hardest ones. What are we missing? She must have *learned how to solve them.* We need a choice that teaches Joy how to solve the puzzles. Only choice A fits.

Let's try another:

Firefighter training prepares you for any danger you may face. The program can be expensive, and [6] you will immediately know how to safely and effectively react to it.

6. Assuming that all the choices are accurate, which provides the most effective transition from the preceding sentence to this one:

F. NO CHANGE
G. When you're in a life-threatening situation,
H. While it's exciting to be a firefighter,
J. You get to ride the truck, where

What's the relationship between these sentences? The first has to do with firefighter training. Well, *all* the choices are about being a firefighter. But what does it say *about* firefighter training? It prepares you for *danger*. The second sentence is about how you "safely and effectively react to it." What's *it*? A *danger!* So we want a choice that says something about *dangers*. Only choice G works.

The key to both these examples is that the transition phrase is **relevant to both sentences**, the one before it and the one after it.* That's the point of a transition—to connect the things on either side. Sentences that are *next to* each other should *refer to* each other in some way.

* Notice that all the wrong choices are *irrelevant* to the other two sentences. We'll talk more about this in a minute.

Introductions and conclusions

Similarly, a question might ask you to provide an **introductory sentence** to a paragraph. An introductory sentence often serves as a transition between the previous paragraph and the new one. But sometimes an introductory sentence simply gives you the *topic* of the paragraph. So you need to know what the paragraph is *about*—the **main idea** of the paragraph.*

<u>While not as diverse as dogs, cats come in many different breeds.</u>[7] Having a sleepy cat purring on your lap can relax you and relieve stress. Cats can be playful and fun, making adventures using normal household objects. In addition, cats can catch mice and other household pests.

7. **Given that all the choices are true, which one most effectively introduces the subject of this paragraph?**
   - A. NO CHANGE
   - B. **Cats were first domesticated thousands of years ago.**
   - (C.) **Owning a cat has both personal and practical benefits.**
   - D. **Some cats can live to be over 15 years old.**

In order to answer the question, we need to figure out the main idea of the paragraph. It's obviously about cats, but all the choices are about cats. We need to be more specific. What does it say *about* cats? It tells us why it's *good* to have cats—they're relaxing, they're fun, and they catch pests. That's choice C.

If you have trouble finding the main idea of the paragraph, try **eliminating irrelevant choices**. Our introductory sentence should be about the same thing as the rest of the paragraph. Let's check the choices:

A: Is the paragraph about different breeds of cats? No, it doesn't mention any different breeds.

B: Is the paragraph about the history of cats' domestication? No, it doesn't mention any history or the process of domestication.

C: Is the paragraph about benefits of owning a cat? **Yes!** They're relaxing, fun, and they catch pests.

D: Is the paragraph about how long cats live? No, it doesn't mention cats' life spans at all.

Sentence order

Sometimes a paragraph will have all the right sentences, but they'll be in the wrong order. Observe:

[1] Having diverse plant life can be good for an ecosystem. [2] However, sometimes exotic species can cause unexpected destruction. [3] Originally from Asia, it rapidly spread across the American South with devastating results. [4] One such example is the vine-like plant called kudzu. [8]

8. **For the sake of the logic and coherence of this paragraph, Sentence 4 should be placed:**
   - F. **where it is now.**
   - G. **before Sentence 1.**
   - H. **before Sentence 2.**
   - (J.) **before Sentence 3.**

We want to find the best place to put Sentence 4. One thing we **don't** recommend is putting Sentence 4 in each of the four spots in the choices and reading the paragraph four times to see which *sounds best*. That will take forever and won't help you a get an answer.

Instead, look for clues in Sentence 4 itself. It starts with the phrase "one such example": one example of *what*? What is kudzu an example of? It's an example of an exotic species that caused destruction—that's what Sentence 2 mentioned. Since Sentence 4 refers to something mentioned in Sentence 2, we should put Sentence 4 right after Sentence 2.

---

* Similarly, a question may ask you to provide a **concluding sentence**. Conclusions usually work just like introductions: they summarize the main idea of the paragraph.

Furthermore, Sentence 3 says "*it* rapidly spread". What does *it* refer to? *Kudzu!* Thus the mention of kudzu in Sentence 4 should come *before* Sentence 3 so we can tell what "it" is supposed to mean. That's choice J.

The key to sentence order questions is to look for references between sentences. Pronouns like "it" or words like "such" or "this" refer to concepts that came *before* them. Sentences that *refer to* each other should be *next to* each other.

III. WRITING STRATEGY

Writing Strategy questions often overlap with the concepts we saw in Style and Organization questions. They primarily differ in that they *explicitly* ask you what you as the writer should do. Should you add this sentence? Should you delete it? What is the intended purpose of this sentence? Does it achieve that purpose? If you want to achieve a certain goal, what should you do?

Writing Strategy questions commonly ask three questions:

1. Does it fulfill the writer's goals?

Some questions will tell you exactly what the writer wants to do and ask you the best way to accomplish that goal. There are two ways a question may ask you about a writer's goal.

Sentence goal

Look at this:

Cameron lay in his sleeping bag, staring up at the stars, <u>shivering in the cold wind.</u> 9

9. The writer wants to suggest the feeling that Cameron is far from civilization. Which choice best fulfills the writer's goal?

A. NO CHANGE
B. which twinkled in the sky above him.
C. alone with the chirping crickets.
D. worried about scorpions.

Any of these choices would make a fine sentence, depending on the context. The sentence we pick will depend on what the writer wants to say. Ah, but we *know* what the writer wants to say—the question tells us "the writer wants to suggest the feeling that Cameron is far from civilization." We need the choice that comes closest to *that goal*. Choice C fits nicely: Cameron is "*alone*", with only "*crickets*" around him.

These questions are pretty easy to spot. If you encounter one, don't pick the choice that sounds best *to you*; pick the choice that **fulfills the stated goal.**

Essay goal

Often, the last question of a passage will ask you a similar question about the *entire essay*. It will state what the author's goal or assignment was in writing the essay and ask if the writer fulfilled that goal.

Let's use a passage we've already seen as an example. Let's look back at Passage 1, "Bicycling the Copenhagen Way", in the exercise at the end of the Grammar & Usage chapter. Flip back to reread the essay, and then look at this question:

10. Suppose the writer's goal had been to write a brief essay about the benefits of utility cycling. Would this essay successfully accomplish that goal?

F. Yes, because the essay indicates that the author enjoyed bicycling as a child.
G. Yes, because the essay discusses several positive effects of utility cycling.
H. No, because the essay is limited to a discussion of bicycling in Europe.
J. No, because the essay indicates that fitness cycling is more beneficial than utility cycling.

There are two parts to this question. First we have to decide whether the essay fulfilled the stated goal. Then we have to choose the correct *reason* it does or does not fulfill that goal.

Questions like this are asking you for the **main idea** of the passage. Overall, what is the essay *about*? Is this essay about "the benefits of utility cycling"? Absolutely! That's clearly the primary topic of the essay. We know the answer is "yes", so we can eliminate choices H and J.

Choice G is exactly what we want: "positive effects" literally means the same thing as "benefits". The alternative, choice F, not only doesn't reflect the main idea of the passage, it's not even *true!* The essay never discusses the author's own childhood. The reference to children riding bikes with their dads is a generic example, not referring to any particular person.*

That's an important point for this kind of question: **make sure your choice is literally true**. If a choice makes a claim about what the author says, make sure that the author actually said that.

Let's try another. Let's look back at Passage 2, "Scraping the Sky", in the exercise at the end of the Sentence Structure chapter. Flip back to reread the essay, and then look at this question:

11. Suppose the writer's goal had been to write a brief essay about Elisha Otis's invention of the safety elevator. Would this essay successfully accomplish that goal?

A. Yes, because the essay indicates the safety elevator was crucial to the birth of skyscrapers.
B. Yes, because the essay describes the history of elevator safety.
C. No, because the essay does not mention Elisha Otis or the safety elevator.
D. No, because the essay primarily focuses on skyscrapers and their development.

What's the main idea of this passage? Is it about elevators? No, it's about *skyscrapers*. Our answer is "No", so we can eliminate A and B.† We're down to choices C and D.

Choice D perfectly matches our main idea—the essay is about *skyscrapers*. Choice C is *false*—the essay *does* mention Otis and the safety elevator in the third paragraph.

Questions like this show why you should **actually read the passage**. Students often focus on individual sentences because that's what most questions ask about. But don't lose sight of the big picture. You *will* see questions about the essay as a whole.

Essay goal questions are twice as likely to have an answer of "No" than "Yes". Of course, the yes-or-no answer alone isn't enough. You'll still have to find the main idea.

2. Should you add it?

Take a look at this paragraph:

Heather has come to a crossroads: she has been accepted into four colleges and must choose which one she wants to attend. [12] She has to decide what's most important to her: the school's location, its academic standing, or the size of the scholarship it offers.

12. At this point, the writer is considering adding the following true sentence:

Heather had the highest grades in her high school graduating class.

Should the writer make this addition here?

F. Yes, because it provides background on Heather that may influence her decision.
G. Yes, because Heather's grades were a factor in her acceptance to these colleges.
H. No, because the sentence does not tell us what colleges the rest of her class got into.
J. No, because it is not relevant to Heather's decision about which college to attend.

* Notice that choices C and D are also false. The essay is not just about Europe; it's about American cycling, too. And the author does not say that fitness cycling is better than utility cycling.

† Choice A may be tempting. It is *true*—the essay does say that the safety elevator was important to the development of skyscrapers. But that was just one detail in one paragraph. That's not what the whole essay is about.

Like the "essay goal" questions, these questions have two parts. First we have to determine whether to add the sentence, then we have to provide a reason for our decision. And like essay goal questions, we need to understand the main idea of the paragraph to determine if the sentence belongs here.

What's going on in this paragraph? Heather is deciding which college to go to. Would it help to know how good her high school grades were? No! Her high school grades don't matter anymore—she's already been accepted into college. Choice J is our answer: the sentence is **irrelevant** to the rest of the essay.

On questions like this, it's more than twice as likely for the answer to be "No", that you should not add the sentence. And in almost all those questions, it's because the sentence is irrelevant to the rest of the paragraph.

Irrelevant details

Irrelevant details pop up in wrong answers all over the ACT. We've already seen several examples of them (such as questions 6 and 7 above).

Take a look at this question:

Cameron had just woken up in his tent when he noticed a scorpion sitting in his boot. <u>Scorpions are actually arachnids, like spiders.</u>[13] He froze, paralyzed with fear.

13. A. NO CHANGE
B. Scorpions' bodies are segmented into three parts.
C. Scorpions can be found on every continent except Antarctica.
D. OMIT the underlined phrase.

This looks similar to some of the questions we've already seen, like the questions about redundancy or wordiness. But these choices are slightly different. Choices A, B, and C give specific, detailed information. Yet *none* of those details are relevant to the rest of the paragraph. Do you think that Cameron cares how many segments scorpions' bodies have? No! *There's a freaking scorpion in his boot!* Since all these choices are irrelevant, our best bet is to OMIT the phrase entirely.

3. What would the essay lose?

We've seen questions about eliminating sentences that don't contribute anything to the passage. But some questions will *assume* that the sentence contributes something, and you have to figure out what that is.

Hank found an old figurine while hiking in the mountains of Mexico. He noticed a strange inscription on the artifact, so he showed it to his friend Larissa, a linguist who specializes in ancient languages. [14] At first, she thought the inscription looked like a very common form of hieroglyphics. But try as she might, Larissa couldn't decipher its meaning.

14. The writer is considering deleting the phrase "a linguist who specializes in ancient languages." If the writer were to make this deletion, the paragraph would primarily lose:
F. information suggesting that Larissa will not be able to read the inscription.
G. details that explain Hank's motivation for showing Larissa the figurine.
H. evidence supporting Hank's idea about the artifact.
J. a description of the writing on the figurine.

This question tells us that deleting that part of the sentence would make the essay lose something. That's good: that means we know that it contributes something. But what does it add? Basically, the question is asking the **purpose** of the phrase.

Let's look at the *literal meaning* of the phrase in question. That phrase gives us background information about Larissa. Larissa is an expert on ancient languages, so Hank thinks she'll be able to read the inscription on the figurine. Therefore, the fact that she's an expert tells us *why* Hank showed her the figurine. That's choice G.

Let's look at another example in the same paragraph:

Hank found an old figurine while hiking in the mountains of Mexico. He noticed a strange inscription on the artifact, so he showed it to his friend Larissa, a linguist who specializes in ancient languages. At first, she thought the inscription looked like a very common form of hieroglyphics. But try as she might, Larissa couldn't decipher its meaning. [15]

15. If the writer were to delete the phrase "try as she might" (and the comma), the paragraph would primarily lose:

A. a sense of how difficult the task was for Larissa.
B. a humorous comment that lightens the mood.
C. an explanation of how to understand hieroglyphics.
D. nothing, since this information was given earlier in the paragraph.

Here, the phrase in question doesn't give *information* the way that the phrase in the last question did. Instead, it modifies the description in the last sentence. In that sentence, the main clause tells us that Larissa couldn't figure out what the inscription said, and this phrase tells us she was *trying hard* to figure it out. Which choice talks about trying hard? Only choice A.

The key to answering questions like this is figuring out the *meaning* of the phrase in question, and seeing how it *relates to* the rest of the paragraph.

RHETORICAL SKILLS SUMMARY

Here are the key rules to look out for on ACT Rhetorical Skills questions:

1. **Style**
   - Be **concise**. Avoid *redundant* or *wordy* choices.
   - Be **specific**. Avoid *vague* choices and vague *pronouns*.
   - Choose **the right word**. Make sure it has the right *meaning* and *tone*.
2. **Organization**
   - Choose the right **transition word** to connect *similar or contrasting* sentences.
   - Choose the right **transition phrase** to connect the *topics* of adjacent sentences.
   - An **introductory or concluding sentence** should state the *main idea* of the paragraph.
   - Find the right **sentence order** by looking at references within the sentences.
3. **Writing Strategy**
   - Does a choice **fulfill the writer's goal**?
     - For a sentence, focus on the *stated goal*, not your opinion.
     - For the essay, find the *main idea* of the essay and eliminate choices that are *false*.
   - Should the writer **add or delete** a sentence? Look out for *irrelevant* choices.
   - If the writer deleted a phrase, **what would the essay lose**? Find the *meaning* of the phrase and how it *relates* to the paragraph.

RHETORICAL SKILLS EXERCISE

This exercise contains a full passage with 15 questions, just like an ACT passage. Unlike a real ACT passage, it only features ***Rhetorical Skills*** *questions. Look out for all the rules discussed above. Enjoy!*

PASSAGE V

Margaret Mitchell's First Novel

[1] It was clear from a young age that Margaret Mitchell had a knack for storytelling. [2] As a child growing up in Atlanta, she would make up tales by the hundreds, writing them in homemade books, which she made herself.[1] [3] After spending one year at Smith College,[2] she eventually got a job as a columnist for the *Atlanta Journal*. [4] As she got older, she would write plays that she would act out with her friends. [5] Instead,[3] she was a literary editor of her high school yearbook and founded a drama society. [6] She became one of the first women to write for a major newspaper in the South. [4]

1. A. NO CHANGE
   B. books by herself in her youth.
   C. books she assembled by herself.
   D. books.

2. F. NO CHANGE
   G. College, which was founded in 1875,
   H. College, a school for women only,
   J. College, named after founder Sophia Smith,

3. A. NO CHANGE
   B. However,
   C. Later,
   D. In contrast,

4. For the sake of the logic and coherence of the paragraph, Sentence 3 should be placed:
   F. where it is now.
   G. after Sentence 1.
   H. after Sentence 4.
   J. after Sentence 5.

While working at the newspaper, an accidental injury[5] launched her literary career. In 1926, she broke her ankle and was forced to stay home while it healed.

5. Which choice provides the most specific and detailed information?
   A. NO CHANGE
   B. a freak occurrence
   C. a life-changing episode
   D. the occasion of an unexpected event

Her bed rest became the cause of her boredom, and she[6] began to occupy herself by writing chapters for a novel.

6. F. NO CHANGE
   G. Bored with her bed rest,
   H. Given that bed rest was boring for her,
   J. With the time she spent in her bed beginning to make her bored,

She kept writing after her ankle healed, and the [7] manuscript soon evolved into her masterpiece, the Civil War epic *Gone with the Wind.*

She got some of the ideas for the book from her grandfather, a Civil War veteran. [8] She was too humble and too bashful to show it to anyone or even to acknowledge that she had written anything. One day, when an editor from New York came to Atlanta looking for talented new authors, she graciously showed him around town without even mentioning her own book. [9] It was quickly accepted and finally published the following year.

Gone with the Wind received near universal praise both from the general public and from critics: the book sold millions of copies and won the Pulitzer Prize. [10] The film adaptation, premiering in Atlanta three years later, was just as popular as the book. It won ten Academy Awards, and, when prices are adjusted for inflation, it still holds the record as the highest-grossing movie of all time, weirdly. [11]

7. The writer wishes to indicate that writing the manuscript took a great deal of work. Which of the choices provides a vivid and specific detail that accomplishes that goal?
   - A. NO CHANGE
   - B. Three years and one thousand pages later,
   - C. Written with exquisite prose,
   - D. A story about the daughter of a Georgia plantation owner,

8. Given that all the choices are true, which choice would provide the most effective transition from the previous paragraph while introducing the topic of this one?
   - F. NO CHANGE
   - G. She wrote the last chapter first and filled in earlier chapters in a random order.
   - H. It wasn't until 1936, however, that the book was actually published.
   - J. While most of the book was finished, she had not yet given the book a title.

9. Assuming that all the choices are accurate, which provides the most effective transition from the preceding sentence to this one?
   - A. Later that night, she changed her mind and decided to show him the manuscript.
   - B. Most publishing houses were based in the northeast.
   - C. Besides, at the time it was difficult for a woman to get a novel published.
   - D. Her job at the newspaper made her rather well known around town.

10. If the writer were to delete the phrase "and won the Pulitzer Prize" from the preceding sentence, the paragraph would primarily lose:
    - F. a detail that explains why Mitchell decided to write the book.
    - G. a contrast to the phrase "sold millions of copies" in the same sentence.
    - H. a statement that reveals how the book was made into a film.
    - J. a detail supporting the idea that the book was well received.

11.
    - A. NO CHANGE
    - B. time. Isn't that crazy?
    - C. time.
    - D. time. That blows my mind!

Despite the success of *Gone with the Wind*, Mitchell never published another novel. In fact, the success of her first book may have prevented her from writing another. She had immediately become an international celebrity almost overnight, but the constant demands of fame were overwhelming for her. [14] When a reporter once asked her whether she had been writing anything, she said she was too busy responding to mail about her last book to work on anything new. But even without writing any other books, she had secured literary immortality. Upon her death in 1949, her obituary described *Gone with the Wind* as "the most phenomenal best seller ever written by an unknown author of a first novel." [15]

12. F. NO CHANGE
G. Consequently,
H. Therefore,
J. On the other hand,

13. A. NO CHANGE
B. celebrity incredibly quickly,
C. celebrity at once,
D. celebrity,

14. At this point, the writer is considering adding the following true statement:

A steadfast humanitarian, she dedicated herself to volunteering with the American Red Cross upon the start of World War II.

Should the writer make this addition here?

F. Yes, because it provides evidence of Mitchell's international fame.
G. Yes, because it helps clarify Mitchell's reasons for writing the book.
H. No, because it repeats information given earlier in the essay.
J. No, because it is irrelevant to the focus of the paragraph.

15. Suppose the writer had wanted to write an essay that discusses the importance of the book *Gone with the Wind* in American culture. Would this essay fulfill the writer's goal?

A. Yes, because the essay details the way that the book came to be published.
B. Yes, because the essay describes why the book was so popular with the public.
C. No, because the essay focuses on the author rather than the work she created.
D. No, because the essay argues that Mitchell was not a significant figure in American literature.

ACT MATH

INTRODUCTION TO ACT MATH

Welcome to ACT Math! I think you'll like it here. Let's take a look around.

Many people consider the ACT to be much more of a content-based test compared to its cousin, the SAT. While it is true that the ACT requires slightly more math knowledge than the SAT does, it's still a *reasoning test* at heart.

ACT math is not exactly the same as the math you do in school. Yes, a lot of your old favorites will show up here (ratios, two-variable equations, the Pythagorean Theorem, and many more!) but the questions are a little bit different. In school, you learn *content*. For example, you learn *algebra* and then you're tested on *how well you use algebra*. The ACT gives you a *problem* and asks you to solve it *any way you can*. That could mean algebra or it could mean arithmetic or geometry. On any given problem, there's no one way that's "the right way" to do it. Now, some ways are faster or safer than others, so our job is to show you *the best way* to do a given problem.

Throughout the next chapters, we'll be talking about two types of things: content and techniques. *Content* is the literal stuff you need to know (like the Pythagorean Theorem). *Techniques* are methods for doing lots of different kinds of problems (like Plug In). Both are equally important. However, a lot of the content you'll already be familiar with from your adventures in school; it's the techniques that will be new for you, so that's where we will concentrate.

> The appendices at the end of this book contain a quick guide to all the formulas and definitions you need for the ACT Math Test.

GENERAL FORMAT

Here are a few notes about the format of the ACT Math Test:

- It consists of **60 multiple-choice questions** in **60 minutes**. The timing here can be a little rough. Don't freak out. It'll be okay. We'll talk more about timing strategies in the Math Techniques chapter.
- All questions are **ordered by difficulty**—questions at the beginning of the section are easy and questions at the end are hard.*
- All questions are multiple choice. But unlike in the other ACT tests, math questions will have **5 choices per question** instead of 4.
- Calculators are allowed, but not required.
- Like all ACT questions, there is **no penalty for wrong answers**. That means you should **NEVER LEAVE ANY QUESTION BLANK.** If you're not sure of an answer, guess one. If you don't do all the questions, pick random choices for the ones you didn't finish.

* This is approximate, of course. Difficulty is a subjective thing; what's hard for one student isn't always what's hard for another. But it will be true *in general*. Question #37 will not necessarily be harder than question #36. But it will certainly be harder than question #17. And question #57 will be harder than both.

QUESTION TYPES

The ACT groups math questions into six categories. The number of questions in these categories is fixed, so every test will always have the same number of questions of each type, though they will be mixed up in any order. Below is a chart outlining how many questions will appear for each type:

QUESTION TYPE	NUMBER OF QUESTIONS	PERCENT OF TEST
Pre-Algebra	14	23%
Elementary Algebra	10	17%
Intermediate Algebra	9	15%
Coordinate Geometry	9	15%
Plane Geometry	14	23%
Trigonometry	4	7%

In addition to your overall Math score (1–36), you will get three subscores (1–18) based on the different topics that appear in the math questions:

- Pre-Algebra & Elementary Algebra (24 questions)
- Intermediate Algebra & Coordinate Geometry (18 questions)
- Plane Geometry & Trigonometry (18 questions)

Here's an outline of the concepts included in each category, as defined by the ACT. This roughly corresponds to the order in which they're presented in this book, though we may have switched some around to make things easier to follow.

Pre-Algebra

Pre-Algebra questions include any question that deals with only numbers (not variables), word problems that don't require writing equations, and simple equations with only one variable. Major topics include:

- One-variable equation solving
- Basic operations
- Manipulating fractions and decimals
- Basic roots & exponents
- Ratios & percents
- Multiples, factors, and primes
- Probability and combinatorics
- Mean, median, and mode
- Data interpretation
- Basic manipulation of absolute value

Elementary Algebra

Elementary Algebra questions involve more advanced algebraic manipulation. Over 40% of these questions can be done with a Math Technique like Plug In or Backsolve. Major topics include:

- Multi-variable equations
- More advanced nonlinear equations
- Translating word problems into algebraic expressions
- Evaluating equations with a given value
- Substitution of expressions
- FOIL, polynomials, and factoring expressions

Intermediate Algebra

Intermediate Algebra questions involve higher-level algebra questions and more advanced topics. Over 50% of these questions can be done with a Math Technique like Plug In or Backsolve. Major topics include:

- Algebraic expressions using exponents and exponent rules
- Functions, $f(x)$ format, combining functions
- Quadratic manipulation and quadratic inequalities
- Absolute value equations and inequalities
- Arithmetic and Geometric sequences
- Imaginary numbers
- Matrices
- Logarithms

Coordinate Geometry

Coordinate Geometry questions include anything and everything related to graphing and the *xy*-coordinate plane. Major topics include:

- Understanding the *xy*-coordinate plane and its quadrants
- Locating coordinates of geometrical figures
- Slope & intercepts
- Graphing linear equations
- Intersection of graphs
- Equations of circles and ellipses
- Graphs of inequalities
- Midpoint & distance formulas
- Transformation of functions

Plane Geometry

Plane Geometry questions include anything and everything related to geometry and figures, excluding figures graphed on the coordinate plane (which are included in Coordinate Geometry). Students will be expected to know some basic formulas (area of a triangle, circumference of a circle, etc.) Some higher-level formulas when necessary will be given in the problems. Major topics include:

- Angle rules and properties
- Pythagorean theorem and special triangles (3–4–5, 30–60–90, 45–45–90 triangles)
- Similar triangles & rules of congruence
- Properties of triangles, rectangles, parallelograms, trapezoids, circles
- Perimeter and length
- Area, shaded area, and irregular shapes
- Surface area and volume
- Rotation and reflection
- Logic and logical consequence

Trigonometry

Most trigonometry questions will require a basic understanding of trigonometric terms. Some questions may involve higher-level formulas, such as the law of cosines, but in those cases the formulas will be given to you in the problem. Major topics include:

- Definitions of basic trigonometric ratios (sin, cos, tan, sec, csc, cot)
- Basic identities
- Graphing trigonometric functions and their transformations
- Law of sines and law of cosines
- The Unit Circle
- Radians and degrees

CALCULATORS

Here are some frequently asked questions about calculators:

1. Can I use one?

Yes! Calculators are allowed on the ACT. Only on the Math Test, though. You may not use a calculator on the English, Reading, or Science tests (not that you'd need one).

2. *Any* calculator?

For the most part. You may use a four-function, scientific, or graphing calculators. Certain calculators are not allowed. According to the ACT guidelines, you may NOT use:

- calculators on cell phones or smart phones
- calculators with built-in algebra systems (like the TI-89)
- handheld, tablet, or laptop computers
- electronic writing pads or pen-input devices
- calculators with typewriter-style ("QWERTY") keypads.

Some calculators are allowed with modifications: for example, calculators with infrared ports are allowed only if you cover up the port.

Calculators that possess human emotions, can feel pain, or are armed with any kind of weapons systems are also forbidden. Cybernetic implants are allowed on a case-by-case basis.

Do I really need one?

Strictly speaking, calculators are **allowed but not required**. That means that every question *can* be done without a calculator. Most of the time, the only actual calculation you'll need to do is basic addition, subtraction, multiplication, and division.

If a question involves a concept that can't be done by hand, the question itself will give you the necessary calculations. In fact, if a question has such calculations, that's a clue telling you what you need to solve the problem. But you may not need every calculation they give you. For example, if a question says:

Note: $\sin 25° \approx 0.42$, $\cos 25° \approx 0.91$, $\tan 25° \approx 0.47$.

You know you're going to need at least *one* of those calculations in the problem. But you probably won't need *all* of them.

That said, just because a question *can* be done by hand doesn't mean you *want* to. Calculators are useful when you have big computations to do, and **you should definitely get one**.

But don't leap for the calculator *every* time you have to do math. Don't use a calculator to do 7 + 5.[*] The better you are at doing simple math in your head, the faster you will work. This sounds counterintuitive, but yes, **it is faster to do simple math in your head**. I promise. Some people have no faith in their abilities and insist on punching everything into their calculators because "the calculator is always right." These people are cowards. And guess what? While the calculator is always right, there's a chance *you* might make a mistake typing stuff into your calculator. Especially if you have trouble doing 7 + 5 in your head.

Do I need a graphing calculator?

You certainly don't *need* one. Again, the test is calculator-optional, so everything you need to do can be done with a cheap-o four-function drug-store calculator that's missing the 7-key.[†]

Now, there are some questions on which a graphing calculator can help you, particularly Coordinate Geometry questions. These questions are not common, but there are some fancy tools that can sometimes help you—if you know how to use them. Of course, if you don't know how to use them, they won't be helpful at all.

So if you don't already have a graphing calculator, you don't have to go out and get one. If you have one, sure, use it. If know how to use it well, it might work to your advantage every once in a while. But if not, don't sweat it. You'll be fine. Just learn 7 + 5. That's all we ask.

---

[*] It's 12.

[†] Well, okay, you probably need the 7-key.

MATH TECHNIQUES

AS we mentioned earlier, there are two components to our ACT Math materials: *content* and *techniques*. The content is all the *stuff* you need: all the rules and basic math you learned in school (hopefully). In this chapter, we'll talk about the techniques, the *ways of doing problems*. They can be used on just about any type of problem: on hard problems or easy problems, arithmetic or algebra, with triangles or circles, <u>anywhere</u>. They are powerful, versatile, and very, very easy.

I. GENERAL STRATEGIES

We'll start with two quick and easy things you can do to help organize your time, be more efficient, and cut down on careless mistakes:

1. Circle the Question

2. Show Your Work

Circle the Question

This takes all of two seconds to do but can significantly help you.

- It can help reduce the number of careless mistakes you make (more about this in the next section).
- It will help you understand how to do the problem. By focusing on the thing you're trying to find rather than the things they give you, it's easier to think about what you need in order to find it.

Do this on every problem. No exceptions.

Show Your Work

You're probably tired of hearing math teachers to tell you to "Show your work!" Well, too bad.

SHOW YOUR WORK!

We can already hear you complaining:

"Why bother? It's not like you get partial credit for doing it correctly."

True, you don't get partial credit, and there is no single "correct method". But that's not the point at all.

The point is that not writing down your steps is ***the single greatest reason*** for students' careless mistakes. We are astounded by how often we see students do an entire test worth of math problems without writing a thing on any page. These students are not getting the scores they want.

This is not a memory test. You can't possibly keep track of everything in your head, and you should never have more than one step in your head at any moment. By just writing down what you're doing as you do it, you can turn a complex problem into a series of small, basic steps. And you can *significantly* reduce your odds of making a careless mistake, like adding instead of subtracting, or solving for the wrong variable.

Furthermore, showing your work gives you a record of what you've done. This makes it easier to find mistakes when you're checking your work during a test. And it makes it easier to look over your performance when you're reviewing a practice test you just finished. This way, when you want to know why you got #10 wrong, you'll see what you did to get your answer.

"But I don't need to write stuff down. I'm good at math and can do it all in my head."

No, you can't.

"No, really, I can."

No, really, you can't. ACT problems are <u>complicated</u>. You can't hold every step in your head at once. And you know what? You don't have to! If you write stuff down, you don't have to remember everything.

And these questions are designed to fool you. Many students' biggest problem *isn't* that they don't know enough math—it's that they're missing questions *that they already know how to do*, because they make careless, stupid mistakes.

"That just slows me down. I don't have time to show my work."

You don't have time to write down numbers? That's ridiculous. What, are you writing with a calligraphy pen? We're not asking you to write out every single step in complete sentences and perfect penmanship. Don't write out annotated Euclidean proofs; just keep track of which variable is which.

Seriously, we're not kidding around. Just write stuff down.

Let's look at a sample problem to see how this works:

13. Points A, B, C, and D lie on a line in that order. The length of $\overline{AB}$ is 8, and the length of $\overline{CD}$ is 7. Point C is the midpoint of segment $\overline{BD}$. What is the length of segment $\overline{AD}$?

A. 7
B. 14
C. 15
D. 22
E. 23

> ACT Math questions are numbered by difficulty. Accordingly, all sample questions throughout this book reflect that numbering. This question, for example, would be #13 on a 60-question section, so it should be relatively simple.

First thing to do: **circle the question**. Not the whole problem, smart guy; just circle the thing that they're asking you to find.

Points A, B, C, and D lie on a line in that order. The length of $\overline{AB}$ is 8, and the length of $\overline{CD}$ is 7. Point C is the midpoint of segment $\overline{BD}$. What is the length of segment $\overline{AD}$?

Wrong.

Points A, B, C, and D lie on a line in that order. The length of $\overline{AB}$ is 8, and the length of $\overline{CD}$ is 7. Point C is the midpoint of segment $\overline{BD}$. What is the length of segment $\overline{AD}$?

Right.

Okay, now what?

ACT questions are complicated. There's often a lot going on within a question, and it's easy to take your eye off the ball. There might be so much information that you're not sure what to do with it. If you're not sure how to get started, **ask yourself two questions**:

1. **What do I *want*?** That is, what is the question asking me for?
2. **What do I *know*?** That is, what information does the problem give me?

Then your goal is to **connect these questions**. Look at what you want and work backwards to see what you need in order to get it. Or use what you already know and see what else that tells you.

What you want: The length of $\overline{AD}$.

That's why we circled the question—to find out what we want.

What you know: $AB = 8$, $CD = 7$, C is midpoint of $\overline{BD}$.

Write down what you know. This question is about a line, but no figure is given. So **draw the figure**.

First draw the points in order:

Then label the lengths you're given:

And since C is the midpoint of $\overline{BD}$, $BC = CD$:

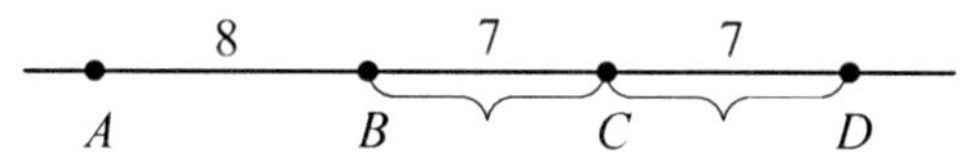

$\overline{AD}$ is the whole length, so we have everything we need: $AD = 8 + 7 + 7 = \mathbf{22}$.

Our answer is **choice D.**

This is an addition to our rule about showing your work: if a geometry problem doesn't already have a picture, **DRAW A PICTURE!** It doesn't have to be perfect; even a rough sketch can help you understand the problem and catch careless mistakes.

Notice that we didn't know where we were going when we started. We just played with the stuff we knew until we got what we needed. The point here is to not be scared. There's always *something* that you know, and something that you can figure out. If you work forward from what you know or backwards from what you want, chances are you can connect them in the middle. Even if you're not sure where you're going, the more you write down, the easier it will be to make a connection.

II. Common Mistakes

The people who make the ACT aren't chumps. They know how high school kids think. More importantly, they know how high school kids mess up. Therefore, when they write the test they intentionally include wrong answer choices that kids who make certain common mistakes will choose. However, once you know what these mistakes are and how to avoid them, you will be much less likely to make them.

RTFQ

Take a look at this question:

15. A certain bookstore gets a shipment of 24 copies of a new book and sells 18 of them. What percentage of the books was NOT sold?

A. **75%**
B. **67%**
C. **50%**
D. **33%**
E. **25%**

Okay, so 18 over 24 is 0.75, which is 75%. That's choice A, right?

WRONG! That's the number of books that were ***sold***; the question is asking for those that were ***not sold***. They even put it in CAPITAL LETTERS! Pay attention!

We call choice A the **RTFQ** choice. "RTFQ" stands for "Read the full question." It's what happens when all of your math was correct, but you didn't solve for the thing they were asking for.

RTFQ choices show up *all over* the test. They could show up on question #60 or on question #1. It is a very easy mistake to make. But it's also a very easy mistake to avoid: *just read the question.* Take an extra two seconds to make sure that the number you're choosing is the number they want.

In fact, we've already given you two ways to help cut down on RTFQ mistakes: **Circle the Question** and **Show Your Work**. Both of these things will significantly help you keep track of what you're doing.

Some students don't put enough weight on these mistakes when they make them on practice tests. "Oh, I *knew* how to do that one," they say. "I just wrote down the wrong answer." What? That's *so much worse!* If you don't know how to do the math, fine. We can teach you how to do math. But you don't know how to write down what they're asking for? **You are throwing away points by missing questions that you already know how to do.**

Here's a harder one. Give it a shot, and make sure you *read every word of the question.*

44. If a is a number selected from the set {1, 2, 3} and b is a number selected from the set {3, 5, 7}, how many different values for $a + b$ are possible?

F. 5
G. 6
H. 7
J. 8
K. 9

Fool's Gold

Take a look at this problem:

60. Scott drives to Bob's house at a speed of 30 miles per hour and drives back at a speed of 50 miles per hour. If he takes the same route both ways, what was his average speed, in miles per hour, for the whole trip?

F. 35
G. 37.5
H. 40
J. 42.5
K. **Cannot be determined from the given information**

We want the average speed for the trip. His two speeds are 30 and 50. So the average is 30 + 50 divided by two. That's 40. Choice H.

Wow, that was easy. Hmm. A little *too* easy.

Wait a minute. This is question number 60 out of 60. Questions are ordered by difficulty. That means this is the *hardest* question on the test. There's *no way* that the hardest question on the test can be done by just taking the average of two numbers *that they give me!* That can't possibly be right.

Look at it this way:

1. We know for a fact that ACT Math Test questions are ordered by difficulty.
2. A question's difficulty is determined by looking at the percentage of students who get it right.
3. Most kids probably had the same instinct I did: take the average of the speeds.
4. But I <u>know</u> that most kids get it wrong. *That's why it's number 60.*
5. Therefore, taking the average of 30 and 50 is wrong. If it were right, most kids would get it right. *So it wouldn't be number 60.*
6. Therefore, I can eliminate choice H.

We call this a ***Fool's Gold*** choice. It's when a hard question has a choice that's so easy and so obvious that it can't possibly be right. We *know* the question must be harder than this. It must be a trap.

So if you see an easy choice on a hard question—***eliminate it***. You know most people get it wrong. So the obvious answer *can't* be right.* Sometimes we see students who even *recognize* a choice as a Fool's Gold choice, and then pick it anyway because they can't think of any other way of doing the problem. They wind up choosing the one choice that they *know* is wrong. That's madness. Utter, utter madness.

Let's go back and take another look at that #60 above. We eliminated H as Fool's Gold. Hmm. But if that's not right, how else would you do the problem? All it tells us is the two speeds; we don't know the distance traveled or the time it took. So maybe there isn't enough information. That's Choice K. Right?

> Choice K, "Cannot be determined", isn't *always* wrong. It's often Fool's Gold on hard questions, but perfectly plausible on easy questions.

Wrong! "Cannot be determined" is a *classic* Fool's Gold choice. Number 60 is not going to be as easy as, "Well, uhh, they don't tell me anything, so I guess I dunno." Don't be a quitter.

So we've eliminated H and K. Worst-case scenario, we can guess from the three remaining choices. Remember, **you may not leave any questions blank.**

So how do we do actually do this? The reason you can't just take the average of 30 and 50 is because those are already rates. In order to find the average speed for a trip, you have to take the rate of the *total* distance over the *total* time. Hmm. If we knew the distance traveled, we could find the time it took, but we don't know either. But the answer can't be K—that's too easy. So it probably *doesn't matter* what the distance is. You probably get the same answer no matter what.

So let's **make up a value for the distance**. Let's say it's **150 miles** from Scott's house to Bob's house. Since $d = rt$, we can use the distance to find the time each leg of Scott's trip took:

To Bob's:	$150 = 30t_1$	From Bob's:	$150 = 50t_2$
	$5 \text{ hours} = t_1$		$3 \text{ hours} = t_2$

So Scott's trip took 5 hours one way and 3 hours back for a total of **8 hours**. His total distance traveled is **300 miles** (*two* trips, 150 each). So:

$$\text{Average Speed} = \frac{\text{Total Distance}}{\text{Total Time}} = \frac{300}{8} \quad \boxed{= \mathbf{37.5\ mph}}$$

That's **Choice G**! We're done! Wait, but we only got G after using a number we made up. How do we know we won't get a different answer if we chose another number? Well, try it. Make the distance 300 miles and see what you get.†

* Obviously, Fool's Gold choices only occur on the hardest questions—about the last third of the test. If there's a choice on question #3 that looks really easy, it probably really is that easy.

† You've just seen a sneak preview of Plug In, one of our fundamental Math Techniques. We'll see a lot more of this very soon…

III. Target Numbers

This is one of the most powerful strategies that we have, so much so that it gets its own section. If you ignore everything else we say, at least pay attention to this.

Most students have trouble with timing on the ACT. You've got 60 questions to do in 60 minutes. That's a lot of questions in a short amount time and a lot of students feel rushed trying to finish. But ACT Math Test questions are ordered by difficulty—number 1 is easy, and number 60 is hard. So students rush through early questions, making a lot of careless mistakes on questions they should be getting right. Then they spend a lot of time on hard questions, which they get wrong because they're hard. So they're getting nailed on both ends of the test.

But here's the thing: *the easy questions are worth the same number of points as the hard ones.*

The solution? **Target Numbers**. It's really easy to do. It's just one rule: ***DON'T DO THE WHOLE TEST***. You don't have to get *every* question in order to get the score that you want. The biggest problem most kids have isn't that they don't know enough math; it's that **they're missing questions *that they already know how to do.***

Here's a chart to figure out your target numbers:

If this is your starting score...	...do these questions...	...and get this target score
13 and below	Questions 1–23	20
15	Questions 1–29	22
17	Questions 1–34	24
19	Questions 1–40	26
21	Questions 1–45	28
23	Questions 1–50	30
25	Questions 1–54	32
27	Questions 1–57	34
29 and above	Do all questions	36

Use the chart above to find your target score and the number of questions you have to do to get that score. Do those questions, and those questions only. For example, let's say you're scoring around a 21 right now. From now on, you should do questions 1 to 45. Do all of these questions and *only* these questions; do not attempt the last 15 questions. If you get all or most of them right, you will get a 28 on the test. That's your target score.* That's 7 points higher by doing less work! Nice!

For those last 15 questions you didn't do, **guess something**. Don't leave them blank. It doesn't matter what you pick, just pick something. You don't lose points for wrong answers, so you'll pick up a few points by chance. **The points you pick up by random guessing are factored into the final score listed here.**

Okay, so you're doing fewer problems, but how do you know you'll do any better on those problems than you were doing before? Because now you've got *fewer questions* to do *in the same amount of time*, so you can spend **more time per question**. The more time you spend on a question, the less likely it is you'll make a careless mistake.

* This is **an approximation** of course. You may not get *exactly* the score listed here. Every scoring table is different. Your random guessing might be particularly lucky or unlucky. And the listed target score is an upper limit, assuming you get all or most of these questions right. If you miss some, then you won't hit the target. But you should get into the ballpark.

People tend to think about ACT scores in the wrong context. People tend to think of them like *figure skating* scores—there's a perfect ten and then points deducted for your flaws.* Instead, think of them like *basketball* scores—you're just trying to get as many points as possible. As such, your *shooting percentage* is much more important than the number of shots you take.

This strategy is amazing. You can get a score increase by literally doing *less* work, not by learning new things but by nailing all the things you already know how to do. It's miraculous.

Frequently Asked Questions about Target Numbers

1. **Why are you making me do this? What, you think I'm too *dumb* to get #60? Jerk.**

   Let's say this right upfront: *we're not saying you're too dumb to get #60.* We firmly believe that *anyone* could get #60 if given enough time for it. **This isn't about skipping questions that are too hard for you.** The goal here is simply to **do fewer questions**. That's it. So if we're doing fewer questions, we're not going to skip the easy ones; we're going to skip the hard ones. That's just common sense.

   Yes, if you did the whole test, you *might* get number #58. But why worry about #58 when you're still missing #3? We *know* you can get #3. That's the goal here—to nail *all* the easy questions. Why worry about the hard stuff when you're still missing points on the easy stuff? Let's nail those down before we do anything else.

2. **I finished my target numbers, but I've still got some time left. Should I move on to more questions?**

   NO! If you finish your target numbers and still have time, *go back and check your work.* Again, **the point here is to make sure that you get the easy questions.** If you have time left over, don't keep going, and don't stare blankly at the wall for five minutes. Go back and check your work.

3. **I stuck to my target questions, but there were still some hard ones in there, so I left them blank too. Is that okay?**

   NO! **Never leave anything blank!** First of all, there's no penalty for guessing. Secondly, the goal here isn't to "skip hard questions". We're telling you exactly how many questions you need to do to get a good score increase. That means you have to do *all* the questions within your target numbers.

   Yes, there will still be some hard ones in there. They aren't all as easy as #2. *But that's why we have a hundred pages worth of Math chapters!* You didn't think we'd just stop here, did you? There's a lot more we have to go through, and we're going to show you some great techniques that will help you with those hard questions that are within your target numbers.

   If you can't do a question within your target, try a technique like Plug In or Backsolve. If you *really* have *no idea* what to do, don't spend five minutes staring at the page. Guess randomly and move on. But honestly, that shouldn't happen very frequently.

4. **I'm supposed to stop at #50, but I don't know how to do it. But I think I can do #53. Can I skip #50 and do #53 instead?**

   The very fact that you're asking this question means you've thought about two questions. **That takes time**, time you could've spent checking your work on the easy questions. Again, the point here is timing—we want you to spend time making sure you get the easy questions. We do NOT want you to spend time on trying to figure out which questions to do. We want your game plan to be set before you go to the test.

   Now, we do realize that there is a wide variety of question types on the test, and some people really are better at some types than others. Maybe #50 is a weird logarithm question, but #53 is a function question and you're really good at functions. Or it's a question that can be really easy with a technique like Plug In. That seems okay. But be careful: it may only *look* like you can do #53. It might be more complicated than it seems. Maybe there's a trick you didn't see. Maybe there's a Fool's Gold choice. Who knows?

---

* Wait, is that how figure skating is scored? I have no idea.

But you know what we do know? **That you can do #2.** If you've done everything you can on #50 and still can't even eliminate one choice, ***GO BACK AND CHECK QUESTION NUMBER TWO!*** Yes, there may be questions beyond your target numbers that you are capable of doing. But the goal of this technique is to **make sure you get the easy questions**. The questions past your target numbers are not there. They do not exist. We would tell you to rip those pages out of the test book if you were allowed to do that.*

This isn't about picking which *types* of questions you're good or bad at. It's about doing fewer questions, period. Yes, you certainly *could* get some of the later questions right if you had the time. But you don't. And you can *definitely* get the easy questions.

5. **I nailed my target numbers on this practice test. Can I do more on the next one?**

   First of all, if you nailed all your target numbers, congratulations! Your math score has probably increased substantially. Fantastic. But for the next practice test, keep the same numbers. We want to see you do it again. Once might have been a fluke—maybe you were in the zone that day or just happened to get a lot of question types that you're really good at. If you nail all your target numbers *twice*, then we can start to talk about raising them.

   But then again, you might not want to raise them. If you really do nail your target numbers, you might be happy where you are. I think you'll be pleasantly surprised by what it does for your score.

6. **I work really slowly and I never finish the test. What should I do?**

   Congratulations! We were going to tell you not to finish the test anyway. You're one step ahead of us. Are you psychic?

   Again, the goal here is to be *accurate* on the questions that you *do*. If you're not quite making it through all of your target numbers, that's okay—as long as you've got a high shooting percentage on the ones you *do* get to. Plus, once we get to work on the nuts and bolts of the math, you should be able to get through those easy problems much faster.

7. **Do these pants make me look fat?**

   Of course not. You look great. Now stop thinking about your outfit and pay attention.

8. **I have extended/unlimited time for the ACT. Do I still have to do this?**

   Hmm… are you still making careless mistakes, even with extra time? Then yes. Yes you do.

9. **Do I have to do this on the real test too?**

   What? Of course you do! Is that a serious question? Why would we tell you to do this only on practice tests? For fun? You think we're just messing with you? Everything we tell you to do in this book is something you should do on the real test.

10. **Should I do this on the English, Reading, or Science as well?**

    Not exactly. The reason we do this for the math is that we know the first questions are the easy questions. Students make careless errors on early questions, so they're missing questions they know how to do. Questions on the English, Reading, and Science tests are not ordered by difficulty, so there's no guarantee that skipping the last questions means skipping the hard questions.

    On the other hand, timing certainly can be an issue on the other tests (especially the Reading Test). Remember that the same principle applies everywhere: **it's more important to be accurate on the questions you do than to do a lot of questions**. So if you are having trouble finishing the other tests, take heart. You can still get a good score there without answering all the questions, as long as you're accurate on the questions you do.

* You're not. Please do not rip pages out of your test book.

IV. The Techniques

So far we've talked about common mistakes and general strategies. Now we're getting to the good stuff: *how to actually solve problems.*

We're going to show you three techniques for ACT Math problems: Plug In, Backsolve, and Guesstimate. Collectively, these three techniques can be used on about **a third of all math problems** on the ACT. That's a lot. While each technique is different, they all have the same fundamental principle—**they turn abstract problems into concrete problems**. The goal is to turn every problem into arithmetic, to get rid of vague unknowns, intangible ideas, and long equations and make every problem into simple stuff you can punch into your calculator.

> These techniques appear most often on Elementary Algebra and Intermediate Algebra questions, but they might show up anywhere on the test.

Plug In

Let's take a look at this problem:

27. Bob has 4 dollars more than Lisa does. If Lisa has x dollars, how much would Bob have if he doubled his money?

A. $x + 4$
B. $x + 8$
C. $2x$
D. $2x + 4$
E. $2x + 8$

Notice that this question is a number 27—not too hard, but not too easy, just in the middle of the pack. We can see what they want us to do here. They give us a word problem and expect us to translate from sentences into mathematical expressions. I don't want to do that.

Take a look at the answer choices here. They all have x's in them, and x is a variable. That means it can stand for any number. Let's say the answer turned out to be choice A. Well, if the answer is A, then that's the answer. That's how much money Bob has: $x + 4$ dollars. So it will *always* be $x + 4$, *no matter what x is.* If x is 5, if x is 10, if x is 953,234,124.5255, the answer would always be A.

So let's pick an x. If the answer comes out the same no matter what number x is, we can choose any value for x that we like and we'll always get the same thing.

This is ***Plug In***. It has three steps.

1. Pick a number.

What should we choose? Something small, something manageable, preferably something that isn't already in the problem (to avoid confusion). Try to avoid weird numbers that have special properties like 0, 1, negatives or fractions. Just a nice easy counting number. I like 3. Let's say x is 3.

Once you choose a number, make sure you *write it down* and *put a box around it*, so you remember that's the number you made up.

$\boxed{x = 3}$

2. Do the problem with your number.

Read the problem again, but instead of x, use 3.

27. Bob has 4 dollars more than Lisa does. If Lisa has **3 dollars**, how much would Bob have if he doubled his money?

Lisa has x dollars, so now we'll say Lisa has 3 dollars. Bob has 4 more, so Bob has 7 dollars. So if Bob doubled his money, he'd have **14 dollars**. That's our answer: 14. Once you have an answer, circle it.

14

Wait, but 14 isn't an answer choice. Ah, one more step:

3. Put the numbers into the choices.

Our answer isn't a choice, but all the choices have x's. Aha! We have an x now. Let's put 3 in for x in the choices and see which one comes out to 14.

A.	$x + 4$	$3 + 4 = 7$ ×
B.	$x + 8$	$3 + 8 = 11$ ×
C.	$2x$	$2(3) = 6$ ×
D.	$2x + 4$	$2(3) + 4 = 6 + 4 = 10$ ×
E.	$\mathbf{2x + 8}$	$\mathbf{2(3) + 8 = 6 + 8 = 14}$ ✓

Only **Choice E** works. That's our answer. We got the problem by adding one-digit numbers.

Think of the problem as a little function, a series of steps. If I put in this number, I get out that number. When I put in 3, I got 14. The right answer choice should give me the same function. When I put in 3, I should get out 14.

Don't believe me? Try a different number for x. You should still get E as your answer.

Frequently Asked Questions about Plug In

1. Do I have to test every choice?

Yes, just to be safe. It is possible that two answer choices both give you the answer you're looking for. This could happen if you choose a number with special properties (like 1) or a number that was already in the problem. Or it could happen purely by chance. So you should check all the choices to make sure there aren't two choices that work.

2. So what do I do if I get two choices that work out?

First of all, eliminate everything else. You know it's going to be one of those two. Worst-case scenario, guess one; you've got a 50-50 chance.

But before you guess, why not try a different number? If two choices work, it's probably because you happened to pick a weird number. Pick a different one and test the choices that are left. Try different *kind* of number. If you picked a small one before, try a big one now, and vice versa.

> If a question asks what "MUST" be true, that's a sign you might want to try several different numbers.

If you *keep* getting the same two answers, try a *weird* number, like 0, 1, a fraction, or a negative.* These numbers have special properties, so they can help you notice scenarios that you might miss otherwise.

3. Why do I have to do this? That seemed like a lot of work for a #9.

First of all, we're demonstrating the technique on an easier problem so you can see how it works. The problems only get harder from here, yet Plug In is still little more than adding one-digit numbers. Heck, we already saw a Plug-In question—the Fool's Gold example about Scott driving to Bob's house. Try doing *that* sucker with algebra. It ain't pretty.

Second, Plug In may seem weird because *it's new for you.* The more you do it, the more you'll get the hang of it. Pretty soon, you'll be able to churn out problems in a fraction of the time.

Third, algebraic methods are fraught with possible careless mistakes—even on #27. Let's try some algebra on that #27 just for kicks. Bob has 4 more than Lisa, so Bob has $x + 4$. He doubles his money, so that's 2 times $x + 4$. That's D, right? Two times x plus 4? Of course not. It's not $2x + 4$; it's $2(x + 4)$. That comes out to $2x + 8$, which is E, just like we got with Plug In.

As brilliant as we all are with algebra, it's *really* easy to make a small stupid mistake like forgetting the parentheses—*especially if you don't write down your work.* But with Plug In, you're *much* less likely to make that mistake because you're working with concrete numbers. You understand what all these terms represent; they're not just abstract letters on the page. Choice D is no more tempting than any other wrong choice; it's just another choice that doesn't come out to 14.

---

* Conveniently, Fraction, One, Negative, and Zero spell *FONZ.*

There are other ways you can mess this up, too. If you forget to double Bob's money, you get A. If you double Lisa's money instead of Bob's, you get C. None of these mistakes are likely with Plug In because all you're doing is simple arithmetic.

So it's not just that Plug In is faster or easier than algebra; it's also <u>*safer*</u> than algebra. You're much less likely to make an RTFQ or Fool's Gold mistake with Plug In.

Types of Plug In Problems

1. Explicit Variables

As we've already seen, having a *variable in the answer choices* is the first sign of a Plug In problem. But it also works when there is *more than one variable.*

Sometimes you can Plug In for each variable **independently**:

26. How many hours are there in d days and h hours?

F. $24h + d$
G. $h + 24d$
H. $24(h + d)$
J. $\frac{h+d}{24}$
K. $h+\frac{d}{24}$

Because there's no relationship between h and d here, we can come up with totally different numbers for each of them. To make things easy, let's use $\boldsymbol{d = 1}$ and $\boldsymbol{h = 3}$.* One day has 24 hours, plus 3 gives a total of **27 hours**. Which choice matches 27?

F.	$24h + d$	$24(3) + 1 = 73$ ×
G.	$\boldsymbol{h + 24d}$	$3 + 24(1) = \boldsymbol{27}$ ✓
H.	$24(h + d)$	$24(3 + 1) = 96$ ×
J.	$\frac{h+d}{24}$	$\frac{3+1}{24}=\frac{1}{6}$ ×
K.	$h+\frac{d}{24}$	$3+\frac{1}{24}$ ×

On the other hand, sometimes the problem will give you some **restrictions** on the variables. In these cases, you can Plug In for one variable, and then use that value to figure out the other variable:

31. If $x + 5$ is 3 less than y, then $x - 2$ is how much less than y?

A. 2
B. 3
C. 7
D. 8
E. 10

Here we have two variables, but this time, if we pick an x, we can use that number to find y. Let's say $\boldsymbol{x = 4}$. Read the beginning of the problem with our number for x: "If 4 + 5 is 3 less than y". 4 + 5 = 9. That means "9 is 3 less than y," so y is 3 more than 9. So $\boldsymbol{y = 12}$. Picking an x allowed us to find y.

* Picking 1 makes things nice and quick on a problem like this. But because multiplying and dividing by 1 each give you the same answer, picking 1 can sometimes give you two choices that work. Therefore, if your question has a lot of division in the choices, particularly if you see the variable on the bottom of the fraction, you probably shouldn't pick 1. And *any* time you get more than one choice that works, just eliminate and pick a different number.

We're not done yet. The question asks "$x - 2$ is how much less than y?" $4 - 2 = 2$. So 2 is how much less than 12? 2 is **10** less than 12. That's **choice E.** Notice also that we could still use Plug In even though there weren't any variables in the answer choices.

2. Implicit Variables

36. Larry cuts a piece of paper into two equal pieces. He takes one of those pieces and cuts it into three equal pieces. The area of one of the smallest pieces is what fraction of the area of the original piece of paper?

F. $\frac{1}{2}$

G. $\frac{1}{3}$

H. $\frac{1}{5}$

J. $\frac{1}{6}$

K. $\frac{1}{12}$

There's no variable anywhere in the problem or the answer choices, so we can't use Plug In, right?

Wrong! Even though no variable was explicitly mentioned, there is an **implicit** variable—the area. There's no way for us to find the area of the original piece of paper, right? It doesn't tell us the length or width or any numbers at all (we don't even know whether it's a rectangle!), but we're still expected to get an answer. So it *must not matter* what the starting area is—we'll get the same answer no matter where we start. There's no actual letter, but we *could* assign it a variable if we wanted.

Let's not. Let's say the original piece has an area of **12**.

- He cuts it into *two* pieces, so each has an area of 6. ($12 \div 6 = 2$)
- He cuts one of those into *three* pieces, so each of the smaller pieces has an area of **2**. ($6 \div 3 = 2$)
- So each smaller piece is $\frac{2}{12}$ or $\mathbf{\frac{1}{6}}$ of the original. That's **choice J.***

We already saw a problem with implicit variables in the Fool's Gold section. Remember this?

60. Scott drives to Bob's house at a speed of 30 miles per hour and drives back at a speed of 50 miles per hour. If he takes the same route both ways, what was his average speed, in miles per hour, for the whole trip?

F. 35
G. 37.5
H. 40
J. 42.5
K. Cannot be determined from the given information

* The "normal" way of doing this problem is to multiply one half times one third. *But that's still Plug In*—it's just assuming that the page starts with an area of 1 instead of an area of 12.

Even though there are no variables at all, the distance is an implicit variable. We can make up a value for the distance and do the problem with that number. That's Plug In.

3. Geometry

Take a look at this problem:

33. In the figure below, if $y = 90 - x$, what is z in terms of x?

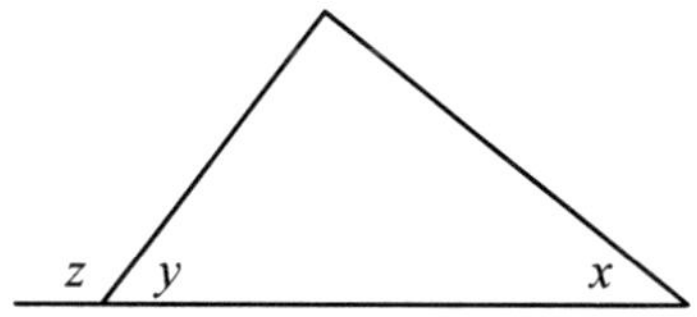

> Whenever a question contains the words **"in terms of"** as in "what is z in terms of x", you can almost always use Plug In.

A. $90 + x$
B. $90 - x$
C. $90 - 2x$
D. $180 + x$
E. $180 - x$

Geometry can be scary for a lot of kids, and we'll talk a lot more about it in a later chapter. But look: we've got variables in the answer choices! That means we can Plug In for x, just like any other normal problem.

Let's say $\mathbf{x = 30}$. We know $y = 90 - x$, so $\mathbf{y = 60}$.

We can tell from the picture that z and y make a straight line; that means $z + y = 180$. Since $y = 60$, we know $\mathbf{z = 120}$. So when $x = 30$, $z = 120$. Put 30 in for x in the answer choices and see which gives you 120:

A.	**$90 + x$**	$90 + 30 = \mathbf{120}$	✓
B.	$90 - x$	$90 - 30 = 60$	×
C.	$90 - 2x$	$90 - 60 = 30$	×
D.	$180 + x$	$180 + 30 = 210$	×
E.	$180 - x$	$180 - 30 = 150$	×

Don't be scared off by figures. If you're confused, don't worry: we'll talk about geometry rules soon enough. But at its heart, this problem is no different than any other Plug In. As soon as you see all those variables in the choices, you know you can Plug In.

And keep in mind that Geometry Plug Ins come in all the same flavors that we've already seen: there may be explicit variables or implicit variables; sometimes you plug in for different variables separately; sometimes you plug in for one and figure out the others (as we just did in #32).

PLUG IN DRILL

14. If p, q, r, and s are consecutive even integers such that $p < q < r < s$, then how much greater is $s - p$ than $r - q$?

F. 0
G. 1
H. 2
J. 3
K. 4

23. Garth has x books, which is 20 more books than Henrietta has. If Garth gives Henrietta 7 books, how many books does Henrietta now have?

A. $x - 27$
B. $x - 20$
C. $x - 13$
D. $x - 7$
E. $x + 6$

26. If $a^2b = c$ and $b \neq 0$, then $\frac{1}{b} =$

F. a^2c

G. $\frac{a^2}{c}$

H. $\frac{c}{a^2}$

J. $\frac{1}{a^2c}$

K. $\frac{1}{c - a^2}$

33. A number p is divided by 3 and the result is increased by 3. This result is then multiplied by 3. Finally, that result is decreased by 3. In terms of p, what is the final result?

A. p
B. $p + 6$
C. $p - 6$
D. $3p$
E. $3p + 6$

GO ON TO THE NEXT PAGE.

36. Lisa uses 2 pieces of copper wire, each 9 feet long, for each robot she builds. If she started with a 500-yard roll of copper wire, which of the following represents the number of yards of wire left on the roll after Lisa built r robots? (3 feet = 1 yard)

F. $500-\frac{1}{6}r$

G. $500-\frac{1}{3}r$

H. $500-2r$

J. $500-6r$

K. $500-9r$

41. Hot dogs cost h dollars and pretzels cost p dollars. How much would it cost, in dollars, to buy $h+1$ hot dogs and $p-1$ pretzels?

A. $h+p$

B. $hp-h+p-1$

C. h^2+p^2

D. $h^2+2hp+p^2$

E. h^2+h+p^2-p

44. The sum of 3 consecutive integers is s. What is the greatest of these integers, in terms of s?

F. $\frac{s}{3}-1$

G. $\frac{s}{3}$

H. $\frac{s}{3}+1$

J. $\frac{s}{3}+2$

K. $\frac{s}{3}+3$

49. If $t \neq 0$ and $s=\frac{1}{t}$, which of the following must be true?

A. $s<t$

B. $s>t$

C. $st<1$

D. $st>1$

E. $st>0$

GO ON TO THE NEXT PAGE.

56. If Leslie gives away k celery sticks, she will have $\frac{1}{n}$ times as many as she had originally. In terms of k, and n, how many celery sticks did Leslie have originally?

F. $k+\frac{1}{n}$
G. $k+n$
H. $kn+k$
J. $\frac{kn}{n-1}$
K. $\frac{k}{n+1}$

59. According to the information below, z is what percent of w?

w decreased by 40% of w yields x
x increased by 50% of x yields y
y decreased by 10% of y yields z

A. 27%
B. 60%
C. 81%
D. 90%
E. 100%

STOP!

BACKSOLVE

Take a look at this one.

33. Gerry's age is 5 more than three times Carol's age. If the sum of their ages is 45, how old is Carol?

A. 10
B. 12
C. 14
D. 16
E. 18

Here, we can't just make up a number for Carol's age because that's the whole point of the question. The value *does* matter—there's only one number that works for Carol's age. So Plug In is out.

However, like we did with Plug In, we can still turn this into a simple arithmetic problem. But instead of picking *random* numbers, let's use the numbers *in the answer choices*. We know one of these 5 numbers is Carol's age, so let's try them until we find one that works.

That's ***Backsolve***. It also has three steps.

1. Make the middle number the answer to the question.

When there are numbers in the answers like this, the choices are always in order, so choice C or H will be the middle number. If we try it and it doesn't work, we can figure out if it was too small or too big and eliminate three answer choices in one fell swoop.

Okay. So let's say that C is the answer. C is **14**. So what does that mean? What's 14? Well, 14 is the answer to the question. In this case, the question is "how old is Carol?" That means if C is right, then Carol is 14.

2. Do the problem and see if it fits.

What else do we know? We know that Gerry's age is 5 more than three times Carol's age. Again, we're saying Carol is 14, so:

C. **Carol = 14.**

$3 \times 14 = 42$	"Gerry's age is 5 more than 3 times 14"
$42 + 5 =$ **47 = Gerry**.	So if Carol is 14, then Gerry is **47**.

How do I know if C is the right answer, then? Well, what *else* does the problem tell us? Their ages should add up to 45. Do they? Of course not. Gerry's age *alone* is bigger than 45. So C is too big.

3. If C fails, figure out if you need a bigger or smaller number and repeat.

Well, C was definitely too big, so we'll need a smaller number. So we'll move on to B.

B. **Carol = 12.**

$12 \times 3 + 5 = 36 + 5 =$ **41 = Gerry**.

$12 + 41 =$ **53 ×**

Still too big. Their ages should add up to 45. Let's move on to A.

A. **Carol = 10.**

$10 \times 3 + 5 = 30 + 5 =$ **35 = Gerry**.

$10 + 35 =$ **45 ✓**

Bingo! **Choice A** is our answer.

That was a word problem. Just like we saw before when we were discussing Plug In, this problem didn't have any explicit variables mentioned, but it did have **implicit** variables. There were no actual letters assigned to Carol or Gerry's age, but we could still put numbers in for them all the same. That's one of the strengths of these techniques. We don't need to worry about variables; we can work directly with the underlying concepts in the problem.

But Backsolve works just as well when there are **explicit** variables. Observe:

42. If $a+b=9$ and $a^2+ab=36$ then $b=$

F. **3**
G. **4**
H. **5**
J. **6**
K. **7**

Any time a problem asks for the value of a variable, we can Backsolve. Just put the numbers in the choices in for the variable and see if it works.

We'll start with H, that's 5. They're asking for *b*, so we'll say $\mathbf{b = 5}$. We know that $a + b = 9$. Since $b = 5$, $\mathbf{a = 4}$. So far, so good. Now let's put *a* and *b* into that big equation and see if it comes out to 36.

$$a^2+ab=4^2+4(5)=16+20=\mathbf{36}\ \checkmark$$

It works! Since H worked, I don't have to look at anything else. The answer is **Choice H: 5**. I'm done!

Let's take a minute to think about how to do this problem with algebra. First of all, you could solve one equation for *a,* and then substitute that into the other equation. Ugh. I guess we could do that, but it's a lot of work and easy to mess up. Backsolve is much quicker and easier.

Now, if you've got a really good eye, you might notice this:

$a+b=9$ and $a^2+ab=36$	We're given two equations.
$a^2+ab=a(a+b)$	The second equation is just the first equation times *a*.
$a(9)=36$	So we can just substitute the values we know,
$\mathbf{a=4}$	And our answer is 4. That's Choice G.

Wait a minute: 4? G? Didn't we get H: 5? Aha! $a = 4$, but they're asking us for *b*. **RTFQ!** So even if we're really clever with our algebra, the algebra easily leads to an RTFQ. You're much less likely to make an RTFQ mistake with Backsolve because you're working *directly* from the question. You pick H, and then make H *the answer to the question.* It's the first step!

So there are basically two algebraic ways of doing this problem. One is slow and painful. The other almost inevitably leads you to an RTFQ mistake. Like Plug In, Backsolve is faster, easier, and *safer* than algebra.

Frequently Asked Questions about Backsolve

1. If C or H works on my first try, should I try the other choices to be safe?

No. Unlike Plug In, with Backsolve there's no way that more than one choice will work out. Once you find a choice that works, stop. That's your answer.

2. What if I'm not sure whether I want a higher or lower number?

Then just pick one! Don't go crazy trying to deduce which way to go. Part of the point of Backsolve is to work quickly and methodically. If C fails and you're not sure whether you should go to B or D, just pick one. You're just doing simple math here. The worst-case scenario is that you go the wrong way and wind up having to test all five choices. But really, that's not very much work. And you know that eventually you'll find the answer.

BACKSOLVE DRILL

6. If $\frac{x+10}{12}=\frac{8}{3}$, then $x =$

F. 10
G. 22
H. 54
J. 66
K. 96

G

15. If the average of 2 and p is equal to the average of 1, 6, and p, what is the value of p?

A. 3
B. 5
C. 6
D. 7
E. 8

E

26. Allen is reviewing his receipts from three different visits to a spa, trying to determine the individual costs of his favorite spa treatments. From his receipts he knows:

A manicure and a back rub together cost \$18.
A back rub and a facial together cost \$19.
A manicure and a facial together cost \$21.

What is the cost of a back rub?

F. \$7
G. \$8
H. \$9
J. \$10
K. \$11

G

27. If $(x+4)^2 = 49$ and $x < 0$, what is the value of x?

A. −53
B. −45
C. −11
D. −3
E. 3

C

30. The product of four consecutive odd integers is 9. What is the least of these integers?

F. −3
G. 1
H. 3
J. 5
K. 7

F

GO ON TO THE NEXT PAGE.

33. Erica had a stack of firewood on Monday. On Tuesday she used $\frac{1}{2}$ of the logs, and on Wednesday she used 110 logs, leaving Erica with $\frac{1}{3}$ of her original supply. How many logs of firewood did Erica originally have on Monday?

A. 220
B. 440
C. 500
D. 570
E. 660

40. Vladimir sold 18 books on Monday. He sold paperback books for $7.50 each and hardcover books for $15 each. If he made a total of $210, how many paperback books did he sell?

F. 12
G. 11
H. 10
J. 9
K. 8

43. The sum of five consecutive integers *a*, *b*, *c*, *d*, and *e* is 55. What is the median of the five integers?

A. 9
B. 10
C. 11
D. 12
E. 13

52. Marion brought some biscuits to a tea party. If everyone at the party takes 5 biscuits, there will be 10 remaining. If 4 people do not take any and everyone else takes 8, there will be none remaining. How many biscuits did Marion bring to the party?

F. 56
G. 70
H. 80
J. 95
K. 104

55. It took Adam 6 hours to canoe upstream from his campsite to the lake and back again. While paddling upstream, he averaged 2 miles per hour; while paddling back, he averaged 4 miles per hour. How many miles was it from his campsite to the lake?

A. 4
B. 8
C. 10
D. 12
E. 16

STOP!

GUESSTIMATE

Take a look at this problem:

57. In the figure below, *c* is equal to 5 less than twice *b*. What is the value of *a* + *b*?

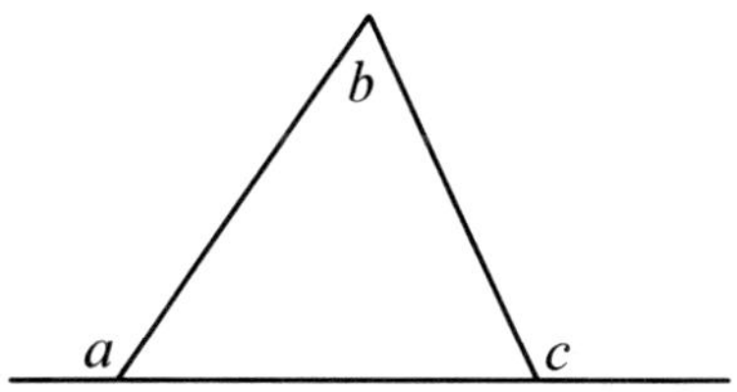

A. 60
B. 90
C. 100
D. 135
E. 185

Okay, this is a pretty hard one. There are all sorts of Geometry rules that you could use here to set up equations and cancel out variables. Those can get pretty nasty, though. Plus we haven't talked about Geometry rules yet. Let's not do that. Let's find an easier way.*

One of the rules given on the first page of every ACT Math Test states that "**Illustrative figures are NOT necessarily drawn to scale.**" That means that the lines and angles don't necessarily have the values that they appear to. It might look like a square, but maybe its dimensions are actually 8 by 97.

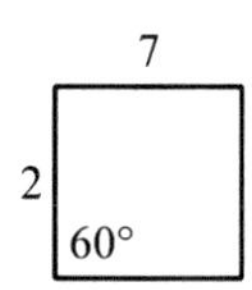

Figure **not** drawn to scale.

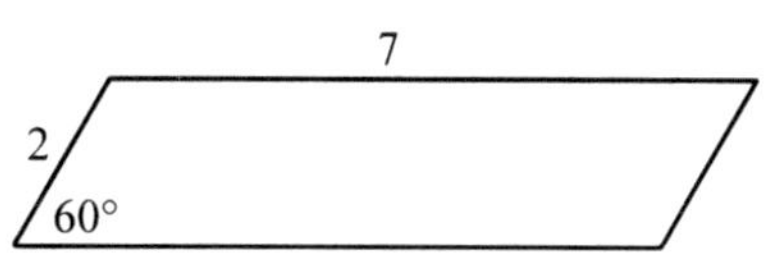

Figure drawn to scale.

The first drawing *looks* like a square, but it's not to scale, so we can't assume it's a square. In fact, we know it's definitely *not* a square because it has a 60° angle and 2 by 7 dimensions. The second drawing is the same figure drawn to scale. That means that if we measured that angle with a protractor it would come out to 60°, and if we measured those sides with a ruler, they would be in a 2 to 7 ratio.

So you can't use the size and shape of the figure to get information. You *can* use the numbers they tell you, but the picture won't necessarily look right.

However, we have discovered a secret. This rule just means is that ACT figures *might* not be to scale. It doesn't mean they're *never* to scale. In fact, we did a study and found that **ACT MATH FIGURES ARE ALMOST ALWAYS DRAWN TO SCALE.**†

---

* You could Plug In. Make up a number for *b*, say, and use it to find all the other angles. That's a pretty good way to do it, but we want to show you a third option.

† Here are the details: we looked at 19 past ACT Math tests, containing a total of 1,140 problems, of which 314 had figures. Of those 314, only 19 figures (that's *six percent*) were not drawn to scale. That means **94% of the figures were drawn to scale**.

Furthermore, some of those 19 figures were drawn *almost* to scale—if you measure them precisely, they're not quite perfect, but they're close enough that you can still use Guesstimate. For some others, scale doesn't matter. The questions are asking for something where Guesstimate won't work anyway, like the volume of a cylinder. That leaves *four questions* in which the fact that it's not to scale might actually mess you up. That's 4 of 314 figures. That's *one percent*. So on **99% of the figures,** either they're drawn to scale or scale is irrelevant.

That means that if it *looks* like two lines are the same length, then they *really are* the same length. If it *looks* like an angle is 60°, then it *is* 60°, or at least really close to 60°.

This is ***Guesstimate***. It has one step:

1. Look at the picture and guess the values you want.

In our example above, they're asking us for $a + b$. So let's take a look at those angles. Angle a is pretty big. Let's say… 120? 130? Let's say **130**. Angle b is smaller, maybe 50 or 60. Let's say **60**. So $a + b$ must be about 130 + 60 or about $\boxed{190}$. So our answer should be pretty close to 190. Hmm, 190 isn't a choice, but 185 is! That's pretty darn close. We'll take it. The answer is **Choice E.**

Look how easy that was! We didn't do a thing other than just look at the picture. I got #57 in all of 10 seconds and all I did was add two numbers.

Frequently Asked Questions about Guesstimate

1. That's all well and good, but how do I know that's right? I just made up those numbers. I could have been wrong.

That's true, but you didn't *randomly* make up those numbers; you measured the angles in the problem, the angles they give you.

Seriously, just look at the other choices they give you. A? 60? Could $a + b$ be 60? Angle a is ***obtuse!*** Angle a alone has to be bigger than 90! So A and B are out right away. C is still too small—angle a is still probably bigger than 100, and when you add b to the mix, there's no way the two of them come out that small. Choice D seems plausible, but it's still too small. Look: the unmarked angle next to a looks to be about the same size as b. They're not exactly the same size, but they're close. And a makes a straight line with that unmarked angle, so together they're 180. So $a + b$ must be pretty close to 180. None of these choices make *any* sense at all. Only Choice E is plausible.

And here's the thing: if you do this problem algebraically, there are ways you can mess it up that will make you pick one of those wrong answers. If you add instead of subtract or forget to distribute across parentheses, you might think that choice A is a plausible answer because of your flawed algebra. But if you look at the picture, you can see there's no way those angles add up to 60. It just doesn't make sense.

2. Okay, I see that. But what's the *real* math way to do this problem?

Are you kidding? *This is real math.* There's nothing mathematically illegitimate about doing this. In math, as in all the sciences, there are two ways of solving any problem: *analytically*, by using pure logic and deduction (that's algebra), or *empirically*, by gathering evidence and measuring (that's Guesstimate).

Say you have a dining-room table and you want to figure out how tall it is. Well, one way I could figure out the height of the table is to construct a line from my eye to the top of the table and a line from my eye to the bottom of the table, measure the angle of declination, and use the law of cosines to find the third side of the triangle. ***OR I COULD GET A @#%$!*! RULER AND MEASURE IT!***

Here are your choices for how tall the table is:

A. 2.5 inches
B. 3 feet
C. 7.8 miles

But how do I *know* the table isn't 7.8 miles tall? Because it's in my living room. And I'm looking at it.

3. Does this only work with angles?

Of course not! You can use Guesstimate on just about any problem that has a picture. For example, we can use it to find ***lengths***. Take a look at this one:

56. In the figure below, $\overline{ST}$ is a chord and $\overline{OP}$ connects the centers of the two circles with equal radii. If $ST = 4$ and $OP = 4\sqrt{3}$, what is the radius of circle O?

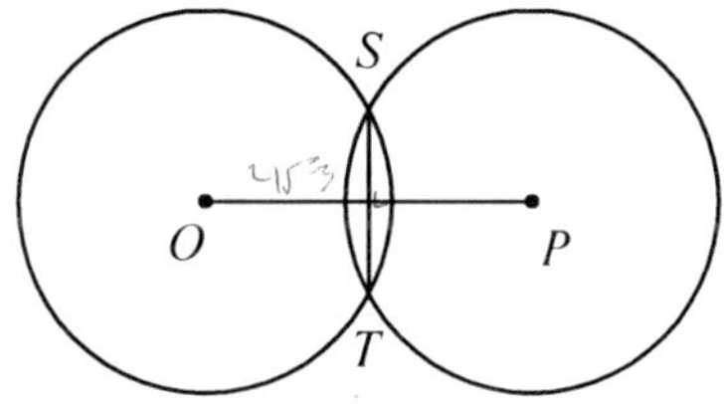

F. 2

G. $2\sqrt{3}$

H. 4

J. $4\sqrt{3}$

K. 8

Hmm. That's a tricky one. Well, let's think.

What do we want? We want the radius of *O*. Hmm, we don't have a radius in the figure. So let's draw one in. Just draw a line from the center to anywhere on the side.

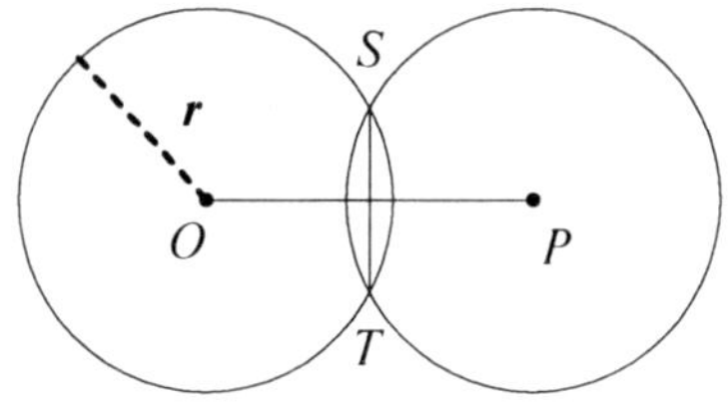

So that *r* is the length we're looking for.

What do we know? We know *OP* is $4\sqrt{3}$ (Not sure what that means? Punch it out on your calculator! It's about 6.92.) Well, *r* definitely looks smaller than *OP*, so it must be smaller than 6.92. So J and K are out. Good so far.

We also know that *ST* is 4, so let's compare *r* to *ST*. They look pretty close to each other. Choice F, 2, is *half* of *ST*—that's definitely too small. Choice F is out.

So we're down to two choices—if all else fails I've got a 50-50 guess. Choice G would mean *r* is a little less than *ST* ($2\sqrt{3}$ is about 3.46) and choice H would mean it's equal to *ST*. How can I tell? **Measure it!** Take a piece of paper (try using your answer sheet) and lay the side of the paper against *r* and mark off its length. Then lay that paper you marked off against *ST*. What do you find? ***They're exactly the same!*** We're done! So the radius is 4 and the answer is **Choice H.**

At the very least, if we go purely by our eyes, we know right away that the radius should be *close* to 4, so only G and H make sense. If we actually measure it out, we can see that the radius is *exactly* 4. Perfect.

It's not just for angles and lengths; it works for ***area*** questions too.

43. In the figure below, square $ABCD$ is circumscribed about circle O. If square $ABCD$ has sides of length 4, what is the area of the shaded region?

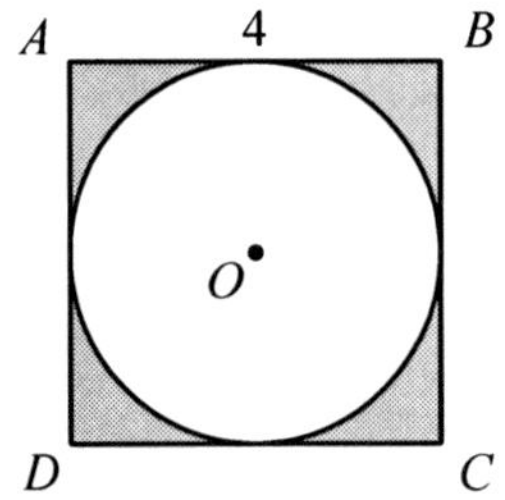

A. $4-2\pi$
B. $4-4\pi$
C. $16-2\pi$
D. $16-4\pi$
E. $16-16\pi$

Let's try to get in the ballpark of what we're looking for.

What do we know? The only value we're given is that the side of the square is 4.

What can we do with that? We can find the area of the square: $4 \times 4 =$ **16**.

How does that help us answer the question? The shaded area is much smaller than the square so our answer must be **a lot less than 16**. Okay, let's eliminate.

But how can we eliminate? All the choices have that stupid π thingy. What do we do? Ah, but wait! What *is* that stupid π thingy? It's not a variable—***it's a number!*** So we can punch all those choices out on our calculators and see which ones come close to what we want.

Even better, let's approximate: π is approximately 3, so we can just do out the choices with 3 instead.

A.	$4-2\pi$	$\approx 4-2(3)$	$=-2$	× That's **negative**! Areas can't be negative!
B.	$4-4\pi$	$\approx 4-4(3)$	$=-8$	× That's even *more* negative!
C.	$16-2\pi$	$\approx 16-2(3)$	$=10$	× Too big. This is more than half of 16.
D.	$16-4\pi$	$\approx 16-4(3)$	$=$ **4**	✓ Okay, that might work.
E.	$16-16\pi$	$\approx 16-16(3)$	$=-32$	× That's *hugely* negative!

Look! **Choice D** is the only one that made sense.

4. Will Guesstimate work on 3-D figures?

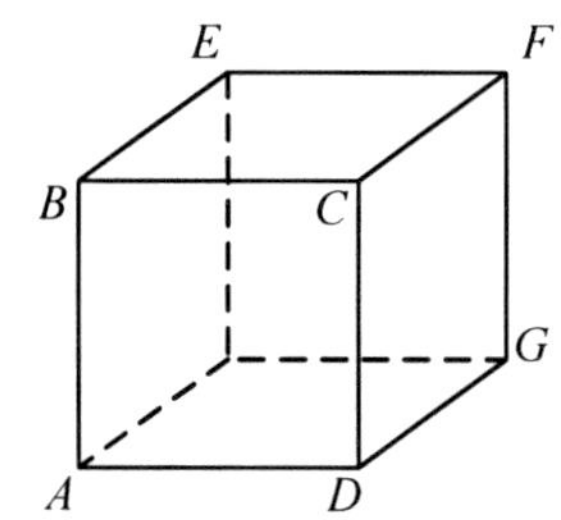

Not exactly. Three-dimensional figures like cubes are drawn using *perspective*, so we can't literally measure the lines as they're drawn to see which one is bigger. In the cube shown here, segment BE is literally shorter than segment BC as the figure is drawn. But we know that in a cube, the top face is supposed to be a square. Therefore, $BE = BC$, even though the lines on the page are not actually equal.

However, if you have a good eye, you might be able to use your imagination to figure this stuff out. Some of you may be good at imagining 3-D objects in your head. For example, you may be able to see that $ED = AF$, even though they're not equal in the drawing. If you can, that's great. Remember: the point of Guesstimate is to use what you know about the figure along with your common sense.

5. Does Guesstimate always work?

Unfortunately, Guesstimate isn't always going to work as beautifully as it did on these questions. You're not always going to be able to home in on the right answer like this. For example, if the answer choices are too close together, you won't be able to distinguish them. Your guess probably wasn't that exact.

However, you can usually eliminate *something*, even if it's only one choice. And once you eliminate something, your odds of getting the problem increase. Even if you can't figure out any other solution, you can guess from what's left.

So *any time* you see a problem with a diagram, ***try Guesstimate first***. Before you do anything else, try to get a ballpark figure for the thing they're asking for, and **eliminate** anything that doesn't make sense.

GUESSTIMATE DRILL

Use Guesstimate for every question in this drill. *To help, we've taken normal SAT questions and blacked out most of the information given. That means you have no choice but to Guesstimate!*

5. In the figure below, [blacked out]. What is the value of x?

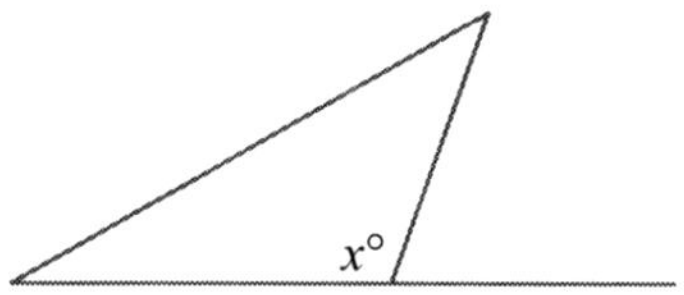

A. 30
B. 50
C. 70
D. 110
E. 150

18. [blacked out]. What is the length of AD?

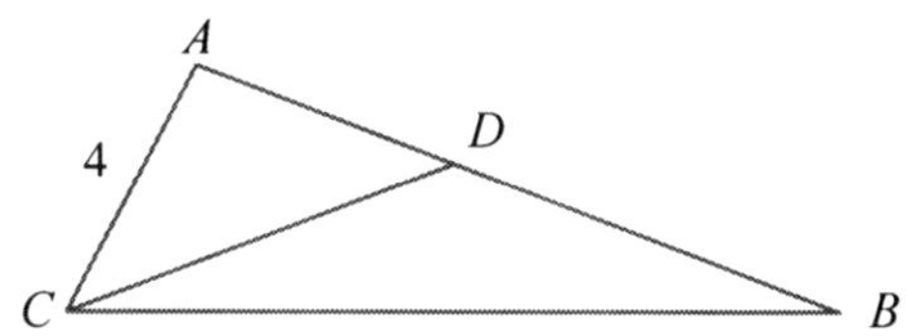

F. 4
G. 6
H. 8
J. 10
K. 12

25. The figure below shows [blacked out], what is the area of the shaded region?

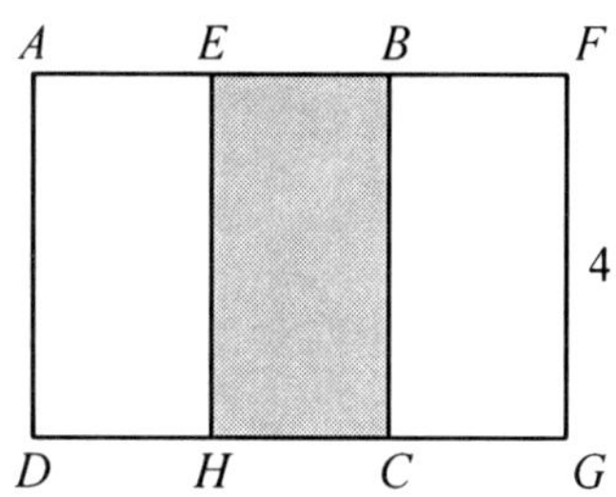

A. 6
B. 8
C. 12
D. 16
E. 24

38. In the figure below, [blacked out] and [blacked out]. What is the length of DC?

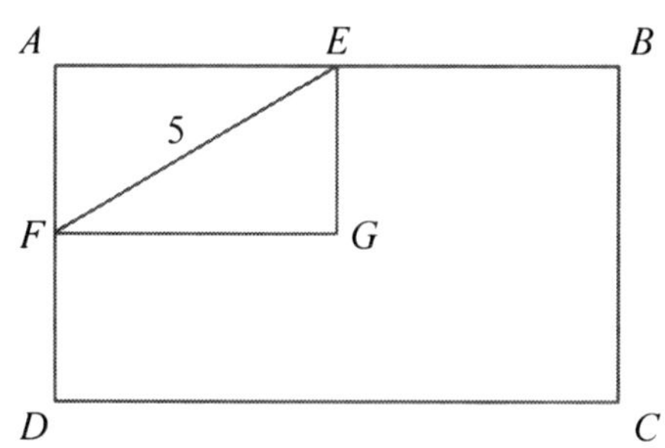

F. 5
G. $5\sqrt{3}$
H. 10
J. $10\sqrt{3}$
K. 12

GO ON TO THE NEXT PAGE.

43. In the figure below, . What is the area of the shaded region?

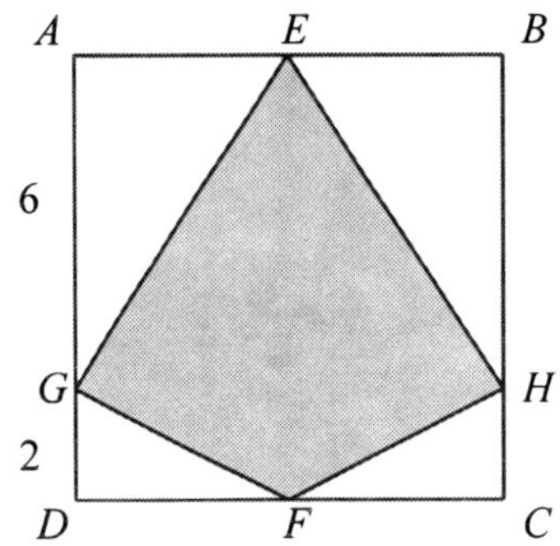

A. 12
B. 16
C. 32
D. 52
E. 64

STOP!

IV. Using the Techniques

It's one thing to understand how these techniques work. It's another to be able to use them and use them effectively in a real-test situation. It's incredibly difficult to change your habits. These techniques are a fundamentally different approach than what you're used to doing in school. Therefore, you have to make a *conscious* effort to use them on your practice tests. ***Every* time you do a problem, your *first* thought should be "Can I use a technique here?"** Even if you see another way of doing the problem. Even if you think that other way is better than the technique. You must try to use the techniques every chance you get.

We can already hear you complaining, but trust us: it's for your own good. Clearly, your old ways of doing problems aren't working for you—if they were, you wouldn't be reading this now. Your old methods have gotten you the score you have now. If you want a different score, you have to try different things.

Of course, you can't use the techniques on every single problem you see. And sometimes there will be problems where the algebra isn't so bad and you can get the problem without the techniques. But here's the thing: *you're not qualified to make that call yet.* The techniques are still new for you, so you don't know whether or not they're the best method on this or that problem. The only way you can *become* qualified is to **try to use the techniques every time you possibly can**. Then when you get to the real test, you can decide when to use the techniques and when not to.

This is no different from any time you learn something new. In sports or in music, the only way to get good at something is to do it a thousand times in a row. The more you practice, the better you become.

Techniques and Target Numbers

As we've seen already, techniques can turn a really hard problem into a really easy problem. But techniques can't be used on every question. There will be some legitimately tough questions that can't be done with Plug In, Backsolve, or Guesstimate. Some of those tough questions will be past your target numbers, so you'll never see them. But it's not unusual for the last question in your target numbers to be a legitimately tough non-technique question.

Therefore, if the last question in your assigned set is **not** a technique question, and you see a question past your target numbers that's **obviously** a technique question, you may do the technique question instead of one of your target questions.

This exception is *only* for technique questions. If you see a non-technique problem—even if you think you can do—it's not worth your time. Remember that one of the dangers of the harder questions is the possibility of a Fool's Gold choice, a wrong choice that looks like an easy answer. But we've already seen that using the techniques actually *reduces* your chances of making those mistakes.

And this doesn't mean you can do *all* technique questions past your target numbers. Remember: **the goal of target numbers is *do fewer questions***. Your first goal should still be to do your target questions and *only* your target questions. But at the end of the section, if you notice a Plug In past your assignment, it's okay to swap it with one of your assigned questions.

So how can you tell if you can use a technique on a problem? Glad you asked.

Identifying the Techniques

Circle the Question

This bears repeating. It's quite remarkable, but a simple act like circling the question—that is, the thing they're actually asking you to solve for—can do wonders for your performance.

We already saw how it can help you avoid RTFQ mistakes. Circling the question helps you remember what the point of the problem is, and will clear your mind on everything you do. But more importantly, it can help you decide *which* technique, if any, is applicable on a question.

Here's a general rule of thumb:

> **If the question asks for a *VALUE*, use Backsolve.**
> **If the question asks for a *RELATIONSHIP*, use Plug In.**

While it may seem like the test asks you about a million different things, it actually repeats the same kinds of question over and over again. The more you use Plug In and Backsolve, the easier it will be to spot them.

Let's recap some common characteristics of the Three Fundamental Techniques:

Plug In

Make up numbers for the variables. Do the problem with your numbers until you get a number for an answer. Then see which answer choice gives you that same number.

Here are some common characteristics of Plug-In problems, with examples from problems we've seen:

- Any time you see a problem that has *variables in the answer choices*, you can definitely use Plug In. If the answer is $x + 4$, it will always be $x + 4$, no matter what x is.
- In particular, look out for questions that ask for "x in terms of y". That's a big sign that Plug In is possible.

27. Bob has 4 dollars more than Lisa does. If Lisa has x dollars, how much would Bob have if he doubled his money?

A. $x + 4$
B. $x + 8$
C. $2x$
D. $2x + 4$
E. $2x + 8$

- Sometimes you can also use Plug In when there are variables in the question but not in the choices. Sometimes if you plug in for one variable you can figure out the other variables.

31. If $x + 5$ is 3 less than y, then $x - 2$ is how much less than y?

A. 2
B. 3
C. 7
D. 8
E. 10

- You can use Plug In on problems with *implicit* variables. You can use Plug In any time there's some concept in the problem and:
  1. You don't know its value.
  2. There's no way to figure out its value.
  3. They still expect you to get an answer.
  4. So it doesn't matter what that value is; you'll get the same answer no matter what.

60. Scott drives to Bob's house at a speed of 30 miles per hour and drives back at a speed of 50 miles per hour. If he takes the same route both ways, what was his average speed, in miles per hour, for the whole trip?

F. 35
G. 37.5
H. 40
J. 42.5
K. Cannot be determined from the given information

Backsolve

Test the numbers in the answer choices. Start with the middle number, put it through the problem, and see if it matches what you know. If it doesn't, pick a bigger or smaller choice until you find one that works.

Some common characteristics of Backsolve problems:

- There are whole numbers in the answer choices. Any time you need to find some kind of single value or quantity, you've got five options for that value right here. Four of them are wrong, one of them is right. Test them.

33. Gerry's age is 5 more than three times Carol's age. If the sum of their ages is 45, how old is Carol?

A. 10
B. 12
C. 14
D. 16
E. 18

- If they're asking you for the *value of a variable* (i.e., what number does x equal), you can usually use Backsolve. They want to know x? Well, here are five options. Try 'em until you find one that works.

42. If $a + b = 9$ and $a^2 + ab = 36$ then $b =$

F. 3
G. 4
H. 5
J. 6
K. 7

Often, Backsolve questions have **two pieces of information**. When you test an answer choice, you run the choice through one piece of information and see if it matches the other. In #33 above, we started with "5 more than three times" and checked that the resulting sums were 45. In #42, we started with the first equation and checked that the second came out to 36.

Guesstimate

Look at the picture. Use the numbers you know to get an approximate value for the thing that you want. Eliminate any choices that don't make sense.

Any time you see a problem that has a picture your *first* instinct should be Guesstimate.

- Obviously, there has to be a picture. Duh.
- Even though the ACT says the figures *might* not be to scale, 99% of the time they *are* to scale.
- You can do this for any kind of value: angles, lengths, or areas.
- Try to eliminate as many implausible answers as you can. Maybe you can eliminate four choices, maybe only one. But get rid of any choice that doesn't make sense.
- Don't worry about being too exact. Start with a broad guess and eliminate choices that are obviously wrong. Then try to get more precise with the choices that are left.
- Remember that you are guessing here, so you can't eliminate choices that are too close together. If you guess an angle is 60 but 55, 57, 60, 63 and 65 are all choices, don't just pick 60. Those choices are too close to make a call; you're not that good at guessing.
- For three-dimensional figures, you can't literally measure the figure as it's drawn, though you may still be able to judge relative values if you have a good eye for figures.

MATH TECHNIQUE EXERCISE

Please enjoy this Big Technique Exercise! ***You must use one of the three Techniques—Plug In, Backsolve, or Guesstimate—on every problem on this exercise.*** *If you get a question right, but did not use a technique, you will get no credit.*

DO YOUR FIGURING HERE.

3. In the correctly worked addition problem below, each $\triangle$ represents the same digit. What is the value of $\triangle$?

$$\begin{array}{r} \triangle 1 \\ \triangle 5 \\ \triangle 7 \\ + \triangle 9 \\ \hline 182 \end{array}$$

A. 3
B. 4
C. 5
D. 6
E. 7

6. If $a \neq 0$, then 25% of $12a$ equals

F. $3a$
G. $4a$
H. $8a$
J. $9a$
K. $12a$

9. Rita has 5 fewer than 4 times the number of peaches that Sal has. If R represents the number of Rita's peaches and S represents the number of Sal's peaches, which of the following expressions correctly relates R and S?

A. $R = 4S - 5$
B. $R = 4(S - 5)$
C. $R = 5(S - 4)$
D. $R = 5S - 4$
E. $R = 5S + 4$

12. What is the <u>greatest</u> of four consecutive integers whose sum is 26?

F. 5
G. 6
H. 7
J. 8
K. 9

GO ON TO THE NEXT PAGE.

DO YOUR FIGURING HERE.

15. If x is a positive integer and $\frac{x+3}{2^x} = \frac{1}{4}$, then $x = ?$

A. 2
B. 3
C. 4
D. 5
E. 6

18. In the figure below, one side of the rectangle lies on the diameter of the circle. If C is the area of the circle and R is the area of the rectangle, which of the following *must* be true?

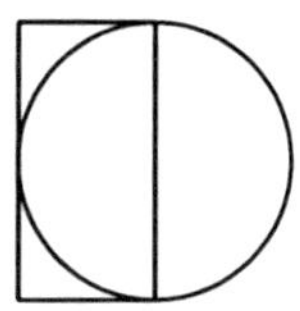

F. $C < R$
G. $C = R$
H. $C > 2R$
J. $C = 2R$
K. $C < 2R$

21. Last month Company A sold 200 more copy machines than Company B. This month, Company A sold 75 fewer than Company B. Which of the following must be true about Company A's total sales for the two months compared to Company B's?

A. Company A sold 275 fewer machines than Company B.

B. Company A sold 125 fewer machines than Company B.

C. Company A sold 125 more machines than Company B.

D. Company A sold 275 more machines than Company B.

E. Company A sold $\frac{3}{10}$ as many machines as Company B.

24. To steam rice, Paul uses m cups of water for every p cups of rice. Which of the following expressions is equivalent to the number of cups of water needed to steam $p + 2$ cups of rice?

F. $m + 2$
G. $m(p + 2)$
H. $\frac{m}{p+2}$
J. $\frac{m(p+2)}{p}$
K. $\frac{p}{m(p+2)}$

GO ON TO THE NEXT PAGE.

DO YOUR FIGURING HERE.

27. In the figure below, what is the value of a?

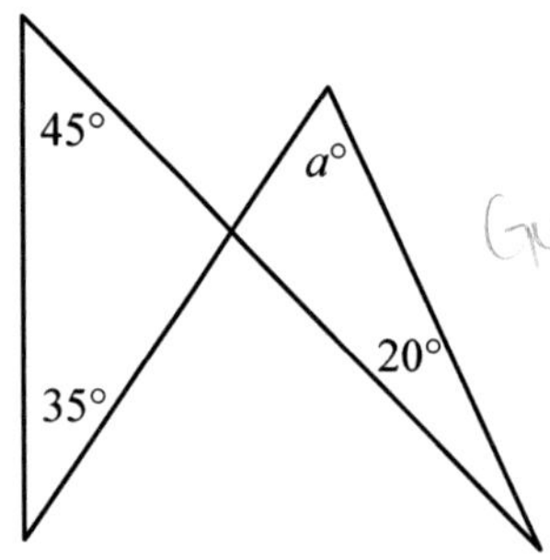

A. 90
B. 70
C. 60
D. 35
E. 20

30. When $\dfrac{x-2}{x^2+x-6}$ is defined, it is equivalent to which of the following expressions?

F. $-\dfrac{2}{x-6}$

G. $\dfrac{1}{x^2+3}$

H. $\dfrac{1}{x+3}$

J. $\dfrac{1}{6-2x}$

K. $\dfrac{1}{3}$

33. The width of a rectangular rug is one-sixth of the length. If the perimeter is 56, what is the rug's width?

A. 4
B. 7
C. 12
D. 15
E. 24

36. The combined price of a pair of pants and a shirt is 100 dollars. If the pants cost 14 dollars less than 2 times the shirt, what is the price, in dollars, of the shirt?

F. 28
G. 38
H. 46
J. 62
K. 70

GO ON TO THE NEXT PAGE.

DO YOUR FIGURING HERE.

39. Let j, k, and m be integers, where $j > k > m > 1$. If $j \times k \times m = 120$, what is the greatest possible value of j?

A. 15
B. 20
C. 30
D. 60
E. 120

42. If $4^a = b$, which of the following equals $16b^2$?

F. 4^{4a}
G. 4^{a^4}
H. 4^{2a+2}
J. 4^{2a^2}
K. 16^a

45. Which of the following would yield the same result as multiplying by $\frac{6}{7}$ and then dividing by $\frac{2}{7}$?

A. Multiplying by 3
B. Multiplying by $\frac{1}{3}$
C. Multiplying by 2
D. Dividing by 2
E. Dividing by $\frac{1}{2}$

48. In the figure below, what is the sum of the measures of the marked angles?

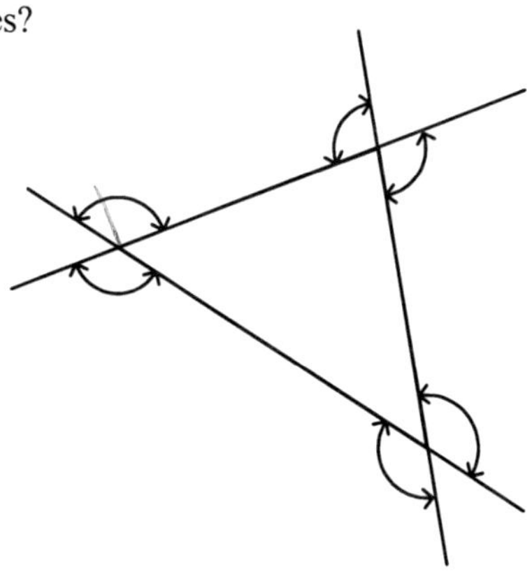

F. 180
G. 360
H. 540
J. 720
K. 900

GO ON TO THE NEXT PAGE.

DO YOUR FIGURING HERE.

51. If $x \neq 0$, which of the following expressions is equivalent to $\dfrac{3}{\frac{2}{x}} + \dfrac{1}{\frac{4}{10x}}$?

A. $\dfrac{1}{4x}$

B. $\dfrac{4}{x}$

C. $\dfrac{x}{4}$

D. $\dfrac{15x}{4}$

E. $4x$

54. At a certain gym, 18 people take an aerobics class and 24 people take a karate class. If 32 people take only one of the two classes, how many people take both classes?

F. 5
G. 10
H. 13
J. 15
K. 19

57. The length and width of a rectangle are both reduced by 60%. Its length and width are then both increased by 50%. The area of the rectangle is what percent of its original area?

A. 10%
B. 36%
C. 40%
D. 81%
E. 90%

60. In the figure below, $AB = AC$ and E is the midpoint of $\overline{AC}$. If $\angle AED = 60°$, what is the length of $\overline{DE}$?

F. 4
G. $4\sqrt{3}$
H. 8
J. $8\sqrt{2}$
K. $8\sqrt{3}$

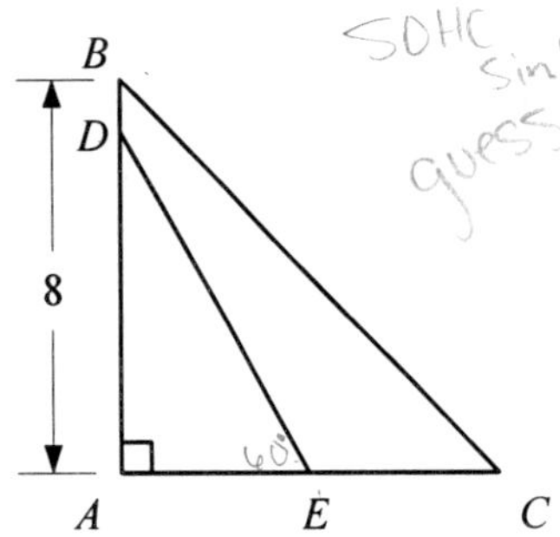

STOP!

PRE-ALGEBRA

THE three fundamental techniques—Plug In, Backsolve, and Guesstimate—can be applied to a lot of different problems. However, the techniques won't work on every problem. We need to talk about *content*—the actual rules of math you have to know on the ACT.

Let's begin at the beginning, as one should. Pre-Algebra deals with most of the nuts and bolts that make up the basic rules of arithmetic and algebra. Since we're talking about the basics here, much of this will probably not be new to you. Therefore, you may be tempted to skip over this part. "This is so boring! Why do we have to talk about fractions? We did this in, like, seventh grade! I hate you!"

Ah, but it's because this is stuff we've seen before that we must make sure we know it well. There are 14 Pre-Algebra questions on every ACT—**that's almost a quarter of the test.** Remember: most students' problem *isn't* that they don't know enough math; it's that they're missing questions that they already know how to do. Therefore, we've got to make sure we know all this stuff backwards and forwards.

I. NUMBER CONCEPTS AND DEFINITIONS

Let's get some terminology out of the way to avoid confusion down the line.

Integer: Any number that does not have a fraction or decimal part: ... −3, −2, −1, 0, 1, 2, 3...

> Note that zero is an even integer but it is neither positive nor negative.

Factor: An integer that can be divided into another integer without a remainder. For example, 3 is a factor of 12 because 12 ÷ 3 = 4. We say the larger number "*is divisible by*" the smaller number, so here 12 is divisible by 3.*

Multiple: An integer that has another integer as a factor. For example, 12 is a multiple of 3 because 3 × 4 = 12.

Prime Number: A number that is divisible only by 1 and itself. 1 is not a prime number. The only even prime number is 2. Examples of prime numbers include 2, 3, 5, 7, 11, and 13.

Remainder: The integer left over when an integer is divided by an integer that is not its factor. For example: 13 ÷ 5 = 2 with a *remainder of 3*. That means you can fit two fives in 13, but there will be 3 left over: 5 × 2 = 10, and 10 + 3 = 13.

Remainders are whole numbers, **NOT** decimals. If you punch "13 ÷ 5" on your calculator you'll get 2.6. The remainder is NOT 6.

Say you wanted to find a number that gives a remainder of 3 when it's divided by 4. Just take a multiple of 4 and add 3 to it. Any these numbers would fit:

4 + 3 = **7** 8 + 3 = **11** 12 + 3 = **15** 16 + 3 = **19**

Properties of Positive and Negative numbers: Bigger digits give smaller negative numbers. That is, −10 is *smaller* than −2.

(Pos) × (Pos) = Pos (Neg) × (Pos) = Neg (Neg) × (Neg) = Pos

Properties of Odd and Even Integers:

(Even) × (Even) = Even	Even + Even = Even
(Even) × (Odd) = Even	Even + Odd = Odd
(Odd) × (Odd) = Odd	Odd + Odd = Even

* Here's a trick to help you find factors: if the sum of the number's digits is divisible by 3, then the number is divisible by 3. 12 is divisible by 3 because 1 + 2 = 3. And 945 is divisible by 3 because 9 + 4 + 5 = 18, and 18 is divisible by 3. The rule is true for 9, too: if the sum of the digits is divisible by 9, the number is divisible by 9.

Decimal places: In the number **25.97**

- 2 is the "tens digit" and is in the "tens place"
- 5 is the "units digit" and is in the "units place"
- 9 is the "tenths digit" and is in the "tenths place"
- 7 is the "hundredths digit" and is in the "hundredths place"

Scientific Notation: Because decimal numbers are based on powers of ten (hundreds, tens, tenths, hundredths, etc), you can express *any number* as a decimal multiplied by a power of ten. So the number 43,500 becomes 4.35×10^4, and 0.00524 becomes 5.24×10^{-3}. This is just a way to make it easier to write really big or really small numbers. Instead of 8,000,000,000 we write 8.0×10^9.

You don't have to know much about this notation. ACT questions may ask you to manipulate numbers in this form, but usually that's easy to do on your calculator.* Just remember that the exponent next to the "10" has the biggest effect on the value of the number: 2×10^9 is much, much bigger than 9×10^2.

Prime Factors

As we said above, integers can be broken down into *factors*, and a *prime number* is one that can't be broken down into factors. Therefore, a *prime factor* is a factor that can't be broken down into smaller factors. Any number that isn't prime can be reduced to a unique set of prime factors. And *all* that number's factors are just different combinations of its prime factors.

➤ **What are the prime factors of 12?**

All we have to do is break 12 up into any factors, then keep splitting up the factors until we can't anymore.

➤ We know 3 × 4 = 12, so 3 and 4 are factors of 12.

➤ 3 is prime, so it can't go any further.

➤ 4 is not prime, so we can break it up into 2 and 2.

➤ 2 is prime, so it can't go any further.

➤ So the prime factors of 12 are **3, 2, and 2**. (Because we found two 2's, we list both of them in our list of prime factors.)

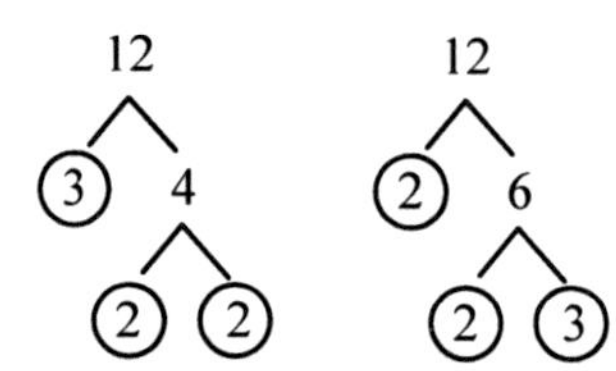

If we had started with a different pair of factors—say, 2 and 6—we'd still get the same set of prime factors. All the factors of 12 can be produced by multiplying the prime factors together:

Factor	2	3	4	6	12
Prime factors	2	3	2 × 2	2 × 3	2 × 2 × 3

The branching diagram shown here makes it easy to find the prime factors of any integer. Split up the number into any factors. If one of the factors is prime, circle it. Otherwise, keep factoring. It helps to start with a small prime numbers on the left, so you only have to expand the tree on the right. This diagram shows that the prime factors of 180 are 2, 2, 5, 3, and 3.

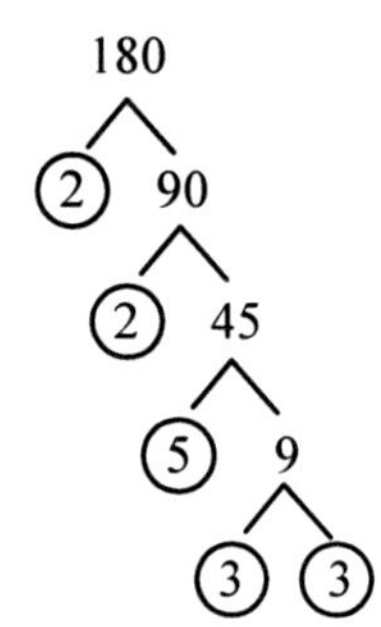

* On some calculators, the "EE" button is shorthand for this notation. Typing "4.24 EE 4" gives you 4.24×10^4 (though it's often displayed with one "E" as "4.24 E4").

TRY SOME:

- **In the number 379.045, what digit is in the units place?**

- **If x is an odd positive integer, which of the following expressions must be *even*?**
  - I. $2x$
  - II. $x + 2$
  - III. $3x + 1$

- **If x has a remainder of 5 when divided by 6 and $x > 10$, what is the smallest possible value of x?**

- **If j is the largest prime factor of 42, and k is the largest prime factor of 36, what is the value of $j + k$?**

- **If x and y are integers such that $xy = -12$ and $x > 0$, what is the greatest possible value of y?**

II. FRACTIONS

A fraction is nothing more than one number divided by another. As such, to convert a fraction to a decimal, just divide the numbers. The top number is called the *numerator*; the bottom number is called the *denominator*.

- $\frac{3}{4} = 3 \div 4 = 0.75$

An *improper fraction* is one in which the numerator is larger than the denominator. A *mixed number* contains a whole number and a fraction.

- $3\frac{1}{4}$ (Mixed number) $= \frac{3\times 4}{4} + \frac{1}{4} = \frac{12}{4} + \frac{1}{4} = \frac{13}{4}$ (Improper fraction)

You must know how to add, subtract, multiply and divide fractions.

To **add or subtract** fractions, you must find a *common denominator*. This just means that you can't add or subtract fractions that have different numbers on the bottom.

- $\frac{3}{4} - \frac{2}{3} = \frac{3\times 3}{3\times 4} - \frac{4\times 2}{4\times 3} = \frac{9}{12} - \frac{8}{12} = \frac{1}{12}$

To **multiply** fractions, you don't have to do any preparation. Just multiply *straight across*: top × top; bottom × bottom.

- $\frac{2}{9} \times \frac{3}{4} = \frac{(2\times 3)}{(9\times 4)} = \frac{6}{36} = \frac{1}{6}$

Notice that our answer could be **reduced** because the top and bottom had a **common factor**. We also could have taken out the common factors before we multiplied:

- $\frac{\overset{1}{\cancel{2}}}{9} \times \frac{3}{\underset{2}{\cancel{4}}} = \frac{1}{\underset{3}{\cancel{9}}} \times \frac{\overset{1}{\cancel{3}}}{2} = \frac{1}{3} \times \frac{1}{2} = \frac{1}{(3\times 2)} = \frac{1}{6}$

To **divide** fractions, you must take the *reciprocal* of the second fraction, and then multiply. "Reciprocal" just means to flip the fraction over.

- $\frac{3}{10} \div \frac{2}{5} = \frac{3}{\underset{2}{\cancel{10}}} \times \frac{\overset{1}{\cancel{5}}}{2} = \frac{3}{2} \times \frac{1}{2} = \frac{3}{4}$

A *compound fraction* is one in which the numerator and/or denominator contain fractions. This is equivalent to dividing fractions. Remember: fractions just mean "divide".

- $\frac{\frac{1}{3}}{\frac{1}{2}} = \frac{1}{3} \div \frac{1}{2} = \frac{1}{3} \times \frac{2}{1} = \frac{2}{3}$

Manipulating fractions is a lost art. With the advent of calculators, a lot of problems that used to require knowledge of fractions can now be done quickly with decimals, since fractions can be easily converted to decimals on your calculator.

That's fine. We're all for doing problems quickly. But don't forget about fractions. Often, using fractions effectively can actually make a problem *faster* than typing the problem out on your calculator.

- First of all, some fractions become repeating decimals, so the calculator will give *approximate* answers—this can be deadly if you have a long computation.
- Secondly, you must be careful of parentheses. If you try to do (1/3) ÷ (1/2) by typing in "1 ÷ 3 ÷ 1 ÷ 2", you'll get it wrong. You must type "(1 ÷ 3) ÷ (1 ÷ 2)".*
- Third, using fractions is often easier than it seems when you can cancel out common factors, thus turning hard math into easy math.
- Finally, you may see some algebra problems with fractions composed of variables. You won't be able to do those on your calculator, so you'd better know how to deal with fractions.

TRY SOME:

- $\frac{5}{4}+\frac{10}{3}=?$

- $\frac{1}{3}+\frac{5}{6}=?$

- $2\frac{2}{5}-\frac{1}{2}=?$

- $\left(\frac{28}{15}\right)\left(\frac{3}{7}\right)=?$

- $\frac{\frac{9}{4}}{\frac{3}{10}}=?$

* Fun fact: the technical name for a division symbol (÷) is an *obelus.*

III. Ratios

A ratio is just a relationship between two or more quantities. Ratios are usually expressed as fractions, but there are many ways of describing them. All of the following mean the same thing:

The ratio of boys to girls is 2:3.

The ratio of boys to girls is 2 to 3.

The ratio of boys to girls is $\frac{2}{3}$.

There are two boys for every three girls.

Take a look at this problem:

- **A recipe calls for 3 cups of sugar for every 7 cups of flour. If Bill uses 28 cups of flour, how many cups of sugar should he use?**

You can set this up as two fractions equal to each other, then solve the equation by cross-multiplying the terms across the equals sign.*

$$\frac{x\text{ sugar}}{28\text{ flour}} = \frac{3\text{ sugar}}{7\text{ flour}}$$

$$\frac{x\text{ sugar}}{28\text{ flour}} = \frac{3\text{ sugar}}{7\text{ flour}}$$

$$7x = 28 \times 3$$

$$7x = 84$$

$$\mathbf{x = 12}$$

The only tricky thing about ratios is that you must make sure your *units match.*

- **A certain park contains only maple and elm trees in a ratio of 2 to 3, respectively. If there are a total of 40 trees, how many maple trees are there in the park?**

You may be tempted to set up the ratio like this:

✗ $$\frac{x\text{ maple}}{40\text{ total trees}} = \frac{2\text{ maple}}{3\text{ elm}}$$

But look: the units in the denominators don't match. The left ratio is "maple" to "total trees", but the right ratio is "maple" to "elm". That's bad.

Luckily, we can fix the right ratio rather easily—just add. If there are 2 maple trees and 3 elm trees, then there are 5 total trees. So there are 2 maple trees for every 5 total trees.

✓ $$\frac{x\text{ maple}}{40\text{ total trees}} = \frac{2\text{ maple}}{5\text{ total trees}}$$

> To avoid mismatching units, always **write the fraction with the quantity you're looking for FIRST.** Then set up a second fraction with matching units.

Now we can cross-multiply:

$$5x = 2 \times 40$$

$$5x = 80$$

$$\mathbf{x = 16}$$

* Another way to solve equations like this is to look across the equals sign. Notice that 28 is *four times* 7, therefore x will be *four times* 3. Which is 12. This doesn't always work easily, but when it does it can save you some time.

Once again, circling the question will help you on ratio problems. Here, the question is "If there are a *total* of 40 trees, how many *maple* trees are there in the park?" That tells us the ratio we're looking for is "maple" to "total trees", so we should set up our fractions using those units.

Ratios like the ones above are also called **direct proportions**. It just means that one quantity divided by the other always comes out to the same number, so we can set two fractions equal to each other. Saying one quantity "**varies directly**" with the other means the same thing.

x varies directly with y: $\qquad x = cy \qquad \frac{x}{y} = c \qquad \frac{x_1}{y_1} = \frac{x_2}{y_2}$

TRY SOME:

- **Bob makes some fruit punch that contains apple juice and mango juice in a 1:5 ratio. If he uses 15 pints of the mango juice, how many pints of apple juice will he need?**

- **An animal shelter has 2 cats for every 3 dogs. If there are 45 animals in the shelter, how many dogs are there?**

- **At a certain school, the ratio of boys to girls in the seventh grade is 3 to 5. If there are 56 total seventh-graders, how many of them are girls?**

- **Two numbers x and y are in a direct proportion such that when $x = 2, y = 9$. What is the value of y when $x = 7$?**

IV. PERCENTS

By now, we should all at least be familiar with percents. The simplest way to do percents is by pure division.

➹ **8 is what percent of 32?**

All you do is divide, then multiply by 100:

$$\frac{8}{32} = 0.25 \qquad 0.25 \times 100 = \mathbf{25\%}$$

Do you want to know a secret? Percents are really nothing more than glorified ratios. Percent literally means "out of one hundred". So you're just converting a ratio into another ratio out of 100. This problem is the same thing as cross-multiplying:

$$\frac{8}{32} = \frac{x}{100}$$

"8 out of 32" is the same thing as "25 out of 100", or 25 "percent".

Of course, percent problems on the ACT can get more complicated than that. We've devised the following table for percent problems:

Read	Write
what	n
is	$=$
percent	$\overline{100}$
of	× (multiply)

Whenever you see one of the words in the left column, write the corresponding symbol in the right column. If you see a number, just write the number. For example:

➹ **12 is 40% of what number?**

becomes $12 = \frac{40}{100} \times n$

You know, a lot of students freak out about word problems. But really, the language we use to describe problems is exactly the same stuff as all the signs and symbols we use in equations. So as long as you can speak English, you can write equations; the words mean exactly what you think they mean.

The advantage of using the table is that it makes percent problems automatic and robotic. You can go directly from words to an equation without thinking about anything.

There are other similar ways of doing percent problems (some of you may know the "is-over-of" method), but this table is particularly effective on certain difficult problems. Take a look at this problem:

➹ **If 25 percent of 12 percent of *s* is 18, *s* = ?**

This can be really nasty with other ways of doing percents. But with the table, we don't care. Do it robotically; when you see a word, write its symbol. So this question becomes:

$$\frac{25}{100} \times \frac{12}{100} \times s = 18$$

Now we have a one-variable equation and we can solve for *s*. We didn't have to think about a thing. The equation came almost instantly.

Here's another toughie:

- **If x is $\frac{1}{2}$ percent of 600, x = ?**

Oh, well half of 600 is 300. Right? WRONG! It doesn't say x is half of 600; it says x is one-half percent of 600. That is, half of one percent. RTFQ!

With the table, we don't make this mistake because we just write what we see:

$$x = \frac{\frac{1}{2}}{100} \times 600$$

Because we aren't *thinking* about the problem—we're just automatically writing down what we read—we're much less likely to make the RTFQ.

Percent Increase and Decrease

A percent increase or decrease just means:

The amount of the *change* is what percent of the *original* amount?

Or:

$$\textbf{Percent Change} = \frac{\textbf{Change}}{\textbf{Original}} \times 100$$

- **Joe made 150 dollars last week and 180 dollars this week. What was the percent increase in his pay?**

In this problem, the amount of the change is **30** (that's 180 – 150) and the original amount is **150**. So the question is "30 is what percent of 150?" Now we can just use the table to set up an equation:

$$30 = \frac{n}{100} \times 150$$

You can also think of percent change as just the *change* divided by the *original*.

$$\frac{30}{150} = \frac{1}{5} = 0.2 = \frac{20}{100} = \mathbf{20\%}$$

TRY SOME :

- **What is 42% of 50?**

- **18 is what percent of 200?**

- **5 is what percent of 4?**

- **21 is 35% of what number?**

- **What is 15% of 75% of 80?**

- **A school had 30 reported absences one week and 27 reported absences the following week. What was the percent decrease in the number of absences between the two weeks?**

V. AVERAGES

There are three types of calculations that concern us here:

Arithmetic Mean

This is what we mean when we say **average**. Find the average by taking the **sum of the numbers** divided by the **number of terms**.

➢ **What is the average (arithmetic mean) of 2, 4, 7, 9 and 18?**

The sum is $2 + 4 + 7 + 9 + 18 = 40$. There are 5 terms, so the average is $40/5 =$ **8**.

Median

You must put the terms **in numerical order** before finding the median.

The median is the **middle** number, <u>when you put the terms in order</u>.*

➢ **What is the median of 7, 18, 4, 9 and 2?**

Write them in order, you get 2, 4, 7, 9, 18. The one in the middle is 7, so the median is **7**.

If there are an *even* number of terms, such that there is no one number in the middle, the median is **the average of the two middle numbers**.

➢ **What is the median of 9, 2, 7, 8, 4 and 18?**

Write them in order and you get 2, 4, 7, 8, 9, 18. The two middle numbers are 7 and 8, so the median is **7.5**.

Mode

The mode is the number that occurs **most frequently**.

➢ **What is the mode of 5, 2, 7, 2 and 9?**

Each number occurs once, except for 2, which occurs twice. So the mode is **2**.

Using the Sum

Let's take a closer look at arithmetic mean (which we'll just call "average"). We all know pretty well how to take the average of a list of numbers they give us. *If you're given a list of numbers*, just add them all up and divide by how many there are. As we already saw:

➢ **What is the average (arithmetic mean) of 2, 4, 7, 9 and 18?**

The sum is $2 + 4 + 7 + 9 + 18 = 40$. There are 5 terms. So the average is $40/5 =$ **8**.

But often on ACT questions *we don't know what the individual numbers are*. Let's look at one:

➢ **The average of 5 numbers is 15. If the average of 3 of those numbers is 19, what is the average of the other two numbers?**

It looks like we don't have enough information. Since we don't know the terms, we can't add them up. What do we do??

Ah, we know more than we think. Let's look again at the definition of average:

$$\text{Average} = \frac{\text{Sum of the terms}}{\text{How many terms}}$$

If we multiply both sides of this equation by the number of terms, we get:

(How many terms) × (Average) = Sum of the terms

* Note that the value of the median doesn't change if you make the highest term higher or the lowest term lower. For example, if we changed the sequence above to 2, 4, 7, 9, 157, the median would still be 7.

This equation is very important. Even if we don't know the *individual* numbers, we can still work directly with their sum. In our problem, we know we have 5 numbers that have an average of 15, so their sum *must* be 5 × 15 = 75. Regardless of what the individual numbers are, they must have a sum of 75.

We can fill out a chart to help us organize this information:

How many terms	Average	Sum of terms	
5	15	75	5 numbers with an average of 15, so their sum is 5(15) = 75
– 3	19	– 57	3 numbers with an average of 19, so their sum is 3(19) = 57
2		**18**	There are **2** numbers we don't know, so their sum must be **18**.

First, we multiplied across each row. The number of terms times the average gives you the sum of the terms.

Then, as we can see in the first column, we should subtract to find the two remaining terms. Since we subtracted in the first column, we'll subtract the sums as well. (Don't try to subtract the average column; just focus on the sum.)

Once we know that those two numbers have a sum of 18, we can find the average:

$$\text{Average} = \frac{\text{Sum of terms}}{\text{How many terms}} = \frac{18}{2} = \mathbf{9}$$

This chart is very useful for questions like this. But again, you only need to use it when you don't know the individual terms involved. If you're given a list of numbers, just add them up and divide by how many there are.

TRY SOME :

$\{ 4, 6, 9, 17, 24 \}$

- **What is the average (arithmetic mean) of the numbers in the set above?**

- **A set contains 3 consecutive integers that have a sum of 78. What is the median of the set?**

- **The 12 trees in John's backyard have an average height of 135 inches. If 7 of the trees have an average height of 100 inches, what is the average height of the other 5 trees?**

- **In a certain class, a student's final grade is determined by taking the average of his or her scores on six tests, each of which is scored on a scale from 0 to 100. If Bob got an average score of 85 on his first 4 tests, what is the highest possible final grade he can get in the class?**

VI. Combinatorics

Combinatorics is a fancy word that just refers to **the mathematics of possible arrangements**. There are several different kinds of problems that deal with possible arrangements.

1. Two or more separate groups

Take a look at this problem:

- **An ice cream shop is having a sale on a cup of one flavor of ice cream with one topping. If the shop sells 4 flavors of ice cream and 3 kinds of toppings, how many different combinations of flavor and topping are possible?**

There are four options for the flavor, and each of those has three options for the topping. So all you have to do to solve this problem is **multiply** 4×3. That's **12**.

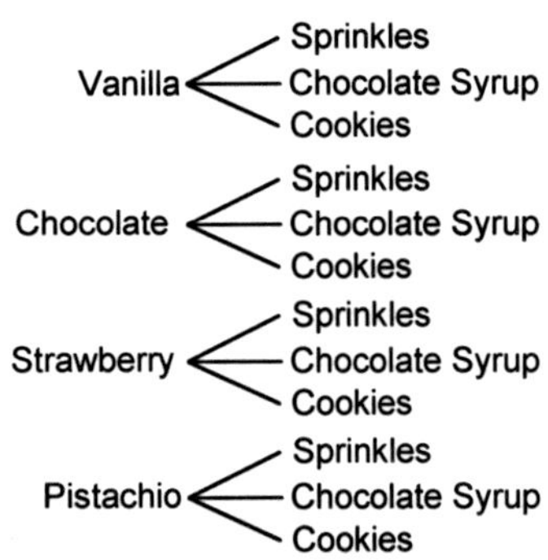

If you get confused by problems like this, it sometimes helps to list all the possible arrangements that can be made. Let's say the flavors are *vanilla*, *chocolate*, *strawberry*, and *pistachio*. And let's say the options for toppings are *sprinkles*, *chocolate syrup*, and *cookies*. The figure to the left shows all the possible combinations.

For each of the four flavors, there are three options for toppings. Therefore, we can get the total number of combinations simply by multiplying 4 times 3.

So if you're just pairing members of one group with members of another group, just multiply the groups together to get the total number of possible combinations.

2. Single group: order matters

- **Roberto has three paintings he wants to hang in a straight horizontal line on his bedroom wall. How many different arrangements of the paintings are possible?**

Here, instead of pairing together two groups, we're putting a single group of things into a certain order. As in the last problem, we could count all the possible arrangements. Since the paintings don't have names, let's just call them A, B, and C. Write them out: there are **six** possible arrangements:

A-B-C	B-A-C	C-A-B
A-C-B	B-C-A	C-B-A

	First	**Second**	**Third**
Think about these problems according to **SLOTS**. There are three slots that we want to fill: first, second, and third.			
Start with the first slot. There are **3** possible paintings for the first slot.	**A, B, C** 3 options	____	____
Let's say we put painting A in the first slot. Now, there are **2 options** left for the second slot, B and C.	A	~~A,~~ **B, C** 2 options	____
Let's put painting B in the second slot. Now, there's only **1 option** left for the third slot, painting C.	A	B	~~A, B,~~ **C** 1 option
We can figure out how many possible orders there are by **multiplying** the options for each slot: $3 \times 2 \times 1 =$ **6 options**.	**3 options** ×	**2 options** ×	**1 option**

At heart, this is the same concept as the ice cream problem, where we had 4 options for the "ice cream slot" and 3 options for the "topping slot". The only difference is that now we're using the same group to fill all the slots, and once we put a painting into a slot, it's no longer eligible for the other slots.

Try another one:

- **A school club wants to appoint a president and a vice president. If there are 5 students in the club and no student can hold both positions, how many different assignments of students to positions are possible?**

This problem works just like the last one. There are **five** candidates for president. Once we choose a president, there are **four** candidates for vice president. $5 \times 4 = 20$. There are **20** total possibilities.

3. Single group: order doesn't matter

- **At a certain detective agency, each case is handled by a team of two detectives. If a total of four detectives work at the agency, how many different teams are possible?**

> Problems where order matters are sometimes called *Permutations*, while problems where order doesn't matter are called *Combinations*. But don't worry, you don't have to know these terms.

This problem is a lot like the last two, but with one important difference: *order doesn't matter*.

This is pretty easy to do if we just write out all the possible teams. To make things easier, let's give them names: **Andre**, **Bob**, **Carlos**, and **Dietrich**.

Andre–Bob	Bob–Carlos
Andre–Carlos	Bob–Dietrich
Andre–Dietrich	Carlos–Dietrich

There are **6 possible teams**.

Wait a minute. Six? If we do the multiplication we did before, we would get 4 options for the first slot and 3 for the second, and 4×3 is 12. How did we get 6?

This problem is different because unlike the painting problem, *order doesn't matter*. In the previous problem, having Andre as president and Bob as vice president was different than having Bob president and Andre vice president, so we want to count each scenario separately. Here, a team of Andre–Bob *is the same* as a team of Bob–Andre, so we don't want to count them separately.

If we multiply 4×3, this is what we're doing:

Andre–Bob	~~Bob–Andre~~	~~Carlos–Andre~~	~~Dietrich–Andre~~
Andre–Carlos	Bob–Carlos	~~Carlos–Bob~~	~~Dietrich–Bob~~
Andre–Dietrich	Bob–Dietrich	Carlos–Dietrich	~~Dietrich–Carlos~~

We are counting each team *twice*; we're counting Andre–Bob *and* Bob–Andre. Since that gives us 12 possibilities, if we divide that by two, we'll get our answer. $12/2 = 6$. There are **6 possible teams**.

TRY SOME :

- Walter's café offers 3 different types of salad, 5 different entrées, and 2 different desserts. Walter's offers a dinner special that consists of a choice of exactly 1 salad, 1 entrée, and 1 dessert. How many different dinner specials are possible?

- From the senior class, 1 boy will be chosen to be homecoming king and 1 girl will be chosen to be homecoming queen. If the senior class has 20 boys and 35 girls, how many different pairs of king and queen are possible?

- Four people live on a city block and each person has exactly one car. If there are four parking spots on the street, how many different assignments of cars to parking spots are possible?

- A company assigns each employee a 4-digit ID number. The first digit of each number must be 3, the last digit must be either 0 or 1, and the 2 middle digits can each be any of the digits 0–9. How many different employee ID numbers are possible?

VII. PROBABILITY

"Probability" means exactly what it sounds like: how "probable" is this event. The probability of an event is defined as:

$$\text{Probability} = \frac{\text{number of "winners"}}{\text{total possible events}}$$

Say the probability of winning the lottery is "one in a million". That just means there's *one* winning number out of *a million* possible numbers. Since probabilities are fractions, most probability questions just boil down to the question: what **part of the whole** is the thing you're looking for?

- **A jar contains 32 marbles, and each marble is either red or blue. If the jar contains 8 red marbles, what is the probability that a marble randomly chosen from the jar will be blue?**

We're looking for the probability of choosing a blue marble. So all we have to find is:

$$\frac{\text{number of blue marbles}}{\text{total number of marbles}} = \frac{\text{blue}}{32}$$

We know there are 32 total marbles, so 32 will go on the bottom. We don't know how many blue marbles there are, but we do know there are 8 red marbles, and there are only red and blue marbles. So if we subtract the red from the total, we'll be left with the blue.

$$\frac{32-8}{32} = \frac{24}{32} = \frac{\mathbf{3}}{\mathbf{4}}$$

We're done! The probability of choosing a blue marble is 3/4.

Note that instead of solving for the blue marbles, we could've found the probability of choosing a red marble and subtracted from 1.

$$\frac{\text{red}}{\text{total}} = \frac{8}{32} = \frac{1}{4}$$

There's a 1/4 chance of picking a red marble...

$$1 - \frac{1}{4} = \frac{3}{4}$$

...so there's a 3/4 chance of picking a blue marble.

We can see from this that **the probabilities of all events surrounding a given problem must add up to 1.** You can think about probability as similar to *percents*. If there's a 3/4 chance of picking a blue marble, then 75% of the marbles are blue. Just as percents add up to 100%, all probabilities add up to 1.

TRY SOME

- **Freddy has only 4 green cars and 5 white cars. What is the probability that a car selected at random is green?**

- **A bag contains 3 fuchsia marbles, 7 hyacinth marbles, and 8 chartreuse marbles. What is the probability that a marble selected from the bag at random is hyacinth?**

- **A bag contains 24 cats, 3 of which are Siamese. What is the probability that a cat randomly selected from the bag is NOT Siamese?**

- **A bag contains 4 blueberry pancakes, 2 strawberry pancakes, and 6 blueberry waffles. If an item is drawn at random from the bag, what is the probability that it is blueberry flavored?**

- **An integer from 11 to 100, inclusive, is chosen at random. What is the probability that the number chosen has 9 as at least one digit?**

PRE-ALGEBRA EXERCISE

DO YOUR FIGURING HERE.

3. Which of the following numbers has the digit 4 in the thousandths place?

A. 0.004
B. 0.040
C. 0.400
D. 4.0
E. 40.0

6. What is the value of $\frac{1}{2}\times\frac{2}{3}\times\frac{3}{4}\times\frac{4}{5}$?

F. $\frac{1}{5}$

G. $\frac{5}{6}$

H. $\frac{4}{5}$

J. 1

K. $\frac{51}{30}$

9. Four randomly chosen employees at Dave's company will win large cash prizes. If there are 100 employees at the company, what is the probability that Dave will not win?

A. $\frac{1}{100}$

B. $\frac{1}{25}$

C. $\frac{1}{4}$

D. $\frac{24}{25}$

E. $\frac{99}{100}$

12. Which of the following numbers is greatest in value?

F. 2.1×10^{1}
G. 0.33×10^{2}
H. 1.2×10^{9}
J. 89,000
K. 49.0×10^{-6}

GO ON TO THE NEXT PAGE.

19. If as many 5-inch strips of ribbon as possible are cut from a ribbon that is 4 feet long, what is the total length of the ribbon that is left over? (12 inches = 1 foot)

A. 1 inch
B. 2 inches
C. 3 inches
D. 4 inches
E. 5 inches

DO YOUR FIGURING HERE.

30. If a is directly proportional to b and if $a = 30$ when $b = 21$, what is the value of a when $b = 10\frac{1}{2}$?

F. $\frac{20}{3}$
G. $\frac{147}{20}$
H. 10
J. 15
K. 30

33. What number is 175 percent of 16?

A. 12
B. 20
C. 24
D. 28
E. 32

34. Gretchen has 8 shirts, 3 skirts, and 10 hats. If an outfit consists of one shirt, one skirt, and one hat, how many different outfits can Gretchen wear?

F. 21
G. 24
H. 34
J. 120
K. 240

39. Loretta had 60 roses and 80 daffodils. If she sold 40% of her roses and 75% of her daffodils, what percent of her flowers remain?

A. 40%
B. 50%
C. 56%
D. 60%
E. 80%

GO ON TO THE NEXT PAGE.

42. The average of three numbers is 10. The average of just two of them is 6. What is the third number?

F. 2
G. 6
H. 10
J. 18
K. 20

DO YOUR FIGURING HERE.

45. A multi-colored candy is sold in a ratio of 7:3:2 of blue, red, and brown candies, respectively. How many pounds of red candies will be found in a 4-pound bag of this multi-colored candy?

A. $\frac{1}{2}$

B. $\frac{2}{3}$

C. 1

D. 2

E. 3

50. The average (arithmetic mean) of a, b, c, d, e, f, and g is 50. If the average of a, b and c is 30, what is the average of d, e, f, and g?

F. 40
G. 44
H. 55
J. 65
K. 70

55. A box contains a shipment of stuffed bears, of which 14 are red, 30 are green, 40 are blue and the rest are yellow. If the probability of selecting a yellow bear from this box at random is $\frac{1}{4}$, how many yellow bears are in the box?

A. 21
B. 28
C. 31
D. 56
E. 168

GO ON TO THE NEXT PAGE.

56. There are 15 consecutive numbers in a list. Which of the following operations would change the value of the median?

F. Increasing the smallest number by 7
G. Increasing the smallest number by 8
H. Increasing the largest number by 8
J. Decreasing the smallest number by 5
K. Decreasing the largest number by 5

DO YOUR FIGURING HERE.

59. A certain car cost c dollars in August. In September, the price was cut by 20 percent. In October, the price increased by 40 percent of the previous month's price. The price of the car at the end of October was what percent of the price in August?

A. 48%
B. 80%
C. 100%
D. 112%
E. 120%

STOP!

ELEMENTARY ALGEBRA

This chapter discusses the bulk of what we generally call *algebra*: solving equations, substituting values, factoring polynomials, and all sorts of other fun stuff like that. Strictly speaking, the ACT doesn't categorize all of these topics as Elementary Algebra—for example, solving one-variable equations is considered Pre-Algebra, and solving inequalities is Intermediate Algebra—but we've grouped them all together here to help keep things simple.

Of course, in the real world there's a lot more to algebra than what's in this chapter. You could spend a whole year on these concepts (many of you probably have!), but here we're focusing only on the algebraic concepts that appear on the ACT Math Test. This chapter gives you everything you need to know.

I. TECHNIQUES!

While this chapter will show you how to solve various types of algebra problems, don't forget the Math Techniques! Plug In and Backsolve were created to help you *avoid* algebra. **Over half of the Elementary Algebra problems can be done with techniques**, so they should always be in your mind and your heart.

Obviously, problems that are swimming in variables are good candidates for both techniques. If a question has variables in the choices, it doesn't matter what their values are, so we can use Plug In. If a question asks you for the value of a variable, you can use Backsolve and test the choices for that variable.

Techniques are also useful on **word problems** that involve **translation**. That is, the problem will describe mathematical relationships in normal English words and expect you to turn those words into algebraic equations. In problems like this, it's often much easier to use real numbers and bypass the equations altogether. We saw a ton of questions like this in the Math Techniques chapter, remember?

27. Bob has 4 dollars more than Lisa does. If Lisa has x dollars, how much would Bob have if he doubled his money?

You will still need to learn some algebra; the techniques won't work on every question, and on some problems techniques are possible but algebra is faster. In this chapter we're going to emphasize algebraic solutions over technique solutions. But don't forget that the techniques are here to help you.

II. BASIC MANIPULATION

1. Evaluating an expression

When we talk about "algebra", we generally mean problems that involve *variables*—letters that can stand for an unknown value.* The simplest algebra problems on the ACT will give you an expression containing a variable and ask you to evaluate the expression when the variable has a certain value. Observe:

➶ **What is the value of the expression $\frac{10x-4}{x-1}$ when $x = 7$?**

We know that the value of x is 7, so we can replace every x in the expression with a 7 and solve:

$$\frac{10(7)-4}{7-1} = \frac{70-4}{6} = \frac{66}{6} \boxed{= 11}$$

* It is sometimes said that algebra was invented by Arabic mathematicians, but that's not true. The *word* "algebra" does come from the Arabic word *al-jabr*, meaning "the completion" or "bone-setting" (yes, bone-setting). But algebraic problems date as far back as ancient Babylonia, over 3,500 years ago, and algebra involving symbols and letters began in 17th century Europe.

Problems like this may involve more than one variable:

- **If $a = 3$, $b = -4$, and $c = 8$, what is the value of $ac - ab$?**

Substitute the values for the corresponding letters. Just be careful to put the numbers in the right spots:

$$ac - ab = (3)(8) - (3)(-4) \quad = 24 - (-12) \quad = 24 + 12 \quad \boxed{= 36}$$

Sometime these questions may seem complicated:

- **The volume of a right circular cone is given by the formula $V = \frac{1}{3}\pi r^2 h$, where r is the radius of the base and h is the height. What is the volume of a right circular cone whose base has a radius of 3 and whose height is 10?**

Wait a minute—why are we looking at a geometry problem in the algebra chapter? Because all the problem asks you to do is substitute values into a given expression. Don't worry about what a cone is; just stick the numbers in for the letters in the formula:

$$V = \frac{1}{3}\pi(3)^2(10) \quad = \frac{1}{3}\pi(9)(10) \quad = \frac{1}{3}\pi(90) \quad \boxed{= 30\pi}$$

TRY SOME:

- **If $x = 5$ and $y = 4$, what is the value of $3x - 4y$?**

- **What is the value of $\frac{8x-9}{x}$ when $x = \frac{1}{2}$?**

- **If $x = 3$ and $k = 12$, what is the value of $x^2 + kx + 6$?**

2. Solving an equation

Most of the examples above were *expressions,* not *equations*. That just means that they have no equals sign. But a lot of algebra involves equations. When an equation has one variable in it, there will usually be only one value for the variable that makes the equation true.*

➤ **If $3x + 5 = 23$, $x = ?$**

You can solve an equation by **getting the variable by itself on one side of the equation**. That means we have to move all the stuff next the x to the other side of the equals sign. You can do this by **doing the opposite** of anything you see to **both sides of the equation**:

$3x + 5 = 23$ — To move "+ 5", subtract 5 from both sides.

$3x + 5 - 5 = 23 - 5$

$3x = 18$ — To move "× 3", divide both sides by 3.

$$\frac{3x}{3} = \frac{18}{3}$$

$$\boxed{x = 6}$$

This, my friend, is the heart of algebra: to get x by itself, do the opposite of anything you see to both sides. We'll see more complicated concepts, of course, but this is pretty much it. Sometimes an equation may seem more complicated, but just remember to do the opposite to get rid of something:

➤ **If $\frac{\sqrt{x-3}}{2} = 4$, $x = ?$**

$\frac{\sqrt{x-3}}{2} = 4$ — To remove "÷ 2", multiply both sides by 2.

$\sqrt{x-3} = 8$ — To remove the square root, square both sides.

$x - 3 = 64$ — To remove "−3", add 3 to both sides.

$$\boxed{x = 67}$$

How do you know which operations to do first? Think of an equation as a package with many layers of ribbons, wrapping paper, and boxes, and the variable is your birthday present inside the package.† To unwrap the package, you've got to start with the outermost ribbon, then the wrapping paper, then the box underneath. Each layer you remove is covering all the layers below it.

When solving an equation, **start with the operations that apply to *everything* else on that side of the equation.** In the first equation above, $3x + 5$, the "× 3" only applies to the x, not the 5. But the "+ 5" applies to everything before it, so we start there. In the second equation above, the square root only applies to the "$x - 3$", not to the 2. The "÷ 2" applies to everything else on that side, so we start there.

---

* Why is x always the first variable we use? There are several theories, but this is my favorite. This notation started in 1637 with the French mathematician and philosopher René Descartes in his book *La Géométrie*. Originally, he wanted to use z as the first variable, y as the second, x as the third, etc. But when the book went to be published, the publisher didn't have enough z's (back then, books were printed using individual blocks of metal for each letter). He had plenty of x's though—very few French words use x. So we use x as our variables because the French language uses too many z's.

† Surprise! It's just what you wanted!

x in terms of *y*

Not every algebra problem will just deal with numbers. Observe:

- **If $y = 5x + 3$, what is x in terms of y?**

Right now, the equation gives "y in terms of x". That means the equation defines y and uses x's in its definition: y is by itself on one side of the equation, and its value is $5x + 3$. But we want "x in terms of y". That means that we want to get x by itself on one side of the equation and nothing but y's and numbers on the other side. We do this **exactly the same way** we solved for x above. But now instead of a number, our answer will have a bunch of y's.

$y = 5x + 3$ Subtract 3 from both sides.

$y - 3 = 5x + 3 - 3$

$y - 3 = 5x$ Divide both sides by 5.

$\frac{y-3}{5} = \frac{5x}{5}$

$\boxed{\frac{y-3}{5} = x}$

> Most ACT questions that ask for "x in terms of y" can be done with Plug In.

TRY SOME:

- **If $4u + 11 = 3$, $u = ?$**

- **If $13 - 3z = 15z + 4$, $z = ?$**

- **If $\frac{5x+6}{6} = 11$, $x = ?$**

- **If $P = 5(a + 8)$, what is a in terms of P?**

- **If $\frac{2}{3}x - 6 = y$, what is x in terms of y?**

3. Multiple equations

Each problem above dealt with a single equation, but some problems may give you multiple equations with multiple variables. The most straightforward way to solve these problems is **substitution**. For example:

- **If $a = 3x - 6$, and $5x + a = 10$, then $x = ?$**

We're given two equations with two variables, x and a. Notice that the first equation has a on one side of the equation by itself. Since "a" is equivalent to "$3x - 6$", we can **substitute** "$3x - 6$" into the second equation wherever we see an "a".

$$5x + a = 10$$

$$5x + (3x - 6) = 10$$

$$8x - 6 = 10$$

$$8x = 16$$

$$\boxed{x = 2}$$

Try another:

- **When $x + y = 4$, what is the value of $5(x + y) - 6$?**

It might seem like we have to solve for x or y individually, but we don't. The first equation gives a value for "$x + y$", and the second equation also contains "$x + y$". So we can substitute 4 for that whole expression:

$$5(x + y) - 6 \qquad = 5(4) - 6 \qquad = 20 - 6 \qquad \boxed{= 14}$$

These examples were pretty simple, but more complicated problems can get quite intricate. If a problem has two or more variables in it, **don't forget the techniques**. Being able to solve intricate algebra problems is a good skill to have, but Plug In and Backsolve can help turn complicated problems into simple ones.

TRY SOME:

- **If $j = 3x - 5$ and $k = 6x + 1$, then $2j + 3k = ?$**

- **If $\frac{a}{b} = 5$ and $4a + 7b = 9$, what is the value of b?**

- **If $x - y = 10$ and $z = 3x - 3y - 8$, then $z = ?$**

III. POLYNOMIALS

1. What's a polynomial?

A **polynomial** is any mathematical expression with terms that are added or subtracted together. These terms will usually contain variables taken to different powers multiplied by a number called its **coefficient**. A polynomial containing two terms is a **binomial**.

In the following expressions, all the terms contain the same variable taken to the same power, so they can be added together directly:

$5+7$	$5y+7y$	$5x^2+7x^2$
$=12$	$=12y$	$=12x^2$

But in the following expressions, the terms are all different, so they can't be added together:

$5x+7$ $\quad$ $5x+7y$ $\quad$ $5x^2+7x+xy$

To simplify a long polynomial with a lot of different terms, find any terms that have the same combination of variables and powers:

$\mathbf{x^2}+4x+2xy+\mathbf{7x^2}-10x+5+9xy-1$	Add the terms containing x^2.
$8x^2+\mathbf{4x}+2xy-\mathbf{10x}+5+9xy-1$	Subtract the terms containing x.
$8x^2-6x+\mathbf{2xy}+5+\mathbf{9xy}-1$	Add the terms containing xy.
$8x^2-6x+11xy+\mathbf{5-1}$	Subtract the terms with no variables.
$\boxed{8x^2-6x+11xy-4}$	

2. FOIL

Take a look at this:

- **6(x + 5)**

Here we have a number multiplied by an entire binomial. To do this, just multiply 6 by each term inside the parentheses. We sometimes call this *distributing* the 6 inside the parentheses.

> Watch out for negatives! If you multiply a polynomial by a negative number, you must distribute the negative inside the parentheses.

$6(x+5) \quad = 6\times x+6\times 5 \quad \mathbf{= 6x+30}$

Great. Sometimes we want to multiply two binomials together:

- **(x + 5)(x + 4) = ?**

Just like we did above, we want to multiply *each* term in the first binomial with *each* term in the second. To help you keep track of the terms, remember the acronym "FOIL". Multiply:

First two terms	$x\times x$
Outside terms	$x\times 4$
Inside terms	$5\times x$
Last terms	5×4

Then add them all together and combine similar terms:

$=x^2+4x+5x+20 \quad \boxed{=\mathbf{x^2+9x+20}}$

TRY SOME:

- $(x + 8)(x - 3) = ?$

- $(a - 7)(a - 2) = ?$

- $(2y + 3)(y - 4) = ?$

- $(x + y)^2 = ?$

- $(x^2 + y)(3x^2 + 2y) = ?$

3. Factoring

FOIL involves multiplying two binomials to get a larger polynomial. But some ACT problems might want you to go the other way. Look at this expression:

➶ $\mathbf{2x + 6}$

Notice that each term in this expression contains a multiple of two. We can "pull out" that two and put it off to the side:

$2x + 6 \qquad = (2 \times x) + (2 \times 3) \qquad \boxed{= 2(x+3)}$

We call this process **factoring**. In this case, 2 was a factor of each term, so we "factored out" the 2. We can do the same thing with variables:

$x^2 - 3x \qquad = (x \times x) - (3 \times x) \qquad \boxed{= x(x-3)}$

What if we want to factor a polynomial into two binomials? Look at this expression:

➶ **What is the factored form of $x^2 + 7x + 12$?**

We know that there must be two binomials that multiply together to make that expression:

(? + ?)(? +?)

The first term here, x^2, was the result of the first two terms of the binomials multiplied together. So each of the binomials must start with an x:

$(x + ?)(x + ?)$

The last term, 12, was the result of the last two terms of the binomials multiplied together. So we know the **product** of our last two numbers is 12. That could be 1 and 12, 2 and 6, or 3 and 4.

The middle term, $7x$, was the result of each of the last terms multiplied by x and then added together. So we also know the **sum** of the last two numbers must be 7. What two numbers have a product of 12 and a sum of 7? Only 3 and 4 fit both requirements.

$\boxed{(x+3)(x+4)} \qquad = x^2 + 4x + 3x + 12 \qquad = x^2 + 7x + 12$

This can be easier when you have answer choices:

23. Which of the following expressions is equivalent to $x^2 - 2x - 15$?

A. $(x-2)(x+1)$
B. $(x-3)(x+5)$
C. $(x+3)(x-5)$
D. $(x-3)(x-5)$
E. $(x-7)(x-8)$

One option here is **Backsolve**: It's often easier to FOIL than to factor, so FOIL out the answer choices and see which one equals the polynomial we want:

A.	$(x-2)(x+1)$	$= x^2 + x - 2x - 2$	$= x^2 - 2x - 2$	×
B.	$(x-3)(x+5)$	$= x^2 + 5x - 3x - 15$	$= x^2 + 2x - 15$	×
C.	$\mathbf{(x+3)(x-5)}$	$= x^2 - 5x + 3x - 15$	$\mathbf{= x^2 - 2x - 15}$	✓
D.	$(x-3)(x-5)$	$= x^2 - 5x - 3x + 15$	$= x^2 - 8x + 15$	×
E.	$(x-7)(x-8)$	$= x^2 - 8x - 7x + 56$	$= x^2 + 15x + 56$	×

Even better, you could **Plug In** a number for x. Say $\mathbf{x = 6}$.

$(6)^2 - 2(6) - 15 \quad = 36 - 12 - 15 \quad = \mathbf{9}$

A.	$(6-2)(6+1)$	$=(4)(7)$	$=28$	×
B.	$(6-3)(6+5)$	$=(3)(11)$	$=11$	×
C.	$\mathbf{(6+3)(6-5)}$	$=(9)(1)$	$\mathbf{=9}$	✓
D.	$(6-3)(6-5)$	$=(-3)(1)$	$=-3$	×
E.	$(6-7)(6-8)$	$=(-1)(-2)$	$=2$	×

Difference of Squares

Try this problem:

- $(x+y)(x-y)=?$

Both binomials contain the same terms, except one binomial is a sum and the other is a difference. To do this, we can just FOIL as we did before:

$$(x+y)(x-y) \quad = x^2 - xy + xy - y^2 \quad \boxed{= x^2 - y^2}$$

Notice that the middle terms cancelled out, so the result was just the first term squared minus the second term squared. This equation is called the **difference of squares identity**. That just means it's an equation that shows up a lot that's always true for any variables, so it's good to remember it.

$$\boxed{x^2 - y^2 = (x+y)(x-y)}$$

When you see two squares subtracted from each other, you can easily factor the expression. For example:

- $x^2 - 64 = ?$

Both terms here are squares, so we can immediately factor it into the sum and difference of their roots:

$= (x+8)(x-8)$

TRY SOME: *Factor the following expressions:*

- $x^2 - 2x - 8$

- $x^2 - 14x + 24$

- $2x^2 + 11x + 5$

- $9x^2 - 49$

- $x^4 - 16$

4. Dividing polynomials

So far we've been multiplying polynomials, but ACT questions may ask you to divide polynomials, too.

- $$\frac{x+3}{x^2+x-6}$$

What do we do? Remember that a fraction can be reduced when the top and bottom have a common term:

$$\frac{2}{8}=\frac{2\times 1}{2\times 4}=\frac{1}{4}$$

The same concept applies to polynomials. Let's factor the denominator and see if we can cross out some terms common to the top and bottom.

When factoring, our ultimate goal is canceling out terms. Don't factor blindly: *try to factor out the term that's in the numerator.* In this problem, we want to cancel out "$x + 3$", so we'll try to get "$x + 3$" on the bottom. The bottom ends in "−6": what times 3 gives −6? −2. So the other term will be "$x - 2$". Now $x + 3$ cancels out on the top and bottom:

$$\frac{x+3}{x^2+x-6} = \frac{x+3}{(x+3)(x-2)} \boxed{= \frac{1}{x-2}}$$

PLEASE NOTE: whenever a problem involves division, there will be some values of x that are not allowed. As a rule, **you can never divide anything by zero**. Any values that make the denominator zero will not be allowed. The fancy math way of saying that is to say the expression is **undefined** for that value of x. In the problem above, the denominator is zero when $x + 3 = 0$ or when $x - 2 = 0$. So the expression is undefined when $x = -3$ and when $x = 2$.

TRY SOME: *Divide the following expressions (assuming the denominator is not zero in all cases).*

- $$\frac{x}{x^2+7x}=?$$

- $$\frac{x+5}{x^2-25}=?$$

- $$\frac{x^2+6x-40}{x-4}=?$$

5. Quadratic equations

All the polynomial problems we've seen so far have been expressions, not equations. That means almost any value of x will make it work. But we might also see polynomials involved in *equations*, where only certain values of x will make the equation true.

> **For what values of x does $x^2 + 7x + 12 = 0$?**

Any equation in the form $ax^2 + bx + c = 0$ is a **quadratic** equation—a polynomial containing one squared variable, set equal to zero.* So how do we solve it?

Well, we already factored this expression before, so let's do it again:

$$x^2 + 7x + 12 = (x + 3)(x + 4) = 0$$

Remember that zero has a special property: anything times zero is equal to zero. If we know $ab = 0$, then we know either a or b (or both) *must* equal zero. Since we know that $(x + 3)$ times $(x + 4)$ equals zero, we know that one or both of those terms must equal zero:

$x + 3 = 0$ or $x + 4 = 0$

$\mathbf{x = -3}$ **or** $\mathbf{x = -4}$

Beware of the change in sign! We factored the expression to $x + 3$ and $x + 4$, but the values of x are -3 and -4.

Note that **a quadratic equation must be set equal to zero.** If it's not, you'll have to make it equal to zero.

> **For what values of x does $x^2 - 3x + 2 = 20$?**

Here we have 20 on the right side. That's no good; we want 0 there. So we'll just subtract 20 from both sides before we factor:

$$x^2 - 3x + 2 - 20 = 20 - 20$$

$$x^2 - 3x - 18 = 0$$

$$(x - 6)(x + 3) = 0$$

$x - 6 = 0$ or $x + 3 = 0$

$\mathbf{x = 6}$ **or** $\mathbf{x = -3}$

The Quadratic Formula

In your math class at school, you may have been exposed to the quadratic formula. This is a special formula you can use to find the solutions for a quadratic equation. You can use it for any quadratic equation, but it's especially useful for polynomials that can't be factored into happy integers.

For the equation $ax^2 + bx + c = 0$, the solution for x is: $x = \dfrac{-b \pm \sqrt{b^2 - 4ac}}{2a}$

Generally, you will not need to know the quadratic formula on the ACT**.** You should be able to do any problem involving quadratics by factoring or with Plug In and Backsolve. If you *really* prefer the formula you *can* use it, but we generally don't recommend it. It's way too easy to mess it up.†

* If the variable is only taken to the *second* power, why is it called *quadratic*? Doesn't "quad" mean "four"? Indeed it does. The term comes from the Latin word "quadratus", meaning "square" (as in "*x squared*"). And a square has *four* sides.

† One way the formula can help is if you have a graphing calculator that allows programs. You can program the formula into your calculator so that you just have to input *a*, *b*, and *c*, and the program does the calculations for you. If you know how to do this, it can be nice and quick. But if you don't, don't worry about it.

TRY SOME:

- **What are the solutions for $x^2 - 12x = 0$?**

- **What are the solutions for $x^2 - 11x + 30 = 0$?**

- **What are the solutions for $x^2 - 7x - 8 = 0$?**

- **What are the solutions for $x^2 - 81 = 0$?**

- **What are the solutions for $x^2 - 13x = -42$?**

IV. INEQUALITIES

Number lines

Inequality questions often involve **number lines**. Number lines are a simple way to show the range of possible values for a single variable. For example, $x > 2$ can be graphed on a number line like so:

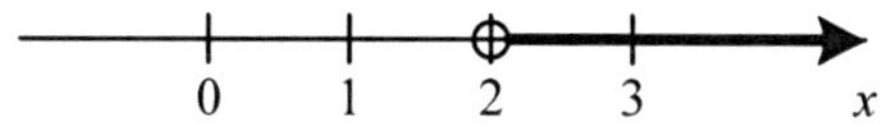

Note that the circle around the "2" mark means that x cannot *equal* 2. In contrast, $x \leq 2$ looks like this:

And you can graph multiple inequalities on the same number line. This graph shows $x < 1$ or $x \geq 3$:

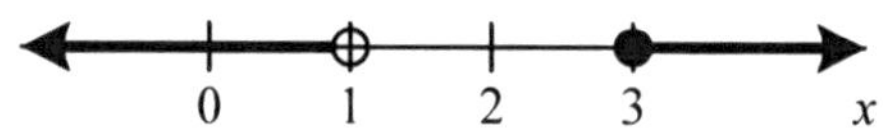

Algebraic manipulation

Inequalities work just like equations for the most part. You can solve for variables just like you do with equations. The only difference is that **if you multiply or divide by a negative number, you have to flip the inequality**. Permit us to demonstrate:

$$7 - 3x > 16$$

$$7 - 3x - 7 > 16 - 7$$

$$-3x > 9$$

$$\frac{-3x}{-3} < \frac{9}{-3}$$ ←Watch out here. This is where the sign flips.

$$\boxed{x < -3}$$

More complicated inequality questions—particularly those involving multiple variables—are often difficult to solve with algebraic manipulation. Don't forget: techniques like Plug In and Backsolve are here to help!

TRY SOME: *Solve these inequalities for x:*

- **$3(x + 2) < 12$**

- **$17 - x > 23$**

- **$x + 4 > \frac{x}{5}$**

ELEMENTARY ALGEBRA EXERCISE

DO YOUR FIGURING HERE.

3. If $x = -4$, what is the value of $\frac{x^2 - 4}{x - 2}$?

A. -6
B. -3
C. -2
D. 0
E. 2

6. If $9(x - 8) = -12$, $x = ?$

F. $-\frac{28}{3}$
G. $-\frac{4}{3}$
H. $-\frac{3}{2}$
J. $\frac{20}{3}$
K. $\frac{69}{9}$

11. If $3x - 5 = 5x + 3$, then $x = ?$

A. 4
B. 1
C. -1
D. -4
E. -8

14. Which of the following is equivalent to $(x - a)(x + b)$?

F. $x^2 - (b - a)x - ab$
G. $x^2 + (b - a)x - ab$
H. $x^2 + (a - b)x + ab$
J. $x^2 + (a + b)x - ab$
K. $x^2 + (a + b)x + ab$

17. The expression $(4p + 3)(5p - 6)$ is equivalent to:

A. $9p^2 - 18$
B. $20p^2 - 18$
C. $20p^2 - 3p - 18$
D. $20p^2 - 9p - 18$
E. $20p^2 + 39p - 18$

GO ON TO THE NEXT PAGE.

22. If $3(3x-5)+1<2x+7$, which of the following expressions gives the solution set for x?

F. $x<-1$
G. $x>-1$
H. $x>3$
J. $x<3$
K. $x>9$

DO YOUR FIGURING HERE.

25. For all nonzero values of m, n and p, which of the following expressions gives the solution set for x of the equation $mx+n=p$?

A. $\frac{p+n}{m}$

B. $\frac{p-n}{m}$

C. $\frac{n-p}{m}$

D. $\frac{p}{m}-n$

E. $\frac{p}{mn}$

30. The expression given below is equivalent to which of the following expressions?

$$(3x^4-2x^3-5)-2(x^4-2x^3+3x^2-2x+2)$$

F. $-8x^{17}$
G. $x^{17}-9$
H. $x^4+2x^3-6x^2+4x-9$
J. $x^4-4x^3+3x^2-2x-3$
K. $x^4-6x^3+6x^2-4x-1$

33. If $x^2\neq 16$, $\frac{(x+4)^2}{x^2-16}=?$

A. -1

B. $8x$

C. $-\frac{1}{4}$

D. $\frac{1}{x-4}$

E. $\frac{x+4}{x-4}$

GO ON TO THE NEXT PAGE.

DO YOUR FIGURING HERE.

38. The solution set for x for the equation $x^2 + kx - 12 = 0$ is $\{-3,4\}$. What does k equal?

F. -12
G. -7
H. -1
J. 1
K. 7

41. Interest can be calculated using $I = Prt$, where I is the interest, P is the initial amount of money, r is annual interest rate expressed as a decimal, and t is the time, in years. If Raoul invests $1,000 with a 4% interest rate, how much interest will he earn after 5 years?

A. $200
B. $400
C. $2,000
D. $4,000
E. $20,000

46. Which of the following expressions is equivalent to $6x^2 + 15x - 36$?

F. $(2x - 6)(3x + 6)$
G. $(2x + 9)(3x - 4)$
H. $(6x - 3)(x + 12)$
J. $3(2x + 3)(x - 4)$
K. $3(2x - 3)(x + 4)$

49. Which of the following number line graphs shows the solution set of $x^2 < 2x + 3$?

A.
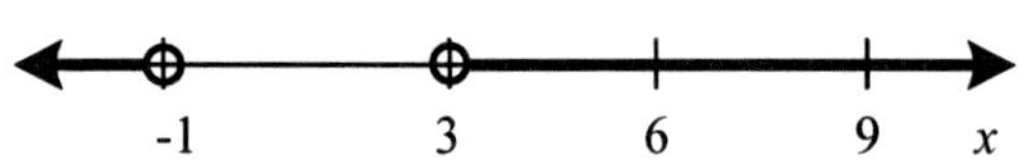

B.
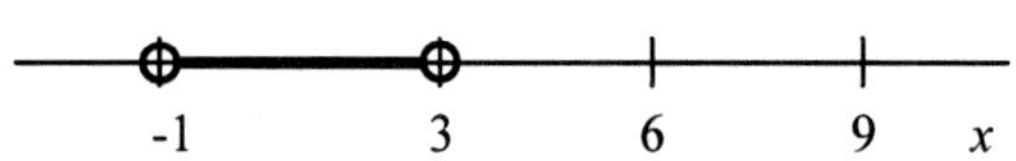

C.
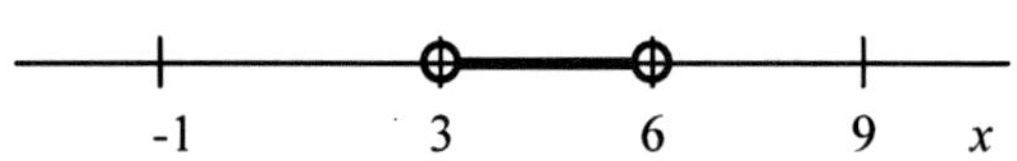

D.
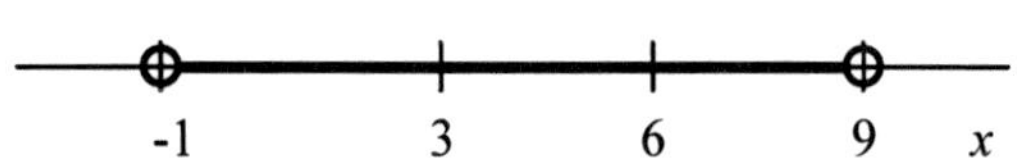

E.
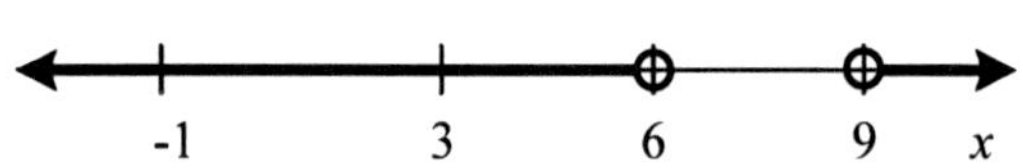

GO ON TO THE NEXT PAGE.

54. Which of the following quadratic expressions has solutions $x = -8m$ and $x = 2n^2$?

F. $x^2 - 16mn^2$

G. $x^2 + (8m - 2n^2)x - 16mn^2$

H. $x^2 + (8m + 2n^2)x + 16mn^2$

J. $x^2 - (8m + 2n^2)x + 16mn^2$

K. $x^2 - (8m - 2n^2)x - 16mn^2$

DO YOUR FIGURING HERE.

57. For all real numbers a and b such that a is the sum of b and 5, which of the following expressions represents the product of b and 5 in terms of a ?

A. $5(a - 5)$

B. $5(a + 5)$

C. $5a$

D. $5a - 5$

E. $\frac{a-5}{5}$

STOP!

INTERMEDIATE ALGEBRA

Now we're getting to the interesting stuff. Intermediate Algebra problems start to introduce some more difficult math concepts like functions, exponents, and absolute value. Intermediate Algebra doesn't occur as frequently as the previous two categories—only 9 questions per test, compared with 14 Pre-Algebra and 10 Elementary Algebra questions. Furthermore, since these problems tend to be harder, they will appear more often on the later questions on the test. That means that if you've got strict Target Numbers, you'll be skipping a lot of these questions. So the concepts in this chapter are not going to have as large an effect on your score as those in the previous chapters. However, if you're hoping for a higher score, these concepts will be crucial.

Keep in mind, again, that the math techniques are still important and widespread. On average, **65% of Intermediate Algebra questions can be done with Plug In or Backsolve.** That's a lot. And they're particularly helpful on difficult questions that can be otherwise confusing. So keep an eye out for them.

I. FUNCTIONS

1. Funny Symbols

Look at this:

$$5^2$$

What does that mean? Duh. Obviously:

$$5^2 = 5\times 5$$

The little "2" tells us to multiply the big number times itself. We all know that. Similarly:

$$7^2 = 7\times 7$$

$$(-23)^2 = (-23)\times(-23)$$

$$y^2 = y\times y$$

$$\Omega^2 = \Omega\times\Omega$$

$$(\text{donkey})^2 = (\text{donkey})\times(\text{donkey})$$

This should not be news to you. Any time you see a little "2" next to *anything*, multiply it by itself.

That's a function. It's a symbol (the "2") with a rule attached to it (multiply by self). *Everything* we do in math is a kind of function: a symbol with a rule attached to it.

On the ACT, sometimes there will be new, made-up symbols Take a look at this problem:

27. The operation ♥ is defined as ♥$x = 2x + 5$. What is the value of ♥7 – ♥6 ?

A. 1
B. 2
C. 6
D. 7
E. 9

Some of you are thinking, "Huh? What's up with the little heart? I've never seen a little heart symbol before. So how am I supposed to know what the little heart means?"

Because they just told you what it means! It's the first thing they say in the problem! Do you really think you're expected to know what ♥ means before the test? Can you show me the ♥ button on your calculator? Of course not. They just made it up. It's a random, arbitrary function, and they *tell you* exactly what it means. The only difference between this and 5^2 is that the exponent is a common math function, while ♥ is just one they made up randomly.

So. The function they give us is defined as:

♥$x = 2x + 5$

The x here is just a **placeholder**; it's a variable that stands for *any number*, an example of how to use the function. Just as the little "2" meant "multiply the number by itself", the little heart here means "multiply by 2 and add 5".

That means: ♥$2 = 2(2) + 5$

and: ♥$3 = 2(3) + 5$

therefore: ♥$18 = 2(18) + 5$

so: ♥$1979 = 2(1979) + 5$

also: ♥$y = 2y + 5$

ergo: ♥$(omg) = 2(omg) + 5$

this too: ♥$\pi = 2(\pi) + 5$

why not: ♥(☺) = 2(☺) + 5

one more: ♥(*fluffybabypandabear*) = 2(*fluffybabypandabear*) + 5

Get the point? Whatever you see next to the ♥, stick it in for x in $2x + 5$.

Now, let's get back to the original problem:

27. The operation ♥ is defined as ♥$x = 2x + 5$. What is the value of ♥7 – ♥6 ?

A. 1
B. 2
C. 6
D. 7
E. 9

So let's just stick 7 and 6 into the function and subtract our answers.

♥$7 = 2(7) + 5 = 14 + 5 = \mathbf{19}$

♥$6 = 2(6) + 5 = 12 + 5 = \mathbf{17}$

♥7 – ♥6 $= 19 - 17 = \boxed{2}$

So our answer is **2**. That's **B.**

2. $f(x)$ notation

We've just seen some examples of new functions being defined with funny symbols:

$$\heartsuit x = 2x + 5$$

But in reality, they don't use funny symbols all that often on the ACT. More often, they simply use a letter.

$$f(x) = 2x + 5$$

This means *exactly* the same thing as the little heart did. The only difference is that here they used an "f" instead of a "♥". The function itself behaves in exactly the same way. This means that:

$$f(2) = 2(2) + 5$$

$$f(-5) = 2(-5) + 5$$

$$f(q) = 2(q) + 5$$

$$f(g(k)) = 2(g(k)) + 5$$

$$f(x + 1) = 2(x + 1) + 5$$

You get the picture: "$f(x)$" doesn't mean "multiply f by x". The f isn't a variable; it's the name of a *function*.

We can do a lot with functions, but it all comes down to **substitution:**

Take whatever you see inside the parentheses and stick it in for *x*.

Let's look at some examples:

Evaluation

- **If $f(x) = x^2 + 3x - 10$, then $f(-4) = ?$**

The expression "$f(-4)$" means "the value of the $x^2 + 5x - 24$ when $x = -4$". So just stick -4 in for x:

$f(-4) = (-4)^2 + 3(-4) - 10 \qquad = 16 - 12 - 10 \qquad \boxed{= -6}$

TRY SOME:

- **If $f(x) = x^2 + 3x - 10$, then $f(10) = ?$**

- **If $f(x) = x^2 + 3x - 10$, then $f\left(\frac{1}{2}\right) = ?$**

- **If $f(x) = x^2 + 3x - 10$, then $f(2x) = ?$**

Multiple variables

➤ **If $f(x, y) = 2x + 3y - xy$, what is the value of $f(5,-1)$?**

This function has *two* variables inside the parentheses, but it also has two variables in the equation. Whenever we see two numbers inside the parentheses, we'll make the *first* number equal to x and the *second* equal to y.

$$f(5, -1) = 2(5) + 3(-1) - (5 \times -1) \quad = 4 - 3 - (-5) \quad = 4 - 3 + 5 \quad \boxed{= 6}$$

Composite functions

➤ **If $f(x) = 3x + 4$ and $g(x) = x^2$, what is the value of $f(g(3))$?**

We're given two functions, $f(x)$ and $g(x)$, and we have equations for both. This may seem scary, but it works exactly the same way the previous problems did. Remember: take whatever you see inside the parentheses and stick it in for x. Here, "$g(3)$" is inside the parentheses, so that will go in for x:

$$f(g(3)) = 3 \times g(3) + 4$$

That doesn't help: what does $g(3)$ mean? Ah, that's just a different function. We can put 3 in for x in the equation for $g(x)$:

$$g(3) = (3)^2 = 9.$$

Now we'll substitute 9 back into the first function:

$$f(g(3)) = f(9) \quad = 3 \times 9 + 4 \quad = 27 + 4 \quad \boxed{= 31}$$

Note that **the order is important**: do the function inside the parentheses first. Here, g was inside the parentheses for f, so we did g first. If the question had asked for $g(f(3))$, we'd first put 3 into the equation for f, then put the result into the equation for g:

$$g(f(3)) = (f(3))^2$$

$$f(3) = 3 \times 3 + 4 \quad = 9 + 4 \quad = 13.$$

$$g(f(3)) = g(13) \quad = 13^2 \quad \boxed{= 169}$$

FUNCTION DRILL

17. If $f(x) = \dfrac{2x-5}{x^2}$ for all nonzero values of x, then $f(3) =$

A. $\dfrac{11}{6}$
B. $\dfrac{11}{9}$
C. $\dfrac{1}{6}$
D. $\dfrac{1}{9}$
E. -1

26. If $x \Omega y = x^2 + y$, what is $(3 \Omega 4) \Omega 5 = ?$

F. 12
G. 18
H. 60
J. 149
K. 174

31. When Troy jumps off a bridge, the distance d, in feet, that he travels from his starting point after t seconds is given by the function $d(t) = 25t - 2t^2$. How far will Troy have traveled after 2 seconds?

A. 8 feet
B. 17 feet
C. 42 feet
D. 50 feet
E. 58 feet

44. If $f(x) = x^2 + 4$, what is $f(f(-2))$?

F. 0
G. 4
H. 8
J. 20
K. 68

51. If $f(x) = x^2 - 14$, then $f(x + c) = ?$

A. $c^2 - 14$
B. $x^2 + c - 14$
C. $x^2 - 14cx + c^2$
D. $x^2 + 2cx + c^2$
E. $x^2 + 2cx + c^2 - 14$

STOP!

II. EXPONENTS

You should be somewhat familiar with exponents by now. Exponents in some form have shown up in the question types we've already seen—Pre-Algebra questions may ask you to calculate the value of exponential numbers, and Elementary Algebra questions may ask about polynomials that contain exponents. However, Intermediate Algebra questions introduce some more complex rules and properties about exponential numbers.

1. Properties

Exponents tell you how many times to multiply a number or term by itself. The number that is being multiplied is called the "base". Giving a number an exponent is also called taking it to that "power".

$$\textit{base} \rightarrow 4^2 \leftarrow \textit{exponent}$$

Here are a few definitions and properties of exponents to remember:

- An exponent tells you how many times to multiply a number by itself.

  $5^2 = 5 \times 5$ $\qquad h^4 = h \times h \times h \times h$

- A **negative base** taken to an *even* exponent will become *positive*.
  A negative base taken to an *odd* exponent will stay *negative*.

  $(-2)^2 = (-2)\times(-2) = 4$ $\qquad (-2)^3 = (-2)\times(-2)\times(-2) = -8$

- When taking a positive **fraction** to a power, the result is *smaller* than the original number.

  $\left(\frac{1}{2}\right)^2 = \frac{1}{4}$ $\qquad \frac{1}{2} > \frac{1}{4}$

- A **negative exponent** is the same as the reciprocal of the base with a positive exponent (that is, 1 divided by the number with a positive exponent).

  $x^{-3} = \frac{1}{x^3}$ $\qquad \frac{1}{x^{-3}} = x^3$

- Any number to the **zero power** equals one.

  $x^0 = 1$

- A **root** is the inverse (the opposite) of its corresponding power. A square root is the inverse of a square, a cube root is the inverse of a cube, the fourth root is the inverse of the fourth power, etc. That means that doing both at the same time will cancel them out.

  $\sqrt{x} \times \sqrt{x} = x$ $\qquad \sqrt{x^2} = x$ $\qquad \sqrt[3]{x^3} = x$ $\qquad \sqrt[4]{x^4} = x$

- A **fractional exponent** is the same as a root.

  $x^{\frac{1}{2}} = \sqrt{x}$ $\qquad x^{\frac{1}{3}} = \sqrt[3]{x}$ $\qquad x^{\frac{1}{n}} = \sqrt[n]{x}$ $\qquad x^{\frac{2}{3}} = \sqrt[3]{x^2}$

A word about parentheses

On exponent problems, it's especially important to pay attention to what's inside and outside the parentheses.

If an exponent is next to parentheses, it applies to the *entire* expression *inside* the parentheses.
If there are no parentheses, the exponent applies *only* to the number or variable *right next to it*.

ab^2: Only b is squared, not a.

$(ab)^2$: Both a and b are squared.

$-2x^2$: Only x is squared.

$-(2x)^2$: $2x$ is squared. This equals $-4x^2$.

$(-2x)^2$: -2 and x are both squared. This equals $4x^2$.

2. Combining exponents

There are a few rules for dealing with exponential numbers that you should know:

1. To multiply exponential numbers with the same base, add the exponents.

$$2^5 \times 2^3 = 2^{5+3} = 2^8$$

2. To divide exponential numbers with the same base, subtract the exponents.

$$\frac{2^5}{2^3} = 2^{5-3} = 2^2$$

3. To raise an exponential number to another exponent, multiply the exponents.

$$\left(2^5\right)^3 = 2^{5\times 3} = 2^{15}$$

WARNING: You can add variables with the same exponent, but you **cannot** add bases with different exponents:

OK: $2x^2 + 7x^2 = 9x^2$ NOT OK: $2^5 + 2^3 \neq 2^8$

Variables in exponents, Different bases

If an equation has variables in its exponents, you can usually set the exponents equal to each other.

➤ **If $2^{a+10} = 2^{3a}$, then $a = ?$**

Both sides of the equation have the same base, so we can just set the exponents equal to each other:

$a + 10 = 3a$ $10 = 2a$ $\boxed{5 = a}$

If we're given numbers that don't have the same base, we should try to put them in the same base:

➤ **If $3^x = 9^5$, then $x = ?$**

We can't just set x equal to 5 because one base is 3 and the other is 9. But look: 9 is a power of 3. If we rewrite 9 as 3^2, we'll have the same base on both sides.

$3^x = \left(3^2\right)^5 = 3^{10}$ $\boxed{x = 10}$

TRY SOME:

- $\left(3^2\right)^{\frac{1}{2}} = ?$

- $2x^2 - (3x)^2 = ?$

- $\dfrac{x^4 x^3}{x^5} = ?$

- $\left(a^3 b^4 c^{10}\right)\left(a^8 b^{-1} c^2\right)^3 = ?$

- If $8^{13} = 2^x$, then $x = ?$

3. Logarithms

A **logarithm** is just a way of writing an exponent problem in a different order. Usually logarithm problems just require you to understand the definition of a logarithm:

$$\boxed{\log_a b = c \textbf{ means that } a^c = b}$$

As with exponential numbers, the "a" here is called the base.

How about an example?

➤ **What is the value of $\log_3 9$?**

Let's set that expression equal to a variable, x. Using the definition above,

$$\log_3 9 = x \qquad \text{means} \qquad 3^x = 9$$

The question is basically asking: 3 taken to what power gives you 9? Clearly, 3^2 is equal to 9, so $\boldsymbol{x = 2}$.

Logarithms don't appear often, and when they do appear, it's only on the hardest questions (the last 10 on the test). So this is not a very valuable concept—you'll see about one logarithm question for every three tests you take. If you're shooting for a very high score on the ACT, you'll want to get cover every concept that might show up. Otherwise, just worry about the basic exponent rules.

Logarithm problems often just require understanding the definition shown above.* However, you may also need to know some logarithm identities, rules for combining and simplifying logarithms. Note that these identities are just logical consequences of the exponent rules discussed in the previous section.

$$\log_a(mn) = \log_a m + \log_a n \qquad \log_a(a) = 1 \qquad \log_a(m^n) = n(\log_a m)$$

$$\log_a(m/n) = \log_a m - \log_a n \qquad \log_a(a^x) = x$$

* You may have noticed that your calculator has two buttons to perform logarithms, but they won't help you on ACT questions. The "LOG" button gives the logarithm with base 10, and the "LN" button gives the "natural logarithm", the logarithm with base e. The letter e is a constant, like π, which is important for certain types of Fancy Math. What types? Don't worry about it. You will not need to know anything about natural logarithms or e on the ACT.

Exponent Drill

20. For all $x > 1$, the expression $\frac{2x^3}{2x^6}$ equals:

F. $\frac{1}{2}$

G. $x^{\frac{1}{2}}$

H. $x^{\frac{1}{3}}$

J. $\frac{1}{x^2}$

K. $\frac{1}{x^3}$

29. For all x, $\left(-2x^2\right)^3$ is equivalent to:

A. $-8x^6$
B. $-8x^5$
C. $-6x^6$
D. $6x^5$
E. $8x^6$

36. Which of the following is a value of x that satisfies $\log_x 16 = 2$?

F. 2
G. 4
H. 8
J. 12
K. 16

43. For all nonzero x and y, $\frac{\left(5xy^3\right)\left(-2x^3y\right)}{x^2y^{-2}} = ?$

A. $\frac{3y^4}{x^4}$

B. $\frac{x^2y^2}{10}$

C. $-10x^2y^2$

D. $-10x^4y^4$

E. $-10x^2y^6$

50. If $x^2y^3 < 0$, then which of the following *must* be true?

F. $x < 0$
G. $x > 0$
H. $y < 0$
J. $y > 0$
K. $xy < 0$

STOP!

III. Absolute Value

The **absolute value** of a number is its numerical value without its sign. That means that *negative numbers become positive and positive numbers stay positive*. The symbol for absolute value is two straight lines on either side of the number:

$$|5| = 5 \qquad |-5| = 5$$

When you want to compute expressions with absolute value, do whatever is inside the lines first, then strip away any negatives between the lines:

$|10-8|-|5-11|$ First, do the stuff inside the lines.

$=|2|-|-6|$ Now, strip away the negatives inside the lines, so −6 becomes 6.

$= 2 - 6$ $\boxed{= -4}$

Solving for a variable

Take a look at this:

- $|x| = 7$

The variable x is inside the absolute value lines, and its absolute value is 7. There are two possible solutions:

- Ether $\mathbf{x = 7}$ and the absolute value keeps it positive 7,
- or $\mathbf{x = -7}$ and the absolute value strips its negative to make it positive 7.

The key to absolute value problems is: ***DON'T FORGET ABOUT THE NEGATIVES***.

- **If $|n-12| = 7$, what is one possible value of n?**

If $|n-12| = 7$, then we have two options:

$n - 12 = 7$ or $n - 12 = -7$

$\boxed{n = 19}$ $\boxed{n = 5}$

It's sometimes helpful to think of absolute value as **distance**: *The absolute value of a difference gives the distance between the two points.* That is:

$$|\text{Point A} - \text{Point B}| = \text{distance between points}$$

A simple subtraction will always tell us the distance. If we want to find the distance between 19 and 12, we'd subtract 19 – 12. But if we want the distance between 5 and 12, subtracting 5 – 12 gives us −7, and we generally don't like to use negative distances. The nice thing about the absolute value is that it gives us the distance *in either direction.*

In the problem above, the expression "$|n-12| = 7$" means "point n is a distance of 7 away from 12". That is, n is either 7 more than 12 or 7 less than 12.

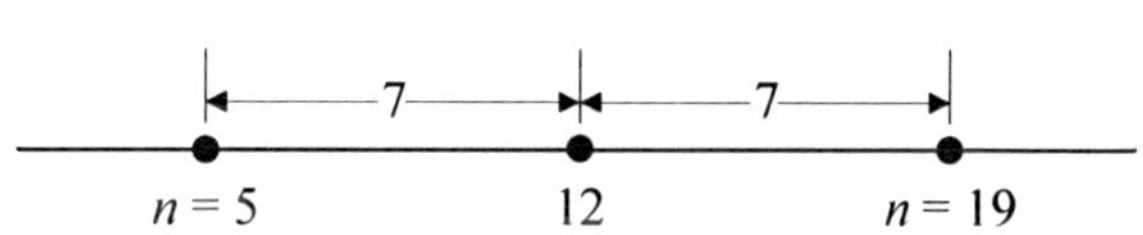

Inequalities

A lot of absolute value questions also involve inequalities. Take a look at this:

> Absolute value questions can be tricky when they involve multiple variables or inequalities. **Don't forget about the math techniques!** Plug In and Backsolve can be a big help when things start to get complicated.

- **If $|2x-5|>9$, what is the solution set for x?**

As we saw in the Elementary Algebra chapter, inequalities can be solved just like equations. Like the equation above, this inequality will have two solutions, one positive and one negative. But there's one trick to solving inequalities with absolute values: **you have to flip the inequality sign for the negative solution**:

$|2x-5|>9$ means	$2x-5>9$	or	$2x-5<-9$
	$2x>14$	or	$2x<-4$
	$x>7$	or	$x<-2$

Remember we said that, when solving inequalities, you have to flip the sign if you multiply or divide by a negative. This is the same concept. Here's another way to think about it:

$|2x-5|>9$ means	$2x-5>9$	or	$-(2x-5)>9$.

If we divide the second equation by -1, we flip the sign to get $2x-5<-9$.

ABSOLUTE VALUE DRILL

13. $|6-15|-|5(-4)|=?$

A. -29
B. -11
C. 1
D. 11
E. 29

26. If $|x+11|=23$, what are the possible values of x?

F. -34 and 12
G. -23 and 23
H. -12 and 12
J. -12 and 34
K. 12 and 34

33. Which of the following is the solution set for the inequality $|x-2|<7$?

A. $x<-5$ or $x>9$
B. $x<-7$ or $x>7$
C. $x<-9$ or $x>5$
D. $x>-5$ and $x<9$
E. $x>-7$ and $x<9$

42. If $a>0$ and $|ab|>ab$, which of the following MUST be true?

F. $b>a$
G. $b>0$
H. $b<0$
J. $a^2<b^2$
K. $a^2>b^2$

55. Which of the following is a graph of the solution set for the inequality $|x|\geq 8$?

A.

B.
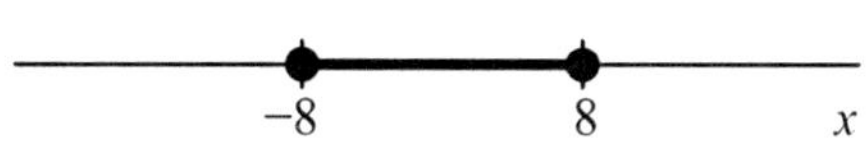

C.

D.

E.
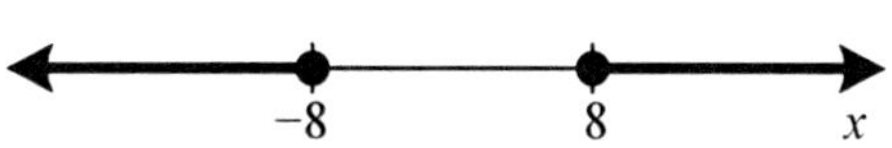

STOP!

IV. MISCELLANY

There are a few more concepts left that don't quite fit into any of the topics we've covered so far, so we threw them all together into a big grab bag of math. All of the following topics are at the bottom of the ACT Math totem pole: they don't appear often, maybe on one question for every three tests. If you're going for a 36, you'll want to know this stuff well. Otherwise, don't lose sleep over it.[*]

1. Sequences

A **sequence** is a fancy term for a list numbers (which continues infinitely, unless otherwise specified) where each next term is obtained by applying some sort of rule. In theory, this rule can be anything, but there are two types of sequences that concern us on the ACT.

Arithmetic sequences

An **arithmetic sequence**[†] is a sequence in which each term is obtained by **adding** a certain number to the previous term. To define a sequence, you need to know where the sequence starts and what number is added to each term (called "the common difference"). For example:

5, 8, 11, 14, 17, 20, 23, 26, 29, 32 ...

This arithmetic sequence starts with 5 and the common difference is 3.

> Sequence questions sometimes define terms like "arithmetic sequence" or even provide equations in the questions themselves. But they don't always, so you should still learn these terms and formulas.

- **The second term of an arithmetic sequence is 31 and the third term is 48. What is the first term of the sequence?**

We know two consecutive terms, so we can subtract them to find the common difference. 48 – 31 = 17. So each term is 17 more than the one before it. So the second term, 31, must be 17 more than the first term. To get the first term, subtract again: 31 – 17 = **14.**

But arithmetic sequence questions can get more complicated:

- **The first term of an arithmetic sequence is 5 and the common difference is 3. What is the 10th term of the sequence?**

We could just count out 10 terms (which we already did above, so we know the 10th term is 32). But we could also use this formula:

$$a_n = a_1 + (n-1)d$$

- a_n is the last term of the sequence (the term we want)
- a_1 is the first term of the sequence
- n stands for the number of terms we want
- d is the amount added to each term

In this problem, $a_1 = 5$, $d = 3$, and $n = 10$. Therefore:[‡]

$$a_n = 5 + (10 - 1)3 \qquad = 5 + (9)3 \qquad = 5 + 27 \qquad \boxed{= 32}$$

---

[*] All of these topics can get much more complicated, but our focus here is what you need on the ACT, and on this test you'll only get a taste of them.

[†] When talking about a sequence, it's pronounced <a-rith-MEH-tic>, not <a-RITH-muh-tic>

[‡] This formula isn't too difficult to understand. We're starting with 5 (that's a_1) and we're adding 3 (that's d) a bunch of times until we get to the 10th (that's n) term. But we're not adding it 10 times—we're adding it 9 (that's $n - 1$) times. (Think about it: to get to the *2nd* term we'd add 3 *once*; to get to the *3rd* term, we'd add 3 *twice*)

Arithmetic sum

Sometimes a question will ask us for the sum of the terms, not just the terms themselves.

- **The first term of an arithmetic sequence is 3 and the common difference is 2. what is the sum of the first 18 terms of this sequence?**

We could literally count out all the terms and add them up. The numbers are pretty small, so we could do it:

$$3 + 5 + 7 + 9 + 11 + 13 + 15 + 17 + 19 + 21 + 23 + 25 + 27 + 29 + 31 + 33 + 35 + 37 \boxed{= \mathbf{360}}$$

But that's a lot of numbers, and the chances of making a careless mistake are pretty high. If you prefer, you can remember another formula. To find the sum of the first *n* terms of an arithmetic sequence:

$$s_n = \frac{n(a_1 + a_n)}{2} \qquad \text{where } s_n \text{ is the sum of first } n \text{ terms.}^{*}$$

To use this formula we need a_n, the last term in the sequence. We can use the formula we learned before to find it:

$$a_n = a_1 + (n-1)d \qquad = 3 + (18 - 1)2 \qquad = 3 + (17)2 \qquad = 3 + 34 = \mathbf{37}$$

Now we can stick 37 in for a_n

$$s_n = \frac{n(a_1 + a_n)}{2} \qquad = \frac{18(3+37)}{2} \qquad = \frac{18(40)}{2} \qquad = \frac{720}{2} \qquad \boxed{= \mathbf{360}}$$

We could also combine the sum equation with the equation for a_n to get: $s_n = \dfrac{n(2a_1 + (n-1)d)}{2}$

Note that the *sum of consecutive numbers* is just an arithmetic sequence where $d = 1$.

Geometric sequences

A **geometric sequence** is a sequence in which each term is obtained by **multiplying** a certain number to the previous term. The number you multiply each time is called the "common ratio". Here's an example:

1, 2, 4, 8, 16, 32

In this geometric sequence, the first term is 1, and the common ratio is 2.

Geometric sequence questions often simply require you to understand this definition.

- **What is the next term after −1 in the geometric sequence 27, −9, 3, −1, ... ?**

First, we'll find the common ratio by dividing the *second* term by the *first* term: $\dfrac{-9}{27} = -\dfrac{1}{3}$

Each term is obtained by multiplying by $-\dfrac{1}{3}$.[†] Multiply −1 by $-\dfrac{1}{3}$ to get the next term in the sequence:

$$-1 \times -\frac{1}{3} \qquad \boxed{= \frac{\mathbf{1}}{\mathbf{3}}}$$

---

* This formula is just the average of the first term and the last term, multiplied by the number of terms.

† Geometric sequences on the ACT often use fractions as their common ratio, meaning the terms get smaller as the sequence goes on. If you prefer, rather than thinking of this as multiplying each term by a fraction, you can think of it as dividing by −3. It's the same thing.

2. Matrices

Think of a matrix as a set of data. It's like a table, with numbers organized into rows and columns. Take any table, take away the grid lines and put in some big brackets, and bam! You have a matrix. Unlike tables, matrices can be directly added, subtracted, and multiplied. Here are some examples of matrices, with their dimensions labeled:*

1×1: $\begin{bmatrix} 0 \end{bmatrix}$ 1×2: $\begin{bmatrix} 0.5 & 0.75 \end{bmatrix}$ 3×2: $\begin{bmatrix} a & b \\ c & d \\ e & f \end{bmatrix}$ 3×3: $\begin{bmatrix} 1 & 0 & 0 \\ 0 & 1 & 0 \\ 0 & 0 & 1 \end{bmatrix}$

2×1: $\begin{bmatrix} 1/2 \\ 3/4 \end{bmatrix}$ 2×3: $\begin{bmatrix} -4 & h & 2.5 \\ 900 & 6 & j \end{bmatrix}$

Addition and subtraction

To add or subtract matrices of the same dimensions, just add or subtract the corresponding entries with each other. For example:

$$\begin{bmatrix} 1 \\ 2 \end{bmatrix} + \begin{bmatrix} 3 \\ 4 \end{bmatrix} = \begin{bmatrix} 1+3 \\ 2+4 \end{bmatrix} = \begin{bmatrix} 4 \\ 6 \end{bmatrix} \qquad \begin{bmatrix} 1 \\ 2 \end{bmatrix} - \begin{bmatrix} 3 \\ 4 \end{bmatrix} = \begin{bmatrix} 1-3 \\ 2-4 \end{bmatrix} = \begin{bmatrix} -2 \\ -2 \end{bmatrix}$$

$$\begin{bmatrix} 10 & 4 \end{bmatrix} + \begin{bmatrix} 7 & 20 \end{bmatrix} = \begin{bmatrix} 10+7 & 4+20 \end{bmatrix} = \begin{bmatrix} 17 & 24 \end{bmatrix} \qquad \begin{bmatrix} 10 & 4 \end{bmatrix} - \begin{bmatrix} 7 & 20 \end{bmatrix} = \begin{bmatrix} 10-7 & 4-20 \end{bmatrix} = \begin{bmatrix} 3 & -16 \end{bmatrix}$$

$$\begin{bmatrix} a & b \\ c & d \end{bmatrix} + \begin{bmatrix} e & f \\ g & h \end{bmatrix} = \begin{bmatrix} a+e & b+f \\ c+g & d+h \end{bmatrix} \qquad \begin{bmatrix} a & b \\ c & d \end{bmatrix} - \begin{bmatrix} e & f \\ g & h \end{bmatrix} = \begin{bmatrix} a-e & b-f \\ c-g & d-h \end{bmatrix}$$

Multiplication

Multiplying two matrices is a more complicated process involving some weird rules.† Let's try one:

$$\begin{bmatrix} 1 & 2 & 3 \\ 4 & 5 & 6 \end{bmatrix} \times \begin{bmatrix} 1 & 4 \\ 2 & 5 \\ 3 & 6 \end{bmatrix} = ?$$

To multiply the matrices, take the entries in the **first *row* of the first matrix**, *multiply* each term with the corresponding entry in the **first *column* of the second**. Then *add* all those products. That gives you one entry in your new matrix. It goes in the first row and first column of the resulting matrix.

$$\begin{bmatrix} 1 & 2 & 3 \\ 4 & 5 & 6 \end{bmatrix} \times \begin{bmatrix} 1 & 4 \\ 2 & 5 \\ 3 & 6 \end{bmatrix} \qquad (1 \times 1) + (2 \times 2) + (3 \times 3) = 1 + 4 + 9 = \mathbf{14} \qquad \begin{bmatrix} \mathbf{14} & ? \\ ? & ? \end{bmatrix}$$

Do this with every row and column pair:

$$\begin{bmatrix} 1 & 2 & 3 \\ 4 & 5 & 6 \end{bmatrix} \times \begin{bmatrix} 1 & 4 \\ 2 & 5 \\ 3 & 6 \end{bmatrix} \qquad (4 \times 1) + (5 \times 2) + (6 \times 3) = 4 + 10 + 18 = 32 \qquad \begin{bmatrix} 14 & ? \\ \mathbf{32} & ? \end{bmatrix}$$

$$\begin{bmatrix} 1 & 2 & 3 \\ 4 & 5 & 6 \end{bmatrix} \times \begin{bmatrix} 1 & 4 \\ 2 & 5 \\ 3 & 6 \end{bmatrix} \qquad (1 \times 4) + (2 \times 5) + (3 \times 6) = 4 + 10 + 18 = 32 \qquad \begin{bmatrix} 14 & \mathbf{32} \\ 32 & ? \end{bmatrix}$$

---

* The plural of matrix is "matrices" (pronounced "MAY-trih-sees"). The "dimensions" of the matrix are just the number of rows and columns. Rows are always listed first. A matrix with, for example, 3 rows and 4 columns is a 3×4 ("three by four") matrix. An $n \times m$ matrix has n rows and m columns.

† Note that if you have a graphing calculator (and you know how to use it), it can multiply matrices for you.

$$\begin{bmatrix} 1 & 2 & 3 \\ \mathbf{4} & \mathbf{5} & \mathbf{6} \end{bmatrix} \times \begin{bmatrix} 1 & \mathbf{4} \\ 2 & \mathbf{5} \\ 3 & \mathbf{6} \end{bmatrix} \qquad (4 \times 4) + (5 \times 5) + (6 \times 6) = 16 + 25 + 36 = 77 \qquad \begin{bmatrix} 14 & 32 \\ 32 & 77 \end{bmatrix}$$

Do this same process for matrices of any dimensions. Match the first *row* of the first matrix to the first *column* of the second matrix:*

$$\begin{bmatrix} 100 & 10 \end{bmatrix} \times \begin{bmatrix} 3 & 6 & 9 \\ 4 & 5 & 7 \end{bmatrix} = \begin{bmatrix} 340 & 650 & 970 \end{bmatrix} \qquad \begin{bmatrix} a & b & c & d \end{bmatrix} \times \begin{bmatrix} e \\ f \\ g \\ h \end{bmatrix} = \begin{bmatrix} ae + bf + cg + dh \end{bmatrix}$$

3. Imaginary and Complex numbers

You know how sometimes a problem will start by saying "For all real numbers"? Why do they say that? Are there any numbers that aren't real?

Yes there are! **Imaginary numbers** are numbers that contain i, defined as $i = \sqrt{-1}$. Questions involving imaginary numbers often give the definition as $i^2 = -1$, but that's the same thing. Usually you're not allowed to take the square root of a negative, which is why numbers that do so are called "imaginary". Often an imaginary number will have a coefficient, such as "$8i$" or "$3i$".

Most imaginary numbers on the ACT involve **complex numbers**. A complex number is a polynomial in the form $a + bi$, a real number plus or minus an imaginary number. Let's look at an example:

- **$(3 + 2i)(5 + 3i) = ?$**

Complex numbers work like any other polynomial and can be multiplied using FOIL:

$$(3+2i)(5+3i) \qquad = 3(5) + 9i + 10i + 6i^2 \qquad = 15 + 19i + 6i^2$$

We're not done. Remember that $i^2 = -1$, so we can substitute -1 in the last term:

$$= 15 + 19i + 6(-1) \qquad \boxed{= \mathbf{9 + 19}\boldsymbol{i}}$$

Occasionally you may be asked about higher powers of i. If you multiply i by itself a bunch of times, you'll see that the powers of i show a repeating pattern:

$i^1 = \sqrt{-1} = i$ $\qquad i^2 = \sqrt{-1} \times \sqrt{-1} = -1$ $\qquad i^3 = i^2 \times i = -1 \times i = -i$ $\qquad i^4 = i^3 \times i = (-i) \times i = -i^2 = 1$

$i^5 = i^4 \times i = i$ $\qquad i^6 = i^5 \times i = i \times i = -1$ $\qquad i^7 = i^6 \times i = -1 \times i = -i$ $\qquad i^8 = i^7 \times i = (-i) \times i = -i^2 = 1$ etc...

4. Factorial (*n*!)

Very, very rarely a question might ask you about factorials. Taking the factorial of n (symbol is "$n!$") means finding the product of all the consecutive numbers up to n.

$3! = 1 \times 2 \times 3$ $\qquad 10! = 1 \times 2 \times 3 \times 4 \times 5 \times 6 \times 7 \times 8 \times 9 \times 10$ $\qquad n! = 1 \times 2 \ldots \times (n - 1) \times n$

You might see a question that expects you to know what this symbol means. Other times, the definition will be given to you in the text of the question. This is at the bottom of the list of important things for you to know.

* This means you can only multiply matrices if the number of rows in the first matrix matches the number of columns in the second. Here we're multiplying a 2 × **3** matrix with a **3** × 2 matrix, so we're good.

INTERMEDIATE ALGEBRA EXERCISE

DO YOUR FIGURING HERE.

4. $5y^2 \cdot 2x^4 y \cdot 3x^3 y^2$ is equivalent to:

F. $10x^7 y^5$
G. $10x^{12} y^4$
H. $30x^7 y^5$
J. $30x^{12} y^4$
K. $30x^{12} y^5$

7. If the second term of an arithmetic sequence is −9 and the third term is −23, What is the first term?

(Note: In an arithmetic sequence, consecutive terms differ by the same amount.)

A. −37
B. −14
C. 5
D. 14
E. 37

10. Let a function of two variables be defined by

$f(x,y) = y - \frac{y}{x}$ when $x \neq 0$. What is the value of $f(1,5)$?

F. −4

G. 0

H. $\frac{4}{5}$

J. $\frac{24}{5}$

K. 4

15. If the function $g(x)$ is defined by $g(x) = x^3 + 2x$, what is $g(-2)$?

A. −12
B. −4
C. 0
D. 4
E. 12

GO ON TO THE NEXT PAGE.

22. Emily's Bakery sells three sizes of coffee (S, M, and L). The matrices below show the number of each size of coffee sold on two days of a certain week and the price of each size. What is the total cost of all the coffee sold over these two days?

DO YOUR FIGURING HERE.

$$\begin{array}{c} \\ \text{Monday} \\ \text{Tuesday} \end{array} \begin{array}{c} \begin{array}{ccc} \text{S} & \text{M} & \text{L} \end{array} \\ \begin{bmatrix} 130 & 150 & 120 \\ 90 & 100 & 70 \end{bmatrix} \end{array} \qquad \begin{array}{c} \text{Price} \\ \begin{array}{c} \text{S} \\ \text{M} \\ \text{L} \end{array} \begin{bmatrix} \$3 \\ \$4 \\ \$5 \end{bmatrix} \end{array}$$

F. \$1,020
G. \$1,590
H. \$2,040
J. \$2,610
K. \$3,120

27. If $5^{2x+1} = 125$, what is the value of x?

A. 1
B. 2
C. 3
D. 4
E. 5

30. The height, h, in inches, of a student in the twelfth grade of a certain school satisfies the inequality $|h - 66| < 8$. Which of the following could be the height in inches of the student?

F. 58
G. 59
H. 74
J. 75
K. 76

35. For all values of x, the function f is defined by $f(x) = x^2 - 5$, What is the value of $f(f(4))$?

A. 11
B. 44
C. 116
D. 121
E. 251

GO ON TO THE NEXT PAGE.

38. The first term of an arithmetic sequence is 1 and the common difference of the sequence is 1. What is the sum of the first 50 terms of this sequence?

DO YOUR FIGURING HERE.

F. 50
G. 100
H. 250
J. 1275
K. 2550

41. If $a = b^2c^3$ and $c = j^2k^5$, which of the following is a correct expression for a in terms of b, j, and k?

A. $b^2j^2k^8$
B. $b^2j^2k^{15}$
C. $b^2j^5k^8$
D. $b^2j^5k^{15}$
E. $b^2j^6k^{15}$

44. What is the set of all real values of x that solve the equation $|x|^2 + 3|x| - 10 = 0$?

F. $\{2\}$
G. $\{-2, 5\}$
H. $\{-2, 2\}$
J. $\{-5, 2\}$
K. $\{-5, -2, 2, 5\}$

47. For $i^2 = -1$, what does $(i + 1)^2$ equal?

A. 0
B. $2i$
C. $2i + 2$
D. $2i - 2$
E. $4i - 4$

50. $\left(\sqrt[3]{2x}\right)^6$ is equivalent to:

F. $2x^2$
G. $4x^2$
H. $6x^6$
J. $8x^3$
K. $64x^6$

GO ON TO THE NEXT PAGE.

55. If $|a - b| > a - b$, which of the following *must* be true?

DO YOUR FIGURING HERE.

- **A.** $a > b$
- **B.** $a < b$
- **C.** $a = 0$
- **D.** $a < 0$
- **E.** $b < 0$

60. If $\log_5 10 = b$ and $\log_5 15 = c$, what is 5^{b+c} ?

- **F.** 25
- **G.** 125
- **H.** 150
- **J.** 3125
- **K.** 5^{25}

STOP!

COORDINATE GEOMETRY

Coordinate Geometry, like Plane Geometry, can be a love-it-or-hate-it field. Some students get easily confused and scared by all these lines and formulas, and the problems tend be toward the hard end of the test. Other students love the logic and consistency of the plane, and the order that it brings.

It's okay to hate Coordinate Geometry. We're not here to judge you.* But we are here to help you understand a few of the basic principles behind these problems. As we saw in all the other chapters, Math Test questions ask the same things over and over again, so a little bit of knowledge can go a long way.

Before we go any further, it's important to emphasize that graphs are *pictures*. Therefore, **you can use *Guesstimate* on graphing problems**. You'd be astounded how many graphing problems can be done just by looking at the picture they give you. If this line *looks* equal to that line, then they *are* equal.

In fact, Guesstimate is often *easier* on coordinate geometry questions because coordinates have values you can use as references. Once you become familiar with the coordinate plane, it's easy to quickly glance at a point and see "oh, that point has a negative x and a y bigger than 7, so I can eliminate A, B, and E." Don't forget Guesstimate.

I. THE COORDINATE PLANE

This is the standard (x,y) coordinate plane (or "coordinate plane" or "grid" or whatever you want to call it):

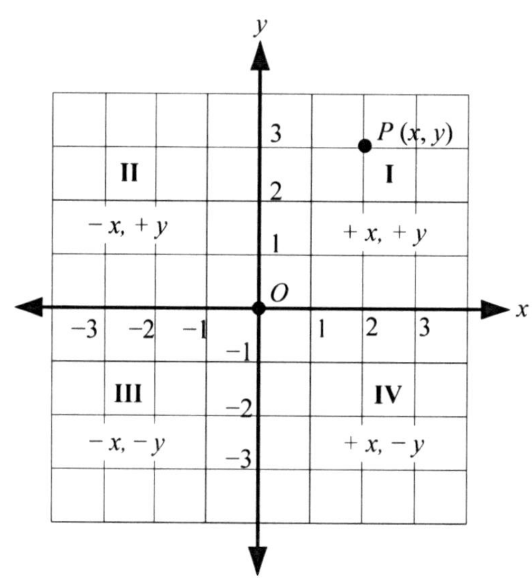

A lot of you probably already know your way around this guy, but here are some definitions for those who are new to it:

The ***x*-axis** is the horizontal line; it tells you the x-value of a point. Values of x are positive to the right and negative to the left.

The ***y*-axis** is the vertical line; it tells you the y-value of a point. Values of y are positive at the top and negative at the bottom.

The two axes† divide the coordinate plane into four **quadrants**, often labeled with Roman numerals. The sign of the x- and y- value of a point will determine which quadrant the point lies in.

1. Plotting Points

Points on the graph are given as (x,y). Point P shown here is (2,3), since it has an x-value of 2 and a y-value of 3. You can tell the x- and y-values by looking at where the point lies with respect to the axes. The **origin** (labeled "O" here) is the point where the axes cross; it has coordinates (0,0).

So what can we do with these points?

Geometry

Coordinate geometry is still geometry—it deals with shapes and pictures. The only difference between regular geometry and coordinate geometry is that the coordinate plane gives specific locations for every point. You'll see coordinate geometry questions that ask about traditional shapes like rectangles and triangles plotted onto a coordinate plane. For example:

➢ **Rectangle *ABCD* has vertices *A*(−3,6), *B*(4,6), *C*(4,1), and *D*(*a*,*b*). What are the coordinates of point *D*?**

---

* Well, maybe a little.

† Yes, the plural of "axis" is "axes". It rhymes with "taxis", not with "faxes".

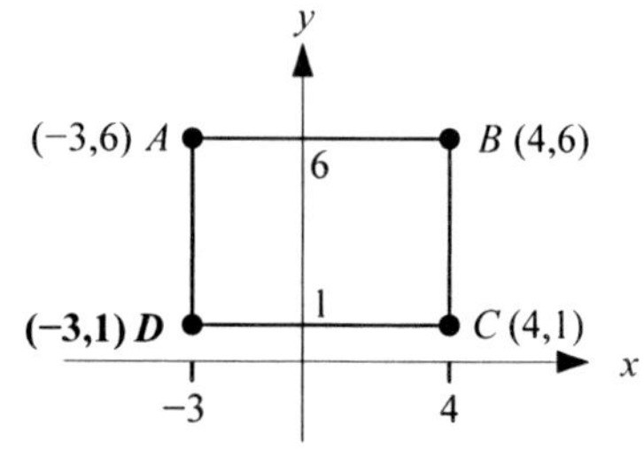

Any time a question asks you about points without giving you a figure, **DRAW THE FIGURE.** It doesn't have to be perfect; just sketch it out.

In this question, you can see that point *D* will have the same *x*-value as point *A* and the same *y*-value as point *C*. So point *D* must be **(−3, 1).**

You can also use these points to figure out length. And once you know lengths, you can calculate perimeter, area, and all those other fun things we'll talk about in the next chapter. For example:

- **Rectangle *ABCD* has vertices *A*(−3,6), *B*(4,6), *C*(4,1), and *D*(−3,1). What is the perimeter of *ABCD*?**

This question asks us about the same rectangle we just looked at. But now we want the perimeter. so we need the lengths of the sides.

Let's start by looking at $\overline{BC}$, the right side of the rectangle. Its two endpoints have the same *x*-value but different *y*-values. So we can calculate the length by just subtracting the *y*-values. 6 – 1 = 5.

Now let's look at $\overline{AB}$, the top of the rectangle. Its two endpoints have the same *y*-value but different *x*-values. So we can calculate the length by subtracting the *x*-values. 4 – (−3) = 4 + 3 = 7.

Opposite sides of a rectangle are equal, so the perimeter is 5 + 5 + 7 + 7 = **24.**

You can easily find the length of horizontal or vertical line segments by subtracting their *x*- or *y*-values. That's the whole point of having a grid! But what about points that don't share a value? How do we find their distance?

> Coordinate questions like these often require you to know some of the properties of shapes like triangles or parallelograms. We'll discuss those properties in the Plane Geometry chapter.

Distance

If you want to find the ***distance*** between two points on a graph, just use **the Pythagorean Theorem**:

- **What is the distance in coordinate units between *P* (2,2) and *Q* (6,5)?**

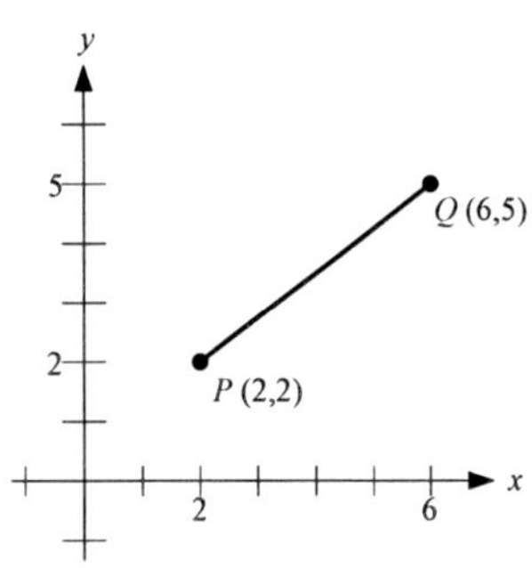

We don't have a good way of measuring diagonal lines like that directly. But we *do* have a good way of measuring horizontal and vertical lines. Let's draw point *R* to make a triangle that has $\overline{PQ}$ as its hypotenuse. We can easily measure its legs because we know the coordinates of the points.

$PR = 6 - 2 = 4$ $\qquad$ $QR = 5 - 2 = 3$

The legs of the triangle are 3 and 4, so we can use the Pythagorean Theorem to find the hypotenuse:*

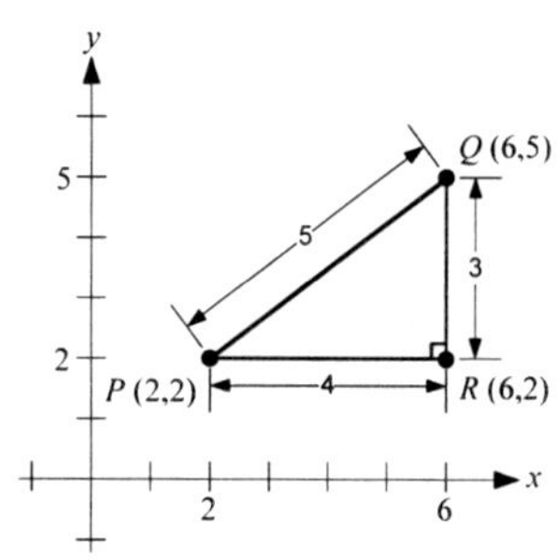

$3^2 + 4^2 = (PQ)^2$ $\qquad$ $9 + 16 = (PQ)^2$ $\qquad$ $25 = (PQ)^2$ $\qquad$ $\boxed{5 = PQ}$

If you prefer, you can use **The Distance Formula**. The distance, *d*, between points (x_1, y_1) and (x_2, y_2) is

$$d = \sqrt{(x_2 - x_1)^2 + (y_2 - y_1)^2} \qquad \text{or} \qquad d^2 = (x_2 - x_1)^2 + (y_2 - y_1)^2$$

Note that this is *exactly* the same thing we just did. **The distance formula is nothing more than the Pythagorean Theorem.** Any two points on the coordinate grid can form a right triangle: $(x_2 - x_1)$ is one leg of the triangle, $(y_2 - y_1)$ is the other leg, and the distance between the points is the hypotenuse.

* If you don't know what the Pythagorean Theorem is, don't worry. We'll talk about it more in the Plane Geometry chapter. Some of you may be able to see right away that it's a 3-4-5 triangle.

Midpoint

- **What is the midpoint of (2,2) and (6,5)?**

This question asks about the same points we just looked at. To find the coordinates of the midpoint between two points, *take the average of the x's and the average of the y's.*

The average of the x-values, 2 and 6, is $\frac{2+6}{2} = 4$. The average of the y-values, 2 and 5, is $\frac{2+5}{2} = 3.5$.

So the coordinates of the midpoint are **(4, 3.5).**

TRY SOME

- **Rectangle $ABCD$ has vertices $A(-1,7)$, $B(6,7)$, $C(x,y)$, and $D(-1,-1)$. What are the coordinates of vertex C?**

- **Triangle ABC has vertices $A(-2,-2)$, $B(7,10)$, and $C(7,-2)$. What is the length of $\overline{AB}$?**

- **What is the distance, in coordinate units, from (3,2) to (6,4) in the standard (x,y) coordinate plane?**

- **What is the midpoint of the line segment with endpoints (3,1) and (7,5) in the standard (x,y) coordinate plane?**

- **What is the midpoint of the line segment with endpoints (−2,−3) and (4,9) in the standard (x,y) coordinate plane?**

2. Graphing Functions

A graph on the coordinate plane is nothing more than **a picture of a function**. Take the equation $y = 2x$. We could plug in any number we like for x and we'll get a value for y as a result. Below we have a table of x's and their respective y's, along with a graph of those points plotted on the grid.

x	y
-3	-6
-2	-4
-1	-2
0	0
1	2
2	4
3	6

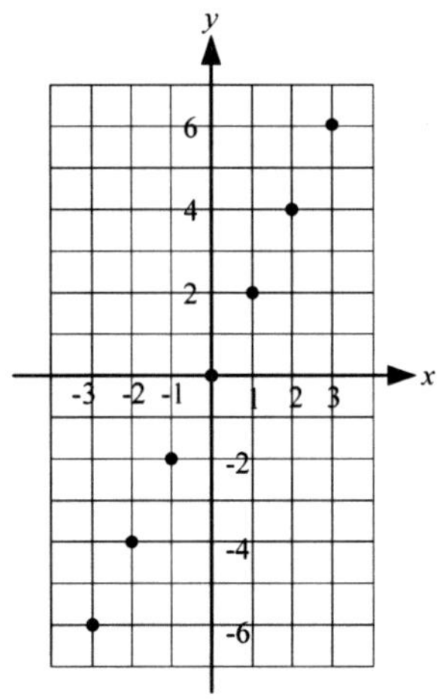

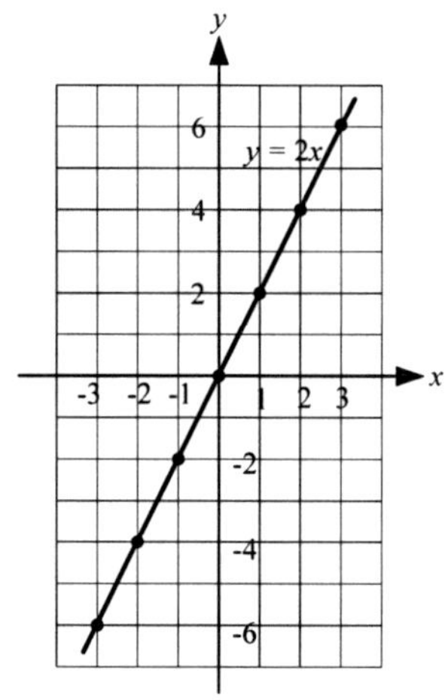

We can see that the points we chose start to make a straight line. If we fill in *all* the possible x's and their corresponding y's, including all the nasty decimal numbers, that's exactly what we'd get. The graph of $y = 2x$ is a picture of *all* the possible solutions to the equation—every x paired with its corresponding y. Rather than defining our equation as $y = 2x$, we could call it $f(x) = 2x$ and say that $y = f(x)$ in the graph. Don't get bogged down with all the different letters.

The most important thing to remember is: **If a point lies on the graph of a function, the coordinates of that point will satisfy the function's equation.** And vice versa. Even if you don't know the equation of the function, you can learn a lot just from the picture. For example:

- **The figure to the right shows the graph of $y = f(x)$. What is the value of $f(1)$?**

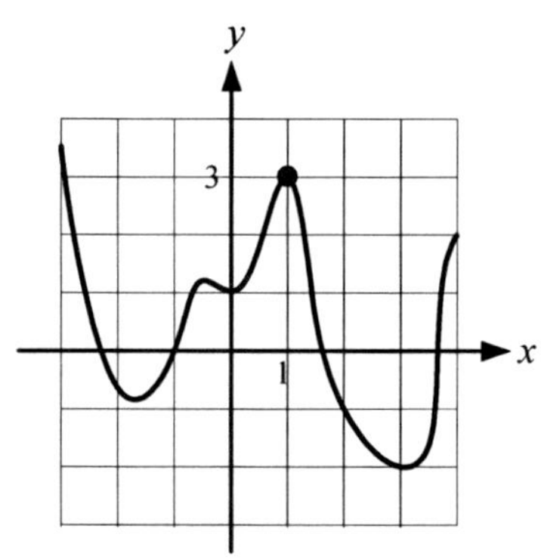

If they'd given you an equation for $f(x)$, you could find $f(1)$ by substituting "1" for "x" in the formula. No problem. But here we don't have an equation. Hmm. That's a crazy, crazy looking function. We'll never be able to write an equation for it.

But we don't need an equation because we have a graph of the function! A graph is a picture of the function. Every point on that squiggly line is a set of numbers that satisfies the equation, whatever that may be.

We want the value of $f(1)$. So we just have to find the value of y when $x = 1$. That's 3! The squiggly line crosses point (1,3). When $x = 1$, $y = 3$. So **$f(1) = 3$.**

This is an important point, so it bears repeating:

If the point (a, b) is on the graph of f, then $f(a) = b$.

If $f(a) = b$, then the point (a, b) is on the graph of f.

TRY SOME: Find these points on the graph above:

- **$f(-1) = ?$**
- **$f(2) = ?$**
- **$f(0) = ?$**
- **$f(3) = ?$**

A lot of people get confused by this notation, so here's a trick to help you remember. If you **draw in some parentheses**, the equation looks just like a coordinate pair. So:

$f(1) = 3$ becomes $f((1), 3)$

$f(x) = y$ becomes $f((x), y)$

Intersection

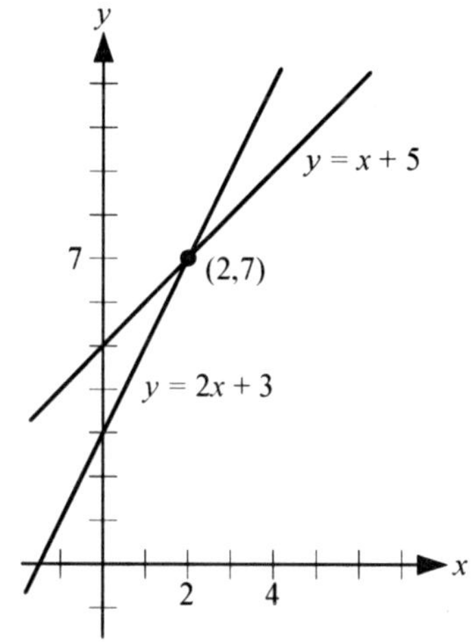

This fact about points and functions has an interesting consequence: If a point on a graph is a solution to that function's equation, then a point where **two graphs intersect** is a solution to *both* functions' equations.

For example, consider these functions:

$$y = 2x + 3$$
$$y = x + 5$$

When we have two equations together like this we call it a "system of equations". Each equation has an infinite number of (x,y) pairs that make the equation true. But there's only one pair that makes both equations true at the same time: (2,7).[*]

The graph of each of these functions is a straight line. If we draw both lines in the same plane, we can see that the two lines intersect at the point (2,7). Point (2,7) is the solution for the system of equations and the place where the two lines intersect.

Inequalities

Most graphs you'll see on the ACT have equations that describe them. But you can also graph *inequalities*. The graph of an inequality looks just like the graph of the corresponding equation—a line or a curve of some kind—but with a shaded region above or below the line.

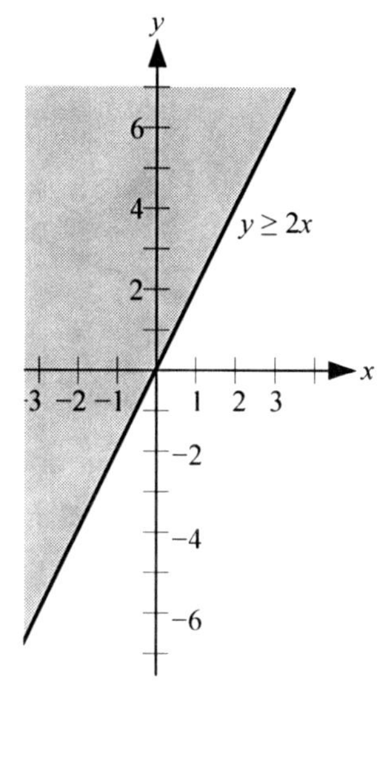

For example, the figure to the right shows the graph of $y \geq 2x$. Notice that the line running through the middle looks exactly like the line for $y = 2x$ that we saw earlier, but now the region above the line is shaded. That means that *all the points within the shaded region satisfy the inequality*.[†]

For this graph, it should be easy to understand why the area above the graph is shaded. The line shows all the points where y equals $2x$, so all the points *above* the line have a y-value greater than $2x$.

But if you're not sure which region you want to shade, you can always **try some test points.** Pick a point above the graph, let's say (0,2).[‡] Now let's plug $x = 0$ and $y = 2$ into the inequality $y \geq 2x$ and see if it works:

$2 \geq 2(0)$ $2 \geq 0$ ✓ It works!

Let's check a point from the other side of the line, say (0,–2), just to be sure.

$-2 \geq 2(0)$ $-2 \geq 0$ × That doesn't work!

After trying those points, we can see we must shade the area above the graph. (Hmm… using real numbers to test an algebraic expression. Haven't we done that before? Oh yeah! That's **Plug In!**)

---

[*] There are several ways we can solve this system algebraically. Since both have y by itself, we could set the two equations equal to each other: $2x + 3 = x + 5$, thus $x = 2$. Or we could subtract the equations directly to get $0 = x - 2$, thus $x = 2$. Then put $x = 2$ back into either equation to get $y = 7$.

[†] Because the inequality says y is greater than *or equal to* $2x$, the line is solid. If the inequality were $y > 2x$ without allowing them to be equal, the line would be dashed.

[‡] Points on the axes are generally easier to test because it's easy to plug 0 into your inequality.

II. LINES

The most basic function on Coordinate Geometry questions is a straight line. There are several characteristics that define a line.

1. Slope

As the name implies, slope, abbreviated "m" for some reason,* is a way to measure the "steepness" of a line. Looking from left to right, a ***positive* slope goes <u>up</u> and a *negative* slope goes <u>down</u>**. As you can see from the examples below, the more the line goes up, the larger its slope; the more the line goes down, the smaller its slope.

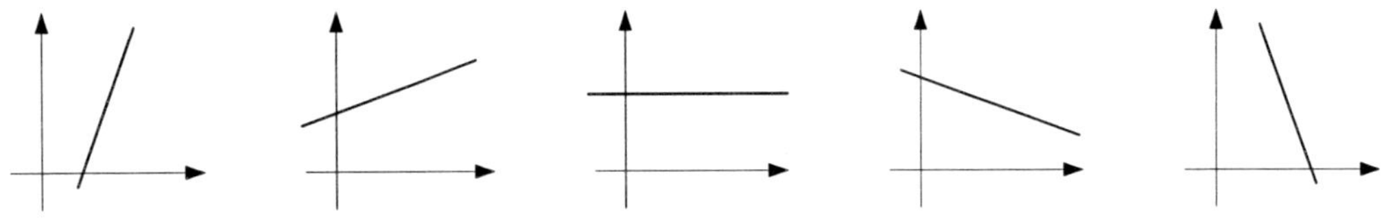

$m = 3$ $\quad m = \frac{1}{3}$ $\quad m = 0$ $\quad m = -\frac{1}{3}$ $\quad m = -3$

There are many ways to define slope, but they all mean the same thing:

$$\frac{\text{change in } y}{\text{change in } x} \qquad \frac{\text{rise}}{\text{run}} \qquad \frac{\Delta y}{\Delta x} \qquad \frac{y_2 - y_1}{x_2 - x_1}$$

If you know two points on a line, you can find its slope. All you have to do is take the difference of the y's over the difference in the x's:

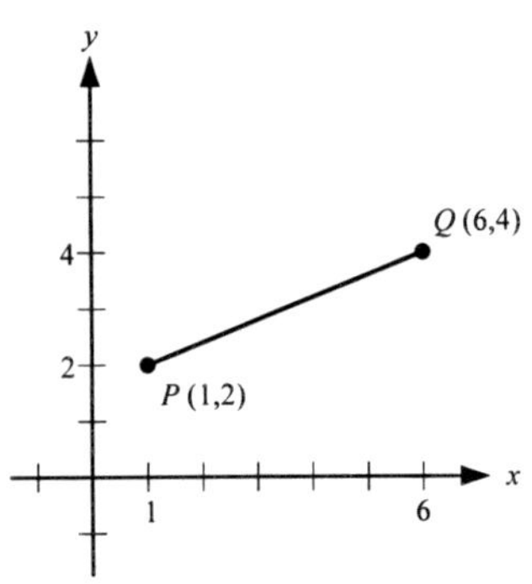

In the figure to the left, $(x_1, y_1) = (1,2)$ and $(x_2, y_2) = (6,4)$

$$m = \frac{y_2 - y_1}{x_2 - x_1} = \frac{4-2}{6-1} \qquad \boxed{m = \frac{2}{5}}$$

Don't get bogged down by all those letters. It doesn't matter which point we use first. We could say that $(x_1, y_1) = (6,4)$ and $(x_2, y_2) = (1,2)$ and get the same thing

$$m = \frac{y_2 - y_1}{x_2 - x_1} = \frac{2-4}{1-6} = \frac{-2}{-5} = \frac{2}{5}$$

> When the axes of a graph measure distance and time, the slope of a line gives the speed of the object.

There are several things to remember when calculating slope:

- Make sure y is on top. We repeat: **make sure [Y] is on top**. You will <u>not</u> be given the formula for slope. You have to remember it.
- Be consistent with x and y. You can start with either point, but you have to start with the same point on the top and the bottom. In the example above, when we use 4 first on the top, we must use 6 first on the bottom.
- *Parallel* lines have equal slopes.
- The slopes of *perpendicular* lines are the "negative reciprocals" of one another. Take the first slope, make it negative, and flip the fraction to get the second slope.

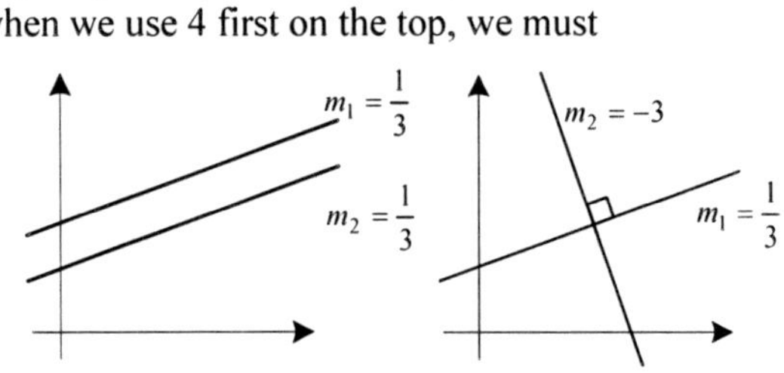

* No one knows how "m" became the symbol for slope. Over the years, different people in different countries have used a, k, l, p, and s for slope. Descartes, who invented "x", did not use "m". Sometimes this stuff is just random.

2. Intercepts

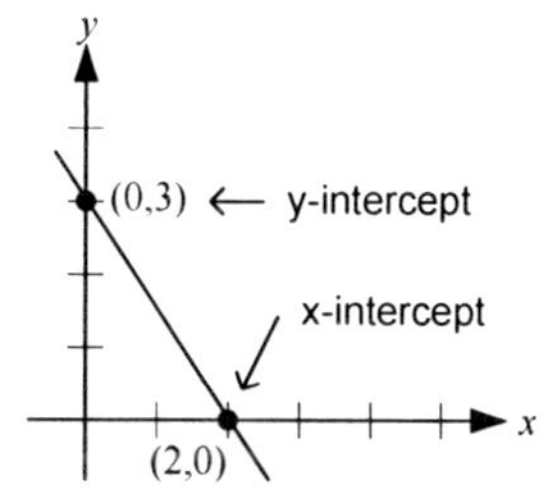

An "intercept" is just the point at which the line crosses one of the axes. So the ***x*-intercept** is the point at which the line crosses the *x*-axis. And the ***y*-intercept** is the point at which the line crosses the *y*-axis.

In the figure to the right, the line has a *y*-intercept of 3, since it crosses the *y*-axis at the point (0,3). **The *y*-intercept always has an *x*-value of zero**.

In the figure to the right, the line has an *x*-intercept of 2, since it crosses the *x*-axis at the point (2,0). **The *x*-intercept always has a *y*-value of zero.**

3. Equations

We can use the slope and intercepts to write an equation of a line, called a "linear equation". Any line will have a corresponding equation that contains one *x* and one *y* with no exponents.* There are several different ways we can write a linear equation.

Slope-intercept form (*y* = *mx* + *b*)

The most useful form of a linear equation is **the slope-intercept form**: $\boxed{y = mx + b}$ The "*m*" stands for the slope, the "*b*" stands for the *y*-intercept, and the "*x*" and "*y*" stand for the coordinates of any and all points on the line.

Let's see this stuff at work:

- **Line *l* passes through the points (4,4) and (2,3). What is the equation of line *l*?**

To find the equation of the line, we need the *slope* and the *y-intercept*. First, since we know two points, we can find the slope.

$$m = \frac{y_2 - y_1}{x_2 - x_1} = \frac{4-3}{4-2} \qquad \boxed{m = \frac{1}{2}}$$

Now we know *m*, so our equation so far is $y = \frac{1}{2}x + b$. To find *b*, let's just stick one of the points we know in for *x* and *y*—we'll use (2,3) here—and then we can solve for *b*.

$$y = \frac{1}{2}x + b$$

$$3 = \frac{1}{2}(2) + b$$

$$\boxed{2 = b}$$

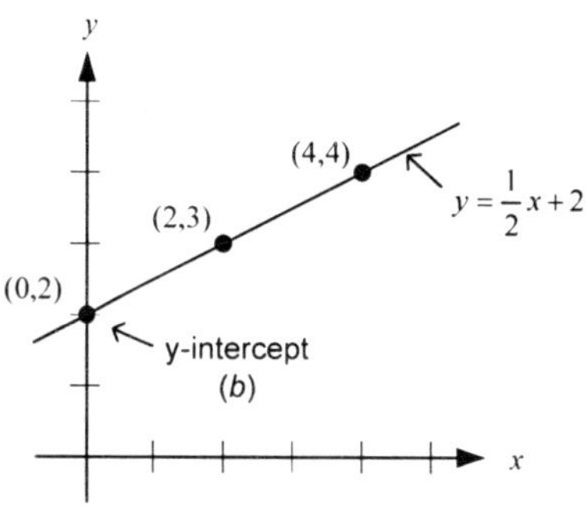

So our equation is $\boxed{y = \frac{1}{2}x + 2}$. The graph of the line can be seen at right.

Standard form (*ax* + *by* = *c*)

The slope-intercept form is great because we can immediately find the slope and *y*-intercept of the line just by looking at the equation. Unfortunately, ACT problems often present lines in the standard form. Don't worry about the name; that's just a fancy word for the form ***ax* + *by* = *c*.**

- **What is the slope of the equation 5*x* + 6*y* = 7?**

---

* Exception: an equation with *no x*, like *y* = 3, is a horizontal line. It has a slope of *zero*. Similarly, an equation with *no y*, like *x* = 3, is a vertical line. It has an *undefined* slope.

Annoyingly, in this form a, b, and c (5, 6, and 7) don't directly correspond to anything about the graph of the line, so the equation doesn't help us much. If we want the slope, we have to convert it to the slope-intercept form. To do that, just solve the equation for y:

$5x + 6y = 7$	Subtract $5x$ from both sides.
$6y = -5x + 7$	Divide both sides by 6.
$y = -\frac{5}{6}x + \frac{7}{6}$	The slope is $-\frac{5}{6}$.

This form of the equation might appear shuffled around: you might see "$6y + 5x = 7$" or "$5x + 6y - 7 = 0$" instead. But no matter how it is given to you, if you can get it into $y = mx + b$ form, you can find anything you need.

TRY SOME:

- **What is the slope of the line that passes through the points (2,6) and (4,1)?**

- **What is the slope of the line that passes through the points (−2,−3) and (−1,5)?**

- **What is the slope of the line represented by the equation $2x - 6y = 7$?**

- **What is the slope-intercept equation of the line that passes through the points (−1,2) and (1,6)?**

- **The equation of line l is $y = 3x + 5$. If line k is perpendicular to line l and passes through the point (0,−3), what is the equation of line k?**

III. CIRCLES

Most graph functions on the ACT are lines. Of course, in the real world, lines are just the tip of the graphing iceberg. On the ACT, we'll mostly just see two types of curved graphs: circles and parabolas.

The most common curve on the ACT is a circle. The equation of a circle is defined as:

$$\boxed{(x-a)^2+(y-b)^2=r^2}$$

where r is the radius, and (a, b) is the center of the circle. If the circle is centered on the origin (0,0), the "$-a$" and "$-b$" won't be there. For the grand majority of Coordinate Geometry circle questions, all you need to know is this equation, **SO LEARN IT!** Let's look at an example:

> We'll talk more about the properties of circles in the Plane Geometry chapter

- **A circle in the standard (x,y) coordinate plane has center (3,2) and radius 5 coordinate units. What is the equation of the circle?**

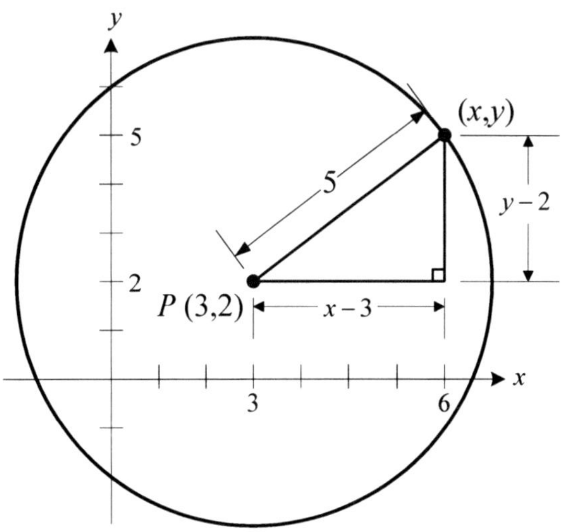

Using the formula above, we know the equation will be $(x-3)^2+(y-2)^2=25$.

Does the form of this equation look familiar? It should. **It's the Pythagorean Theorem again!**

Think about it: what *is* a circle? A circle is defined as the set of all points that are a certain distance (the radius) from a single point (the center). In this case, the curve will define all points that are a distance of 5 away from the point (3,2). How do we find the distance between points? With the distance formula:

$$d^2=(x_2-x_1)^2+(y_2-y_1)^2$$

Here, (x_1, y_1) is the center of the circle, (3,2) and (x_2, y_2) is the general point (x, y). That just means (x,y) refers to any point that's on the actual circle. So the distance between (3,2) and any point on the circle is 5.

We'll discuss circles more in the Plane Geometry chapter. The only other thing you need to know for Coordinate Geometry is the **tangent line**.

Usually, if you draw a line through a circle, it will cross the circle in two points—once where it enters the circle and again when it leaves. A tangent line is a line that touches the circle at exactly one point. In the figure to the right, the y-axis is tangent to the circle at the point (0,1), and the x-axis is tangent to the circle at the point (1,0). Note also that the tangent lines are perpendicular to the radius of the circle.

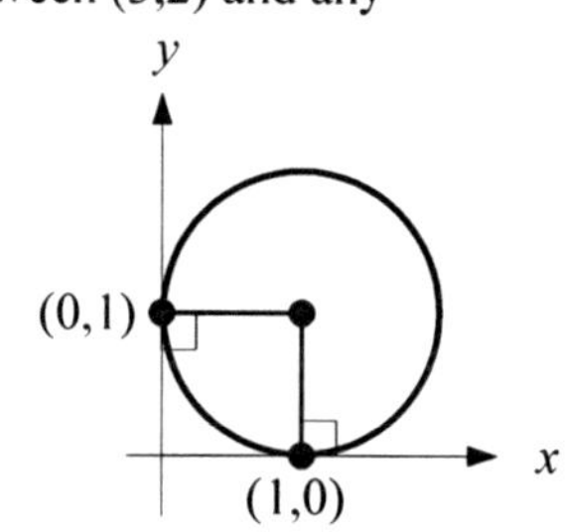

Ellipses

An ellipse is like a circle that's been stretched out in two opposite directions.* The equation of an ellipse is defined by: $\frac{(x-h)^2}{a^2}+\frac{(y-k)^2}{b^2}=1$ where (h, k) is its center of the ellipse, $2a$ is the length of the horizontal axis (along the x) and $2b$ is the length of the vertical axis (along the y).

Ellipses have shown up on the ACT, but **very, very rarely**. If you don't already know how to deal with ellipses, don't worry about them. Your time would be better spent making sure you understand circles.

* Strictly, an ellipse is defined as the set of all points such that the sum of the distance from a point on the ellipse to two points (the foci) is constant.

TRY SOME:

- What is an equation of a circle that has center (2,1) and radius 6 coordinate units?

- What is an equation of a circle that has center (−4,0) and radius 5 coordinate units?

- What is an equation of a circle that has center (5,4) and is tangent to the x-axis?

- What is the center of a circle with equation $(x+8)^2+(y-2)^2=9$?

- What is the radius of a circle with equation $(x-1)^2+(y+2)^2=7$?

IV. PARABOLAS

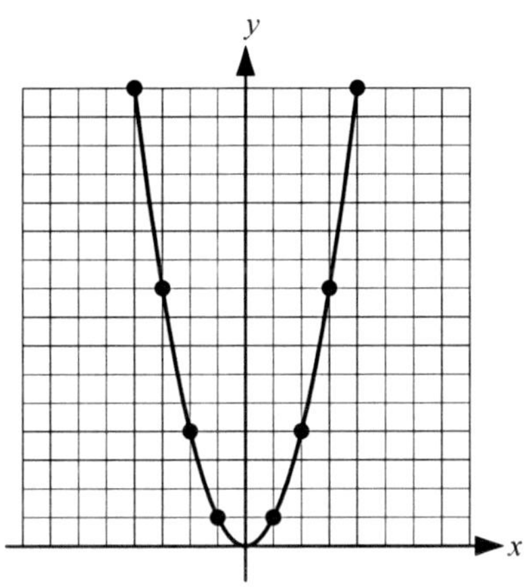

A **parabola** is the graph of a *quadratic function*—that is, an equation containing the square of x and a y with no exponent. This is the graph of $y = x^2$. You can see that the marked points fit the equation: the y value of each point is the square of the x value:

x	–4	–3	–2	–1	0	1	2	3	4
y	16	9	4	1	0	1	4	9	16

The standard form of an equation of a parabola is:

$$\boxed{y = ax^2 + bx + c}$$

where a, b, and c are constants.* For $y = x^2$, $a = 1$, $b = 0$, and $c = 0$.

In the Elementary Algebra chapter, we talked about *quadratic equations*. Previously, we had an equation equal to zero instead of y: there were only one or two values of x that solved the equation. Here, we have a function: we can stick in any value for x and get out a y. A quadratic equation is a quadratic function in which $y = 0$.

What does that mean? It means that **the real solutions to the quadratic equation correspond to the x-intercepts of the parabola**. An x-intercept is a point on the graph where $y = 0$. So you can quickly find the solutions to a quadratic equation by looking at its graph and finding the places where it crosses the x-axis.

Here are some other properties of parabolas:

- The **vertex** of the parabola is the point at the very bottom of the curve (or the very top, if the curve points down). This point is also called the **maximum** or **minimum** of the curve.
- Notice that this parabola is **symmetrical**—the left and right sides of the curve are mirror images of each other. That's because the square of a negative comes out positive (in our example: $y = 4$ when $x = 2$ *and* when $x = -2$.) *All* parabolas are symmetrical, though they may not be centered on the axis like this.

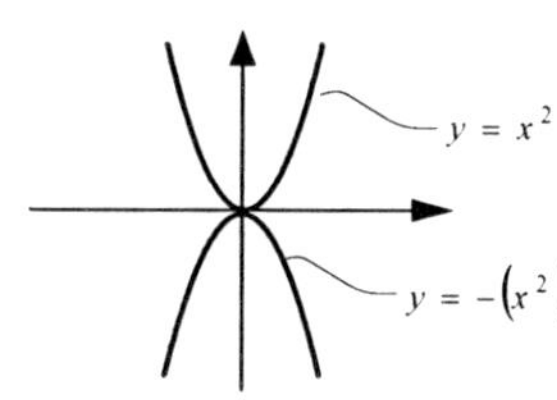

- If a (the number in front of x^2) is *positive*, the parabola will open *upwards*. If a is *negative*, the parabola will open *downwards*.
- The value of a also gives the "squeeziness" of the parabola: a bigger a gives a thinner graph; a smaller a gives a wider graph.
- The value of c (the number that doesn't have any x's next to it) will be the *y-intercept* of the parabola. Just like in a straight line, the y-intercept is the value of y when $x = 0$. Because c is the only term in the equation that doesn't come with an x next to it, if $x = 0$, all that's left is c.†

Parabolas can also be written in equations with different forms, such as $y - h = j(x - k)^2$ where (h,k) is the vertex of the parabola. But most parabola equations will be expressed as a polynomial, as shown above.

---

* Constants are numbers that don't change at all *within a given equation*. You can stick in any numbers you want for x and y and it'll still be the same equation. If you change the values of a, b, or c, it's no longer considered the same equation.

† Don't be confused by the fact that we call the y-intercept for parabolas "c", but we call the y-intercept for lines "b". The letters are entirely arbitrary. We could call them p or q or ¥ for all it matters. We don't even have to put it last; we could say $y = b + xm$. What does matter is that it stands by itself: in each case, the y-intercept is the number that doesn't have an x next to it.

Coordinate Geometry Exercise

DO YOUR FIGURING HERE.

9. What is the slope of the line that passes through the points (1,8) and (3,2) in the standard (x,y) coordinate plane?

A. -3
B. -2
C. -1
D. 2
E. 3

14. Rectangle $ABCD$ has vertices $A(-2,-1)$, $B(-3,2)$, and $C(3,4)$, as shown below. Which of the following could be the coordinates of point D?

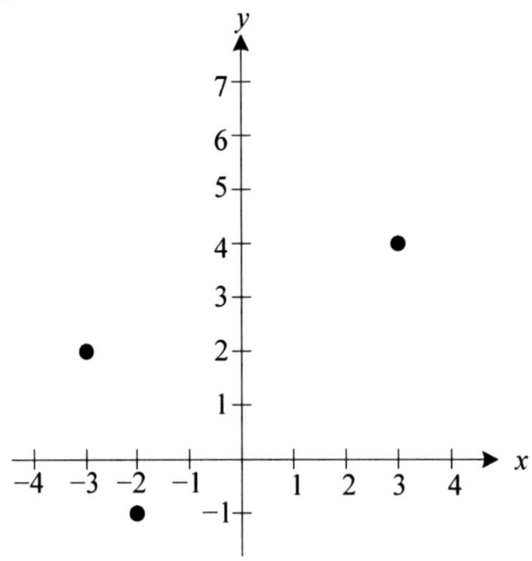

F. $(-4, 0)$
G. $(-3,-1)$
H. $(2, 7)$
J. $(3,-1)$
K. $(4, 1)$

21. In the standard (x,y) coordinate plane, A has coordinates $(-1,7)$ and B has coordinates $(5,3)$. What are the coordinates of the midpoint of $\overline{AB}$?

A. $(2, 5)$
B. $(3, 4)$
C. $(3, 5)$
D. $(6, 4)$
E. $(6,10)$

28. What is the slope of the line that is parallel to the line represented by the equation $3y + 6x = 8$?

F. -2
G. $-\frac{1}{2}$
H. $\frac{1}{2}$
J. 2
K. 3

GO ON TO THE NEXT PAGE.

Use the following information to answer questions 31−33.

DO YOUR FIGURING HERE.

Quadrilateral $ABCD$ is shown below in the standard (x,y) coordinate plane.

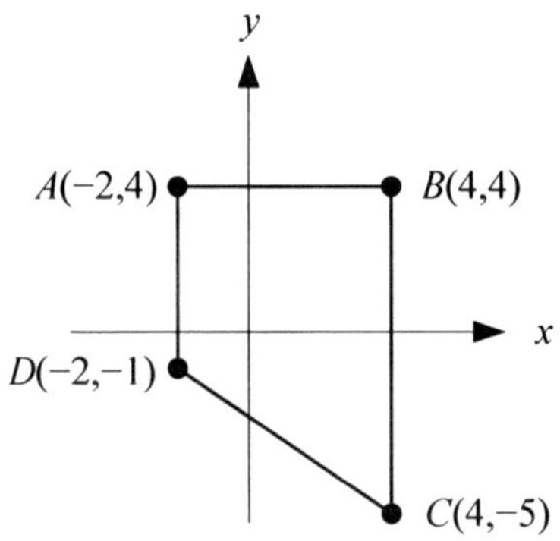

31. What is the area of quadrilateral $ABCD$, in square coordinate units?

A. 10
B. 12
C. 30
D. 42
E. 54

32. Which of the following is closest to the perimeter of quadrilateral $ABCD$, in coordinate units?

F. 17.0
G. 20.0
H. 21.5
J. 25.1
K. 27.2

33. What is the slope of $\overline{DC}$?

A. $-\frac{3}{2}$

B. $-\frac{2}{3}$

C. 1

D. $\frac{2}{3}$

E. $\frac{3}{2}$

GO ON TO THE NEXT PAGE.

36. A circle in the standard (x,y) coordinate plane has center $(5,-7)$ and radius 3 coordinate units. Which of the following is an equation of the circle?

F. $(x+5)^2+(y-7)^2=3$
G. $(x+5)^2+(y-7)^2=9$
H. $(x-5)^2+(y+7)^2=3$
J. $(x-5)^2-(y-7)^2=9$
K. $(x-5)^2+(y+7)^2=9$

DO YOUR FIGURING HERE.

39. Which of the following is the graph of the equation $x + 2y - 6 = 0$ in the standard (x,y) coordinate plane?

A.

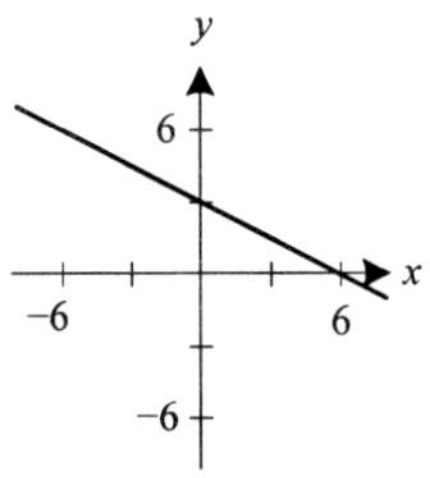

B.

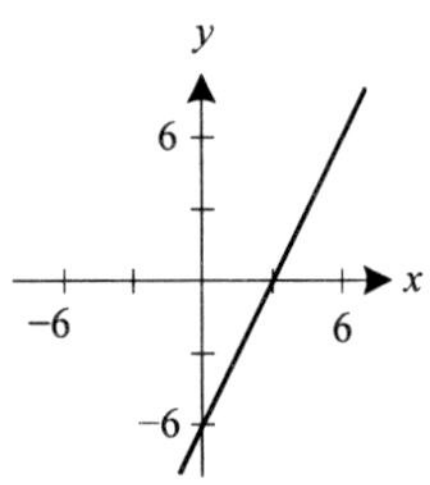

C.

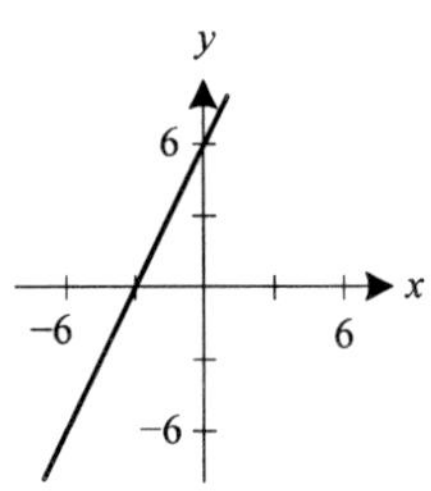

D.

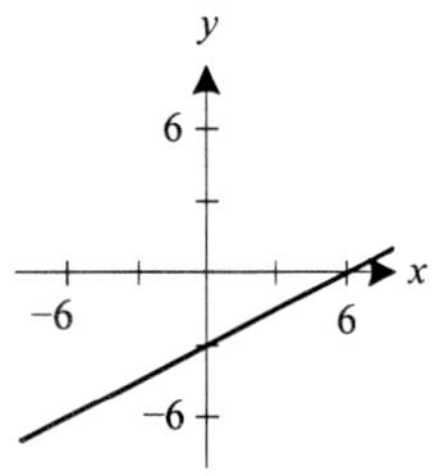

E.

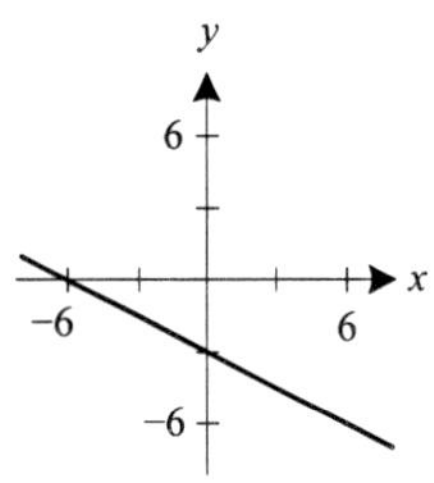

42. The points $(-3,4)$ and $(9,-2)$ are the endpoints of a diameter of a circle. What are the coordinates of the center of the circle?

F. (3,1)
G. (3,3)
H. (5,5)
J. (6,2)
K. (6,3)

GO ON TO THE NEXT PAGE.

43. The graph of $y = ax^2 + bx + c$ in the standard (x,y) coordinate plane is shown below. When $y = 0$, which of the following best describes the real solution set for x?

DO YOUR FIGURING HERE.

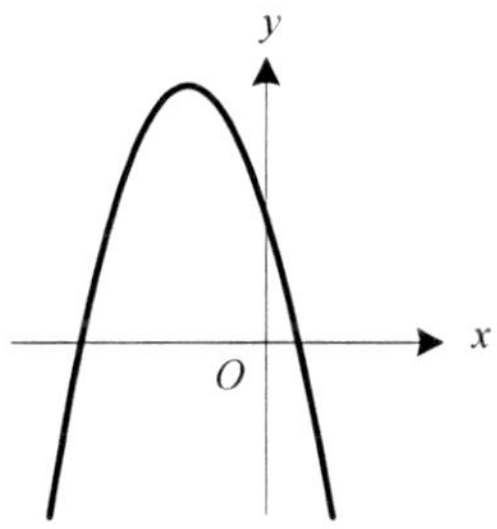

A. 2 positive solutions
B. 2 negative solutions
C. 1 positive and 1 negative solution
D. 1 positive solution only
E. 1 negative solution only

46. In the standard (x,y) coordinate plane below, the area of $\triangle ABC$ is 15, the length of $\overline{OB}$ is 3 and the coordinates of point A are (0, 6). What is the slope of segment $\overline{AC}$?

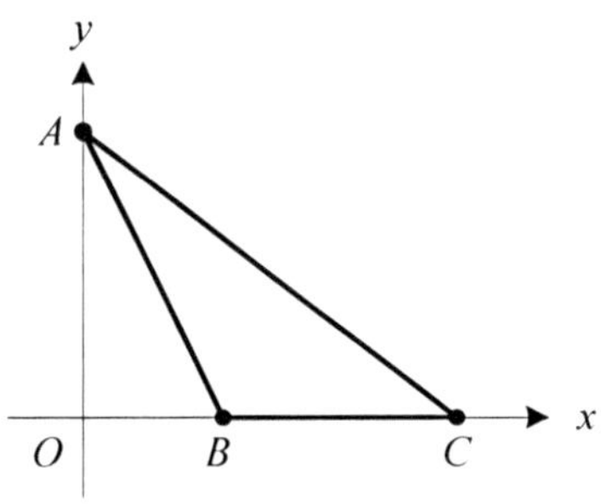

F. -2
G. $-\frac{4}{3}$
H. $-\frac{6}{5}$
J. $-\frac{3}{4}$
K. $-\frac{1}{2}$

49. The points (0,2) and (3,−1) lie on a straight line in the standard (x,y) coordinate plane. What is the slope-intercept equation of the line?

A. $y = -3x + 6$
B. $y = -x + 2$
C. $y = x + 2$
D. $y = 2x - 2$
E. $y = 3x - 1$

52. Which of the following is an equation for a circle that has its center at (6,5) and is tangent to the y-axis in the standard (x,y) coordinate plane?

F. $(x-6)^2 + (y-5)^2 = 25$
G. $(x-6)^2 + (y-5)^2 = 36$
H. $(x+6)^2 + (y+5)^2 = 25$
J. $(x+6)^2 + (y+5)^2 = 36$
K. $(x-6)^2 - (y-5)^2 = 25$

GO ON TO THE NEXT PAGE.

57. What is the distance, in coordinate units, between the points $(-k, k)$ and $(k, k-1)$?

A. 1

B. $2k^2 - 1$

C. $4k^2 + 1$

D. $\sqrt{4k^2 + 1}$

E. $\sqrt{8k^2 - 4k + 1}$

DO YOUR FIGURING HERE.

STOP!

PLANE GEOMETRY

Plane Geometry is a big part of the ACT Math—it makes up almost a quarter of the test. A "plane" is just any two-dimensional surface, so "Plane Geometry" is what we mean when we talk about "geometry" in general. You will occasionally see some three-dimensional solids on the ACT, but it's mostly flat stuff—triangles, squares, circles, and all their friends. We saw some of this stuff in the Coordinate Geometry chapter, but now we won't have any axes or coordinates.

If you've had a rigorous geometry class in school, you probably had to learn a lot of theorems—little rules about angles and lengths and all sorts of weird things. On the ACT, you don't need all those rules. *All* you need is the stuff in this chapter. We're only going to show you a few simple rules and not much else. Any other theorems or rules that you may have heard about are only true *because of* the stuff in this chapter. But if you do need a more complicated rule, you can figure it out from the basic rules.

Of course, that means **you need to learn the basic rules really, really well.** That means memorizing the formulas and definitions discussed in this chapter. The better you know them, the easier life will be for you.

I. INTRODUCTORY REMARKS

Techniques

Don't forget about **Guesstimate**. If you see a question with a picture, *before you do anything else*, check that it's to scale, guess the value they're asking for, and then eliminate any implausible choices.

In this chapter we're going to be talking about a lot of straight math content (rules and formulas). But that doesn't mean you should forget about the techniques. And not just Guesstimate. You can use Plug In and Backsolve on geometry problems, too. So stay alert.

General Strategy for Geometry

While the number of rules you need on the test is relatively small, it may still seem burdensome to you. I mean, how do you know which rule to use on which question? Where do you even begin?

Just like we saw before, there are two questions to ask yourself:

1. What do I *want*? **2. What do I *know*?**

The goal of every geometry problem is to connect these two questions, to play with what you *know* in order to get what you *want*. Take a look at this problem:

> If a geometry problem doesn't already have a picture, DRAW A PICTURE! It doesn't have to be perfect; even a rough sketch can help you understand the problem and catch careless mistakes.

18. In the figure below, a circle is tangent to two sides of a 12 by 6 rectangle. What is the area of the circle?

A. 3π
B. 6π
C. 9π
D. 12π
E. 36π

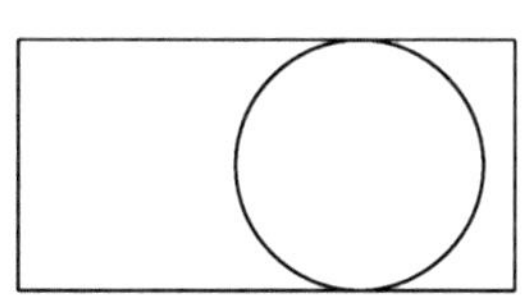

1. **What do we want?** The area of the circle.

As we'll soon see, the formula for the area of a circle $A = \pi r^2$. To find the area, we'll need the radius of the circle (or the diameter, which is just double the radius).

2. **What do we know?** The length of the rectangle is 12 and the width is 6.

So the real key to this problem is: *how can I use the length or width of the rectangle to find the radius or diameter of the circle?*

Aha! The width of the rectangle is equal to the diameter of the circle! How can I tell? By Guesstimate! Don't worry about the weird "tangent" stuff: they *look* equal.

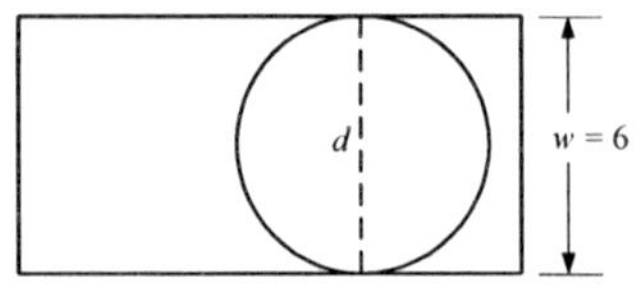

The width of the rectangle is 6, so the diameter of the circle is 6. So the radius is 3, and the area of the circle is 9π, which is **choice C.**[*]

The point here is that *you should never be absolutely stuck on a geometry question.* There's always *something* that you know, something that you can figure out. Don't be scared of the figures, just put down what you know and try to connect it to what you want.

Know your polygons

A **polygon** is any shape with straight edge. You're probably already familiar with some of them:

A **triangle** is a polygon with 3 sides.

A **quadrilateral** is a polygon with 4 sides.

A **pentagon** is a polygon with 5 sides.

A **hexagon** is a polygon with 6 sides.

Polygons can have many more sides with even more complex names, but you probably won't see those on the ACT.

Quadrilaterals in particular come in a lot of different shapes, and each shape has its own funny name. Sometimes an ACT question will define these terms for you, but it's good to understand them in advance:

QUADRILATERAL TYPE	EXAMPLES
A **parallelogram** has two pairs of parallel sides.	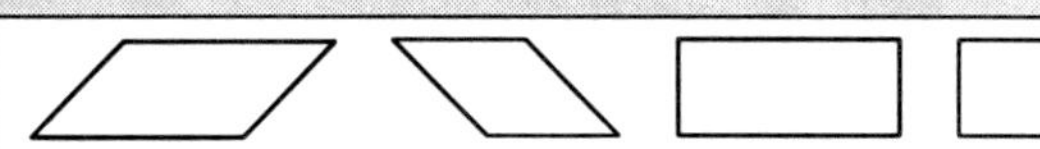
A **rhombus** has four equal sides. All rhombuses are also parallelograms.	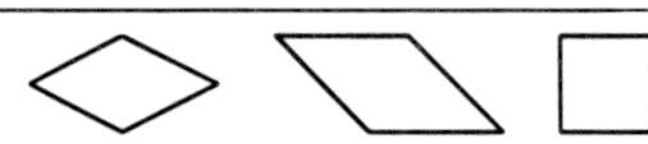
A **rectangle** has four 90° angles. All rectangles are also parallelograms.	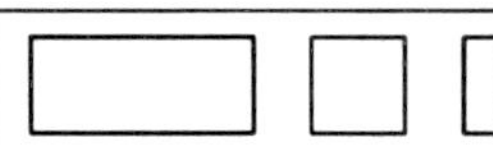
A **square** has four 90° angles and four equal sides. A square is a rectangle and a rhombus.	
A **trapezoid** has only one pair of parallel sides.	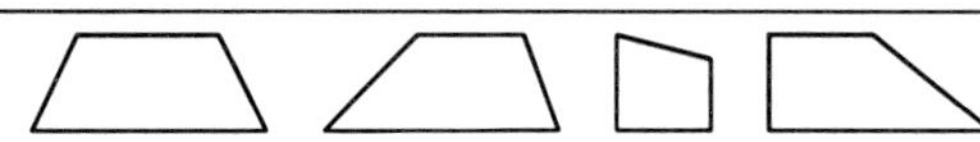

[*] Note that we could also use Guesstimate to get the area of the circle directly. The rectangle is 12 by 6, so its area is 72. The circle looks like a bit less than half the rectangle, so its area should be a bit less than 36. All the answers are in terms of π, so we'll multiply the choices by 3.14 (or use the "π" button if your calculator has one) and see which is closest. D and E are more than 36. A is way too small. B is 18.84, and C is 28.27. C is closest. Bam.

II. ANGLES

There are five things you have to know about angles.

1. A straight line equals 180°.

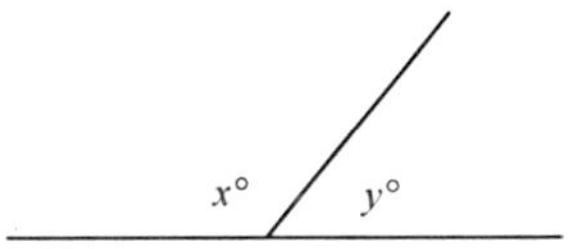

When angles form a straight line, the sum of their measures is 180°. In this diagram, $x + y = 180$.

2. A triangle equals 180°.

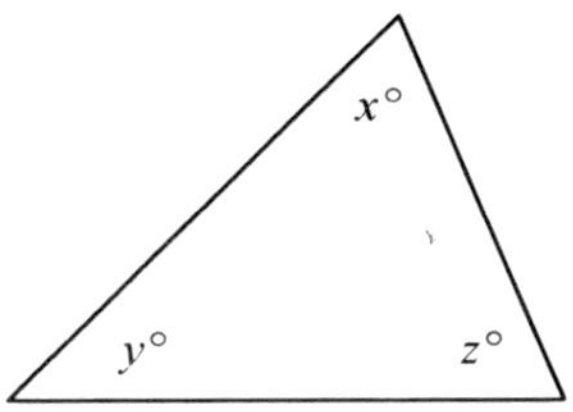

The three angles of a triangle add up to 180°. In this diagram, $x + y + z = 180$.

Here's an example of using one rule to figure out another: An ***equilateral triangle*** has three equal sides and three equal angles. If all angles are equal, and they add up to 180°, each angle of an equilateral triangle is $180 \div 3 = 60°$.

So we have a new rule: every equilateral triangle has three 60° angles.

3. An isosceles triangle has two equal sides and two equal angles.

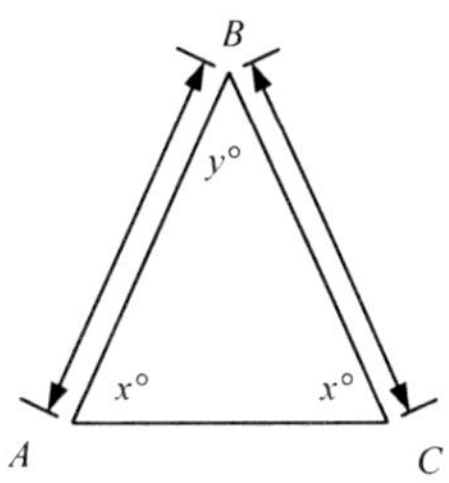

An ***isosceles triangle*** is one in which two of the sides are equal in length. The angles opposite the equal sides will also be equal to each other. (Similarly, an ***isosceles trapezoid*** has two pairs of equal angles.)

In this triangle, since we know that $\angle BAC = \angle ACB$ (both are x) we know $AB = BC$. Conversely, if we know that the sides AB and AC are equal, we can assume that the angles are equal.

4. Vertical Angles are equal.

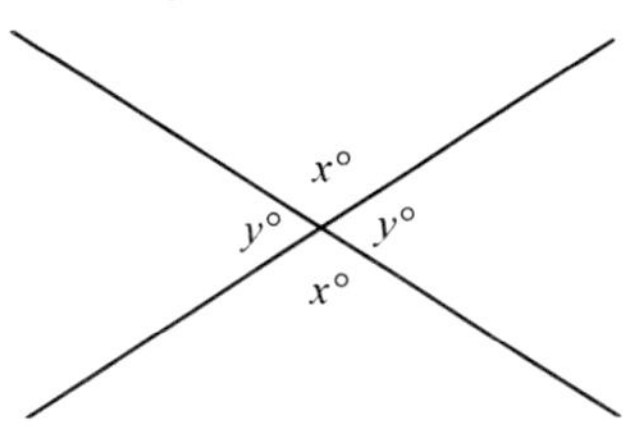

When two straight lines cross, four angles are formed. The angles that are directly across from each other are called "vertical angles" and they are equal to each other.

In this diagram, the angles marked "x" are equal to each other, and the angles marked "y" are equal to each other.

5. Parallel lines with a transversal produce a bunch of equal angles.

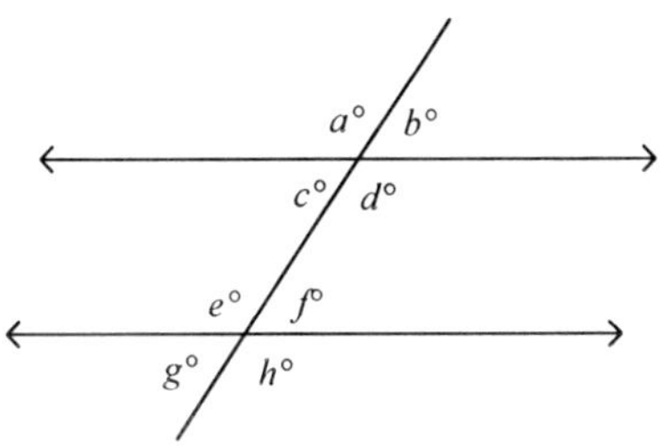

When a third line (a "transversal") cuts through two parallel lines, eight angles are formed. The four at the top are collectively the same as the four at the bottom. Basically, we've got two types of angles: big ones and little ones. All the big ones are equal, and all the little ones are equal. Any big one plus any little one is 180°.

Here, $a = d = e = h$ and $b = c = f = g$. <u>Any</u> of the big ones (a, d, e, h) plus <u>any</u> of the little ones (b, c, f, g) equals 180°.

Note that this is *only* true for parallel lines. If we know that the lines above are *not* parallel, then we know that these rules are not true (e.g., $c \neq f$).

This one's a little bit more complicated than the other four, but it's a great demonstration of what we were saying before about knowing the basic rules. If we just look at the top four angles, we know that $a = d$ and $b = c$ because of rule #4: vertical angles are equal. Similarly, we know that $a + c = 180$ because of rule #1: a straight line equals 180. The only new information we're adding here is that because the lines are parallel, $c = f$. Everything else we can say here is simply a logical conclusion of the rules we already know. So once you know the small rules, you can figure out the larger rules.

Of course, there are other rules that exist about angles, but they're only true *because of* these rules. For example, take a look at this problem:

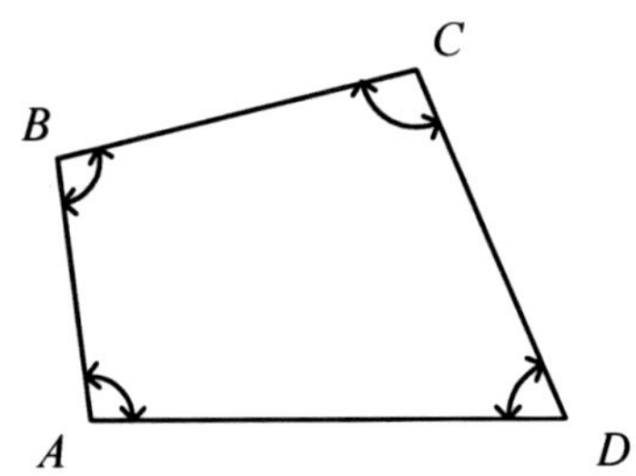

What is the sum of the marked angles in quadrilateral *ABCD* show to the left?

What? They don't tell us anything about this thing! Whatever shall we do? [*]

Fear not. We didn't learn any rules about angles of quadrilaterals. But we *do* know that a triangle has 180°. Let's split this guy up into triangles!

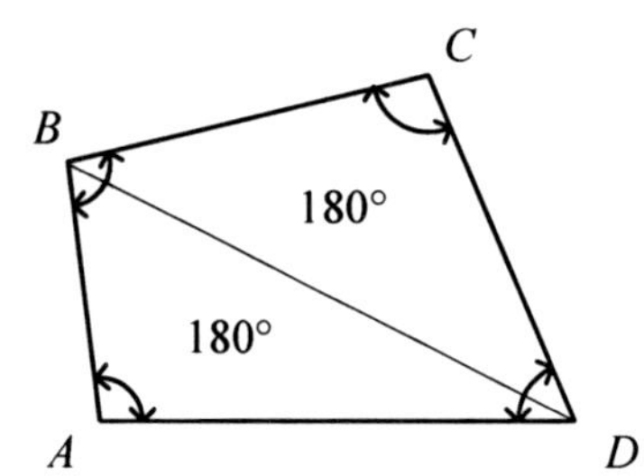

The quadrilateral is made up of two triangles. Each triangle has 180°. So the quadrilateral has 2 × 180 = **360°**. That's it. We're done!

Some of you may have already known that the angles of any quadrilateral add up to 360°. But we can do this with any shape. Draw triangles using only the shape's existing vertices. We can see that a pentagon contains 3 triangles, so its angles add up to 3 × 180 = 540°. And a hexagon contains 4 triangles, so its angles add up to 4 × 180 = 720°. [†]

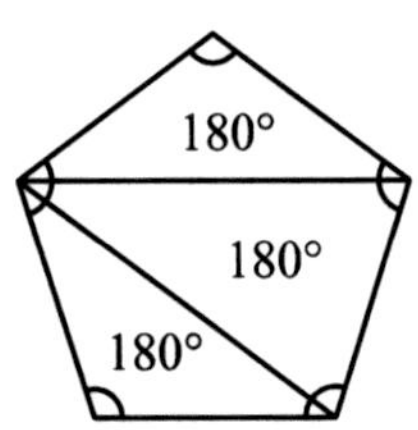

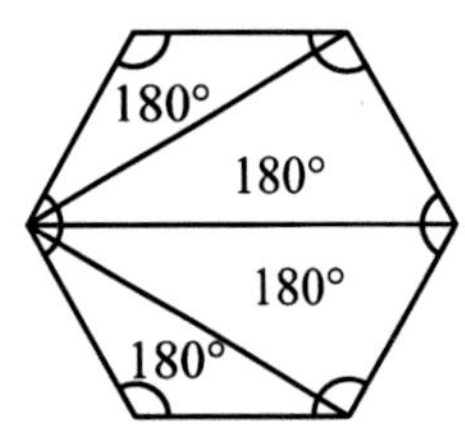

Our point is not to get you to memorize the number of angles in every polygon. The point is that you don't have to memorize a bunch of rules like that. Just know the five basic angle rules and you can figure out anything else you need to know about angles.

You should never be totally stuck on a problem that deals with angles, because there's always *something* you know. More often than not, just putting down what you know based on these rules will lead you to what you're trying to find—even if you don't see where you're going with it. "Okay, I really don't know how to find what they want, but I know that's a triangle, so its angles add up to 180. And I know that's a straight line, so those angles add up to 180…" Et cetera. Just play with these rules and see where it takes you.

And remember: **when in doubt, draw triangles**.

[*] If we had answer choices, this would be a great Guesstimate problem.

[†] If you're interested here's the formula: the angles a polygon with n sides will add up to $(n - 2)180$ degrees. That's because $n - 2$ is the number of triangles you can draw in the shape. When drawing triangles, remember to only connect points in the polygon—don't use the center of the shape as a triangle's vertex.

ANGLE DRILL

15. In the figure below, what is the value of $a + b$?

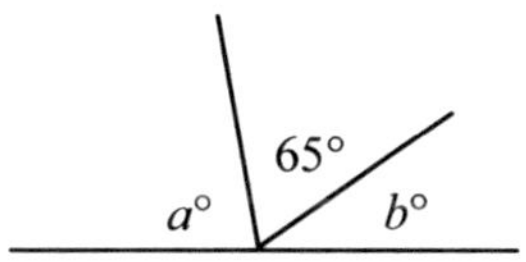

A. 25
B. 115
C. 125
D. 295
E. 305

18. In the figure below, if $y = 50$, then $x = ?$

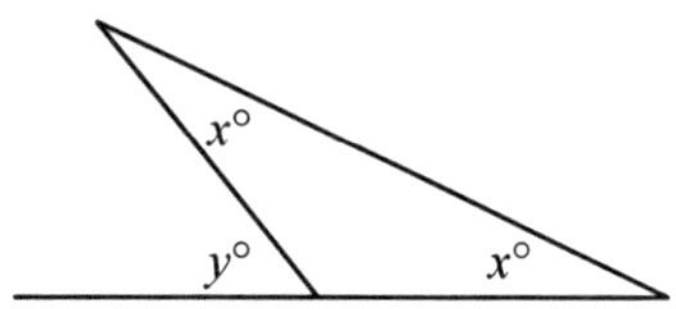

F. 20
G. 25
H. 30
J. 50
K. 65

29. In the figure below, line k is perpendicular to line l and lines l and m are parallel. If $x = 115$, what is the value of $y - z$?

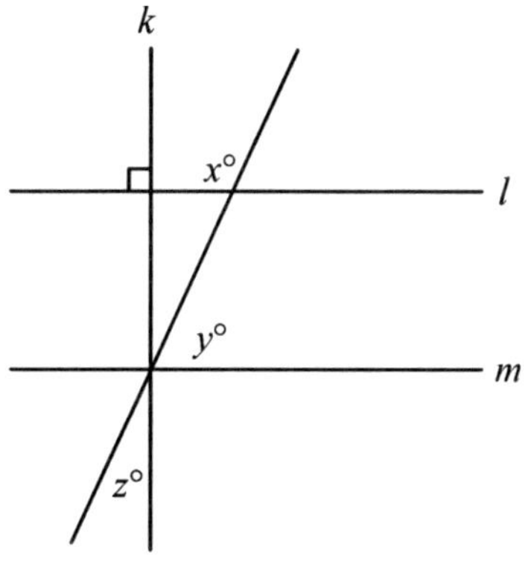

A. 25
B. 40
C. 65
D. 90
E. 115

GO ON TO THE NEXT PAGE.

44. In the figure below, $p = ?$

F. 110
G. 115
H. 120
J. 125
K. 130

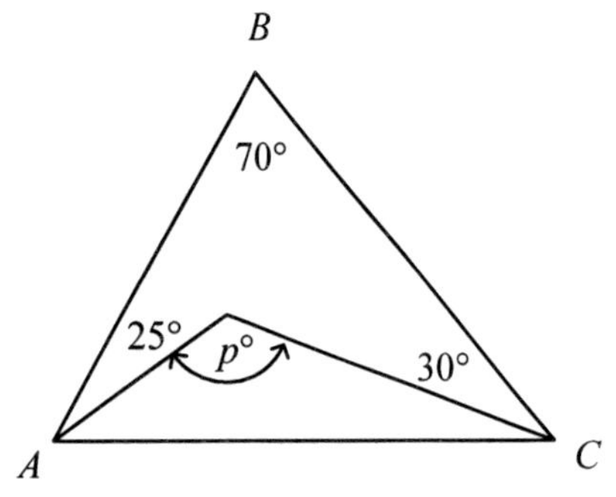

57. In the figure below, $BQ = PQ = RQ$ and $AP = PR$. If $\overline{PQ}$ is parallel to $\overline{AC}$, what is y in terms of x?

A. $180 - 2x$
B. $180 - 4x$
C. $2x - 180$
D. $2x - 360$
E. $4x - 180$

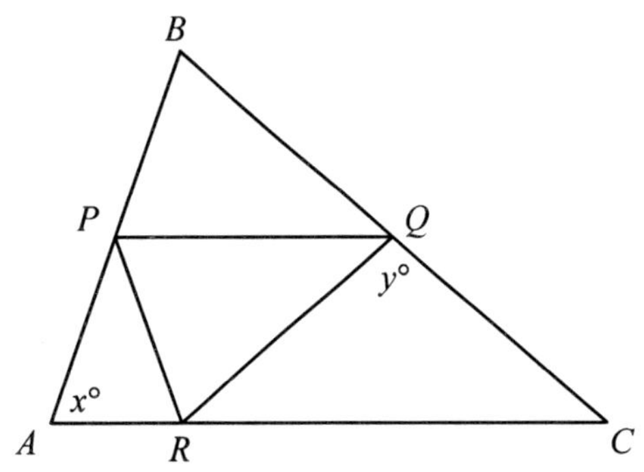

STOP!

III. Triangles

Triangles are the key to a lot of ACT questions; you'll see a lot more triangles than any other shape. In fact, if you're confronted with an odd shape you don't understand, try drawing in a triangle. We already saw an example of that in the quadrilateral problem in the last section. We didn't know anything about quadrilaterals, but we know a lot about triangles, so we drew some triangles. Triangles are your best friend. Trust us.

1. The Pythagorean Theorem

The Pythagorean Theorem is a way to find the third side of **a right triangle**.*

> A *right triangle* is a triangle with a right angle (a 90° angle). The side opposite the right angle is called the *hypotenuse*. The two sides next to the right angle are called *legs*.

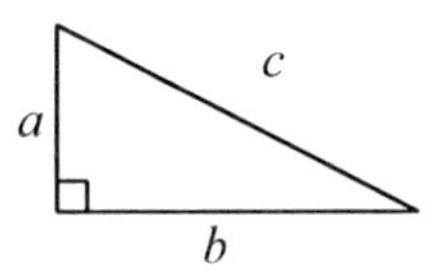

$$a^2 + b^2 = c^2$$

The sum of the squares of the legs of a right triangle is equal to the square of the hypotenuse.

Try this one:

If a right triangle has legs of length 3 and 4, what is the length of the hypotenuse?

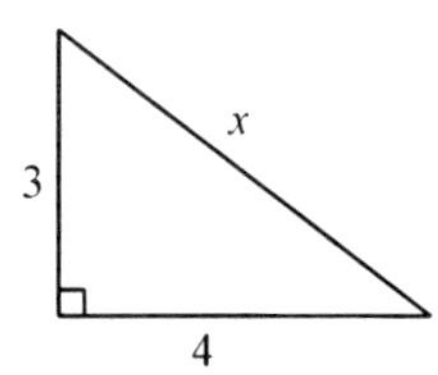

$$3^2 + 4^2 = x^2$$

$$9 + 16 = x^2$$

$$25 = x^2$$

$$\boxed{5 = x}$$

Some of you may have recognized the triangle in the problem above. It's a "Pythagorean Triple". Because the Pythagorean Theorem has all those "squares" in it, most right triangles don't have integer values for all the sides. So the triangles that *do* have all integers show up a lot. The 3-4-5 is a common one.† If you see a triangle that has legs of length 3 and 4, you know immediately that the hypotenuse must be 5.

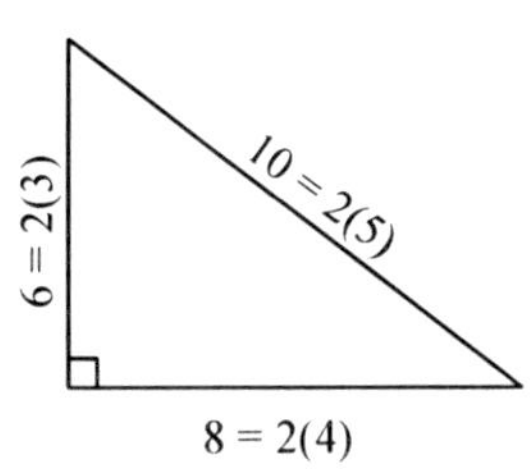

Be on the lookout for multiples of the 3-4-5, as well. For example, a 6-8-10 triangle is just a 3-4-5 triangle with each side multiplied by two.

Being able to spot a 3-4-5 triangle can save you some time. If you see a triangle with legs 6 and 8, you know immediately the hypotenuse is 10, without having to do out the Theorem. But spotting this is really just a bonus; if you can't see the 3-4-5 triangle, don't worry. You can always use the Pythagorean Theorem to find the dimensions of a right triangle.

Warning: Don't be too quick to declare a triangle 3-4-5. The hypotenuse must be the largest side of a triangle. If a triangle has *legs* of 4 and 5, the hypotenuse is *not* 3.

---

* The theorem is named for the Greek philosopher Pythagoras and his cult, the Pythagoreans, but the fundamentals of the theorem were known hundreds of years before him by the Babylonians, Indians, and Chinese among others. There is little evidence that he or his followers ever proved the theorem. Why it was named for him, we have no idea. The Pythagoreans did a lot of important work in mathematics, but they also thought eating beans was sinful.

† There are other Pythagorean Triples, too. The 5-12-13 is fairly popular, but there's also the 7-24-25, 8-15-17, and more (to say nothing of the multiples of each).

2. The Isosceles Right Triangle (45-45-90)

An *isosceles* right triangle has two legs of equal length, and two 45° angles.* The dimensions of these triangles are always in the same proportion:

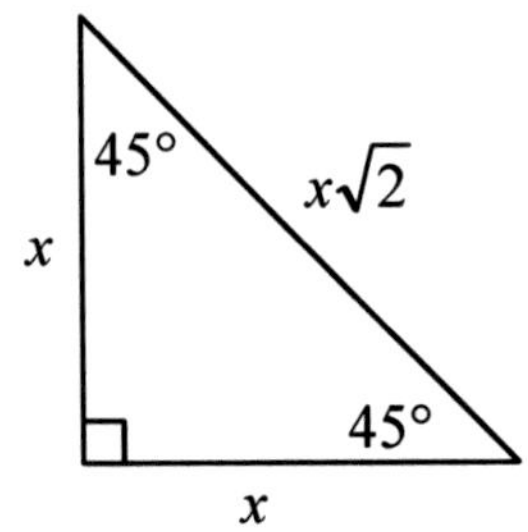

$$a^2 + b^2 = c^2$$

$$x^2 + x^2 = c^2$$

$$2x^2 = c^2$$

$$\sqrt{2x^2} = \sqrt{c^2}$$

$$\left(\sqrt{2}\right)x = c$$

This means that if you know the length of a leg of the triangle, you can immediately find the hypotenuse—it's just the leg multiplied by $\sqrt{2}$.

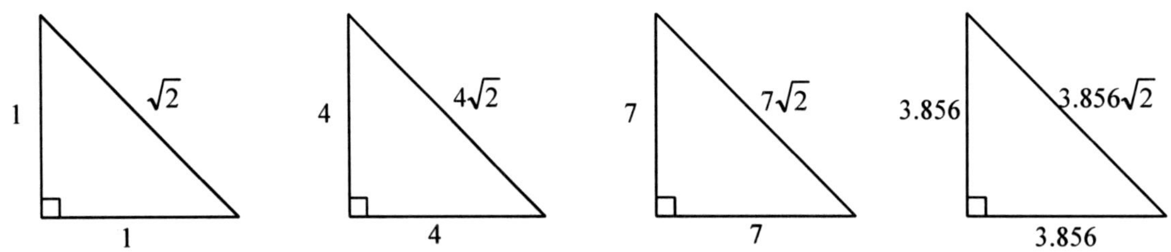

Notice that we know all of these triangles are 45-45-90 even though they didn't tell us the angles are 45°. That's because we know each has two equal sides—and that alone is enough to make them isosceles.

3. The 30-60-90 Triangle

Any triangle with angles of 30°, 60°, and 90° will always have the same dimensions.

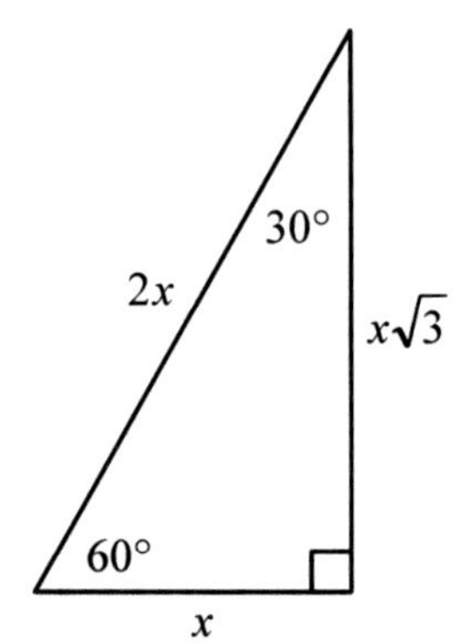

It's the same concept as the 45-45-90 triangle: if I know just a few things about the triangle, I can just fill in all the values for the rest of the triangle without doing a lot of calculations or bothering with the Pythagorean Theorem.†

Remembering these triangles

It can be tough to remember all these dimensions. The 45-45-90 is a bit easier since two of the sides are the same. But in the 30-60-90 since each side has a different value and it's easy to mix up where everything goes. Here's a tip for remembering which angle and which length goes where:

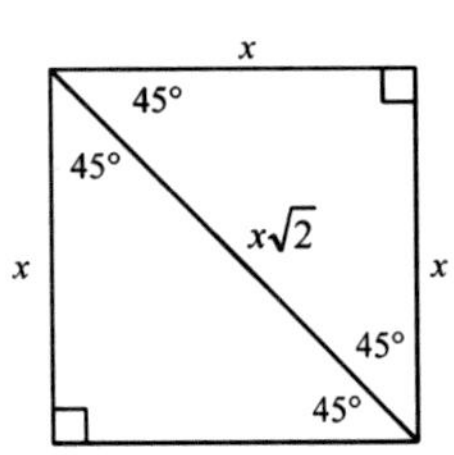

- The 45-45-90 triangle is **half a square**. The diagonal of the square cuts two right angles into 45° angles. The two x's are the sides of the square and the hypotenuse is the diagonal.
- The 30-60-90 triangle is **half an equilateral triangle**. A line divides one of the 60° angles into two 30° angles, and then cuts the opposite side in half as well.

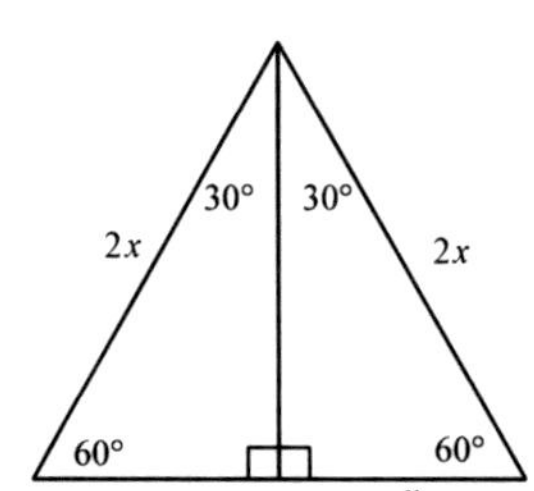

---

* Plus a 90° angle. Thus "right triangle".

† You could prove these dimensions with the Pythagorean Theorem the same way we did above with the 45-45-90 triangle. We didn't, because we don't feel like it and we don't think any of you care. But if you do, knock yourself out.

But again, if you're not sure where to put everything—*check the front of the section.* They *give* you this. You don't have to remember it.

Sometimes, it may not be obvious that a triangle in a problem is 30-60-90 or 45-45-90. But notice that these triangles involve two **happy magic numbers**: $\sqrt{2}$ and $\sqrt{3}$. These numbers don't show up very often in other situations. In fact, they rarely show up in other situations. So if you're doing a problem and notice $\sqrt{3}$ in the answer choices, there's a pretty good chance that there's a 30-60-90 triangle in the problem. The same goes for $\sqrt{2}$; if you see it in the answers, there's a good chance there's a 45-45-90 triangle in the problem. Of course, this isn't *always* true. But if you're stuck on a problem, look for these happy magic numbers. They could help you spot something you would have missed otherwise.*

4. Similar Triangles

If all the angles of one triangle are equal to all the corresponding angles of a second triangle, then they are *similar triangles*. That means that all their sides are in the same ratio with each other.

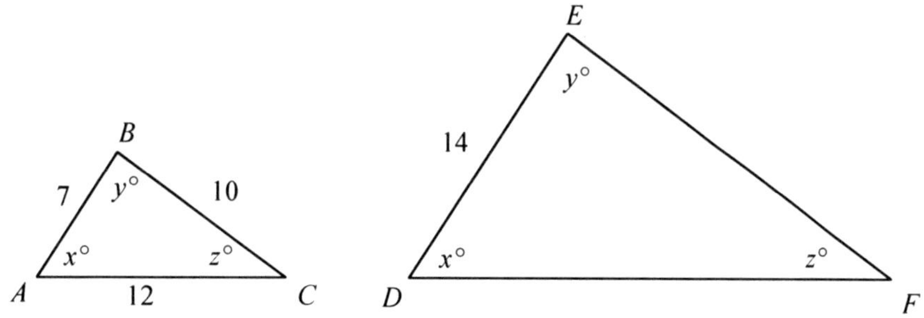

Here, $\triangle ABC$ has all the same angles as $\triangle DEF$, so they are similar triangles. $AB = 7$ and $DE = 14$, so DE is double AB. Since the triangles are similar, each side of $\triangle DEF$ will be double the corresponding side of $\triangle ABC$. So $EF = 2(10) = 20$, and $DF = 2(12) = 24$.

When dealing with similar triangles, it's important to keep track of which side is which. AB will be proportional to DE because each of them is across from the "z" angle.

This, by the way, is exactly why we can do that stuff with the 30-60-90 triangles we just saw. All 30-60-90 triangles have the same angles, therefore their sides are in the same ratio—$1:\sqrt{3}:2$.

Similar triangles don't have to be next to each other. Often these questions will feature *a triangle inside of a triangle.* In the figure to the left, if DE is parallel to BC, then $\angle ADE = \angle ABC$. Therefore $\triangle ABC$ is similar to $\triangle ADE$ because all of their corresponding angles are equal.

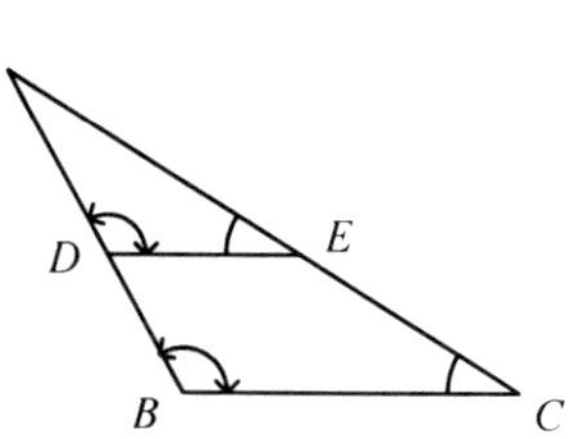

5. Lengths of the sides of a triangle

There are several additional points to be made about the relationship between sides in a triangle.

- **The hypotenuse must be the longest side of a right triangle.**

Well, that makes sense, since the Pythagorean Theorem says a and b together contribute to c. So if someone tells you a right triangle has sides of 7, 24, 25, you know right away that the hypotenuse is 25 and the legs are 7 and 24.

---

* $\sqrt{2}$ is certainly a magic number. It was the first "irrational number"—a decimal that can't be expressed as a fraction. It was first discovered by Hippasus of Metapontum, a Pythagorean mathematician. He was at sea when he discovered it, and some of his Pythagorean shipmates were so angered and offended by the idea of an irrational number, they threw him overboard and drowned him. The Pythagoreans were nuts. If you know any Pythagoreans, don't mention $\sqrt{2}$ to them.

In a right triangle, the 90° angle must always be the largest angle, so the side opposite (the hypotenuse) must be the longest side. But this same rule holds for *any* triangle:

- **The largest angle of a triangle must be opposite the longest side.**

Or, more generally, "the larger the angle, the larger the opposite side." There's a definite relationship between the lengths of the sides of a triangle and the angles opposite them.* That's exactly why an isosceles triangle has two equal sides *and* two equal angles opposite them.

Let's look at this in action:

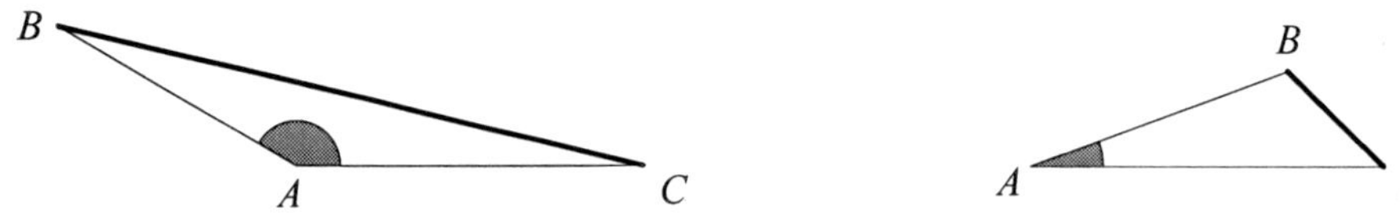

As you can see from these figures, when we make angle A bigger, side BC opposite it also becomes bigger. Ditto, when A is smaller, BC is smaller.

But are there limits to how big or small that third side can get? Yes, there are:

- **The third side of a triangle must be *smaller* than the *sum* of the other two sides.**
    - $BC < AC + AB$
- **The third side of a triangle must be *larger* than the *difference* of the other two sides.**
    - $BC > AC - AB$

Let's see how far we can stretch these triangles. On the left, we'll make angle A bigger and bigger; on the right, we'll make angle A smaller and smaller. Let's see what happens to side BC.

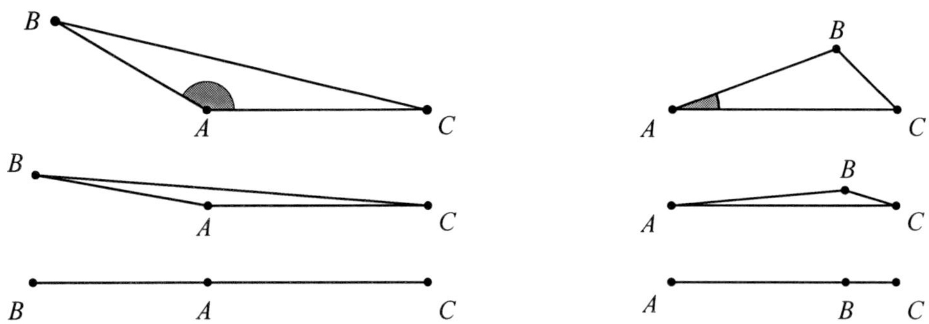

We can keep stretching angle A until it reaches 180°—a straight line. In that case, BC is exactly equal to BA and AC combined. But if we do that, *it's not a triangle.* It's just a straight line now. So if we want it to be a triangle, angle A has to be less than 180°, so the third side has to be less than the sum of the other two.

On the right, we can see the same thing happening in the opposite direction. Angle A can keep shrinking until it gets to 0°. Now we have a straight line again, this time with AB lying on top of AC. So BC is equal to the difference of the other two: $AC - AB$. But again, if we do that, *we don't have a triangle*. So if we want it to be a triangle, angle A has to be greater than 0°, so the third side has to be greater than the difference of the other two.

Similarly, we can see that if the third side were bigger than the sum of the other two, the two smaller sides wouldn't be able to reach each other:

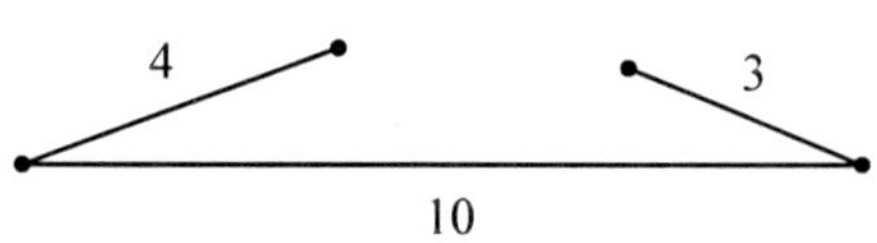

* There's actually a whole field of math that deals with the relationships between angles and sides of triangles. It's called trigonometry, and we'll be doing some very, very soon.

TRIANGLE DRILL

11. What is the area of a square that has a diagonal of length $3\sqrt{2}$?

A. 3
B. 4
C. 9
D. $9\sqrt{2}$
E. 18

30. Mariano lives 12 miles due south of school and Nancy lives 16 miles due west of school. If Chris walks in a straight line from Nancy's house to Mariano's house, what is the distance, in miles, that he will have walked?

F. 12
G. 16
H. 20
J. 25
K. 28

35. Triangle $\triangle ABC$ is similar to $\triangle XYZ$. $AB = 6$, $BC = 12$, and $AC = 15$. If the shortest side of $\triangle XYZ$ is 10, what is the perimeter of $\triangle XYZ$?

A. 22
B. 35
C. 45
D. 55
E. 66

54. In quadrilateral $ABCD$ below, $\angle ABC = 150°$ and $\overline{BD}$ bisects $\angle ADC$. What is the perimeter of $ABCD$?

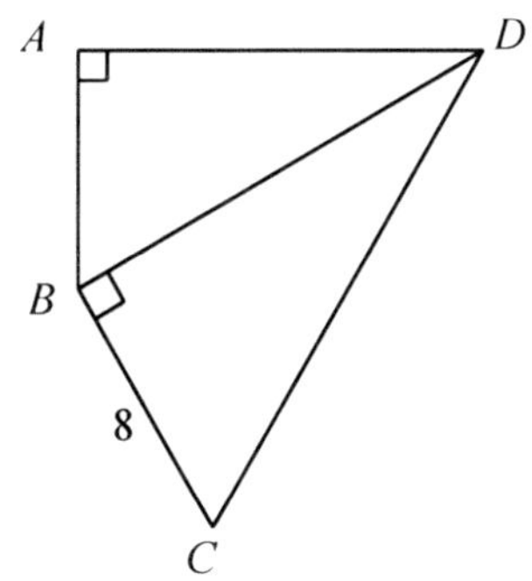

F. $8 + 24\sqrt{3}$
G. $24 + 8\sqrt{3}$
H. $32 + 8\sqrt{3}$
J. $36 + 4\sqrt{3}$
K. $36 + 12\sqrt{3}$

GO ON TO THE NEXT PAGE.

59. The figure below shows a cube with edges of length 2. What is the length of diagonal AB?

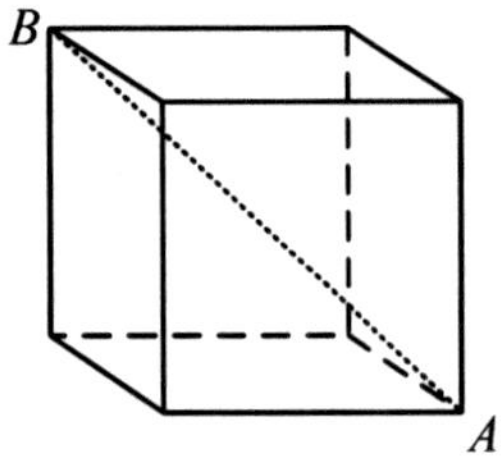

A. $\sqrt{2}$
B. $2\sqrt{2}$
C. $\sqrt{6}$
D. $2\sqrt{3}$
E. 4

STOP!

IV. PERIMETER, AREA & VOLUME

Let's start with a few definitions and formulas. Note that this is *all* you need to know for the ACT about perimeter, area, and volume. If you want to find the area or volume of a shape that isn't listed here (like a pentagon or a pyramid), either:

- you can find it by using some combination of the shapes listed here, ***or***
- you don't actually need that area (you only *think* you do).

1. Perimeter

The perimeter of any figure is the sum of the lengths of all the outside edges.

Okay? Okay.

2. Area

Some ACT questions will give you formulas in the questions. But you'll be expected to know the formulas for basic shapes **You will not be given these formulas.** You have to know them. If you don't, **learn them now.**

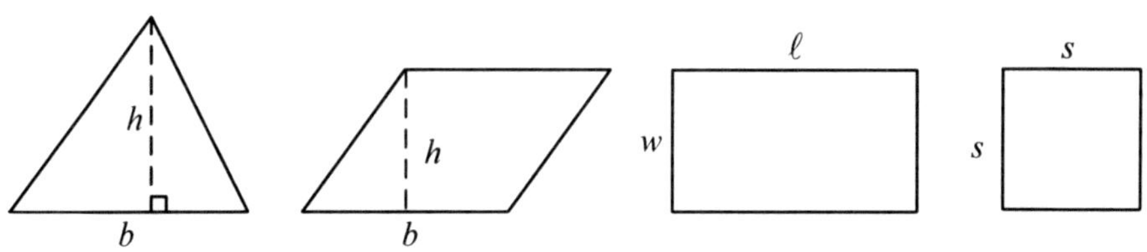

$A = \frac{1}{2}bh$ $A = bh$ $A = \ell w$ $A = s^2$

AREA:

Triangle: $A = \frac{1}{2}bh$

Parallelogram: $A = bh$

Rectangle: $A = \ell w$

Square: $A = s^2$

Some notes:

- In a triangle, the *base* is just whatever side happens to be lying flat on the ground. The *height* is a line from the topmost point of the triangle extending perpendicular to the base. Sometimes that's just a side of the triangle, sometimes it's inside the triangle, sometimes it's outside the triangle. All three of the following triangles have identical areas, because they have the same base and height:

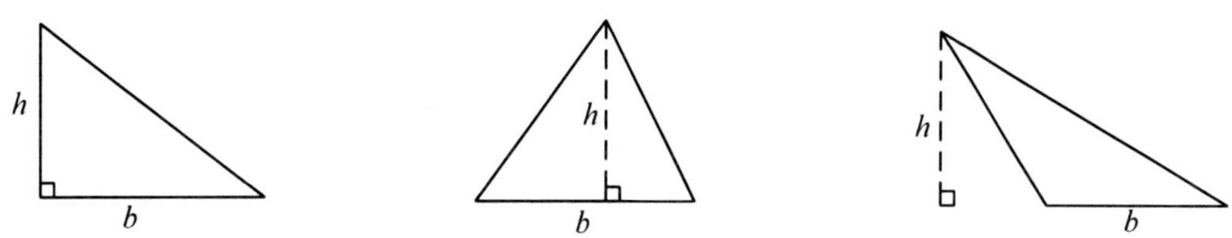

- Notice that the formula for a parallelogram is base times **height**, not the *side*.
- The formulas for squares and rectangles say the same thing. A square is just a rectangle with equal sides, so $s = \ell = w$. Similarly, a rectangle is just a parallelogram whose height is equal to one side.
- Notice that the area of a triangle is half the area of a rectangle. Imagine cutting a rectangle in half along the diagonal; you'd get two right triangles. And for each triangle, the base and height are equal to the length and width of the original rectangle. The same is true for any parallelogram: it is made up of two identical triangles, so its area is twice the area of a triangle

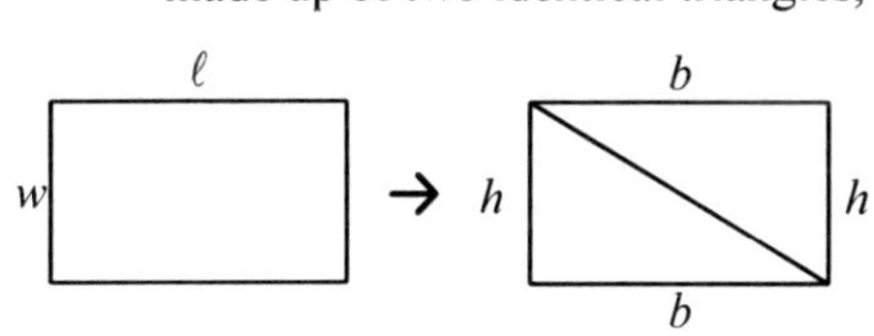

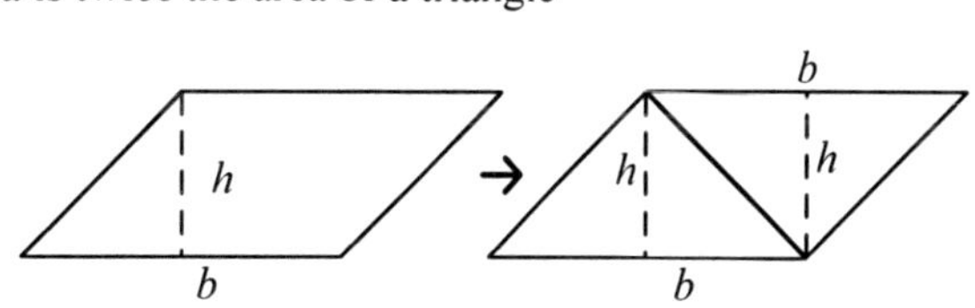

- You can also use triangles to find the area of other shapes that aren't shown here. For example, the area of a trapezoid is the height times the average of the two bases. But you can also see this by **dividing the trapezoid into a rectangle and one or two triangles**, as seen below. Again, we use the rules we know to figure out the rules we don't.

$A = \frac{1}{2}h(b_1 + b_2)$ $\quad$ $A = \frac{1}{2}ha + hw + \frac{1}{2}hb$ $\quad$ $A = hw + \frac{1}{2}hb$

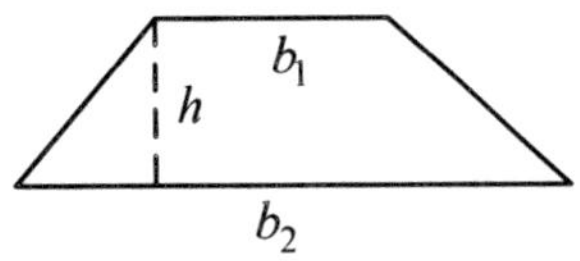

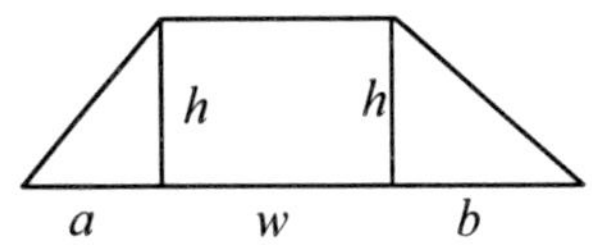

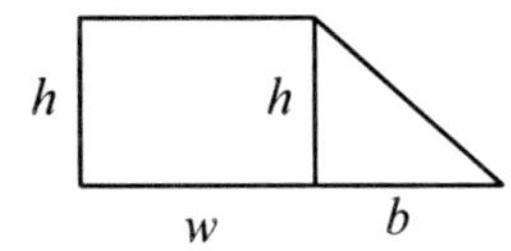

Shaded Area Problems

Shaded area problems are best done by ***subtraction***. Find the area of the whole figure and take away what you don't need.

Take a look at this one:

- **In the figure below, a small square is inside a larger square. What is the area of the shaded region?**

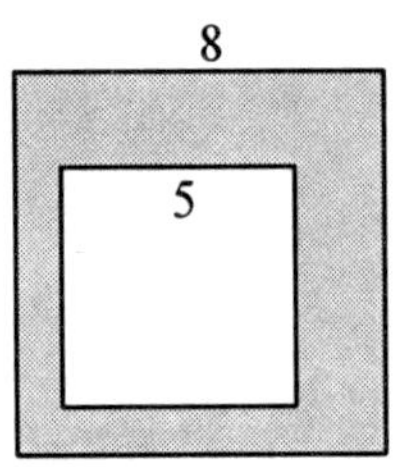

It may be tempting to try to find the area directly by dividing up the shaded region into four rectangles. But we can't find those areas because we don't know all of their dimensions. Plus it's kind of tedious.

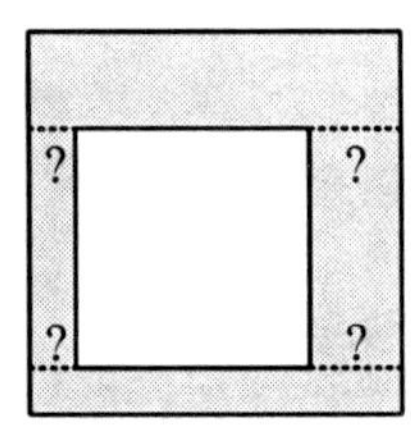

Instead, let's just find the area of the **whole** square and subtract the area of the **unshaded** square. Whatever's left will be the area of the shaded region.

$$A_{whole} = s^2 = 8^2 = 64$$

$$A_{unshaded} = 5^2 = 25$$

$$A_{shaded} = A_{whole} - A_{unshaded}$$

$$= 64 - 25 \boxed{= \mathbf{39}}$$

3. Surface Area

We find the "surface area" by finding the *area* of the *surface.*[*] That means we have to find the areas of all the shapes on the outside of the box. A box is made up of a bunch of rectangles; we'll find the area of the rectangles and add them all up. That's it.

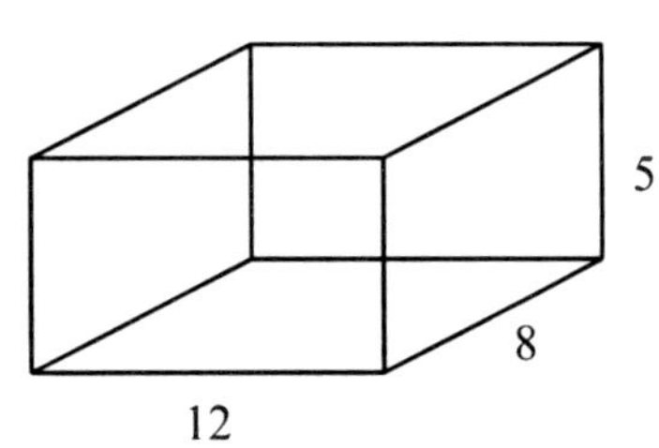

This box has dimensions 12, 8, and 5. To find the surface area, we'll take the areas of all the rectangles on the outside and add them up.

[*] Brilliant.

We can see that there are three types of rectangles in this box:

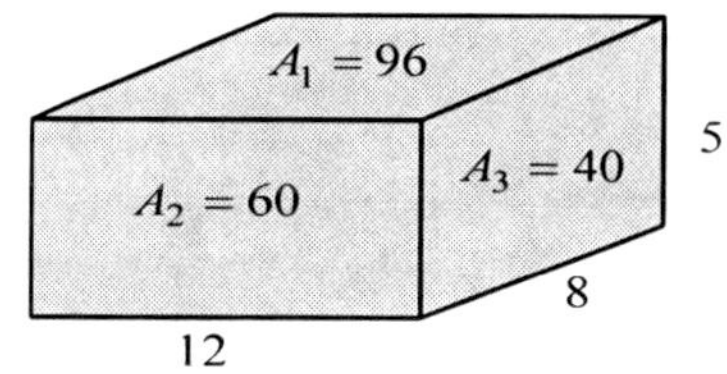

$A_1 = 12 \times 8 = 96$

$A_2 = 12 \times 5 = 60$

$A_3 = 8 \times 5 = 40$

BUT, each of these sides shows up *twice* in the box (top and bottom, front and back, side and side.)

$$SA = 2(A_1 + A_2 + A_3)$$

$$SA = 2(96 + 60 + 40) = 2(196)$$

$$\boxed{SA = 392}$$

Again, a cube is just a special type of box. Since it's made up of 6 squares, we'll just find the area of one face and multiply by 6. This square has edges of length 4.

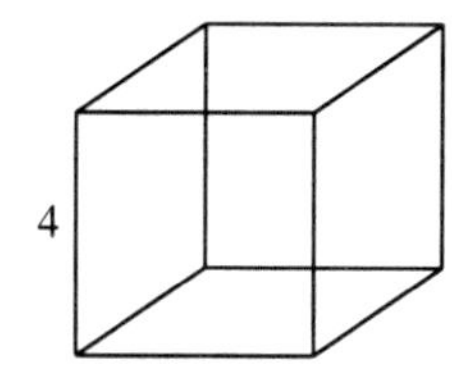

$$SA = 6(A_{\square})$$

$$SA = 6(s^2) = 6(4^2) = 6(16)$$

$$\boxed{SA = 96}$$

4. Volume

Just like with area, you'll be expected to know some formulas for volume, while more complicated formulas will be given in the question.

Learn these:

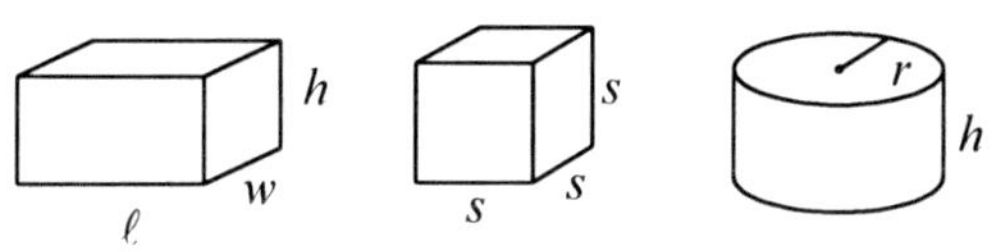

$V = \ell wh$ $\quad V = s^3$ $\quad V = \pi r^2 h$

> VOLUME:
>
> Box: $V = \ell wh$
>
> Cube: $V = s^3$
>
> Cylinder: $V = \pi r^2 h$

- Sometimes the formula for a cylinder may be given to you in the question, but not always.
- Just as the area of a rectangle is found by multiplying its two dimensions, the volume of a box is found by multiplying its three dimensions.
- Just as a square is a rectangle with equal sides, a cube is a box with equal sides.
- Notice that the volume of a cylinder works under the same principle as the volume of a box. For a box, the base is a rectangle, so its area is length times width; get the volume by multiplying that by the height. For a cylinder, the base is a circle, so its area is πr^2; get the volume by multiplying that by the height.

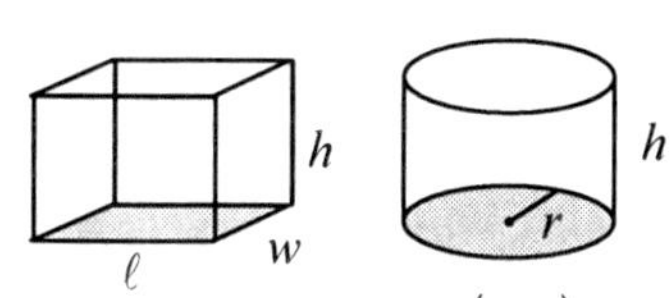

$V = (\ell w) \times h$ $\quad V = (\pi r^2) \times h$

PERIMETER/AREA/VOLUME DRILL

7. The width of a rectangular quilt is 1 foot less than its length. If the width of the quilt is 3 feet, what is the area of the quilt in square feet?

A. 4
B. 6
C. 7
D. 10
E. 12

34. Orestes has a rectangular block of cheese with dimensions 15 inches by 21 inches by 24 inches. If he cuts this block entirely into cubes with a side of length 3, how many such cubes are produced?

F. 27
G. 42
H. 96
J. 280
K. 480

39. What is the area of a right triangle whose sides are x, $x + 4$, and $x - 4$ and whose perimeter is 48?

A. 48
B. 96
C. 144
D. 192
E. 210

42. In the figure below, $\triangle EFD$ is an isosceles triangle inscribed in a square of side 6. What is the area of the shaded region?

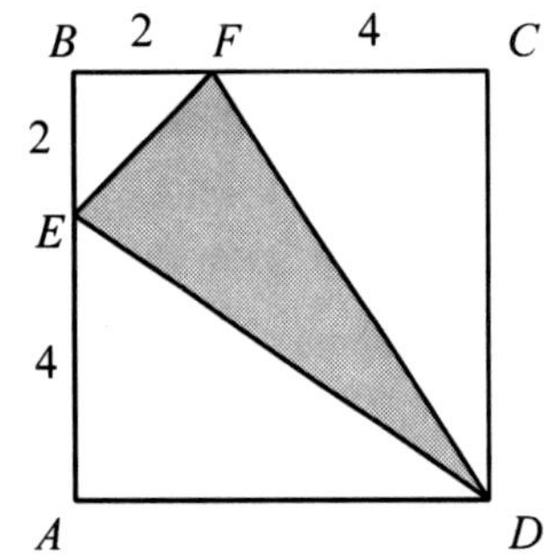

F. 8
G. 10
H. 12
J. 24
K. 36

45. What is the area of the trapezoid below, in square feet?

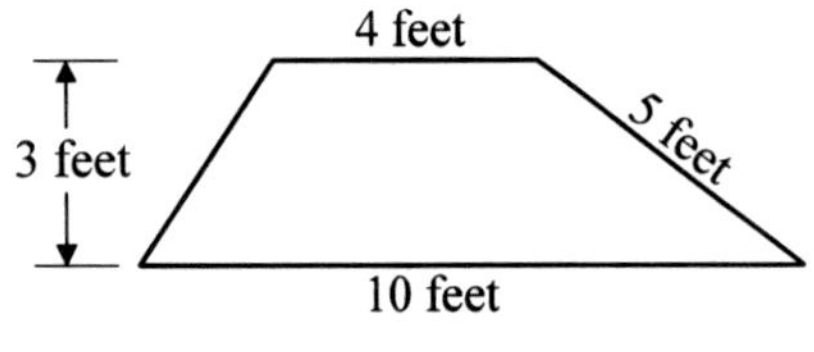

A. 21
B. 24
C. 30
D. 42
E. 50

STOP!

V. CIRCLES

1. Definitions

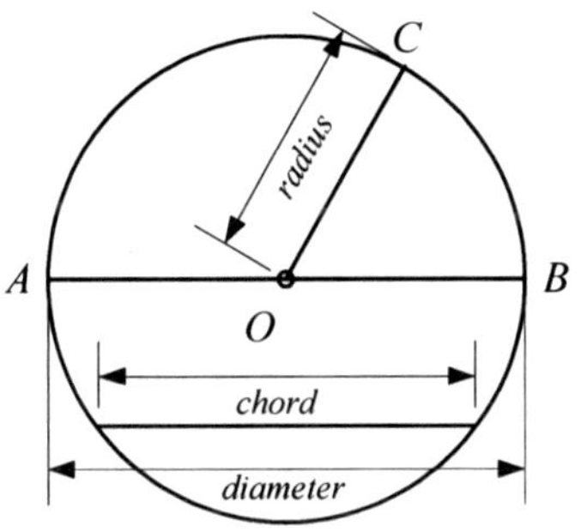

Some fun circle facts:*

- A circle has ***360°***. In the figure to the left, all angles surrounding point O will add up to 360°.†
- The ***diameter*** of a circle is a line segment from one end of the circle to the other, passing through the center. In the figure, AB is a diameter. The diameter by definition is the longest segment you can draw through a circle.

> Circles are named for their center points, so this circle is circle O. A lot of circles are named "O". Can you guess why?

- The ***radius*** of a circle is a line segment from the center to the end of a circle. The radius is half of the diameter. In the figure, OA, OB, and OC are all radii. All radii of a circle are equal.
- A ***chord*** is *any* line segment from one end of the circle to the other. The longest chord in a circle is a diameter.

Almost everything we do with a circle requires knowing its radius (or diameter, which is just double the radius). If you're given a circle and you don't know its radius, before you do anything else **try to find the radius**. You'll probably need it, even if you don't yet know why.

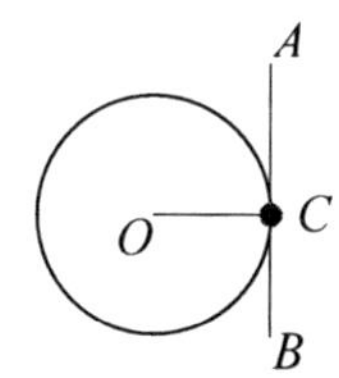

- When a line is ***tangent*** to a circle, that means it touches the circle at exactly one point. In the figure to the right, segment AB is tangent to circle O at point C. Note that a tangent line is always perpendicular to the radius of the circle at the point of intersection. Here, radius OC is perpendicular to segment AB.

- When one shape is ***inscribed*** inside another shape, that means it fits exactly within the larger shape, touching its edges at one point on each side.‡ If you encounter a question involving circles and inscribed shapes, the radius or diameter of the circle likely corresponds with a key element of the other shape. In the first figure to the right, the circle's diameter is the same length as the side of the square. In the second, the diameter is the same as the diagonal of the square.

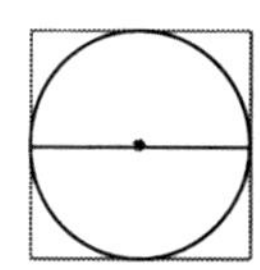

A circle inscribed in a square

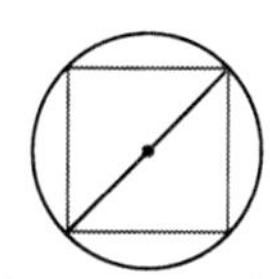

A square inscribed in a circle

2. Formulas

- The perimeter of a circle is called its ***circumference*** (***C***). The circumference is equal to the diameter times π, which is the same as two times the radius times π (since the diameter equals two radii).
- Note that the distance a wheel travels in one revolution is equal to the circumference of the circle.
- The ***area*** of a circle is equal to the radius squared times π.

$$C = \pi d = 2\pi r$$

$$A = \pi r^2$$

- π (pronounced "pi") stands for a special number whose value is approximately 3.14. For most ACT problems, you don't have to calculate the number; you can just leave it as the symbol π.

---

* Well, not that fun.

† Actually, we can already figure this out from our angle rules. The diameter is a straight line, so the angles above it add up to 180° and the angles below it add up to 180°. Put them together and you've got 360°.

‡ The opposite of inscribed is *circumscribed*. To say that a circle is inscribed within a square means the same thing as saying the square is circumscribed about the circle.

The circle shown here has a radius of 3. Therefore:

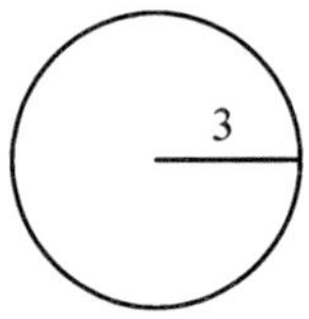

$$C = 2\pi r \qquad A = \pi r^2$$

$$C = 2\pi(3) \qquad A = \pi(3^2)$$

$$\boxed{C = 6\pi} \qquad \boxed{A = 9\pi}$$

Almost everything we do with a circle requires knowing its radius (or diameter, which is just double the radius). If you're given a circle and you don't know its radius, before you do anything else **try to find the radius**. You'll probably need it, even if you don't yet know why.

3. Slices

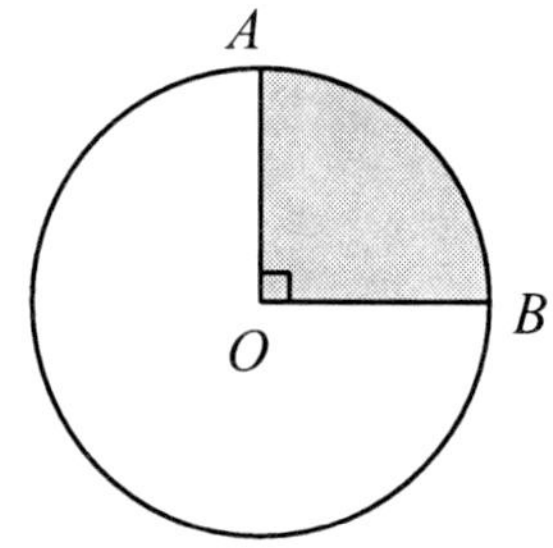

A wedge or slice of a circle is nothing more than a *part* of a circle. Problems dealing with them can be done with simple ratios. Take a look at this circle:

Obviously, the shaded section is one fourth of the circle. How can I tell? First of all, because it *looks* like a fourth of the circle (Guesstimate!)

Secondly, we know central angle, $\angle AOB$, is 90°. 90 is one fourth of 360. So that central angle is one fourth of the whole angle (360).

Let's say the circle has a radius of 10. So its area is 100π. The area of the slice is one fourth of that: 25π.

If the circle has a radius of 10, its circumference is 20π. The length of minor arc AB is one fourth of it: 5π.

This is pretty easy to see. Since that slice is one fourth of the circle, everything about that slice is one fourth of the corresponding characteristic of the circle: the angle is one fourth of 360, the area is one fourth of the circle's area, and the arc length is one fourth of the circumference.

$$\frac{1}{4} = \frac{90°}{360°} = \frac{25\pi}{100\pi} = \frac{5\pi}{20\pi}$$

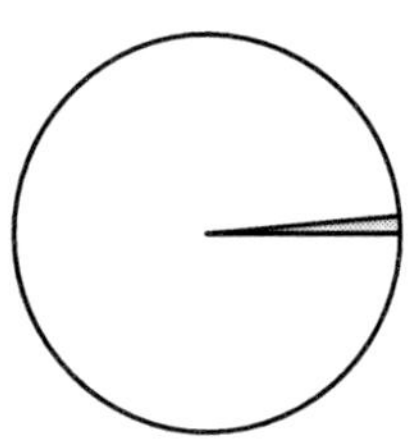

This is true of *all* slices. The slice shown to the left is 1/60 of the circle, so that angle is 1/60 of 360, the arc is 1/60 of the circumference, and the area of the slice is 1/60 of the whole area.

So if you know any one thing about a slice, you can figure out what fraction of the circle it is. Once you know what fraction of the circle it is, you can find anything else about that slice.

You can set up any such problem with a series of ratios:

$$\frac{\text{part}}{\text{whole}} = \frac{\text{angle}}{360°} = \frac{A_{\text{slice}}}{A_{\text{O}}} = \frac{\text{arc}}{C}$$

TRY ONE:

- **Circle O has a radius of 12. If $\angle AOB$ is 60°, what is the length of minor arc AB?**

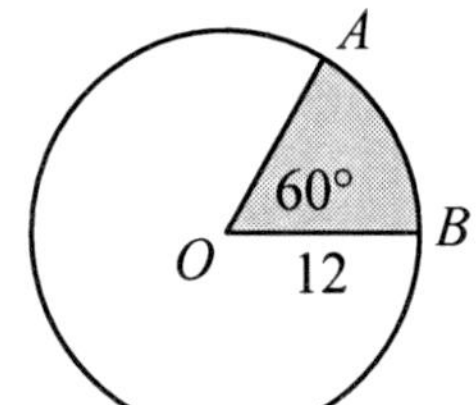

CIRCLE DRILL

17. If the radius of a circle is doubled, by what factor does the circle's area increase?

A. 2
B. 4
C. 6
D. 8
E. 16

28. Through how many degrees does the hour hand of a clock turn from 4:00 PM to 8:00 PM of the same day?

F. 20
G. 40
H. 80
J. 90
K. 120

43. In the figure below, both circles have their centers at point O, and point Q lies on segment OP. If $OQ = 4$ and $PQ = 2$, what is the ratio of the circumference of the smaller circle to the circumference of the larger circle?

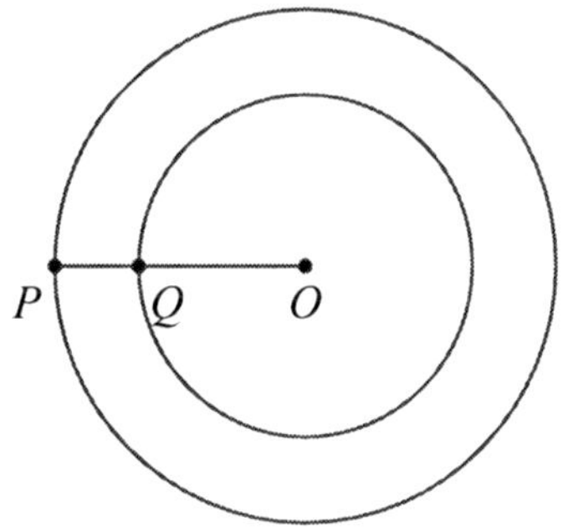

A. 1:3
B. 1:2
C. 2:3
D. 3:5
E. 4:5

48. In the figure below $ABCD$ is a square with sides of length s and AD and BC are both diameters of semicircles inscribed in square $ABCD$. What, in terms of s, is the area of the shaded region?

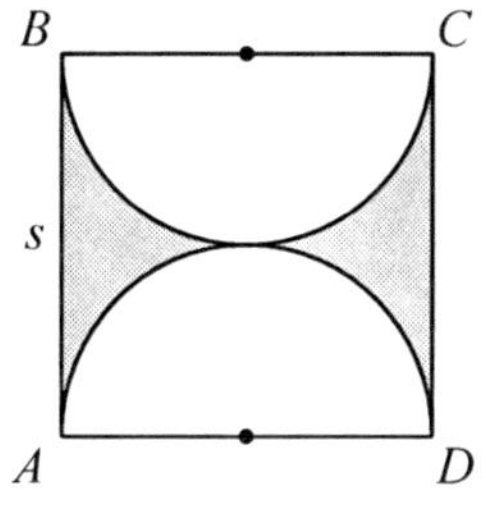

F. $s^2 - \pi s^2$

G. $\dfrac{s^2 - \pi s^2}{4}$

H. $s^2\left(1 - \dfrac{\pi}{4}\right)$

J. $s^2\left(1 - \dfrac{\pi}{16}\right)$

K. $2s^2\left(1 - \dfrac{\pi}{4}\right)$

GO ON TO THE NEXT PAGE.

59. The circle in the figure below with center O is inscribed in square $ABCD$. Which of the following measures for the figure would be sufficient by itself to determine the area of the circle?

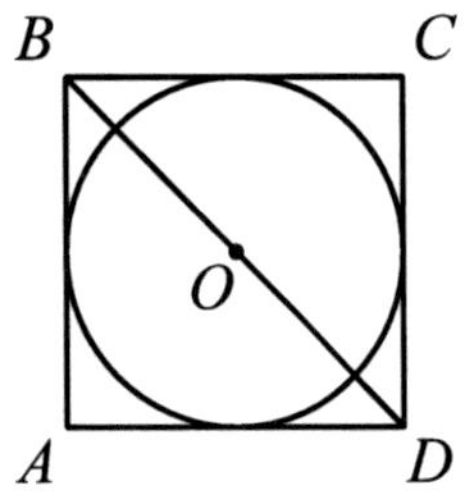

I. The perimeter of square $ABCD$
II. The area of square $ABCD$
III. The length of diagonal BD

A. None
B. I only
C. III only
D. I and II only
E. I, II, and III

STOP!

PLANE GEOMETRY EXERCISE

DO YOUR FIGURING HERE.

1. In the figure below, $\overline{OZ} \perp \overline{OX}$ and $\overline{OY} \perp \overline{OW}$. If $a = 50$, what is the value of c?

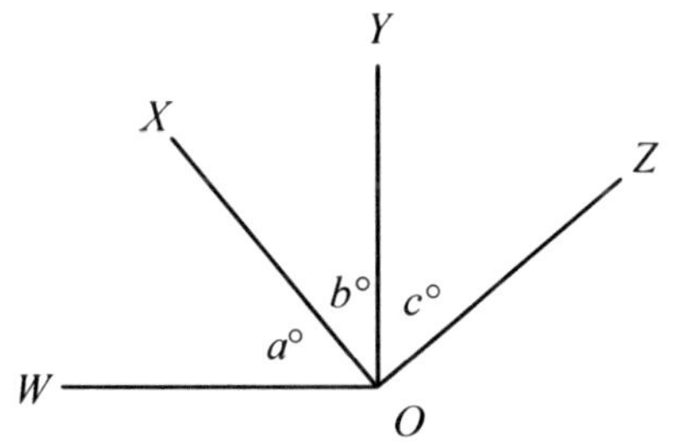

A. 50
B. 45
C. 40
D. 35
E. 30

4. In the figure below, if line k is parallel to line l, the sum of which of the following pairs of angles must equal 180°?

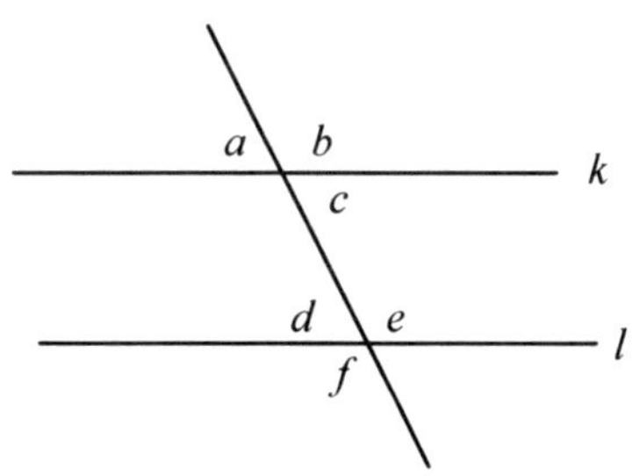

F. a and c
G. a and d
H. b and d
J. c and d
K. e and f

7. A rectangle has a perimeter of 200 and a width of 40. What is the length of the rectangle?

A. 40
B. 50
C. 60
D. 70
E. 80

10. Circles O and P have radii of 3 and 4 respectively. How much greater is the area of circle P than the area of circle O?

F. π
G. 3π
H. 5π
J 7π
K. 9π

GO ON TO THE NEXT PAGE.

13. In the figure below, what is the value of $x + y$?

DO YOUR FIGURING HERE.

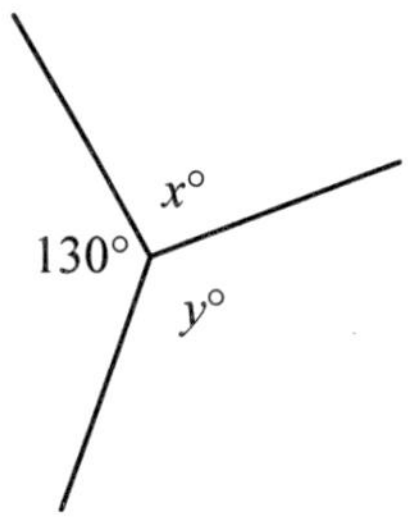

A. 260
B. 230
C. 210
D. 180
E. 130

16. What is the area of the figure below?

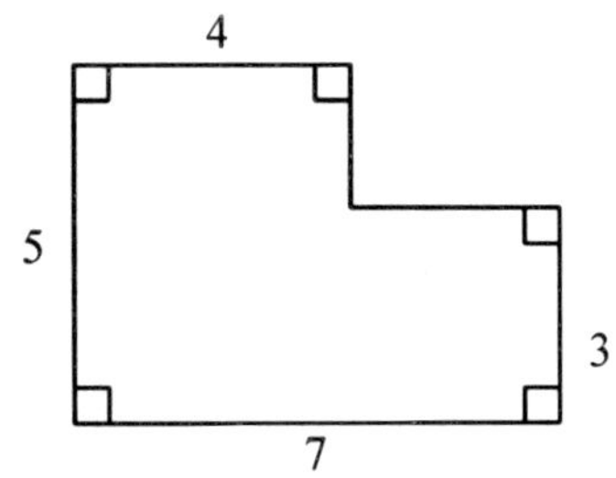

F. 20
G. 24
H. 26
J. 29
K. 35

19. How many more degrees of arc are there in $\frac{1}{3}$ of a circle than in $\frac{1}{4}$ of a circle?

A. 15°
B. 20°
C. 25°
D. 30°
E. 35°

24. In $\triangle ABC$ below, what is the length of $\overline{AC}$?

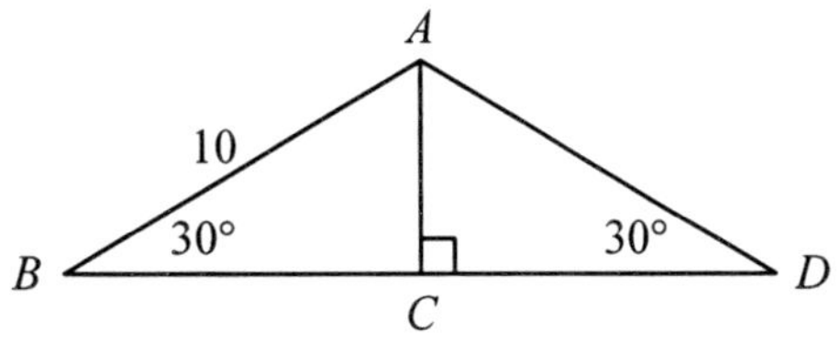

F. 5
G. $5\sqrt{3}$
H. 10
J. $10\sqrt{3}$
K. 20

GO ON TO THE NEXT PAGE.

DO YOUR FIGURING HERE.

29. In the figure below, $AB = BC$. What is the area of $\triangle ABC$?

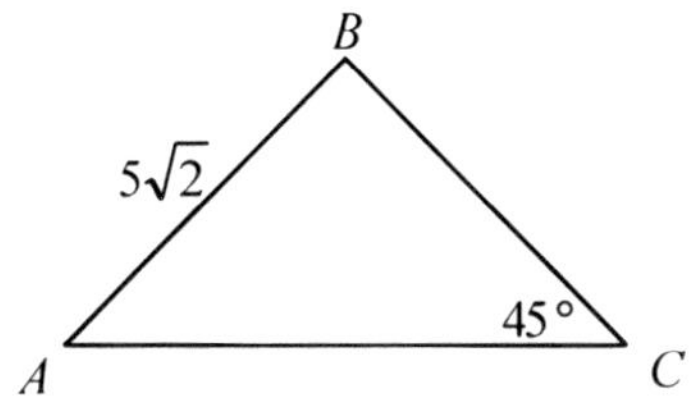

A. 5
B. 10
C. 15
D. 20
E. 25

34. In the figure below, P, Q, R, and S are midpoints of the sides of the square. If the square has sides of length 12, what is the area of the shaded region?

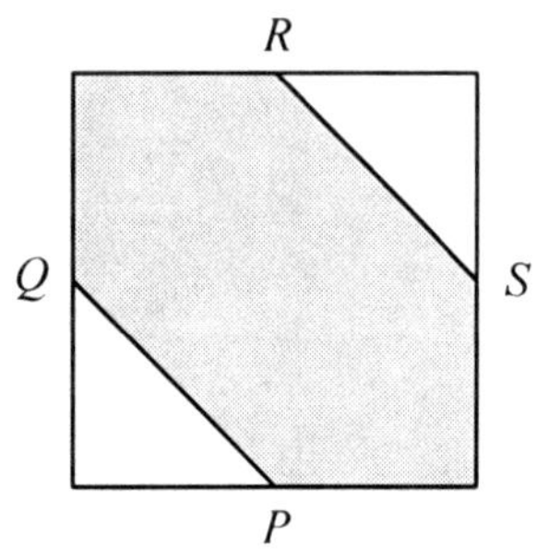

F. 144
G. 126
H. 108
J. 72
K. 36

37. What is the volume of a cube that has a surface area of 54?

A. 3
B. 9
C. 27
D. 36
E. 81

40. In the figure below, P is the midpoint of $\overline{AB}$ and Q is the midpoint of $\overline{AC}$. If $\overline{AP}$ is 5 and $\overline{PQ}$ is 3, what is the area of $\triangle ABC$?

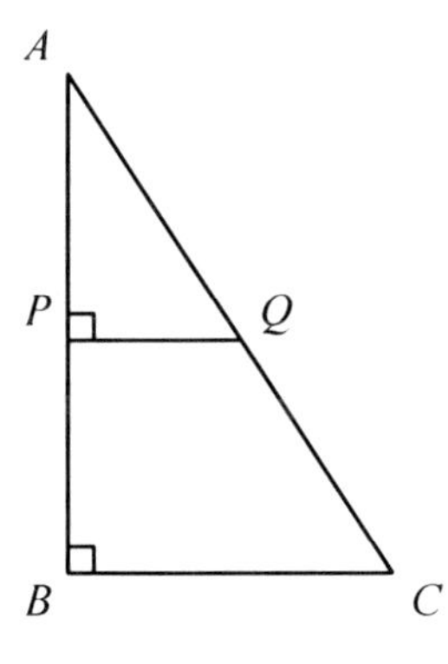

F. 7.5
G. 8
H. 15
J. 30
K. 60

GO ON TO THE NEXT PAGE.

DO YOUR FIGURING HERE.

45. A right circular cylinder has a volume of 64π. If the height of the cylinder is 4, what is the circumference of the base?

A. 8π
B. 12π
C. 16π
D. 20π
E. 24π

50. The figure below is composed of four semicircles on the sides of a square. If the square has an area of 64, what is the length of the darkened outline of the figure?

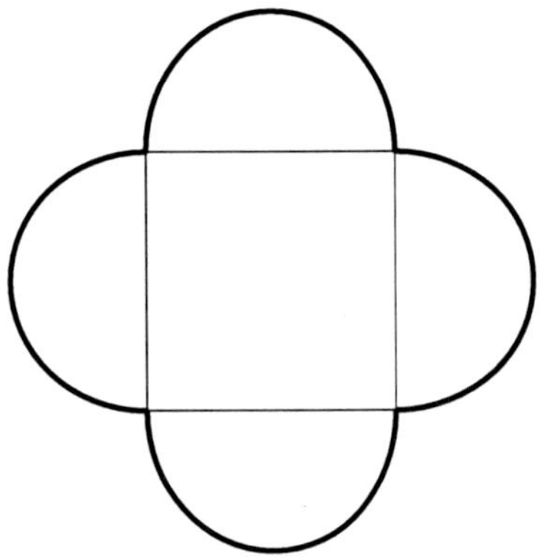

F. 8π
G. 16π
H. 24π
J. 32π
K. 64π

55. In the figure below, a square with side of length $\sqrt{18}$ is inscribed in a circle. What is the circumference of the circle?

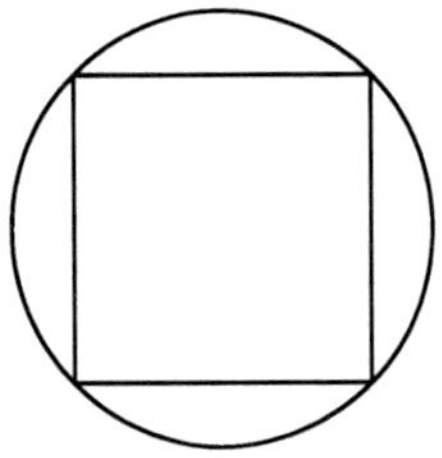

A. 3π
B. 6π
C. 9π
D. 18π
E. 36π

STOP!

TRIGONOMETRY

Trigonometry can be the scariest topic on the ACT because it's the most advanced. Some of you may not have done any trigonometry in school, so this will be entirely unfamiliar to you. There are a lot of weird symbols and Greek letters involved, and it can be quite intimidating. But trigonometry isn't nearly as bad as you think it's going to be.

First of all, **there will only be 4 trigonometry questions on each test**. That's right: four. This is by far the least significant of all the major topics we've covered. So if you really don't understand what's going on here, your time would probably be better spent on some of the other concepts and techniques that appear more frequently.

Second, because trigonometry questions are so difficult for students, they tend to appear at the end of the test. That means that a lot of trigonometry questions will be past your target numbers, so you won't even read them at all.

Third, while some trig questions do involve some tricky concepts, most of them just test your knowledge of the definitions of the basic trigonometric functions. Once you learn those, you'll be able to do more than half of all ACT trigonometry questions without breaking a sweat.

I. TRIGONOMETRY FUNCTIONS

1. Basic Functions

What is trigonometry and why do we need it? It all begins with right triangles.

Remember when we were talking about 45-45-90 triangles? We said that every triangle whose angles measure 45°, 45°, and 90° have dimensions in the same proportion, $1:1:\sqrt{2}$.

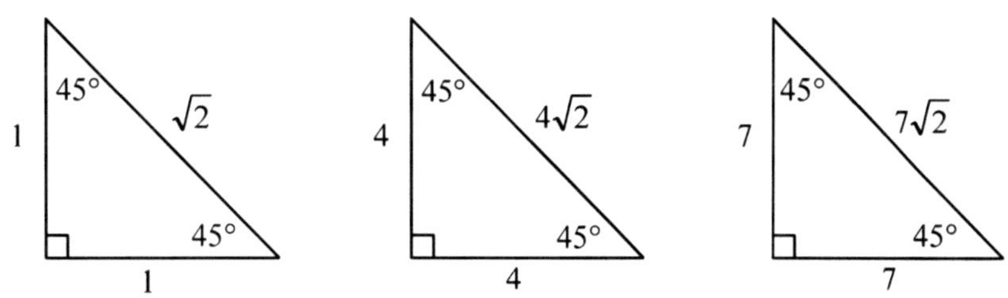

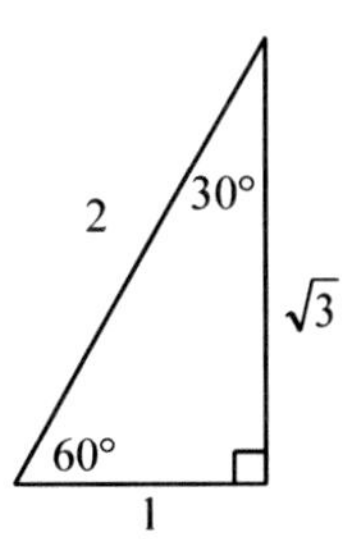

The same was true of the 30-60-90 triangle. Every triangle whose angles measure 30°, 60°, and 90° have sides in the ratio $1:\sqrt{3}:2$. We call triangles like this *similar triangles*—if their angles are all the same measure, their sides will be in the same ratio.

Rather than looking at the ratio of all three sides at the same time, it's easier to look at two sides at a time. If a right triangle has a 45° angle, the ratio of the side opposite the angle to the side next to it will be 1:1. If a right triangle has a 60° angle, the ratio of the side across from it to the hypotenuse will be $\sqrt{3}:2$.

These ratios are the whole point of trigonometry. There are three basic trigonometry functions: **sine**, **cosine**, and **tangent** (abbreviated "sin", "cos", and "tan"). These functions do exactly what we just did: they take the ratios of the sides of a right triangle in relation to a specific angle.

Here are the definitions for these functions:

For any given angle of a triangle:

- the **SINE** of the angle is equal to the length of the **opposite** side over the length of the **hypotenuse**. $\sin\theta = \dfrac{Opposite}{Hypotenuse} = \dfrac{y}{r}$
- the **COSINE** of the angle is the length of the **adjacent** side over the **hypotenuse**. $\cos\theta = \dfrac{Adjacent}{Hypotenuse} = \dfrac{x}{r}$
- the **TANGENT** of the angle is the length of the **opposite** side over the **adjacent**. $\tan\theta = \dfrac{Opposite}{Adjacent} = \dfrac{y}{x}$

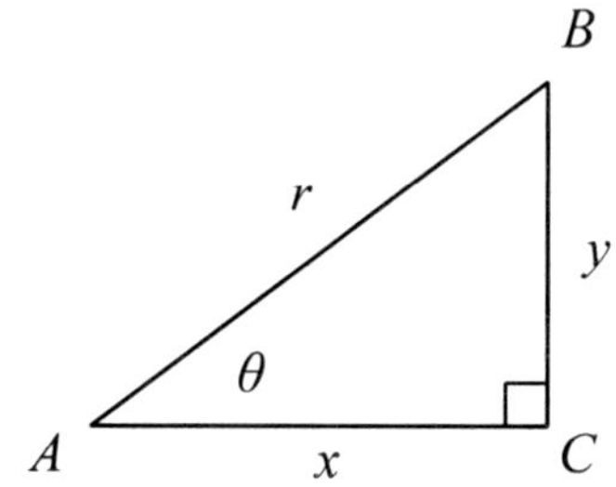

The symbol "θ" is the Greek letter "theta". It's often used to describe angles in trigonometry problems. Note that these functions only work with *right triangles*—triangles that contain a right angle.

MEMORIZE THESE DEFINITIONS. Over half of all ACT Trigonometry questions require nothing more than knowing these three definitions. You can remember these ratios via the acronym **SOHCAHTOA** :

Sine = **O**pposite over **H**ypotenuse, **C**osine = **A**djacent over **H**ypotenuse, **T**angent = **O**pposite over **A**djacent

Calculating the ratios

Let's look at an example:

- **In $\triangle ABC$ to the right, what is the value of $\sin A$?**

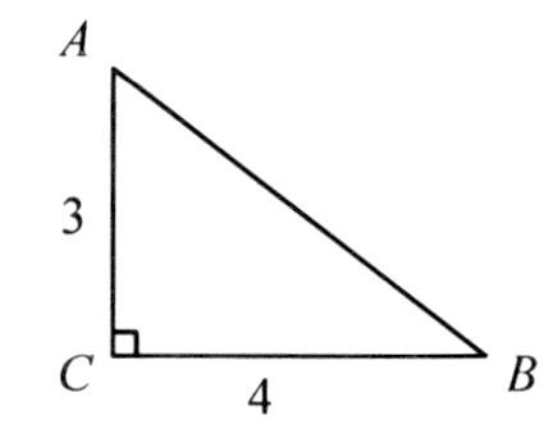

We know that sine is equal to the opposite side over the hypotenuse. The side opposite angle A is 4, but we don't know the hypotenuse. We can use the Pythagorean Theorem to find it, or we can see that it's a 3-4-5 triangle, so the hypotenuse is 5. Therefore, $\sin A = \frac{4}{5}$.

In fact, once we have all the lengths of the sides, it's easy to find all the ratios:*

$\sin A = \frac{4}{5}$ $\cos A = \frac{3}{5}$ $\tan A = \frac{4}{3}$ $\sin B = \frac{3}{5}$ $\cos B = \frac{4}{5}$ $\tan B = \frac{3}{4}$

Let's try one that has answer choices:

35. If $0° < x < 90°$ and $\tan x = \frac{5}{8}$, what is $\cos x$?

A. $\dfrac{5}{\sqrt{89}}$

B. $\dfrac{\sqrt{89}}{5}$

C. $\dfrac{\sqrt{89}}{8}$

D. $\dfrac{8}{\sqrt{89}}$

E. $\dfrac{8}{5}$

* Notice that $\sin A = \cos B$, and $\cos A = \sin B$. That's because the side that's opposite one angle is adjacent to the other.

This question doesn't give us a figure, so **we should draw one**. It doesn't have to be to scale, just draw a triangle and call one angle x.

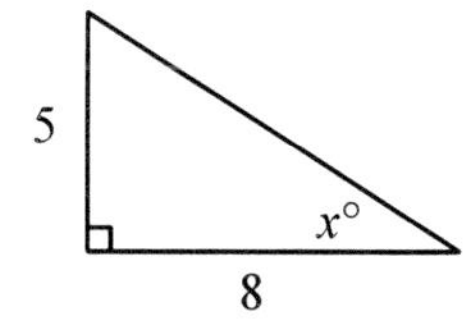

Tangent is *opposite* over *adjacent*, so the side opposite x is 5 and the side next to x is 8.

We want cos x: that's *adjacent* over *hypotenuse*. We know that the adjacent side is 8, but we don't know the hypotenuse. We could use the Pythagorean Theorem to find it. But look—all the answer choices contain combinations of 5, 8, and $\sqrt{89}$. So the hypotenuse ***must*** be $\sqrt{89}$. We don't have to do out the work. Nice!

The side adjacent to x is 8, the hypotenuse is $\sqrt{89}$, so cos x is $\frac{8}{\sqrt{89}}$. That's **choice D.**

TRY SOME:

These questions refer to $\triangle ABC$ shown at right.

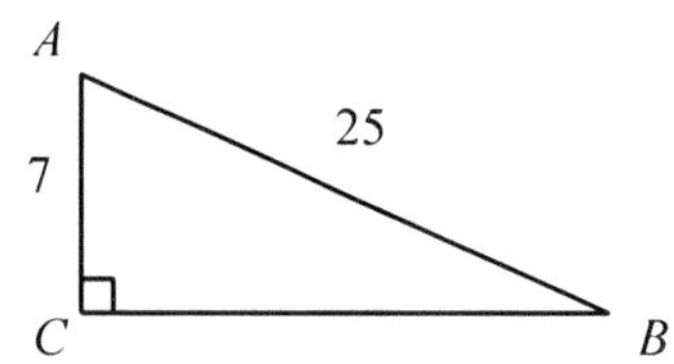

- **sin ($\angle A$) = ?**

- **tan ($\angle B$) = ?**

- **cos ($\angle B$) = ?**

Using the ratios to find lengths

28. In the triangle shown below, which of the following is an expression for the height, h, of the triangle?

F. $12 \sin 25°$

G. $\frac{12}{\sin 25°}$

H. $12 \cos 25°$

J. $\frac{\cos 25°}{12}$

K. $12 \tan 25°$

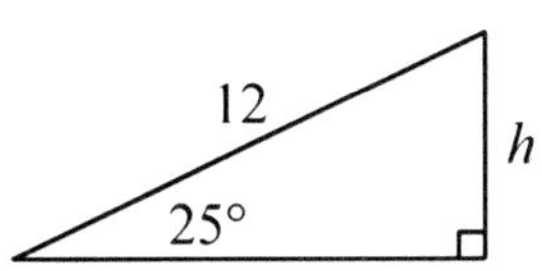

Here we don't have to actually find the value for h. We just have to set up the solution.

We know our answer will involve a trig function using the 25° angle. We know the hypotenuse is 12.

We want h, which is the side *opposite* the 25° angle. Therefore, we'll need a trig function that involves the *opposite* side and the *hypotenuse*. Which one does that? Sine! We can set up the ratio this way:

$\sin 25° = \frac{h}{12}$ To solve for h, multiply both sides by 12.

$\boxed{12 \sin 25° = h}$ That's **choice F.**

Let's try another:

35. In $\triangle ABC$ below, lengths are measured in inches. Which of the following is closest to the length, in inches, of AC?

(Note: $\sin 65° \approx 0.906$, $\cos 65° \approx 0.423$, $\tan 65° \approx 2.144$)

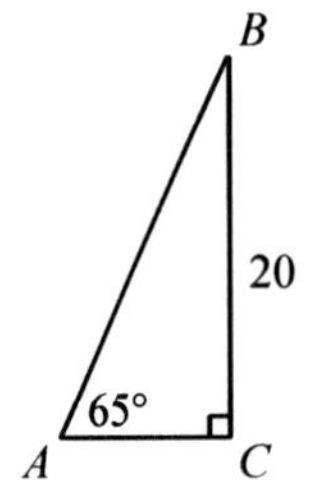

> Hey, look! Guesstimate can eliminate choices C, D, and E!

A. **8.5**
B. **9.3**
C. **18.1**
D. **22.1**
E. **42.9**

This time we want to find an actual value for the length. We'll start the same way we did before.

We know our answer will involve a trig function using the 65° angle. We know the side opposite is 20.

We want *AC*, which is the side *adjacent* to the 65° angle. Therefore, we'll need a trig function that involves the *opposite* side and the *adjacent*. Which one does that? Tangent! We can set up the ratio this way:

$$\tan 65° = \frac{20}{AC}$$

The problem *tells us* the value of tan 65°! It's 2.144. Stick it in and solve for *AC*.

$$2.144 = \frac{20}{AC} \qquad AC = \frac{20}{2.144} \qquad \boxed{AC = 9.3}$$

That's Choice B.

2. Secondary Functions

Reciprocal functions

The three basic functions show three ratios of sides of a right triangle. But those are not the only combinations of sides. We could also flip the fractions to get the *reciprocal functions*. These are called **cosecant** (csc), **secant** (sec), and **cotangent** (cot).

COSECANT: $$\csc\theta = \frac{1}{\sin\theta} = \frac{Hypotenuse}{Opposite} = \frac{r}{y}$$

SECANT: $$\sec\theta = \frac{1}{\cos\theta} = \frac{Hypotenuse}{Adjacent} = \frac{r}{x}$$

COTANGENT: $$\cot\theta = \frac{1}{\tan\theta} = \frac{Adjacent}{Opposite} = \frac{x}{y}$$

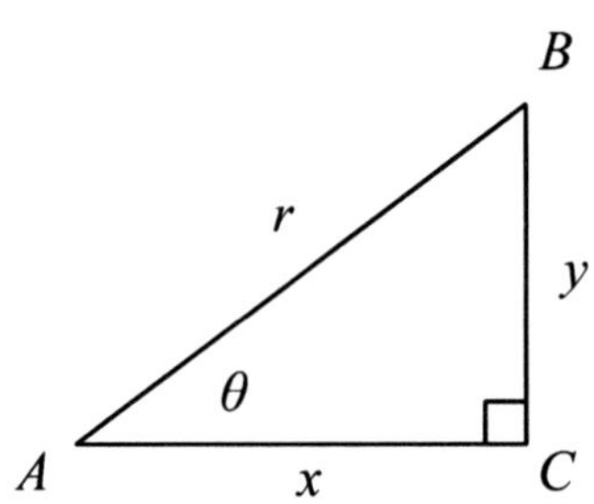

It's easy to mix these up because the "co-"s don't match: *co*secant is the reciprocal of *sine*, and *secant* is the reciprocal of *co*sine.

On the ACT, the reciprocal functions don't show up nearly as much as the basic functions, but you will see them occasionally, so it's still important to learn them.

Inverse functions

So far we've been solving for lengths or the ratios of lengths. But what if we want to solve for the angles?

- **If $0° < x < 90°$, and $\sin x = 0.529$, $x = ?$**

We can solve that directly for x by using **inverse sine** (abbreviated $\sin^{-1}$). This is *not* the same thing as the reciprocal functions mentioned above. It's purely a way to solve an equation like this for the angle. It asks "the sine of what angle comes to 0.529?" You can solve this by punching it out on your calculator:*

$\sin x = 0.529 \qquad x = \sin^{-1}(0.529) \qquad x \approx 32.$

All trigonometric functions have inverse functions like this. On the ACT these functions are not very useful—questions rarely ask you to solve for angle values like this. But the symbols may occasionally show up, so it's good to understand what they mean.

3. Identities

In the Elementary Algebra chapter, we spoke about identities. These are equations that show up frequently, like the "difference of squares" identity, so that you can memorize their forms and do the algebra quickly.

There are a *lot* of rules and identities related to trigonometry functions. They can get complicated and hard to remember. Luckily, if an ACT question requires one of these rules, it will almost always be given in the question. However, there are two identities you won't be given that you should remember:

- $\dfrac{\sin\theta}{\cos\theta} = \tan\theta$ This is easy to prove: $\left(\dfrac{opp}{hyp}\right) \div \left(\dfrac{adj}{hyp}\right) = \left(\dfrac{opp}{hyp}\right) \times \left(\dfrac{hyp}{adj}\right) = \dfrac{opp}{adj} = tan$

- $(\sin\theta)^2 + (\cos\theta)^2 = 1$ Sometimes this is written "$\sin^2\theta + \cos^2\theta = 1$"

If a question asks you to algebraically manipulate an expression that contains a trig function, chances are you'll need one of these identities.

4. Laws

All the trig functions we've seen only apply to right triangles. But what if you have a triangle that *doesn't* contain a right angle? There are two "laws" that can help you: the Law of Sines and the Law of Cosines.

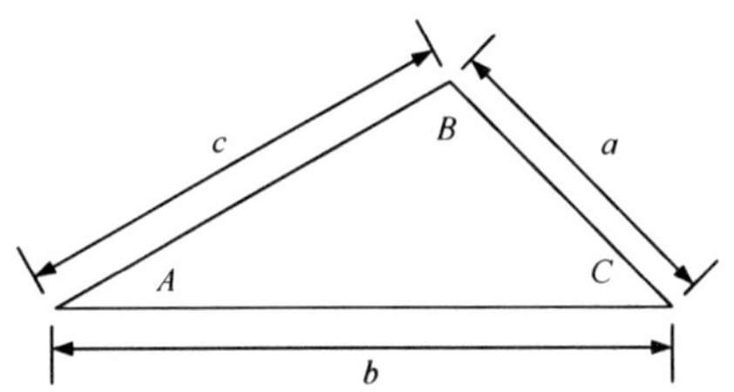

Law of Sines: $\dfrac{\sin A}{a} = \dfrac{\sin B}{b} = \dfrac{\sin C}{c}$

Law of Cosines: $c^2 = a^2 + b^2 - 2ab\cos(C)$

The nice thing about these laws is that **you don't have to remember them**. If you need either of these laws on an ACT question, *it will be given to you.* But even though you don't need to *memorize* the formulas, it's still a good idea to be familiar with the principles.

The **law of sines** states that in *any* triangle, the ratio of the sine of an angle to the side opposite is always constant. If you know two sides and an angle, or two angles and a side, you can set up a simple ratio to solve for any other side or angle.

The **law of cosines** gives a relationship between three sides and one angle in any triangle. If you know three sides, you can use the formula to solve for an angle. Or if you know two sides and an angle, you can use it to solve for the third side.

* Just make sure that your calculator is set to degrees, not radians. We'll talk more about radians in a minute.

TRIGONOMETRY FUNCTION DRILL

21. In $\triangle JKL$ shown below, $JK = 17$ and $JL = 8$. What is $\cos(\angle K)$?

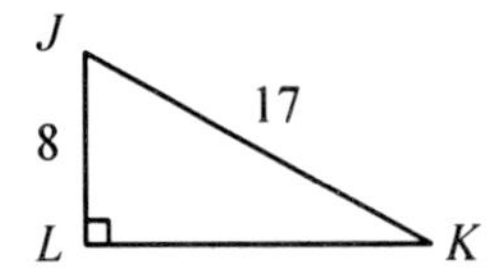

A. $\frac{8}{15}$

B. $\frac{8}{17}$

C. $\frac{15}{17}$

D. $\frac{17}{8}$

E. $\frac{17}{15}$

28. In $\triangle DEF$ below, $\sin F = \frac{5}{9}$. Which of the following expressions equals $\sin D$?

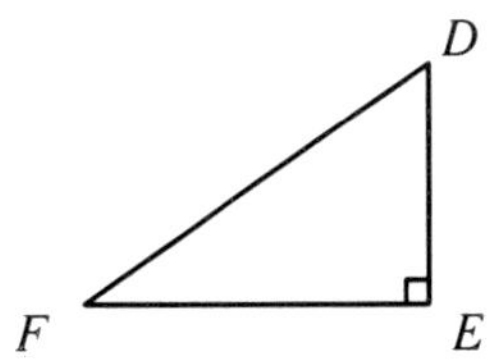

F. $\frac{5}{9}$

G. $\frac{\sqrt{56}}{9}$

H. $\frac{\sqrt{106}}{9}$

J. $\frac{\sqrt{56}}{5}$

K. $\frac{\sqrt{106}}{5}$

33. A surveyor stands on level ground 22 meters away from a tree and determines the angle of elevation to the top of the tree to be 51°. Which of the following expressions correctly gives the height of the tree?

A. 22 sin 51°
B. 22 tan 51°
C. 22 sec 51°
D. 22 cot 51°
E. 22 cos 51°

GO ON TO THE NEXT PAGE.

40. Sherwyn is installing a ramp to the entrance of his office. The front door is elevated 3 feet above ground level. If the ramp is inclined at an angle of 12° to the level ground, which of the following is closest to the length, in feet, of the ramp?

(Note: $\sin 12° \approx 0.208$, $\cos 12° \approx 0.978$, $\tan 12° \approx 0.213$.)

F. 2.9 ft
G. 3.1 ft
H. 8.7 ft
J. 14.1 ft
K. 14.4 ft

45. Triangle $\triangle ABC$ shown below has legs of length a and b, as shown. In terms of a and b, what is the value of $\cos A$?

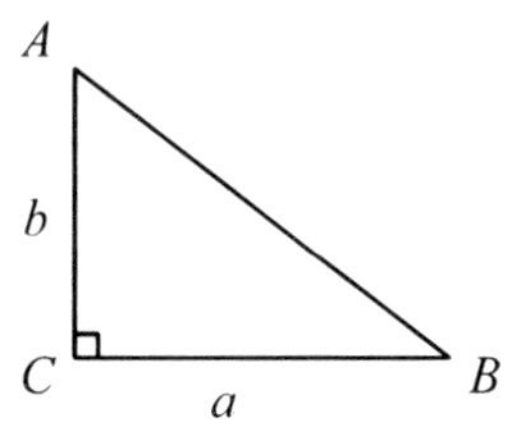

A. $\dfrac{b}{\sqrt{a^2+b^2}}$

B. $\dfrac{a}{\sqrt{a^2+b^2}}$

C. $\dfrac{b}{\sqrt{a^2-b^2}}$

D. $\dfrac{\sqrt{a^2+b^2}}{b}$

E. $\dfrac{\sqrt{a^2-b^2}}{a}$

STOP!

II. Graphing Trigonometric Functions

1. Sine and cosine waves

The graphs of $y = \sin x$ and $y = \cos x$ have distinctive wave-like shapes:

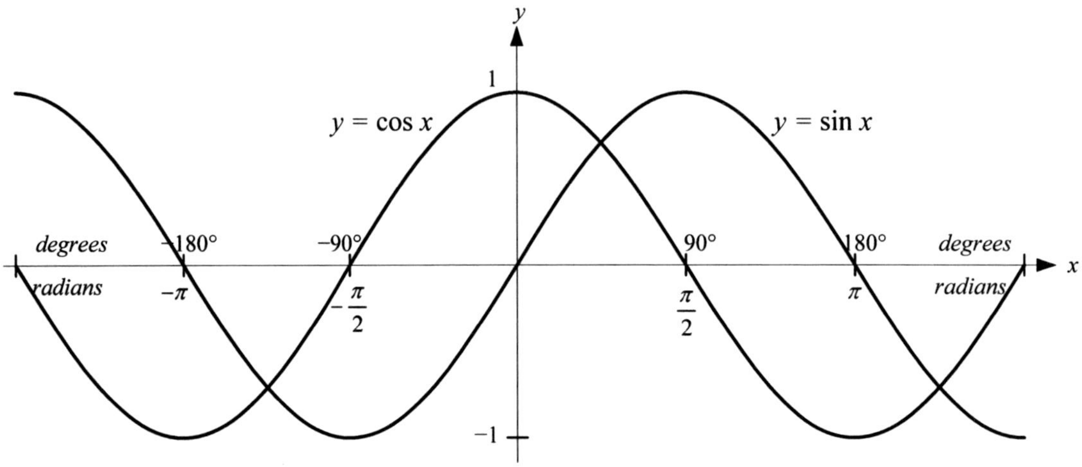

A few notable characteristics of these curves:

- The x-value gives the value of the angle, and the y-value gives the value of the ratio of the sides.
- If you see a graph and you're not sure whether it shows $\sin x$ or $\cos x$, check the y-intercept. In the graph of $y = \cos x$ the curve crosses the axis in the middle of a hump at (0,1). The graph of $y = \sin x$ crosses between humps at the origin.
- All the trig problems we've done so far have involved values of x between 0° and 90°. But notice that both x and y can have negative values. That means that we can have negative values for the angle measures and that we can have negative values for the ratios themselves.

Domain and Range

If you look at the y-values of the graphs above, you can see that they never get above 1 or below −1. The fancy word for this is **range**. The range of a function gives all the possible values of that function. Here, the range of $y = \sin x$ and $y = \cos x$ is $-1 \leq y \leq 1$.

That's the range for the entire function, but we can also find the range of a part of the function if we only focus on a certain group of x values. We call that selection of x-values the **domain**. For example:

- **What are the ranges of $y = \sin x$ and $y = \cos x$ in the domain $0° \leq x \leq 180°$?**

Look at the graphs above but only look at x-values from 0° to 180°. Find the highest and lowest y-values in that span. The y-values of $y = \sin x$ go from 0 to 1 and back to 0. The y-values of $y = \cos x$ go from 1 to 0 to −1. So the range of $y = \sin x$ is $0 \leq y \leq 1$, while the range of $y = \cos x$ is $-1 \leq y \leq 1$.

Radians

The graph above actually shows two different scales for the x-axis mapped on top of each other: the top labels are in degrees and the bottom labels are in **radians**. Graphs of trig functions are often shown in radians—they're simply a different way of measuring angles instead of degrees. It's like the difference between miles and kilometers. You can convert degrees to radians using this formula:

> Any time you do any trig functions on your calculator, be sure to check whether your calculator is set to radians or degrees.

$2\pi \text{ rad} = 360°$

You won't have to convert units often on the ACT, but you will see angles expressed as radians, so it's important to understand what they mean. If you just remember the values shown here, you'll be fine for most questions.*

Degrees:	90°	180°	270°	360°
Radians:	$\frac{\pi}{2}$	π	$\frac{3\pi}{2}$	2π

Periods

You can see that the sine and cosine waves repeat themselves over and over again. The length of one wave from start to finish—both a top hump and a bottom hump—is called the **period** of the function. Both $\sin x$ and $\cos x$ have a period of 360° or 2π radians.†

Transformations

These graphs show the simplest versions of the functions, but there's a lot you can do to them to alter their shapes. We call these changes **transformations** of the function.

Let's see what happens when we add or multiply things to the function. We'll use $y = \sin x$ for our examples, but these rules hold equally true for $y = \cos x$. Compare $\mathbf{y = \sin(x)}$ to $\mathbf{y = a\sin(bx + c) + d}$:

Function	Effect	Graph
$y = a(\sin x)$ $y = -a(\sin x)$	Graph is **stretched vertically** by a factor of a. A negative a will reflect the graph across the x-axis so the humps point the other way.	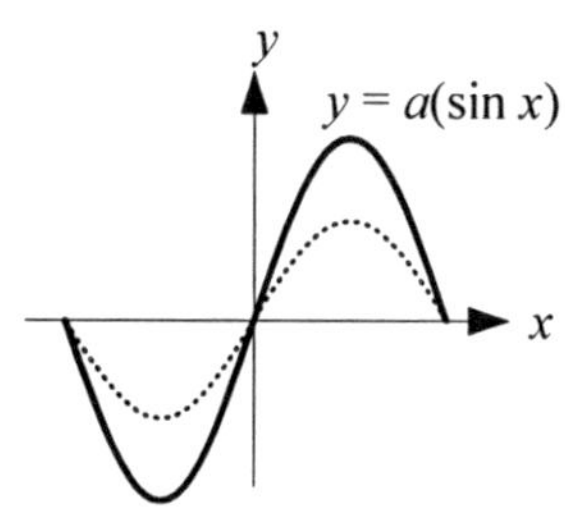
$y = \sin(bx)$	Graph is squashed horizontally by a factor of b. The **period** of the function is changed to $\frac{2\pi}{b}$.	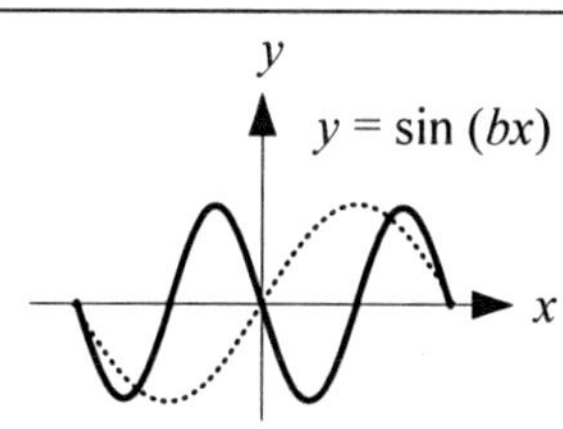
$y = \sin(x + c)$ $y = \sin(x - c)$	Graph is **shifted left** by c units. Graph is **shifted right** by c units. This is the *opposite* of what you might expect. [Note: this is true of *any* function $f(x + c)$]	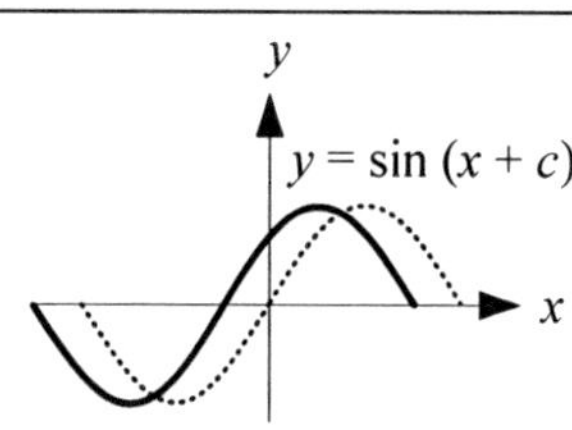
$y = \sin(x) + d$ $y = \sin(x) - d$	Graph is **shifted up** by d units. Graph is **shifted down** by d units [This is true of any function $f(x) + d$]	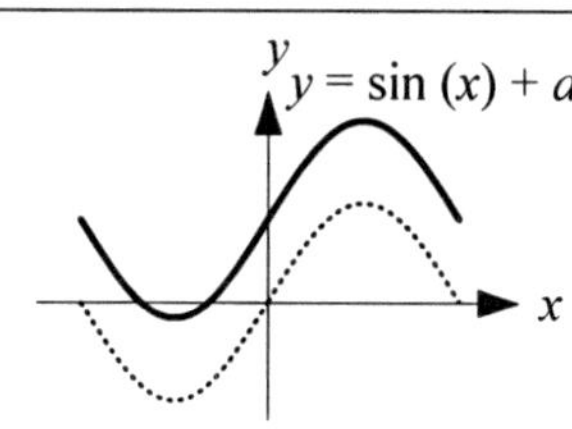

* Remember back in the Plane Geometry chapter when we said that every part of the slice of a circle was proportional to every other part? That's the idea with radians. Imagine an angle as a slice of a circle with radius 1. The measure in radians is the arc length of the slice. 360° is 2π radians because 2π is the circumference of the whole circle. Similarly, and π radians is half the circumference and 180° is the angle of a semicircle, etc.

† The graph of $\tan x$, which looks somewhat different, has a period of 180° or π radians. You generally will not be asked about the graph of $\tan x$ on the ACT.

If you forget these rules and you have a graphing calculator, you can always test them by graphing the transformed equation and the original function together on your calculator. Type these equations into "Y="

$$Y_1 = \sin(x) \qquad Y_2 = \sin(x+1)$$

You can see that the graph of the second equation looks just like that of the first equation, but shifted slightly to the left.*

2. The Unit Circle

The Unit Circle is a convenient way to look at all these trigonometric functions. Here it is, in all its glory:

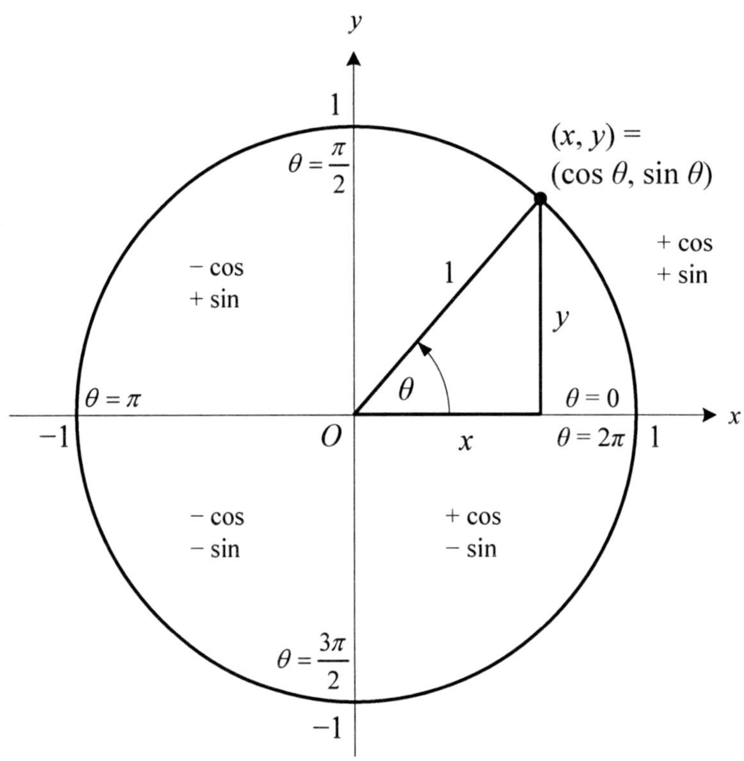

Imagine a circle with radius 1 plotted on the xy-coordinate plane, centered on the origin. As we saw in the Coordinate Geometry chapter, for any point (x, y) on the circle we can draw a right triangle. The legs of the triangle will have length x and y, and the hypotenuse will be 1.

The triangle makes an angle, θ, between the x-axis and the radius. As θ gets bigger, the angle moves counterclockwise around the circle. If we take the normal trig ratios of that angle θ, we get

$$\cos\theta = \frac{x}{1} \quad \text{and} \quad \sin\theta = \frac{y}{1} \quad \text{or}$$

$$\cos\theta = x \quad \text{and} \quad \sin\theta = y$$

That means the coordinates of any point (x,y) on the circle are equal to $(\cos\theta, \sin\theta)$.

* That's assuming your calculator is set to radians. If it's set to degrees, try a more "degree-ish" number, like $\sin(x + 30)$. If you're having trouble seeing the curve when you graph trig functions, you may have to reset the dimensions of your window. On a TI calculator, there's often a "ZTrig" option in the "ZOOM" menu that automatically sets your window to trigonometry-happy settings.

The equation for this circle is $x^2 + y^2 = 1$. If we substitute the trig functions for x and y, we get $(\cos\theta)^2 + (\sin\theta)^2 = 1$. That's the same identity we saw earlier! ***All this stuff is connected!***

This figure shows radian angle measures, though we could also use degrees. But look: the radian measure of an angle is simply equal the length of the arc at that point.

There are lots of ways the unit circle can help you. It's perhaps most useful for finding range of the functions over various domains. That is, which angle values give negative and positive sine and cosine. For example:

- $\cos\theta$ will be negative wherever the x-value of the circle is negative. That's in Quadrant II and III, where $90° < \theta < 270°$ or $\frac{\pi}{2} < \theta < \frac{3\pi}{2}$.
- $\sin\theta$ will be negative wherever the y-value of the circle is negative. That's in Quadrant III and IV, where $180° < \theta < 360°$ or $\pi < \theta < 2\pi$.
- Since $\tan\theta = \frac{\sin\theta}{\cos\theta}$, $\tan\theta$ will be negative wherever cos and sin have different signs. That's in Quadrant II (−cos, +sin) and Quadrant IV (+cos, −sin).

The unit circle also helps emphasize the **periodic** nature of the graphs. On the graphs we saw earlier, the wave repeated the same shape infinitely as angles got bigger. But it wasn't immediately obvious how big the period is—we just have to know that it's 2π. On the unit circle, it's easy to see that sine and cosine have a period of 360° because that's the angle of one trip around the circle. For angles bigger than 360°, the trig values cycle back over themselves: sin 450° gives the value as sin = 90°, because 450 – 360 = 90.

Negative values of θ arise from going **clockwise** instead of counterclockwise: $\theta = -90°$ gives the same value as $\theta = 270°$, because –90 + 360 = 270.

From this we can deduce that $\sin(-\theta) = -\sin(\theta)$ and $\cos(-\theta) = \cos(\theta)$. A negative angle moves below the axis into Quadrant IV. The y-value becomes negative, so the value of sine is negative. But the x value in Quadrant IV is still positive, so cosine remains positive, too.*

You don't have to remember everything about the unit circle for the ACT, but you may encounter some problems that use it. If you just remember that **the points on the circle represent (cos θ, sin θ)**, you should be able to handle anything you see.

* Of course, if you have a negative angle that's less than −90°, it'll go beyond Quadrant IV into Quadrant III or beyond. You can keep rotating around the circle as long as you like.

TRIGONOMETRY EXERCISE

DO YOUR FIGURING HERE.

23. In $\triangle ABC$ given, $\overline{AC}$ is 30 centimeters long. If the tangent of $\angle B$ is $\frac{12}{5}$, what is the length, in centimeters, of $\overline{BC}$?

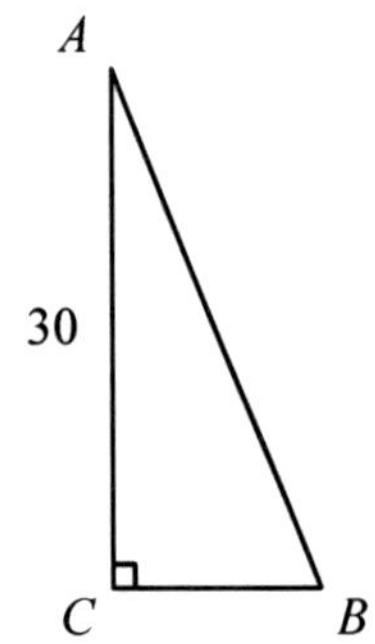

A. 5.0
B. 10.6
C. 12.5
D. 15.0
E. 22.7

30. There are two trees on the same side of Maple Street at points *M* and *N* as shown below. Pooja is standing at point *P*, directly across the street from one of the trees. She determines that $\angle MPN$ is 62° and the street is 78 feet wide. Which of the following expressions can be used to determine the distance in feet between the trees?

F. $78 \tan 62°$
G. $\frac{78}{\cos 62°}$
H. $78 \sin 62°$
J. $\frac{78}{\tan 62°}$
K. $78 \cos 62°$

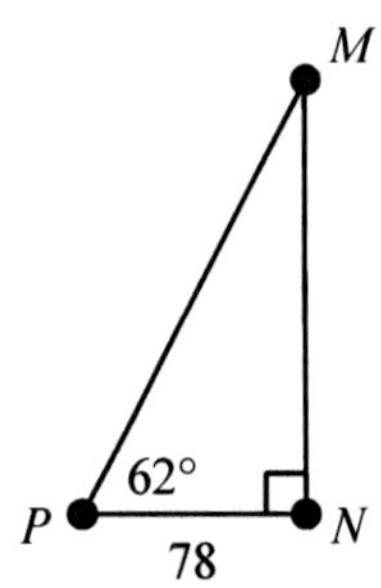

35. For $\triangle TUV$ below, what is $\cos \angle T$?

A. $\frac{7}{11}$
B. $\frac{11}{7}$
C. $\frac{\sqrt{72}}{7}$
D. $\frac{\sqrt{72}}{11}$
E. $\frac{7}{\sqrt{72}}$

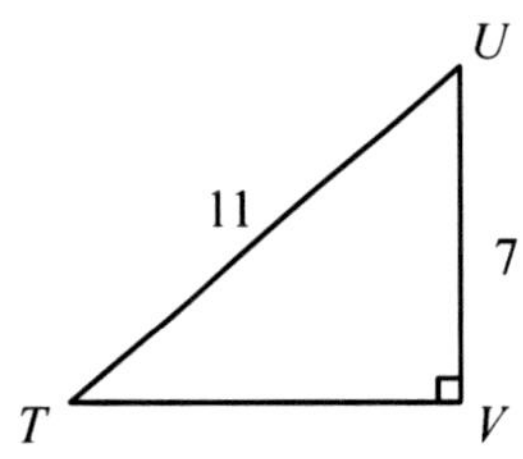

GO ON TO THE NEXT PAGE.

DO YOUR FIGURING HERE.

42. When an 18-foot ladder leans against a building on level ground, it makes an angle of 20° with the outside wall. If the top of the ladder just reaches the roof, which of the following expressions correctly gives the height of the building?

F. $18 \sin 20°$
G. $\dfrac{18}{\sin 20°}$
H. $18 \cos 20°$
J. $\dfrac{18}{\cos 20°}$
K. $18 \cos 70°$

45. In $\triangle ABC$, shown below, angle measures are as marked and the length given is in inches. Which of the following gives the length, in inches, of $\overline{BC}$?

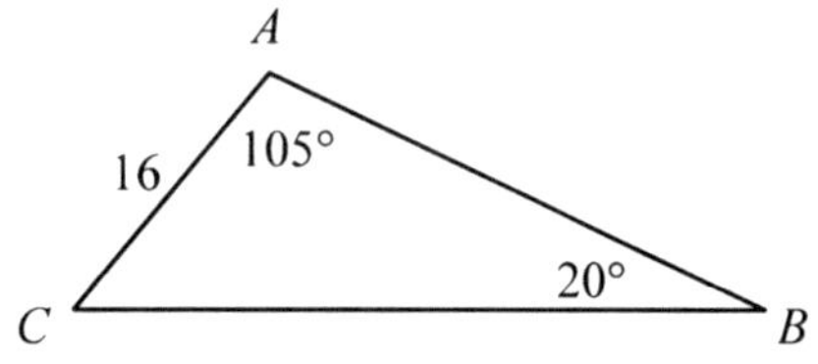

(Note: the *law of sines* states that the ratio between the length of the side opposite any angle and the sine of that angle is equal for all interior angles in the same triangle. Note also that $\sin 20° \approx 0.342$, $\sin 55° \approx 0.819$, and $\sin 105° \approx 0.966$.)

A. 6
B. 12
C. 19
D. 38
E. 45

50. If $0 < x < \dfrac{\pi}{2}$, which of the following expressions is equivalent to $\dfrac{\sqrt{1-\cos^2 x}}{\cos x}$?

F. 1
G. $\tan x$
H. $\tan^2 x$
J. $\tan x \sin x$
K. $\cos x$

GO ON TO THE NEXT PAGE.

DO YOUR FIGURING HERE.

53. If $0 < \theta < 2\pi$, $\tan\theta < 0$, and $\sin\theta = \frac{5}{13}$, then $\cos\theta = ?$

A. $\frac{5}{12}$

B. $\frac{12}{13}$

C. $-\frac{12}{13}$

D. $-\frac{5}{12}$

E. $-\frac{13}{12}$

58. The domain of the function $f(x) = 5\sin(3x) - 2$ is the set of all real numbers. What is the range of the function?

F. $-7 \le f(x) \le 3$
G. $-5 \le f(x) \le 1$
H. $-5 \le f(x) \le 5$
J. $-3 \le f(x) \le 3$
K. $-3 \le f(x) \le 7$

STOP!

ACT Reading

READING

The ACT Reading Test is one of the most hated parts of the ACT. Nobody likes to read. Ugh… so many words… it's not fair! Well, suck it up. We're going to have to do some reading. If the hardest thing you do on this test is read, you'll do fine.

However, the thing about these passages is that they involve *so much* less thought than most people realize. The point of this section is to understand something you just read. Sometimes this is *really easy* and *really dumb*. It's literally a question of whether you read the passage. Not whether you understand it, not whether you know where to find a thesis, not whether you know what a thesis is, not whether you caught the nuances of the author's biting satire on the bourgeoisie—no: *can you read English*? That is all.

Here's your passage:

Passage 1

I like cats.

End of passage.

And here's your question:

---

1. Which of the following statements would the author most likely agree with?

A. The U. S. government must dedicate more time and resources to preserving its native wildlife.
B. Pet ownership has therapeutic effects on people recovering from traumatic events.
C. I like cats.
D. Cats are dangerous creatures that are a threat to modern society.

It's a tough one, I know. Do you need extra time?

Obviously this is a joke, but it's not *that* much of a joke. You'd be astounded by how much of this section can be done with little more than knowing *what* the passage says. Not any fancy interpretations: literally "what does it say?"

I. FORMAT

You will have 35 minutes for the ACT Reading Test, which will consist of 4 passages with 10 questions each, for a total of 40 questions. The passage types are rigorously fixed. There will be one passage on each of these topics: **Prose Fiction, Social Science, Humanities,** and **Natural Science.*** The passages will always appear in that order and their topics will be labeled.

In addition to the main Reading score out of the usual 36 points, students will receive two subscores out of 18 points each:

- Arts/Literature (based on the Prose Fiction and Humanities passages) and
- Social Studies/Sciences (based on the Social Science and Natural Science passages).

All questions will be multiple-choice questions with four possible choices. Unlike the Math Test, the questions will *not* be ordered by difficulty. Unlike the English Test, the questions will *not* be ordered according to the order the information is presented in the passage. **ACT Reading questions will not be in any particular order at all.** The order will be random.

---

* Occasionally, the first passage will be called "Literary Narrative" instead of "Prose Fiction". That happens when the passage is a narrative that sounds like fiction, but is actually nonfictional, like a memoir. This is pretty rare, though.

Timing

So you've got 4 passages with 40 questions to do in 35 minutes. If you remember your math,* you can see that's just 8 minutes and 45 seconds per passage. For most students, **that is not enough time.** So what can you do?

Accuracy is more important than bulk.

On the Math Test we recommended Target Numbers—doing only a certain amount of questions and guessing randomly on the remainder. That way, you have more time to do each question, so you have a better chance of being accurate on the ones you do and you'll get more points in the end.

The same idea holds true on the Reading Test, but there's a catch. On the Math test, it was easy to figure out which questions to skip because they're ordered by difficulty. Reading questions are ordered randomly within a passage, so you won't be able to tell which questions are hard and which are easy.

Rather than focusing on a number of questions to skip, focus on **how much time you spend per passage.** Here are some options for how much time to spend, depending on how fast you can work while still being effective. The target scores shown are the scores you can get if you get most of the questions you do correct and you pick up a few extra points from guessing randomly.†

TARGET TIME PER PASSAGE	TARGET SCORE	NOTES
Under 9 minutes	33 & up	Do all passages and questions. This is really tough to do. Try to finish the whole section on your first practice test or two, just to see how it goes. If you can pull it off, great. If not, try a different target time.
10 minutes	29–32	You'll get through 3 passages and 30 questions in 30 minutes. That leaves 5 minutes for the last passage. **Don't** try to read the remaining passage; you won't have time to read and answer questions. Instead, **do the questions that have line references**. There should be a few questions that mention specific lines—you can jump to those lines and answer the questions without reading the passage. You should have enough time to do about 3 questions and guess randomly on the rest.
11–12 minutes	25–28	You'll get through 3 passages and 30 questions with no time remaining. Guess randomly on the ones you don't get to.
13-14 minutes	22–24	You'll get through almost 3 passages but not quite. You'll do 2 full passages with 8-10 minutes left. That's enough to get half of a third passage. Do questions with line references first.
15 minutes	19–21	You'll get through 2 passages and 20 questions with 5 minutes remaining. Do remaining questions with line references.

* *Do* you remember your math?

† The scores listed here are *approximations*. These are not guarantees; they're goals—the high end of what you *can* achieve if you do the specified number of questions effectively. But remember that every test has a different scoring table, you won't always get 100% of the questions you try, and your success at randomly guessing is pure luck.

The key here is finding an equilibrium between speed and accuracy. You want to do as many questions as you can without being so rushed that you work carelessly. When you first start taking practice tests, don't worry about timing; just try to get through as much as you can. Then, take a look at how well you did and use the results to determine a speed you're comfortable with. It might take a couple of practice tests before you find the right pace.

Time yourself.

Literally. As you practice—either in full-length proctored practice tests or sections you do at home by yourself—get a stopwatch and time yourself. Jot down your start and end time for reading the passage and for doing each question. Figure out how long it takes you to do a full 10-question passage. Once you set your target time from the chart above, you'll need to time yourself to make sure you're on track.

Regardless of exactly how much time you spend on a passage, the ratio of time spent reading to time spent on the questions should be about 40:60. That means if you spend 10 minutes on a passage, you should spend 4 minutes reading and 6 minutes doing the questions. This is a guideline, not a rule; you may find your ideal ratio is slightly different. But again, the point is to find an equilibrium. Spend too much time on the passage and you won't have enough time for the questions. Spend too little time on the passage, and you won't understand it well enough to do the questions effectively.

Do your strongest passage type first.

You don't have to do the passages in the order they're presented. Use your knowledge of passage types to your advantage. Try to figure out if you have a particular strength or weakness on a particular type of passage—not everyone does, but a lot of people do. Say you take a few practice tests and find that you tend to do well on the Natural Science passages and tend to do poorly on Prose Fiction passages. You'll want to make sure that you do the Natural Science passage *first* and save the Prose Fiction for last—otherwise you might run out of time before you get to the problems you're best at.*

Just like all the other sections, there's no penalty for wrong answers on the Reading Test. **Don't ever leave anything blank. Guess randomly** on the questions you didn't answer. You don't even have to read the questions—just fill in bubbles at random. Since there are four choices per question, on average you'll get about one fourth of those guesses right, so you'll pick up a few extra points. The ones you guess wrong are scored the same as a blank, so there's no harm done.

Skip "Black Hole" questions.

As we mentioned, questions do not appear in any particular order. You may have a question about paragraph 5 followed by a question about paragraph 1, then one on paragraph 3. Then there might be some questions that ask about details from *all over* the passage. It can be maddening.

Sometimes you'll encounter a question where you just can't figure out what's going on. The question asks about cats, and you remember it said something about cats, but you look and you look and you just can't find it. Or, even worse, it asks about a detail that you don't remember seeing at all, and you have no idea where to look for it. And it's driving you crazy and freaking you out.

We call these **Black Hole questions**, because they suck up all your time and you cannot escape their pull. Don't get trapped. Don't spend 5 minutes on single question: **skip it**. That one question can mess up your timing for the entire section. You might run out of time and skip questions you'd otherwise be able to do.

When you skip it, you have a few options. Or you could leave it aside and come back to it at the end. Maybe, as you do the other questions in the passage, you'll stumble across the detail you're looking for. If you don't, and you have time at the end of the test, you can come back to it and try again to look for the detail. Or you can just give up on it and guess randomly. (Don't ever, *ever* leave a question blank.) The important thing is to not let one question ruin the whole test.

---

* Don't just rely on your gut when figuring out what topics you're best at—look at actual results, too. It's easy to say "oh, I'm bad at science," but that doesn't mean you should skip the Natural Science passages. Just because you don't *like* a topic doesn't mean you're *bad* at it (and you won't have to actually do science here). That's not to say you should ignore your gut. Use a combination of your personal preference and the results of your practice tests to determine the order you do the passages.

II. Reading the Passage: Main Ideas

Before we get into specifics, here are three "don'ts" to remember when reading the passages:

1. Don't enjoy yourself.

None of the passages will be fun. You will not like them. They will be on subjects you don't care about. They will not be things you will want to read on the beach in your leisure time. Get used to it.

2. Don't know anything.

Just because the passage is about particle physics doesn't mean you have to know anything about particle physics. This is a *reading* test. You're being tested on *what you just read*. Everything you need to answer the questions is *in the passage*, written on the page itself. In fact, it's actually counterproductive to know anything about the topic, because you may be tempted to use your existing knowledge or beliefs to help you answer the question. Don't do that. No one cares what *you* think about the topic. We only care what the *author* thinks about the topic.

3. Don't remember anything.

You don't have to memorize the passage. It's all on the page and it's going to stay on the page. If you can't remember what the author said, *you can go back and check!* It's right there! Don't waste a lot of time trying to memorize all the details of the passage; just get a sense of what it's about and move on to the questions. This brings us to our first strategy: ***Main Ideas***

One of the biggest problems kids have with the passages is that reading them takes a loooong time. Kids try to memorize every point and understand every subtle detail and convoluted sentence in the passage. That's bad. It's a waste of time—it takes forever and it doesn't actually help you.

Instead, read the passage quickly and just get the **Main Ideas**. Every paragraph is nothing more than a collection of sentences that have some common theme. That common theme is the Main Idea of the paragraph. It's the answer to this question:

What's it about?

That's it. For each paragraph, just get a sense of the topic of that paragraph. Paraphrase the idea into a short phrase. It doesn't have to be a quote from the passage or even be a complete sentence. It's a note to yourself about what the paragraph is about.

Here are a few tips on finding Main Ideas:

Skim the details.

Don't worry about all the piddly little details. We don't care about *every* idea, just the *Main* Idea. All those details are confusing and unnecessary.

The goal here is to **spend less time reading the passage** so that you can spend more time on the questions, since the questions are the things that actually matter. Therefore, when you read the passage, you just want to get a sense of what it's about. We'll worry about the details later.

You may be asking yourself, "But wait, don't I need those details?" Surprisingly, no. For two reasons:

1. The questions might never ask you about the details.

Why would you spend five minutes trying to understand a sentence *that they never ask you about!* That's five minutes you wasted and won't get back. Yes, you'll need *some* of the details to answer the questions. But *every* passage has *huge* chunks of information that never show up in the questions. And when you're reading the passage, you don't know which details are important and which ones aren't.

2. If a question *does* ask you about details, you can go back and check.

This is an open-book test. If a question asks you about a detail, *go back to the passage and see what it says!* Even if a detail *is* important to a question, you don't have to worry about it while you're reading the passage. Worry about it when they ask you about it, not before.

If the question gives you a specific line reference, going back to look up details is a piece of cake. The problem is that questions don't always tell you where to go in the passage, so it can sometimes be difficult to find the detail you need. But that's another advantage of writing down your Main Ideas: it makes it easier to narrow down the location of a detail. When a question asks you about cats, you can glance at your main ideas to find the paragraph that mentions cats.

Not all questions are about specific details; some are about entire paragraphs or the passage as a whole. But if that's the case, *you can use your Main Idea to answer the question.*

Skip hard sentences.

Passages will *often* contain difficult writing. Sentences can be long, intricate, or convoluted. They may use subtle or confusing metaphors. The vocabulary can be difficult. With Main Ideas, if you encounter a sentence you don't immediately understand, **skip it**. You don't need to understand every single sentence to understand the paragraph. If the details of that sentence are important, you can deal with them if and when a question asks you about them.

Check the first and last sentence.

The difficulty of finding the Main Idea for a paragraph can vary depending on the particular passage. Sometimes it's really obvious, sometimes not so much. If you're having trouble finding the Main Idea, **check the first and last sentence of the paragraph**. They're often the introduction and the conclusion to the topic, so they can help you find the theme of the paragraph.

<u>This is a guideline, not a rule</u>. The Main Idea is *often* in the first and last sentence, but not always. If the main idea *isn't* there, but that's all you've read, you'll be confused, you'll have to backtrack, and it'll be a mess. So you should read the whole paragraph. But if you're having trouble finding the Main Idea, the first and last sentences are a good place to look for it.

Underline key words and phrases.

When you get to the questions, you're often going to have to do a bit of searching to find where to find certain information in the passage. So it's a good idea to underline key words and phrases as you read: that includes names, dates, numbers, italicized text, or anything that seems like an important concept.

Let us be clear: we're only talking about underlining words, not full sentences. **Underlining is not a replacement for writing down Main Ideas**. If you try to underline as a way to find Main Ideas, you'll wind up underlining every other sentence, and it will be much, much harder to find things quickly when you need them. You must write Main Ideas in the margins.

Look for transitional language.

By "transitional language" we mean all the words that connect clauses and sentences to each other, words like *but*, *however*, *furthermore*, etc. Words like this signal a shift in the topic, which can often affect the overall point of the sentence or paragraph.

For example, here is the first beginning of a paragraph:

- **David, you have been a wonderful boyfriend for several years now. You have been kind and caring towards me, and you're always a lot of fun to be with.**

Aww, thanks honey! I love you, too. It's nice to know I'm apprecia—oh, I'm sorry, you weren't finished?

- David, you have been a wonderful boyfriend for several years now. You have been kind and caring towards me, and you're always a lot of fun to be with. **However,**

Uh oh…

- David, you have been a wonderful boyfriend for several years now. You have been kind and caring towards me, and you're always a lot of fun to be with. **However, I've met someone else and we're going to have to break up.**

Now, if you were to ask David what the Main Idea of this paragraph was, which part of it do you think he's going to focus on? Would he say this is my girlfriend talking about how great I am? Or would he say this is what she said when she dumped me? That "however" was a big warning sign that the paragraph was about to be transformed into a whole new set of ideas. So if you see transitional words like this, **circle them**. They can be important clues about the author's ultimate point.

Don't spend too much time on this.

Remember that the point of this is to *spend less time reading the passage.* Don't spend a lot of time trying to get your Main Ideas absolutely perfect. Don't struggle with the precise wording or try to capture all the nuances of the paragraph. This is supposed to be quick and dirty.

- You Main Ideas should be short. Don't even use complete sentences. Something like "author likes cats" or "cats are cute and smart" or "dogs = not as good".
- If a paragraph is so confusing that you can't figure out the Main Idea at all, just skip it. Move on. You can even make your Main Idea some sort of vague placeholder ("something about cats?").
- If single paragraph has several different ideas in it, you can split up the paragraph and give two Main Ideas. Maybe the first half of the paragraph is about one thing and the second half is about something else. That's fine.
- If it's a fiction passage that has long stretches of dialogue, each line of speech will technically be its own paragraph. Here, you can split the dialogue arbitrarily to assign Main Ideas. In the first 10 lines they're arguing about where to eat; in the second 10 lines they're trying to find the restaurant; etc.

Main Idea Drill

Read the following passage and write the Main Idea for each paragraph in the space on the right. Be sure to also write down the time you start and stop reading so you can see how long it takes you to get through the passage.

START TIME: 00:00

HUMANITIES

When three of Philip K. Dick's science fiction novels were inducted into the Library of America, a series devoted to "to publishing, and keeping in print, authoritative editions of America's best and most significant writing," many were stunned. To his fans, Dick is a master of tackling grand philosophical questions about what is real and what makes us human. They treasure his insight and inventiveness. But his critics argue that his prose is clunky, his plots convoluted and his characters flat. One review accused Dick of having "three, at most four, characters." An overview of his career in *Newsweek* noted that, "reading his prose can feel like being assaulted with a blunt instrument." Even Dick's greatest admirers admit that much of his work is deeply flawed and, in the words of the novelist Jonathan Lethem, "howlingly bad".

MAIN IDEA: Novels were inducted into the Library of America.

Dick's literary reputation cannot be separated from his legendarily tragic and bizarre life. In large part, the weaknesses Dick's novels suffer from are a reflection of the intense financial pressures he was under as he wrote them. Throughout his life he lived in extreme poverty and was forced to churn out cheap pulp paperbacks at a fantastic rate. In total, he wrote 51 books, some in as little as two weeks, along with countless short stories. Dick clearly didn't have the luxury of slowly mulling over each sentence or making time-consuming revisions to his work. His words had to fly onto the page.

MAIN IDEA: Can't be seperated from tragic + bizarre life
flew word onto page

Dick's frenzied life, which included massive drug abuse, five marriages, and long bouts of insanity, has also clearly shaped the way both Dick's boosters and his opponents view his stories and novels. The delusions that overwhelmed the author mid-life—that CIA agents were spying on him and aliens were controlling his mind—sound like they belong in one of his novels, and, indeed, his final works were directly inspired by these visions. To some, Dick's apparent insanity adds to his fascination; to others they prove him a crackpot.

MAIN IDEA: his Insanity adds facination (drugs)

However, the factor that shapes Philip K. Dick's reputation today more than any other is probably the genre he chose to write in. Science fiction has traditionally been kept out of classrooms and excluded from the lists of "classics". Readers of science fiction were viewed as immature and nerdish, and science fiction was classified with children's adventure stories and romance novels as literary junk food.

MAIN IDEA: Science fiction genre

GO ON TO THE NEXT PAGE.

For this reason, Dick's contemporaries whose work included science fiction elements were careful to keep themselves out of the science fiction ghetto. The novelist Kurt Vonnegut frequently wrote about space aliens, time travel and outlandish technologies, but his work was sold not as science fiction but as "literature with science-fiction elements". Today, Vonnegut's *Slaughterhouse-Five,* which describes a character who has "come unstuck from time" and creatures from the planet Tralfamadore, is seen as one of the great works of American literature. One wonders if Dick's best works would have won recognition sooner had his publishers used the "literature with science-fiction elements" label that Vonnegut adopted.

MAIN IDEA:

Science fiction elements kept out

literature with science fiction elements

Due to these circumstances, Dick's meditations on the nature of reality and human consciousness found relatively few interested listeners and no place in the mainstream literary establishment during his lifetime. But today, advances in technology make us increasingly sensitive to his themes. What observer of the advance of computer technology hasn't wondered when the machines will outsmart us? (If that hasn't already happened.) And as we live more and more of our lives online, we are all bound to ask ourselves: how can we tell the difference between the artificial and the real?

MAIN IDEA:

reality + human consiousness few interests

artifical – real

Many have tackled these questions, but few have done so with the energy and sincerity of Philip K. Dick. "This kind of speculation," Charles McGrath writes, "takes on genuine interest in Mr. Dick's writing because he means it and because he invests the outcome with longing. His characters … desperately want something authentic to believe in, and the books suggest that the quality of belief may be more important than the degree of authenticity."

MAIN IDEA:

degree of authenticity

Dick himself may have had mixed feeling about his recent surge in popularity. Clearly, he was hungry for respect and a wider audience during his lifetime. But in many ways Dick's writings have been overshadowed by the movies based on them, including *Blade Runner*, *Total Recall* and *Minority Report*. Initially he was highly critical of the script for *Blade Runner* and fought the studio over it. He died in 1982 just before the film's release, but he was ultimately pleased with the footage he had seen, saying that it perfectly captured the mood of the book.

MAIN IDEA:

mixed feelings of recent surg in popularity

Fans of Dick's works hope that the movies will help his books find their ways into the hands of readers, and that those works will be judged not by the author's life or the genre he chose to write in, but by the words between the covers. Others feel it does not matter whether people are exposed to him through film or print. The medium is not as important as his universal message about humanity. As he wrote in 1978, analyzing his own work: "I don't write beautifully—I just write reports about our condition."

MAIN IDEA:

Movies will make them bigger

END TIME:

6:25

III. ANSWERING THE QUESTIONS

There's often more than one way to do a reading question. Sometimes it's easier to get the answer directly from the passage, sometimes it's easier to eliminate from the answer choices, and sometimes you'll want to do both. Here we'll outline a number of different strategies for tackling all types of passage questions.

1. Go Back to the @#&*%$! Passage!!

We told you not to worry about the details when reading the passage. Now that you're actually asked about the details, you can worry about them. Luckily, you don't have to rely on what you remember about the passage. *This is an open-book test. You can look it up.*

> Remember: the questions on the ACT Reading Test ARE NOT IN ANY PARTICULAR ORDER. They are not in order of difficulty, and they do not correspond to the order of the information in the passage.

Some questions will give specific line references. Those are easy. Once you read the question, before you do anything else, **go back to the passage and check the line reference**. If they ask you a question about line 35, go back to line 35 and see what it says, *before you even look at the choices*.

Don't just read the literal line mentioned in the question: **read the whole sentence that includes that line.** Most sentences stretch over a couple of lines, and you'll need the full sentence to understand the context.

Keep in mind that even if the question gives you a line reference, it might not tell you *exactly* where the answer is; it might just point you to the ballpark. If you don't find the answer in the line you're given, **check one sentence before or after the line reference** to get a fuller context.

Word search

The biggest problem with ACT Reading questions is that you don't always know where to go to find the information you need. **Only about 40% of the questions will tell you where to go in the passage.** About a quarter give specific line references. Another 15% give broader references (such as "in the fifth paragraph"). The rest of the time, you have to find the information in the passage yourself.*

First of all, this makes writing down your Main Ideas doubly important. Now that we wrote down our Main Ideas for the Philip K. Dick passage, it's easy to find which paragraph talked about which topics.

Second, as we said before, when you read through the passage, underline key words and phrases like names, dates, and numbers. Names in particular are important, as it's very likely that any person mentioned in the passage will come up later in the questions.

Finally, when you do have to go back for information, **don't read the whole passage over again**. Before you go to the passage, look in the question for a **key word or phrase** to search for. Then *scan* the passage looking for that word. It's not reading—it's like a word search or an Easter egg hunt. Think of that key word more like a picture than a word, and scan the text looking for that picture.

* Whether or not a question has a line reference strongly correlates with the question type. You're much more likely to get a line reference in a Meaning question (95% have references) or a Strategy question (80% have references) than an Explicit question (20%) or a Generalization question (15%). We'll talk more about these types soon.

Word Search Drill

Look in the previous passage for the following words and phrases. Either circle them in the passage or write the line numbers of their locations in the passage in the spaces below. Some may appear more than once. ***Work quickly.***

- ***Total Recall:*** 83
- **Charles McGrath:** 71
- **Kurt Vonnegut:** 48
- **CIA agents:** 31
- **financial pressures:** 19
- **Jonathan Lethem:** 15
- **literary junk food:** 44
- **cheap pulp paperbacks:** 21
- ***Newsweek*:** 11
- **meditations on the nature of reality and human consciousness:** 59

2. Anticipate

Okay, you found the information in the passage. Now what? Now you can see what those lines say about the question. Try to answer the question yourself before looking at the choices. We call that your **anticipation**—you're *anticipating* what the answer is going to be. Then look at the choices and see which one most closely matches your anticipation. Remember: **all the information you need to answer the question is in the passage**. That's why we look in the passage, not in the choices, for our answers.

When you go back, think about what the lines say and what they mean. Try to **paraphrase** the lines in your own words. Sometimes the right answer will be a direct quote from the passage—it's awesome when that happens—but sometimes it won't. Your anticipation should give you the *meaning* you're looking for. The right answer will have the same meaning as your anticipation, but may be worded differently.

Let's look at a sample question about the previous passage:

1. **According to the passage, how did Dick feel about the movie *Blade Runner*?**

   A. He thought it brilliantly tackled grand philosophical questions.
   B. He was unhappy with the script at first but liked the footage he saw from it.
   C. He was upset that it wasn't as popular as the book on which it was based.
   D. He did not think it was as well done as other film adaptations of his work.

First, we'll ignore the answer choices and just focus on the question:

1. **According to the passage, how did Dick feel about the movie *Blade Runner*?**

Now we have to find where in the passage it discusses the movie *Blade Runner*. Can you find it? It might help to notice that the title is *italicized*; look for italicized words in the passage. You can also check your Main Ideas—which paragraph talked about movies?

There it is: the first mention is in line 82 in the eighth paragraph. Let's start there and keep reading to the next sentence. We'll reproduce that part of the passage here:

> *Initially he was highly critical of the script for* Blade Runner *and fought the studio over it. He died in 1982 just before the film's release, but he was ultimately pleased with the footage he had seen, saying that it perfectly captured the mood of the book.*

Okay! So how did he feel about the movie? ***Initially* he didn't like the script, but *ultimately* he liked the footage he saw**. That's our anticipation.

Is there a choice that says something like that? Yes! That's almost exactly what it says in **choice B!**

B. He was unhappy with the script at first but liked the footage he saw from it.

Perfect. Let's try another:

2. **The passage gives all of the following as reasons that critics dislike Dick's books EXCEPT the books':**

   F. complicated plots.
   G. awkward prose.
   H. predictable endings.
   J. poor characterization.

We'll start the same way we did before. First, we'll ignore the answer choices and just focus on the question:

2. **The passage gives all of the following as reasons that critics dislike Dick's books EXCEPT the books':**

This question has a twist: now *three* of the choices are mentioned in the passage, and we want the one that *isn't* mentioned. So we'll go back to the passage and look for any reasons that critics dislike Dick's books. As soon as we find one, we'll look for it in the choices and cross it off.

First we need to find the relevant place in the passage. Our key word here is **critics**; where does the passage talk about **critics**? Several places mention some kind of criticism, but most of it is in the first paragraph. Indeed, we can see the word "critics" in line 8. Let's take a look:

> *But his critics argue that his prose is clunky* **[that's choice G]**, *his plots convoluted* **[that's choice F]** *and his characters flat* **[that's choice J]**. *One review accused Dick of having "three, at most four, characters".* **[that's also choice J]**

Great! We eliminated all three choices from the same sentence![*] Our answer is **choice H**: the passage doesn't mention the books' endings at all.

Use your Main Ideas

Sometimes a question will ask you about a whole paragraph, or a large chunk of text that includes several sentences. In that case, we can use the Main Ideas themselves as our anticipations. For example:

3. **The main idea of the fourth paragraph (lines 37-44) is that:**

   A. Dick's writings were never good enough to be considered classics.
   B. schools should not be encouraging children to read romance novels.
   C. adventure stories are more popular with children than with adults.
   D. Dick wrote in a genre that was not well respected.

Here, the question is asking about the entire sixth paragraph. Ugh. We still want to anticipate, but that's a lot of text to go back, read, and paraphrase. If only we had a summary of this paragraph…

Wait, we do! We already got the **Main Idea** of each paragraph. We can just use our Main Idea as our anticipation.

Your Main Idea for paragraph 6 may have differed from ours, but it should be something like "**sci-fi viewed as immature**" or "**sci-fi not taught in school**". Let's look at our choices and see what fits:

A. × Dick's writings ~~were never good enough~~ to be considered classics.
This paragraph doesn't say Dick wasn't a good writer.

B. × schools ~~should not~~ be encouraging children to read ~~romance novels~~.
The paragraph says what schools *do*, not whether they *should do*. Also, while it does mention romance novels, the main focus of the paragraph is science fiction.

---

[*] This question turned out to move pretty quickly. However, questions like this have the potential to be very time consuming if the relevant pieces of information are scattered in different parts of the passage. If you see an "EXCEPT" question, see if you can find the information quickly. But if you can't and if timing is an issue for you, you might consider skipping it and moving on to the next question.

C. **× adventure stories are more ~~popular with children~~ than with ~~adults~~.**
The paragraph never says what's popular with children and never mentions adults.

D. **✓ Dick wrote in a genre that was not well respected.**
Perfect! The paragraph says that he wrote science fiction and that science fiction was not respected. **Choice D** is our answer.

Notice that we can pinpoint very specific reasons why each of the wrong answers is wrong. When you find something in an answer choice that makes the choice obviously wrong, you should **literally cross those words out**. This may seem silly, but just like circling the question on math problems, the act of writing on a choice can help you focus your thoughts and be more certain of your elimination.

No matter what, once we read the question we'll go back to the passage to see what it says. But what we do when we get there depends on the question.

- If the question asks about a **single line or sentence**, we'll read the line and get an **anticipation**.
- If it doesn't give you a line reference at all, **search for key words** to try to get an anticipation.
- If the question asks about a **paragraph or chunk of text**, we'll use our **main idea** as our anticipation.

But sometimes passages are hard to understand. What if we can't figure out what the passage says? That's were the third strategy comes in…

3. Eliminate Nonsense

When you anticipate successfully, you can jump right to the correct answer. But it's not always that easy. Sometimes when you go back to the passage, you can't get an anticipation. Maybe you don't understand what the line says. Maybe you understand the line, but you don't understand what it has to do with the question. Maybe you do anticipate, but none of the choices match your anticipation.

That's okay. There's still *a lot* we can do even if we don't understand what the passage says. All reading passages are loaded with nonsense choices—choices that are obviously wrong. If we can **eliminate the nonsense** and guess from what's left, we can greatly increase our odds of getting the question. If we can get each tough question down to two choices, we'll get half of them right.

There are three main ways that a choice can be wrong:

1. **Random** The choice talks about things that the passage doesn't even mention. You'd be *astounded* to learn how often this happens. (In question 1 above, all three wrong choices were random.)
2. **False** The choice is explicitly contradicted by the passage.
3. **Irrelevant** The choice is something the author *says*, but it doesn't actually *answer the question.*

Here are some tips to keep in mind:

- As before, you should **literally cross out** the words that make a choice wrong. This will greatly help you keep track of what you're doing.
- You're not looking for the right choice, **you're looking for wrong choices**. On every question, three out of four choices are wrong. If you think a choice is wrong, there's a 75% chance you're right.
- Again, the key here is to **work quickly**. Don't spend too much time agonizing over every choice. If you're not sure whether a choice fits, or if you can't find a specific reason to eliminate it, leave it in for now. Go through the choices, get rid of the ones that are *obviously* wrong, and see what you have left.
- Once you get down to two or three choices, you can go back to the passage again to see which is better. If you really can't decide which is better, **guess one**.

Let's look at an example:

4. The passage states that Dick's financial pressures:

- **~~F. drove him~~ to get his books adapted into movies.**
- **~~G. forced him~~ to write slowly and carefully.**
- **H. caused his marital trouble and mental instability.**
- **J. contributed to his writing style.**

We'll start just like we did before. First, we'll ignore the answer choices and just focus on the question:

4. The passage states that Dick's financial pressures:

Now we have to find where in the passage it discusses his financial pressures. Well, if you've done the Word Search drill above, you've already found the words "financial pressures" in line 19. You also might have mentioned financial pressures in your Main Idea for paragraph 2. Go back to line 19 and see what it says. Read the whole sentence, not just the lines mentioned. We'll reproduce that sentence here:

> *In large part, the weaknesses Dick's novels suffer from are a reflection of the intense financial pressures he was under as he wrote them.*

What does this sentence say about his financial troubles? Hmm. That's a bit of a complicated sentence, and it may be tough to come up with an anticipation here. Let's do this one by *Eliminating Nonsense* instead.

F. × ~~drove~~ him to get his books ~~adapted into movies~~.
<u>*Random!*</u> The passage does not say that he actively tried to get his books adapted into movies. It does mention movies *six paragraphs later*, but it doesn't say anything about his financial troubles there.

G. × forced him to ~~write slowly and carefully~~.
<u>*False!*</u> That's the opposite of what he did. It says he "was forced to churn out cheap pulp paperbacks *at a fantastic rate*."

H. × ~~caused~~ his marital trouble and mental instability.
<u>*Irrelevant!*</u> It does say that he had marital trouble and mental instability in the next paragraph, but it doesn't connect those problems to his financial problems. We cannot assume that the one caused the other if the passage doesn't say so.

J. ✓ contributed to his writing style.
<u>*Bingo!*</u> The line we quoted above connects his financial problems to the "howlingly bad" prose that the first paragraph mentioned. His financial problems forced him to churn out books quickly, which meant that he couldn't take time to edit or think about sentences, which made the quality of his writing suffer.

Even if we don't understand why choice J is right, we can still easily see that the other three choices are all wrong. Beautiful.

Let's try another one:

5. As used in line 71, the phrase "This kind of speculation" most nearly refers to:

- **~~A.~~ questions about the nature of reality.**
- **B. the accurate predictions of the future in Dick's books.**
- **C. intense energy and sincerity of the characters.**
- **~~D. Dick~~'s reliance on advanced computer technology.**

Ahh, finally! A line reference! Okay, let's go to line 71 and see what it says:

> *"This kind of speculation," Charles McGrath writes, "takes on genuine interest in Mr. Dick's writing because he means it and because he invests the outcome with longing.*

Hmm. Not sure what's going on here. We can see that this guy McGrath is talking about Dick's writing. It seems like he's probably saying good things, but it's not entirely clear. Let's just look at the choices.

A. **questions about the nature of reality.**
Not sure what this means. Let's skip it.

B. **× the ~~accurate predictions~~ of the future in Dick's books.**
<u>*Random!*</u> The passage never claims that Dick's books predict the future.

C. **intense energy and sincerity of the characters.**
Not sure what this means. Let's skip it.

D. **× Dick's ~~reliance on~~ advanced ~~computer technology~~.**
<u>*Random!*</u> Did Dick use computer technology at all? The passage doesn't say that. For all we know he used a typewriter.*

We eliminated B and D so we're down to A and C. What do we do? Leave it blank? Panic? Cry?

No! **Guess one!** If you're down to two and you can't figure out which is better, just pick one and move on. If you do this on every hard question, you'll get half of them right. If you guessed choice C… nice try, but that's not it. The correct answer is **choice A.**

Let's take a closer look at what's going on here. Our original quote from line 71 was this:

> *"**This kind of speculation,**" Charles McGrath writes, "takes on genuine interest in Mr. Dick's writing because he means it and because he invests the outcome with longing.*

Look at the phrase "**this** kind of speculation"—the word "this" must be referring to something mentioned earlier. So let's go **one sentence earlier**, starting at line 69:

> ***Many have tackled these questions**, but few have done so with the energy and sincerity of Philip K. Dick.*

Aha! "This kind of speculation" must be referring to the act of **tackling these questions**. The mention of "questions" should already be drawing us to choice A. But look: "*these* questions" must also be referring to something earlier in the text. Was there a question before this line? Let's go back again, starting at line 67:

> *…how can we tell the difference between the artificial and the real?*

Bingo! That's **choice A, questions about the nature of reality.** In fact, the entire sixth paragraph is about "Dick's meditations on the nature of reality and human consciousness" (lines 58-59).

Notice that choice C may be tempting because it does sound like something mentioned in the above quote. But "speculation" means "thought or meditation"; "energy and sincerity" aren't a "kind of speculation".

This was a tough question, and you may still have some trouble understanding why A is right. But that's not the point. The point here is that it's easy to see why the other choices are wrong. **Even on hard questions, there are a lot of choices that you can easily eliminate.** If you narrow every hard question down to two choices, the odds are in your favor—you can get half of them right just by guessing.

Whether you do a question by anticipating or eliminating nonsense is entirely up to you. If you understand the lines in the passage perfectly, then you'll be able to jump to the correct answer. But if you didn't understand the lines, or if there isn't a choice that matches you first anticipation, *you can still get the question right*. Just eliminate aggressively and you'll make progress.

And remember: if you can't eliminate *all* the wrong choices, **guess from what's left.** The key is to **eliminate choices quickly**. If you're not sure whether a choice works, just skip it and check the next one. If you're having trouble, try to get it down to two choices and see which one is better. Go through the choices in several waves: first get rid of the choices that are obviously wrong, then go back to what's left and look for nuances.

* Which is pretty likely, considering he died in 1982.

Working together

Almost every question on the Reading Test can be done with some combination of Anticipation and Elimination, but the exact ratio is flexible. You'll often do both: you'll anticipate easily, no choices perfectly match your anticipation, so you'll eliminate the ones that are obviously wrong.

The point is that both these strategies are working together for you. On any given question, the more you use one, the less you'll use the other. If one fails, look to the other. They complement each other into a harmonious unity of test-taking peace and perfection.

IV. QUESTION TYPES

Knowing the common types of questions can help you learn how to approach the test more efficiently, both in the way you answer the questions and in the way you read the passage. However, it's important to understand that these types are just a guideline and these categories overlap. It's not always obvious whether a particular question is an Explicit Question or a Meaning Question or a Strategy Question or what have you. Don't worry about it. These are just suggestions to help you recognize patterns and see that future tests are going to resemble past tests. Don't waste time trying to categorize.

Let's take a closer look at the different types of questions you'll see with the passages.

1. Explicit Questions

These are the questions that ask you **what the passage literally says**. Go back, anticipate the answer, then match your anticipation to the choices.

It's important to see that every answer you put to explicit questions must be grounded in the passage. Don't pick a choice unless you can show us *exactly* where in the passage it says that. Don't just say, "Well, somewhere in the middle the author kinda says something about how cats are good." Say, "*Look*: in line 23 he says QUOTE 'I like cats.'"

> Explicit Questions are the most common question type on the ACT: over a third of all reading questions are explicit. They appear throughout the test, but they are somewhat more common on Social Studies/Sciences passages than Arts & Literature passages.

The bad news is that explicit questions rarely have line references—fewer than 1 in 5 do. But the good news is that once you *do* find the reference, the right answer often matches the wording of the passage very closely. That means that once you do find the information in the passage, you're almost home free.

Most of the questions we've already seen were explicit questions:

1. According to the passage, how did Dick feel about the movie *Blade Runner*?

   A. He thought it brilliantly tackled grand philosophical questions.
   B. He was unhappy with the script at first but liked the footage he saw from it.
   C. He was upset that it wasn't as popular as the book on which it was based.
   D. He did not think it was as well done as other adaptations of his work.

2. The passage gives all of the following as reasons that critics dislike Dick's books EXCEPT the books':

   F. complicated plots.
   G. awkward prose.
   H. predictable endings.
   J. poor characterization.

4. The passage states that Dick's financial pressures:

   F. drove him to get his books adapted into movies.
   G. forced him to write slowly and carefully.
   H. caused his marital trouble and mental instability.
   J. contributed to his writing style.

These questions varied in difficulty, but all focused on what the passage literally said.

2. Inferential Questions

Rather than asking about what's literally in the passage, these will ask you to make conclusions and inferences based on the information in the passage.

It may sound like Inferential Questions are harder than Explicit Questions, but that's not always the case. Inferential Questions can sometimes be quite easy. Sometimes a question will *technically* require an inference—the passage doesn't *literally* say the correct answer—but the information stated in the passage is so close to the correct choice that it's virtually explicit.

> Inferential Questions are the second most common question type, making up about a fifth of the questions.

6. It can reasonably be inferred from the passage that one reason Vonnegut was more widely accepted than Dick was that Vonnegut:

F. was a much better writer than Dick was.
G. did not have financial or mental problems.
H. was less preoccupied with film adaptations of his work.
J. had a publisher who marketed his books effectively.

We can treat this just like we did the previous questions. First, the key word here is **Vonnegut**. Vonnegut was discussed in the fifth paragraph (lines 45-58). There are many clues in that paragraph hinting at what we want. Let's paraphrase the sentences in that paragraph:

- Lines 45–47: Other writers distanced themselves from science fiction.
- Lines 48–51: Vonnegut wrote science fiction but his work was sold as "literature with science-fiction elements."
- Lines 51–54: Vonnegut's book is accepted as great literature.
- Lines 55–57: Dick might have had better recognition if his publishers also sold his work as "literature with science-fiction elements".

All these things lead us to **choice J:** Vonnegut's publisher marketed his books as literature, not as science fiction. The passage never quite comes out and *says* that Vonnegut was more accepted *because* his work was sold as "literature". But it's strongly implied based on the way the paragraph strings its statements together.

The wrong answers here are also things that the passage doesn't literally say. The difference is that the passage gives us *no reason to believe* any of them are true.

F. × was a ~~much better writer~~ than Dick was.
This *might* be true—much of the passage talks about how bad a writer Dick was. But it doesn't say that Vonnegut was any better. It doesn't say anything about Vonnegut's writing style. For all we know, Vonnegut had all the same issues that Dick did (but with better marketing).

G. × did not have ~~financial or mental problems~~.
The passage says nothing about Vonnegut's personal life.

H. × was less ~~preoccupied with film adaptations~~ of his work.
The passage says nothing about whether or not Vonnegut was involved in film adaptations. It also never says that Dick was "preoccupied with" film adaptations, just that adaptations were made.

J. ✓ had a publisher who marketed his books effectively.
Bam. "Marketing" just means the way that a book is sold to an audience. It's not science fiction; it's "literature with science fiction elements".

TRY ONE:

7. **It can be inferred that the group of people mentioned in line 88 believe that Dick's works are:**

   A. **best appreciated after watching the film adaptations.**
   → B. **more rewarding than the circumstances around them might suggest.**
   C. **more beautiful that Dick believes them to be.**
   D. **concerned about the pace of technological development.**

3. Main Idea Questions

Main Idea Questions ask you for the main idea of a paragraph, a group of paragraphs, or the entire passage. These questions might also ask you for the "function", "theme", "conflict" or "purpose" of a paragraph. They will usually give a specific reference to which paragraph or paragraphs they are asking about.

We've already seen an example of one:

3. The main idea of the fourth paragraph (lines 37-44) is that:

   A. Dick's writings were never good enough to be considered classics.
   B. schools should not be encouraging children to read romance novels.
   C. adventure stories are more popular with children than with adults.
   D. Dick wrote in a genre that was not well respected.

This is another reason why it's important to write your main ideas down—there's a good chance a question will literally ask you about them.

4. Generalization Questions

Generalization Questions ask you to make a short generalization about a large amount of information in the passage. These questions may use phrases like "*is characterized by*" or "*is best described as*".

Generalization Questions are similar to Main Idea questions in that they ask about large chucks of the passage. But they don't necessarily point to specific paragraphs or sections of the passage. Rather they're about themes and ideas that run throughout. Therefore, the answer to these questions may not be in a single place, and the questions rarely give line references. Generalization Questions may also ask about the tone, opinions, beliefs, actions, or attitudes of any character in the passage.

> Generalization Questions make up about 12% of the questions overall. They are more common on Arts & Literature passages than Social Studies/Sciences passages.

Let's look at one:

8. **Based on the passage as a whole, the author would most likely characterize Dick's writing as:**

   F. **flawed yet insightful.**
   G. **unsophisticated and worthless.**
   H. **pessimistic yet pragmatic.**
   J. **poetic and restrained.**

Here we can see that the question asks about the author's general opinion of Dick's writing. There are clues about that throughout the passage. We can use our Main Ideas to help us, too. What sort of things does the author say about Dick's writing?

Generalization Questions will sometimes ask you about the *tone* of a passage, that is, the emotional character of the text. How does the author or narrator *feel* about a particular subject, and what feeling is conveyed in the language? It's the difference between saying "Cats are popular" and "I adore cats!"

> Some passages are **informative**, giving you facts of a situation, while others are **persuasive**, arguing for a particular position or opinion.

Tone questions are somewhat infrequent, but they can often throw you for a loop. To help you determine the tone of a passage, we here at A-List have spent millions of dollars in research using the most advanced computer analytic technology to develop the ***A-List Passage Tone Scale*™.**

☺	😐	☹

Let's take a minute to explain this complicated terminology:

☺ means the author **likes** the subject. This could mean he's arguing *in favor of* something, that he's saying someone is a good person, or just telling a happy anecdote.

☹ means the author **does not like** the subject. This could mean he's arguing *against* something, that he's giving a warning about something, or that he's telling a sad or angry anecdote.

😐 means the author **does not have an opinion** about the subject. This means the author is *just presenting the facts* without saying if they're good or bad. Think of this author as a *historian* or a *scientist*. Imagine that he has little glasses and a pipe.*

We can use this scale for question 8 above. How does the author *feel* about Dick's writing? Where on the scale does this passage fall?

This passage will fall somewhere in the middle. The passage mostly *reports* on other people's opinions about him. It certainly says a lot of bad things about him—about his writing in paragraph 1 and his personal life in paragraphs 2 and 3. But it says some good things about him too, especially in paragraphs 6, 7, and 9.

So his tone should be somewhere around 😐. Each choice has two words, so we'll rate both of them:

F.	**flawed yet insightful.**	☹/☺	✓ Some good, some bad, it averages to 😐.
G.	unsophisticated and worthless.	☹/☹	× Too much bad .
H.	pessimistic yet pragmatic.	☹/😐	× Needs some good.
J.	poetic and restrained.	☺/😐	× Too much good. Needs some bad.

The Tone Scale is a useful tool but it won't work on all generalization questions. It is an oversimplification, and some questions will require a deeper and more specific understanding of the passage. But because generalization questions don't refer to specific places in the passage, it can be really tough to know where to find your answer. Anything you can do to narrow down your choices will be to your benefit.

* Despite our vast technology budget, it's very difficult to draw a little pipe. You'll have to use your imagination.

5. Meaning Questions

Meaning Questions, as the name implies, ask you the meaning of a full line or sentence in the passage. It may be the literal meaning of the sentence in the context of a larger argument. Or it may ask for the figurative or metaphorical meaning of the sentence.

> Meaning questions almost always give a line reference, so you'll know exactly where to look.

Meaning Questions are similar to Explicit Questions, but they require an additional level of interpretations. Explicit Questions ask "what does the author say?" or "when the author says X, what does X *refer* to?" Meaning Questions, however, ask "when the author says X, what does he *mean* by X?" This may require an inference, it may require knowledge of the main idea, or it may just require that you look in the line above or below.

9. The sentence "His words had to fly onto the page" (line 26) most nearly means that:

- **A. he had to write quickly and carelessly.**
- **B. his stories involved fantastic themes.**
- **C. he expected his books would become movies.**
- **D. his mental instability caused hallucinations.**

Whenever you see a question like this, make sure you **go back and check the context.** The sentence in question might seem to mean one thing by itself but actually mean something else in the context of the paragraph. So let's go back.

This line comes at the end of paragraph 2. We already talked about this paragraph back on question 4 when we talked about Dick's financial pressures. Let's look at the sentence just before this one.

> *Dick clearly* ***didn't*** *have the luxury of* ***slowly*** *mulling over each sentence or making* ***time-consuming*** *revisions to his work.*

He couldn't work slowly; therefore he **had to work fast**. That's **choice A.** If this line isn't clear enough for you, look at lines 20–22:

> *Throughout his life he lived in extreme poverty and was forced to churn out cheap pulp paperbacks* ***at a fantastic rate****.*

Vocab-in-Context Questions are a sub-category of Meaning Questions. They work exactly the same way but ask about a single word. For example:

10. As used in line 43, the word *classified* most nearly means:

- **F. encoded.**
- **G. categorized.**
- **H. exalted.**
- **J. promoted.**

Again, it's *doubly* important to go back and anticipate. Don't just go by what you think the word means; go back and look at what it means *in the context of the sentence.* Let's go back, starting at the beginning of the sentence in line 41:

> *Readers of science fiction were viewed as immature and nerdish, and science fiction was* ***classified*** *with children's adventure stories and romance novels as literary junk food.*

Can you anticipate the meaning of the word in the blank? We want to say it was **grouped** with adventure stories and romance novels. **Choice G, categorized**, matches nicely.

Note that in other contexts, the word "classified" can mean something like choice F, encoded, when it means "secret". Like when the CIA has classified files about spies and weapons systems. *But that has nothing to do with the context of this sentence.* That's why it's important to actually go back and check the passage.

6. Strategy Questions

Strategy Questions ask you about the author's intentions or techniques. These questions could ask about the literal structure of the passage, its organization, the author's motivation for presenting information in a certain way, or why the author uses a particular rhetorical strategy. Any "meta" question—a question that asks about the *form* of the passage instead of its *content*—can be classified as a Strategy Question. That is, why does the author or narrator write what he writes?

Strategy Questions are the least frequent major question type, occurring only about 5% of the time. Here's an example.*

11. Which of the following best describes how the fifth paragraph functions in relation to the fourth paragraph?

A. It gives historical background for the events described in the fourth paragraph.
B. It provides an exception to the phenomenon described in the fourth paragraph.
C. It attacks those who hold the beliefs presented in the fourth paragraph.
D. It moves to a new topic and is only indirectly related to the fourth paragraph.

Let's start, as we often do, with our Main Ideas. By now we've already discussed the fourth and fifth paragraphs a few times, so they should be somewhat familiar.

- Paragraph 4 said that Dick's reputation suffered because science fiction is not considered serious literature.
- Paragraph 5 said that Kurt Vonnegut wrote science fiction but his work is considered serious literature.

The paragraphs are saying **opposite things**, to some extent. Okay, let's look at our choices.

A. × It gives historical background for the events described in the fourth paragraph.
There's no historical background here. Paragraph 5 says we're talking about "Dick's contemporaries"—that means people who lived at the same time as him.

B. ✓ It provides an exception to the phenomenon described in the fourth paragraph.
Bingo! The fourth said sci-fi authors aren't legit. But the fifth gives an example of a sci-fi author who is legit. That, my friends, is an exception.

C. × It attacks those who hold the beliefs presented in the fourth paragraph.
Too strong. There is a contrast between the paragraphs, but no one is being attacked here.

D. × It moves to a new topic and is only indirectly related to the fourth paragraph.
No, no, no. The paragraphs are clearly both about science fiction and literary acceptance.

* Yes, we realize this is the eleventh question and ACT passages only have 10 questions. We threw in an extra question—*AT NO ADDITIONAL COST!*—just because we like you.

READING PASSAGE FLOW CHART

The Passage

- Read quickly and get the **Main Ideas** of the passage, paragraph by paragraph.
- To find the main idea, just ask yourself: **what's it about?**
- If you're not sure what the main idea is, check the **first and last sentences** of the paragraph.
- Don't spend too much time. Don't overanalyze. If you're not sure, move on.

The Question

- Read the question, **ignore the choices.**
- *Does the question have a line reference?*
  - Yes: Go back to that line reference.
  - No: Look for **key words** from the question to find the information in the passage. Use your **Main Ideas** to help find the information.
- *Can you answer the question with what you just learned?*
  - Yes: That's your **anticipation**. Go to the choices.
  - No: Read the **sentence before** and/or the **sentence after** to understand the context.
- *Now can you answer the question?*
  - Yes: That's your **anticipation**. Go to the choices.
  - No: Go to **elimination**.

The Choices

Anticipation

- *How many choices match your anticipation?*
  - None: Your anticipation wasn't good enough. Go back to the passage and try again, or go to elimination.
  - One: **That's your answer! Pick it!**
  - Two:
    - **Eliminate** the ones that fail.
    - Ask yourself: what's the difference between the choices?
    - Go back and check the line again to see which is better.
    - If you can't decide, **guess one**.
  - Three or four: Go to Elimination.

Elimination

- Go through the choices looking for wrong answers.
  - Don't look for the right answer, **look for the wrong answers**.
  - **Work quickly**. If you can't eliminate a choice, skip it and come back to it later.
  - As you eliminate, **cross out** the words that make a choice wrong.
- Eliminate for three reasons:
  1. Is the choice *mentioned* in the passage? If not, it's **random**.
  2. Is the choice *true* according to the passage? If not, it's **false**.
  3. Does the choice *answer the question*? If not, it's **irrelevant**.
- After you eliminate, how many choices do you have left?
  - None: Run through them again. Don't eliminate choices you don't understand.
  - One: **That's your answer! Pick it!**
  - Two or three:
    - **Eliminate** the ones that fail.
    - Ask yourself: what's the difference between the choices?
    - Go back and check the line again to see which is better.
    - If you can't decide, **guess one**.
  - Four:
    - You didn't eliminate enough. Run through them again and look more closely.
    - If you really can't eliminate anything else, move on to the next question.

READING EXERCISE

35 Minutes—40 Questions

DIRECTIONS: There are four passages in this test. Each passage is followed by several questions. After reading a passage, choose the best answer to each question and fill in the corresponding oval on your answer document. You may refer to the passages as often as necessary.

Passage I

PROSE FICTION: This passage is adapted from the short story "The Guitar Lesson" by Nicholas DiMichele.

When I was a teenager in Texas, I took guitar lessons from a man named Bobby Crawford. Bobby was a middle-aged, mild-mannered acoustic rock star with a good ear and a fast hand. Despite (or perhaps because of) his outward appearance as a charming Southern bluesman, Bobby had mysterious qualities that became more pronounced the longer I knew him. He was like the murky pond in my backyard: familiar, tranquil, and unknowable. Every Tuesday evening after school I would cautiously travel to Bobby's little guitar shack on the outskirts of town to learn his secrets.

He began by showing me finger-picking patterns: various orders and rhythms for plucking the strings to produce the guitar's more dulcet tones. He would often refer to artists I had never heard of; his look of disappointment at my confusion always quickly turned into enthusiasm for their techniques. I slowly learned patterns of the rock, blues, and folk canon at a stuttering pace to match my scattered and distinctly adolescent lifestyle.

I never knew what I truly wanted to get out of these lessons. I was always excited to be exposed to something new, but my appetite for developing an artistic skill was not as great I thought it was. I would learn what I could while I was there and then respectfully, but neglectfully, tuck the tougher material away in my notebook for later. Week after week, I would come back, eager for something new without having mastered the techniques from the previous lessons. And Bobby knew it. The glimmer in his eye would fade when I demonstrated my "progress". I would put on a little dance about how I was stuck on some particular aspect of the technique. He responded with difficulty, trying to walk a thin line between encouragement and admonishment.

Instead of actually practicing more, I went about showing my dedication in other ways. I always showed up on time. I bought a new, expensive guitar from his shop. I always put on my best listening face so he would see I was a good student. I kept all his handouts so organized and pristine, so obviously valued. But I did not practice.

Bobby was not fooled. One day, he cut me loose. He broke it to me simply and without much fanfare, cloaked in his usual unreadable disposition. "I don't have anything more to teach you," he said.

"Of course you do!" I protested. "I still can't do any of the things you can! If you don't teach me, how will I learn?"

"You've got all the materials now," he said. "You'll make do."

Just like that. I felt like a flood victim: the marbled, far-off stare picturing a home that had been washed away suddenly in the night. I had not expected someone in the arts to willfully dismiss a source of income. I had not expected a teacher to give up on a student, especially a student like me. I was so dutiful, so willing, so *nice*! And yet there I sat, rejected. Somehow, I was a failure.

I comforted myself with the notion that he was simply unprepared to go further. I tried to convince myself that I was too special for him, and I had to go my own way. Perhaps he didn't know how to teach a student as *skilled* as I was. I had put him to shame. Perhaps I had out-gunned my teacher in great, fiery bursts of natural talent. I was not a failure—I was a monumental success!

Years later, in college, I began teaching guitar myself. Searching for material to give to my students, I stumbled across the old notebook I had used with Bobby. I photocopied all the pages and distributed them as my own. I started teaching my students all those beautiful picking patterns I had learned years before.

As I taught the old lessons to the new students, something peculiar started to happen. The students would take Bobby's lessons, only to have completely forgotten them by the next week. They wanted the next lesson right away, regardless of whether they had mastered the previous subject. Flustered, I gave out the next page and then the next. Within several weeks I was totally depleted of all course material, and the students showed less and less progress. I offered to help the students perfect the many techniques which had gone flying through their brains without sticking. They were not interested. They could always practice them at home, later. I was devalued, so they abandoned me.

I never saw a single student execute the maneuvers I had taught them, yet they all thought they had finished. I then realized that Bobby was wise for having cut me off. Had I studied further with him the way I was going, I would have grown dissatisfied, too. What I thought he was hiding from me was not his to give. He knew he couldn't just give it to me on a sheet of paper. I had to learn the guitar for myself, just as he had. Learning art is the process of developing patience.

1. The passage is written from the point of view of:

A. a teenager preparing to enter college.
B. an adult reminiscing about two different experiences from his youth.
C. an aging musician lamenting the events that prevented him from becoming successful.
D. a college student recalling a tragic event that occurred when he was a young child.

2. When the narrator says Bobby was "trying to walk a thin line between encouragement and admonishment" (lines 32–33), he most nearly means that Bobby:

F. was giving the narrator contradictory advice.
G. tried to correct the narrator without disheartening him.
H. wanted to praise the narrator's progress while maintaining his stern demeanor.
J. became frustrated with the narrator's disrespectful behavior.

3. The narrator was flustered by his students because they:

A. were much more skilled than he was.
B. did not understand the lessons he gave them.
C. thought Bobby was a better teacher than the narrator.
D. went through lessons more quickly than he had expected.

4. Bobby can most accurately be characterized as:

F. judgmental and cruel.
G. forgetful and lazy.
H. charming yet mysterious.
J. naïve yet pretentious.

5. Lines 70-82 most strongly suggest that the narrator's students:

A. did not sufficiently practice between sessions.
B. did not fully appreciate the importance of Bobby's handouts.
C. were too focused on unrealistic dreams of being famous musicians.
D. became technically proficient on the guitar but did not achieve emotional expressiveness.

6. As it is used in line 7, the word *pronounced* most nearly means:

F. ominous.
G. spoken.
H. noticeable.
J. affected.

7. According to the passage, as the narrator had more and more sessions with Bobby:

A. his technique grew more refined.
B. his skills did not improve.
C. he grew bored with Bobby's anecdotes.
D. his abilities surpassed Bobby's.

8. Which of the following best describes the narrator's reaction to being rejected by Bobby?

F. Delight combined with hopefulness
G. Anger mixed with fear of the future
H. Shock followed by reassurance
J. Devastation caused by shame

9. The narrator does all of the following to show his dedication to Bobby EXCEPT:

A. buying a new guitar.
B. keeping his handouts in good condition.
C. putting on an attentive appearance.
D. studying the work of artists Bobby mentioned.

10. Which of the following best describes the ideas expressed in lines 57-63?

F. They explain why the narrator was more successful in teaching his own students than Bobby was with him.
G. They are thoughts that consoled the narrator but that he no longer believes to be true.
H. They are the reason that the narrator decided to start teaching other students.
J. They demonstrate why the narrator never became a successful guitarist.

Passage II

SOCIAL SCIENCE: This passage was adapted from the article "Are All Calories Created Equal?" by Rebecca Erenrich.

Obesity has been a growing problem in the United States for decades. Historically, obesity rates have been fairly stable, but starting around 1980, rates began to skyrocket, doubling from 15% to 30% in the period from 1980 to 2005. Obesity is hardly just an aesthetic problem; it has been linked to a number of serious illnesses, such as heart disease, diabetes, and even cancer. Everyone agrees this is a national problem, yet no one quite knows how to solve it.

For years nutritionists have argued that a low-fat diet is the key to weight management. The USDA developed a "food pyramid", a nutrition guide recommending a diet consisting primarily of grains and vegetables, and light on fats and proteins. The many food products offering "healthy" low-fat or fat-free alternatives are a testament to the success of the anti-fat campaign. Yet the period in which the low-fat fad has taken off coincides exactly with the period in which obesity rates have sharply increased.

For this reason, some scientists think we're looking in the wrong place. In his book, *Good Calories, Bad Calories*, science journalist Gary Taubes argues that it's not fat that's making us fat; it's carbohydrates, a class of foods including sugars, like sucrose and fructose, and starches, like bread and pasta. This idea is hardly revolutionary: the carbohydrate-restricting Atkins diet has been popular since the 1970s, and theories about the hazards of starches have existed since the nineteenth century. But if the carbohydrate theory is correct, it could mean that the USDA recommendation of a grain-heavy diet is the source of the very obesity crisis it intended to thwart.

Taubes argues that the reason carbohydrates are uniquely pernicious is insulin. Insulin is a hormone that regulates the level of sugar in your blood, either delivering it to cells to be turned into energy or storing excess sugar in fat cells. Consuming excess carbohydrates, be they actual sugars or starches which are broken down into sugars when they pass through the intestines, will increase the blood-sugar level, which in turn stimulates higher insulin production, which in turn makes fat accumulate. Hence Taubes calls sugars and starches the "primary nutritional evil". He believes that the rise in obesity rates has been caused by increased carbohydrate consumption, and one can lose weight by switching to a diet low in carbohydrates and high in proteins and fats.

This all might sound like a persuasive theory, but the majority of the scientific community does not accept this picture. The evidence simply has not substantiated the thesis that carbohydrates are uniquely fattening. This lack of evidence is not due to lack of research on the subject. There have been literally hundreds of studies comparing various diets, including diets that restrict carbohydrate consumption, as well as several meta-analyses—studies that combine and compare the results of multiple studies. The consensus of this research is that there is no correlation between restricting carbohydrates and weight loss, nor is there any evidence of a correlation between elevated insulin levels and weight gain.

That doesn't mean it's impossible to lose weight on a low-carbohydrate diet. On the contrary, many people have successfully lost weight on the Atkins diet. Low-carbohydrate diets might be effective, but not for the reasons that Taubes and his colleagues claim. The research suggests that a diet high in fats and low in starches can result in weight loss because people who force themselves to eat less carbohydrate-rich food consume less food overall. They remove a whole class of food from their menus without replacing it with anything else. In other words, these diets work not because they reduce consumption of the supposedly hazardous starches and sugars, but because they reduce the total consumption of calories, period.

The current scientific consensus instead blames weight gain primarily on consuming too many calories. Food is our fuel, and calories are a measure of the energy it contains. Things go haywire when we take in more energy than we spend. Overeating creates an energy surplus, which is stored in the form of fat deposits. In this model, weight gain or loss depends purely on caloric intake and expenditure. Sugars and fats should both be avoided because they are calorie dense and nutrient poor. But it doesn't matter if you consume 500 calories of protein or 500 calories of sugar: a calorie is a calorie. Stanford endocrinologist Gerald Reaven concludes: "One can lose weight on a low-calorie diet if it is primarily composed of fat calories or carbohydrate calories or protein calories. It makes no difference!"

11. Which of the following most closely summarizes the viewpoint of Gary Taubes?

A. Obesity is a national problem that has no obvious solution.
B. One can lose weight by switching to a diet with fewer total calories of any type of food.
C. Consumption of carbohydrates is a significant cause of weight gain.
D. The best diet is one that is heavy on grains and light on fats.

12. The passage states that, according to the current scientific consensus, sugars should be avoided because:

F. they are calorie dense and nutrient poor.
G. they increase insulin production.
H. they are uniquely worse than proteins and fats.
J. they are the chief ingredient in bread and pasta.

13. According to Taubes, which of the following most directly causes weight gain?

A. Increased insulin production
B. Excess fat consumption
C. Decreased blood-sugar levels
D. Insufficient carbohydrate consumption

14. It can be reasonably be inferred from the passage that Reaven would agree that a low-carbohydrate diet:

F. will decrease the level of insulin in the blood.
G. is unlikely to result in weight loss in any way.
H. would be effective only if balanced with increased consumption of fat and protein.
J. can be effective if it also restricts total calorie consumption.

15. According to the passage, which of the following does the food pyramid recommend as a primary component of one's diet?

A. Fats
B. Sugars
C. Proteins
D. Grains

16. It can be inferred from the second paragraph that:

F. the USDA recommendations do not place enough emphasis on proteins.
G. the widespread promotion of low-fat diets has not quelled the rise in obesity rates.
H. the rise in obesity can be directly attributed to the increased consumption of carbohydrates.
J. most people do not choose to buy healthy low-fat alternatives to fattening foods.

17. In the context of the passage, the author's statement "This idea is hardly revolutionary" (line 25–26) most nearly means that the carbohydrate theory:

A. is rejected by a majority of scientists.
B. has been held by people in the past.
C. has had a significant effect on the obesity rate.
D. is irrelevant to the popular Atkins diet.

18. Which of the following statements best describes how the fifth paragraph (lines 46–58) functions in relation to the rest of the passage?

F. It gives a possible solution to the problem presented in the first paragraph.
G. It gives additional support for the argument presented in the fourth paragraph.
H. It identifies potential problems with a view presented earlier in the passage.
J. It gives historical background to introduce the issue presented in the second half of the passage.

19. The author characterizes obesity as an issue that:

A. was once a major problem but has become fairly stable in the past few decades.
B. most scientists believe is caused by excess carbohydrate consumption.
C. is recognized as a major problem that has not yet been solved.
D. has not been conclusively linked to any major health problems.

20. Lines 59–72 suggest that an alternate explanation for the success of the Atkins diet is that:

F. decreased carbohydrate consumption causes increased blood-sugar levels.
G. the Atkins diet also recommends an increase in exercise and physical activity.
H. restricting carbohydrates may cause a decrease in overall caloric consumption.
J. the obesity crisis is not as severe as scientists previously suspected.

Passage III

HUMANITIES: This passage was adapted from the essay "Who Owns a Dance?" by Julia Lindpaintner.

Choreographers, like all artists, have the right to protect their work from being unlawfully reproduced. The creation of intellectual property is the basis upon which artists or inventors may demand financial remuneration for the use of their material by others. In the United States, where originality and entrepreneurship are prized above all, intellectual property law has been such a hallmark that copyright protection is addressed in the U.S. Constitution. Copyright protection is the simple idea that an artist or inventor owns the artwork or idea that he or she devised, and other people cannot use or reproduce it without permission. Copyright protection is important in the arts because without the right to control the distribution of a work, it is difficult for authors to reap the financial rewards of creativity, which may act as a disincentive for future creative endeavors.

But in spite of the good intentions and value placed on protection of the arts, dance has remained largely uncharted territory in intellectual property. The passage of the 1976 Copyright Act was a notable event in the dance community, as it marked the official inclusion of choreographic works to the subject matter of copyright. Before 1976, dancers and choreographers who were integral to American art and popular culture such as Gene Kelly, Martha Graham, and Madonna had no legal means of protecting their choreographies from being stolen or of charging money for their use. Yet despite this protection, modern media have made copyright infringement easier. A search on YouTube returns over 7,000 videos of people performing the dance from Beyoncé's "Single Ladies" music video, but few if any of them acknowledge her choreographers, Frank Gatson and JaQuel Knight, let alone Bob Fosse's original 1969 routine on which it is based.

The problem with copyrighting choreography is that a dance performance is ephemeral. The 1976 Copyright Act requires a work to be "fixed in any tangible medium" in order to be protected; this means that no live performance is copyrightable, but the basis of the performance is. For example, though the production of any given play may vary immensely based on scene design, costume design, and directorial vision, the script for a play is protected under copyright law. The work of a choreographer is similar to that of a playwright, but the playwright has a tangible script, while a dance routine is nearly impossible to document. While video revolutionized dance by permitting the capture of movement for the first time, dance is still largely preserved and transmitted through age-old oral traditions. Older generations of dancers teach the younger generations, who are expected to pass on their knowledge to the next.

Most attempts to document dance in writing have failed. Some notation forms exist, most notably a system called "Labanotation" created by Rudolf Laban, but these forms are too intricate to be generally accessible. A choreographer dictates not just the motion of body parts and the pattern of bodies moving together, but also the quality of these movements, just as a composer labels a sequence of notes as *mezzo piano* or *staccato*. A notation system must capture this, but the qualitative directions in dance are far more complex than those of music. Think, for instance, about how different the simple movement of one arm could be when petting a cat versus throwing a baseball. Now imagine the utter mess of lines and symbols involved in notating a jump series in which the choreographer demands precise, quick footwork accompanied by slow, undulating arms. Even if it could be notated, who would be able to read it and recreate that dance in the absence of the choreographer or a firsthand account? It is for this reason that dance notations such as Labanotation exist only in elitist academic circles, serving more as status symbols for their users than as practical tools for preserving choreography.

Perhaps innovations in other realms will aid dancers and choreographers in better documentation of their work. The development of 3-D video technology, for example, has powerful potential for documenting dance in a new way. Wim Wenders used this technology in a recent film about the work of German choreographer Pina Bausch. The dancers of MOMIX have collaborated with scientists to track movements electronically, creating digital dance scores. These new avenues will undoubtedly advance the abilities of choreographers to preserve their work, and raise awareness for the importance of its preservation. Though the subtleties of choreography may never be fully transmittable without human contact, a continued effort to document and protect dance is essential to fostering the development of dance in the United States.

21. The main idea of the third paragraph is that:
    - **A.** copyrighting choreography is difficult because it is difficult to document.
    - **B.** oral traditions in dance have contributed to the richness of the medium.
    - **C.** the 1976 Copyright Act made it harder for dancers to protect their work.
    - **D.** dance performances do not require as much preparation as theatrical performances.

22. The author compares choreographers to all of the following EXCEPT:

F. playwrights.
G. actors.
H. composers.
J. inventors.

23. Which of the following is NOT given in the passage as a reason that copyright protection is important?

A. It gives artists control over reuse and reproduction of their works.
B. It helps artists receive financial remuneration for use of their works.
C. It encourages future creative endeavors.
D. It protects artists against expensive lawsuits and legal battles.

24. It can reasonably be inferred that the author believes Labanotation:

F. is widely used as an effective tool for preserving choreography.
G. uses complex symbols to denote qualitative distinctions in pieces of music.
H. is useful in helping choreographers secure intellectual property rights for their works.
J. is often learned for reasons other than documentation of choreography.

25. The author characterizes intellectual property protection for choreographers as:

A. gratifying but ultimately unnecessary.
B. vital but historically neglected.
C. less important than it is for other artists.
D. well-meaning but ultimately futile.

26. As it is used in line 60, the word *qualitative* most nearly means:

F. methodical.
G. transcribed.
H. instinctive.
J. stylistic.

27. The author states that the 1976 Copyright Act was significant because it:

A. extended copyright protection to choreographic works.
B. inadvertently caused copyright infringement to become easier.
C. provided a means for putting choreographic works into a tangible medium.
D. helped otherwise obscure choreographers to expose their works to a large audience.

28. The function of the first paragraph with respect to the rest of the passage is to:

F. present an argument the author will later attempt to refute.
G. provide a general introduction to the topic to explain its importance.
H. give statistics to support the author's main thesis.
J. describe a situation that is only tangentially related to the rest of the passage.

29. It can be inferred from lines 64–70 that, for some choreographies, Labanotation:

A. would help express the emotional character of the work.
B. can concisely convey complex gestures in a few strokes.
C. would become too unwieldy to be of practical use.
D. is not detailed enough to capture their intricacies.

30. The fifth paragraph (lines 74–89) suggests that new technological innovation:

F. will ultimately make oral traditions obsolete.
G. can improve documentation but will never replace written systems like Labanotation.
H. allow choreographers to convey a greater range of emotional expression in their dances.
J. may facilitate securing intellectual property protection for choreographers.

Passage IV

NATURAL SCIENCE: This passage was adapted from the article "Apes and Speech" by St. John McKay.

The ability to use language is perhaps the one characteristic that most distinguishes humans from the rest of the animal kingdom. The cognitive scientist and linguist Noam Chomsky has argued that language is an innate and distinctly human skill, standing against the views of behaviorists like B. F. Skinner who believe that language is an acquired behavior that can theoretically be taught even to animals. But some believe that one group of animals has already demonstrated this capacity: apes.

Scientists have been studying the potential for language among primates for decades, with mixed results. While apes lack the necessary oral and laryngeal mechanisms to be able to speak the way humans do, there have been several famous attempts to teach sign language to apes, including gorillas, orangutans, and a chimpanzee playfully named "Nim Chimpsky". But the apes' "sign language" was hardly that. The apes would merely make random gestures until they found one that overzealous researchers would interpret as a word, thus rewarding them with a treat. Nim Chimpsky's own trainer, Herbert Terrace, said that the animal was simply "going through a bag of tricks in order to get things."

Recent work by primatologist Susan Savage-Rumbaugh is more promising. Her research has focused on bonobos, a kind of ape from central Africa most closely related to chimpanzees. Aware of flaws in earlier studies with chimpanzees, she has gone to great lengths to ensure the accuracy of her results. For example, the bonobos communicate via keyboards with symbols representing words to prevent trainers from interpreting gestures more meaningfully than they were intended. After years of study, she firmly believes that bonobos' communicative behavior does constitute language.

Her star pupil is a bonobo named Kanzi, who has been documented displaying communicative abilities far more impressive than any seen in previous studies. Perhaps most remarkable is his seeming ability to produce novel assertions, rather than just repeating things learned previously. In one instance, Kanzi, without being prompted, pushed the buttons on his keyboard for "marshmallow" and "fire". She gave him matches and marshmallows, and he started a fire with some twigs and cooked the marshmallows. Similarly, he has been documented correctly interpreting original statements from trainers. On one occasion, a trainer asked him "Can you make the dog bite the snake?" Despite never having heard that question before, Kanzi promptly took his toy snake and put it in the mouth of his toy dog.

While Kanzi might be seen as an outlier, Savage-Rumbaugh reports that bonobos use similarly sophisticated communication on their own in the wild. She found that, when traveling in the forest, they would leave markers in the form of broken leaves at the crossroads of two paths showing where they had gone. "What they are doing is leaving little notes in the vegetation. Those notes are signals about where they are going to go."

There is no doubt that apes have been shown to communicate in some ways, both with humans and among themselves. But does this count as *language*? Chomsky says no. He believes that human language is a specific neurological phenomenon that animals are simply incapable of producing. Humans acquire language effortlessly simply by being exposed to it as children. If apes really have the capacity for language, he asks, why haven't they used it themselves, instead of waiting for humans to teach it to them? Teaching apes to use language as humans do is akin to teaching humans to fly as birds do.

The argument also revolves around how one defines "language". Linguist Geoffrey Pullum believes that there is much more to language than what Kanzi does. There is a difference between indicating an emotional state, like hunger or fear, and communicating propositionally, one of the defining characteristics of language. Pullum notes that no ape has ever been shown to "state opinions, or ask what your opinions are, or comment in even the most trivial way on what it's like to be an ape.... If a bonobo or any other ape would even just say, 'How are you feeling today?', I would sit up and take notice."

Chomsky further argues that the subject itself is not worthy of debate. Even if apes could perfectly mimic human behavior, it would add nothing of value to our understanding of apes or humans. But Savage-Rumbaugh believes the bonobos force us to question our conception of ourselves, of what is innate and what is learned. "Many people think the animal world is hard wired and there's something special about man," she said. "As we look at culture, we come to understand how we got to where we are. And I don't think it's in our biology."

31. The passage states that bonobos are most closely related to:

A. humans.
B. gorillas.
C. chimpanzees.
D. orangutans.

32. Chomsky's attitude to the debate about ape language can best be described as:

F. optimistic.
G. amused.
H. infuriated.
J. dismissive.

33. Chomsky's views most closely agree with those of:

A. Pullum.
B. Savage-Rumbaugh.
C. Kanzi.
D. Skinner.

34. In line 55, the phrase "little notes" refers to:

F. broken leaves.
G. hand-written messages.
H. physical gestures.
J. symbols representing words.

35. The author italicizes the word *language* in line 59 most likely to:

A. question the significance of the discovery of apes using sign language.
B. underscore the certainty that Terrace felt in the results of his experiments.
C. deride Chomsky's vacillation on the question of ape language.
D. emphasize a distinction between different types of communication.

36. As used in line 38, the phrase *novel assertions* most nearly means:

F. original statements.
G. new arguments.
H. inventive discoveries.
J. spoken instructions.

37. According to the passage, Savage-Rumbaugh thinks the question of ape language is an important one because it:

A. can raise awareness about the apes' threatened habitats.
B. raises questions about the innate capacities of humans.
C. will vindicate Terrace's earlier work of chimpanzees.
D. proves the existence of a genetic connection between humans and apes.

38. It can be inferred from the second paragraph (lines 10–22) that the scientists chose sign language to teach to apes because sign language:

F. is little more than a series of random gestures.
G. is easier to understand than spoken languages.
H. does not require the ability to speak.
J. is cheaper than using keyboards and other devices.

39. The main idea of the passage is that:

A. language is an innate and distinctly human skill.
B. bonobos and other apes have been shown to use human language.
C. debate exists about whether apes can use human language.
D. human biology has not been the primary factor behind human culture.

40. It can reasonably be inferred that Savage-Rumbaugh believes bonobos in the wild:

F. show no evidence of human comprehension.
G. possess a rudimentary capacity for language.
H. have been trained to make original utterances.
J. lack sophisticated communication seen in captive bonobos.

ACT Science

SCIENCE

The Science Test on the ACT is a unique experience. For many students, science is already an intimidating subject, and the wide scope of concepts that might appear on the ACT can make it quite scary. Furthermore, the entire format will be new for students who are transitioning from the SAT to the ACT, as the SAT has no counterpart similar to ACT Science. But once you get to know it a bit better, the Science Test won't seem nearly so frightening. Soon, you and Science will grow to understand each other, respect each other, perhaps even love each other.

FORMAT

The Science Test is composed of 40 questions in 35 minutes. It has no subscores, so you will only get a single score, from 1 to 36.

The test is divided into 7 passages. Each passage will focus on concepts taken from one of four major fields of science taught in high school: Biology, Chemistry, Earth Science, and Physics. There will be at least one and no more than two passages from each field.*

The passages will be made up of collections of data, results of experiments, or sets of hypotheses, and the questions will ask you to identify, analyze, or draw conclusions from that data. Usually a passage will be accompanied by some set of tables, graphs, or other figures. Each passage will be one of three types: Data Representation, Research Summaries, or Conflicting Viewpoints. These passages may appear in any order, but the number of questions and passages will always be the same:

PASSAGE TYPE	NUMBER OF PASSAGES	QUESTIONS PER PASSAGE	TOTAL QUESTIONS
Data Representation	3	5	15
Research Summaries	3	6	18
Conflicting Viewpoints	1	7	7

- ***Data Representation:*** These will present either a single set of data or several sets of data referring to the same situation or set of facts. Questions about these passages are often fairly straightforward and simply require you to read and interpret the information presented.
- ***Research Summary:*** These will present a series of different experiments which share a common topic of investigation. In addition to questions about the data, you will find questions asking about the design of the experiment and how a hypothesis is tested, confirmed, or refuted.
- ***Conflicting Viewpoints:*** This passage will present a single set of circumstances and give several competing hypotheses that attempt to explain those circumstances. Questions will ask you to understand the hypotheses, both on their own and in relation to each other.

* Of course, the sciences all overlap, so it may not be obvious which subject a given passage belongs to. For example, say you have a passage about the atomic structure of enzymes: does that count as biology? Chemistry? Physics? Nobody cares. You won't be asked to categorize the passages. Just know that they will be on a variety of topics.

I. General Strategies

Science Facts

Students often associate the Science Test with the Math Test. After all, math and science are best friends, right? They go together. There's English & reading, then there's math & science, right?

But in terms of the way you do questions, the ACT Science Test is vastly different from the Math Test. Sure, you'll see *numbers* here. The tables and graphs will be covered with numbers. But you won't have to *do math* very much. Calculators are neither allowed nor necessary on the Science Test. There will be no algebra, no arithmetic, no geometry. You won't have to solve equations for x or cross-multiply ratios or find the length of the third side of a triangle. While you might occasionally have to do some light addition or multiplication, usually the most you'll have to do with all these numbers is to judge *relative quantity.* Questions such as:

- Can you find a point on a graph?
- Given two numbers, which one is bigger?
- Given a list of numbers, do the values go up or down?
- Which answer choice is between two numbers?

In fact, the Science Test is a lot more like the *Reading Test.* Like reading passages, science passages will present some information and ask questions about the information presented. And like on the Reading Test, questions can be answered simply by **going back to the passage** and looking up the information you need.*

Furthermore, questions on the Science Test *will tell you where to go.* Most questions will specifically mention which figure, table, or experiment contains the information you have to find. And even those that don't will have clues that can help you find the answer.

That brings us to the big secret: For the grand majority of questions on the Science Test, ***YOU DO NOT NEED TO KNOW SCIENCE.*** Very few questions expect you to know facts about science other than what's actually presented in the passage. And even these questions don't require a nuanced, sophisticated understanding of a concept; usually you don't need to know much beyond the definition of a word. Questions that require outside knowledge generally make up 5–10% of all questions. That means **90–95% of the questions can be done *purely* based on the information on the page.**†

In fact, you often don't even have to understand the passage itself! Because so many of the questions simply ask you to look up values in a table or graph, you don't have to understand what those values mean. You just have to **match** a weird word in the question to the same weird word in the figure.

> To demonstrate the fact that actual scientific truth is irrelevant to your ability to do the problems, the science in this chapter's practice problems is mostly made up. Don't be alarmed if you see words you've never seen before.

Why is that? Why would they give me a science test that doesn't require me to know science? Well, there's too much science in the world to be able to test it all in one 35-minute section. If you've ever taken a science AP test or SAT Subject test, you know how many concepts are involved. And those tests each cover just one topic—the ACT Science Test covers four: biology, chemistry, physics, and earth science.

Instead, the ACT tests *scientific thinking.* You don't have to know specific concepts, but you have to know how to read the results of an experiment. You have to be able to tell whether the data supports a particular hypothesis. You have to understand why an experiment was set up in this way, not that way.

---

* They're even called the same thing: *passages!*

† Examination of recent tests seems to suggest that questions requiring some outside knowledge have been getting more common. There used to be around 2 such questions per test, but since 2009 or so it has been more like 4 or 5 questions per test. (The overall average of all tests we've studied remains around 6–7%.) But don't worry. These questions still just require very basic outside knowledge. And 35 or 36 questions per test require no outside knowledge at all.

But so many of those things simply require *looking at the data*. That's the very definition of science. You have a theory about the world, so you look at the world and see what happens. Then you write down what you saw and check whether it matches your theory. *Bam! You just did science!*

> See **APPENDIX D** for a glossary of some key concepts and terms that have shown up on past tests.

Now, we don't want to mislead you: you will most likely see *some* questions that expect you to know facts of science that are not given in the passage. And there will be some questions for which the necessary facts are given to you in the passage—so you don't *need* to know them—but the question is a lot easier if you already do. Yes, the more you remember from your science classes, the more comfortable you'll be. Our point is that unless you're trying to score above 32, your knowledge of science facts is not what will make or break your score on this test. Because the test draws from so many different fields, there's no way of knowing which topics will be the ones you see. **Don't study for this test by cramming three years' worth of science textbooks.** Your ability to read and interpret data will have a much greater impact on your score.

Timing

As we saw on the Reading Test, timing on the Science Test can be very tight. You've got 40 questions to do in 35 minutes. Many questions involve nothing more than looking up a number in a table and can be done very quickly, but even easy questions can take time when they're surrounded by *Fancy Science Words*. And the pressure of tight timing can lead to careless mistakes. There are several things that can help you move faster and improve accuracy.

1. Don't read the passage.

One reason science passages take so long is that reading the passages is a burden. They're long, they use confusing words, and they discuss complex issues that can go completely over your head. But most questions on the ACT simply ask you to retrieve or analyze the data on the tables and figures, so you don't *need* a deep understanding of the concepts involved.

When you first get to a new passage, **don't read it**. Dive into the questions. You can get *a lot* of questions just by matching the values and key words given in the question to the same values and terms in the figures. We realize that sometimes it can be scary to jump into the questions without knowing what the passage is about. If you like, you can **skim it** to get a sense of what going on, but do so *quickly*. Just get a general sense of what's going on. If you don't understand some concept or detail, *skip it and move on*.

Obviously, not every question will just rely on looking up numbers; sometimes you will have to read and understand the content of the passage. But when that happens, you can always **go back**. Don't try to absorb all the information from the beginning—worry about that information when you need it, when you're asked about it. You don't have a lot of time on this test. Don't spend time trying to understand something unless a question asks you to understand it.

One slight exception here is the **Conflicting Viewpoints** passage. These passages tend to be more text-heavy and use far fewer tables and figures than the other passage types. Instead, they present several different hypotheses and explanations for a given set of facts and circumstances.

For questions on these passages, you will generally need some understanding of the difference between the various hypotheses. But often you just need a bare understanding of what the hypotheses are—*the main ideas*. These passages are written in clear, direct language, so the main idea is usually given in the first sentence. So just **underline the first sentence of each viewpoint**. Skim or ignore the rest. That should give you a good summary, and you'll be ready to start the questions.*

* For example: There's a mysterious crater. What caused it? Scientist 1 thinks it was an asteroid. Scientist 2 thinks it was a volcano, and Scientist 3 thinks it was dug by a swarm of large rabbits. Those are your main ideas. Ignore the rest of the passage and get to the questions.

2. Use Target Numbers.

Our general rule for the ACT as a whole still applies: **accuracy is more important than bulk**. This is the idea behind Target Numbers: only do a certain number of questions and guess randomly on the remainder. That way, you'll have fewer questions to do in the same amount of time. Therefore, you'll have more time for each question, you'll have a better chance of being accurate on the ones you do, and you'll get more points overall.

On the Science Test, that means it may be to your benefit to skip an entire passage. The following table shows you the **target scores** you can get if you skip 1 or 2 entire passages on the Science Test.

TARGET SCORES		
NOTES	SKIP 1 PASSAGE	SKIP 2 PASSAGES
Get all questions right, plus guesses on skipped passages.	**29–31**	**25–28**
Get 1 wrong question on each passage you do.	**25–26**	**22–24**

The scores listed here are *approximations*. These are not guarantees; they're goals. Here are a few things to keep in mind about this table:

- As always, **you must never leave any questions blank**. The above calculations assume that you **guessed randomly** on the questions you skipped and got about 25% of them right. These numbers may vary depending on how lucky you were in these guesses. Remember: *there is no penalty for guessing. There is no possible drawback to guessing randomly on questions you skip.*
- The first row in the table shows the high end of what you can achieve, assuming you get **all the questions you do correct**, plus a few random guesses. But you probably won't get 100% of them right. The second row shows what your scores will look like if you miss 1 question in each passage you do.
- The scores are shown as ranges because different passages have **different numbers of questions**, so the total number of questions you skip may vary. If you skip more questions, you have a lower maximum possible score, but you'll have more time to get the questions you do.
    1. In the Skip 1 column, the low number assumes you skip a Conflicting Viewpoints (7 questions) and the high number assumes a Data Representation (5 questions).
    2. In the Skip 2 column, the low number assumes you skip a Conflicting Viewpoints and a Research Summaries (7 + 6 = 13Q) and the high assumes two Data Representation passages (5 + 5 = 10Q).*
- Remember that each test form has its own particular **scoring table**. We computed these figures by looking at past real tests and finding the *average* final score for a given raw score. But the scoring table for the real ACT you take will vary. A raw score of 30 (that is, getting 30 questions right) might give you a final score of 25 on one test but a final score of 27 on another test.

To repeat: these numbers are not exact. They are *approximations.*

So how many passages should you skip? Think about your starting score and your goal. For example:

- Say you're currently getting around a 17 on the Science Test. You can skip 13 questions over 2 passages, get a bunch of questions wrong, and *still* get a 22, a 5-point score increase. That's great!
- Say you're getting a 21. You could skip 1 passage, miss 5-6 questions, and end up with a 26. You could skip 2, but you would have to be sure you get most of them right to get up to that range.
- Say you're getting a 25. You can skip 1 passage, get nearly all of them right, and get a 30.

* You can skip passage types in any combination of 5, 6, and 7 questions. But you can't skip 2 Conflicting Viewpoints passages, because there's only one per test.

- If you want to get above a 30, you need to do all the passages. But you may consider doing the passages in a different order in order to maximize your chances.

So which passage should you skip? There are a few possibilities:

1. Skip the last passage.

This is the easiest method to remember. Don't worry about the content or structure of the passage, just skip the last one. While the ACT does not release information about how it orders individual questions on the Science Test, our anecdotal evidence seems to suggest that *passages* (not the questions) are ordered by difficulty. That is, the last passage often features the most complicated reasoning, unconventional graphs, or difficult subject matter. So that might make it a good passage to skip.

2. Skip the Conflicting Viewpoints passage.

The Conflicting Viewpoints passage—the one with 7 questions that asks about multiple theories on the same topic—is generally very light on figures and heavy on text. That means it will generally have fewer questions involving simple data lookup or comparison. As a result, even if the Conflicting Viewpoints passage isn't necessarily *harder* than other passages, it will be more of a time suck.

The downside to skipping the Conflicting Viewpoints passage is that it means you will skip more questions—7 instead of 5 or 6. That extra skipped question means you're saving more time, but it also means your maximum possible score will be a bit lower. If you're trying to get a score above 29, you may not want to skip that many questions. Consult the chart above for more details.

3. Skip the passage on the subject you like the least.

The passages will draw from the fields of biology, chemistry, physics, and earth science. Within these subjects are a variety of sub-topics; for example, a biology passage could be about genetics, zoology, cellular structure, or other topics. If say, you particularly hate, fear, or are bad at genetics, you may want to skip a passage that discusses genetics.

However, it's dangerous to use this to decide what to skip because you can't predict which sub-topics will appear on any given test. You might not see any genetics on the test. You might see two passages on two different topics that you hate. Unless you're a science enthusiast (i.e. nerd), chances are there will be multiple passages on topics that you struggle with. That's okay! Again, this is not a test of your science knowledge. But if you're not sure which passage to skip, you can use your love and/or knowledge of a subject as a tie-breaker.

You may also want to use these guidelines to consider doing the passages **in a different order**. For example, say you're having timing problems, but you're trying to get a score above 30. You might want to skip the Conflicting Viewpoints passage and *come back to it at the end.* The other passages will feature more data questions that can be done quickly and easily. That way you'll make sure you get to those questions before you spend a large chunk of time reading a dense passage.

Similarly, if you're low on time and have a whole passage left that you want to do, **do the data questions first**. Questions that just ask you to look up values in figures and tables can be done quickly without any kind of deep understanding of the passage. One way to tell is to look for questions that have numbers in the choices. Those generally go more quickly than questions involving a lot of reading.

Answering the questions

Here is a basic four-step method for answering just about any Science question. Below, we outline the steps along with some *frequently asked questions* about what to do when the steps don't work as well as you planned. Keep in mind that these steps can be followed *robotically.* Don't think too much. The point of these steps is to demonstrate that for most questions you don't have to understand the passage or the deep meaning of the question.

1. Identify and underline which Figure or Table you need.

Most questions will specify which table or figure you're talking about. **Underline the figure's name in the question** and find it in the passage. Make sure you're looking at the right figure when you answer the question.

Q: Do I have to do this? Like, do I have to actually underline it?

YES. You have to actually underline it.* If this seems unnecessarily specific and meticulous, you're half right. Yes, it's meticulous, but *it is entirely necessary*. So much of the test is just about locating the information you need, so you must be doubly, triply, and quadruply sure that you do so accurately. Careless mistakes can and will happen.

Q: What if the question lists two figures?

Underline both of them: you'll probably need both! One of them might wind up being more important than the other, but both should be relevant.

Q: What if the question doesn't list any figures or tables?

This does happen. Sometimes instead of listing a figure, the question will say something like "Based on the information provided". That is usually a clue that the information you need will be in the introductory paragraphs, not in the figures and tables.

Also, sometimes a passage will only have one figure or table. In those cases, the figure or table often won't be listed in the questions. They'll assume you know where to go.

For Conflicting Viewpoints passages, rather than listing the name of a table or figure, questions will specify which students or scientists they're asking about. If a question doesn't name a student or scientist, it's often because the point of the question is to ask *which* student or scientist would agree or disagree with a piece of information. For these questions, continue on to step 2.

2. Identify and underline any key words in the question.

Look for words that give you information you need to answer the question. These are words that tell you what you **know**, or what you **want**. For example, if the question is:

- **According to <u>Table 1</u>, when the chamber had a temperature of 10°C what was the volume of nitrogen?**

I notice that you already underlined "Table 1". Well done.

The words that tell us what we know are "temperature" and "10°C". We want the "volume" of "nitrogen". These are all key words that tell us where in Table 1 to look. When you find words that look like they will help you, <u>underline them</u>. You will need these words later.

- According to <u>Table 1</u>, when the chamber had a **<u>temperature</u>** of **<u>10°C</u>** what was the **<u>volume</u>** of **<u>nitrogen</u>**?

Don't worry about what these words mean yet. We're just identifying which words are important. We don't care what they mean yet. For example, if the question is:

- **According to Table 1, when the chamber had a tinstaffle of 10 gorr, what was the gravilax of flextane?**

---

* Well, okay, you don't have to underline: if you want, you can circle it instead.

You probably don't know what these words mean. That's because we made them up. But we can still tell that "tinstaffle", "10 gorr", "gravilax", and "flextane" are the key words. We'll go to Table 1 and look for those words.

Q: How do you know if a word is a key word?

Some students get a little too happy with underlining. Don't underline *everything* in the sentence, just the key words. Questions will often be padded with extra words that don't actually help you find the answer.

Anything that sounds like an Important Science Word (like "volume" or "capacitance" or "propanoic acid") might be a key word that helps you. Ask yourself: what do you **know**, and what do you **want**? Find any information in the question that might help you when you go back to the figures.

Certainly anything with *a number* attached to it is potentially important. But not every number winds up being important. Sometimes questions give you extra information that isn't necessary to solve the question. For example, the example question above mentioned "the chamber had a temperature of 10°C." That seems important. But if *everything* in Table 1 is at 10°C, that information doesn't actually add anything new. In that case, we'd just want to find the volume of nitrogen, period.

Ultimately, the point is to try to highlight the important information and ignore the filler. You won't always know right away what the important stuff is, and some things you underline may not be important in the end. But you'll get better with practice.

Q: This question is total nonsense. I'm really confused. What do I do if I can't find any key words?

If the question is too confusing, try **reading the choices**. Sometimes the question will be densely phrased or will rely on a deep understanding of the passage, but the choices are a simple list of values or statements. Look for key words in the choices: units, names of variables, or anything that might help you figure out where in the passage to look.

Q: That didn't help. Now what?

Go on to step 3. Look in **the figure or table**. Check the labels in the relevant figure to see if they match any words in the sentence. Look at the labels on the axes, the headers on the table, the names associated with different lines in the graph, or any other words that appear.

If that still doesn't help, certain types of questions have to be done in different ways. See the discussion of question types below.

3. Go to the Figure or Table identified in step 1 and circle the key words identified in step 2.

We've identified the key words. We know where in the passage to look for them. Now we have to find them. **Circle or underline the key words in the Figure or Table itself**. If the question gave you a specific value, find that value.

For example, let's return to the earlier question:

- **According to <u>Table 1</u>, when the chamber had a <u>temperature</u> of <u>10°C</u> what was the <u>volume</u> of <u>nitrogen</u>?**

Table 1 is shown below. Let's look for the relevant key words:

Table 1				
Time (s)	Temperature (°C)	y (mm)	Volume (L)	Balloon color
50	10	7.5	0.85	Blue
100	15	8.8	1.28	Green
150	20	10.1	1.70	Green

We can see columns labeled "Temperature" and "Volume". Under "Temperature" we can find a value of 10. Circle them. Circle all of them.

Table 1				
Time (s)	**Temperature (°C)**	*y* (mm)	**Volume (L)**	Balloon color
50	10	7.5	0.85	Blue
100	15	8.8	1.28	Green
150	20	10.1	1.70	Green

Again, it's very important to *actually* circle or underline the words and numbers *on the table itself.* Figures and tables are often dense jumbles of information, and it's *very* easy to be careless and look at the wrong numbers. Use a double line, squiggly lines, whatever. Just highlight them.

Q: The key words aren't in the figure.

That's not a question.

Q: What do I do if the key words aren't in the figure?

Excellent question! Sometimes you'll find a key word in the question, but the words on the figure won't literally match. If so, there are several other places to look for your key word.

- Maybe **you don't need that word**. Note that "nitrogen" was one of the key words we underlined, but it doesn't appear in the table. That's okay. We found all the other key words here, so we probably have all the information we need. If we read the introductory paragraph before the table, it will likely tell us that the entire table refers to nitrogen.
- Check the **units**. "Units" are the thing that the quantity is measured in, like meters, kilograms, seconds, etc. Perhaps there's one key word in the question and a different key word on the axis in the figure, but both give values in "*g/L*". That's a clue. The two words might refer to the same thing.
- Use **common sense**. Think about what the axes on the represent, and think about what your key word means. For example, say the question asks you for the temperature at sea level in Figure 3. You go to Figure 3 and find "temperature" on the horizontal axis, but the vertical axis just says "depth of ocean (m)". The words "sea level" don't appear anywhere.

  Well, what does "sea level" mean? It's the level of the surface of the sea. The vertical axis gives the *depth*: that means how far *below* the ocean you are. Therefore, "sea level" means you have a depth of 0, so we want a point with a value of 0 on the vertical axis.
- Look in the **passage**. When Fancy Science Words are used in a passage, the introductory paragraphs often define them for you. Look in these paragraphs—both in the first introductory paragraphs and in the paragraphs directly above your figure—to find the key words you need. You don't necessarily have to read the passage in detail; just skim the paragraphs to see if your key word shows up (much like we did in the "Word Search Drill" in the Reading chapter). The passage even helps you: when key words are defined in the paragraphs, they are often *italicized*, which makes them much easier to find.

  Similarly, if a key word is *italicized in the question*, then it's probably defined for you right there in the question. In these cases, the question is introducing a new term that you're not expected to know; you're just expected to use that new information with respect to the passage.
- If a simple word search doesn't help, you might have to **read the passage** in more detail. Sometimes you really do need a deeper understanding of the passage. It's unfortunate, but it happens.
- You might need **outside knowledge**. Some questions do require you to know the definitions of terms that aren't defined. If a question asks you about the "density" of the objects in the experiment, and the word "density" wasn't mentioned anywhere in the graphs or tables or the

descriptive paragraphs, the question is probably just testing whether you know what "density" means. As we said, these questions are a small fraction of the test, but they do occur.

Keep in mind that even if you don't know the definitions of these outside words, you can often still *eliminate*. Look at the choices and check if any are clearly false based on the data you know.

4. Match values you know to the value you want.

Okay, we're almost done. Here's where you actually answer the question. You know where to look, you know what you're looking for. Match the value of the key word you know to the value of the key word you want. Bam. You're done.

To return to our previous example, we already found the temperature of 10°C. We want to know the volume. We'll continue along the row that has 10 until we get to the volume column.

Table 1				
Time (s)	**Temperature (°C)**	y (mm)	**Volume (L)**	Balloon color
50	**10**	7.5	**0.85**	Blue
100	15	8.8	1.28	Green
150	20	10.1	1.70	Green

The volume is **0.85 L**.

That's your basic method for most questions. Underline, underline, circle, matchy-matchy, done. But there are some types of questions that may make things slightly more complicated.

Q. The value given in the question (or choices) isn't on the figure. What do I do?

This is an **Inferred Data question**. Rather than looking up data points that are on the graph, it asks you to look up points that *aren't* on the graph. Where *would* a given data point go if it had been included on the graph. We'll talk more about these when we get to the discussion of question types.

Inferred data questions don't usually involve math. They're just a matter of taking the value in the question and seeing if it's bigger, smaller, or in between the values in the table. However, you may see some questions where you'll have to do a little bit of **math**. Don't freak out: it's just light math that you can do in your head. You'll have to take the values in the table and cut them in half, or multiply them by 10. If you're adding a string of five two-digit numbers, you're probably doing it the hard way.

Q. The value I know is not on the same figure as the value I want. What do I do?

This is a **Combination question**. The thing you know and the thing you want occur on different figures; you'll have to find a way to connect them. Look for a value you can use as a bridge between the two. We'll talk more about these when we get to the discussion of question types.

Q: The choices are all say "Yes" or "No" in them. What do I do?

This is a **Reasoning question**. The question presents you with a statement or hypothesis about the subject of the passage, and the question asks whether the data in the figures supports this statement. The choices first say "Yes" [the data supports the statement] or "No" [the data does not support the statement], followed by evidence that demonstrates why the data does or doesn't support the statement.

You can do these questions in two steps. First, *ignore the statement in the question.* Just look at the choices and **eliminate choices that are *false***. That is, they give information that does not match the information in the figures and tables. If you have more than one choice remaining, *then* you can worry about whether that information proves or disproves the statement in the question. . We'll talk more about these when we get to the discussion of question types.

Techniques

Although the Science Test does not involve very much actual math, some of the techniques we discussed for the Math Test can also help you here.*

Backsolve

As we said in the four-step method, many of the questions involve going back to the passage, looking up the information we know, and matching it to the information we have.

But we can also work the other direction. Start with the choices, look up those values in the passage, and then see which one matches the information given in the question. For example:

➤ **In Experiment 2, the gases in tanks 3 and 7 had the same pressure at which of the following temperatures?**

A. 30°C
B. 45°C
C. 60°C
D. 75°C

Obviously we can't actually do this problem since we don't have the results of Experiment 2 handy. Regardless, we can tell that one way to do this problem is to look at the figures associated with Experiment 2 and find the temperatures at which the tanks had the same pressure.

But what if it's not that easy? What if the data in Experiment 2 is spread across two figures? It may be hard to compare tanks 3 and 7 directly. So instead, we can work directly off the values in the choices. Look up the pressure of tank 3 at the temperatures listed and write them next to the choices. Then do the same for tank 7 and see which choice gives the same values. Something like this:

	tank 3	tank 7
A. 30°C	80	50
B. 45°C	85	70
C. 60°C	**90**	**90**
D. 75°C	95	110

Backsolve can show up all over the test on all sorts of different question types. It may or may not be faster than looking up the values directly. More often than not, it takes about the same amount of time to do it in either direction, so ultimately it comes down to whatever you're more comfortable with. So if you're having trouble dealing with the information in the question, try using the choices instead.

Guesstimate

On the Math test, the idea behind Guesstimate was that we can learn a lot by looking at the figure. Well, half of the Science Test involves nothing more than looking at figures! Practically everything we do with figures is a kind of Guesstimate. We look at the picture, look at the numbers on the picture, and find the values we need.

Like Guesstimate on the Math Test, when you look at figures on the Science Test, *you do not have to be exact*. Look at the figure and get a **range** of possible answer for the value you need. This point looks like it's between 40 and 50. Look at the choices and eliminate anything that's not between 40 and 50.

If more than one choice works out, then you can go back and try to be more precise. *Where* between 40 and 50 is it? Is it right in the middle, like 45? Closer to 40, like 42? Closer to 50, like 48? How can you tell? *Visually*. Look at the picture and see where the point is.

Obviously, if the data is in a Table instead of a Figure, you're not going to be able to solve it visually. And when you look up a value on a table, the exact number you need is already written down for you. However, even with tables there are times when you should *approximate*. For example, inferred data questions ask

* Because there's no algebra on the Science Test, Plug In, sadly, will not help you much.

you where on a table a new point would occur. These questions don't ask for precise numbers, just ranges of values. Whenever possible, start with broad values and get more precise only when necessary.

RTFQ (and friends)

RTFQ stands for "Read the Full Question." It's a common mistake on the Math Test, a mistake that's based on *carelessness*. You're working too quickly and accidentally solve for x instead of y, or find the percent of books that *were* sold instead of the percent that were *not* sold.

Carelessness is very much a problem on the Science Test. We often talk about how easy many of these questions are at heart—just look up the number on the table *that they give you*! But if it's all so easy, why do so many students struggle with the test? Because there's *a lot* of information, and it's incredibly easy to lose track of it all.

RTFQ mistakes occur frequently on the Science Test, but it's not just the question that's the problem. Other common mistakes include **RTFT** (Read the Table), **RTFF** (Read the Figure), and **RTFP** (Read the Passage).

Here are some common careless mistakes that students make:

- Reading the wrong column in a table
- Reading the wrong row in a table
- Looking at the wrong axis in a figure
- Looking at the wrong curve or line on a figure with multiple lines
- Looking at the wrong figure entirely
- Thinking the values in the figure go up when they actually go down (or vice versa)

And many, many more. These kinds of mistakes are the main reason that we stressed underlining key words and figure names when doing the question. Just taking a few extra seconds to be sure of yourself on every question can make a big difference on your score.

Breathe!

It's very easy to get overwhelmed on the Science Test, especially if you don't have a strong science background. If you start to feel overwhelmed by a question, a figure, a passage, or anything, just take a second to stop and compose yourself. There may be some hard stuff on the test, but there is a lot of stuff that you can get.

As we mentioned on the Reading Test, sometimes there'll be a question that just gets to you. You can't figure out what it's asking. You can't figure out how it relates to the passage. You can't figure out what the passage means. And it's driving you crazy and freaking you out. We call these **Black Hole Questions**, because they suck up all your time and you cannot escape their pull.* Don't get trapped. If you've been spending 5 minutes on a single question, **skip it**. Just guess something (randomly, if necessary) and move on to the next one. You don't want to ruin an entire section because of one question.

* It should be mentioned that we mean "Black Hole" metaphorically here. Since this is the Science Test, you may also see questions that are literally about actual black holes. Don't skip those. (Unless, of course, those black hole questions are also Black Hole Questions).

II. Figure Types

Since so much of the test depends on tables and figures, let's take a closer look at how they work. There are many different types of tables and figures that may appear in ACT Science passages. All of them are simply ways of representing information. The key to almost all figures is ***matching***—match a row to a column, match one axis to another.

1. Tables

Tables are the most common way of presenting data on the ACT. In general, the test will have about as many tables as all other figures combined. You probably have some experience with tables already, and most of them are straightforward. Just match up the rows and the columns:

Table 2

Time (min)	Temperature (°C)	Volume (mL)
0	50	85
5	57	83
10	64	80

When the time was 0 minutes, the temperature was 50°C and the volume (of whatever it is we're talking about) was 85 mL. At 5 minutes, the temperature was 57°C and the volume 83 mL. And at 10 minutes, the temperature is 64°C and the volume 80 mL.

Some tables might group together columns or rows that are similar in some way:

Table 3

Ball Substance	Mass (g)	Launch distance (m)	
		First launch	Second launch
Metal	68	4.0	1.8
Wood	52	8.3	3.1
Plastic	44	12.3	7.7

TRY SOME:

- **Which had a greater mass, the metal ball or the plastic ball?**
- **What was the distance of the second launch of the wood ball?**
- **What was the mass of the ball whose first launch went the farthest?**

Most tables will show numbers in their fields. But some might give verbal descriptions instead:

Table 4

Dog	Size	Color	Coat	Personality
Britney	Large	Brown	Thick fur	Friendly
Fido	Medium	Black	Short hair	Friendly
Robespierre	Medium	Black and white	Short hair	Friendly
Nelson	Small	Brown	Long hair	Aggressive

Even though there aren't any numbers, the table can be read exactly the same way. Britney is a large, friendly dog with thick brown fur. The only small dog is Nelson. Fido and Robespierre both have short hair. Just match up rows and columns.

Some tables might just "check off" a characteristic. In Table 5, an "×" indicates a topping is present:

Table 5			
	Topping		
Pizza Sample	Pepperoni	Sausage	Mushrooms
A			
B	×	×	
C		×	×
D	×	×	×

Table 5 presents four types of pizza. Pizza A has no toppings. Pizza B has pepperoni and sausage but no mushrooms. Pizza C has sausage and mushrooms but no pepperoni. Pizza D has all three toppings.

Really, there's not a lot of variation in how tables are presented. They're all pretty much the same—if you can read one of them, you can read all of them. Figures, on the other hand, come in lots of different shapes and sizes, with lines, dots, areas, and drawings, among others. Let's take a look at a few.

2. The Coordinate Plane

Lines, Curves, and Points

The majority of figures on the ACT can be read just like the *xy*-coordinate plane we saw on the math questions. There are two axes, one horizontal (the "*x*-axis") and one vertical (the "*y*-axis"). Sometimes questions will refer to the *x*- or *y*-axis, but they'll usually just use labels. The axes will correspond to different values that are discussed in the passage. Each axis will be labeled, so you can easily see what the numbers mean.

Questions do occasionally ask about the SLOPE of a line. Slope is the ratio of the change in *y*-value over the change in *x*-value. That corresponds to the line's *rate of change*. A horizontal line has a slope of zero.

When we deal with graphs on the Math Test, we have a lot to think about. The axes are labeled *x* and *y*, there are equations and slopes and intercepts, there are lines and parabolas and all sorts of algebra, and it's easy to get overwhelmed. However, on the Science Test, graphs won't feature variables and equations the way Math Test problems do. Don't be scared: *there won't be any algebra.* As with tables, the key to reading a graph is **matching**. Let's look at an example:

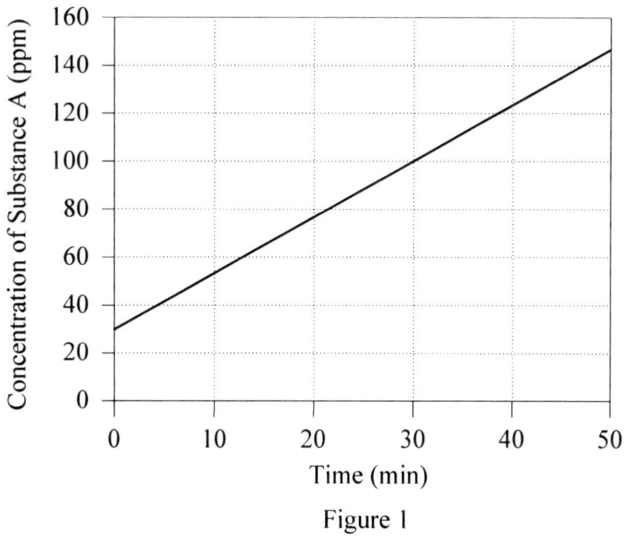

Figure 1

Try this question:

- **What is the concentration of Substance A at 30 minutes?** 100

As we said, before doing anything else, *circle the key words:*

What is the concentration of Substance A at 30 minutes?

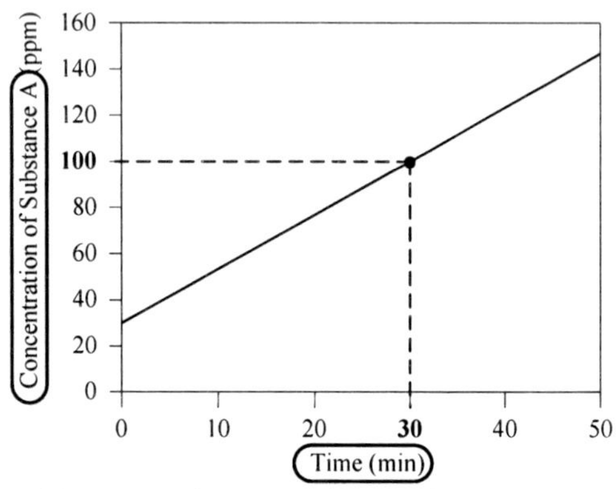

In Figure 1, the horizontal axis represents *time* in minutes and the vertical axis represents the *concentration of Substance A* in ppm.* We know the time in minutes—that's the horizontal axis. Find the mark for 30 on the horizontal axis. Follow it straight up and mark the spot where it hits the line. Now go straight left to see where that spot lies on the other axis. It's at the 100 mark. So when the time is **30 minutes**, the concentration is **100 ppm**.

Figure 1 has **gridlines** that help you follow the values from the axis to the graph line, but not every figure will. And the point that we're looking for won't always be lying along those grid lines. If you have trouble connecting the value on the axis with the point on the line, **use the edge of your answer sheet to draw a straight line**.

We can put even more information in the figure. Graphs will often feature more than just one line:

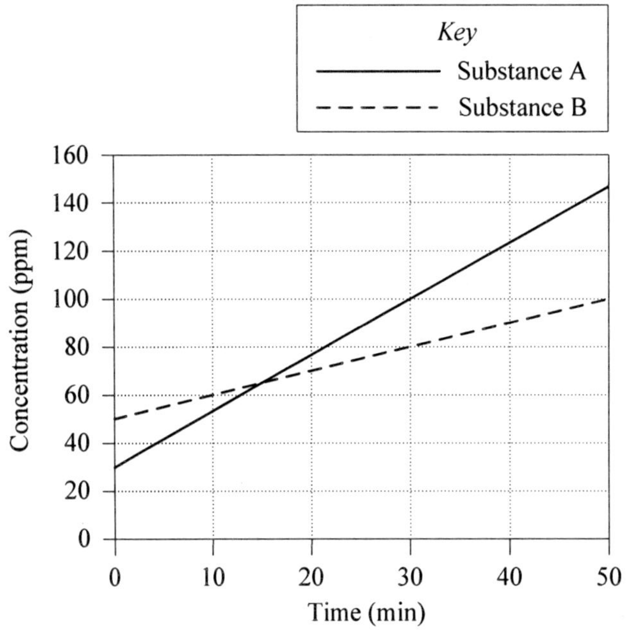

Figure 2

In Figure 2, the vertical axis now just shows "concentration", and there are two lines representing different substances. The key above the graph tells us which line is which: the solid line refers to Substance A and the dashed line refers to Substance B. Now you have to match three things: time, concentration, and substance. The different substances have different concentrations at any given time:

- When the time is 30 minutes, Substance A has a concentration of 100 ppm, but Substance B has a concentration of 80 ppm.
- The two substances have the same concentration when the time is about 15 minutes. Because the lines cross, the same point occurs on both lines. So both substances have the same concentration.
- For all times less than 15 min, Substance B has a greater concentration. For all times greater than 15, Substance A has a greater concentration.

* Here, "ppm" stands for "parts per million". But you know what? It doesn't matter. The ACT doesn't often pull tricks about units or conversion, so you don't have to worry about it. For all we care, ppm could stand for "pie pan monsters" or "pretty penguin manicures" or "please paint, monkeys". All that matters is that you match the thing the question wants to the correct axis in the figure.

And of course, the graphs don't always just show straight lines. Often figures will show lines that are curved in any number of crazy ways, as in Figures 3 and 4 below:

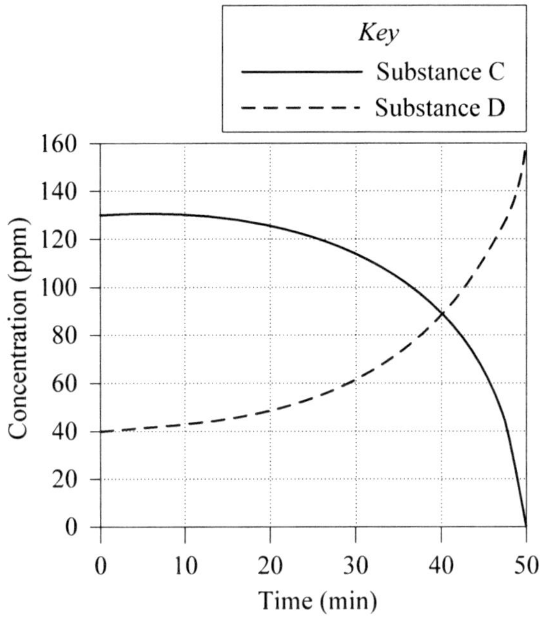

Figure 3

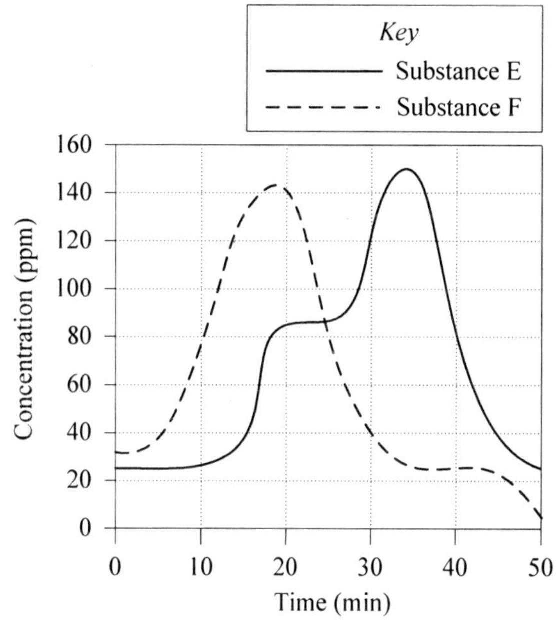

Figure 4

TRY SOME:

- **In Figure 3, when does the concentration of Substance C equal the concentration of Substance D?**
- **At approximately what time does Substance C have a concentration of 120 ppm?**
- **In Figure 4, what is the concentration of Substance E at a time of 30 minutes? Of Substance F?**
- **At approximately what time does Substance E have its highest concentration?**

These graphs all show continuous graphs. But sometimes a graph will show only a few data points. These can be shown as individual points or as connected points:

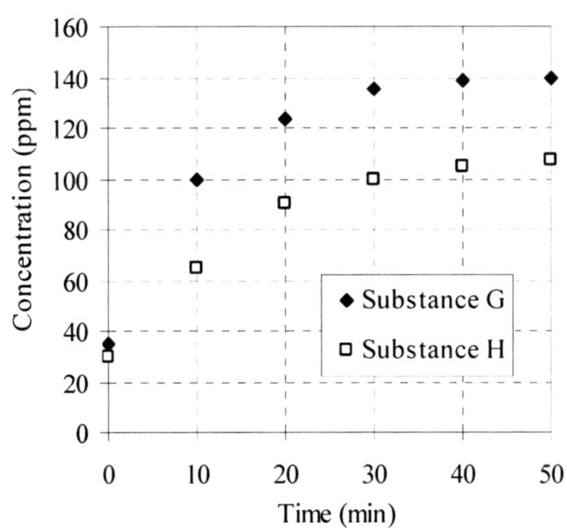

Figure 5

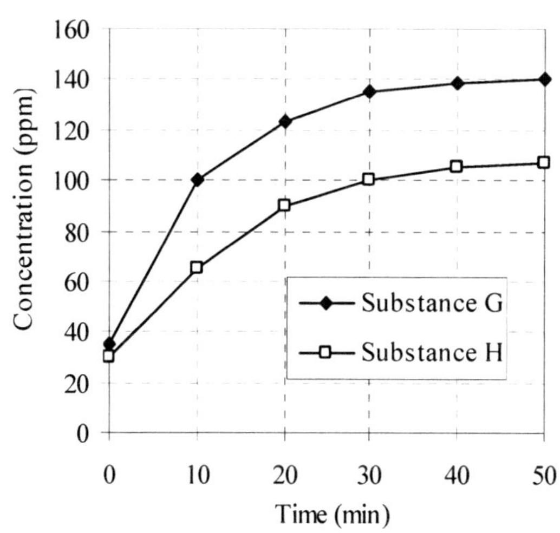

Figure 6

Here we can see the connection between a graph and a table a bit more clearly. Table 5 shows the values of the points in Figures 5 and 6. The graphs work exactly the same way the table does. Each point on the graph matches a *time* (the horizontal axis) to a *concentration* (the vertical axis) of a given *substance* (the type of point).

Table 5		
	Concentration (ppm)	
Time (min)	Substance G	Substance H
0	35	30
10	100	65
20	123	90
30	135	100
40	139	105
50	140	108

The main difference between graphs and tables is that graphs are *graphic*—they can be grasped visually. A table only shows numbers. On figures, a lot of information is immediately obvious. Just by looking at the picture we can see:

- Concentration always increases as time increases.
- The concentrations do not increase at a constant rate but taper off at the end.
- The concentration of Substance G is always greater than that of Substance H.

And so on. On the table, you can still figure that out, but you have to do some mental arithmetic to see it.

Trend lines

In Figures 5 and 6 above, each set of points seems to make a relatively smooth curve. We could probably draw that line using some kind of equation if we wanted (but we don't). However, collections of points don't always look that smooth. They could be scattered more randomly, as in Figure 7. If we connect the points, we get a jagged line, sometimes going up and sometimes going down, as in Figure 8.

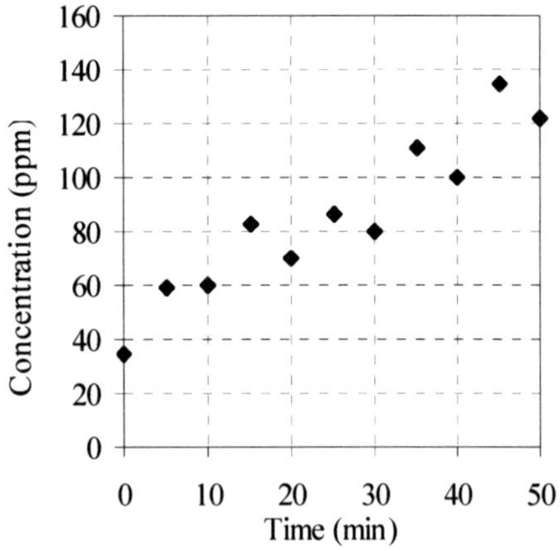

Figure 7

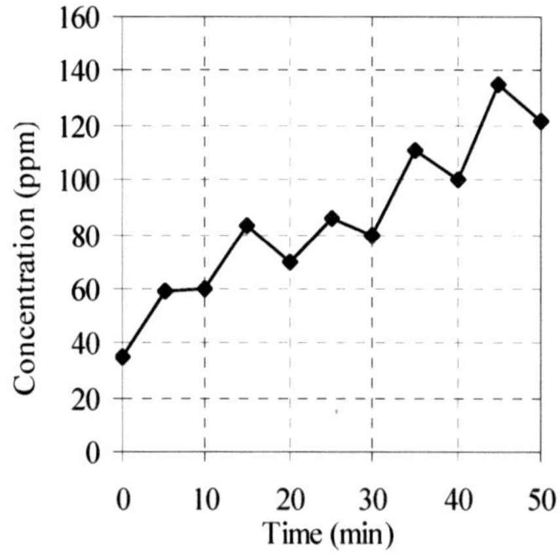

Figure 8

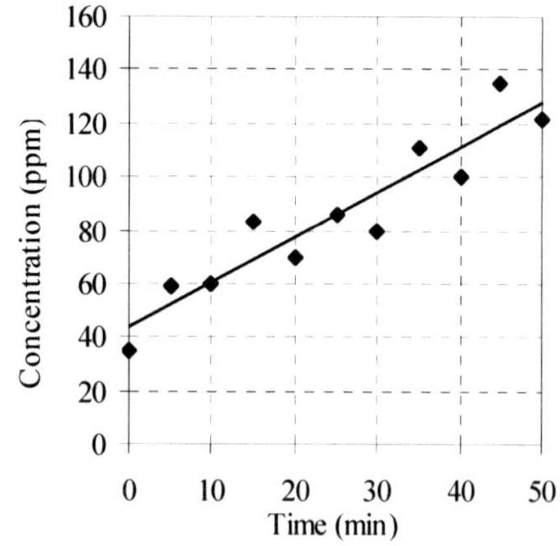

Figure 9

But even though the line goes up and down from point to point, we can see that, overall, the line *generally* goes up. The points with low values for time have low values for concentration. The points with high values for time have high values for concentration. So the values show a *general upward trend.*

Figure 9 shows this by adding something called a **trend line** or a **line of best fit**. This is a straight line that most closely *approximates* the path of all the points. It's the line that fits the points best. Again, this line is an approximation; if you want to look up actual values, look at the points, not the line.

You may see graphs with a trend line on the ACT, but you don't have to know anything special or do anything differently. It's just a way to show that even though the values go up and down from point to point, there's still a noticeable relationship; as one value increases, the other also increases.

Nonlinear scales

All the figures we've seen have had *linear scales*. That means that each space you move on the axis represents the same amount. In Figure 9, for example, each gridline on the x-axis represents an increase of 10 minutes: 0, 10, 20 ... Each gridline on the y-axis represents an increase of 20 ppm: 0, 20, 40 ... This is how the grand majority of ACT graphs are drawn.

But there's no rule that says we have to use a linear scale on our axis. We could use a *nonlinear scale.*

Look at the points in Figure 11. This graph seems to show constant growth: the points look like they make a straight line. But look at the vertical axis! Here, *the gridlines are not equally spaced.* The first space on the vertical axis goes from 1 to 10, but the next goes from 10 to 100! Even though they appear the same size, the axis tells us each segment on the vertical axis is bigger than the one before it.* Figure 12 shows the same points, but with a linear scale—each line represents 20,000 bacteria. You can see the points certainly do not make a straight line.

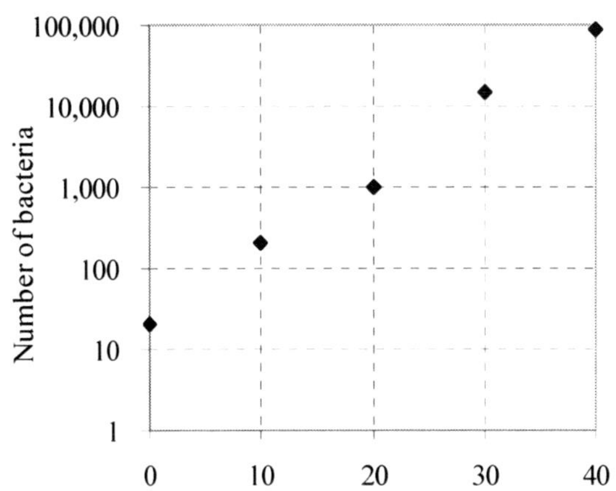

Figure 11

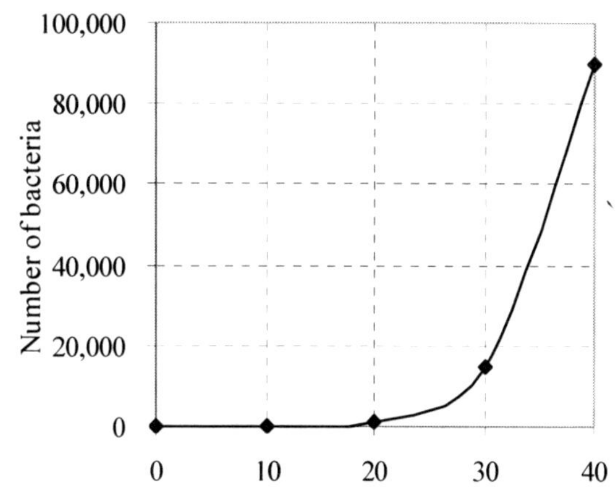

Figure 12

This may seem weird, but it really changes very little about your approach to a graph. We can analyze points here the same way we did on other graphs: just match up the two axes. So at 20 days, there were 1,000 bacteria.

Be careful about approximating with nonlinear scales. Figure 11 makes it look like at 40 days, there were 100,000 bacteria. But Figure 12 shows that there were only 90,000 bacteria. Why the difference? The truth is that Figure 11 *also* shows 90,000 bacteria at 40 days; it's just that on this scale 90,000 is a only a teeny tiny smidge under the line for 100,000.

As long as you always read carefully, you shouldn't have any trouble getting the data you need.

Multiple axes

All the graphs we've seen so far have two axes: one horizontal and one vertical. Sometimes a graph may reproduce the values on both sides of the graph, putting the same vertical axis on the left and the right. This

* Figure 11 shows a *logarithmic* scale: the tick marks each show a number raised to a higher power. Here, the marks are all powers of 10. But you don't have to know that word.

doesn't change the graph at all; it just makes it easier to read. For larger graphs in particular, it can be tricky to follow a point on the rightmost side all the way over to the left axis to get the value.

But sometimes a graph will have *entirely different axes* on opposite sides of the graph. This is a way to get additional information on the same graph. There are several ways this can happen.

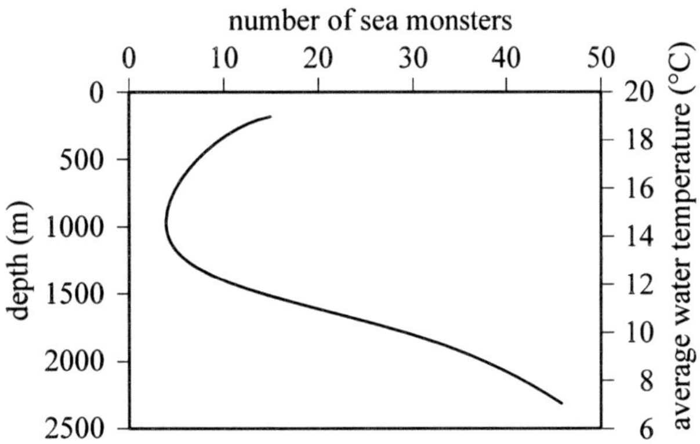

Figure 13

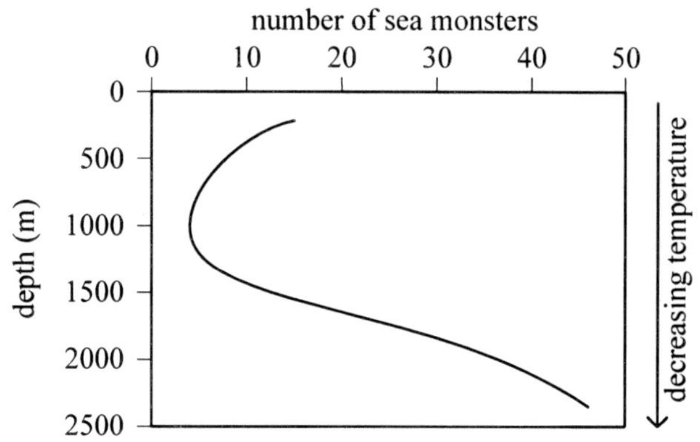

Figure 14

Figure 13 presents a survey of a particular part of the ocean and gives a count of the number of sea monsters (or *krakens*) found there. Note that there are *two different vertical axes* here: depth and temperature. So each point on the line relates the number of sea monsters to a certain depth *and* temperature. In fact, the two axes always correspond to the given scales. At a depth of 0 m, the water is an average of 20°C. At 2500 m, the water is 6°C.

Figure 14 gets the same idea across but without specific values for temperature. Here, all we know is that as you go deeper, the temperature gets lower.*

In contrast, take a look at Figures 15 and 16:

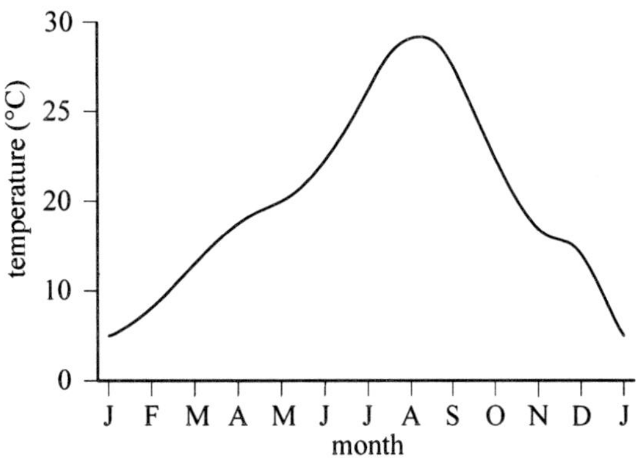

Figure 15

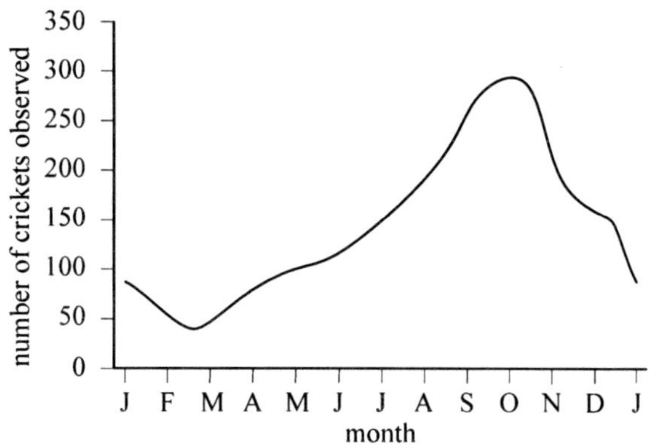

Figure 16

These figures refer to the same experiment. In Figure 15, the temperature at a particular site was recorded throughout the year. In Figure 16, the number of crickets was recorded at the same site. Those two graphs seem to have a similar shape, but it's a bit hard to compare them. What would happen if we combined the two, laying one graph on top of the other? The two graphs both have the same horizontal axis, so it's easy to line up the graphs. But they had different vertical axes, so the new graph will have two vertical axes, one on each side.

* Notice that the numbers on two axes do not go in the same direction. As you go down the line, the depth numbers get bigger but the temperature numbers get smaller. If there are two axes, don't assume they go the same direction. Look at the numbers.

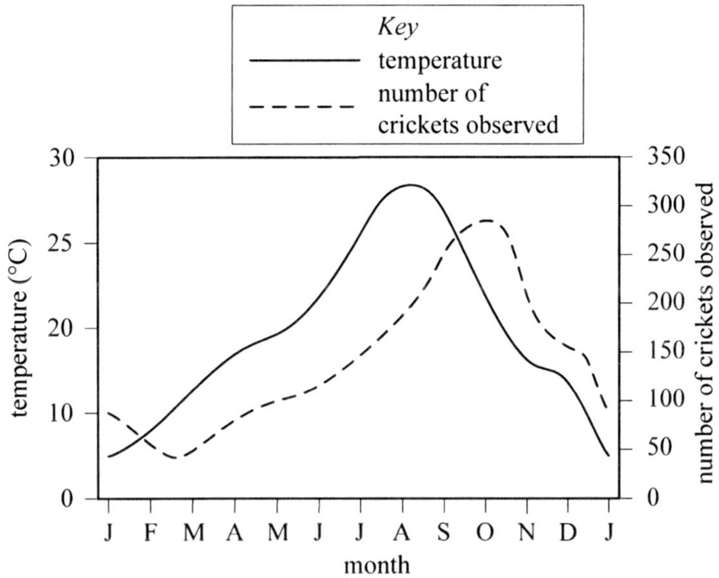

Figure 17

There are two curves drawn in Figure 17, each one corresponding to a different vertical axis. The key at the top tells us which is which:

- The *solid* curve corresponds to the *temperature*, so we match it to values on the *left* axis. In January, the temperature was about 5°C. In August, it was about 28°C.
- The *dashed* curve corresponds to *crickets*, so we match it to values on the *right* axis. In January, there were about 100 crickets. In August, there were a little less than 200 crickets.

By laying one graph on top of the other, we can look at the relationship between the change in crickets and the change in temperature. The number of crickets increases and decreases along with the temperature, but the crickets change about a month or two after the temperature changes.

It's important to remember is that, unlike in Figure 13, *the two axes are not connected to each other*. We cannot match axis to axis. We cannot assume there will always be 350 crickets when it's 30°C. We cannot look at the solid curve and assume there were 50 crickets at the end of the year; that point only tells us the temperature at the end of the year was 5°C. The dashed curve shows there were 100 crickets at the end of the year. We can only match each curve to the axis it's defined for. The solid curve *only* shows temperature. The dashed curve *only* shows crickets.

Sometimes the two axes are connected to each other and sometimes they aren't. How can we tell the difference? By looking at *the key*. In Figure 17, the labels of the curves in the key exactly correspond to the labels of the two vertical axes. That tells us each curve corresponds to one axis. In Figures 13 and 14, there was no such key, so we can assume that the two axes correspond to each other.

3. Layers and Shaded Areas

Not all graphs have to depict lines or points. With a line graph, there's usually a one-to-one correspondence between the axes. Each point on the horizontal axis corresponds with one and only one point on the vertical axis (or occasionally, vice versa). With area graphs, we can look at large regions of points at the same time.

In the simplest cases, a normal line graph has *layers* on it. These layers can add more information about the graph without changing the basic shape of the graph. In Figure 18, there are three layers that correspond to the ocean depths depicted:

- The epipelagic layer, from 0 to about 250 m
- The mesopelagic layer, from 250 m to 1000 m
- The bathypelagic layer, from 1000 m to 2500 m

Just like a second axis, these layers are tied to depth, so when we know the depth of a point, we also know which layer it's in. *All* points below 1000 m are in the bathypelagic layer.

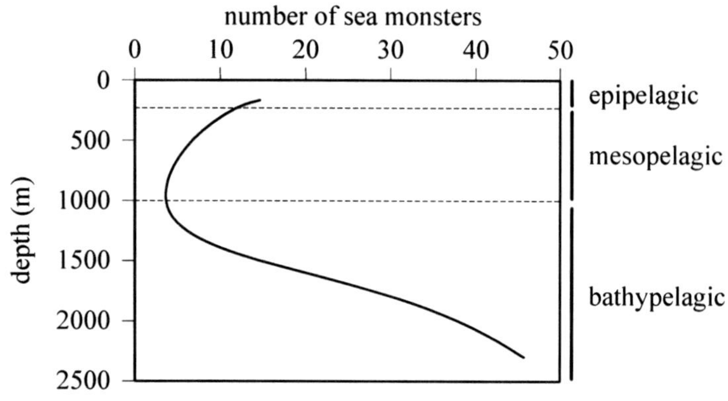

Figure 18

Here, the regions are only defined with respect to one axis, the depth. Sometimes, however, a graph can define regions using both axes, as in Figure 19.

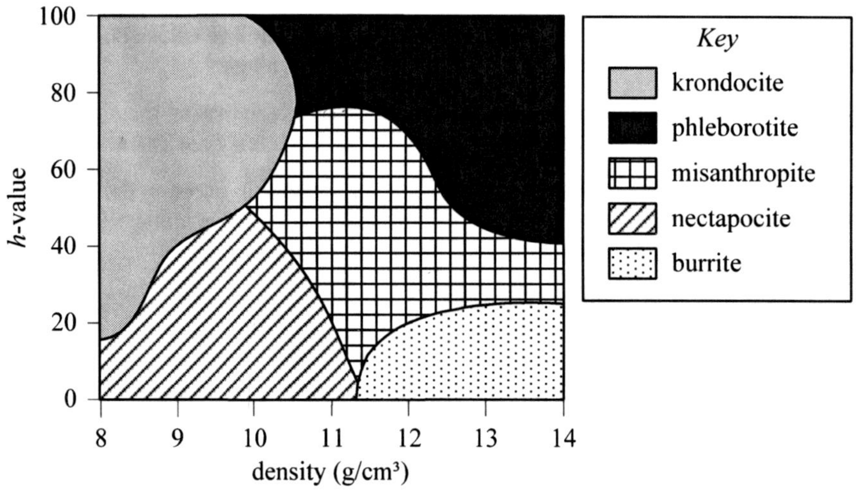

Figure 19

Figure 19 shows 5 fictitious minerals, organized by density and something called "*h*-value". Each differently shaded region corresponds to a type of mineral, so *any* point within that region refers to that mineral. *Every* point with an *h*-value lower than 20 and a density greater than 12 g/cm³ must be burrite. If a mineral has a density of 9 g/cm³ and an *h*-value above 40, it's krondocite. If its *h*-value is below 40, it's nectapocite.

TRY SOME:

- **If a mineral has a density of 10 g/cm³ and an *h*-value of 20, what type of mineral is it?**

- **If a sample of misanthropite has an *h*-value of 70, what is one possible value for its density?**

- **All samples of krondocite are less dense than all samples of which mineral?**

- **Which mineral's *h*-values are always higher than any *h*-value of burrite?**

4. Bar Graphs

We can read bar graphs exactly the same way we do any other graph: matching, matching, matching.

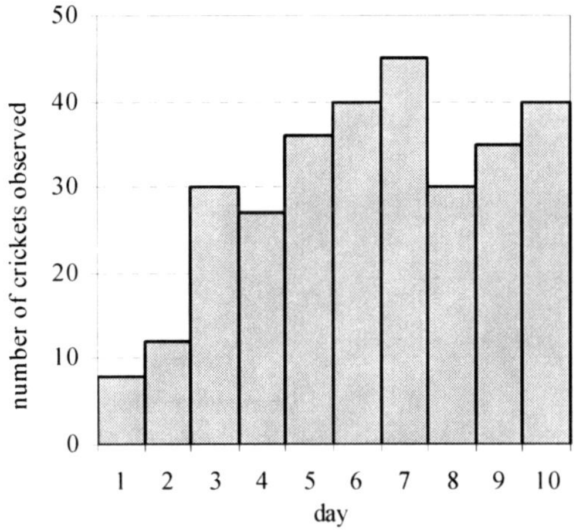

Figure 20

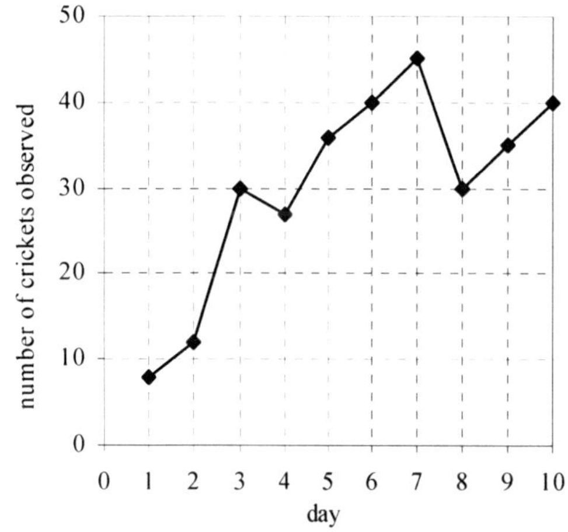

Figure 21

Figure 20 and Figure 21 show exactly the same data. In Figure 20, instead of a point for each day, there's a solid bar that extends to the value in question.

- On day 1, just under 10 crickets were observed.
- On day 6, 40 crickets were observed.
- The greatest number of crickets were observed on day 7.

Just as we can plot more than one set of points on the same graph, we can also plot more than one set of bars. In figure 22, data from two different locations, Site A and Site B, are shown side by side. On day 1, Site A had just under 10 crickets, while Site B had about 15. Day 4 was only day in which Site A had more crickets than Site B.

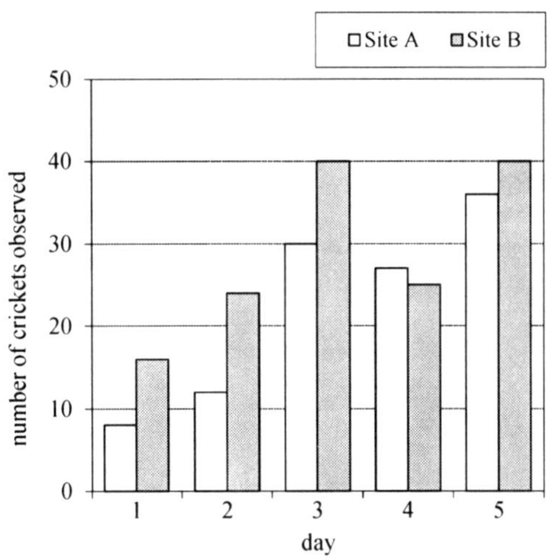

Figure 22

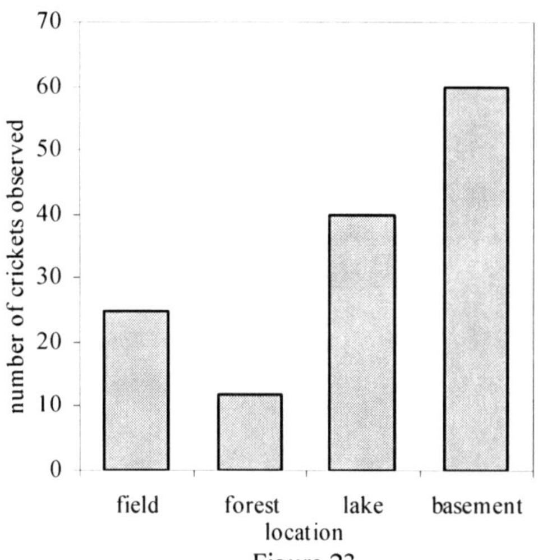

Figure 23

We also don't have to use numbers for each axis. In Figure 23, each bar refers to a different location. There were about 25 crickets observed in the field, and about 60 observed in my basement.*

* Based on a true story.

5. Setup Diagrams

Finally, sometimes a figure won't provide data; it will just explain the setup of the experiment. Experiments will often involve special or elaborate equipment—tube A is connected to tank B, which releases gas C, launching the car down ramp D, etc. When there's a lot going on, pictures and diagrams can make things clearer. You usually don't have to spend a lot of time analyzing these diagrams; they're only useful if you're asked about them, and you're rarely asked about them.

Here are a few examples of what setup diagrams might look like:

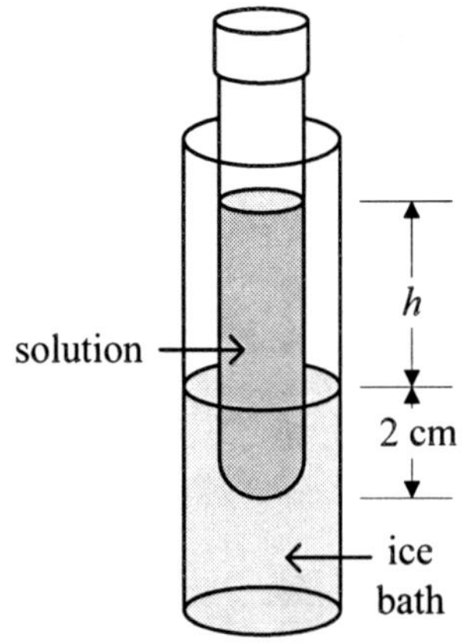

Figure 24

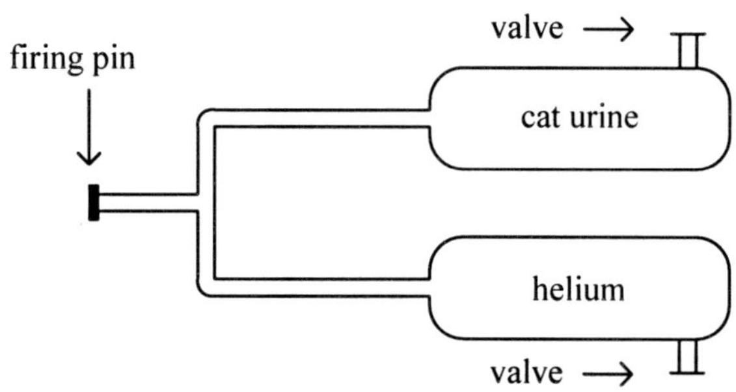

Figure 25

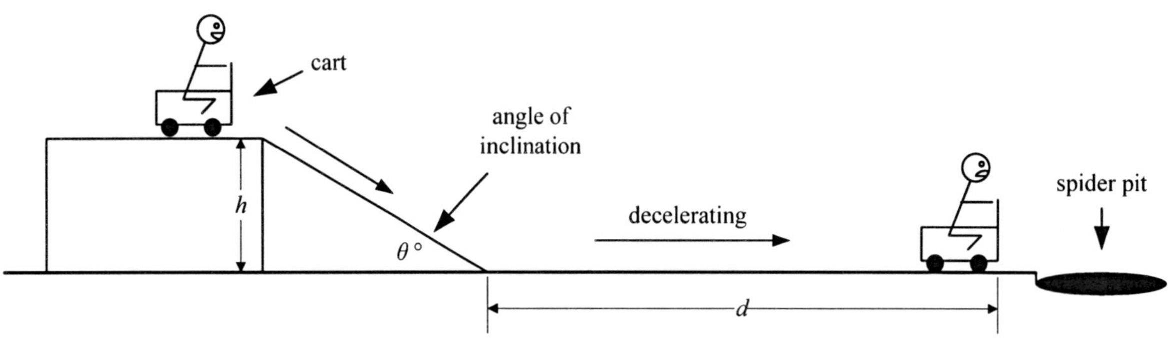

Figure 26

III. QUESTION TYPES

ACT Science questions tend to fall into categories based both on the form of the question and on where to find the answer.

1. Data Questions

These question types all have to do with the data presented in the figures and tables. Let's take a brief look at the categories, and then look at some examples on a sample passage. All these question types can be done using the same basic four-step method we discussed earlier.

Data Lookup questions

Data Lookup questions are the most common type of question on the Science Test. They're also the most straightforward: they simply require you to retrieve a value given in one of the tables or graphs provided. In fact, most of the time you don't even have to understand what it is you're looking up. All you have to do is match the name of the quantity the question asks for with the headings and labels in the figure. Ask yourself two questions: *what do we know?* and *what do we want?* Simply take what you know and match it to what you want in the data given.

Combination questions

Combination questions require you to pull information from more than one part of the passage. These questions are similar to Data Lookup questions, but the data you need is spread across multiple tables or figures. These questions usually don't require any additional understanding of the meaning of the data; they just require an additional lookup step. You have to find a bridge between the two figures. For example, say a question asks you to connect volume on Table 1, with temperature on Table 2. Ask yourself: what do the tables have in common? What columns or rows are **the same on both tables**? Find what they have in common and use that variable to compare the values you need.

Relationship questions

Instead of asking you to retrieve specific data values, these questions ask you about the relationship between fields. Usually this is just a matter of figuring out **up** vs. **down**: when one value increases, does the other value increase, decrease, do both, or stay the same? Sometimes these questions might be slightly more mathematically sophisticated (for example, one value is always *triple* another value), but any math you may need will be very simple.

Don't confuse the direction of the values with the direction on the page. If the numbers in a column go physically *down* the page, that's not the same thing as the *values* of the numbers going down. We care about whether the numbers increase or decrease; they may be written in either direction on a table. On graphs it's a bit easier to tell visually whether numbers are going up, but some graphs don't act the way you think they will. Be sure to look at the actual numbers on the axes.

Sometimes questions may ask you to **produce your own graph** based on the data provided. This could involve converting a table to a graph, or converting one type of graph to another (say, a line graph to a bar graph). But these are essentially just like other Relationship questions: you just have to know whether one factor increases or decreases with respect to another factor.

Inferred Data questions

These questions are similar to Data Lookup questions with one important twist: the data point that the question is asking for does not literally appear in the figure. You must infer the value based on the data that does appear. This may sound difficult, but it's not so bad: the point will either be right *in between points that are given*, or it will be *higher or lower than any values given*. Inferred Data questions usually don't ask for a single value but for a range of possible values based on the information you know. This is basically a game of **higher**, **lower**, or **in-between**.

On the next page is a **Data Representation passage**: it presents one set of information about a topic. Data Representation passages tend to have questions involving literal interpretation of charts and graphs. First we'll present the passage and questions, and then we'll discuss the answers.

Data Representation Drill

NOTE: *On the real ACT, Data Representation passages will always have* ***5 questions each****, but this passage will have more in order to demonstrate the different question types more fully.*

Passage I

Certain organic substances can undergo a process called *mimeticization.* The *cromulence* of a substance determines the rate at which it becomes mimeticized. Cromulence is measured in peccaries (pec). The *grittiness* of a substance is the factor by which the substance can be syllogized when mimeticization is taking place. Grittiness is measured in ecksteins (eck). Table 1 identifies the cromulence and grittiness of several liquids at 20°C.

Table 1

Substance	Density (g/cm^3)	Cromulence (pec)	Grittiness (eck)
pentane	0.626	16.54	0.102
hexane	0.659	30.84	0.772
heptane	0.684	46.19	1.442
octane	0.703	60.41	2.121
nonane	0.718	73.99	2.873

A substance's *heat of bonification* (ΔH_b) identifies the amount of energy needed to completely bonify the substance while mimeticization is occurring. Once bonified, the substance can be rebonified through the opposite process. Its receptiveness to rebonification is called its *vagrancy*, measured in anapests (ap). Table 2 shows values for vagrancy and ΔH_b.

Table 2

Substance	ΔH_b (kJ/g)	Vagrancy (ap)
pentane	21.4	48.1
hexane	98.9	40.1
heptane	170.0	28.6
octane	255.2	19.9
nonane	327.1	9.3

Figure 1 shows the progress of mimeticization reactions of 100 mL of each substance according to the percent volume of the substance that is mimeticized over time.

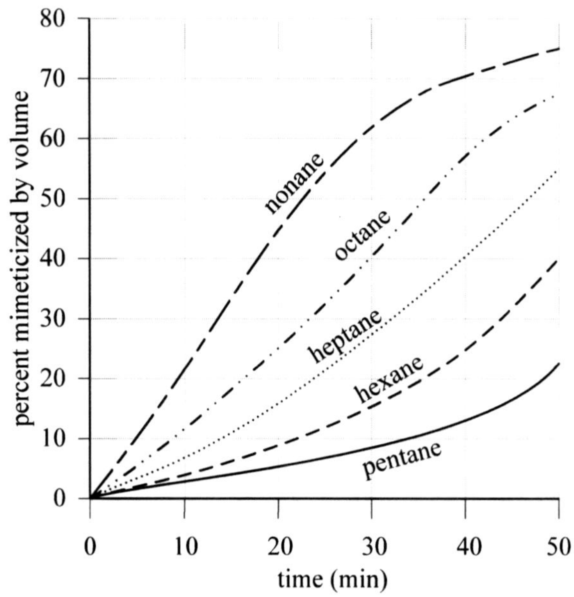

Figure 1

Data Lookup questions

1. According to Table 1, at 20°C heptane has a grittiness of:

   A. 0.772 eck.
   B. 1.442 eck.
   C. 2.121 eck.
   D. 2.873 eck.

2. Based on the information in Figure 1, after 15 minutes what percent of nonane had been mimeticized?

   F. Less than 20%
   G. Between 20% and 40%
   H. Between 40% and 60%
   J. More than 60%

3. In order to synthesize a certain type of stigmagated plastic, engineers need a mimeticized chemical that has a grittiness between 2.0 eck and 2.5 eck. Based on the information in Table 1, which of the following substances would be suitable for making this plastic?

   A. Pentane
   B. Hexane
   C. Heptane
   D. Octane

Combination questions

4. An unidentified substance has a cromulence of 30.84 pec. Based on Table 1 and Table 2 which of the following is most likely its vagrancy?

F. 8.3 ap
G. 17.9 ap
H. 27.6 ap
J. 40.1 ap

Relationship questions

5. Which of the following best describes the relationship between cromulence and grittiness shown in Table 1? As cromulence increases, grittiness:

A. increases only.
B. decreases only.
C. increases, then decreases.
D. stays constant.

6. Consider the information presented in Table 2. Across the substances shown, as heat of bonification increases, vagrancy:

F. increases only.
G. decreases only.
H. decreases, then increases.
J. increases, then decreases.

7. Which of the following graphs best illustrates the relationship between density and cromulence shown in Table 1?

A.

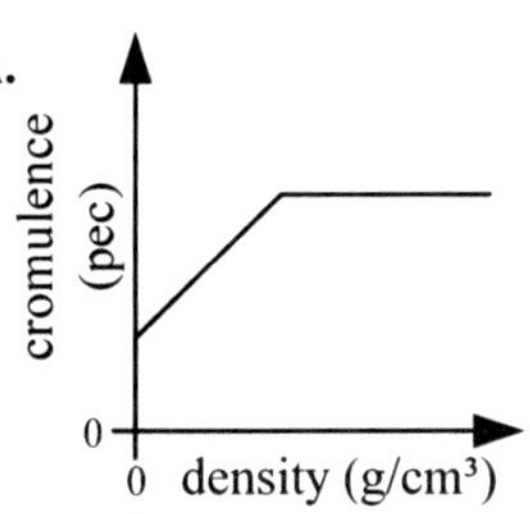

C.

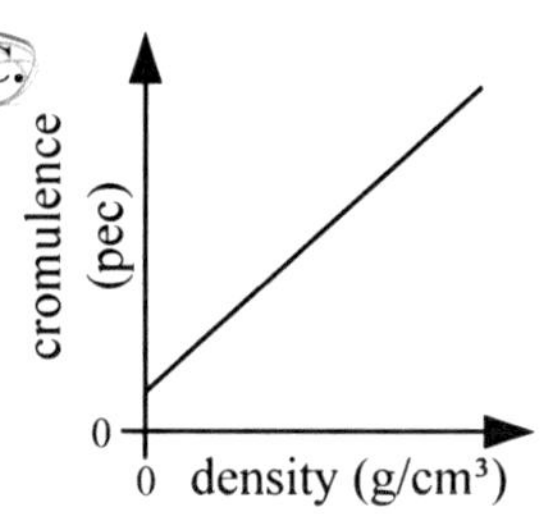

B.

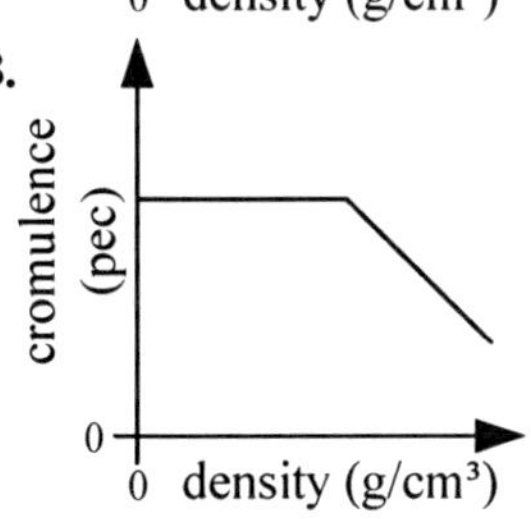

D.

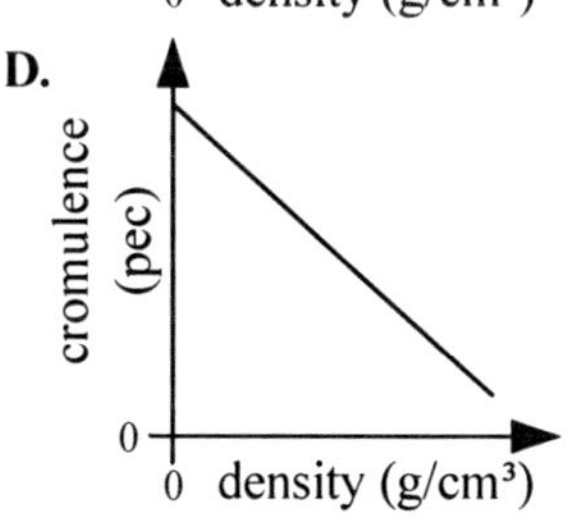

8. Which of the following graphs best illustrates the relationship between cromulence and grittiness?

F.

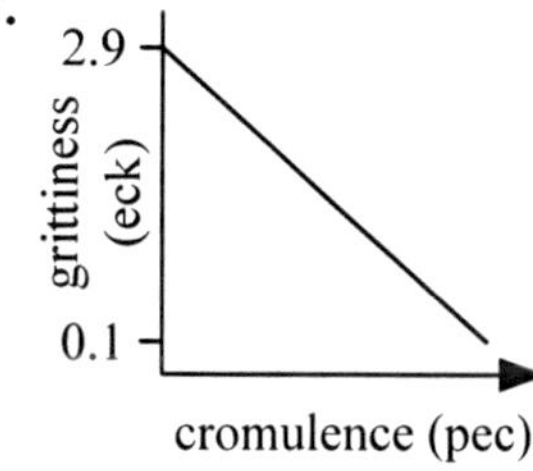

H.

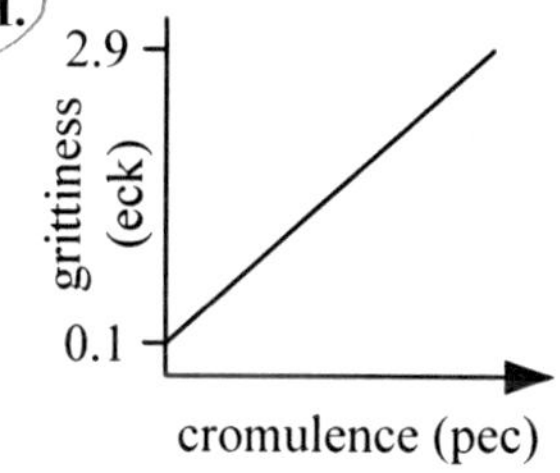

G.

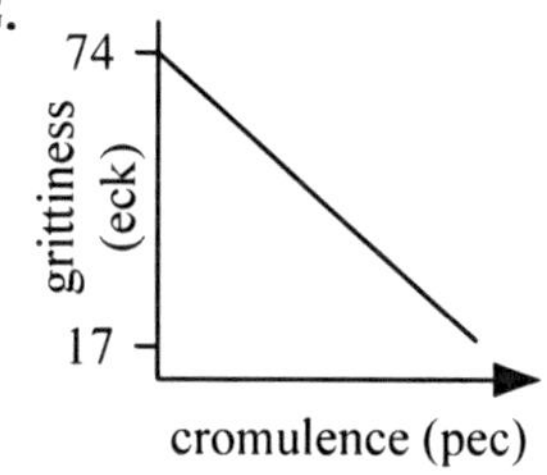

J.

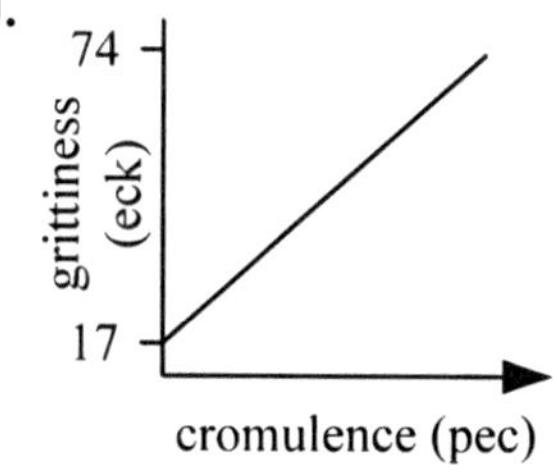

Inferred Data questions

9. *Dodecane* has a density of 0.749 g/cm³ at 20°C. According to Table 1, the grittiness of dodecane is most likely:

A. less than 0.102 eck.
B. between 0.102 eck and 1.442 eck.
C. between 1.442 eck and 2.873 eck.
D. greater than 2.873 eck.

10. An unknown substance is found to have a vagrancy of 44 ap. Based on the information in Table 2, its heat of bonification is most likely closest to:

F. 30 kJ/g.
G. 60 kJ/g.
H. 100 kJ/g.
J. 150 kJ/g.

ANSWERS AND EXPLANATIONS

By now you should have discussed the basic concepts behind mimeticization and rebonification in your regular chemistry class, so you should remember how to convert ecksteins to anapests… Nah, just kidding. We made it all up. But we made it up to prove a point. All of you are no doubt confused by what this passage is supposed to mean. Are these even real words? But for some of you, *every* passage looks like this. The passage might as well have been written in an alien moon language. But don't worry! There's still a *lot* we can do, *even if we don't understand what the passage is talking about.* Data questions in particular do not always require that you understand the concepts; they often only require you to be able to read the tables and figures.

Let's take another look at those questions and discuss the how to do them.

Passage I (repeated)

(We're repeating the text of the passage here so you don't have to flip the pages back and forth.)

Certain organic substances can undergo a process called *mimeticization.* The *cromulence* of a substance determines the rate at which it becomes mimeticized. Cromulence is measured in peccaries (pec). The *grittiness* of a substance is the factor by which the substance can be syllogized when mimeticization is taking place. Grittiness is measured in ecksteins (eck). Table 1 identifies the cromulence and grittiness of several liquids at 20°C.

Table 1

Substance	Density (g/cm^3)	Cromulence (pec)	Grittiness (eck)
pentane	0.626	16.54	0.102
hexane	0.659	30.84	0.772
heptane	0.684	46.19	1.442
octane	0.703	60.41	2.121
nonane	0.718	73.99	2.873

A substance's *heat of bonification* (ΔH_b) identifies the amount of energy needed to completely bonify the substance while mimeticization is occurring. Once bonified, the substance can be rebonified through the opposite process. Its receptiveness to rebonification is called its *vagrancy*, measured in anapests (ap). Table 2 shows values for vagrancy and ΔH_b.

Table 2

Substance	ΔH_b (kJ/g)	Vagrancy (ap)
pentane	21.4	48.1
hexane	98.9	40.1
heptane	170.0	28.6
octane	255.2	19.9
nonane	327.1	9.3

Figure 1 shows the progress of mimeticization reactions of 100 mL of each substance according to the percent volume of the substance that is mimeticized over time.

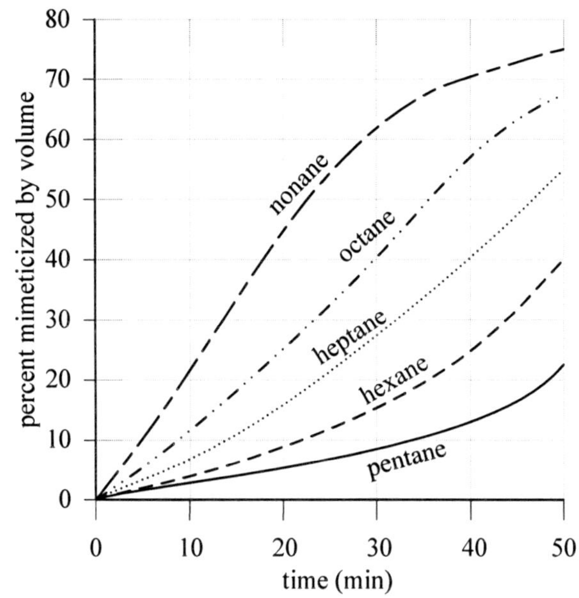

Figure 1

Data Lookup questions

1. According to Table 1, at 20°C heptane has a grittiness of:

A. 0.772 eck.
B. 1.442 eck.
C. 2.121 eck.
D. 2.873 eck.

1. This question couldn't be more straightforward. We know we need to look in Table 1. We know we're talking about heptane—that's the third row of the table. And we want grittiness—that's the fourth column of the table. The intersection of the third row and the fourth column gives us 1.442 eck, **choice B**.

(Don't be distracted by the "20°C" stuff. The paragraph before Table 1 tells us that *all* the values in the table are for 20°C. So that doesn't tell us anything new.)

2. Based on the information in Figure 1, after 15 minutes what percent of nonane had been mimeticized?

F. Less than 20%
G. Between 20% and 40%
H. Between 40% and 60%
J. More than 60%

2. Here we need Figure 1. We know we're talking about nonane—that's the topmost line. We know we want 15 min—that's not marked on the axis, but it's right in the middle between 10 and 20. Start there, move your pencil straight up until you hit the nonane line, and mark the point. Then go straight left until you get to the axis to find the percent mimeticized. It's right between 30% and 40%, so it's about 35%. That's just an estimate, but all the choices are ranges anyway. Where does 30% fall? Between 20% and 40%, **choice G**.

3. In order to synthesize a certain type of stigmagated plastic, engineers need a mimeticized chemical that has a grittiness between 2.0 eck and 2.5 eck. Based on the information in Table 1, which of the following substances would be suitable for making this plastic?

A. Pentane
B. Hexane
C. Heptane
D. Octane

3. This question looks more complicated, but it isn't. It starts with some new information with some new big words. *Don't get distracted.* What do we know? We want something with a grittiness between 2.0 and 2.5. Look at Table 1. Which substance fits that range? Only 2.121, octane, **choice D**.

Combination questions

4. An unidentified substance has a cromulence of 30.84 pec. Based on Table 1 and Table 2 which of the following is most likely its vagrancy?

F. 8.3 ap
G. 17.9 ap
H. 27.6 ap
J. 40.1 ap

4. What do we know? The cromulence is 30.84 pec. What do we want? Vagrancy. But cromulence is only shown on Table 1, and vagrancy is only shown on Table 2, so we can't connect them directly. We'll have to find a way to connect the tables, so we must ask ourselves: *what column do the two tables have in common?* The substance. Looking at Table 1, if the substance has a cromulence of 30.84, it must be *hexane*. Looking at Table 2, hexane has a vagrancy of 40.1, **choice J**.

Relationship questions

5. Which of the following best describes the relationship between cromulence and grittiness shown in Table 1? As cromulence increases, grittiness:

A. increases only.
B. decreases only.
C. increases, then decreases.
D. stays constant.

5. In Table 1, cromulence is the third column. The values increase as we go down the table, from pentane (16.54 pec) to nonane (73.99 pec). Grittiness is the fourth column. If we go down the table from pentane to nonane, the grittiness values *increase*, from pentane (0.102 eck) to nonane (2.873 eck). And we can see that the values *only* increase: as we go down the table, each grittiness value is higher than the one before it. So while cromulence increases, grittiness increases only, **choice A**.

Passage I (repeated)

(We're repeating the text of the passage here so you don't have to flip the pages back and forth.)

Certain organic substances can undergo a process called *mimeticization*. The *cromulence* of a substance determines the rate at which it becomes mimeticized. Cromulence is measured in peccaries (pec). The *grittiness* of a substance is the factor by which the substance can be syllogized when mimeticization is taking place. Grittiness is measured in ecksteins (eck). Table 1 identifies the cromulence and grittiness of several liquids at 20°C.

Table 1			
Substance	Density (g/cm^3)	Cromulence (pec)	Grittiness (eck)
pentane	0.626	16.54	0.102
hexane	0.659	30.84	0.772
heptane	0.684	46.19	1.442
octane	0.703	60.41	2.121
nonane	0.718	73.99	2.873

A substance's *heat of bonification* (ΔH_b) identifies the amount of energy needed to completely bonify the substance while mimeticization is occurring. Once bonified, the substance can be rebonified through the opposite process. Its receptiveness to rebonification is called its *vagrancy*, measured in anapests (ap). Table 2 shows values for vagrancy and ΔH_b.

Table 2		
Substance	ΔH_b (kJ/g)	Vagrancy (ap)
pentane	21.4	48.1
hexane	98.9	40.1
heptane	170.0	28.6
octane	255.2	19.9
nonane	327.1	9.3

Figure 1 shows the progress of mimeticization reactions of 100 mL of each substance according to the percent volume of the substance that is mimeticized over time.

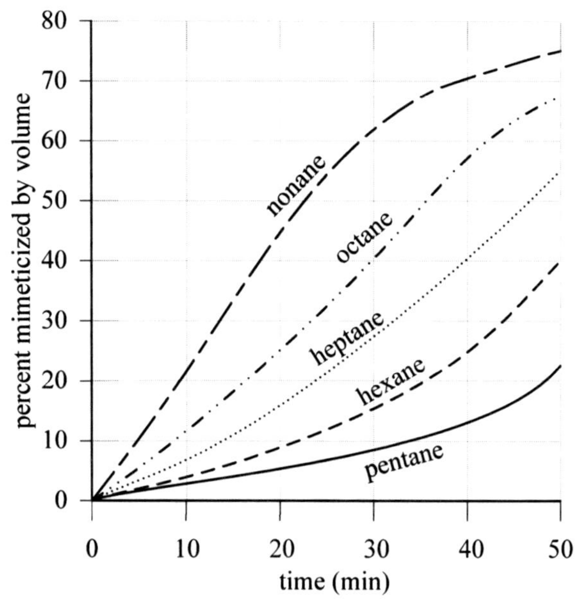

Figure 1

---

6. Consider the information presented in Table 2. Across the substances shown, as heat of bonification increases, vagrancy:

F. increases only.
G. **decreases only.**
H. decreases, then increases.
J. increases, then decreases.

6. In Table 2, heat of bonification is the middle column. The values increase as we go down the table, from pentane (21.4 kJ/g) to nonane (327.1 kJ/g). Vagrancy is the third column. If we go down the table from pentane to nonane, the vagrancy values decrease, from pentane (48.1 ap) to nonane (9.3 ap). So while heat of bonification increases, vagrancy decreases, **choice G**.

7. Which of the following graphs best illustrates the <u>relationship</u> between <u>density</u> and <u>cromulence</u> shown in <u>Table 1</u>?

A.

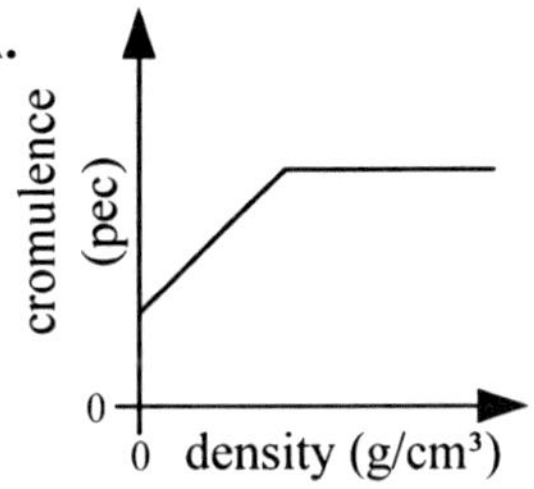

C.

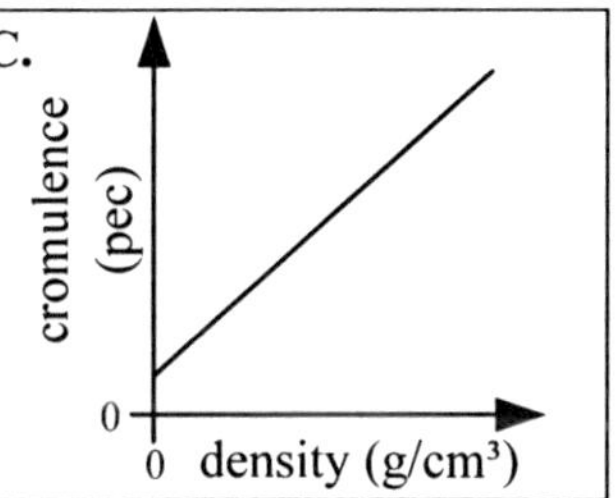

B.

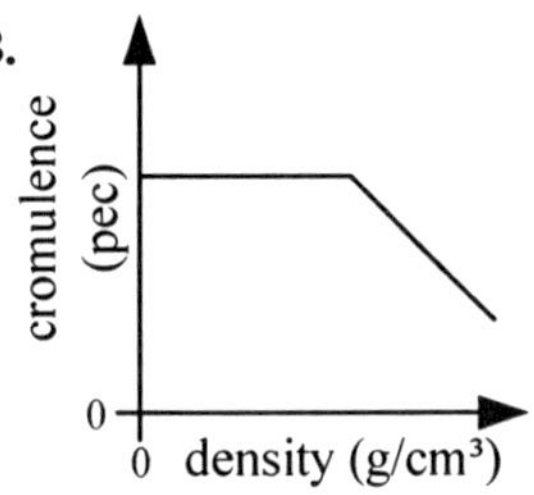

D.

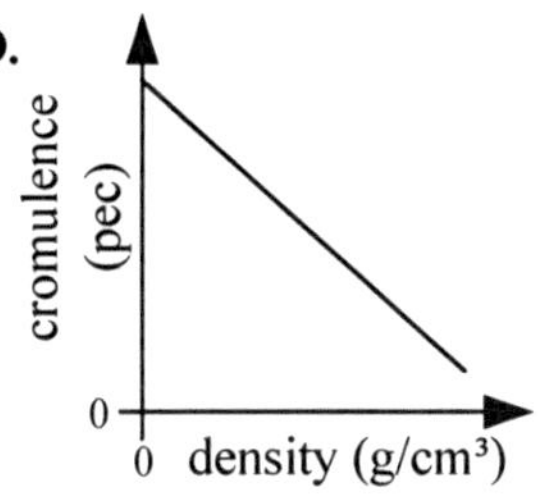

> **7.** This a special type of relationship question where we must show the relationship graphically. If we look at Table 1, we can see that density increases as we go down the table, from pentane (0.626 g/cm³) to nonane (0.718 g/cm³), and cromulence also increases, from 16.54 pec to 73.99 pec. So our graph must show a line that goes up from left to right. Eliminate B and D. In choice A, the graph starts to go up but then flattens out. That's no good. We can see in the table that both values *always* go up, **choice C**.

8. Which of the following graphs best illustrates the <u>relationship</u> between <u>cromulence</u> and <u>grittiness</u>?

F.

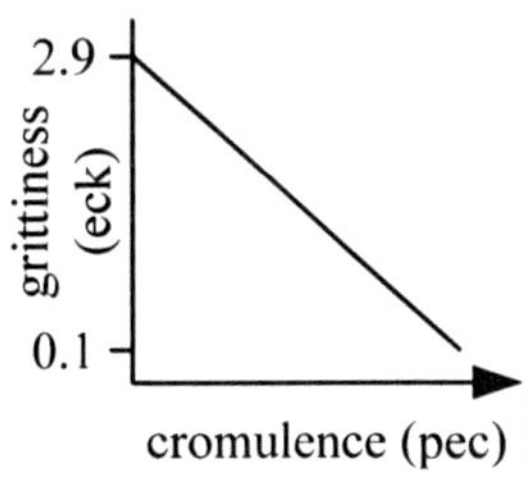

H.

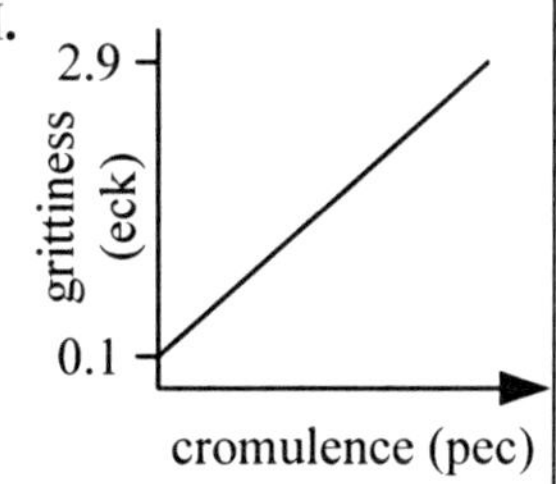

G.

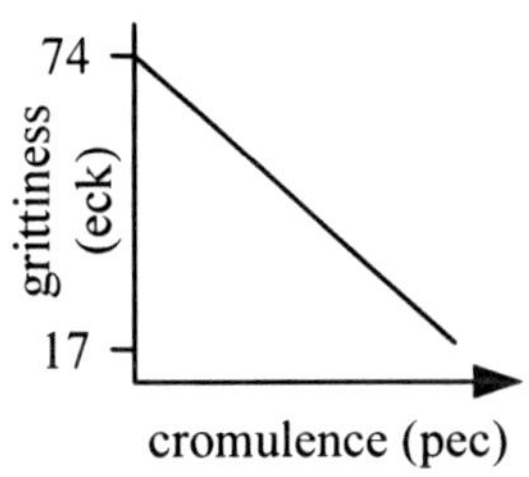

J.

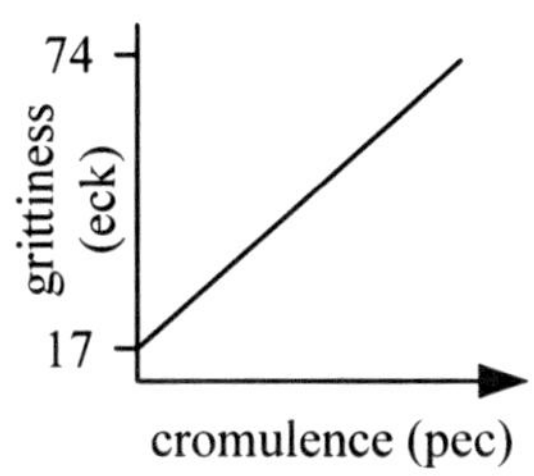

> **8.** We can begin just as we did on question 7. We already saw in question 5 that grittiness increases as cromulence increases. So we know the line must go up, thus we can eliminate F and G. But the graphs in H and J both have the same shape. The only difference between them is the *scale*. We must find out not only the relationship, but the range of values for grittiness. In Table 1, grittiness goes from 0.102 eck to 2.873 eck, **choice H**.

Inferred Data questions

9. Dodecane has a <u>density</u> of <u>0.749 g/cm³</u> at 20°C. According to <u>Table 1</u>, the <u>grittiness</u> of dodecane is most likely:

A. less than 0.102 eck.
B. between 0.102 eck and 1.442 eck.
C. between 1.442 eck and 2.873 eck.
D. greater than 2.873 eck.

> **9.** Dodecane isn't shown on Table 1, but there is a column for density. Density increases as we go down the table, from pentane (0.626 g/cm³) to nonane (0.718 g/cm³). A value of 0.749 g/cm³ would be *greater than any of the values shown.* We want to know its grittiness. Grittiness also increases as we go down the table, from pentane (0.102 eck) to nonane (2.873 eck). So density is directly related to grittiness: the higher the density, the higher the grittiness. Since dodecane's density is greater than nonane's density, its grittiness will also be greater than nonane's grittiness. Nonane's grittiness is 2.873 eck, so dodecane's grittiness will be greater than 2.873 eck, **choice D**.

10. An unknown substance is found to have a <u>vagrancy</u> of <u>44 ap</u>. Based on the information in <u>Table 2</u>, its <u>heat of bonification</u> is most likely closest to:

F. 30 kJ/g.
G. 60 kJ/g.
H. 100 kJ/g.
J. 150 kJ/g.

> **10.** Vagrancy is the third column in Table 2. A value of 44 ap would be between the first two rows, pentane (48.1 ap) and hexane (40.1 ap). So its heat of bonification will also be between those of pentane and hexane, so it will be between 21.4 kJ/g and 98.9 kJ/g. Eliminate H and J: they're both larger than 98.9.
>
> However, F and G are both within our range. So we'll have to be a bit more precise. 44 is right in the middle between 48 and 40. So our value for heat of bonification should be right in the middle of 21 and 99. F is too close to 21 The closest is 60, **choice G**.

2. Non-data Questions

Of course, not all questions will just ask about the figures and tables. Here are some question types that require you to go beyond the numbers in the pictures.

Passage questions

These are questions for which you need more information than what's in the figures and tables themselves. In addition to looking at the figure, you'll have to read the introductory material in the passage or the definitions of terms used.

Usually it's pretty easy to tell whether you need to go back to the passage: if the key words in the question do not appear in the figure, look for them in the passage. Remember that key words in the passage are often *italicized.* If you're looking for the definition of a word, just quickly scan the paragraphs and look for italicized words.

These questions vary in their difficulty. If all you need is the definition of a term, they're really no more difficult than Data Lookup questions. You just go back to the passage instead of the figure. Other times they can be trickier—you can't just know what the fields in the figures say, you have to understand what they *mean.* In that case you'll have to read the paragraphs more closely. But don't spend time doing that unless you really have to.

It's also important to use information you learn in one question on later questions. Multiple questions may ask about the same parts of the passage. You don't always have to get a deep understanding of the experiment, but if you *do* learn something, remember it. It might show up again later.

Experiment Design questions

These questions ask you about the *design* of the experiment. These questions will *only* appear in Research Summaries passages, which feature several different experiments around the same topic or line of investigation. Questions may ask how an experiment was literally set up, why things were set up a certain way, what factors were varied, or what might happen if we change the experiment.

A word about variables

It's worth spending a bit of time here discussing how experiments (and science in general) work. The purpose of any experiment is to test a hypothesis. In order to check whether one thing affects something else, you run a bunch of tests and write down what happened. Usually this means doing the same thing several times, keeping some things the same and other things different. We say that the things that are the *same* across the tests are **controlled**, and things that are *different* are **varied**.

The thing that you vary is the thing that you want to test. If you change something and the results are the same, then the thing you changed had no effect on the results. On the other hand, if the results are different and you *only* changed *one* thing, the thing you changed was probably the cause of the difference.

Let's take a specific example. Say you want to figure out whether a certain fertilizer makes plants grow bigger. You could test it by getting two plants. Give one the fertilizer and the other one no fertilizer and measure how big they grow. If the one that got the fertilizer grew bigger, you might conclude that the fertilizer worked.

However, if everything else was *not* the same, then you can't make that conclusion. What if the one that grew bigger *also* got more sunlight? Or got more water? Or it was a different kind of plant that naturally grows bigger. If there are too many differences between the two plants, you can't tell which factor caused the extra growth. But if you keep everything the same except the factor you want to test, then you know that factor caused the growth. These factors that you *don't* change are **controlled**.

The factors that we vary are called **independent** variables, and the results we get are called **dependent** variables. They're "independent" because we can choose any values at all we want for them. We can give the plant 10 grams, 100 grams or 500 grams of fertilizer if we want. The others are "dependent" because the values depend on all the other factors in the experiment. We can't choose how big the plant gets—it *depends* on how much fertilizer it gets. In fact, when there is a relationship between variables, we say that one variable *depends* or *is dependent* on the other.

Reasoning questions

These questions ask you to make conclusions about hypotheses based on the results of the experiments. They may ask whether a certain conclusion is justified, whether a certain fact weakens or strengthens a hypothesis, or what assumptions are necessary to make an argument. Sometimes these questions may require extended reasoning, but often they require little more than looking up data and can be done by elimination.

Most Reasoning questions take the same form. The question presents you with a statement or hypothesis about the topic of the passage, and the question asks whether the data supports this statement. The choices will have two components to the answer choices: the *answer* (yes or no) and the *evidence* for that answer (usually a description of the data). So there are two questions: whether the given statement is correct, and what part of the data shows whether it's correct.

You can do these questions in two steps. First, *ignore the statement in the question.* Just look at the choices and **eliminate choices that are** ***false***. Look at the *second* part of the choices, after the "Yes" or "No" and see if it matches what we know. The second part could be actual numbers from the figures and tables, or just a description of the results. Eliminate anything that isn't true. If a choice says "Yes, because the plants all got bigger," *go back and make sure the plants actually got bigger.* You'll be surprised to see how often this elimination is enough to get the whole question.

If you have more than one choice remaining, *then* you can worry about whether that information proves or disproves the statement in the question. Often this means you'll be left with two choices that describe the same data in the passage, the only difference being whether it's a "Yes" or a "No". Sometimes seeing the relationship between the hypothesis and the data can be tricky, but often it just comes down to asking: *are these things saying the same thing or different things.* If the hypothesis said "the fertilizer will make the plants grow" and the data showed that the plants got bigger, then *yes*, the data proved the hypothesis. Sometimes it's really that simple.

Knowledge questions

These questions require additional scientific knowledge that is not given in the passage. Sometimes this may be something as simple as knowing what a word means (like "mammal"). Other times you may need an understanding of certain properties or concepts (like "density") that aren't explicitly defined in the passage. These questions can be the most annoying, since they rely on information that isn't present, but they are also the least common question type.

If you don't know the facts or definitions you need for a question, you'll probably be stuck and might freak out a little. It's okay. First, look at the choices and see if you can **eliminate** any that are clearly **false** based on what you do know from the passage. Once you've eliminated what you can, just guess something and move on to the next question. Remember: *never ever leave any question blank for any reason ever ever.**

Let's take a closer look at these question types by looking a sample passage on the next page. This passage is a **Research Summaries passage**, presenting several different experiments about the same topic. First we'll just show the passage and the questions, and then we'll repeat them alongside answers and explanations.

On this passage we will only present non-data questions for the sake of illustrating the question types. In reality, however, questions on Research Summaries passages aren't significantly different from those on Data Representation passages. Both passage types can have data and non-data questions. The biggest difference is that Experiment Design questions will only appear on Research Summary passages, not on Data Representation passages.

NOTE: On the real ACT, Research Summaries passages will always have 6 questions each, but this passage will have more than that in order to demonstrate these question types.

* Ever.

RESEARCH SUMMARIES DRILL

NOTE: *On the real ACT, Research Summaries passages will always have 6 questions each, but this passage will have more than that in order to demonstrate the different question types.*

Passage II

The height an object will bounce is dependent on the height from which it was dropped and the composition of the object. An object's bounciness can be shown through its *coefficient of restitution* (COR). The higher the value of the COR, the higher the object will bounce when dropped from a given height. The maximum possible value of COR is 1. Researchers have developed a polymer that, when applied to an object, is intended to increase its COR.

Several badgers were collected and each was placed on a platform 10 m above a concrete floor. A trap door opened and the badger immediately fell to the ground. Using high-speed photography, the maximum height of the badger's first bounce was measured and recorded. The arrangement of the badger and the platform is shown in Figure 1.

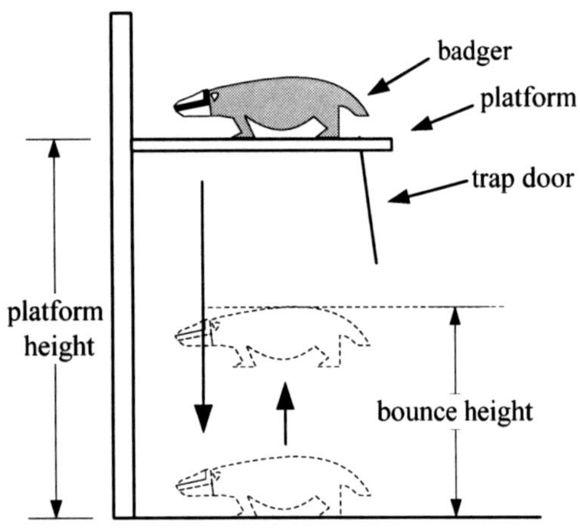

Figure 1

Four badgers of different species were used for the experiments, as outlined in Table 1. Each badger had a mass of 10 kg and was roughly the same size and shape.

Table 1

Specimen	Species	Common name
A	*Mellivora capensis*	Honey badger
B	*Taxidea taxus*	American badger
C	*Arctonyx collaris*	Hog badger
D	*Meles meles*	Eurasian badger

Experiment 1

The specimens in Table 1 were each dropped from the 10 m platform shown in Figure 1. Their maximum bounce height was recorded and shown in Table 2.

Table 2

Trial	Specimen	Bounce height (m)
1	A	1.92
2	B	2.19
3	C	4.02
4	D	3.34

Experiment 2

Experiment 1 was repeated with 100 g of the polymer applied to each of the specimens. The polymer was applied to each specimen in liquid form, and then allowed to dry until it hardened. The specimens were then dropped from the platform in the same manner already described.

Table 3

Trial	Specimen	Bounce height (m)
5	A	3.12
6	B	3.56
7	C	6.53
8	D	5.43

Experiment 3

Experiment 2 was repeated using only specimen C. Additional amounts of the polymer were applied in the same manner in 100 g increments, thus increasing the total amount of polymer on the specimen with each test.

Table 4

Trial	Total amount of polymer (g)	Bounce height (m)
9	200	8.26
10	300	9.22
11	400	9.67

Passage questions

1. According to the information in the passage, which specimen had the highest coefficient of restitution in Experiment 1?

   A. Specimen A
   B. Specimen B
   C. Specimen C
   D. Specimen D

2. According to the information in the passage, which of the following could be the coefficient of restitution for specimen D in Experiment 1?

   F. 0.6
   G. 1.7
   H. 3.3
   J. 5.4

Experiment Design questions

3. Which of the following was kept constant in all three experiments?

   A. Species
   B. Amount of polymer
   C. Coefficient of restitution
   D. Platform height

4. The purpose of Experiment 3 was to determine the dependence of bounce height on which of the following variables?

   F. Species
   G. Platform height
   H. Mass of specimen
   J. Amount of polymer applied

5. A scientist hypothesizes that bounce height is dependent on the composition of *both* objects involved in a collision. Which of the following experiments, if performed alongside the experiments described, would best test this hypothesis?

   A. Repeat Experiment 1 using a 20 m platform for all trials.
   B. Repeat Experiment 1 using a wooden floor instead of a concrete floor for all trials.
   C. Repeat Experiment 2 using a different polymer for all trials.
   D. Repeat Experiment 2 using raccoons instead of badgers for all trials.

6. Based on the information provided, if Experiment 1 was repeated with a platform height of 20 m, how would the results differ from those in Table 2? Compared to values in Table 2:

   F. all bounce heights would be the same.
   G. all bounce heights would be greater.
   H. all bounce heights would be less.
   J. some bounce heights would be different and some would be the same.

Reasoning questions

7. It was hypothesized that adding the polymer to the specimens would increase their coefficient of restitution. Do the results of Experiments 1 and 2 support that conclusion?

   A. Yes, because each specimen had a greater bounce height in Experiment 2 than in Experiment 1.
   B. Yes, because each specimen had a smaller bounce height in Experiment 2 than in Experiment 1.
   C. No, because each specimen had a greater bounce height in Experiment 2 than in Experiment 1.
   D. No, because each specimen had a smaller bounce height in Experiment 2 than in Experiment 1.

8. One researcher hypothesizes that the bounciness of a specimen is dependent on the mass of the specimen. Do the results of Experiment 1 support that conclusion?

   F. Yes, because the bounce height varied with specimen type.
   G. Yes, because the bounce height increased as the amount of polymer added increased.
   H. No, because the bounce height increased as the mass of polymer added increased.
   J. No, because the mass of the specimens was kept constant.

Knowledge questions

9. In each trial of Experiment 1, the specimen had the greatest gravitational potential energy:

   A. before the trap door was released.
   B. just before it hit the ground.
   C. at the moment it hit the ground.
   D. at the maximum point of the first bounce.

Passage II (repeated)

(We're repeating the text of the passage here so you don't have to flip the pages back and forth.)

The height an object will bounce is dependent on the height from which it was dropped and the composition of the object. An object's bounciness can be shown through its *coefficient of restitution* (COR). The higher the value of the COR, the higher the object will bounce when dropped from a given height. The maximum possible value of COR is 1. Researchers have developed a polymer that, when applied to an object, is intended to increase its COR.

Several badgers were collected and each was placed on a platform 10 m above a concrete floor. A trap door opened and the badger immediately fell to the ground. Using high-speed photography, the maximum height of the badger's first bounce was measured and recorded. The arrangement of the badger and the platform is shown in Figure 1.

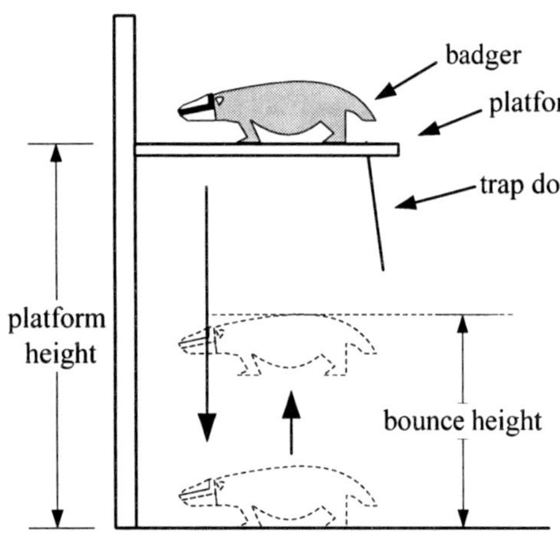

Figure 1

Four badgers of different species were used for the experiments, as outlined in Table 1. Each badger had a mass of 10 kg and was roughly the same size and shape.

Table 1

Specimen	Species	Common name
A	*Mellivora capensis*	Honey badger
B	*Taxidea taxus*	American badger
C	*Arctonyx collaris*	Hog badger
D	*Meles meles*	Eurasian badger

Experiment 1

The specimens in Table 1 were each dropped from the 10 m platform shown in Figure 1. Their maximum bounce height was recorded and shown in Table 2.

Table 2

Trial	Specimen	Bounce height (m)
1	A	1.92
2	B	2.19
3	C	4.02
4	D	3.34

Experiment 2

Experiment 1 was repeated with 100 g of the polymer applied to each of the specimens. The polymer was applied to each specimen in liquid form, and then allowed to dry until it hardened. The specimens were then dropped from the platform in the same manner already described.

Table 3

Trial	Specimen	Bounce height (m)
5	A	3.12
6	B	3.56
7	C	6.53
8	D	5.43

Experiment 3

Experiment 2 was repeated using only specimen C. Additional amounts of the polymer were applied in the same manner in 100 g increments, thus increasing the total amount of polymer on the specimen with each test.

Table 4

Trial	Total amount of polymer (g)	Bounce height (m)
9	200	8.26
10	300	9.22
11	400	9.67

Passage questions

1. According to the information in the passage, which specimen had the highest coefficient of restitution in Experiment 1?

A. Specimen A
B. Specimen B
C. Specimen C
D. Specimen D

> **1.** The question tells us to check Experiment 1, so let's look at the results. Hmm… "coefficient of restitution" isn't mentioned there at all. Let's check the passage for that phrase. Aha! The first paragraph mentions coefficient of restitution (COR). It's even italicized! The third sentence says, "The higher the value of the COR, the higher the object will bounce when dropped from a given height." Specimen C bounced the highest. **Choice C** is our answer.

2. According to the information in the passage, which of the following could be the coefficient of restitution for specimen D in Experiment 1?

F. 0.6
G. 1.7
H. 3.3
J. 5.4

> **2.** This question asks us to get an actual value for the coefficient of restitution. But the passage never tells us how to calculate it, and it doesn't give any values for it in Table 2. Hmm. What *do* we know about the value of COR? Aha! The first paragraph says "The maximum possible value of COR is 1." The only choice less than 1 is **choice F**.

Experiment Design questions

3. Which of the following was kept constant in all three experiments?

A. Species
B. Amount of polymer
C. Coefficient of restitution
D. Platform height

> **3.** We want something constant in *all* tests, so we can eliminate any value that differed in *any* of the tests.
> *Eliminate A:* Experiments 1 and 2 each used four different species (Table 1 tells us each is a different species).
> *Eliminate B:* Experiment 3 used three different amounts of the polymer. Experiment 1 used none.
> *Eliminate C:* We learned in question 1 that COR shows bounciness, and every trial had a different bounce height.
> The only thing that was the same in all experiments was *platform height*. The second paragraph says the platform is 10 m high, and each experiment uses the same platform. **Choice D** is our answer.

4. The purpose of Experiment 3 was to determine the dependence of bounce height on which of the following variables?

F. Species
G. Platform height
H. Mass of specimen
J. Amount of polymer applied

> **4.** As we said before, the thing that you want to test is the thing that you *vary*. So the question is: which of these factors changed across the trials in Experiment 3? In Experiment 3, the same specimen was used each time, so species and mass were kept constant. The platform is the same one used in all the experiments, 10 m high, so platform height is constant. The only thing that's different is the *amount of polymer applied*: 200 g in Trial 9, 300 g in Trial 10, and 400 g in Trial 11. **Choice J** is our answer.

5. A scientist hypothesizes that bounce height is dependent on the composition of *both* objects involved in a collision. Which of the following experiments, if performed alongside the experiments described, would best test this hypothesis?

A. Repeat Experiment 1 using a 20 m platform for all trials.
B. Repeat Experiment 1 using a wooden floor instead of a concrete floor for all trials.
C. Repeat Experiment 2 using a different polymer for all trials.
D. Repeat Experiment 2 using raccoons instead of badgers for all trials.

> **5.** This question asks how to set up a new experiment in order to test a hypothesis. Just like before, the thing that you want to test should be the thing that you *vary* in the experiment. Here, we want to test the effect of the composition of both objects involved in a collision. Well, we've already been testing the effect of the composition of the falling object: we used different specimens and different amounts of polymer. What's the *other* thing involved in the collision? The floor! So let's do the exact same experiment again with a *different floor*. If the bounce heights are significantly different, the new floor must have been the cause. **Choice B** is our answer.

Passage II (repeated)

(We're repeating the text of the passage here so you don't have to flip the pages back and forth.)

The height an object will bounce is dependent on the height from which it was dropped and the composition of the object. An object's bounciness can be shown through its *coefficient of restitution* (COR). The higher the value of the COR, the higher the object will bounce when dropped from a given height. The maximum possible value of COR is 1. Researchers have developed a polymer that, when applied to an object, is intended to increase its COR.

Several badgers were collected and each was placed on a platform 10 m above a concrete floor. A trap door opened and the badger immediately fell to the ground. Using high-speed photography, the maximum height of the badger's first bounce was measured and recorded. The arrangement of the badger and the platform is shown in Figure 1.

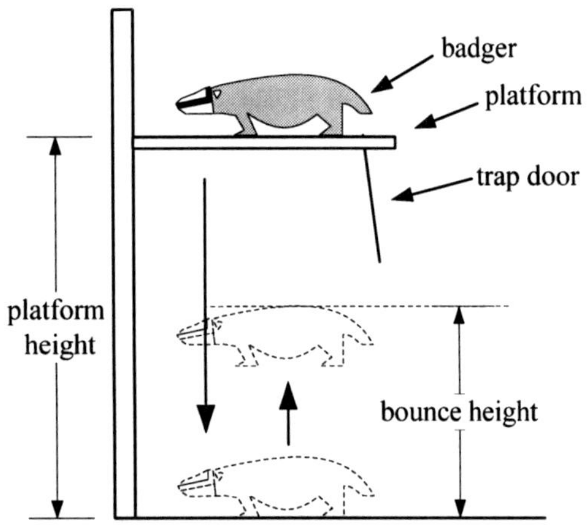

Figure 1

Four badgers of different species were used for the experiments, as outlined in Table 1. Each badger had a mass of 10 kg and was roughly the same size and shape.

Table 1		
Specimen	Species	Common name
A	*Mellivora capensis*	Honey badger
B	*Taxidea taxus*	American badger
C	*Arctonyx collaris*	Hog badger
D	*Meles meles*	Eurasian badger

Experiment 1

The specimens in Table 1 were each dropped from the 10 m platform shown in Figure 1. Their maximum bounce height was recorded and shown in Table 2.

Table 2		
Trial	Specimen	Bounce height (m)
1	A	1.92
2	B	2.19
3	C	4.02
4	D	3.34

Experiment 2

Experiment 1 was repeated with 100 g of the polymer applied to each of the specimens. The polymer was applied to each specimen in liquid form, and then allowed to dry until it hardened. The specimens were then dropped from the platform in the same manner already described.

Table 3		
Trial	Specimen	Bounce height (m)
5	A	3.12
6	B	3.56
7	C	6.53
8	D	5.43

Experiment 3

Experiment 2 was repeated using only specimen C. Additional amounts of the polymer were applied in the same manner in 100 g increments, thus increasing the total amount of polymer on the specimen with each test.

Table 4		
Trial	Total amount of polymer (g)	Bounce height (m)
9	200	8.26
10	300	9.22
11	400	9.67

6. Based on the information provided, if Experiment 1 was repeated with a platform height of 20 m, how would the results differ from those in Table 2? Compared to values in Table 2:

F. all bounce heights would be the same.
G. all bounce heights would be greater.
H. all bounce heights would be less.
J. some bounce heights would be the greater, some would be less.

6. This question asks what would happen if we *changed* the experiment. The key words are "platform height". What do we know about platform height? The first paragraph tells us that bounce height "is dependent on the height from which it was dropped", so changing the height should affect all specimens in the same way. Experiment 1 used a platform height of 10 m, so 20 m would be an *increase* in platform height, so bounce height should also increase. **Choice G** is our answer.

Reasoning questions

7. It was hypothesized that adding the polymer to the specimens would increase their coefficient of restitution. Do the results of Experiments 1 and 2 support that conclusion?

A. Yes, because each specimen had a greater bounce height in Experiment 2 than in Experiment 1.
B. Yes, because each specimen had a smaller bounce height in Experiment 2 than in Experiment 1.
C. No, because each specimen had a greater bounce height in Experiment 2 than in Experiment 1.
D. No, because each specimen had a smaller bounce height in Experiment 2 than in Experiment 1.

7. This is a Reasoning question: it presents a hypothesis and asks you whether the data supports that hypothesis. The first thing to check the *evidence*: which choices are *literally true*? If we look at Tables 2 and 3, we see that each specimen had a *greater* bounce height in Table 3—specimen A went from 1.92 m to 3.46 m, B went from 2.19 m to 3.94 m, etc. So we can eliminate B and D right away.

The next question is: given that the bounce height is higher with the polymer, does that support the conclusion? Yes, it does. As we saw in question 1, the passage tells us that a higher coefficient of restitution means a higher bounce height. **Choice A** is our answer.

8. One researcher hypothesizes that the bounciness of a specimen is dependent on the mass of the specimen. Do the results of Experiment 1 support that conclusion?

F. Yes, because the bounce height varied with specimen type.
G. Yes, because the bounce height increased as the amount of polymer added increased.
H. No, because the bounce height increased as the mass of polymer added increased.
J. No, because the mass of the specimens was kept constant.

8. We'll approach this question the same way we did question 7: which choices are *literally true*. But the problem is that all four choices here are true according to the passage. What can we do?

First, eliminate anything that's unrelated to Experiment 1. Choices G and H are about the polymer, which wasn't added until Experiment 2. We're down to choices F and J.

Things *depend on* each other when one changes along with the other. The first paragraph says the all badgers had *the same mass*, 10 kg. If it doesn't change, we can't conclude that mass had any effect on bounce height. It might, but we don't know. If we wanted to test this, we could do another experiment using badgers of the same species and different masses and see if they a difference in bounce height. But Experiment 1 doesn't do that, so we can't make that conclusion. **Choice J** is our answer.

Knowledge questions

9. In each trial of Experiment 1, the specimen had the greatest gravitational potential energy:

A. before the trap door was released.
B. just before it hit the ground.
C. at the moment it hit the ground.
D. at the maximum point of the first bounce.

9. The question tells us to check Experiment 1, so let's look at the results. Hmm… "potential energy" isn't mentioned there at all. What do we do? Let's check the rest of the passage for that phrase. Hmm… It's not mentioned *anywhere*. That means we have to know the definition of "potential energy".

In brief: potential energy is stored energy that has the *potential* to become motion (as opposed to kinetic energy, which is the energy of motion). Objects at *higher points* have more potential energy because they have more room to fall, thus more potential motion. So the potential energy was greatest *before the trap door was released*. **Choice A** is our answer.

3. Conflicting Viewpoints Questions

Data Representation and Research Summary passages tend to have similar questions types following them. However, the Conflicting Viewpoints passages are noticeably different. The passage will present a topic or situation followed by several different theories that seek to explain the situation. Unlike the other types, there will be only one Conflicting Viewpoints passage per test.

The Passages

The biggest difference is that this passage usually involves less data and more *reading*. As a result, it can take longer to do, which is why many students may want to skip it entirely or save it for the end.

The dense reading also means that you can't gloss over the passage the same way you can with the other passage types. For other types, you can dive straight into the questions and start looking up data without reading a word from the paragraphs. Here, you have no choice: you have to read the paragraphs.*

However, you don't have to memorize *everything* in the passage. All you need are the **Main Ideas**.

First, skim the opening paragraph to get a general sense of what it's about. No details, just the topic: it's about bird migration, or the structure of atoms, or double black holes. Sometimes the passage will begin by listing a series of specific known facts about the situation. Ignore these. Only read them if and when a question refers to them.

Then move on to the viewpoints. The viewpoints will usually be labeled in terms of the people presenting the views: Scientist 1 and Scientist 2, or Student 1 and Student 2. Usually there are 2-3 viewpoints per passage, but there could be as many as 5. (The more viewpoints there are, the shorter each will be.)

Get the *main ideas* of the different viewpoints presented. More often than not, you can just **underline the first sentence of each viewpoint** to get the main idea. These passages may contain some dense science content, but they're written in an unadorned, direct language. Each viewpoint will usually start by stating its hypothesis, followed by an explanation of why they think that, and how it fits in with the known facts. So the first sentences should tell you what the hypotheses are.

If you've done this right, your Main Ideas will look something like this:

> **TOPIC:** Dogs smell weird when they get wet.
>
> *Scientist 1:* The smell is caused by oil in dog fur that chemically reacts with water.
>
> *Scientist 2:* The smell is caused by microbes on the dogs' skin that release chemicals into the air.
>
> *Scientist 3:* The smell is caused by a pheromone the dogs release because they are afraid of the bath.

Now move on to the questions. Don't worry about the rest of the paragraphs. Yes, there is a lot of information in there, and yes you may be asked about it later. But you can worry about it if and when you're asked about it, not before.

Please note: when you read the viewpoints, *don't worry about who's right.* Most of the time we don't actually care which viewpoint turns out to be correct. Sometimes the passage will end with an experiment that will ultimately prove which viewpoint is correct (and the questions will certainly address this). Other times, there might be information in the questions themselves that imply one viewpoint is correct. But we only have to worry about that if it specifically comes up in a question, not before.

* That's not to say that these passages *never* contain figures and tables. They certainly can, but far less frequently than other passage types, which almost *always* have at least one figure or table.

The Questions

You can use the same basic four-step method on Conflicting Viewpoints questions that you do for all other question types. Things will be a little different when there aren't tables or figures, but the general structure is the same.

1. In the question, underline any **specific viewpoints mentioned** (e.g. "Scientist 1", "Student 3", etc). Also underline any figure or table mentioned. If no viewpoints or figures are mentioned, move on to step 2.
2. In the question, underline any **key words**, just like on any other question.
3. Go back to the passage to find the key words:
    a. If one or more viewpoints were mentioned, look for those key words **in the viewpoints**.
    b. If no viewpoints were mentioned, look for the key words in the passage. **Use your Main Ideas** (the first sentences you underlined) to help you figure out which viewpoints to check.
4. Read what the passage or viewpoints say about the key words to answer the question.

The question types we've already discussed show up on Conflicting Viewpoints passages to varying degrees, sometimes in slightly different form. Most common are:

- **Passage questions**: These are questions that literally ask what the introduction or one of the hypotheses says. They occur quite frequently.
- **Reasoning questions**: These may occur in the "Yes" or "No" format we saw before. Other times, a question will ask which viewpoints would be supported or weakened by a given statement.
- **Combination questions**: Instead of asking you to compare data or figures, these questions will ask you to directly compare and contrast different viewpoints.

On the next page you'll find a sample **Conflicting Viewpoints passage** and some questions. Try it on your own:

Conflicting Viewpoints Drill

Try one! This drill has **7 questions**, *just like a real Conflicting Viewpoints passage. Enjoy!*

Passage III

Tree Disintegration Syndrome (TDS) is a disease that affects several species of maple and elm trees in North America. TDS is characterized by the rapid disintegration of the woody interior of the tree and the subsequent failure of the tree's vascular system.

The presence of the Asian imaginary beetle (*anoplophora sporkazola*) has been detected in areas that have been affected by TDS. Table 1 shows the duration of each stage of the beetle's life cycle.

Table 1

Stage	Duration (days)
Egg	3-5
Larva	10-15
Pupa	15-20
Adult	15-20

Three scientists discuss the Asian imaginary beetle's role in TDS.

Scientist 1

TDS is caused by the life cycle of the Asian imaginary beetle. The adult beetle bores into the trees, through the bark into the xylem, in order to lay its eggs. When the eggs hatch, the larvae feed on the tree's interior, destroying the tree's vascular system. In the process, the larvae secrete a chemical in their saliva that helps them digest the wood. As the larvae become pupae, they stop feeding, but the salivary chemical continues to damage the tree's interior, causing the extensive interior deterioration that is characteristic of TDS. The tree dies by the time the adult matures and leaves the tree.

Scientist 2

TDS is caused by a fungus that has a symbiotic relationship with the Asian imaginary beetle. The fungus requires the Asian imaginary beetle to spread its fungal spores. The spores are carried on the beetle's body and become deposited inside the tree when the beetle lays its eggs. Once the spores make it to the interior, the fungus spreads throughout the entire tree, decomposing the wood, which in turn helps larval digestion. When the adult beetle leaves the tree, it picks up new spores and spreads them to the next tree.

The beetle larvae do cause damage to the interior of the tree, but TDS cannot be caused by the beetles alone because each beetle only lays 1-2 eggs in a single tree, far too few to cause the extensive destruction observed in trees with TDS.

Scientist 3

TDS is caused by a fungus that thrives in specific environmental conditions. Instances of TDS have all been observed in areas that have low soil nitrogen and poor drainage, and have experienced a recent heavy rainfall. These soil conditions allow the fungal spores to grow, and the rainfall stirs them into the air. The spores stick to the trees and enter through wounds in the bark.

The Asian imaginary beetle does not cause TDS. While the beetle can make trees more susceptible to the fungus by providing wounds in the bark, the fungus does not specifically require the presence of the beetle. Trees that show signs of TDS fully succumb to the disease at varying rates, sometimes in less than a week. The disease would not spread so rapidly if it were tied to the life cycle of the beetle.

1. According to Scientist 2, the fungus is transported into the interior of trees that later develop TDS by:

A. rainwater.
B. beetle larvae.
C. beetle saliva.
D. adult beetles.

2 Based on Scientist 1's discussion and Table 1, how much time would likely pass between the beetle laying its eggs and the death of the tree?

F. Less than 10 days
G. Between 10 and 15 days
H. Between 15 and 20 days
J. More than 20 days

3. *Mycangia* are structures on certain insects' bodies that are specially adapted to transport fungi. The discovery of mycangia on the bodies of Asian imaginary beetles would support the viewpoint of:

A. Scientist 2 only.
B. Scientist 3 only.
C. Scientist 1 and Scientist 2.
D. Scientist 2 and Scientist 3.

4. Suppose trees with TDS were found in an area where no evidence of Asian imaginary beetle has been found. This discovery would most support the viewpoint(s) of:

   F. Scientist 1 only.
   G. Scientist 3 only.
   H. Scientist 1 and Scientist 2.
   J. Scientist 2 and Scientist 3.

5. How does Scientist 2's viewpoint differ from Scientist 3's viewpoint with regard to the spread of TDS? Scientist 2 claims that the spread of TDS requires:

   A. a fungus and the Asian imaginary beetle, whereas Scientist 3 claims it only requires the beetle.
   B. only the Asian imaginary beetle, whereas Scientist 3 claims it requires a fungus and the beetle.
   C. a fungus and the Asian imaginary beetle, whereas Scientist 3 claims it only requires the fungus.
   D. only a fungus, whereas Scientist 3 claims it requires a fungus and the Asian imaginary beetle.

6. Based on the information provided, Scientist 1's discussion would be most weakened if which of the following observations were made?

   F. Asian imaginary beetles only lay eggs in one species of elm tree.
   G. Most North American fungi do not thrive in areas with low soil nitrogen.
   H. Most species of fungi are deadly to Asian imaginary beetles.
   J. The saliva of Asian imaginary beetle larvae is highly corrosive to plant cells.

7. Suppose a drought eliminated most of the insect life in a certain area. According to Scientist 3's discussion, would this occurrence affect the chances of trees in this area developing TDS?

   A. Yes, because insects are necessary for the spread of fungus.
   B. Yes, because rainfall is necessary for the growth of the fungus.
   C. No, because insects are not necessary for the spread of the fungus.
   D. No, because rainfall is not necessary for the growth of the fungus.

ANSWERS AND EXPLANATIONS

Passage III (repeated)

(We're repeating the text of the passage here so you don't have to flip the pages back and forth.)

Tree Disintegration Syndrome (TDS) is a disease that affects several species of maple and elm trees in North America. TDS is characterized by the rapid disintegration of the woody interior of the tree and the subsequent failure of the tree's vascular system.

The presence of the Asian imaginary beetle (*anoplophora sporkazola*) has been detected in areas that have been affected by TDS. Table 1 shows the duration of each stage of the beetle's life cycle.

Table 1

Stage	Duration (days)
Egg	3-5
Larva	10-15
Pupa	15-20
Adult	15-20

Three scientists discuss the Asian imaginary beetle's role in TDS.

Scientist 1

TDS is caused by the life cycle of the Asian imaginary beetle. The adult beetle bores into the trees, through the bark into the xylem, in order to lay its eggs. When the eggs hatch, the larvae feed on the tree's interior, destroying the tree's vascular system. In the process, the larvae secrete a chemical in their saliva that helps them digest the wood. As the larvae become pupae, they stop feeding, but the salivary chemical continues to damage the tree's interior, causing the extensive interior deterioration that is characteristic of TDS. The tree dies by the time the adult matures and leaves the tree.

Scientist 2

TDS is caused by a fungus that has a symbiotic relationship with the Asian imaginary beetle. The fungus requires the Asian imaginary beetle to spread its fungal spores. The spores are carried on the beetle's body and become deposited inside the tree when the beetle lays its eggs. Once the spores make it to the interior, the fungus spreads throughout the entire tree, decomposing the wood, which in turn helps larval digestion. When the adult beetle leaves the tree, it picks up new spores and spreads them to the next tree.

The beetle larvae do cause damage to the interior of the tree, but TDS cannot be caused by the beetles alone because each beetle only lays 1-2 eggs in a single tree, far too few to cause the extensive destruction observed in trees with TDS.

Scientist 3

TDS is caused by a fungus that thrives in specific environmental conditions. Instances of TDS have all been observed in areas that have low soil nitrogen and poor drainage, and have experienced a recent heavy rainfall. These soil conditions allow the fungal spores to grow, and the rainfall stirs them into the air. The spores stick to the trees and enter through wounds in the bark.

The Asian imaginary beetle does not cause TDS. While the beetle can make trees more susceptible to the fungus by providing wounds in the bark, the fungus does not specifically require the presence of the beetle. Trees that show signs of TDS fully succumb to the disease at varying rates, sometimes in less than a week. The disease would not spread so rapidly if it were tied to the life cycle of the beetle.

MAIN IDEAS

Let's establish the main ideas of the three scientists, using their first sentences (underlined here). What causes TDS? Beetles or fungus?

Scientist 1: beetles only.
Scientist 2: fungus, in a relationship with beetles.
Scientist 3: fungus only (in specific conditions).

1. According to Scientist 2, the fungus is transported into the interior of trees that later develop TDS by:

A. rainwater.
B. beetle larvae.
C. beetle saliva.
D. adult beetles.

1. Go look at Scientist 2's discussion. Third sentence: "The spores are carried on the beetle's body and become deposited inside the tree when the beetle lays its eggs." That means *adult* beetles transport the fungus into the trees. Note that Scientist 2 never mentions rainwater or saliva. Our answer is **choice D**.

2 Based on Scientist 1's discussion and Table 1, how much time would likely pass between the beetle laying its eggs and the death of the tree?

F. Less than 10 days
G. Between 10 and 15 days
H. Between 15 and 20 days
J. More than 20 days

2. Start with Scientist 1. When does the tree die? "The tree dies by the time the adult matures and leaves the tree." That means the beetle passes through the egg, larva, and pupa stages. Add up the values in Table 1: those three stages take anywhere from 28 to 40 days. Don't like adding? Look: the pupa stage by itself is 15-20 days. If we add 2 more stages, we're definitely over 20. Our answer is **choice J**.

3. *Mycangia* are structures on certain insects' bodies that are specially adapted to transport fungi. The discovery of mycangia on the bodies of Asian imaginary beetles would support the viewpoint of:

A. Scientist 2 only.
B. Scientist 3 only.
C. Scientist 1 and Scientist 2.
D. Scientist 2 and Scientist 3.

3. This question says there's evidence that beetles and fungus work together. Which scientist said beetles and fungus work together? Check the main ideas: *Scientist 2*. Our answer is **choice A**.

4. Suppose trees with TDS were found in an area where no evidence of Asian imaginary beetle has been found. This discovery would most support the viewpoint(s) of:

F. Scientist 1 only.
G. Scientist 3 only.
H. Scientist 1 and Scientist 2.
J. Scientist 2 and Scientist 3.

4. The question supposes that TDS can exist without the beetle. Use your main ideas: which scientist said that the beetle is not necessary for the disease? Scientist 3! Our answer is **choice G**.

5. How does Scientist 2's viewpoint differ from Scientist 3's viewpoint with regard to the spread of TDS? Scientist 2 claims that the spread of TDS requires:

A. a fungus and the Asian imaginary beetle, whereas Scientist 3 claims it only requires the beetle.
B. only the Asian imaginary beetle, whereas Scientist 3 claims it requires a fungus and the beetle
C. a fungus and the Asian imaginary beetle, whereas Scientist 3 claims it only requires the fungus.
D. only a fungus, whereas Scientist 3 claims it requires a fungus and the Asian imaginary beetle

5. Use your main ideas! Look up what each scientist said about the cause of TDS and eliminate as you go. First, Scientist 2 said it was caused by the fungus and the beetle together. Eliminate choices B and D. Scientist 3 said it does not require the beetle, only the fungus. Eliminate A. Our answer is **choice C**.

6. Based on the information provided, Scientist 1's discussion would be most weakened if which of the following observations were made?

F. Asian imaginary beetles only lay eggs in one species of elm tree.
G. Most North American fungi do not thrive in areas with low soil nitrogen.
H. Most species of fungi are deadly to Asian imaginary beetles.
J. The saliva of Asian imaginary beetle larvae is highly corrosive to plant cells.

6. We want a choice that *weakens* Scientist 1's viewpoint. Let's start with our main ideas. Scientist 1 said TDS is caused by beetles alone, not a fungus. Scientist 1 never mentions fungus, so any choice about fungus is irrelevant. Eliminate G and H.

Scientist 1 would *agree* with choice J. Scientist 1 argues that the larva's saliva causes "extensive interior deterioration" in the tree. Our answer is **choice F**.

Why? Scientist 1 argued that the Asian imaginary beetle is the sole cause of TDS. But the first paragraph of the passage said TDS "affects *several species* of maple and elm trees". If the beetle only lays eggs in one type of elm, then *something else* must be causing TDS in the maple trees.

Passage III (repeated)

(We're repeating the text of the passage here so you don't have to flip the pages back and forth.)

Tree Disintegration Syndrome (TDS) is a disease that affects several species of maple and elm trees in North America. TDS is characterized by the rapid disintegration of the woody interior of the tree and the subsequent failure of the tree's vascular system.

The presence of the Asian imaginary beetle (*anoplophora sporkazola*) has been detected in areas that have been affected by TDS. Table 1 shows the duration of each stage of the beetle's life cycle.

Table 1	
Stage	Duration (days)
Egg	3-5
Larva	10-15
Pupa	15-20
Adult	15-20

Three scientists discuss the Asian imaginary beetle's role in TDS.

Scientist 1

TDS is caused by the life cycle of the Asian imaginary beetle. The adult beetle bores into the trees, through the bark into the xylem, in order to lay its eggs. When the eggs hatch, the larvae feed on the tree's interior, destroying the tree's vascular system. In the process, the larvae secrete a chemical in their saliva that helps them digest the wood. As the larvae become pupae, they stop feeding, but the salivary chemical continues to damage the tree's interior, causing the extensive interior deterioration that is characteristic of TDS. The tree dies by the time the adult matures and leaves the tree.

Scientist 2

TDS is caused by a fungus that has a symbiotic relationship with the Asian imaginary beetle. The fungus requires the Asian imaginary beetle to spread its fungal spores. The spores are carried on the beetle's body and become deposited inside the tree when the beetle lays its eggs. Once the spores make it to the interior, the fungus spreads throughout the entire tree, decomposing the wood, which in turn helps larval digestion. When the adult beetle leaves the tree, it picks up new spores and spreads them to the next tree.

The beetle larvae do cause damage to the interior of the tree, but TDS cannot be caused by the beetles alone because each beetle only lays 1-2 eggs in a single tree, far too few to cause the extensive destruction observed in trees with TDS.

Scientist 3

TDS is caused by a fungus that thrives in specific environmental conditions. Instances of TDS have all been observed in areas that have low soil nitrogen and poor drainage, and have experienced a recent heavy rainfall. These soil conditions allow the fungal spores to grow, and the rainfall stirs them into the air. The spores stick to the trees and enter through wounds in the bark.

The Asian imaginary beetle does not cause TDS. While the beetle can make trees more susceptible to the fungus by providing wounds in the bark, the fungus does not specifically require the presence of the beetle. Trees that show signs of TDS fully succumb to the disease at varying rates, sometimes in less than a week. The disease would not spread so rapidly if it were tied to the life cycle of the beetle.

MAIN IDEAS

Let's establish the main ideas of the three scientists, using their first sentences (underlined here). What causes TDS? Beetles or fungus?

Scientist 1: beetles only.
Scientist 2: fungus, in a relationship with beetles.
Scientist 3: fungus only (in specific conditions).

7. Suppose a drought eliminated most of the insect life in a certain area. According to Scientist 3's discussion, would this occurrence affect the chances of trees in this area developing TDS?

   A. Yes, because insects are necessary for the spread of fungus.
   B. Yes, because rainfall is necessary for the growth of the fungus.
   C. No, because insects are not necessary for the spread of the fungus.
   D. No, because rainfall is not necessary for the growth of the fungus.

7. Look at the choices. Ignore Yes/No and focus on the second parts: each mentions *insects* or *rain*. Start with insects. Our main idea said Scientist 3 thinks TDS is caused by fungus only; beetles are *not* necessary. *Eliminate A.* Choice C is okay.

Choice B and D mention *rainfall*. Does Scientist 3 mention rain? Yes: it's part of the "specific environmental conditions" in the first sentence. Scientist 3 says rain *is* necessary. Rain allows the spores to get into the tree. *Eliminate D.* We're down to B and C.

Now answer the question. If rain is necessary for TDS to grow, and there is no rain, then we should see less TDS. So **yes**, the chances are affected. Our answer is **choice B.**

SCIENCE SUMMARY

Here are the keys to the ACT Science section:

1. Timing

- **Don't read the passage.** Skim to see what it's about and get to the questions.
- On *Conflicting Viewpoints* questions, **underline the first sentence** of each viewpoint to get the main ideas.
- Use **Target Numbers**: consider skipping one or two passages to give yourself more time on the others.

2. Answering the questions

- Use the following method for most questions:
    1. In the question, **underline the table, figure, or viewpoint** you need.
    2. In the question, **underline key words**: things you know and things you want.
        - If you can't find key words, look *in the choices*.
    3. In the figure, **circle the key words and values** you found in the question.
        - If you can't find them in the figure, look *in the passage.*
    4. Match! Match! Match!
- Use techniques from the Math Test like **Backsolve** and **Guesstimate**.
- Watch out for **RTFQ** choices and other careless mistakes.

3. Figure types

- Figures come in all sorts of shapes and sizes, but they all boil down to the same thing: **matching** one variable with another.
- **Write on your figure**. Draw in gridlines if you need to. Use your answer sheet to line up values.
- **Check the values on the axes**. They may not be what you think they are.

4. Question types

- **Data Lookup questions**: Look up values in a table or figure.
- **Combination questions**: Connect multiple figures or tables.
- **Relationship questions**: If one variable gets bigger, does the other get bigger or smaller?
- **Inferred Data questions**: If we added new points, where would they go?
- **Passage questions**: Look up stuff in the paragraphs, not just the figures.
- **Experiment Design questions**: Why was the experiment set up the way it was? What if we changed it?
- **Reasoning questions**: Does the data support a statement? First eliminate *false* choices, then answer yes or no.
- **Knowledge questions**: Know things that aren't in the passage.

Passage IV

When added to water, *blergarine* degrades into *snarfine* according to the following equation:

blergarine(s) + $H_2O(l) \rightarrow$ snarfine(s) + $2CO_2(g)$

This reaction can become accelerated in the presence of *2-phenylpenelopane*. Students performed the following experiments to investigate the effects of 2-phenylpenelopane on the above reaction.

Experiment 1

Students added 2 g of powdered blergarine to a beaker filled with 100 mL of water at 20°C. Every 2 minutes, a PKE meter was used to measure the concentration of snarfine. The results are shown in Figure 1.

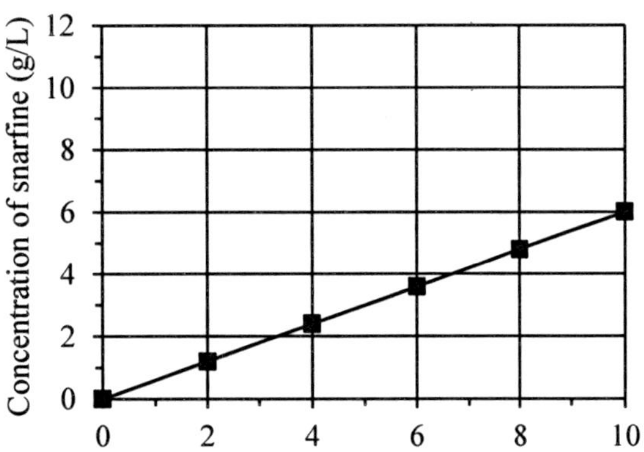

Figure 1

Experiment 2

Experiment 1 was repeated, but 50 mg of 2-phenylpenelopane was added along with the blergarine and water. The students again recorded the snarfine concentration every 2 minutes, as shown in Figure 2.

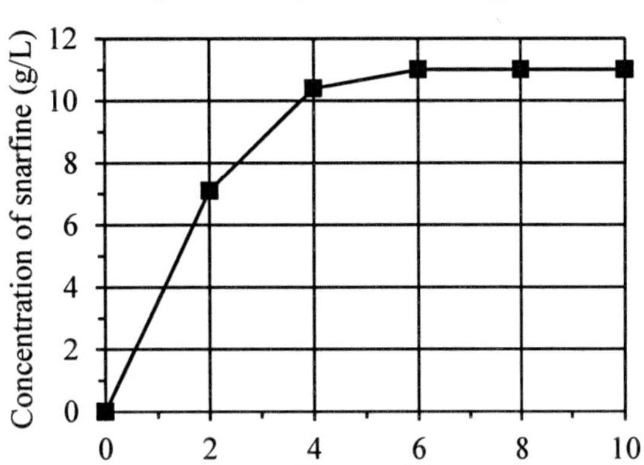

Figure 2

Each time concentration was measured, students also performed a *Manning test* to detect the presence of blergarine. For each measurement, a pink test strip was inserted into the sample. If the sample contained blergarine, the strip turned from pink to blue. The results are shown in Table 1.

Table 1

Time (min)	Manning test
2	Blue
4	Blue
6	Pink
8	Pink
10	Pink

Experiment 3

Several beakers were prepared containing 100 mL of water at 20°C. Students added 2 g of blergarine and different amounts of 2-phenylpenelopane to each beaker. The students observed each sample until it registered a snarfine concentration of 11 g/L. The students then recorded the amount of time that had passed and the temperature of the sample. The results are shown in Table 2.

Table 2

Amount of 2-phenylpenelopane added (mg)	Time (sec)	Temperature (°C)
50	340	31
60	293	38
70	256	52
80	229	79

1. In Experiment 2, when 4 minutes had passed after the blergarine and 2-phenylpenelopane were added to water, the observed concentration of snarfine was closest to:

A. 2.4 g/L
B. 6.5 g/L
C. 7.1 g/L
D. 10.3 g/L

GO ON TO THE NEXT PAGE.

2. In Experiment 3, as the amount of 2-phenylpenelopane increased, the temperature observed when the concentration reached 11 g/L of snarfine:

F. increased only.
G. decreased only.
H. increased, then decreased.
J. remained the same.

3. A student hypothesized that 6 minutes after the 50 mg of 2-phenylpenelopane was added to the sample in Experiment 2, all of the original blergarine had degraded into snarfine. Do the results of Experiment 2 support her claim?

A. Yes, because at 6 minutes the Manning test strip turned from pink to blue.
B. Yes, because at 6 minutes the Manning test strip remained pink.
C. No, because at 6 minutes the Manning test strip turned from blue to pink.
D. No, because at 6 minutes the Manning test strip remained blue.

4. If, in Experiment 1, a measurement had been taken 12 minutes after the start of the experiment, the concentration of snarfine most likely would have been closest to which of the following?

F. 4.2 g/L
G. 5.5 g/L
H. 7.2 g/L
J. 10.8 g/L

5. Suppose an additional trial had been performed in Experiment 3 using 75 mg of 2-phenylpenelopane. How much time would likely elapse from the start of the experiment until the concentration of snarfine reaches 11 g/L?

A. Less than 229 sec
B. Between 229 sec and 256 sec
C. Between 256 sec and 293 sec
D. More than 293 sec

6. In Experiment 3, which of the following was an independent variable?

F. Amount of 2-phenylpenelopane added
G. Time
H. Temperature
J. Concentration of snarfine

GO ON TO THE NEXT PAGE.

Passage V

A mutant is a person who possesses superpowers as a result of genetic mutation. Geneticists have identified mutated alleles of three genes, some combination of which must be present in order for a person to display powers. Table 1 shows how the presence or absence of these mutations results in various types of superpowers. A "+" indicates the mutant allele is present, while a "–" indicates it is absent. Gene 1 has two mutant alleles, labeled A or B when present.

Table 1

Gene 1	Gene 2	Gene 3	Superpower
–	–	–	none
–	–	+	none
–	+	–	none
–	+	+	none
A	–	–	none
A	–	+	none
A	+	–	psychic powers
A	+	+	shape shifting
B	–	–	none
B	–	+	none
B	+	–	super strength
B	+	+	fast healing

The superpowers shown in Table 1 have each been shown to be associated with the presence of certain proteins that are absent in non-mutants. Table 2 shows a correspondence between the powers and the proteins detected, with an "X" indicating the protein was detected.

Table 2

Superpowers	Protein detected: Jonesein	Tantalin	Malachine
Psychic powers	X		
Shape shifting	X		X
Super strength		X	
Fast healing		X	X

Possession of superpowers has also been associated with the presence of an enzyme called *phloxinase*. Concentration of phloxinase is directly proportional to the strength of a mutant's power. Figure 1 shows how the average concentration of phloxinase in the bloodstream changes over a mutant's lifespan.

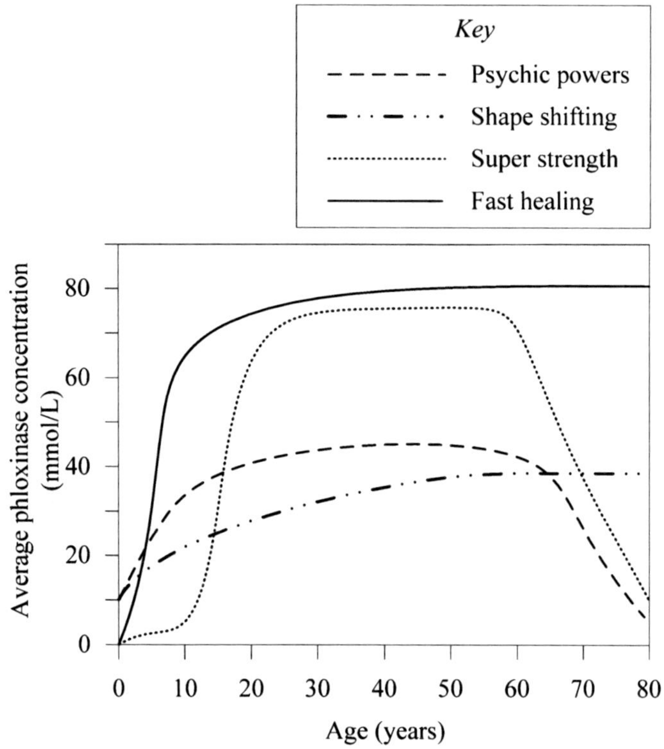

Figure 1

7. In order for any of the superpowers in Table 1 to occur, which of the following combinations of mutations *must* be present?
   - **A.** Mutant allele A of gene 1 and mutant gene 2
   - **B.** Mutant allele B of gene 1 and mutant gene 3
   - **C.** Mutant allele A or B of gene 1 and mutant gene 2
   - **D.** Mutant allele A or B of gene 1 and mutant gene 3

GO ON TO THE NEXT PAGE.

8. According to Figure 1, which of the following graphs best represents the average phloxinase concentration, in mmol/L, of 10-year-old mutants with each of the superpowers shown?

F.

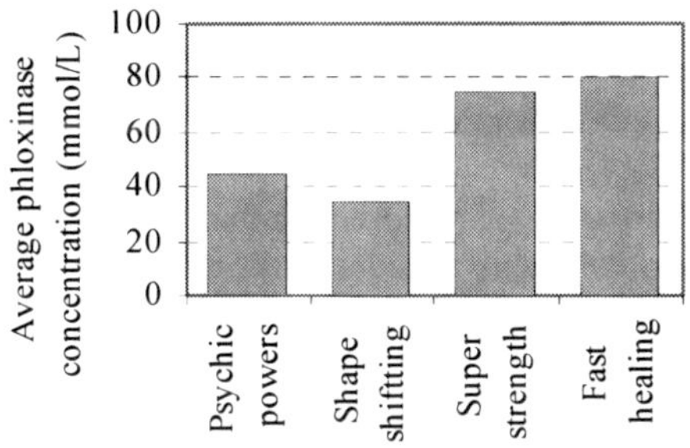

G.

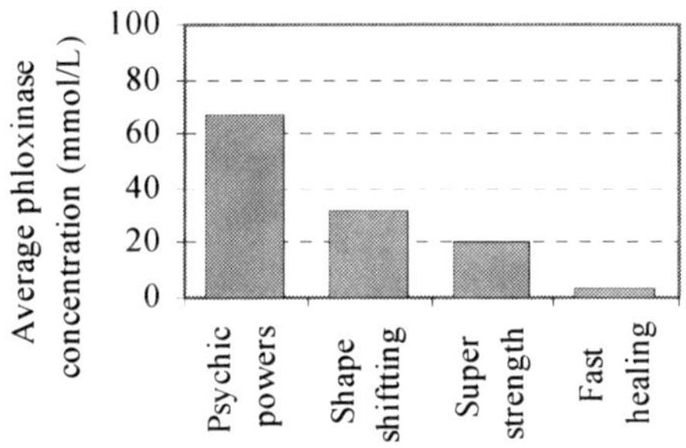

H.

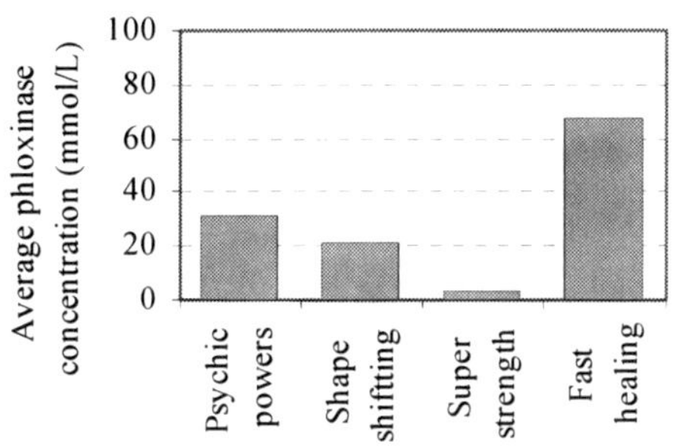

J.

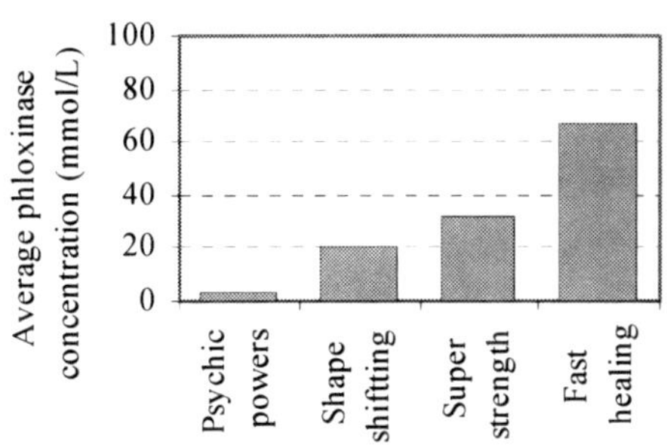

9. A geneticist hypothesizes that malachine causes the strength of superpowers to rapidly decline after a mutant reaches age 60. Does the information in Table 2 and Figure 1 support that hypothesis?

A. Yes, because phloxinase concentration decreases in mutants with super strength and psychic powers after age 60.
B. Yes, because phloxinase concentration decreases in mutants with fast healing and shape shifting after age 60.
C. No, because phloxinase concentration remains constant in mutants with super strength and psychic powers after age 60.
D. No, because phloxinase concentration remains constant in mutants with fast healing and shape shifting after age 60.

10. Based on the information in Table 1 and Table 2, which of the following combinations of mutations most likely results in the presence of jonesein?

F. Mutant gene 2 only
G. Mutant allele A of gene 1 and mutant gene 2
H. Mutant allele B of gene 1 and mutant gene 2
J. Mutant gene 2 and mutant gene 3

11. According to the information in the passage and Figure 1, if a mutant possesses the genes for fast healing, during which of the following age ranges will his or her powers increase in strength most rapidly?

A. Between 0 to 10 years
B. Between 10 to 20 years
C. Between 50 to 60 years
D. Between 60 to 70 years

GO ON TO THE NEXT PAGE.

Passage VI

Thermoregulation refers to an organism's ability to maintain its internal temperature. Organisms can be categorized according to two traits: whether they generate body heat internally and whether they keep their body temperature constant.

- An *endotherm* is an animal that generates its own body heat.
- An *ectotherm* is one that gets heat from its environment.
- A *homeotherm* keeps its body at a constant temperature.
- A *poikilotherm*'s body temperature changes with the environment.

The term "warm-blooded" refers to creatures that are endothermic and homeothermic, while "cold-blooded" creatures are ectothermic and poikilothermic.

Two scientists discuss possible ways that dinosaurs regulated their body heat.

Scientist 1

Dinosaurs were warm-blooded. Evidence for this can be seen in their body shapes. Larger sauropods had long necks that stretched upwards like those of giraffes. In order to force blood up to reach their heads, they would have needed unusually strong hearts that would require an endothermic metabolism. Also, all dinosaurs have upright hind legs, not sideways-sprawling legs like lizards and other cold-blooded reptiles have. All living creatures that have upright legs are endotherms. In fact, the closest living relatives to dinosaurs are birds, which are both endotherms and homeotherms.

Ectotherms generally prefer to live in areas where the climate is warm year-round. Modern ectotherms are more likely to live in hot tropical regions close to the equator. But dinosaur bones have been found in areas with high latitudes, which have colder climates that are not suitable for ectotherms.

Scientist 2

Dinosaurs were not endotherms. Keeping dinosaurs' large bodies warm would have required generating an extreme amount of energy—too much to have been generated internally. The amount of heat needed to warm their extremities would have been too great to bear; they would have boiled from the inside.

While dinosaurs did not produce their own body heat, some of them were able to maintain constant temperature through "inertial homeothermy". Their bodies were so large that it took a long time to change temperature to reach equilibrium with their surroundings. Therefore, fluctuations in environmental temperature would not cause an immediate change in body temperature. This idea is supported by studies that have shown that larger dinosaurs had warmer body temperatures than smaller ones. The large dinosaurs would naturally maintain their temperatures through inertial homeothermy, while the smaller ones would be more vulnerable to fluctuations in the environment.

12. According to Scientist 1, to which of the following creatures are dinosaurs most closely related?

F. Reptiles
G. Fish
H. Giraffes
J. Birds

13. Both scientists would agree that some dinosaurs were:

A. endothermic.
B. ectothermic.
C. homeothermic.
D. poikilothermic.

GO ON TO THE NEXT PAGE.

14. According to the information provided by Scientist 2, which of the following graphs might show the relationship between dinosaurs' body mass and body temperature?

F.

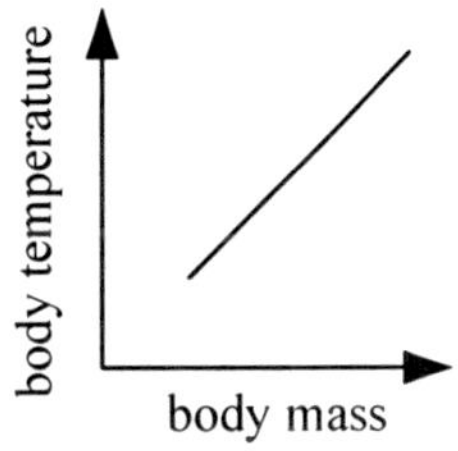

H.

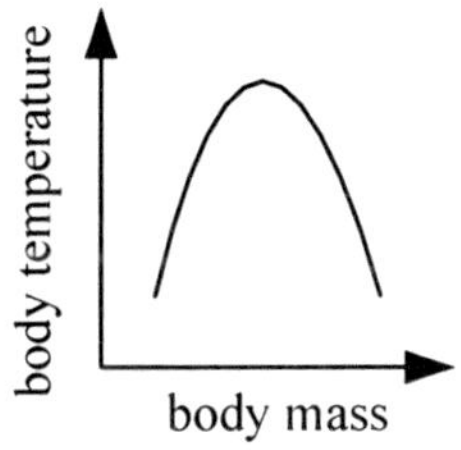

G.

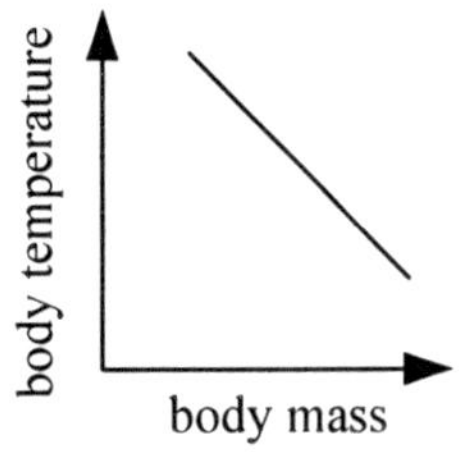

J.

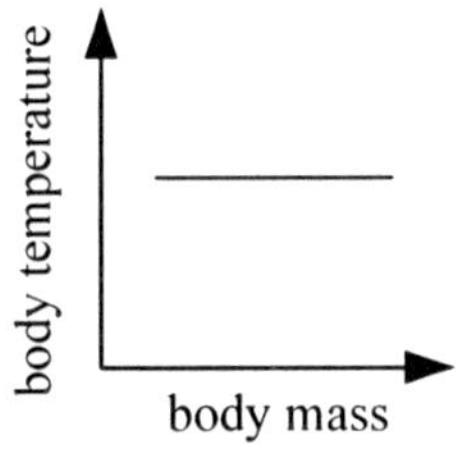

15. By examining the ratio of oxygen isotopes in an animal's bones, researchers can determine its body temperatures over time. The result of one such study of small dinosaurs showed that their body temperatures remained constant throughout the year, despite living in variable climates. This finding would be consistent with which of the scientists' hypotheses, if either?

A. Scientist 1's only
B. Scientist 2's only
C. Both Scientist 1's and Scientist 2's
D. Neither Scientist 1's nor Scientist 2's

16. If it were discovered that sauropods kept their necks held low and parallel to the ground, how would this discovery affect the viewpoints, if at all?

F. It would strengthen the viewpoint of Scientist 1 only.
G. It would weaken the viewpoint of Scientist 1 only.
H. It would strengthen the viewpoint of both scientists.
J. It would weaken the viewpoint of both scientists.

17. Which of the following statements, if true, would *weaken* the argument of Scientist 1?

A. Some mammals have more active lifestyles than some birds.
B. During the time of the dinosaurs, the Earth was hot year-round at high latitudes.
C. Areas of high elevation tend to be colder than areas of low elevation.
D. Some dinosaurs fed on leaves of trees that only grow in dense forests.

18. According to Scientist 1, which of the following traits likely suggests that a creature is cold-blooded?

F. Being closely related to birds
G. Living in a northern climate
H. Having a long neck that stretches upwards
J. Possessing legs that sprawl sideways

STOP!

WRITING

The Writing Test is the essay section of the ACT. It can be quite intimidating to write a coherent essay in just 30 minutes. As with every other section, timing is important. But as with every other section, practice will help you get used to it. And like much of the rest of the test, you don't have to have any *actual knowledge* to do well.

> The Writing Test is the newest section of the ACT. It was added in February 2005.

There is one big thing that makes this section different: **the Writing Test is optional**. It's the only section that you don't *have* to take. It will always be the last section of the test. There will be a break after the multiple-choice sections are over, at which time you're welcome to get the heck out of there if you want.*

In this chapter, we'll take a look at the format of the Writing test, what it takes to write a good essay, and some tips for making your writing sparkle.†

I. ABOUT THE TEST

Format

You will be given **30 minutes** to read the assigned topic write the essay. You'll have **up to 4 pages** available for the essay itself (as well as some scrap pages that won't be graded which you can use to collect your thoughts). You can use as much or as little of this space as you'd like.

The topic will be an issue that is somehow relevant to the life of a high school student. There will be a brief paragraph presenting two sides of a debate. You will be asked to argue in favor of one of the sides given. If you want to argue against both sides presented, you must offer a new position instead.

Your essay will be read by two Official ACT Essay Readers. Each will give your essay a score from 1 (sad) to 6 (happy). So your total score will range **from 2 to 12**.‡ This is your Writing Test score.

In addition, your Writing Test score will be combined with your English Test score to give you the cleverly-named Combined English/Writing score. This is in *addition* to your English score; it won't affect your English Test score in any way. It's calculated using complicated statistical magic and will be presented on the standard ACT scale from 1 to 36. **Neither your Writing Test score nor your Combined English/Writing score will be factored into your Composite score.** Only the four multiple-choice sections affect your Composite score.

Should I take it?

In some ways, the Writing Test is the least important section. It's optional, it doesn't count to your Composite score, and some colleges don't even look at it. For many of you, your time would probably be better spent working on the other four Tests.

> Regardless of whether a college requires the Writing Test, if you write the essay, a copy of it will be included with any scores you send.

On the other hand, many colleges *do* require the Writing Test with any ACT scores you send. If you know which colleges you're interested in, you can check to see if they require it. But there's a pretty good chance that at least one of the colleges you're interested in will require it.

---

* You can't wait until the last minute to decide if you want to take it; you have to specify whether you want to take the Writing Test when you register for the ACT. There is an extra fee for the Writing Test.

† Disclaimer: essay may not literally sparkle.

‡ Essays that are blank, illegible, or off topic will receive no score, and no Writing or Combined English/Writing scores will be reported.

In short, it's probably a good idea to take the Writing Test, but don't sweat it too much. Make sure your scores on the other Tests are at or near where you want them to be before you worry much about the essay.

Scoring

As we mentioned, the essay will be read by two readers, each of which will give it a score from 1 to 6. The essay readers are well trained and know exactly what they're looking for, so in most cases you will get either two of the same score (such as a 3 and a 3) or two scores that are off by one (such as a 3 and a 4). If by some chance the two readers disagree by more than one point (such as a 3 and a 5), then your essay will go to a third reader who will determine your final score. This means that you will never get severely disparate scores. You'll never get a 1 and a 6.

In addition to the score itself, you will get back several **comments** about your essay. These comments are not personalized (sorry); the readers select them from a list of standard comments. The test makers define five categories within which readers evaluate your essay:

Judgment

- Do you understand the **purpose** of the essay? (You're supposed to argue one side of a debate, not tell a story about ponies.)
- Do you take a **clear position** on the topic question? (Most topics have two clear sides—yes this is good, or no this is bad. If you don't agree with either side, what alternative do you propose?)
- Do you offer **context**? (Why are people arguing about this topic?)
- Do you address the **complexity** of the issue and **counterarguments**? (Why would someone argue the other side? How would you defend your position against them?)

Development

- Do you **develop** your ideas? (Do your examples actually support your thesis? Do you explain your reasoning well?)
- Do you **elaborate** on your ideas? (Do you give enough specific detail about your points? Or are they vague, brief, or trite?)

Focus

- Do you **focus** on the issue? (Are you answering the question? Are you making unfounded leaps and assumptions? Do you drift into generalizations that are only slightly related to the topic?)

Organization

- Is your essay **well organized**? (Is your organization clear? Predictable? Logical?)
- Are your **transitions** logical? (Does one idea flow easily to the next? Is your transitional language appropriate?)
- Are your **introduction and conclusion** effective? (Do you have them? Do they appropriately support your thesis and evidence?)

Language

- Do you show competent **command of language**? (Are your sentences well written?)
- Do you show **varied sentence structure**? (Or does your essay read like a *Dick and Jane* book?)
- Do you make **distracting errors**? (Do your subjects and verbs agree? How many spelling mistakes did you make?)

That seems like a lot to think about, but don't be disheartened. The essay is graded **holistically**. That means the reader isn't going through these chili peppers one by one, giving you a grade in each category. Instead, the reader considers all these factors together to judge the *overall* impression that the essay makes.

That means **you don't have to be perfect**. The readers know that you've only got 30 minutes to write and take that into consideration. You can do poorly at *some* of these issues—use some vague language, write a bad conclusion, or make some grammatical errors—and still get a good grade, as long as you do well on the rest of them *overall*.

II. PREPARING THE ESSAY

The Topic

The essay will be on a topic that's generally **content free**. The topic will be somehow relevant to your life—about high school, teenagers, or something that affects everyone's daily lives—so you don't have to know any specific facts to do well on it. You're being judged on your writing style and your argument, not on your knowledge of the world.

The essay is intended to be a ***persuasive* essay**, not a *descriptive* essay. That means you're not just describing the world or telling a story—you're actively arguing a position. That makes it more like a debate topic than an English Literature essay.*

The essay prompt will have several parts to it. There will be an *introduction* that outlines the context of the issue, *two contrasting positions* on the issue, and the *question* that you must answer.

Here's an example:

> Some high schools have debated whether students should be allowed to bring mobile phones to school. Some people think that phones should not be allowed in school because they are a distraction in the classroom. Other people think that phones should be allowed because they are an important way for students to communicate with their parents. In your opinion, should students be allowed to bring mobile phones to school?
>
> In your essay, take a position on this question. You may write about either one of the two points of view given, or you may present a different point of view on this question. Use specific reasons and examples to support your position.

Picking a side

You must present a position on the essay. There's no "right" answer. It doesn't matter which side you pick. But make sure you clearly give a strong thesis statement in your introduction so the reader knows from the beginning which side you're taking. Don't argue both sides. Pick one.

How do you know which side to pick? You could start by picking the side that you actually agree with. But you don't have to. You might actually find that it's easier to argue the other side. So go ahead! You're not on trial here. It's much more important to have a strong argument than to be true to your heart.

Whichever side you decide to argue, you must present some support or evidence for your position. That just means you've got to give some *reasons* why you think you're right. You must provide at least 2, but preferably 3 reasons for your position.

---

* Note that this makes it **very different from the SAT essay**, which tends to give broader, more descriptive topics. If you've been studying for the SAT, you may find that many of the strategies that helped you there will not work on the ACT essay. On the ACT, you generally can't write about books or historical figures; you've got a much more specific topic to address.

So before you start writing, **try to come up with a few reasons to support each side**. This doesn't have to be elaborate, just jot down a few ideas. Make lists of reasons for and against the issue. Which side did you get more reasons for? *That's the side you should pick.*

The topic usually already gives one reason for taking each side. We can see that in the topic above: phones are a "distraction in the classroom", but they also allow students to "communicate with their parents". You can use these reasons as a starting point. You can use them in your essay (with further discussion and elaboration, of course), but you'll need to go beyond them if you want a good score.

SUPPORT EXERCISE

Below we've repeated the topic given earlier. Come up with ***three points of support for each side*** *of this issue and write them in the spaces below. (Note: this is just a practice exercise. On the real test, you don't have to come up with this many points for each side.)*

> Some high schools have debated whether students should be allowed to bring mobile phones to school. Some people think that phones should not be allowed in school because they are a distraction in the classroom. Other people think that phones should be allowed because they are an important way for students to communicate with their parents. In your opinion, should students be allowed to bring mobile phones to school?

PRO: Students should be allowed to bring phones to school.

1. ______________________________

2. ______________________________

3. ______________________________

CON: Students should NOT be allowed to bring phones to school.

1. ______________________________

2. ______________________________

3. ______________________________

Opposing viewpoints

No matter which side you choose, **you must address the opposing view** in your essay. This is important. The official scoring rubric clearly states that you *must* address the opposing viewpoint if you want a 4 or higher.

Not sure what the opposing side would argue? First of all, read the topic question—as we said, it gives you one reason for supporting each side. This is also why it's a good idea to come up with some reasons to support *each* side before you start writing. You want to come up with points to argue for your side *and* points from the other side to argue against. You don't have to spend as much time on the counterargument as you do on your main argument. Just one opposing point is enough. But you want to be sure to include something.

An important warning: **DO NOT *ARGUE* THE OPPOSING VIEW**. Say *what* the opposing argument is, and your **response** to that argument. That is, *why you disagree with it.* All too often, students will spend three paragraphs arguing one side and then say "but you know, the other side is right, too." What? You just spent three paragraphs arguing that they're wrong. You've just undermined your whole essay.

Including a counterargument in your discussion shows you understand the complexity of the issue. You're saying "I know some people think I'm wrong because of X. But here's what's wrong with X." You're showing the reader that you're one step ahead of your opponent.

A Third Position

As we said earlier, you don't actually have to pick one of the two positions presented in the essay prompt. You can come up with your own position if you want. We generally don't recommend coming up with your own position if only because it's usually *harder* than using the positions stated. If done well, this kind of argument can be very effective. But it's really hard to do it well.

The most important thing to keep in mind about taking a third position is that *it still has to be a strong, concrete position.* This does *not* mean you can just say, "Well, both positions kind of have a point." That's not a position. This also does *not* mean you can say that both sides are wrong without presenting a real third alternative.

But you can sometimes come up with a real third alternative to the two choices presented. For example, in the topic given earlier, the question asked "should students be allowed to bring mobile phones to school?" Two positions were given: yes, they should be allowed in school; or no, they should not be allowed. But you could also argue that they should only be allowed in certain circumstances and not in other circumstances. This is a compromise between the two positions, but it can still be a strong, concrete, specific position.

If you're trying to come up with a third position, *make sure you're clear about what your position is from the beginning*. The essay is testing your ability to make an argument, so we want to know what you're arguing right from the start. Don't spend the whole essay arguing one side and then mutate it at the end. That undermines your argument.

Outline

We've already mentioned that it's important to plan your essay before you start writing. The first step is to start jotting down reasons that support your side. But you should go farther than that and actually write an outline for your essay.

This does not have to be elegant. You don't have to number the points or write in complete sentences. Just start taking notes on what reasons you have, what you want to say about them, and what order you want to present them in.

A lot of students don't bother much with planning the organization of their essays, but it's ***incredibly*** important. ***You must write an outline before you begin***.

We know what you're thinking. "An outline? I've only got thirty minutes to write! I can't waste my time on an outline, fool!"

You can and will. It's one thing to have brilliant ideas swimming around in your head; it's another to be able to communicate them to your readers. These essays are not little short stories—they're *arguments*. As such, you must pay close attention to how you present your case. An outline takes very little time and will help the actual writing process go much more quickly and coherently. You must write an outline. You must write an outline.

> You must write an outline.

Writing an outline is incredibly easy. Some English-teacher types often talk about "the five-paragraph essay" as the standard for student essays. Here's an example:

I. Introduction	Give context about what the issue is and say which side you're taking.
II. Reason 1	Give your first reason and *why it proves your point.*
III. Reason 2	Give your second reason and *why it proves your point.*
IV. Counterargument	Discuss an argument from the opposing side and *why it's wrong.*
V. Conclusion	Summarize what you've just said.

That's it! There's your essay. In fact, if you're running out of time, the conclusion is optional. All that matters is that your examples are clearly defined and well argued. Really, your only job now is to figure out what your examples will be and which to use first.

The outline above is a suggestion, not a requirement. If you prefer, here's another example:

I. Introduction/ Counterargument	Give context about what the issue is. Address the counterargument first, then say which side you're going to take instead.
II. Reason 1	Give your first reason and *why it proves your point.*
III. Reason 2	Give your second reason and *why it proves your point.*
IV. Reason 3	Give your third reason and *why it proves your point.*
V. Conclusion	Summarize what you've just said.

You've got a lot of leeway about how you organize your essay. Just be sure to **make separate paragraphs for separate points.** All too often, students will ramble on and on in one big paragraph. Or include several very different points in one paragraph. Or put 5 sentences that have nothing to do with each other in one paragraph. All the sentences in a single paragraph should revolve around one common theme.*

III. WRITING THE ESSAY

Once you've got your side chosen, your reasons set, and your outline jotted, you're ready to start writing. Here are a few things to keep in mind as you go.

Introduction

Some students try to skimp on the introduction, but it is an important part of the ACT essay. It sets the tone for everything that comes after it, and you want to make a good first impression. There are two main things you want to accomplish in the introduction.

- **Establish the context.** This just means setting up what the issue at hand is. Why are you talking about this? Why is this an issue? Basically, just expand and elaborate on the information given to you in the essay prompt.
- **State your position.** You *must* give a firm, clear statement of which side you want to argue. If you're coming up with your own position, you must clearly state what that position is. Failure to do so will significantly weaken your essay.

You may want to use the introduction to address your opponent's point of view. The discussion of the context of the issue is a natural place to discuss it. But depending on how much you have to say about it, you may want to give the counterargument its own paragraph.

Development

People always talk about "development" of an essay, but what does that mean? What does it mean to "develop" an idea? It's essentially a fancy word for "making a *good* point". Now, that can mean many things to many people. There are lots of ways to make a good point (and many more ways to make a bad point). For our purposes, there are two things you *must* include in every paragraph you write:

- **What is your point?** Be specific. Don't write in broad generalizations. Give specific examples and specific scenarios. When you write in broad language, it's hard for a reader to understand what you're trying to say. The more concrete your example, the easier it is to grasp your point.
- **Why is it relevant?** Don't just say what your example is: *tie it to your thesis.* Remember, you're making an argument here, and everything you do should work toward proving your point. No matter how concrete your point is, it won't matter if you don't say how it supports your thesis.

* In the Reading Test, we called that the "Main Idea".

Language

Improving your organization and development is a much more effective way of improving your essay score than trying to improve your actual writing style. First of all, it's really hard to change the language you write with. Secondly, it doesn't have as much of an effect on your score as you'd think.

Nevertheless, there are some things to keep in mind about the way you write.

Vocabulary

Using sophisticated vocabulary can certainly improve your writing. Just be sure to use vocabulary *appropriately.* If you use a difficult word, it can backfire: if you use it in a way that shows you don't know what it means or you don't know its proper usage. Using a hard word incorrectly is worse than using an easy word correctly.

More important than vocabulary is ***concrete language***. This means being *specific* in everything you say. Give us details, give us examples, give us concrete words, not abstract ideas. Say *exactly* what you mean.

Using concrete language is directly related to what we've already been preaching. One of the biggest problems that students have on their essays is that they don't know the difference between *saying* something and *proving* it. You can't assume that your reader will automatically understand why your examples support your point. You've got to *prove* it explicitly.

Sentence structure

If all your sentences sound the same, your writing becomes dull. Varying your sentence structure can help break up the monotony and make you sound like a big shot.

What does that mean? Glad you asked. Here are three different types of sentences:

1. **Simple** Sentence has only one clause.
   - I like cats.
   - My science partner smells like onions.
2. **Compound** Sentence has two or more independent clauses stuck together.
   - I like cats, but John does not.
   - My science partner smells like onions, and his clothes are dirty.
3. **Complex** Sentence has an independent clause and a *subordinate* clause (a clause of lesser importance).
   - Although I like cats, John apparently does not.
   - My science partner, who sits next to me every day in Biology class, smells like onions.

Most students only write in either simple or compound sentences. To shake things up, try to throw at least one complex sentence into your essay. Just make a point of using a sentence with the word "although". That's all you need.

Grammar

Believe it or not, your grammatical competence is probably the *least* important element of the essay. The essay is intended to be a first draft. That means it doesn't have to be totally polished. The essay readers know that you only have 45 minutes for this thing, so you've got some leeway here. They're not looking for Shakespeare here. You can make spelling and grammatical errors and still get a double 6. Your argument is more important than your grammar.

> Your essay doesn't have to be neat. You can cross words out or insert whole sentences with asterisks and arrows pointing here and there. Just don't write in the margins–any text outside the box around the page will not be read.

That said, your mistakes should be within the limits of reason. Every little mistake adds up. A few scattered here and there are okay, but if you consistently butcher every sentence you write, it won't matter how good your examples are— no one will be able to understand what you're saying. So while grammar shouldn't be your *main* concern on the Writing test, you should try to cut down on errors whenever possible.

We've already discussed pretty much all of the major rules of grammar, so we don't have to go over them all again.* Just know that all the grammatical rules we've talked about so far apply to you too.

One way to avoid grammatical problems is to **reread your work**. When you've got a strict time limit, you write quickly, so it's incredibly easy to lose track of what you've already written. In fact, many grammatical mistakes arise because students *literally forget* how they started the sentence by the time they get to the end. Obviously, timing is an issue on the essay, so if you don't have time to re-read, that's okay. But giving your essay another read once you've finished can help you spot errors and clean things up a bit.

* Well, we *shouldn't* have to go over them again.

OUTLINE EXERCISE

Three essay prompts are given below. For each prompt, think about the topic and write a quick outline for an essay. You don't have to write in complete sentences here, but you do have to think about the coherence of the essay as a whole. Make sure the reasons you choose actually support your position, that they're presented in a logical order, and that you come up with both a counterargument and a response to it which supports your position.

Prompt A

> Some schools punish students who violate school policies even when the violations occur out of school. Some people support this kind of punishment because they think bad behavior outside of school can still affect school activities, and it helps promote good behavior overall. Other people believe that this kind of punishment is inappropriate because schools have no right to monitor actions outside of the school day or off school grounds. In your opinion, should schools be allowed to punish students for actions outside of school?
>
> In your essay, take a position on this question. You may write about either one of the two points of view given, or you may present a different point of view on this question. Use specific reasons and examples to support your position.

I. Your Position: ____

II. Reason 1: ____

____

III. Reason 2: ____

____

IV. Reason 3: ____

____

V. Counterargument: ____

Response: ____

Prompt B

> A person in the United States is legally considered an adult at age 18, but the legal age for drinking alcohol is 21. Some groups argue that the higher age limit for drinking is beneficial because it helps reduce the number of traffic fatalities caused by drinking. Other people think that the drinking age should be lowered because the higher age limit makes teens more likely to drink irresponsibly in unsupervised contexts. In your opinion, should the drinking age be changed from 21 to a lower age?
>
> In your essay, take a position on this question. You may write about either one of the two points of view given, or you may present a different point of view on this question. Use specific reasons and examples to support your position.

I. **Your Position:** ______________________________

II. **Reason 1:** ______________________________

____

III. **Reason 2:** ______________________________

____

IV. **Reason 3**: ______________________________

____

V. **Counterargument:** ______________________________

Response: ______________________________

Prompt C

In some states, schools are considering extending the school year by eliminating long summer vacation and replacing it with a shorter break. Some people think this will be beneficial because longer school years generally lead to better academic performance. Other people think that the long vacations should be kept because they allow students opportunities for learning outside the classroom. In your opinion, should schools eliminate long summer vacations?

In your essay, take a position on this question. You may write about either one of the two points of view given, or you may present a different point of view on this question. Use specific reasons and examples to support your position.

I. Your Position: ______________________________

II. Reason 1: ______________________________

____

III. Reason 2: ______________________________

____

IV. Reason 3: ______________________________

____

V. Counterargument: ______________________________

Response: ______________________________

APPENDICES

APPENDIX A MATH DRILLS

PLUG IN DRILL

1. If $a + 3b = 10$, what is the value of $2a + 6b = ?$

A. 12
B. 15
C. 20
D. 30
E. 40

2. The number x is 3 less than 2 times the number y. Which of the following expressions gives y in terms of x?

F. $2x - 3$
G. $3x + 2$
H. $\frac{x-2}{3}$
J. $\frac{x+3}{2}$
K. $\frac{x-3}{2}$

3. A certain two-digit number, n, has a units digit that is three times the tens digit. Which of the following *must* be true?

A. $n > 20$
B. $n < 40$
C. n is odd
D. n is even
E. n is a multiple of 3

4. The length of rectangle B is double that of rectangle A, and the width of rectangle B is half that of rectangle A. If rectangle A is a square, what is the ratio of the perimeter of A to the perimeter of B?

F. 1:1
G. 1:2
H. 1:4
J. 2:3
K. 4:5

5. If $z = x - 3$ and $z = y + 5$, which of the following *must* be true?

A. $x > y$
B. $x < y$
C. $x = y$
D. $z < 0$
E. $z > 0$

6. Three people are eating a box of cookies. Caroline ate half the number of cookies that Sherwyn did, and Sherwyn ate 4 times as many as Laura. What fraction of the cookies did Sherwyn eat?

F. $\frac{1}{2}$
G. $\frac{1}{3}$
H. $\frac{2}{3}$
J. $\frac{3}{4}$
K. $\frac{4}{7}$

7. If $x = 3t - 1$ and $y = t + 4$, what is x in terms of y?

A. $y + 3$
B. $y - 4$
C. $3y + 3$
D. $3y - 5$
E. $3y - 13$

8. Sujit has only white shirts and red shirts. He has four times as many white shirts as red shirts. What percent of his shirts are red?

F. 20%
G. 25%
H. 40%
J. 75%
K. 80%

9. In the figure below, what is z in terms of x and y?

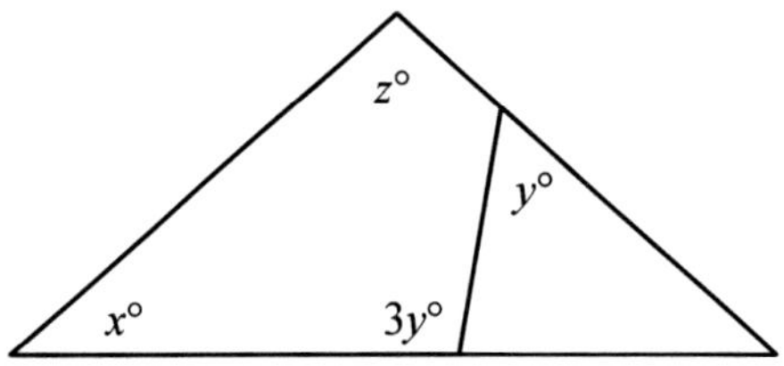

A. $3y + x$
B. $4y - x$
C. $180 - 2y - x$
D. $180 - 3y - x$
E. $180 - 4y + x$

10. Veerle sells waffles for x dollars each. If her expenses total y dollars, which of the following expressions represents the number of waffles she must sell in order to make a profit of $100? (Profit equals total sales minus expenses.)

F. $\frac{100 + y}{x}$
G. $\frac{100 - y}{x}$
H. $\frac{100 + x}{y}$
J. $100x - y$
K. $100 - xy$

BACKSOLVE DRILL

1. If $18-(xy)^2=2$, which of the following could be the value of xy?

   A. -4
   B. 3
   C. 9
   D. 16
   E. 20

2. The number of koalas, k, in a certain colony can be predicted according to the function $k(t)=3125\times 2^{2t}$, where t represents the number of minutes after the start of the observation. After how many minutes will the population reach 50,000 koalas?

   F. 0
   G. 1
   H. 2
   J. 3
   K. 4

3. The length of a certain rectangular box is twice the width, and the width of the box is twice the height. If the volume of the box is 64 cubic inches, what is its height, in inches?

   A. 2
   B. 4
   C. 6
   D. 8
   E. 10

4. Emily's Bakery made some pies for a party. Half of the pies were blueberry, one third were raspberry, and the remaining 21 were pecan. How many total pies did the bakery make for the party?

   F. 42
   G. 63
   H. 72
   J. 108
   K. 126

5. Each term of a certain sequence is formed by adding a positive integer, c, to the term immediately before it. The first term in the sequence is negative and the second term is positive. If the sixth term is 28, what is the value of c?

   A. 3
   B. 4
   C. 5
   D. 6
   E. 7

6. If $x^2 - 6x \leq -8$, which of the following is a possible value of x?

F. −7
G. −5
H. −3
J. 0
K. 3

7. If the measures of the angles of a triangle are in a 1:3:5 ratio, what is the measure of the largest angle?

A. 20°
B. 40°
C. 60°
D. 80°
E. 100°

8. One number is 5 less than half of another number. If the sum of the two numbers is 34, what is the greater of the two numbers?

F. 8
G. 13
H. 24
J. 26
K. 39

9. Of the 68 students in tenth grade, 31 students take Dutch, 45 students take Polish, and 5 students take neither language. How many students take both Polish and Dutch?

A. 8
B. 11
C. 13
D. 18
E. 23

10. There are three integers, x, y, and z, such that $x < y < z$. The median of the three numbers is equal to three times their average (arithmetic mean). If $z = 10$, what is the least possible value of y?

F. −10
G. −9
H. −3
J. 3
K. 9

Fraction Drill

_____ **1.** $\frac{7}{2}+\frac{5}{6}=$

_____ **2.** $\frac{13}{8}-\frac{2}{3}=$

_____ **3.** $\frac{3}{4}\times\frac{2}{3}=$

_____ **4.** $\frac{4}{5}\div\frac{3}{10}=$

_____ **5.** $\frac{1}{2}\left(\frac{8}{9}+\frac{11}{18}\right)=$

_____ **6.** $\frac{1}{3}\times\frac{5}{8}\times\frac{9}{7}=$

_____ **7.** $\frac{\frac{2}{3}+\frac{3}{5}}{\frac{1}{3}}=$

_____ **8.** Bruiser is planning his budget. Daddy Woods gives him an allowance of $200 a month. If he spends one half of his allowance on candy, one quarter on ice cream, and one fifth on dental care, what fraction of his allowance did he spend?

_____ **9.** Elle is trying to plan her monthly budget. She plans to use one fourth of her income on rent, one fourth on shoes, one sixth on hair products, and the rest on food. What fraction of her income is left to spend on food?

_____ **10.** Sweetie and Cutie are making horse treats for the annual pony show. They have a recipe that calls for: $1\frac{1}{2}$ cups of oats, $\frac{3}{4}$ cup of apples, $2\frac{1}{4}$ cups of hay, and $\frac{1}{2}$ cup of carrots. After mixing all the ingredients together, carrots make up what fraction of the mix?

RATIO DRILL

_____ **1.** In Jackson Middle School's 8th grade class, there are 24 boys and 16 girls. What is the ratio of boys to girls in the class? (*Remember to simplify!*)

_____ **2.** A certain recipe for apple pie calls for 3 cups of crust for every 5 cups of filling. If you use 12 cups of crust, how many cups of filling do you need?

_____ **3.** For every 4 hot dogs he eats, Fat Sal drinks 5 Big Sip soda pops. If Fat Sal ate 20 hot dogs on Tuesday, how many sodas did he drink?

_____ **4.** At Pablo's Perfect Petting Zoo, Pablo keeps llamas and goats. There are 3 llamas for every 4 goats. If there are 28 animals, how many llamas does Pablo have?

_____ **5.** Bob's Bookstore stocks books and magazines in a 5 to 3 ratio. If this week Bob stocked 40 total items, how many magazines did he stock?

_____ **6.** If x is directly proportional to y and $x = 6$ when $y = 9$, what is x when $y = 24$?

_____ **7.** Terry's truck has a 20-gallon gas tank. On a full tank, Terry can drive 375 miles. How many tankfuls of gas would Terry need to drive from Boston to Seattle (3000 miles)?

_____ **8.** 20% of the employees at a company are single, childless, and lonely. Of the rest, half are married with children, and half are married without children. What is the ratio of employees with children to employees without children?

_____ **9.** Steve's Grocery Delivery Truck delivers groceries to Sam's Little Grocery Store, and each shipment contains meat, dairy, and produce in a 1:5:10 ratio by weight. If this week's delivery weighs 480 pounds, how many pounds of dairy does it contain?

_____ **10.** A certain type of cotton gin working at a constant rate will separate 3 bushels of cotton in 2 hours. If 3 of these cotton gins work simultaneously, how long, in hours, will it take them to separate 36 bushels of cotton?

PERCENT DRILL

_____ **1.** What is 60 percent of 45?

_____ **2.** 15 is 20% of what number?

_____ **3.** 45 is what percent of 75?

_____ **4.** 16 is 5% of what number?

_____ **5.** 69 is 23% of what number?

_____ **6.** What is 50% of 15% of 240?

_____ **7.** What is $\frac{1}{2}$ percent of 160?

_____ **8.** Holden goes out to dinner at Salinger's Saloon, and his bill is $36 without a tip. What will his total cost in dollars be if he pays his bill with a 15% tip?

_____ **9.** Timmy earns a 5% commission on every vehicle he sells at Lenny's Lemon Lot. On Friday, he sold a car for $450, a truck for $1,300 and a scooter for $200. How much money in dollars did Timmy earn in commissions on Friday?

_____ **10.** In February, Rosie's Flower Shop sold 300 bouquets of roses for $40 each, 250 bunches of tulips for $30 each, and 44 wedding centerpieces at $125 each. In March, Rosie advertised a special St. Patty's Day clover arrangement, and the shop made a total of $30,000 in sales. What was the percent increase in her sales from February to March?

AVERAGE DRILL

_____ **1.** There are five numbers whose average is 16. The average of three of the numbers is 10. What is the average of the remaining two numbers?

_____ **2.** A certain block on 105th Street has 8 buildings with an average height of 62 feet. After a new building is constructed on a formerly empty lot, the average height of all 9 buildings is now 74 feet. What is the height, in feet, of the new building?

_____ **3.** The average of 5, 13, and x is 15. What is the average of 10, 26, and $2x$?

_____ **4.** What is the least of six consecutive even integers whose median is 29?

_____ **5.** Jenny has six weeks to read a 1200-page book for a book report. She reads an average of 150 pages per week for the first four weeks. How many pages per week must Jenny read over the last two weeks in order to finish the book?

Use the following information to answer questions 32–34

Number of students	Grade
7	70
5	100
4	90
2	80
1	50
1	60

The table above shows the grades for 20 students who took Monday's geography test in Ms. Frizzle's class. The test was scored on a range from 0 to 100.

_____ **6.** What was the mode of the scores on the test?

_____ **7.** What was the average (arithmetic mean) score on the test?

_____ **8.** What was the median score on the test?

_____ **9.** Five students were absent on the day of the test so their grades were not included in the table. When they took the test on Tuesday, they each received a score of 100. What is the new average score for all 25 students in the class?

_____ **10.** What is the new median score for all 25 students in the class?

ONE-VARIABLE ALGEBRA DRILL

Solve the following equations for all possible solutions.

_____ **1.** $5x + 3 = 18$

_____ **2.** $4x - 55 + 3x = 2x$

_____ **3.** $13 - 3z = 15z + 4$

_____ **4.** $\frac{5}{x} = \frac{2}{3}$

_____ **5.** $x + 4 > \frac{x}{5}$

_____ **6.** $(p+4)^2 = 36$ and $p > 0$

_____ **7.** $x^2 - x = 0$

_____ **8.** $\frac{r}{8} = \frac{2}{r}$

_____ **9.** $\sqrt{x+4} = 9$

_____ **10.** $\frac{2(q+8.5)}{9} = \frac{5q+5}{10}$

Multi-variable Algebra Drill

_____ **1.** If $y = 5x + 6$, then what is x in terms of y ?

_____ **2.** If $\dfrac{m-15}{4} = n + 3$, then what is m in terms of n ?

_____ **3.** If $z = 10 + 2x$ and $z = x - 5$, then $z = ?$

_____ **4.** If $x = 5t + 13$ and $y = 2 - t$, then what is x in terms of y ?

_____ **5.** If $t = 4u - 24$ and $3v - t = 16$, then what is u in terms of v?

_____ **6.** If $j = k + 1$, $k + 2 = m$, and $m - 5 = n$, then what is j in terms of n ?

_____ **7.** If $2x + 3y = 31$ and $x - 2y = 5$, then what is the value of y ?

_____ **8.** If $3a + b = 12$ and $\frac{2a+2b}{3} = 12$, then what are the values of a and b ?

_____ **9.** If $z = 3x^2$ and $x = y + 5$, then what is z in terms of y ?

_____ **10.** If $a = bc$, $d = b - 5$, and $c = d - 3$, then what is a in terms of d ?

Polynomial Drill

Simplify the following expressions:

_____ **1.** $2x^3 + 5x^2 - 7x + 4 + 3x^3 - 3x^2 + x - 11 = ?$

Answer: ____________________________________

_____ **2.** $(-9x^3 + 3x + 5) - (x^3 + 6x^2 - 4x - 6) = ?$

Answer: ____________________________________

Multiply the following expressions:

_____ **3.** $(x + 3)(x + 4) = ?$

Answer: ____________________________________

_____ **4.** $(x - 5)(x + 1) = ?$

Answer: ____________________________________

_____ **5.** $(3x - 4)(5x - 2) = ?$

Answer: ____________________________________

Factor the following expressions:

_____ **6.** $x^2 - x - 2 = ?$

Answer: ____

_____ **7.** $x^2 - 8x + 12 = ?$

Answer: ____

_____ **8.** $x^2 - 16 = ?$

Answer: ____

Simplify the following expression (when x is defined):

_____ **9.** $\dfrac{x^2 - 3x - 10}{x + 2} = ?$

Answer: ____

_____ **10.** What are the solutions for $x^2 + 14x + 48 = 0$?

Answer: ____

EXPONENT DRILL

Simplify the following expressions:

_____ 1. $(4x^2)(2x^3) =$

_____ 2. $\frac{12x^4}{3x^2} =$

_____ 3. $(3x^2)^3 =$

_____ 4. $\frac{15x^{10}}{5x^5x^2} =$

_____ 5. $(5x^2)(x^{-4}) =$

_____ 6. $(9x^4)^{\frac{1}{2}} =$

_____ 7. $(2^x)(8^{2x}) =$

_____ 8. $(2x^2)^3 + 3x(2x^5) =$

_____ 9. $\left(\frac{(5x)(5x^3)}{x^2}\right)^{\frac{1}{2}} =$

_____ 10. $\frac{10x^2\left(\frac{4x^5}{2x^3} + 6x^2\right)}{4x^3} =$

F(X) DRILL

Use the following information to answer questions 1–20

Let $f(x) = 6x - 8$
Let $g(x) = x^2 - x$

______ **1.** $f(5) =$

______ **2.** $f(-3) =$

______ **3.** $f\left(\frac{1}{3}\right) =$

______ **4.** $f(2a) =$

______ **5.** If $f(3) = w$, what is the value of $f(w)$?

______ **6.** If $f(c) = 46$, what is the value of c ?

______ **7.** If $2f(d) - 4 = 4$, what is the value of d ?

______ **8.** If $f(z - 2) = 10$, what is the value of z ?

______ **9.** $g(8) =$

______ **10.** $g(-3) =$

______ **11.** $g\left(\frac{1}{2}\right) =$

______ **12.** $g\left(-2x^2\right) =$

______ **13.** $g(x + 4) =$

______ **14.** $3g(5) =$

______ **15.** If $g(q) = 0$, what are the two possible values of q?

______ **16.** If $g(4) = v$, what is the value of $f(v)$?

______ **17.** If $f(-1) = k - 8$, what is the value of $g(k)$?

______ **18.** If $g(3) = 4t$, what is the value of $f(t)$?

___ **19.** If $f(2.5) = m$, what is the value of $g\left(\sqrt{m}\right)$?

______ **20.** If $g(-8) = f(-8) + s$, what is the value of s?

Graphing Drill

Use the following information to answer questions 1–10

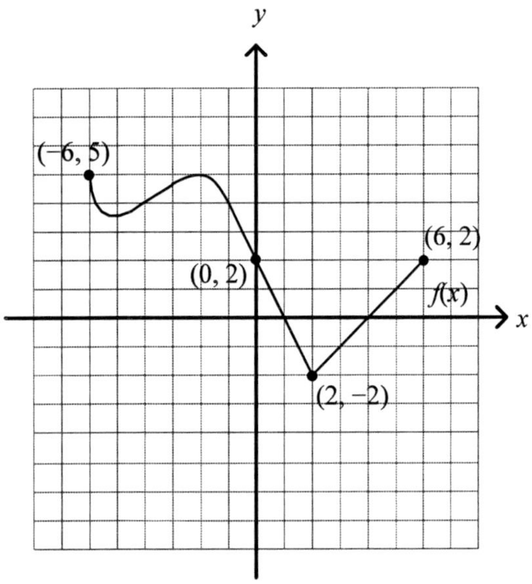

The function f graphed above is defined for $-6 < x < 6$.

_______ **1.** What is the value of $f(-4)$?

_______ **2.** What is the value of $f(5) + 7$?

_______ **3.** What is the value of $4f(3) - 2$?

_______ **4.** If $f(b) = 5$, what is one possible value of b?

_______ **5.** If $f(1) = k$, what is the value of k?

_______ **6.** For what values of x is $f(x)$ negative?

_______ **7.** For how many different values of x does $f(x) = 4$?

_______ **8.** If $f(p) = f(4)$, which of the following could be p?

A. −4
B. 0
C. 1
D. 3
E. 8

_______ **9.** If $g(x) = f(x - 2)$, what is the value of $g(1)$?

_______ **10.** If $h(x) = f(2x) + 3$, what is the value of $h(-2)$

Use the following information to answer questions 11–20

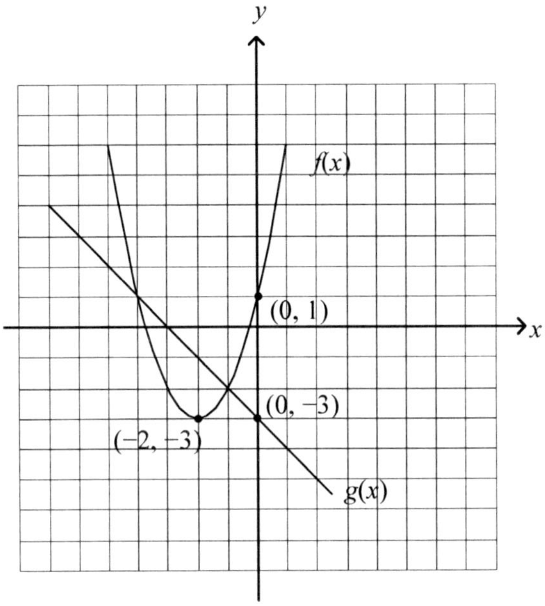

_______ **11.** What is the value of $f(-3)$?

_______ **12.** What is the value of $f(1) + g(-5)$?

_______ **13.** What is the value of $f(-2) - g(2)$?

_______ **14.** If $f(a) = 1$, what could be the value of a?

_______ **15.** If $f(-4) = -k$, what is the value of $g(k)$?

_______ **16.** If $g(0) = m$, what is the value of $f(m) + 6$?

_______ **17.** What is the slope of the graph of $g(x)$?

_______ **18.** If $f(r) = -3$, what is the value of $g(r)$?

_______ **19.** What are all values of x between −7 and 2 for which $f(x) \le g(x)$?

_______ **20.** Which of the following could be the equation of the graph of $f(x)$?

A. $f(x) = -x^2 - 4x + 1$

B. $f(x) = x^2 + 4x + 1$

C. $f(x) = x^2 - 2x + 3$

D. $f(x) = x^2 + 2x - 3$

E. $f(x) = x^2 - 6x + 7$

ANGLE DRILL

_____ **1.** What is the value of x?

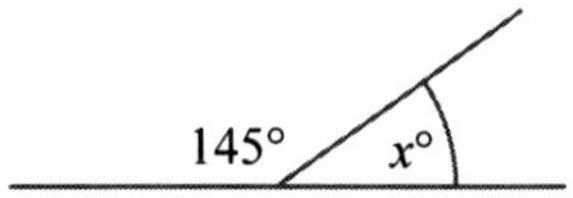

_____ **2.** In the figure below, $AB = BC$. What is the value of x?

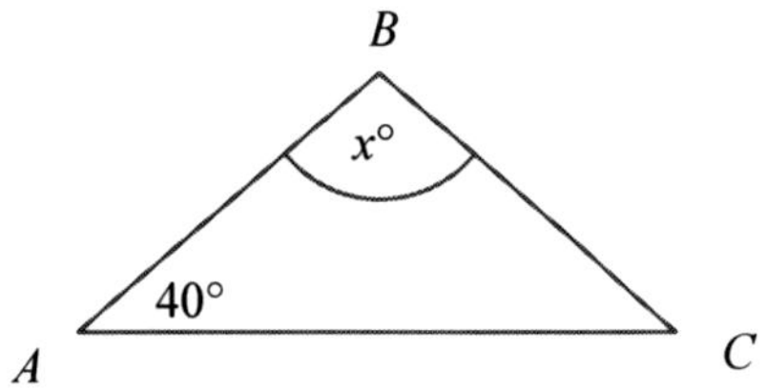

_____ **3.** What is the value of x?

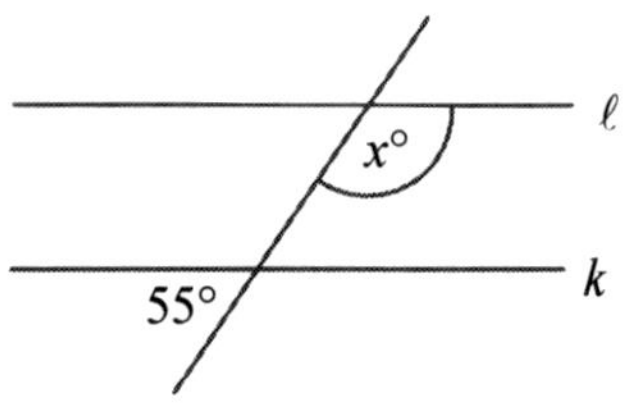

_____ **4.** The figure below shows a rectangle. What is the value of x?

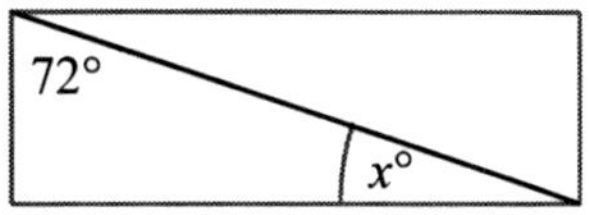

_____ **5.** What is the value of x?

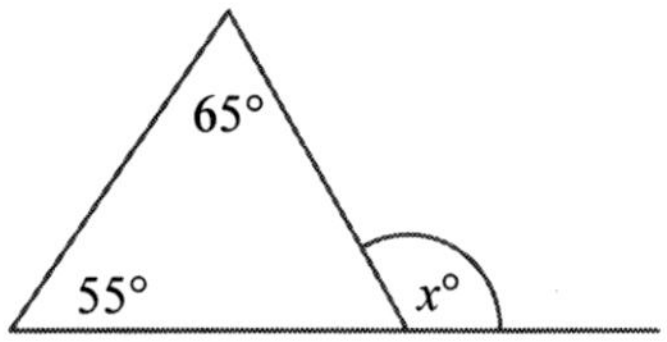

_____ **6.** In the figure below, $AB = AC$. What is the value of x?

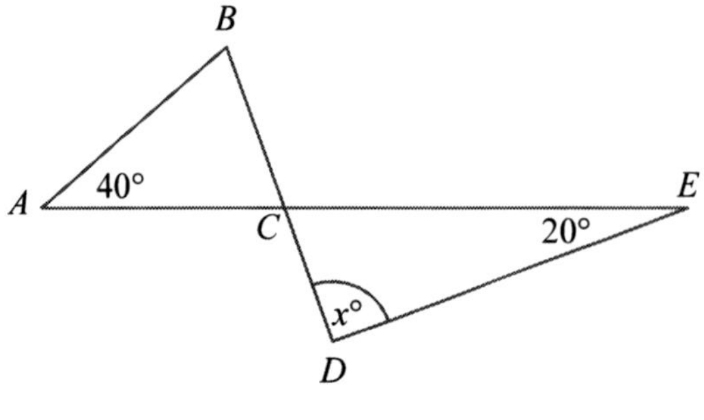

_____ **7.** In the figure below, $ABCD$ is a parallelogram. What is the value of x?

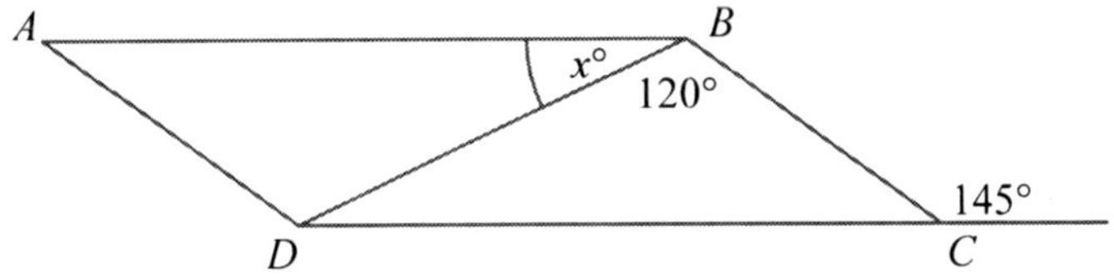

_____ **8.** In the figure below, $AB \parallel CD$ and $BD \parallel AE$. If $x = 65$ and $y = 35$, what is the value of z?

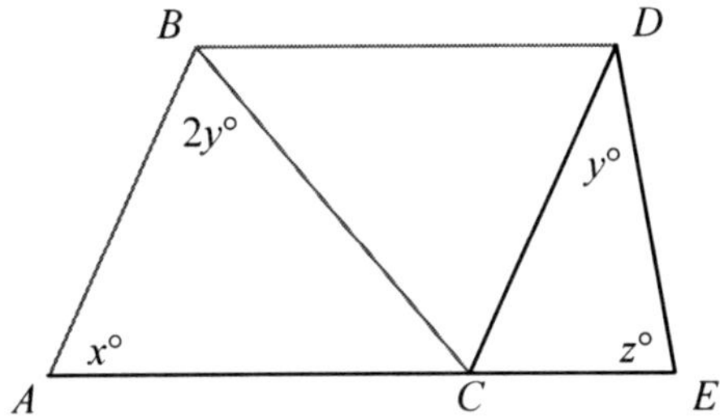

_____ **9.** In the figure below, $ABCDE$ is a regular pentagon. What is the value of x?

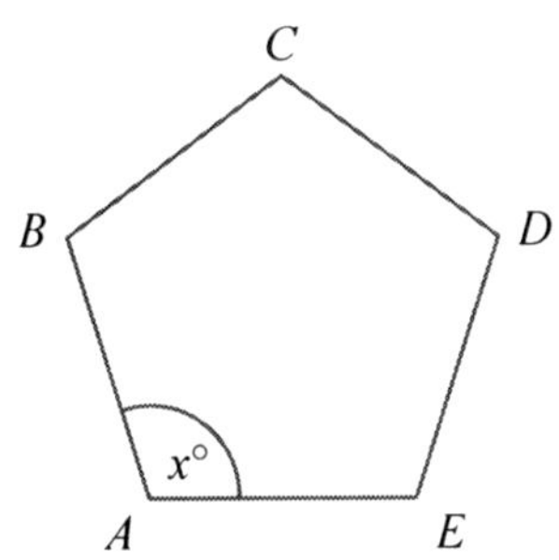

_____ **10.** In the figure below, $BCDG$ is a rectangle and $AF \parallel BE$. If C and F lie on a straight line and $\angle GFE = 115°$, what is the value of x?

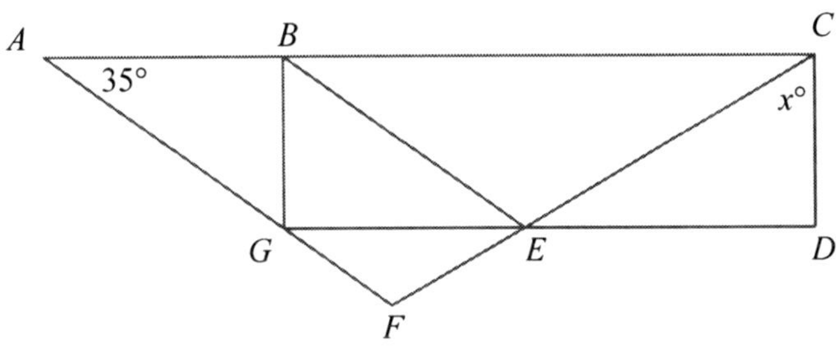

TRIANGLE DRILL

_____ **1.** What is the value of x?

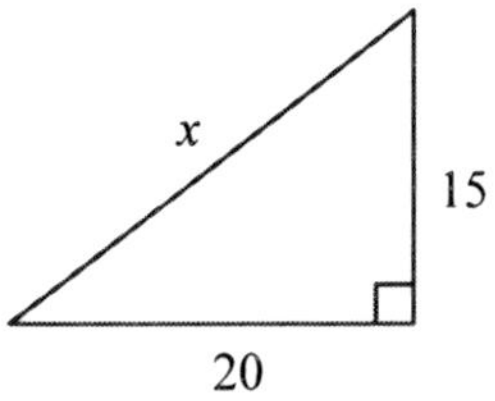

_____ **2.** What is the value of x?

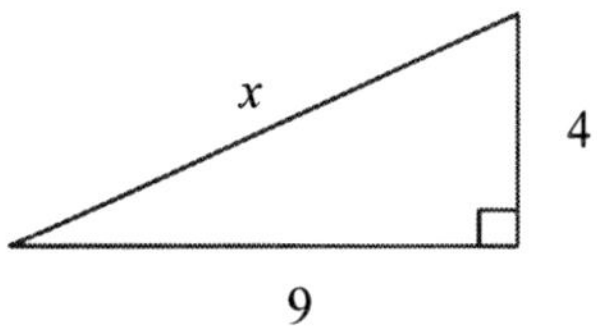

_____ **3.** The figure below shows a square. What is the value of x?

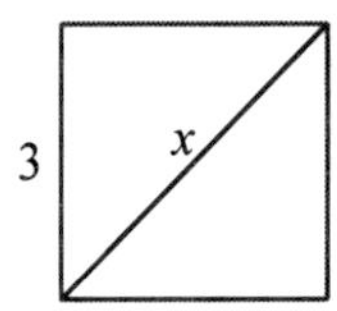

_____ **4.** What is the value of x?

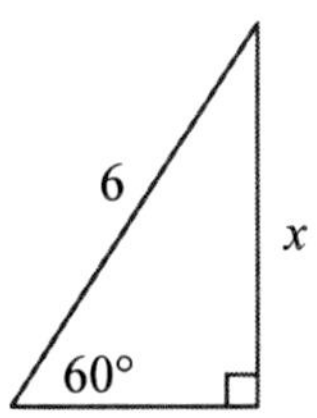

_____ **5.** What is the value of x?

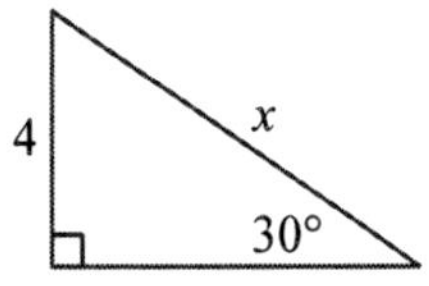

_____ **6.** In the figure below, $AC \parallel DE$. If $AB = 9$, what is the value of CE?

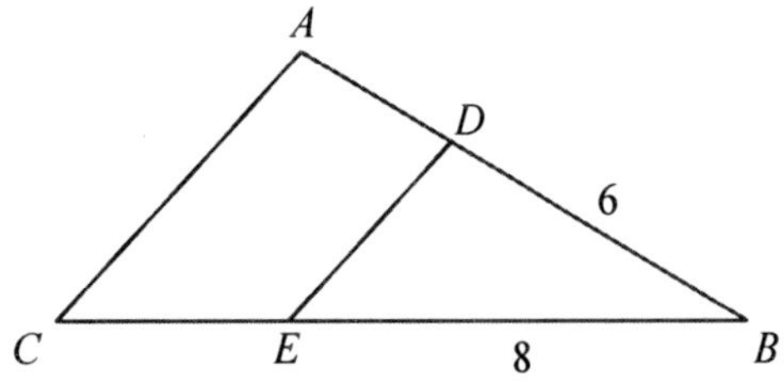

_____ **7.** In the figure below, if $BC = 5\sqrt{2}$, what is the value of AB?

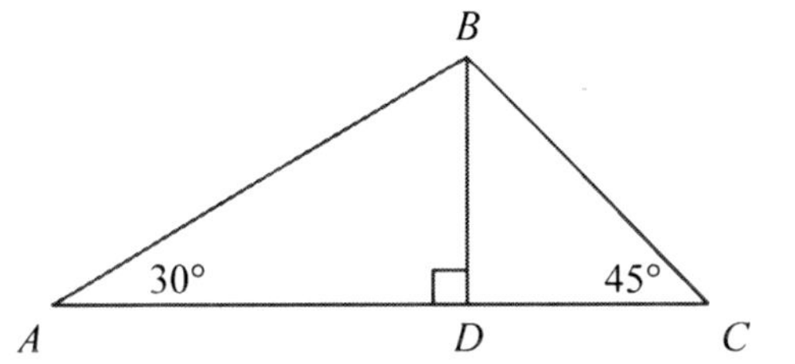

_____ **8.** In $\triangle ABC$, $AB = 3$ and $BC = 7$. If BC is the largest side of the triangle and $\triangle ABC$ is not isosceles, what is one possible value for the length of AC?

_____ **9.** In the figure below, $ABCD$ is a square, $BD = 12\sqrt{2}$ and $BE = 13$. What is the length of DE?

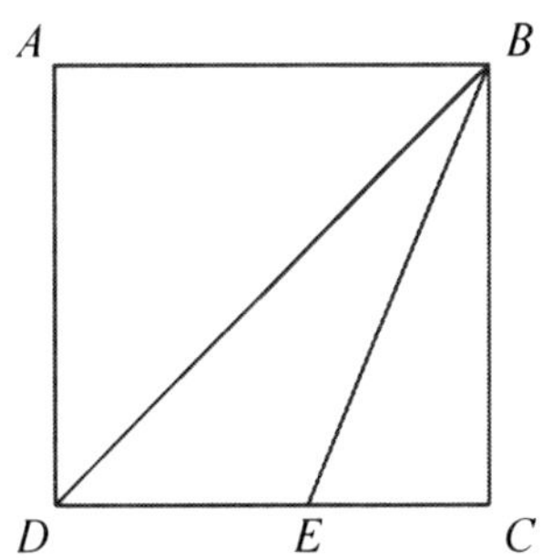

_____ **10.** In the figure below, what is the length of BC?

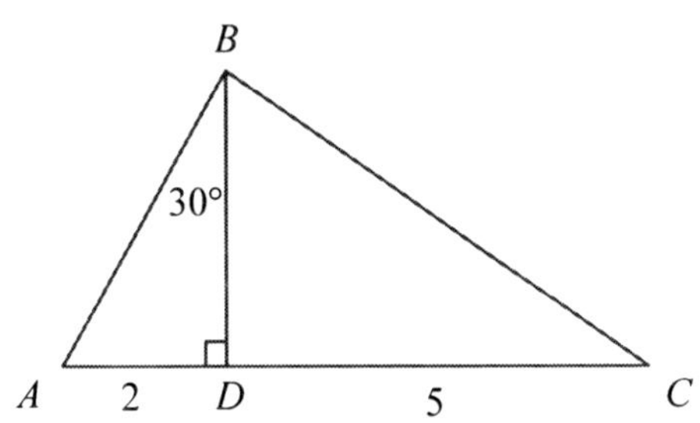

PERIMETER, AREA, VOLUME DRILL

_____ **1.** The rectangle shown below has a perimeter of 20. What is the value of x?

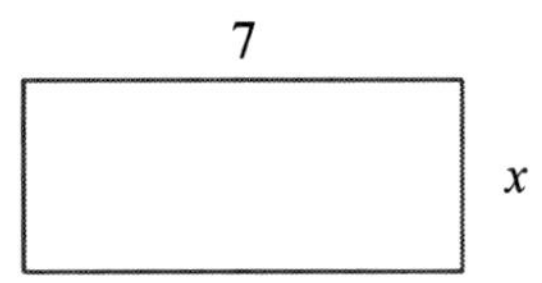

_____ **2.** The rectangle shown below has an area of 30. What is the perimeter of the rectangle?

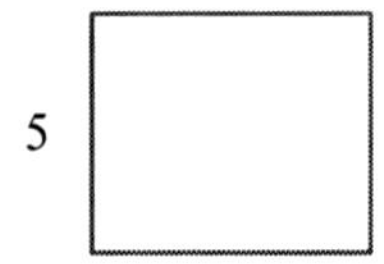

_____ **3.** What is the area of the triangle shown below?

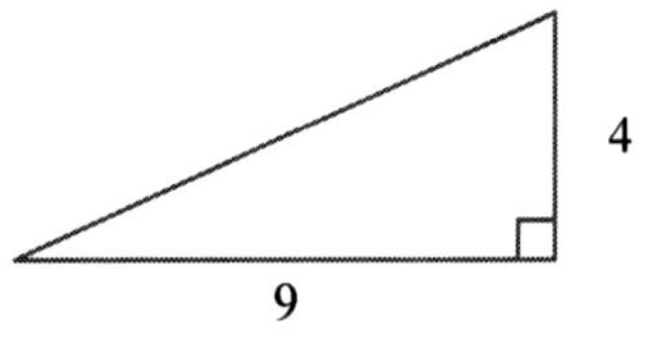

_____ **4.** What is the area of the triangle shown below?

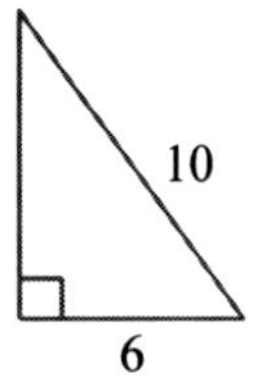

_____ **5.** In the figure below $\triangle ABC$ is equilateral and $BD \perp AC$. What is the area of $\triangle ABC$?

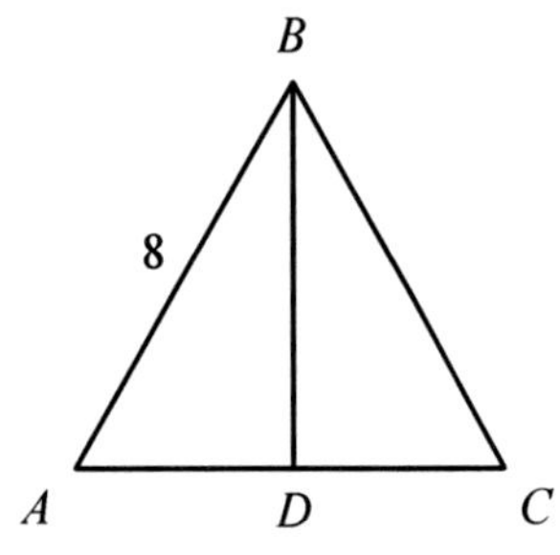

_____ **6.** In the figure below, $ABCD$ is a rectangle and E is the midpoint of DC. What is the area of the shaded region?

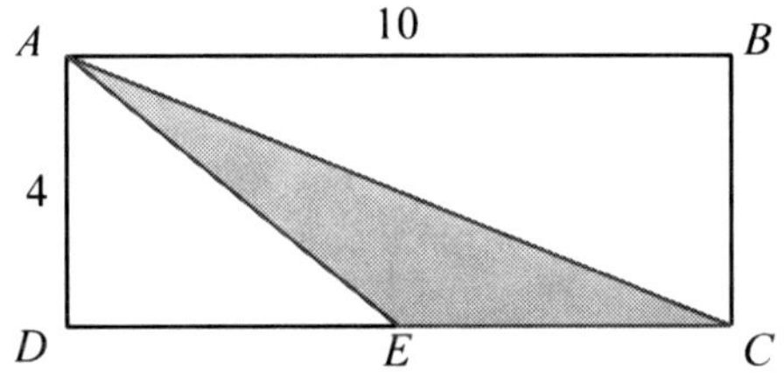

_____ **7.** What is the volume of a right circular cylinder with radius 3 and height 7?

_____ **8.** In the figure below, $ABCD$ is a rectangle. E is the midpoint of AB and G is the midpoint of DC. If $AB = 8$, what is the area of the shaded region?

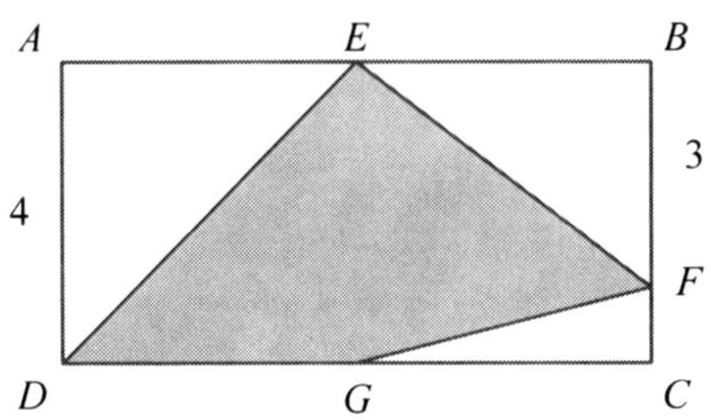

_____ **9.** A rectangular box has dimensions of 3 centimeters by 5 centimeters by 7 centimeters. What is the surface area, in square centimeters, of the box?

_____ **10.** In the figure below, $\triangle ABC$ is an equilateral triangle with area 18 and the shaded region is a regular hexagon. What is the area of the shaded hexagon?

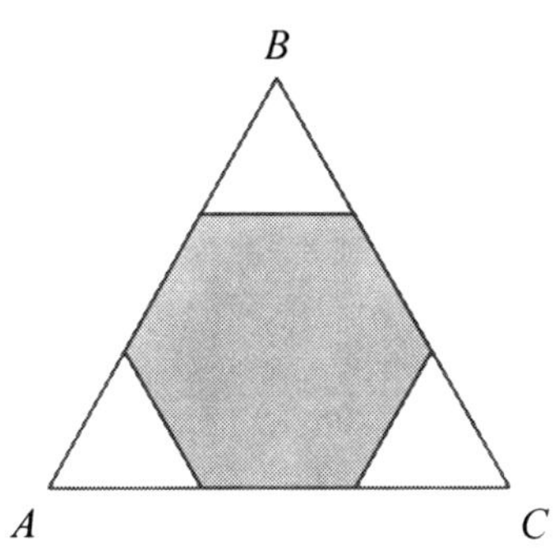

CIRCLE DRILL

_____ **1.** What is the area of a circle with radius 3?

_____ **2.** What is the circumference of a circle with radius 7?

_____ **3.** What is the area of a circle with diameter 10?

_____ **4.** What is the area of a semicircle with radius 6?

_____ **5.** What is the area of a circle with circumference of 16π?

_____ **6.** The figure below shows a circle inscribed within a square. If the square has a side of length 12, what is the area of the circle?

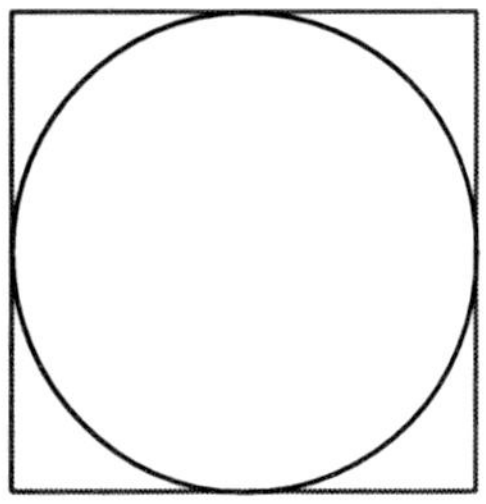

_____ **7.** The figure below is composed of two small circles and one large semicircle. *AB* is a diameter of the large circle, and *AO* and *OB* are diameters of the two small circles. If the radius of the large circle is 6, what is the total length of the darkened edge of the figure?

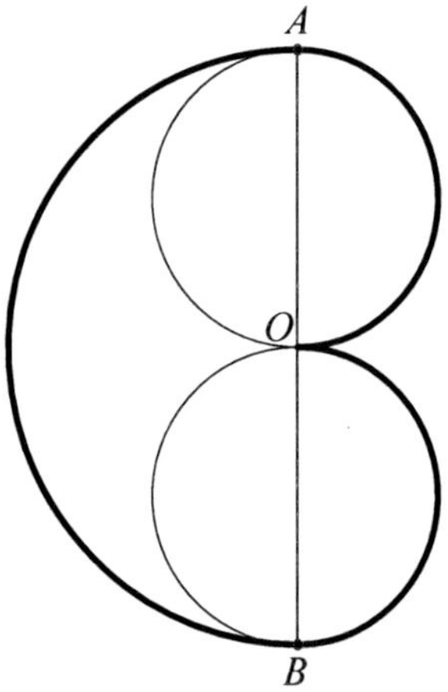

_____ **8.** In the figure below, point A is the center of the large circle and the two circles are tangent at point B. If $AB = 20$, what is the area of the shaded region?

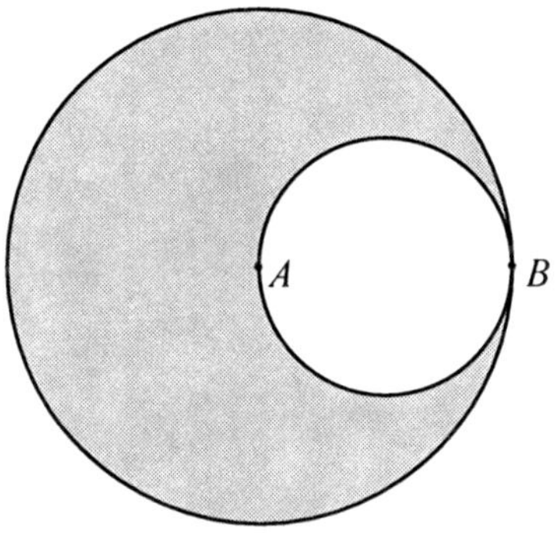

_____ **9.** In circle O shown below, $\angle AOB = 45°$ and the length of arc $ACB = \frac{3}{2}\pi$. What is the radius of the circle?

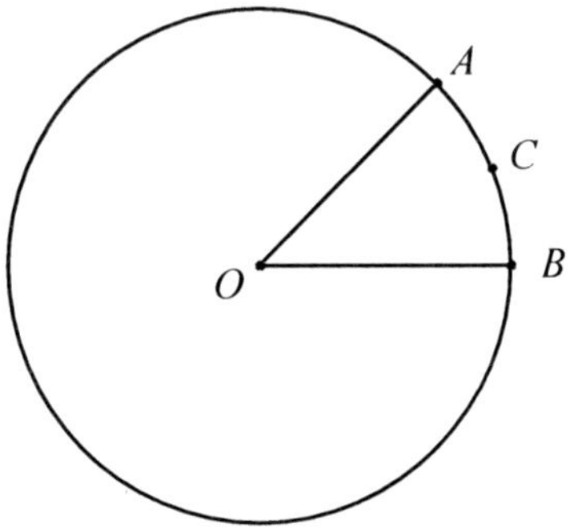

_____ **10.** In the figure below, $\angle BOA = 30°$ and $OB = 8$. What is the area of the shaded region?

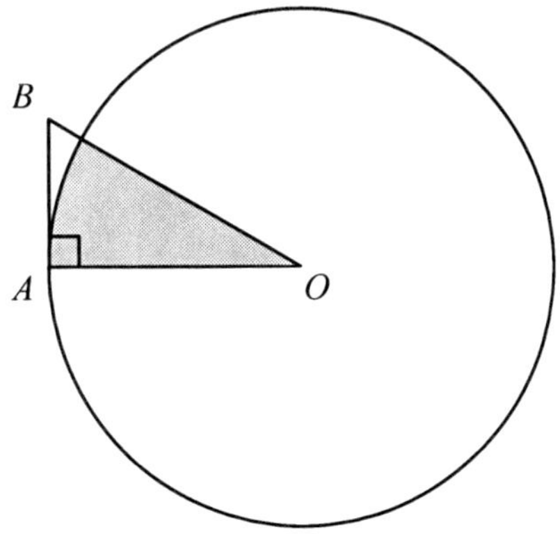

APPENDIX B
STUFF TO KNOW FOR ACT MATH

Here's a guide to some of the rules, concepts, and formulas you may need for the ACT Math Test. Not all of these are *crucial* concepts; some appear relatively rarely on the ACT. This is just a quick guide to concepts you may not be entirely familiar with.

Intermediate Algebra

Exponents

$(x^a)(x^b) = x^{a+b}$ $\frac{x^a}{x^b} = x^{a-b}$ $(x^a)^b = x^{ab}$ $x^0 = 1$ $x^{-a} = \frac{1}{x^a}$ $x^{\frac{1}{a}} = \sqrt[a]{x}$

Logarithms

Usually logarithm problems just require you to understand the definition of a logarithm:

$\log_a b = c$ means that $a^c = b$

Occasionally you may need to know some logarithm properties. Note that these properties are just logical extensions of the exponent rules.

$\log_a(mn) = \log_a m + \log_a n$ $\log_a(m^n) = n(\log_a m)$

$\log_a(m/n) = \log_a m - \log_a n$ $\log_a(a) = 1$, $\log_a(a^x) = x$

Sequences

An ***arithmetic sequence*** is a sequence in which each term is obtained by *adding* a certain number to the previous term.

- n stands for the number of terms
- a_1 is the first term of the sequence
- a_n is the last term of the sequence
- d is the amount added to each term
- s_n is the sum of first n terms

To find the last term of the sequence:

$$a_n = a_1 + (n-1)d$$

To find the sum of the first n terms:

$s_n = \frac{n(a_1 + a_n)}{2}$ or, combined with the first equation: $s_n = \frac{n(2a_1 + (n-1)d)}{2}$

A ***geometric sequence*** is a sequence in which each term is obtained by *multiplying* a certain number to the previous term. Questions about geometric sequences will simply require you to understand this definition.

Imaginary and Complex numbers

Imaginary numbers are numbers that contain i, defined as $i = \sqrt{-1}$ or $i^2 = -1$.

A *complex number* is a polynomial that contains a real number and an imaginary number. They can be manipulated and FOILed just like any other polynomials. For example:

$$(3+2i)(5+3i) = 3(5) + 9i + 10i + 6i^2 = 15 + 19i + 6(-1) = 9 + 19i$$

The powers of *i* show a repeating pattern:

$i^1 = \sqrt{-1} = i$ $\quad i^2 = \sqrt{-1} \times \sqrt{-1} = -1$ $\quad i^3 = i^2 \times i = -1 \times i = -i$ $\quad i^4 = i^3 \times i = (-i) \times i = -i^2 = 1$

$i^5 = i^4 \times i = i$ $\quad i^6 = i^5 \times i = i \times i = -1$ $\quad i^7 = i^6 \times i = -1 \times i = -i$ $\quad i^8 = i^7 \times i = (-i) \times i = -i^2 = 1$ etc...

Matrices

Adding and subtracting:

$$\begin{bmatrix} a & b \\ c & d \end{bmatrix} + \begin{bmatrix} e & f \\ g & h \end{bmatrix} = \begin{bmatrix} a+e & b+f \\ c+g & d+h \end{bmatrix}$$

Multiplying:

$$\begin{bmatrix} a & b \\ c & d \end{bmatrix} \times \begin{bmatrix} e & f \\ g & h \end{bmatrix} = \begin{bmatrix} ae+bg & af+bh \\ ce+dg & cf+dh \end{bmatrix}$$

$$\begin{bmatrix} a & b & c \\ d & e & f \end{bmatrix} \times \begin{bmatrix} g & h \\ j & k \\ l & m \end{bmatrix} = \begin{bmatrix} ag+bj+cl & ah+bk+cm \\ dg+ej+fl & hd+ek+fm \end{bmatrix}$$

Factorial (*n*!)

Taking the factorial of *n* (symbol is "*n*!") means finding the product of all the consecutive numbers up to *n*.

$3! = 1 \times 2 \times 3$ $\quad 10! = 1 \times 2 \times 3 \times 4 \times 5 \times 6 \times 7 \times 8 \times 9 \times 10$ $\quad n! = 1 \times 2 \ldots \times (n-1) \times n$

NOTE:

Logarithms, complex numbers, matrices, and factorials all are fairly rare on the ACT—you might see one question about the topic on every third test or so. However, when considered all together, it's likely that any given test will have one question on one of the three topics. When they do appear, they generally only show up on the hardest questions at the end of the test.

Coordinate Geometry

Quadrants

The two axes divide the *xy*-coordinate plane into four quadrants. The sign of the *x* and *y* value of a point will determine which quadrant the point lies in.

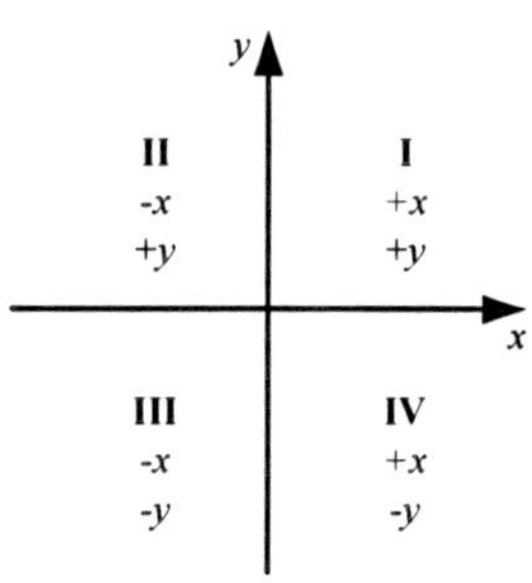

Distance Formula

The distance, *d*, between (x_1, y_1) and (x_2, y_2) is

$$d = \sqrt{(x_2 - x_1)^2 + (y_2 - y_1)^2} \text{ or}$$

$$d^2 = (x_2 - x_1)^2 + (y_2 - y_1)^2$$

Note that the Distance Formula is nothing more than the Pythagorean Theorem. Any two points on the coordinate grid can form a right triangle:

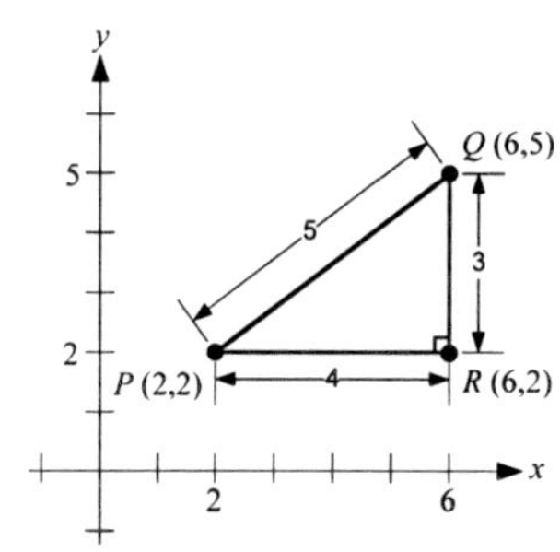

$(x_2 - x_1)$ is one leg of the triangle,

$(y_2 - y_1)$ is the other leg,

and the distance between the points is the hypotenuse.

Midpoint

The Midpoint between two points is just the average of the x's and the average of the y's.

Midpoint of (x_1, y_1) and (x_2, y_2) is $\left(\frac{x_1 + x_2}{2}, \frac{y_1 + y_x}{2}\right)$

Lines

Slope = $\frac{y_2 - y_1}{x_2 - x_1}$

Slope intercept form: $y = mx + b$ where m is the slope, b is the y-intercept, and (x,y) is a point on the line.

Equation of a circle:

$(x-a)^2 + (y-b)^2 = r^2$ where r is the radius, and (a, b) is the center of the circle

Note that this equation is just the *Pythagorean Theorem again!* The distance from the center (a, b) to any point (x, y) on the circle is equal to the radius r. In fact, a circle is defined as the set of all points equidistant to a certain point (the center).

Equation of an ellipse:

Ellipses show up very rarely on the ACT, but they have shown up before.

An ellipse is defined as the set of all points such that the sum of the distance from a point on the ellipse to two points (the foci) is constant.

$\frac{(x-h)^2}{a^2} + \frac{(y-k)^2}{b^2} = 1$ where (h, k) is its center, $2a$ is the length of the horizontal axis (along the x) and $2b$ is the length of the vertical axis (along the y).

Equation of a parabola

$y = ax^2 + bx + c$

- a gives the "squeeziness" of the parabola: bigger a gives a thinner graph; smaller a gives a wider graph.
- Sign of a tells if it opens up or down: positive a opens up; negative a opens down.
- c gives the y-intercept of the parabola.

Quadratic Formula

$$x = \frac{-b \pm \sqrt{b^2 - 4ac}}{2a}$$

- If $b^2 - 4ac > 0$, two solutions occur
- If $b^2 - 4ac = 0$, one solution occurs
- If $b^2 - 4ac < 0$, no real solutions occur

The quadratic formula gives the solutions to a quadratic equation. That is, it's the value of x when $y = 0$. Graphically, the solutions will be the x-intercepts of the parabola (the places where the graph cross the x-axis). The solutions to the quadratic equations are sometimes called "zeroes" or "roots".

You generally won't need the quadratic formula. There will be a number of questions that ask you to solve a quadratic equation, but they can usually easily be done by factoring. However, some students may find using the formula to be easier than factoring.

Plane Geometry

If you've been studying the SAT, please note that all those formulas that are given at the beginning of each SAT section *will not* be given to you on the ACT. You must know the following formulas:

Reference Information

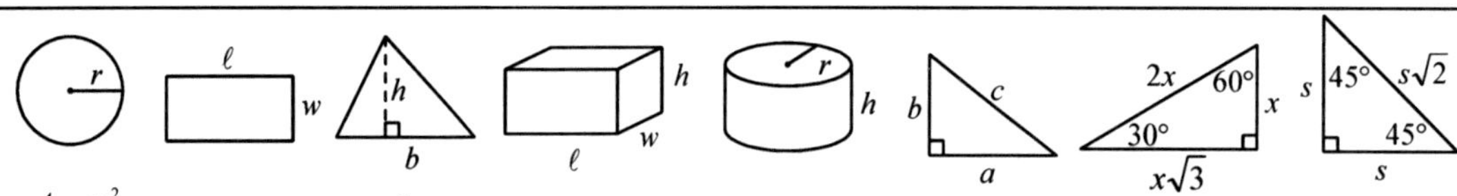

$A = \pi r^2$ $C = 2\pi r$ $A = \ell w$ $A = \frac{1}{2}bh$ $V = \ell wh$ $V = \pi r^2 h$ $c^2 = a^2 + b^2$ Special Right Triangles

The number of degrees of arc in a circle is 360.
The sum of the measures in degrees of the angles of a triangle is 180.

Other area formulas to know:

A **parallelogram** is a quadrilateral with two pairs of parallel sides. $A = bh$

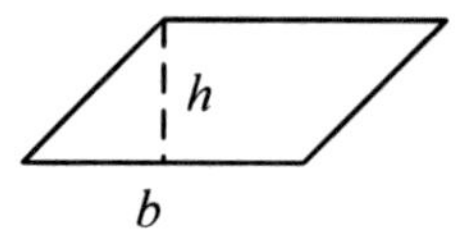

A **trapezoid** is a quadrilateral with only one pair of parallel sides.

Find the area directly with this formula:

$$A = \frac{1}{2}h(b_1 + b_2)$$

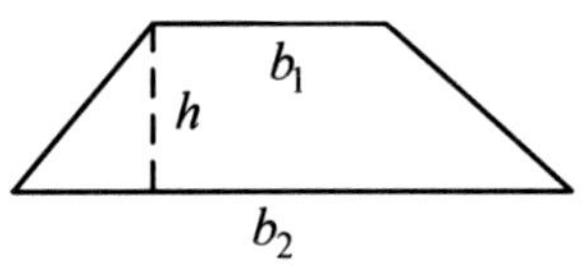

OR: split it up into a rectangle and triangles:

$$A = \frac{1}{2}ha + hw + \frac{1}{2}hb$$

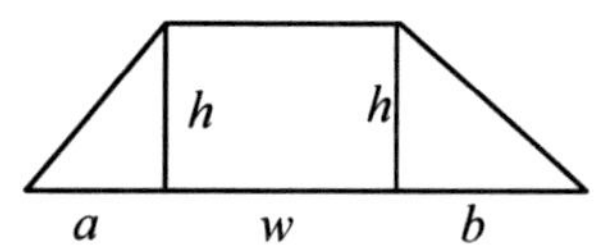

Other formulas for more complicated shapes will usually be given to you in the question.

Trigonometry

Definitions

Learn these ratios! *They will not be given to you.*

$$\sin\theta = \frac{Opposite}{Hypotenuse} = \frac{y}{r}$$

$$\cos\theta = \frac{Adjacent}{Hypotenuse} = \frac{x}{r}$$

$$\tan\theta = \frac{Opposite}{Adjacent} = \frac{y}{x}$$

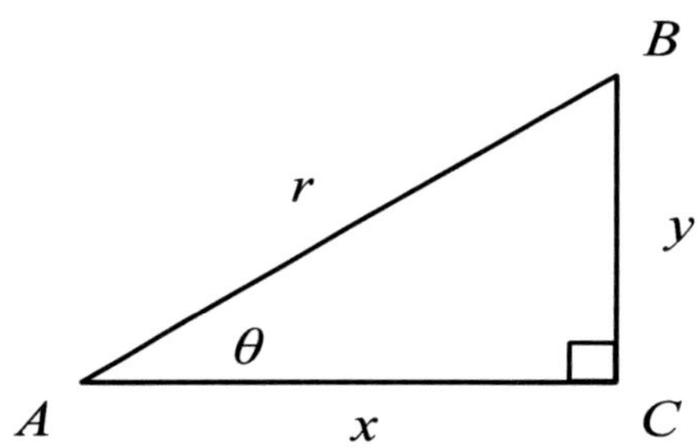

sin A = cos B cos A = sin B

$$\csc\theta = \frac{1}{\sin\theta}$$

$$\sec\theta = \frac{1}{\cos\theta}$$

$$\cot\theta = \frac{1}{\tan\theta}$$

Remember these ratios by remembering the acronym **SOHCAHTOA** :

Sine = **O**pposite **H**ypotenuse, **C**osine = **A**djacent **H**ypotenuse, **T**angent = **O**pposite **A**djacent

Identities:

These will not be given to you. You should learn them.

$$\frac{\sin\theta}{\cos\theta} = \tan\theta$$

$(\sin\theta)^2 + (\cos\theta)^2 = 1$ (This is often written "$\sin^2\theta + \cos^2\theta = 1$")

$\sin(-\theta) = -\sin(\theta)$

$\cos(-\theta) = \cos(\theta)$

Other laws

If you need either of these laws, it will be given to you in the question. However, while you don't need to memorize the formulas, it's still a good idea to be familiar with the principles.

Law of Sines: $\dfrac{a}{\sin A} = \dfrac{b}{\sin B} = \dfrac{c}{\sin C}$

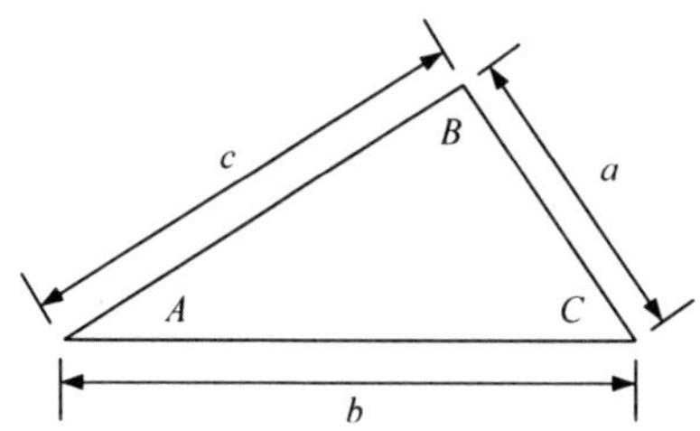

Law of Cosines: $c^2 = a^2 + b^2 - 2ab\cos C$

Radians

2π rad = 360°

To convert radians to degrees, multiply by $\dfrac{360}{2\pi}$. To convert degrees to radians, multiply by $\dfrac{2\pi}{360}$.

Periods

Function	*Period (rad)*	*Period (deg)*
$\sin\theta$	2π	360°
$\cos\theta$	2π	360°

Transformation

$y = \sin(x)$ compared to $y = a\sin(bx + c) + d$:

- a stretches the function ***vertically*** by factor of a. A negative a flips the graph across the x-axis.
- b changes the ***period*** of the function. For sine, new period is $\dfrac{2\pi}{b}$. (In general, it's $\dfrac{\text{old period}}{b}$.)
- c shifts the graph ***left*** by c units. [This is true of any function $f(x + c)$.] A negative c shifts it right.
- d shifts the graph ***up*** by d units. [This is true of any function $f(x) + d$.] A negative d shifts it down.

If you forget these rules, you can always test them by graphing the transformed equation and the original function together on your calculator.

The Unit Circle

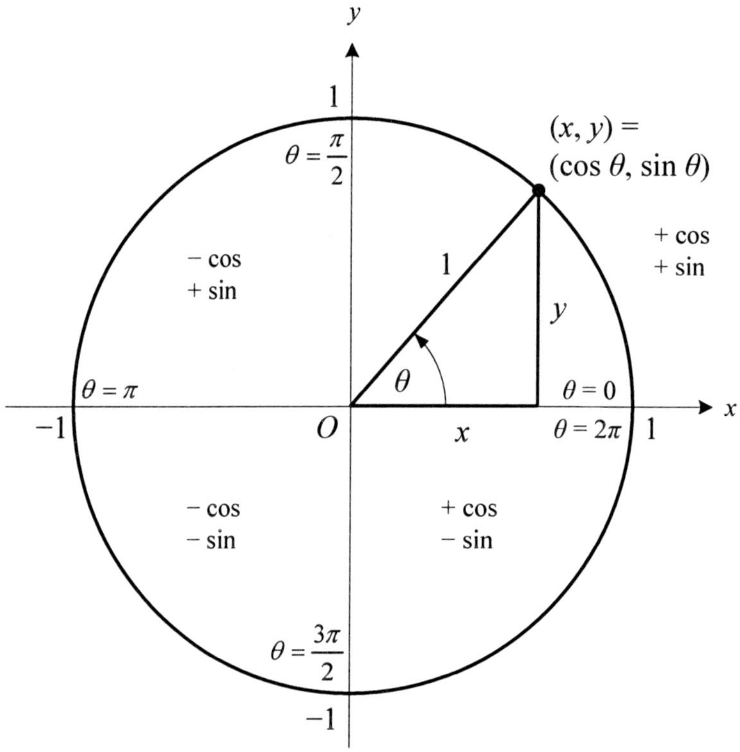

- Imagine a circle with radius 1 plotted on the *xy*-coordinate plane, centered on the origin.
- For any point (x, y) on the circle we can draw a right triangle. The legs of the triangle will have length x and y, and the hypotenuse will be 1.
- The triangle makes an angle, θ, between the x-axis and the radius. If we take the normal trig ratios of that angle θ, we get $\cos\theta = \frac{x}{1}$ and $\sin\theta = \frac{y}{1}$. So $\cos\theta = x$ and $\sin\theta = y$.
- Therefore, the coordinates (x, y) are equal to $(\cos\theta, \sin\theta)$.
- You can use this circle to figure out the domain and range of the major functions:
    - $\cos\theta$ will be negative wherever the x value of the circle is negative. That's in Quadrant II and III, where $90° < \theta < 270°$ or $\frac{\pi}{2} < \theta < \frac{3\pi}{2}$.
    - $\sin\theta$ will be negative wherever the y-value of the circle is negative. That's in Quadrant III and IV, where $180° < \theta < 360°$ or $\pi < \theta < 2\pi$.
    - Since $\tan\theta = \frac{\sin\theta}{\cos\theta}$, $\tan\theta$ will be negative wherever cos and sin have different signs. That's in Quadrant II (cos is neg, sin is pos) and Quadrant IV (cos is pos, sin is neg).
- Radian angle measures are shown on the figure above. Note that the radian measure of an angle is simply equal to the length of the arc at that point.
- Note that θ can cycle to become infinitely large. $\theta = 90°$ gives the same point as when $\theta = 90 + 360 = 450°$.
- Note that negative values of θ arise from going clockwise. So $\theta = -90°$ gives the same point as when $\theta = 360 - 90 = 270°$.

APPENDIX C
GLOSSARY OF FANCY MATH TERMS

Absolute value: The value of an expression without regard to its sign, expressed as a positive number. Symbol is $|x|$. For example, $|-7| = 7$ and $|7| = 7$.

Arc: A portion of the circumference of a circle.

Arithmetic mean: See **Average**.

Arithmetic sequence: A sequence of numbers in which each term is obtained by adding a certain number to the previous term.

Asymptote: A line which a graph approaches but doesn't ever reach. Note that this line is usually not actually drawn in the figure.

Average: Also called "arithmetic mean" or just "mean". For a list of values, the average is the sum of the values divided by the number of terms.

Average speed: The average speed of a trip is the total distance traveled divided by the total time elapsed.

Axis: One of two perpendicular lines that define values in the coordinate plane.

Bisect: To cut into two equal pieces.

Chord: A line segment connecting one point on a circle to another point on the circle. The diameter is the longest chord of a circle.

Circle: The set of all points equidistant to a certain point (called its "center").

Circle graph: Also called a "pie chart". A graph which represents percentages as slices of a circle.

Circumference: The perimeter of a circle. The length all the way around the edge of a circle.

Coefficient: The number that a variable is multiplied by. In the expression $7x$, 7 is the coefficient.

Collinear: Collinear points are points that lie on the same line. Note that the line does not have to be *literally drawn* in the figure; this only means that you *could* connect the points with a single straight line.

Complementary angles: Angles that form a right angle together. Complementary angles add up to 90°.

Complex number: A polynomial in the form $a + bi$, consisting of a real number, a, plus an imaginary number, bi, with a coefficient, b.

Congruent: Equal in measure. Can be said of angles, segments, triangles, or any shape. Symbol for congruence is $\cong$. "$\triangle ABC \cong \triangle DEF$" means that triangles ABC and DEF are congruent, so they have entirely equal angles and lengths.

Coordinate plane: A grid that maps points according to two variables, x and y. Also called the "xy coordinate plane" or "xy plane".

Cosecant: A trig function equivalent to the ratio of the hypotenuse over the leg opposite the angle. The reciprocal of the sine function.

Cosine: A trig function equivalent to the ratio of the leg adjacent to an angle over the hypotenuse. The reciprocal of cosine is secant.

Cotangent: A trig function equivalent to the ratio of the leg adjacent to an angle over the leg opposite the angle. The reciprocal of the tangent function.

Cube: A three-dimensional box in which all the edges are equal. Each of a cube's six faces is a square.

Diagonal: A line segment connecting any two vertices of a polygon, excluding any segment that makes a side of the figure. A quadrilateral has two diagonals; a triangle has none.

Diameter: A chord that passes through the center of a circle. The longest chord of a circle. Composed of two radii.

Direct proportion: A relationship between two variables such that their ratio is constant. That is, one value times a constant gives the second value. Also described as one number "varying directly" with another.

Domain: The set of all possible x-values of a function. All inputs for which the function is defined.

Edge: The edge of a three-dimensional solid is a line segment where two faces touch.

Ellipse: The set of all points such that the sum of the distance from a point on the ellipse to two points (the foci) is constant. It looks like a circle that has been squashed a little in the middle.

Equilateral: Having all sides of equal length.

Exclamation point: See **Factorial**.

Exterior angle: An angle that is supplementary to an interior angle of a polygon.

Face: A two-dimensional figure that makes up part of a three-dimensional solid.

Factor: A number or algebraic expression that can be evenly divided into another number or algebraic expression. Also called a "divisor". The factors of 12 are 1, 2, 3, 4, 6, and 12. The factors of $x^2 + 5x + 6$ are $(x + 2)$ and $(x + 3)$. Also can be a verb meaning to split a number or algebraic expression into its factors.

Factorial: The product of all consecutive integers up to and including a certain integer. Symbol is an exclamation point. $4! = 1 \times 2 \times 3 \times 4$.

Geometric sequence: A sequence of numbers in which each term is obtained by multiplying a certain number to the previous term.

Hypotenuse: The side of a right triangle that is opposite the right angle. The hypotenuse is always the longest side of a right triangle.

Imaginary number: A multiple of i, which is equal to $\sqrt{-1}$. See also: **Complex number**.

Integer: Any whole number; a counting number. Negative numbers and zero are considered integers.

Intercept: The point where the graph of a function crosses an axis.

Interior angle: An angle inside a polygon formed by adjacent sides of the polygon.

Inverse trig function: The inverse of any trig function (written with a "−1" superscript) is a way to solve an equation that has a variable in the trig function. For example, if $\sin x = 7$, then $x = \sin^{-1} 7$.

Irrational number: A number that cannot be expressed as a fraction or ratio of two integers. Examples of irrational numbers include π and $\sqrt{2}$.

Isosceles trapezoid: A trapezoid in which the two non-parallel sides are equal. Isosceles trapezoids are symmetrical: corresponding angles are equal. If you split the trapezoid into a rectangle with two triangles on its sides, the triangles will be congruent.

Isosceles triangle: A triangle in which exactly two sides are equal. The two angles opposite the equal sides are also equal.

Least common multiple: The smallest number that is a multiple of two given numbers. For example, 24 is a multiple of 4 and 6, but 12 is the least common multiple.

Leg: Either side of a right triangle that makes up its right angle. That is, any side other than the hypotenuse.

Line: A line extends infinitely in both directions. Do not confuse with "line segment".

Line segment: A part of a line that is bounded by two endpoints and has a finite length.

Linear function: A function whose graph makes a straight line; a function in which x only raised to the power of 1. See also **Slope-intercept form**.

Logarithm: A way to solve equations with variables in exponents. If $a^c = b$, then the logarithm base a of b equals c, or $\log_a b = c$. The LOG button on your calculator gives the logarithm base 10.

Matrix: (Plural *matrices*) A way to organize a group of numbers in rows and columns, kind of like a table.

Mean: See **Average**.

Median: The middle term of a list of values that have been arranged lowest to highest (or vice versa). If there are an even number of terms such that there is no one term in the middle, the median is the average of the two middle terms.

Midpoint: A point halfway between two endpoints.

Mode: The term that occurs most frequently in a list of values.

Multiple: A number for which a given number or numbers is a factor. The inverse of a factor: 24 is a multiple of 6, just as 6 is a factor of 24.

Number line: A one-dimensional graph. Can be used for graphing one-variable expressions.

Parabola: The shape of the graph of a quadratic function.

Parallel lines: Lines within a single plane that, when extended infinitely, will never touch. Parallel lines have equal slopes.

Parallelogram: A quadrilateral with two sets of parallel sides.

Perimeter: The sum of the lengths of the sides of a polygon.

Period: The length of one cycle of a repeating event. For example, the period of $y = \sin x$ is 2π, because the value of y repeats itself for every 2π values of x.

Perpendicular: Two lines that make a right angle are perpendicular to each other. Symbol is $\perp$. The slope of perpendicular lines are the negative reciprocals of each other.

Plane: A flat two-dimensional surface that extends infinitely in all directions. The 2D counterpart of a line.

Polygon: Any closed two-dimensional figure made up of line segments.

Polynomial: An expression composed of the sum or difference of multiple terms of a coefficient and one or more variables raised to different powers.

Prime: A number that has no factors except for itself and 1, such as 3 or 7. The only even prime number is 2. 1 is not considered prime.

Prime factor: A factor that is prime, thus cannot be broken up into smaller factors. The product of a number's prime factors is the number itself. For example, the prime factors of 18 are 3, 3, and 2, and $3 \times 3 \times 2 = 18$.

Probability: The likelihood of an event occurring. Probability of an event is equal to the number of times the event may occur divided by the total number of possible occurrences.

Product: The result of multiplication. The product of 2 and 3 is 6.

Quadrant: One of four regions into which the coordinate plane is divided by the two axes.

Quadratic equation: A quadratic function in which y equals 0. Can be solved by factoring or by using the quadratic formula.

Quadratic formula: A formula that can be used to solve a quadratic equation (that is, the value of x in a quadratic function when $y = 0$). Quadratic equations can also be solved by factoring.

Quadratic function: A quadratic function is an equation of the form $y = ax^2 + bx + c$. Its graph is a parabola.
Quadrilateral: A polygon with four sides.
Radian: A unit of measuring angles. A full circle is 2π radians.
Radius: A line segment extending from the center of the circle to the edge. Equal to half the diameter.
Range: All possible y-values of a function. The set of all outputs for a given set of inputs. See also: **Domain**.
Rational number: A number that can be expressed as a fraction or ratio of two integers. All integers are themselves rational numbers.
Ray: A part of a line that starts from a point and extends infinitely in one direction.
Real number: Any number that is not imaginary. (In practice, this often just means "any number", since you have no reason to consider imaginary numbers unless the problem specifically asks you to do so.)
Reciprocal: The flip of a fraction. The reciprocal of 2/5 is 5/2.
Regular polygon: A polygon in which all sides and angles are equal.
Rhombus: Any quadrilateral in which all four sides are equal. Every rhombus is also a parallelogram. A square is a type of rhombus.
Right angle: An angle measuring 90°.
Right triangle: Any triangle that contains a right angle.
Secant: A trig function equivalent to the ratio of the hypotenuse over the leg adjacent to the angle. The reciprocal of the cosine function.
Series: A sequence that you take the sum of.
Sequence: An ordered group of numbers.
Set: Any group of numbers.
Similar triangles: Triangles are similar when their corresponding sides are in the same ratio. A 3-4-5 triangle is similar to a 6-8-10 triangle. Corresponding angles in similar triangles are equal to each other. Symbol is "~". "$\triangle ABC \sim \triangle DEF$" means that triangles ABC and DEF are similar. Similar triangles are not necessarily congruent.
Sine: A trig function equivalent to the ratio of the leg opposite an angle over the hypotenuse. The reciprocal of sine is cosecant.
Slope: The rate of change of a line. The change in y over the change in x. The rise over the run.
Slope-intercept form: A linear equation in the form $y = mx + b$, where m is the slope and b is the y-intercept.
Supplementary angles: Two angles that make a straight line. Supplementary angles add up to 180°.
Surface area: The sum of the areas of the faces of a three-dimensional solid.
System of equations: A group of two or more equations with two or more variables. The solution to a system of equations will be the point at which the graphs of the equations intersect.
Tangent: A trig function equivalent to the ratio of the leg opposite an angle over the leg adjacent to the angle. The reciprocal of tangent is cotangent.
Tangent line: A line is tangent to a curve when it touches the curve at exactly one point. A line that is tangent to a circle is perpendicular to the circle's radius at the tangent point.
Trapezoid: A quadrilateral with exactly one set of parallel lines. Looks like a rectangle with a triangle stuck on one end or with two triangles stuck on opposite ends.
Undefined: A function is undefined when no solution can be found for a given x-value. For example, a function is undefined when its denominator is zero because no number can be divided by zero.
Units digit: The "ones place". In the number 459, "9" is the units digit.
Vertex: (Plural *vertices*) 1. A corner of a polygon, where two sides meet. A polygon has as many vertices as it has sides: a triangle has three sides and three vertices. 2. The maximum or minimum of a parabola.
Zero: The boundary between positive and negative numbers. Zero is neither positive nor negative. Zero is a real number, zero is an integer, and zero is even. Zero is not prime. The denominator of a fraction may never equal zero.

APPENDIX D
STUFF TO KNOW FOR ACT SCIENCE

Here are a few terms and concepts that you may be required to know for the ACT Science Test. These are not the only words whose definitions you may need. Nor will you *definitely* be asked about them. These are simply the terms that have appeared multiple times on questions that require outside knowledge.

Boiling Point: The temperature at which a liquid becomes a gas.

Chemical Reaction: A process in which one or more chemical substances change into other chemical substances. The starting substances are called **reactants** and the resulting substances are called **products**. Reactions can be described in an *equation*, such as the following:

$$2H_2 + O_2 \rightarrow 2H_2O$$

In this equation, $2H_2$ and O_2 are the reactants and $2H_2O$ is the product. The "2" in front of H_2 means that this reaction uses two H_2 molecules for every O_2 molecule. Sometimes an equation will indicate whether a substance occurs as a solid (*s*), liquid (*l*), or gas (*g*).

Density: A substance's density is equal to its *mass* divided by its *volume*. Density is related to whether something will *float* or *sink*. If, say, a solid sphere is put into a liquid, it will sink if the sphere is denser than the liquid, and it will float if the solid is less dense than the liquid.

Freezing Point: The temperature at which a liquid becomes a solid. This is usually equal to the *MELTING POINT*.

Gravity: A force of attraction between objects (usually large ones like planets). The larger the object, the stronger the gravitational force. Earth's gravity always pulls down and objects falling due to gravity always accelerate at the same rate.

Electric Charge: Charges can be positive or negative. Substances that have like charges (i.e. both positive or both negative) repel each other. Objects with opposite charges (one positive and the other negative) attract each other. Electrons are negatively charged, so gaining electrons makes an atom more negative, while losing them makes it more positive.

Kinetic Energy: The energy of an object because of its *motion*. See *POTENTIAL ENERGY*.

Melting Point: The temperature at which a solid becomes a liquid. This is usually equal to the *FREEZING POINT*.

pH: pH is the measure of the *acidity* of a solution. The lower the pH of the solution, the more acidic it is. The opposite of an acid is a base. A pH between 0 and 7 is acidic, and a pH between 7 and 14 is basic. A pH of 7 is neutral.

Potential Energy: The energy of an object because of its *position* or *shape*. It is called "potential" because it has the potential for motion. For example, an object elevated above the surface of the Earth (on top of a hill, held in your hand, or resting on your head) has *gravitational* potential energy, because it could fall due to gravity. A spring that has been compressed or stretched has potential energy, because if you let go it will bounce back into shape. In either case, when you let go, the object moves and the potential energy is converted to *KINETIC ENERGY* (and heat due to friction).

Solutions: A solution is a kind of mixture of two substances, such as when salt is mixed in water. The substance added to the mixture (such as the salt) is called the **solute**. The substance that does the dissolving (such as the water) is called the **solvent**. The concentration of the solution tells you how much solute there is per the volume of the whole solution.

Appendix E
How to Compare ACT and SAT Scores

Converting an ACT score to an SAT score isn't like converting miles to kilometers. There's no "right answer", no exact value of what an ACT score is worth in SAT points. They are different tests, testing different skills, taken by different students. There are a lot of factors at work here, and several different ways to look at the data.

The makers of the ACT and The College Board, which administers the SAT, conducted a joint study of concordance between the two tests, available on the website for either program. This study examined the performance of students from the class of 2006 who took the newest versions of both tests, including the new Writing sections. The results were separated into two tables: one compared ACT Composite scores to SAT Critical Reading and Math scores (see **Column B** in the table); the other compared ACT English/Writing combined scores to SAT Writing scores (not shown).

ACT Comp.	Col. A Est. CR + M + W	Col. B SAT CR + M	Col. C Avg. section
36	2390	1600	800
35	2330	1560	780
34	2250	1510	750
33	2180	1460	730
32	2120	1420	710
31	2060	1380	690
30	2000	1340	670
29	1940	1300	650
28	1880	1260	630
27	1820	1220	610
26	1770	1190	590
25	1710	1150	570
24	1650	1110	550
23	1590	1070	530
22	1530	1030	510
21	1470	990	490
20	1410	950	470
19	1350	910	450
18	1290	870	430
17	1230	830	410
16	1170	790	390
15	1100	740	370
14	1020	690	340
13	950	640	320
12	870	590	290
11	780	530	260

Because they're separated into two studies, the results can be difficult to use. Many students want to compare their *final* SAT score (the sum of Critical Reading, Math, and Writing scores) to their ACT Composite score. The ACT developed a formula to estimate a student's final SAT score based on a given Critical Reading and Math score (see **Column A**). For your reference, we've also included the average single-section SAT score based on that Estimated combined score (see **Column C**).

This table is not a predictor of performance. It does not mean that a student who gets a 26 on the ACT will *definitely* get a 1770 on the SAT. That student may not even get *close* to 1770. It just means that those two scores represent, in general, a roughly similar skill level.

However, you can use this chart to see whether you're doing better on one test than on another. Colleges often use charts like this to compare students who have taken different tests. So if you got a 26 on the ACT but a 1530 on the SAT, colleges will know your 26 is a better score and will likely value it more highly. If you're not sure which test you should take, take a practice test of each type before doing any preparation work. If you score *significantly* higher on one of them, that's the test you should focus your prep work on.

It's also important to remember that these tables are *approximations*. SAT scores in particular should be thought of as a **range**, not an absolute number. If you got a 26 on the ACT and a 1740 on the SAT, that does *not* mean you are doing better on the ACT. The concordance considers any score within 20 or 30 points of the SAT scores shown in columns A and B to be equivalent.

Of course, the best source of information is from colleges themselves. Look up the schools you're interested in and find out the SAT and ACT ranges of incoming students. That's the best way you can see how well you stack up against your competition.

APPENDIX F: SUMMARIES

ENGLISH SUMMARY

GRAMMAR & USAGE

Verbs

- The verb must **agree** in number with the subject.
  - Ask: who is performing the action?
  - Ignore **interrupting phrases** and **prepositional phrases**.
  - One verb can have multiple subjects; one subject can have multiple verbs.
- The verb must be in the appropriate **tense**.
  - Look for **time words** or **other verbs** in the sentence or nearby sentences.
  - Watch for special tenses: present perfect, past perfect, and "would".
- **Irregular** verbs may have special forms.
- Don't confuse active and **passive** voice.
  - In a passive verb, the subject does not perform the action.
  - In general, if you know who the actor is, don't use the passive.

Pronouns

- A pronoun must **agree** in number with its antecedent.
  - Ask: what does the pronoun refer to?
  - Watch for **vague pronouns** and **mystery pronouns**, when the antecedent is unclear or missing.
  - Be consistent with **generic pronouns**.
  - Sometimes **nouns** must agree with each other, too.
- A pronoun's **case** is determined by its role in the sentence.
  - Subjects and objects use different forms.
  - Use **reflexive pronouns** when subject and object refer to the same person.
  - Don't confuse **contractions** and **possessive** pronouns.
- **Relative** pronouns (like *who, which,* or *that*) behave similarly to regular pronouns.
  - Their verbs agree with the antecedent of the relative pronoun.
  - Relatives have cases, like regular pronouns.
  - *Who* is for people, *which* is for non-people.

Other issues

- **Adjectives** describe nouns. **Adverbs** describe all other words.
- **Comparatives** compare two things, **superlatives** compare three or more.
- Make sure to use the correct **prepositions**.
- Your choice of preposition may affect the form of the **verb** that follows.
- Beware of **commonly confused words**:
  - Use "would **have**", not "would of".
  - Use "**than**" for comparisons, not "then".

SENTENCE STRUCTURE

Definitions

- An **independent clause** can stand by itself as a sentence. It must have a subject and main verb.
- A **dependent clause** cannot stand by itself as a sentence.
- A **relative clause** is a dependent clause with a relative pronoun that describes a single word in the sentence.
- A **modifier** is a phrase with no main verb that modifies something in the sentence.

Fragments

- Every sentence must have **at least one independent clause** with a subject and verb.
- Fix a fragment by:
  - Turning a *partial verb* into a **main verb.**
  - Removing unnecessary connectors or relative pronouns.
  - **Joining it** to another sentence by *removing the period.*

Run-on Sentences

- **Don't** connect independent clauses with a **comma alone**, or with **no connection** at all.
- Fix a run-on by:
  - Separating the clauses with a **period**.
  - Using a **comma** with a **conjunction**.
  - Making one of the independent clauses a **dependent clause or modifier**.

Modifiers

- A modifier at the *beginning of a sentence* must describe the *subject of the main clause* (the word right after the comma) or else it's a **dangling modifier**.
- A modifier at *the end of a sentence* may describe:
  - the **subject**, if there's a *comma.*
  - the **word next to it**, if there's *no comma.*
- *Prepositional phrases* must be **placed right after** the words they describe.

Parallelism

- Use **parallel forms** for **parallel ideas.** Any words or phrases joined with the word "**and**" must be in parallel forms.
- **Don't** use "and" if the forms **aren't parallel**.

PUNCTUATION

DO use commas:

- between **independent clauses** with a **conjunction**.
- around **parenthetical phrases**.
- in a list of **three or more**.
- with **coordinate adjectives**.
- before a **direct quote**.
- around **sentence adverbs**.

DON'T use commas:

- between **subject and verb**.
- between **verb and object**.
- before **infinitives**.
- before or in the middle of **prepositional phrases**.
- with a **two part list** (two nouns or verbs with a conjunction).
- with a "**that**" clause.
- before **restrictive** clauses.

Apostrophes

- **Plurals** usually take -s.
- **Possessives** take -'s.
- **Plural possessives** take -s'.
- **Contractions** use apostrophes for missing letters.
- **Pronouns** take **contraction** apostrophes but **not possessive apostrophes**.

Other marks

- A **semicolon** separates *independent clauses* (interchangeable with a period).
- A **colon** *strongly* connects phrases.
- A **dash** connects *independent clauses* or *parenthetical phrases*.
- Don't mix up **sentence-final marks**: *periods*, *question marks*, and *exclamation points*.

RHETORICAL SKILLS

Style

- Be **concise**. Avoid *redundant* or *wordy* choices.
- Be **specific**. Avoid *vague* choices and vague *pronouns*.
- Choose **the right word**. Make sure it has the right *meaning* and *tone*.

Organization

- Choose the right **transition word** to connect *similar or contrasting* sentences.
- Choose the right **transition phrase** to connect the *topics* of adjacent sentences.
- An **introductory or concluding sentence** should state the *main idea* of the paragraph.
- Find the right **sentence order** by looking at references within the sentences.

Writing Strategy

- Does a choice **fulfill the writer's goal**?
    - For a sentence, focus on the *stated goal*, not your opinion.
    - For the essay, find the *main idea* of the essay and eliminate choices that are *false*.
- Should the writer **add or delete** a sentence? Look out for *irrelevant* choices.
- If the writer deleted a phrase, what **would the essay lose**? Find the *meaning* of the phrase and how it *relates* to the paragraph.

MATH SUMMARY

MATH TECHNIQUES

General Strategies

- Before you do anything else, **circle the question** you're being asked.
- **Show your work** for every question. Don't do math in your head.
- If you need a figure that isn't given, **draw one**.

Common Mistakes

- **RTFQ**: make sure you answer the question you're being asked!
- **Fool's Gold**: if a choice seems too easy for a hard question, it's probably wrong.

Target Numbers

- **Don't do all the questions!** Guess on the last ones.
- If you take **more time per question**, you'll cut down on carelessness and are more likely to get them right.
- It's not that those questions are too hard for you. It's about doing **fewer questions**, but doing them **more accurately**.

Plug In

- **Pick a number** for the variable.
- Do the problem with that number and get a number for an answer.
- Put the number you chose into the choices and see which gives you the same answer.
- Check all choices. If more than one works, pick a different number.
- Sometimes you have to plug in for more than one variable. Sometimes plugging in for one gives you the value of another.
- Sometimes there are implicit variables—there are no variables with letters, but there is an unnamed value you don't know.
- If a question asks about a **relationship**, try Plug In. That often means **variables in the answer choices**.

Backsolve

- **Start with the middle choice** (choice C or H). Assume that's the answer.
- That's the answer to the question. Put that number through the information given to see if it matches.
- If it matches, that's your answer. If it doesn't pick another one.
- If the choice fails, try to see whether you want a higher or lower number. If you can't, just pick one.
- If a question is asking for a **value**, try Backsolve. That usually means there are **numbers in the answer choices**.

Guesstimate

- While technically some pictures *might* not be drawn to scale, in reality **virtually every figure is drawn to scale**.
- Look at the picture. Compare the value you want with the values you know. Get a **rough guess** of what the value should be based on the picture.
- Eliminate choices that are obviously too big or too small. Then refine your guess with more precise measurement.

PRE-ALGEBRA

- Know some basic **definitions** of numbers: integer, factor, multiple, prime number, remainder, positive/negative, even/odd, prime factor.
- Know how to add, subtract, multiply, and divide **fractions**.
- Solve **ratios** by cross multiplying. Make sure units match across the equals sign.
- A **percent** is a ratio out of 100. Know how to manipulate percents and percent change.
- **Combinatorics** is about arranging groups:
  - When combining two **separate groups**, multiply the two numbers.
  - When arranging things into slots, where **order matters**, multiply the number of possible items for each slot. Once you put something in a slot, you can't use it again.
  - If **order doesn't matter**, do the same thing but divide by two, or just write out all possible groups.
- Probability is the number of **winning events** divided by the **total possible events**.
  - The probabilities of all events associated with a problem must **add up to 1**.
- Know how to compute **averages**. In a list of terms:
  - *Mean* is the sum over the number of terms.
  - *Median* is the number in the middle when written in order.
  - *Mode* is the most frequent number.
  - Average problems can often be solved via the **sum** instead of the terms. The average times the number of terms equals the sum.

ELEMENTARY ALGEBRA

- Solve an algebraic equation by getting the **variable by itself**. Move terms around by doing the opposite of any function (e.g. $x + 7 = 12$ means $x = 12 - 7$).
- Simplify **polynomials** by combining terms with the same exponential terms.
- To multiply binomials, use **FOIL**: Multiply the First terms, the Outside terms, the Inside terms, and the Last terms.
- The reverse of FOILing is **factoring**. Know how to split a polynomial into its constituent factors.
- You can **divide** polynomials by canceling out a factor from the top and bottom.
- Know the **difference of squares**: $(x + y)(x - y) = x^2 - y^2$

- **Inequalities** can be manipulated just like equations. Remember to flip the inequality sign if you multiply or divide by a negative.

INTERMEDIATE ALGEBRA

Functions

- If a problem uses a funny symbol, **follow the directions**: the symbol is defined in the question.
- The notation "$f(x)$" works the same way: **follow the directions**. The value **inside the parentheses** tells you the value of x.
- **Plug that value in** for x. If $f(x) = 2x + 5$, then $f(4) = 2(4) + 5$
- Some functions may use **two variables** in the parentheses.
- You may have to **combine** functions. Do one function and get an answer; then put your answer through the other function.

Exponents

- Know properties of exponents, including negative, zero, and fractional exponents.
- To multiply exponentials, **add** exponents.
- To divide exponentials, **subtract** exponents.
- To raise an exponent to another exponent, **multiply** the exponents.
- To solve for a variable in an exponent, get all exponential numbers in the **same base**.
- Know the definition of **logarithm**: $\log_a b = c$ means $a^c = b$.

Absolute Value

- The absolute value of a term is its value without its sign—that is, **make it positive**.
- If a variable is inside the absolute value signs, don't forget about the negative solution.

COORDINATE GEOMETRY

- Know how to read a **coordinate plane**. The x-axis is horizontal, and the y-axis is vertical.
- A **graph of a function** is a picture of its solutions. Saying "$f(3) = 4$" means that the point (3, 4) appears on the graph of $f(x)$.
- The **slope** of a line is the change in y over the change in x.
- The **equation of a line** can be written $y = mx + b$, where m is the slope and b is the y-intercept.
- A **circle** can be described by the equation $(x - a)^2 (y - b)^2 = r^2$, where (a, b) is the center and r is the radius.
- A **parabola** can be written with the equation $y = ax^2 + bx + c$, where c is the y-intercept.

PLANE GEOMETRY

Angles

- A **straight line** equals 180°.
- A **triangle** equals 180°.
- An **isosceles triangle** has two equal sides and two equal angles.
- **Vertical angles** are equal.
- **Parallel lines** with a transversal produces two kinds of angles: big ones and little ones.
    - All the big ones are equal.
    - All the little ones are equal.
    - Any big plus any little make 180°.

Triangles

- In a right triangle, **the Pythagorean theorem** says $a^2 + b^2 = c^2$, where a and b are legs and c is the hypotenuse.
- A **45-45-90** triangle has dimensions x, x, $x\sqrt{2}$.
- A **30-60-90** triangle has dimensions x, $x\sqrt{3}$, $2x$.
- Any two triangles with the same three angles are **similar**. The lengths of their corresponding sides are in the same ratio with each other.
- The **third side of a triangle** must be smaller than the sum and bigger than the difference of the other two sides.

Perimeter, Area, Volume

- The **perimeter** of a figure is the sum of the lengths of the sides.
- Know some formulas for **area:** triangle = $(1/2)bh$; rectangle = ℓw; square = s^2; parallelogram = bh.
- **Shaded area** problems can best be done by subtraction: find the area of the whole figure and subtract the part you don't need.
- **Surface area** is the sum of the areas of the faces of an object.
- Know some formulas for **volume:** box = ℓwh; cube = s^3; cylinder = $\pi r^2 h$

Circles

- A circle's center has **360°**.
- The **diameter** goes from end to end of a circle, passing through the center.
- The **radius** goes from the center to the end. The radius is half a diameter.
- The **area** of a circle is πr^2.
- The **circumference** of a circle is $2\pi r$.
- A **slice** of a circle is a fraction of the circle. Everything about that slice is the same fraction: angle, area, and arc length.

TRIGONOMETRY

- The trigonometric functions are the ratios of various sides of a right triangle.
    - **Sine** of an angle is the opposite side over the hypotenuse
    - **Cosine** is the adjacent side over the hypotenuse
    - **Tangent** is the opposite over the adjacent.
- You may encounter the law of sines or the law of cosines, but the formulas are usually given to you.
- Familiarize yourself with the graphs of the trig functions.

READING SUMMARY

Timing

- You may consider **skipping a passage** to have more time on the ones you do.
- If you're short on time, do **questions with line references** first.

The Passage

- Read quickly and get the **Main Ideas** of the passage, paragraph by paragraph.
- To find the main idea, ask: **what's it about**?
- If you can't find the main idea, read the **first and last sentences** of the paragraph.
- Don't spend too much time. Don't overanalyze. If you're not sure, **move on**.

The Question

- Read the question, **ignore the choices**.
- When there's a line reference, **go back to the passage** and read the line.
- If there's no line reference:
  - Search the passage for **key words** from the question.
  - Use your **Main Ideas** to help find the information.
- **Read the whole sentence**, not just the line.
- If that line is unclear, read the sentence **before or the sentence after**.
- Try to answer the question with what you just learned. That's your **anticipation**.
- If you can't anticipate, just go to the choices to **eliminate**.

The Choices

- If you find a choice that matches your anticipation, pick it.
- If you don't find a match, or if you don't have an anticipation, don't look for right choice, **look for wrong choices**. 80% of the choices are wrong. You can eliminate even if you don't understand the passage or question.
- **Work quickly**. If you're not sure about a choice, skip it and come back later.
- Eliminate choices that are **random**, **false**, or **irrelevant**.
- As you eliminate, **cross out** words that make a choice wrong.
- If you get down to two or three choices and can't decide, **guess one**.

SCIENCE SUMMARY

Timing

- **Don't read the passage**. Skim to see what it's about and get to the questions.
- On *Conflicting Viewpoints* questions, **underline the first sentence** of each viewpoint to get the main ideas.
- Use **Target Numbers**: consider skipping one or two passages to give yourself more time on the others.

Answering the questions

- Use the following method for most questions:
  1. In the question, underline the table, figure, or viewpoint you need.
  2. In the question, **underline key words**: things you know and things you want. If you can't find key words, look *in the choices*.
  3. In the figure, **circle the key words** and values you found in the question. If you can't find them in the figure, look *in the passage*.
  4. Match! Match! Match!
- Use techniques from the Math Test like **Backsolve** and **Guesstimate.**
- Watch out for **RTFQ** choices and other careless mistakes.

Figure types

- Figures come in all sorts of shapes and sizes, but they all boil down to the same thing: **matching** one variable with another.
- **Write on your figure**. Draw in gridlines if you need to. Use your answer sheet to line up values.
- **Check the values on the axes**. They may not be what you think they are.

Question types

- **Data Lookup questions**: Look up values in a table or figure.
- **Combination questions**: Connect multiple figures or tables.
- **Relationship questions**: If one variable gets bigger, does the other get bigger or smaller?
- **Inferred Data questions**: If we added new points, where would they go?
- **Passage questions**: Look up stuff in the paragraphs, not just the figures.
- **Experiment Design questions**: Why was the experiment set up the way it was? What if we changed it?
- **Reasoning questions**: Does the data support a statement? First eliminate *false* choices, then answer yes or no.
- **Knowledge questions**: Know things that aren't in the passage.

WRITING SUMMARY

Format

- The Writing test is **optional**.
- Essay will get two scores, each 1 to 6. Scores cannot differ by more than 1 point.
- You will get a combined English/Writing score, but only your English score goes into your composite.
- Essay is graded in 5 categories: *Judgment, Development, Focus, Organization,* and *Language*.

Development

- The topic will present a specific issue that has two sides. The issue will somehow relate to normal high school life, so you should not need significant outside knowledge.
- Come up with some reasons for each side of the issue.
- **Choose a specific side to argue**. It doesn't have to be the side you actually believe, just the one you came up with more reasons for.
- You must **address the opposing view** in your essay and why it's wrong.

Organization

- Make an **outline** of your essay:
  - Introduction
  - Reason 1
  - Reason 2
  - Counterargument
  - Conclusion
- For each reason you write argue, you should include two things:
  - **Description** (who, what, when, where)
  - **Relevance** to the topic (why, how)

Language

- Include **vocabulary** you learned for the Critical Reading section.
- Make sure you use **concrete language** whenever possible.
- Use **complex sentences** with a varied structure.
- Watch out for **grammatical mistakes** (like those we discussed in the other chapters).

PERFORMANCE LOGS

ENGLISH

Grammar and Usage

Verb Agreement____________________

Verb Tense____________________

Verb Drill____________________

Pronoun Agreement____________________

Pronoun Case ____________________

Relative Pronouns ____________________

Pronoun Drill ____________________

Grammar & Usage Exercise ____________________

____

Sentence Structure

Fragment Drill ____________________

Run-on Drill ____________________

Sentence Structure Exercise ____________________

____

Punctuation

Comma Drill ____________________

Punctuation Exercise ____________________

____

Rhetorical Skills

Rhetorical Skills Exercise ____________________

____

MATHEMATICS

Math Techniques

Plug In Drill ____________________

Backsolve Drill ____________________

Guesstimate Drill ____________________

Math Technique Exercise ____________________

____

Pre-Algebra

Number Concepts & Definitions ____________________

Fractions ____________________

Ratios ____________________

Percents ____________________

Averages ____________________

Combinatorics ____________________

Probability ____________________

Pre -Algebra Exercise ____________________

____

Elementary Algebra

Basic Manipulation

Evaluating an expression ____________________

Solving an equation ____________________

Multiple equations ____________________

Polynomials

FOIL ____________________

Factoring ____________________

Dividing polynomials ____________________

Quadratic equations ____________________

Inequalities ____________________

Elementary Algebra Exercise ____________________

____

Intermediate Algebra

Functions ____________________

Function Drill ____________________

Exponents ____________________

Exponent Drill ____________________

Absolute Value Drill ____________________

Intermediate Algebra Exercise ____________________

____

Coordinate Geometry

Plotting Points ____________________

Graphing Functions ____________________

Lines ____________________

Circles ____________________

Coordinate Geometry Exercise ____________________

____

Plane Geometry

Angle Drill ____________________

Triangle Drill ____________________

Perimeter, Area, Volume Drill ____________________

Circle Drill ____________________

Plane Geometry Exercise ____________________

____

Trigonometry

Basic functions ____________________

Trigonometry Function Drill ____________________

Trigonometry Exercise ____________________

____

READING

Main Idea Drill ____________________

Word Search Drill ____________________

Reading Exercise ____________________

____

SCIENCE

Tables ____________________

Lines ____________________

Layers ____________________

Data Representation Passage ____________________

Research Summaries Passage ____________________

Conflicting Viewpoints Passage ____________________

Science Exercise ____________________

____

APPENDIX A: MATH DRILLS

Plug In Drill ____________________

Backsolve Drill ____________________

Fraction Drill ____________________

Ratio Drill ____________________

Percent Drill ____________________

Average Drill ____________________

One-variable Algebra Drill ____________________

Multi-variable Algebra Drill ____________________

Polynomial Drill ____________________

Exponent Drill ____________________

F(x) Drill ____________________

Graphing Drill ____________________

Angle Drill ____________________

Triangle Drill ____________________

Perimeter, Area, Volume Drill ____________________

Circle Drill ____________________

NOTES

NOTES

See all of our products at www.alisteducation.com/bookstore

- ***The Book of Knowledge SAT***
  Everything you need for the SAT
- ***The Book of Knowledge SAT Student Solutions***
  Detailed explanations for the SAT book
- ***The Book of Knowledge SAT Teacher Manual***
  All of the regular book alongside explanations

- ***The Book of Knowledge ACT***
  Everything you need for the ACT
- ***The Book of Knowledge ACT Student Solutions***
  Detailed explanations for the ACT book
- ***The Book of Knowledge ACT Teacher Manual***
  All of the regular book alongside explanations

- ***The Unofficial Guide to the Official SAT Study Guide***
  Detailed explanations for every question in the College Board's book of tests
- ***The Vocabulary Box***
  The 500 most important words for the SAT
  Available as a box of flashcards or a workbook
- ***Vocab Videos Flashcards***
  A companion to the Vocab Videos site
  Available as a box of flashcards or a workbook

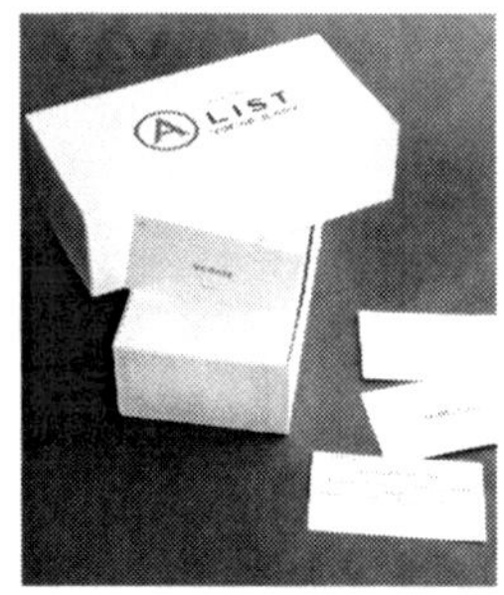

VOCAB VIDEOS

Bringing Vocabulary to Life
www.vocabvideos.com

- Hilarious short videos illustrate the meanings of 500 high value, frequently-tested SAT, ACT, & high school vocabulary words.
- Features entertaining characters, outrageous plotlines, and parodies of your favorite TV shows and movies.
- Contains extensive online review material including:
  - ✓ *Quizzes* for each episode
  - ✓ *Worksheets* to write sentences and mnemonic devices
  - ✓ *Multimedia flashcard maker*: create flashcards for *any* academic subjects (you can even upload your own images and videos!)
  - ✓ *Downloadable crossword puzzles* for a fun review
- **NEW** photo and video uploading functionality allows students to create their own vocab photos and videos!

Get started at <u>www.VocabVideos.com</u>.
Enter coupon code **BOK5** in Step 3 of Checkout to receive **25% off**!

Sample Flashcard

CPSIA information can be obtained at www.ICGtesting.com
Printed in the USA
BVOW03s0859230814

363670BV00003B/3/P

9 780989 160551